Handbook of Data-Based Decision Making in Education

Education has fought long and hard to gain acceptance as a profession and, since professionals by definition use data to shape the decisions they make, education has little choice but to continue moving in this direction. This 3-part, 28-chapter handbook represents a major contribution to the literature of education. It is a unique compendium of the most original work currently available on how, when, and why evidence should be used to ground practice. It is a comprehensive, cross-disciplinary, research-based, and practice-based resource that all educators can turn to as a guide to data-based decision making. The following is a brief overview of its coverage.

Part I: Theoretical and Practical Perspectives
Part II: Building Support for Data-Based Decisions
Part III: Data-Based Applications

The *Handbook of Data-Based Decision Making in Education* is a must-read for researchers who are just beginning to explore the scientifically based nature of educational practice. It is also appropriate for policy makers and practitioners who are confronted with young people who need to be in classrooms where "best practices" are the norm and not the exception.

Theodore J. Kowalski is a former superintendent and college of education dean and is currently the Kuntz Family Chair, an endowed professorship at the University of Dayton.

Thomas J. Lasley II is Dean of the School of Education and Allied Professions at the University of Dayton.

Handbook of Data-Based Decision Making in Education

Edited by
Theodore J. Kowalski and
Thomas J. Lasley II

Routledge
Taylor & Francis Group

NEW YORK AND LONDON

First published 2009
by Routledge
711 Third Avenue, New York, NY 10017

Simultaneously published in the UK
by Routledge
2 Park Square, Milton Park, Abingdon, Oxon OX14 4RN

Routledge is an imprint of the Taylor & Francis Group, an informa business

© 2009 Taylor & Francis

Typeset in Minion by
RefineCatch Limited, Bungay, Suffolk

Library of Congress Cataloging-in-Publication Data
Handbook of data-based decision making in education / Theodore J. Kowalski & Thomas J. Lasley II, editors.
    p. cm.
    Includes bibliographic references and index.
    1. School management and organization–Decision making–Handbooks, manuals, etc.   I. Kowalski, Theodore,
1943–   II. Lasley II, Thomas J. 1947–
    LB2805 .H2862 2008
    371.2 22

ISBN13: 978–0–415–96503–3 (hbk)
ISBN13: 978–0–415–96504–0 (pbk)
ISBN13: 978–0–203–88880–3 (ebk)

Contents

Preface

This book focuses on how educators can use data to make decisions at both the policy and practice levels. The book is written at a time when increasing emphasis is being placed on scientifically based (evidence-based) practice, but it is occurring in an environment that is struggling to both collect and manage all the accumulated data. The *Handbook of Data-Based Decision Making in Education* explores theoretical issues around data usage, establishes conceptual support relative to how to collect and use data, and then outlines the different ways in which data are used to make policy and practice decisions. The book is intended for policy makers who are often pressed to understand the importance of evidence-based environments and practitioners who function in a No Child Left Behind (NCLB) culture, which holds them accountable for student achievement in ways that have never before been evidenced in American education.

Structure

The *Handbook* is divided into three major sections: Theoretical and Practical Perspectives, Building Support for Data-Based Decisions, and Data-Based Applications.

Part I: Theoretical and Practical Perspectives

In this section the chapter authors explore such issues as the ethics of decision making in the professions as well as the legal dimensions associated with using data to make decisions. Ethical and legal considerations are fundamental to how educators use data, especially in their efforts to comply with NCLB requirements. The first part of the text allows readers to see the wide variety of theoretical and practical considerations that need to be taken into account if evidence-based decision making is going to be accomplished in a professionally efficacious manner.

Part II: Building Support for Data-Based Decisions

In this section the chapter authors investigate the wide variety of data collection and data management problems that are confronting decision makers. The more data that are available the more complex it becomes to access, use, and analyze what is known. Many of the current efforts to collect data have been successful, only to discover that the appropriate data management systems were not in place to enable decision makers to use the available data in an effective manner. The second set of chapters examines both at the national and local level how researchers are beginning to identify ways of better accessing and then using data to shape program and instructional decision making.

Part III: Data-Based Applications

In this section the chapter authors describe the ways in which a wide variety of educational stakeholders use data to make decisions. Decision making has always been a part of what administrators do, but in the twenty-first century administrators are expected to make decisions using the best data available. In some cases those data are being used to shape instructional decisions and in other instances the data are being used to document compliance with federal or state mandates. In almost every instance principals and other school leaders are being asked to use data to improve education at the classroom or school level and to do so in ways that are fiscally and functionally effective and efficient.

Special Features

The *Handbook* authors examine both the types of research that have occurred relative to data-based decision making as well as some of the scholarly critiques vis-à-vis using evidence to ground policy or practice decisions. It is important for readers to know both the type of research being conducted as well as the content of the critical reviews of that extant research. Some would argue that over the years practitioners have been too focused on conclusions (and using those conclusions to make specific program decisions about things such as a reading series or a math curriculum) and not sufficiently aware of how those conclusions were reached (i.e., what processes or assumptions were made in the collection of data about salient educational practices?). The text focuses on the types of research that are currently available and the problems associated with each.

The authors contributing to this text developed the chapters with specific attention

(a) to theoretical data-based decision making issues,
(b) to support (or data manage) systems for collecting and synthesizing data,
(c) to the use of data to make educational decisions.

The chapters, each of which is original and created just for the *Handbook*, are authored by the most respected educators associated with the data-based decision making movement. As such, the text represents state-of-the-art practice at all the different levels: theory, data collection and management, and application.

Special Thanks

The editors are especially grateful for the wonderful chapter contributions of all the authors. Special thanks also go to: Ms. Elizabeth Pearn and Ms. Colleen Wildenhaus for their wonderful editorial support; Ms. Mea Greenwood and Brother Michael Amakyi for their management assistance with the manuscripts; Ms. Beth Blanks for her technical assistance; and to all those who read and critiqued chapter contributions.

Introduction

Contextualizing Evidence-Based Decision Making

The use of evidence to make decisions is not new to educators in particular or to other practicing professionals (lawyers, doctors, engineers) in general. For the past century, and especially as professional fields have expanded and matured, evidence has been considered a cornerstone of effective professional practice. Patients expect their doctors to use evidence when making diagnoses and offering prescriptions, and, increasingly, parents want teachers who use instructional practices to utilize interventions that are grounded on evidence.

The often heated debate connected to scientifically based practice is not really about whether evidence should be used in decision making and by professionals, but rather how evidence (data) is collected, analyzed, and then subsequently used to guide practice. As even the most naive professional practitioner knows, it makes a difference how data are collected and who is collecting them. Once collected, it makes a difference how they are analyzed and evaluated (the assumptions made and statistical tests chosen). Finally, once all the data go from a raw to refined form it matters how policy makers and practitioners use what is "known" to decide what should be done in terms of professional "best practices." Unfortunately, it is all too common for the biases of practitioners to determine which studies to use as they make decisions about what constitutes effective classroom practice. The reality of most phenomena suggests that there is sufficient complexity to limit transferability of findings from one context to another without at least some qualifications or adjustments and that transferability becomes even more complicated in highly politicized educational environments.

Researchers tend to rely on a limited number of observations and that fact has import for generalizing to broader populations or multiple settings (Briggs, 2008). School administrators and teachers are desperate for best practice answers in many instances because they feel the political push associated with a high stakes educational environment. The value-added, No Child Left Behind age we now live in is putting pressure on everyone to produce academic growth, and measuring that growth (and reporting findings) is becoming increasingly important and transparent. Some organizations (e.g., What Works Clearinghouse or WWC and Best Evidence Encyclopedia or BEE) focus on (a) establishing criteria for eligible research studies, (b) selecting studies with strong research designs, and (c) making judgments about program effectiveness based on selected studies (Briggs, 2008). Sounds simple and straightforward! As Briggs points out, the rub comes because all too often "what counts as best evidence differs depending on the organization [collecting the data and] doing the synthesis" (p. 15).

Clearly, what counts as "best evidence" is still being debated but equally clear is the fact that the No Child Left Behind legislation is causing everyone to find ways to make transparent the performance of students. The United States Department of Education website now provides "dashboard" data on every state in the U.S. The dashboard data include demographic information as well as specific achievement metrics around the number of schools that are making adequate yearly progress (AYP), the number of schools in need of improvement, and the number of schools in restructuring. The data suggest both how far we have come in efforts to make data about student performance part of the public domain and how far we need to go before all the key stakeholders have the information they need to make sound judgments about the quality of a school. According to the website fully 70% of the schools in the U.S. (or 64,546) are making AYP. On the other hand, 10,676 schools are "in need of improvement" and 2,302 are "in restructuring." The site also indicates the number of highly qualified teachers in both high- and low-poverty schools.

A quick review of the CORE principles guiding the U.S. Department of Education would suggest that the emphasis on evidence-based decision making is just beginning to find its way into the public policy realm. At least three of the CORE principles focus conceptually on the potential use of evidence, whether in making assessments annually on school performance or in helping parents use information to make judgments about the efficacy of different school programs. In addition, a variety of private entities (e.g., see GreatSchools.net) are beginning to use public domain data to help parents and others as they make judgments about school programs. GreatSchools provides achievement data on almost every school in the U.S. and allows parents to electronically access information about both student academic performance and parental attitudes and then to use that information to make judgments about whether their children should attend a particular school. We live in an age of educational choice and as (and if) the choice options expand the demand for data will increase. Obviously, politics will play a part in how choice manifests itself but what seems apparent is that parents and educators, especially those in urban settings and within high-poverty schools, are wanting and even demanding more information so that they can then make decisions consistent with what they believe to be in the best interests of their children.

Of course, all this demand for evidence is also placing unique pressure on the wide variety of researchers who are responsible for generating and providing data. For example, serious scholars who are exploring best practice questions debate nuanced but significant issues around construct validity, causal inferences and generalizabiltiy. What practitioners want are studies with positive effects across settings; what they usually get are, at best, mixed effects or potentially positive effects with relevance to certain types of settings.

The palliatives for dealing with the what-data-to-use conundrum are cumbersome and complex for practitioners. Chatterji (2008), for example, argues that educators can learn much by examining public health policy practices. Specifically: "a commitment to scientific analysis and research . . . [needs to be undertaken in order] to attack complex public health problems in communities" (p. 26). Others (Dynarski,

2008) assert that educators should simply look for interventions that have been broadly tried and tested (in multiple context and settings). Such an approach does not assume success but it does mitigate and moderate potential risks.

Clearly, using evidence to make decisions is emerging as a best practice standard because there is frustration with the perceived instructional inertia of K-12 educational institutions. Hess (2007, p. 80) writes (citing a U.S. Chamber of Commerce document):

> It has been nearly a quarter century since the seminal report *A Nation at Risk* was issued in 1983. Since that time, a knowledge-based economy has emerged, the Internet has reshaped commerce and communication, exemplars of creative commerce like Microsoft, eBay, and Southwest Airlines have revolutionized the way we live, and the global economy has undergone wrenching change. Throughout that period, education spending has steadily increased and rafts of well-intentioned school reforms have come and gone. But student achievement has remained stagnant, and our K-12 schools have stayed remarkably unchanged—preserving, as if in amber, the routines, culture, and operations of an obsolete 1930s manufacturing plant.

What does it mean to be a professional who uses evidence? And, in what ways is the use of evidence an expectation for professionals?

The first question is one that will be addressed directly or indirectly throughout most of the chapters in this book. The second question represents a slightly different but equally relevant matter and will be discussed briefly here. That is, how and why does the use of evidence connect with the expectation for professional behavior? We make two points in this regard. First, professionals make decisions in the service of clients (e.g., teachers for students) and in making those decisions they "use the most valid knowledge [data] available" (Howsam, Corrigan, Denemark, & Nash, 1976, pp. 6–7). Further, they are not simply using data but they are also knowledgeable about why they make the decisions they make given the available data. This nuance of knowing both how and why to use data is important because it represents much of what we and the other authors explore in this book. That is, data-driven decision making is not good in and of itself, but rather it represents a professional good because those using data are endeavoring to identify the best approaches to serve the salient needs of those they serve.

Second, and further, the professional not only uses data but is also able to go beyond them. Evidence-based decision making does not mean that one becomes a slave to the data available, but rather the professional can "see through" the data in ways that transcend facile or simplistic conclusions or labels. May (2001, pp. 46–47) notes a conceptual equivalent with psychiatric care:

> every thoughtful psychiatrist knows that the better you get to know a patient, the more difficult it is to classify the patient under one of the diseases listed in the DSM IV. The patient does not conveniently vanish into the scientist's law. The doctor uses science, but healing also requires practical wisdom in bringing science artfully to bear in order to restore harmony to the patient's universe. That healing is the end purpose of doctoring.

In essence, the professional who uses evidence knows how to access data, how to use that data in the service of clients, and then understands why the decisions made represent the potential for best practice within a particular context or setting. That is, he or she also has the practical wisdom necessary to see beyond the *how* and *why* to the unique contexts being served.

This book focuses on the how, the why and the practical wisdom associated with evidence-based decision making within educational contexts. Readers will see that each of the sections of this text (and all the chapters within each of the sections) connect with these fundamental elements because they enable readers to see the theoretical grounding of evidence-based decision making, the practical actions that practitioners can take and the multiple ways in which the actions taken are a result of considering a wide variety of critical choices.

We necessarily add a caution. Specifically, not all educators embrace the "causal model of professional action" (see Biesta, 2007), whereby professionals "do something [provide some type of intervention] in order to bring about certain effects" (p. 7). That is, although most of the authors contributing to this text implicitly embrace the "causal model" and also envision a certain "technological model of professional action" (p. 8) as the most effective (and efficient) methods of achieving defined ends (i.e., student achievement), some critics, such as Biesta, question such a nexus. He writes:

> This first problem with this approach is the role of causality: apart from the obvious fact that the condition of being a student is quite different from that of being a patient—being a student is not an illness, just as teaching is not a cure—the most important argument against the idea that education is a causal process lies in the fact that education is not a process of physical interaction but a process of symbolic or symbolically mediated interaction. If teaching is to have any effect on learning, it is because of the fact that students interpret and try to make sense of what they are being taught. It is only through processes of (mutual) interpretation that education is possible.
>
> (Biesta, 2007, p. 8)

We present this counter argument to illustrate how important it is to both understand what data-based decision making is, and also to suggest the philosophical volatility of education today, and that volatility demands that educators at all levels evidence a certain practical wisdom in all that they do.

The *Handbook of Data-Based Decision Making in Education* is intended to offer readers the best and most current information available relative to how data and other forms of evidence are being used to shape educational policy and practice. As educators move closer to their goal of assuring that all students are taught by highly qualified teachers and are in schools administered by highly qualified school leaders, it will become imperative that they not only have access to data but also know how to use them in ways that serve a wide variety of stakeholders.

References

Biesta, G. (2007). Why "what works" won't work: Evidence-based practice and the democratic deficit in educational research. *Educational Theory, 57*(1), 1–22.

Briggs, D. C. (2008). Synthesizing causal inferences. *Educational Researcher, 37*(1), 15–22.

Chatterji, M. (2008). Comments on Slavin: Synthesizing evidence from impact evaluations in education to inform action. *Educational Researcher, 37*(1), 23–26.

Dynarski, M. (2008). Bringing answers to educators: Guiding principles for research syntheses. *Educational Researcher, 37*(1), 27–29.

Hess, F. M. (2007, July–August). What is the best way for business to help fix education? *The American,* 78–85.

Howsam, R. B., Corrigan, D. C., Denemark, G. W., & Nash, R. J. (1976). *Educating a profession.* Washington, DC: American Association of Colleges for Teacher Education.

May, W. F. (2001). *Beleaguered rulers.* Louisville, KY: Westminister John Knox Press.

Part I: Theoretical and Practical Perspectives

1

Evidence and Decision Making in Professions

Theodore J. Kowalski
University of Dayton

Professional practitioners are expected to rely on scientific evidence to make crucial decisions affecting their clients or patients. This seemingly innocuous benchmark, however, has generated considerable controversy, especially regarding the extent to which intuition, emotion, politics, and philosophy should influence these choices. Traditionally, science (or more precisely, scientific research) has served the purpose of protecting "practitioners from implementing useless programs" (Mayer, 2003, p. 361). Physicians, for example, have been and still are required to pass comprehensive examinations on the medical profession's scientific knowledge base as a licensing prerequisite. Today, however, the accumulation of massive amounts of data and the development of technology that allows databases to be accessed easily and quickly have spawned an accountability movement that is sweeping across professions. The overall goal of this movement is to make *evidence-based practice* (EBP) normative (Levant, 2005).

The application of EBP in education has not been debated widely and the extent to which educators understand and support the concept is unknown. Even so, administrators and teachers historically have exhibited a proclivity to oppose ideas that conflict with their prevailing beliefs, especially when these ideas emerge in the context of politically coercive change strategies (Bauman, 1996). As an example, critics of the No Child Left Behind Act of 2001 (NCLB)[1] have often reacted negatively to the law's requirements for data-based decision making. More specifically, they have argued that basing consequential decisions solely on research data is demeaning and precarious—demeaning because the wisdom of educators is devalued and precarious because research data are fallible (Kowalski, Lasley, & Mahoney, 2008).

Given the role of schools in society, the future of EBP in education should not be determined solely by political, emotional, or even philosophical discourse. Rather, making the concept normative for administrators and teachers should depend on the extent to which it improves practice and ultimately, school effectiveness. The purpose here is to provide a framework for examining EBP in the context of professional responsibility. First, the topics of problem solving and decision making in schools are addressed. The intent is to (a) clarify the nature of these processes, (b) delineate the nexus between them, and (c) contrast programmed and un-programmed decisions. Next, evidence is defined and multiple types of evidence are identified and incorrect and correct interpretations of EBP, generally and in education, are discussed. Last, the barriers preventing EBP from becoming normative are categorized.

Professional Problems and Decisions

Though there are countless definitions of a profession, they are essentially "occupations with special power and prestige. Society grants these rewards because professions have special competence and esoteric bodies of knowledge linked to central needs and values of the social system" (Larson, 1977, p. x). Recognized professions enjoy a symbiotic relationship with societies; that is, in return for services rendered, their practitioners are granted influence and social status (Kowalski, 2004). Curtis (2000), citing the work of British ethicist, Paul Rowbottom, identified five characteristics of a profession:

(a) a theoretical knowledge base,
(b) protocols of practice,
(c) knowledge is developed via research and transmitted via publications by and among members,
(d) members accept and are held accountable to a service ethic, and
(e) academic preparation and entry are rigorous and controlled.

The scope of professional knowledge required for practice and the manner in which knowledge and skills are acquired have become increasingly important because society has come to expect that practitioners are near perfect in exercising authority. That is, society has become more intolerant of practitioners who err (May, 2001).

If practice in professions merely involved the application of scientific knowledge, pre-service technical training would be sufficient. Schön (1983, 1990) explains, however, that practitioners frequently encounter problems that defy textbook solutions. Studying the treatment of difficult problems, he concluded that highly effective practitioners possessed both theoretical and craft knowledge, the latter being a form of artistry acquired through practice-based experiences. As craft knowledge accumulated, practitioners were increasingly able to resolve or at least manage atypical problems. Scholars generally agree that intuition in the form of craft knowledge plays an important role in practitioner competency, especially with respect to producing and validating evidence. The discovery of penicillin and nylon demonstrates the validity of this conclusion. Both provide "well documented cases of the 'intelligent noticing' of evidence that emerged outside the intellectual infrastructure from which evidence is expected to materialize" (Thomas, 2004, p. 3).

In essence, craft knowledge provides a practitioner with the ability to think beyond the parameters of technical knowledge.

Problem Solving

In professions, practitioners encounter both routine tasks and problems. The former are situations that can be managed successfully by following prescribed or customary actions; they typically require some technical knowledge but little analysis. The latter are perplexing and unique situations characterized by intricate unsettled questions;

they too require technical knowledge but also extensive analysis. Fundamentally, problem solving is an analytical process that entails making and evaluating decisions in relation to problems.

Experiences across professions have demonstrated that practitioners err when they take problems for granted (Nutt, 1989). Unproductive responses are most often rooted in incorrect or superficial perceptions of a situation. According to Heifetz (2006), misdiagnosing problems is one of the five most common mistakes made by administrators and it entails the failure to distinguish between technical and adaptive problems. He explained that the former "have known solutions and can be handled with authoritative expertise. But there are no readily available solutions for adaptive challenges—those that require new ways of thinking and behaving" (p. 512).

When a problem is defined incorrectly or incompletely, subsequent choices (decisions) made in relation to it are likely to be ineffective or possibly counterproductive. Consider a first-grade teacher who described a male student's poor academic performance as "the expected outcome of a limited intellect." Her view of the problem was affected by knowledge of the student's family (e.g., his siblings were not good students and neither of his parents had graduated from high school) and his behavior in the classroom (e.g., he had a low attention span and was socially immature for his age). Her definition of the problem prompted her to make a series of counterproductive decisions. For instance, she decided to ignore or explain away evidence indicating that the student might be dyslexic; she stubbornly refused to refer the student to the school psychologist so that diagnostic tests could be administered; she set low expectations for the student and essentially treated his poor academic performance as being normal.

Because persons have a proclivity to define problems instinctively, cognitive psychologists recommend that three aspects of a situation should guide the framing process: (a) a current state, (b) a desired state, and (c) a lack of a direct obvious way to eliminate the gap between the current state and desired state (Mayer, 1983). In simple terms, a problem exists when something is needed or wanted but the decision maker is unsure what to do in order to attain it (Reys, Lindquist, Lambdin, Smith, & Suydam, 2003). A future state (or desired outcome) should be described using measurable criteria, ensuring that objective and accurate assessment is possible (Clemen, 1996).

After the problem is framed, a practitioner is expected to determine its level of difficulty. One approach for determining difficulty, developed by Reitman (1965), is a four-tier typology. The categories group problems based on current and desired states.

- Category 1 problems include situations in which the current and desired states are well-defined.
- Category 2 problems include situations in which the current state is well-defined but the desired state is poorly defined.
- Category 3 problems include situations in which the current state is poorly defined but the desired state is well-defined.
- Category 4 problems include situations in which both the current and desired states are poorly defined.

Routine problems have low difficulty; therefore, they can usually be addressed successfully by applying technical knowledge and authority. Conversely, difficult problems usually defy textbook solutions. Instead, they require adaptive solutions, actions that lead educators to challenge current practices and to experiment with non-traditional approaches (Heifetz & Linsky, 2002).

Decisions

Decision making, the core process in problem-solving, is basically a three-stage procedure:

1. Identifying choices (alternative decisions), demands (e.g., expectations, job requirements), and constraints (e.g., laws, policy, lack of resources).
2. Evaluating choices in relation to demands and constraints.
3. Selecting the best alternative.

Objective decisions depend on the decision maker's ability to identify and apply criteria that define an acceptable decision (Kowalski et al., 2008). Without criteria, a person cannot rationally determine the merits of each alternative that is being contemplated, and thus, an emotional or political decision becomes more probable.

Ideally, practitioners want to minimize demands (e.g., pressure for a principal to make a decision favorable to one group) and constraints (e.g., eliminating some possible choices because they require additional resources) so that they can identify, assess, and evaluate as many choices as possible (Sergiovanni, 2006). When discretion is eliminated (i.e., a person has only one choice), a practitioner is relegated to functioning as a manager; that is, he or she merely needs to determine *how* a law, policy, or rule will be enforced. As examples, mandatory sentencing laws restrict judges and zero-tolerance policies restrict school administrators. Conversely, discretion (having multiple choices) allows administrators to exert leadership by focusing on *what* should be done to manage a problem (Yukl, 2006).

Decisions, like problems, differ in difficulty. According to Simon (1960), difficulty is determined by three variables and the basic questions they generate.

1. *Frequency—How often is a decision made?* Frequency ranges from "routine" to "unique." Unique decisions are more difficult than routine decisions.
2. *Configuration—To what extent is a problem clear and easily framed?* Configuration ranges from "unstructured" to "structured." Unstructured decisions are more difficult than structured decisions.
3. *Significance—What are the potential consequences?* Significance ranges from "unimportant" to "important." Important decisions are more difficult than unimportant decisions.

Schön (1983, 1990) concluded that decision difficulty was affected by both problems and context. He described three intermediate zones of practice that explain dissimilar levels of difficulty.

1. *Uncertainty*—Problems encountered by practitioners frequently do not occur as well-informed structures. When uncertainty is high, the probability of decision alternatives succeeding or failing is typically unknown; hence, uncertainty increases decision difficulty.
2. *Uniqueness*—Problems encountered by practitioners are frequently unfamiliar in that they were not addressed in textbooks, do not comply with the standards of espoused theories, and do not recur with regularity in practice. When uniqueness is high, the decision maker typically has limited confidence in theoretical knowledge or routine practice; hence, uniqueness increases decision difficulty.
3. *Value conflict*—Problems encountered by practitioners are frequently characterized by competing values and beliefs. When value conflict is high, the decision maker knows that his or her choice is likely to be criticized by some individuals and groups; hence, value conflict increases decision difficulty.

Decision Analysis

Practitioners are expected to engage in *decision analysis*, a process that "provides structure and guidance for thinking systematically about hard decisions" (Clemen, 1996, p. 2). The intent of this scrutiny is to produce prescriptive advice that is especially helpful when a practitioner's overall knowledge is insufficient to make an informed choice intuitively. According to Simon (1960), decision analysis requires an understanding of three different types of decisions.

1. *Programmed*—These decisions are routine, structured, and relatively unimportant; they can usually be made effectively by following pre-established policy and protocols.
2. *Semi-programmed*—These decisions are semi-routine, semi-structured, and moderately important; they can usually be aided by pre-determined policy and protocols.
3. *Un-programmed*—These decisions are uncommon, unstructured, and relatively important; they cannot usually be made effectively by following pre-determined policy or protocols.

A person's understanding of decision difficulty is more complete when he or she evaluates decision choices in relation to contextual variables. Both Table 1.1 and Figure 1.1 summarize decision difficulty based on Simon's (1960) decision characteristics and Schön's (1983, 1990) intermediate zones of practice. Though all the factors are relevant to understanding decision difficulty, uncertainty arguably is the most critical variable because it directly relates to risk—that is, uncertainty increases the likelihood that an alternative will produce negative outcomes (Nutt, 1989).

Models are crucial to decision analysis because they provide both a framework and knowledge that is especially important to making un-programmed decisions (Kowalski, 2008). The literature on decision science identifies three categories of models. Dillon (2006) defined them in the following manner.

Table 1.1 Categorization of decisions based on difficulty.

Decision category	Difficulty factor		
	Programmed	Semi-programmed	Un-programmed
(Simon's decision characteristics)			
Frequency	Routine	Moderately uncommon	Highly uncommon
Configuration	Structured	Moderately unstructured	Highly unstructured
Significance	Unimportant	Moderately important	Highly important
(Schön's intermediate zones)			
Uncertainty	Low	Moderate	High
Uniqueness	Low	Moderate	High
Value conflict	Low	Moderate	High

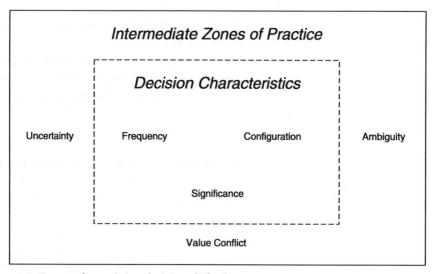

Figure 1.1 Factors determining decision difficulty.

1. *Normative models*—These paradigms stipulate in theory what the decision maker should do.
2. *Prescriptive models*—These paradigms stipulate what the decision maker should and can do.
3. *Descriptive models*—These paradigms describe what decision makers actually have done.

There are a myriad of theories and models across these categories. Identifying and discussing all of them is not practical here; instead, the purpose is to demonstrate their value to practitioners.

Normative Models   Traditionally, decision-making research has been grounded in two assumptions: it is an orderly rational process of choosing from alternative means of accomplishing objectives; it is a logical and sequential process (Owens, 2001). The classical paradigm, the quintessential example of a normative model, is a linear, scientific approach intended to produce the perfect or ideal decision. The classical model was routinely taught to professionals because it was considered to provide:

(a) rules for a potentially disorderly process,
(b) a deductive approach to problem solving, and
(c) predictability, order, technical competence, impersonality, and objective reasoning.

(Tanner & Williams, 1981)

The model was initially designed and deployed in economics in a context in which the decision maker acted as a "maximizer" (Razik & Swanson, 2002); that is, he or she quantified alternatives to determine the absolute best one.

Simon (1997), however, pointed out that the classical approach is based on a number of faulty assumptions. Most notably, it assumes that

(a) all possible decision alternatives can be identified (when in fact only a few can typically be identified),
(b) all consequences that would follow each alternative are known or could be accurately predicted (when in fact such knowledge is only fragmentary), and
(c) quantitative values can be assigned objectively and accurately to each alternative (when in fact values attached to consequences can only be imperfectly anticipated).

Other critics, for example, March (1978), add that decision makers are either unaware of their preferences or they avoid, suppress, or change them when selecting a preferred alternative. Moreover, ideal decisions are uncommon because decision makers typically are unable to (a) frame the problem perfectly, (b) acquire all pertinent information, and (c) devote the time required for extensive analysis (Zey, 1992).

Prescriptive Models   Prescriptive models are scientific and achievable. The *expected utility model* has been one of the most widely studied and used. Its purpose is to produce a "good" decision; that is, it provides a process that helps the decision maker to select a known and plausible alternative that best achieves his or her objective (Baron, 1996). The concept of utility is based on *transitivity* and *connectedness* (Baron, 2000). The former refers to the relative value of alternatives in relation to each other. For example, if a teacher identifies three alternatives for increasing a student's participation in class, she would make paired comparisons of them—that is, the first alternative (A) would be compared with the second alternative (B), the second alternative (B) with the third alternative (C). Connectedness means that in each paired comparison, one alternative is either found to be better or the two are deemed to have equal value. The model stipulates that there is no such thing as a non-answer for a comparison (i.e., concluding the utility relationship cannot be established). The best alternative emerges after the comparisons are completed.

The *behavioral model* has also been one of the most widely studied and used prescriptive paradigms. Often confused with the classical model because it deploys a nearly identical linear approach, this paradigm differs from the classical model in two important ways. First, it rejects the classical model's four flawed assumptions (that decision makers can be unbiased, that they can acquire all pertinent information, that they can identify all plausible alternatives, and that they can make an ideal decision). Second, it is guided by the principle of *bounded rationality*, a concept that features *satisficing* as its core principle. Satisficing entails selecting the first available satisfactory course of action instead of endlessly searching for the ideal course of action (Hellreigel & Slocum, 1996). March and Simon (1958) described the difference between an ideal and satisfactory decision as "the difference between searching a haystack to find the sharpest needle in it and searching the haystack to find a needle sharp enough to sew with" (pp. 140–141).

Descriptive Models   Descriptive models provide insights about actual decision-making behavior, and they are based primarily on research. *Incremental decision making*, for example, is a pragmatic process reflective of political influences commonly found in organizations (Lindblom, 1993). Typically it occurs when the decision maker's intent is to minimize organizational change; thus, he or she analyzes choices in an effort to determine the extent to which each is likely to disrupt the status quo. Values are assigned to alternatives based on the extent they are expected to produce change; that is, alternatives expected to produce considerable change are given low value and those expected to produce little or no change are given high value. For example, consider a committee of teachers that must recommend one of five possible mathematics textbooks. Instead of seeking to select the best text, the members focus on making a choice that will not be disruptive or politically unacceptable to their peers. Thus, instead of valuing each book on its merits, they value each book based on its alignment with current practices.

The *garbage can model* is another popular descriptive model that evolved from observations of organizational decision making. Researchers discovered that traditional decision-making models often got inverted; that is, solutions were proposed before problems were framed (in fact, the model is often described as a decision in search of a problem). Cohen, March, and Olsen (1972) used a garbage can as a metaphor to explain how and why this occurred. They noted that when two conditions were favorable, an administrator could make a decision that otherwise would be unacceptable. One condition was the emergence of a change opportunity and the other was a favorable mix of organizational members showing interest in the situation. As an example, consider a new elementary school principal who attempted to implement cooperative learning. About two-thirds of the faculty opposed the concept and thwarted efforts to implement it. After the school was placed on probation because 42% of the third-grade students fell below the state's benchmark in reading, the principal again proposed cooperative learning. This time, most of the opponents were passive and a few even supported the principal's recommendation. Being placed on probation created a change opportunity and resulted in fluid participation (i.e., the right mix of people showing interest) that allowed the principal to implement his preferred decision. Decisions made in this manner frequently prove to be counter-productive because they (a) involve unproven or ineffective initiatives (Tarter & Hoy, 1998), (b) are inconsistent with previous decisions, and (c) are poorly defined in terms of purpose and expected outcomes (Schmid, Dodd, & Tropman, 1987).

Evidence-Based Practice in Professions

In traditional science, knowledge is constructed through model building and testing intended to invalidate an inaccurate view and replace it with one that is more accurate. Babbie (1998) used an example from astronomy to explain this process. He noted that no modern astronomer believes that the sun revolves around the earth; yet, there was a time when this belief was widely held because it was untested. In the physical sciences, rationality emerged as a reasonable and defensible norm because laboratory research could be isolated substantially from political, economic, and social variables. In the late 1950s and early 1960s, scholars in the social sciences also began embracing pure rationality even though controlled studies outside laboratories are extremely difficult. Even so, the rationalist approach has continued to be prevalent in the social sciences (Carney & Williams, 1997).

In professions, evidence provides the building blocks for constructing and refining knowledge. Evidence-based practice involves the use of evidence underlying knowledge to make important decisions in relation to problem solving. Consequently, our understanding for evidence and EBP are essential.

Evidence

Dictionaries define evidence as something providing proof. Focusing on teaching, Hargreaves (1997) referred to evidence as information that verifies effective practice. The most readily identified (and valued) form of evidence in professions is *empirical evidence*—verification embedded in espoused theories, especially those that were developed from controlled, quantitative studies (Whitehurst, 2007). Argyris and Schön (1974), however, noted that theoretical knowledge is also produced from *in-use theories* (now commonly called *action theories*). In the case of education, these constructs are developed in practice and based on relevant experiences educators have in and out of the schools (Osterman & Kottkamp, 1993).

Whitehurst (2007) posits action theories, which he calls *professional wisdom*, represent the consensus views of teachers regarding normative behavior.[2] Perhaps most important, they constitute the intuitive dimension of practice; that is, they are instinctive dispositions that guide behavior in relation to problems. Mayer (2003), however, believes that validity and reliability of data depend on how they are produced. He contends that all scientific methods, ranging from controlled experiments to systematic observations in natural contexts, are acceptable sources of evidence whereas fads, doctrines (e.g., constructivism), and popular practices are not. Given this perspective, teacher observation reports (developed objectively and consistently) are evidence.

Various types of records routinely maintained in schools also provide valuable data. Examples include student records, such as achievement and ability test scores, student progress reports, and attendance data. National, state, and local demographic reports and accreditation reports may also contain useful data.

Data, including those derived from controlled research studies, do not have equal value in relation to a specific decision. According to Thomas (2004), evidence value is determined by three criteria.

1. *Relevance* involves the extent to which information refutes or supports an assertion. If a piece of evidence is relevant, it is pertinent to the problem and to decisions made in relation to the problem.
2. *Sufficiency* involves corroborating a piece of evidence by interfacing it with other pieces of evidence. From a sufficiency perspective, data are categorized as (a) isolated observations (an inspiration), (b) prima facie evidence (a hunch), (c) corroborative evidence (a rational belief), or (d) conclusive evidence (knowledge).
3. *Veracity* involves determining if a piece of evidence is free of contamination (e.g., errors) and vested interests (e.g., bias).

When data are assessed using these criteria, their value differences become apparent. The relationship between data and the problem being addressed is more important than the methods that were used to produce the data (Mayer, 2003).

Applying Evidence in Practice

Basically, EBP is relying on evidence to shape decisions. The EBP movement is rooted in decision-making research "aimed at improving rather than understanding human capability" (Eraut, 2004, p. 93). The concept originated as a philosophy encouraging practitioners to use current best evidence conscientiously and judiciously to inform their decisions (Sackett et al., 2000). It is grounded in the belief that practitioners are responsible for (a) stating their intended outcomes, (b) providing a rationale for their selected interventions, and (c) identifying the evidence on which they relied (Rosen, 1993). According to Eraut (2004), three conditions are especially relevant to engaging in EBP:

1. Practitioners must have easy and quick access to substantial amounts of information.
2. Professions must facilitate a relevant research and practitioners must integrate research outcomes into practice.
3. Practitioners must use modern technology to access and apply data.

The development of information-based societies has clearly made EBP more possible and popular. As examples, massive amounts of data have been accumulated and stored in the past few decades. These databases have become accessible to practitioners by virtue of modern technologies and the quantity and quality of research being conducted in and for professions has increased substantially (Howard, McMillen, & Pollio, 2003).

Applications of EBP have been especially prevalent in medicine. In the context of this profession, Cordell and Chisholm (2001, p. 13) describe EBP as a four-stage process.

1. Formulating answerable questions.
2. Rapidly searching for best evidence to answer these questions.
3. Critically appraising the evidence for validity and applicability.
4. Integrating this appraisal with clinical expertise and patients' values, and applying it to the individual patient.

Other authors writing about EBP generically (e.g., Peile, 2004; Thyer, 2004) include evaluation of outcomes as a fifth stage.

In order to conduct focused searches, practitioners must be able to identify their evidence needs accurately (Howard et al., 2003). As noted earlier, this is the primary reason why a person's ability to frame a problem accurately is so critical. In addition, practitioners must possess other requisite application skills. Specifically, they include (a) the ability to access, evaluate, and use information in a timely manner, (b) a commitment to rely on multiple sources of evidence, and (c) a commitment to evaluate outcomes objectively (Kowalski et al., 2008). Relationships between the EBP stages and the requisite skills are illustrated in Figure 1.2.

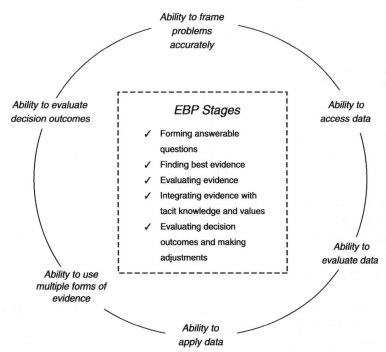

Figure 1.2 Stages of evidence-based practice in the context of required practitioner expertise.

The literature on EBP reveals that not all practitioners support the process, even in scientific and high-status professions such as medicine. Rejection is usually anchored in a conviction that EBP restricts practitioners to using only certain types of evidence. Physicians disparaging EBP, for example, argue that relying entirely on empirical evidence denigrates clinical expertise, artistry, and patient values (Straus & McAlister, 2000). Proponents counter by asserting that the opposite is actually true; that is, they contend that correctly defined and applied, EBP requires the integration of espoused theory, action theories, and patient values (Cordell & Chisholm, 2001).

Barriers to Evidence-Based Practice in Education

Surprisingly little has been written about the potentialities of EBP in education. Negative responses to the data-driven decision-making requirements in NCLB, however, suggest that many educators would oppose or at least be skeptical of the process. Basically, there are three types of potential impediments to making EBP normative in education: barriers to *understanding*, barriers to *accepting*, and barriers to *implementing*.

Understanding

Understanding involves information and knowledge. Opposition to EBP across professions is frequently related to inaccurate interpretations. Most notably, the process has frequently been defined too narrowly as the application of findings derived solely from quantitative experimental studies. A lack of understanding is likely to be highly detrimental in education for two reasons. First, most administrators and teachers have only a limited understanding of research (Sarason, 1996). Second, education scholars have expressed vastly different views about the value of research to practice (Phillips & Burbules, 2000); for example, Mayer (2003) contends that many education professors are skeptical of positivist views, and those who are postmodernists believe all research is hopelessly biased. Recognizing the damaging effects of inaccurate interpretations, proponents of EBP in other professions (e.g., psychology and social work) have predicted that opposition to the concept will persist until it is defined in a profession-specific manner, presented to students in the early stages of their professional studies, and applied consistently in professional studies and practice (Howard et al., 2003).

An accurate conceptualization of EBP among educators may also be thwarted by negative dispositions toward NCLB. Data-based, decision-making provisions in the law have been interpreted by some authors (e.g., Feuer, Towne, & Shavelson, 2002; Ryan & Hood, 2004) as promoting a narrow definition of scientific evidence.[3] More specifically, critics believe that NCLB fails to treat quantitative and qualitative research as being epistemologically similar and equally relevant.

Accepting

Understanding EBP correctly does not ensure philosophical acceptance; even so, knowledge makes it more likely that a practitioner will deploy the concept. Slovic and Tversky (1974) referred to the nexus between personal knowledge and attitudes as the *understanding-acceptance principle*—a belief that the deeper the understanding of a normative standard, the greater the inclination to respond in accord with it. Research on decision making has generally supported this principle (Stanovich & West, 1999). Yet, knowledge does not consistently result in acceptance as evidenced by the fact that staff development often fails to alter teaching or administrative practice.

Historically, educators have been expected to manage; that is, much of what they have been required to do pertained to *how* something should be done. For instance, principals and teachers focus primarily on how to implement a pre-determined curriculum or reform mandates. Rarely, if ever, are they required to decide *what* should be done to improve schools (Talbert & McLaughlin, 1994). By comparison, practitioners in most other professions have been expected to resolve difficult problems requiring them to make un-programmed decisions; thus, they have to decide, individually or collectively with peer practitioners, *what* should be done to resolve such problems. Un-programmed decisions are more difficult than programmed decisions because the outcomes are unknown and risk of failure is relatively high. Consequently, having to make un-programmed decisions socializes practitioners to accept reasonable levels of risk whereas requiring only programmed decisions socializes practitioners to avoid failure (Bassett, 1970).[4]

With few exceptions, educators have not been held accountable for determining what should be done to improve schooling. As a result, their socialization has encouraged them to avoid failure—a proclivity that nurtures an aversion to risk (Darling-Hammond, 1989). Expectedly, traditional socialization in the education profession has become a major impediment to school reform (York-Barr & Duke, 2004), primarily because many of the problems that need to be corrected are adaptive challenges requiring educators to think outside the parameters of their technical knowledge (Heifetz, 2006). In other words, they are problems requiring educators to take some reasonable risks.

Philosophical rejection of EBP has also been due to suspicions about political motives. Disagreement over EBP in the United Kingdom provides an example. Critiquing applications to education in that country, Pirrie (2001) argued that the concept was actually a social and political value promoted by the same individuals who had determined incorrectly that schools were in a crisis situation. Much in the same manner, opponents of NCLB have often characterized data-based decision making as an initiative created and promoted by would-be reformers who view public education as a failed monopoly.

Implementing

Even educators who understand and accept EBP may question whether they have the capacity to implement it. Their doubts center primarily on two issues: their ability to gain public acceptance of them as legitimate professionals and their ability to acquire resources needed to implement the concept effectively.

As political institutions, schools are vulnerable to public opinion. During the last half of the twentieth century most districts in the United States became increasingly diverse; and since philosophical dissonance (competing values and beliefs) is endemic in demographic diversity (Stout, Tallerico, & Scribner, 1994), citizen involvement in education became progressively more politicized (Danzberger & Usdan, 1994). At the same time, however, educators continued to face the seemingly contradictory challenge of providing intellectual leadership while remaining sensitive (and often subservient) to the political will of stakeholders (Wirt & Kirst, 2001). This conundrum is reflective of manifest tensions between democracy and professionalism (Zeichner, 1991). To alleviate the inevitable conflict, society permitted educators to call themselves professionals even though they were denied autonomy and limited authority away from schools (Kowalski, 2004). The public's ambivalence toward the education profession has been demonstrated by political decisions related to school reform. Most notably, many change initiatives over the past few decades have promoted teacher empowerment (a concept providing added status and autonomy) while requiring greater levels of citizen involvement in governance. The interests of the two strategies resulted in inevitable conflict; and when this became apparent, citizen empowerment almost always took precedent. As a result, educators actually lost power (Bauch & Goldring, 1998).

In addition to political barriers, EBP is confronted with economic obstacles. In the aftermath of NCLB, school administrators have discovered that the costs of storing, accessing, and using databases are considerable. They have also realized that many employees are not prepared to engage in EBP, and correcting this problem, either through internal staff development or through external continuing education involves substantial costs. Many of the same policy makers who are demanding data-based decision making and educator accountability have been less than enthusiastic about appropriating additional funding to ensure that educators could actually implement EBP.

Concluding Comments

Much of the school reform literature is consistent on one point: the extent to which schools will improve depends substantially on how educators solve problems and make decisions. In an information-rich society where the production of scientific evidence continues to accelerate, EBP offers a relevant paradigm for both of these essential processes. Yet, there is a distinct possibility that the concept will never be widely adopted in schools, possibly because it is misunderstood, possibly because it is politically or philosophically unacceptable, or possibly because the districts and schools lack required resources. When defined accurately, EBP integrates empirical evidence, tacit knowledge, and values; and though it does not require educators to rely solely on scientific data, it creates a responsibility to identify and consider scientific data. And by taking advantage of multiple forms of evidence, educators almost ensure that their assessments and subsequent decisions will become more effective (Stufflebeam & Shinkfield, 2007).

Separating EBP from the political minefields around NCLB will not be easy; many educators already view data-based decision making and the controversial law as being inextricably intertwined. In truth, the concept is embedded in EBP but presented to educators through NCLB. Therefore, it has become imperative that administrators and teachers view data-based decision making as a professional responsibility separate from political convictions.

Educators are more likely to accept EBP if they come to see school reform as a process of solving adaptive problems (Heifetz, 2006). Practicing in the context of this conceptualization, they are more likely to forge learning communities so that they are able to

(a) accurately define the problems that need to be addressed,
(b) identify their primary information needs,
(c) learn to create, evaluate, and apply evidence,
(d) integrate various forms of evidence and values,
(e) value experimentation and risk, and
(f) evaluate the effectiveness of their decisions.

Notes

1. The reauthorization of the Elementary and Secondary Education Act in 2001 is PL 107–110 and is commonly known as the No Child Left Behind Act of 2001.
2. Though aspects of school culture are considered to be ubiquitous (see, for example, Sarason, 1996), research reveals that cultures actually vary in strength (the degree to which the same values are embraced) and quality (the degree to which shared values are congruous with the professional knowledge base). Consequently, professional wisdom, as expressed in a school culture, also varies in strength and accuracy.
3. NCLB (2001) describes scientific research as a "rigorous, systematic, and objective methodology to obtain reliable and valid knowledge appropriate to the research being conducted, employing systematic, empirical methods that draw on observation or experiment" (p. 116).
4. Work with open-ended (Type B) case studies demonstrates that a considerable number of teacher education students have an aversion to decision making, especially when the decisions are perceived as being risky (Kowalski, 2008). Individuals not inclined to risk taking prefer to be in situations where failure avoidance is rewarded (Bassett, 1970). As an example, teachers who prefer failure avoidance seek close supervision and direction from the principal. The extent to which this disposition is innate or cultural (i.e., produced by an organization's culture) is not precisely known (Kowalski et al., 2008).

References

Argyris, C., & Schön, D. A. (1974). *Theory in practice: Increasing professional effectiveness.* San Francisco: Jossey-Bass.

Babbie, E. (1998). *The practice of social research* (8th ed.). Belmont, CA: Wadsworth.

Baron, J. (1996). Norm-endorsement utilitarianism and the nature of utility. *Economics and Philosophy, 12,* 165–182.

Baron, J. (2000). *Thinking and deciding* (3rd ed.). New York: Cambridge University Press.

Bassett, G. A. (1970). Leadership style and strategy. In L. Netzer, G. Eye, A. Graef, R. Drey, & J. Overman (Eds.), *Interdisciplinary foundations of supervision* (pp. 221–231). Boston: Allyn & Bacon.

Bauch, P., & Goldring, E. (1998). Parent–teacher participation in the context of school restructuring. *Peabody Journal of Education, 73,* 15–35.

Bauman, P. C. (1996). *Governing education: Public sector reform or privatization.* Boston: Allyn & Bacon.

Carney, D. P., & Williams, R. (1997). No such thing as . . . scientific management. *Management Decision, 35*(10), 779–784.

Clemen, R. T. (1996). *Making hard decisions: An introduction to decision analysis* (2nd ed.). Belmont, CA: Duxbury Press.

Cohen, M. D., March, J. G., & Olsen, J. P. (1972). A garbage can model of organizational choice. *Administrative Science Quarterly, 7*(1), 1–25.

Cordell, W. H., & Chisholm, C. D. (2001). Will the real evidence-based medicine please stand up? *Emergency Medicine News, 23*(6), 4, 11–14.

Curtis, E. (2000). Defining a profession. *Inscriptions, 14*(12), 5.

Danzberger, J. P., & Usdan, M. D. (1994). Local education governance: Perspectives on problems and strategies for change. *Phi Delta Kappan, 75*(5), 366.

Darling-Hammond, L. (1989). Accountability for professional practice. *Teachers College Record, 91*, 59–80.

Dillon, S. M. (2006). *Descriptive decision making: Comparing theory with practice.* Retrieved February 6, 2006, from www.esc.auckland.ac.nz/organisations/orsnz/conf33/papers/p61.pdf

Eraut, M. (2004). Practice-based evidence. In G. Thomas & R. Pring (Eds.), *Evidence-based practice in education* (pp. 91–102). Maidenhead, UK: Open University Press.

Feuer, M. J., Towne, L., & Shavelson, R. J. (2002). Scientific culture and educational research. *Educational Researcher, 31*(8), 4–14.

Hargreaves, D. (1997). In defense of research for evidence-based teaching: A rejoinder to Martyn Hammersley. *British Educational Research Journal, 23*(4), 405–419.

Heifetz, R. A. (2006). Educational leadership: Beyond a focus on instruction. *Phi Delta Kappan, 87*(7), 512–513.

Heifetz, R., & Linsky, M. (2002). *Leadership on the line: Staying alive through the dangers of leading.* Boston: Harvard Business School Press.

Hellreigel, D., & Slocum, J. W. (1996). *Management* (7th ed.). Cincinnati, OH: South-Western College Publishing.

Howard, M. O., McMillen, C. J., & Pollio, D. E. (2003). Teaching evidence-based practice: Toward a new paradigm for social work education. *Research on Social Work Practice, 13*(2), 234–259.

Kowalski, T. J. (2004). The ongoing war for the soul of school administration. In T. J. Lasley (Ed.), *Better leaders for America's schools: Perspectives on the Manifesto* (pp. 92–114). Columbia, MO: University Council for Educational Administration.

Kowalski, T. J. (2008). *Case studies in educational administration* (5th ed.). Boston: Allyn & Bacon.

Kowalski, T. J., Lasley, T. J., & Mahoney, J. (2008). *Data-driven decisions and school leadership: Best practices for school improvement.* Boston: Allyn & Bacon.

Larson, M. S. (1977). *The rise of professionalism: A sociological analysis.* Berkeley: University of California Press.

Levant, R. F. (2005). Evidence-based practice in psychology. *Monitor on Psychology, 36*(2). Retrieved August 20, 2007, from http://www.apa.org/monitor/feb05/pc.html

Lindblom, C. E. (1993). *The science of muddling through.* New York: Irvington.

March, J. G. (1978). Bounded rationality, ambiguity, and the engineering of choice. *Bell Journal of Economics, 9*, 587–608.

March, J. G., & Simon, H. (1958). *Organizations.* New York: John Wiley.

May, W. F. (2001). *Beleaguered rulers: The public obligation of the professional.* Louisville, KY: Westminster John Knox Press.

Mayer, R. E. (1983). *Thinking, problem solving, cognition.* New York: W. H. Freeman and Company.

Mayer, R. E. (2003). Learning environments: The case for evidence-based practice and issue-driven research. *Educational Psychology Review, 15*(4), 359–366.

No Child Left Behind Act of 2001, Pub. L. No. 107–110, 115 Stat. 1425 (2002).

Nutt, P. C. (1989). *Making tough decisions: Tactics for improving managerial decision making.* San Francisco: Jossey-Bass.

Osterman, K. F., & Kottkamp, R. B. (1993). *Reflective practice for educators: Improving schooling through professional development.* Newbury Park, CA: Corwin Press.

Owens, R. G. (2001). *Organizational behavior in education* (6th ed.). Boston: Allyn & Bacon.

Peile, E. (2004). Reflections from medical practice: Balancing evidence-based practice with practice-based practice. In G. Thomas & R. Pring (Eds.), *Evidence-based practice in education* (pp. 102–118). Maidenhead, UK: Open University Press.

Phillips, D. C., & Burbules, N. C. (2000). *Postpositivism and educational research.* Lanham, MD: Rowman & Littlefield.

Pirrie, A. (2001). Evidence-based practice in education: The best medicine? *British Journal of Educational Studies, 49*(2), 124–136.

Razik, T. A., & Swanson, A. D. (2002). *Fundamental concepts of educational leadership* (2nd ed.). Boston: Allyn & Bacon.

Reitman, W. R. (1965). *Cognition and thought: An information processing approach.* New York: Wiley.

Reys, R., Lindquist, M., Lambdin, D., Smith, N., & Suydam, M. (2003). *Helping children learn mathematics* (6th ed.). New York: John Wiley & Sons.

Rosen, A. (1993). Systematic planned practice. *Social Service Review, 3,* 84–100.

Ryan, K. E., & Hood, L. K. (2004). Guarding the castle and opening the gates. *Qualitative Inquiry, 10*(1), 79–95.

Sackett, D. L., Straus, S. E., Richardson, W. S., Rosenberg, W., & Haynes, R. B. (2000). *Evidence-based medicine: How to practice and teach EBM* (2nd ed.). New York: Churchill Livingstone.

Sarason, S. (1996). *Revisiting "the culture of school and the problem of change."* New York: Teachers College Press.

Schmid, H., Dodd, P., & Tropman, J. E. (1987). Board decision making in human service organizations. *Human Systems Management, 7*(2), 155–161.

Schön, D. A. (1983). *The reflective practitioner.* New York: Basic Books.

Schön, D. A. (1990). *Educating the reflective practitioner.* San Francisco: Jossey-Bass.

Sergiovanni, T. J. (2006). *The principalship: A reflective practice perspective* (5th ed.). Boston: Allyn & Bacon.

Simon, H. A. (1960). *The new science of management decisions.* New York: Harper & Row.

Simon, H. A. (1997). *Administrative behavior: A study of decision-making processes in administrative organizations* (4th ed.). New York: Simon & Schuster.

Slovic, P., & Tversky, A. (1974). Who accepts Savage's axiom? *Behavioral Science, 19,* 368–373.

Stanovich, K. E., & West, R. F. (1999). Discrepancies between normative and descriptive models of decision making and the understanding/acceptance principle. *Cognitive Psychology, 38*(3), 349–385.

Stout, R. T., Tallerico, M., & Scribner, K. P. (1994). Values: The "what?" of the politics of education. *Journal of Education Policy, 9*(5–6), 5–20.

Straus, S. E., & McAlister, F. A. (2000). Evidence-based medicine: A commentary on the common criticisms. *Canadian Medical Association Journal, 163,* 837–841.

Stufflebeam, D. L., & Shinkfield, A. J. (2007). *Evaluation theory, models, and applications.* San Francisco: Jossey-Bass.

Talbert, J. E., & McLaughlin, M. W. (1994). Teacher professionalism in local school contexts. *American Journal of Education, 102,* 123–153.

Tanner, C. K., & Williams, E. J. (1981). *Educational planning and decision making: A view through the organizational process.* Lexington, MA: D. C. Heath & Company.

Tarter, C. J., & Hoy, W. K. (1998). Toward a contingency theory of decision making. *Journal of Educational Administration, 36*(3–4), 212–228.

Thomas, G. (2004). Introduction: Evidence and practice. In G. Thomas & R. Pring (Eds.), *Evidence-based practice in education* (pp. 1–18). Maidenhead, UK: Open University Press.

Thyer, B. A. (2004). What is evidence-based practice? *Brief Treatment and Crisis Intervention, 4*(2), 167–176.

Whitehurst, G. J. (2007) *Evidence-based education.* Retrieved August 21, 2007, from http://www.ed.gov/nclb/methods/whatworks/eb/evidencebased.pdf

Wirt, F., & Kirst, M. (2001). *The political dynamics of American education.* Berkeley, CA: McCutchan.

York-Barr, J., & Duke, K. (2004). What do we know about teacher leadership? Findings from two decades of scholarship. *Review of Educational Research, 74*(3), 255–316.

Yukl, G. (2006). *Leadership in organizations* (6th ed.). Upper Saddle River, NJ: Prentice Hall.

Zeichner, K. M. (1991). Contradictions and tensions in the professionalization of teaching and the democratization of schools. *Teachers College Record, 92*(3), 363–379.

Zey, M. (1992). *Decision making: Alternatives to rational choice models.* Newbury Park, CA: Sage.

2

Ethics Based Decision Making by Educational Leaders

Paul T. Begley
Pennsylvania State University

Research on school principals' valuation processes (Begley & Johansson, 1998), as well as earlier research conducted on administrative problem-solving processes by Leithwood and Steinbach (1995), demonstrate that administrators tend to consciously employ ethics as a guide to action relatively infrequently and under particular conditions. Ethics based postures tend to be relevant to certain types of administrative decision processes and not always considered by school leaders as an appropriate basis for decision making in other administrative situations, particularly those occurring in culturally diverse contexts or where accountability is a major consideration (Begley & Johansson, 1998). The circumstances where ethics tend to surface are situations of high stakes urgency, when consensus is impossible, when responding to unprecedented situations, and for certain hot-topic social issues that tend to escalate debate to a point where people seek refuge within an ethical posture. These findings appear to be consistent across the practices of school leaders in several countries. Ethics are culturally derived norms and if the context for leadership action is multicultural there can be issues associated with shared interpretations of ethical postures grounded in the experience of one culture and not another.

The implication for school leaders engaged in decision making is the need to understand the ways in which values and ethical frameworks are relevant to their professional work. As will be proposed, valuation processes can be relevant to leadership in quite specific ways as conscious and unconscious influences on the cognitive processes of individuals, as rubrics or codes for responding to problematic situations, and as meta-values around which to establish consensus on shared objectives and purposes.

The Moral Context of School Leadership Situations

The application of any ethic occurs within a normative and cultural context. However, in scholarly settings ethical postures and frameworks are often presented as abstract concepts stripped of the contextual details that would give them relevance and specificity in particular settings and in support of particular roles. This can result in a number of problems. The most obvious problem is that an ethic stripped of context requires interpretation as it is applied to a particular social or cultural context. This can be a serious challenge in culturally diverse societies where, for example, headgear (e.g. Sikh turban) is sometimes more than just a hat, or daggers are religious symbols and not so much a weapon. Or consider how a "focus on mission" as a professional ethical posture would mean radically different things to a school principal as compared to an infantry officer. Moreover, human nature being what it is, individuals, groups, and societies are often inclined to interpret ethics in ways that are appropriate to their preferences and traditions rather than any commitment to the social inclusion of minorities. These interpretations can often extend to preserving self-interests at the expense of the freedom of others. If the moral deliberation is being carried out by a person in a professional role, the process becomes even more complicated because professionals are also expected to be agents of society or of their profession. So, their pursuit of ethical decision making must involve more than addressing their own belief systems.

The sheer austerity and abstractness of many ethical frameworks poses a second challenge for those interested in employing ethics as a component of educational decision making. Practitioners tend to be attracted to practicality and relevance. By their nature, philosophically based discussions about ethics and valuation processes may not be very appealing in terms of relevance because of the context-stripped manner in which they are usually portrayed. For example, the ethics of administration, as proposed by Strike, Haller, and Soltis (1998), identify maximizing benefits and respecting individual rights through protocols of due process as key notions associated with an ethic of justice perspective. However, the task of clarifying the inherent benefits associated with a situation, and the fair distribution of benefits among an a priori identified set of potential recipients, all sorted according to degree of entitlement and need, is something that requires contextual knowledge as well as skill. Indeed, this is one of the reasons why the use of context-rich case problems, critical incidents, and dilemmas of practice is probably the most successful way to teach and study ethical analysis and valuation processes with practitioners.

For these reasons there is a lot of merit in speaking of ethical actions within a specific professional context or through the use of heuristic applications of ethical postures appropriate to a professional or personal context. There are several examples of this that can be used as illustrations. Furman (2003) uses the "ethic of community" as a focus point for ethical educational practice in North American schools. Stefkovich (2006) adopts the notion of "best interests of students" as a focus for her professional ethics in education. Begley (2006) speaks of "authentic leadership" as an approach to presenting ethical leadership practices and moral literacy in a manner that has relevance for people working in school leadership situations. However, even these context grounded heuristic applications require definition and the establishment of consensus on meaning. Fortunately, there is literature that can be helpful in this regard. Stefkovich and Begley (2007) and Stefkovich and O'Brien (2004) have identified and explored the various meanings associated with the concept of "best interests." When it comes to "authentic leadership," Begley (2006) points out that this perspective that has been explored in recent years by several other scholars beyond himself, including Taylor (1991), Duignan and Bhindi (1997), and Starratt (2004). Authentic leadership, as Begley defines it, is the outcome of self-knowledge, sensitivity to the orientations of others, and a technical sophistication that leads to a synergy of leadership action (Begley, 2001, 2003, 2006). It is in this context that Begley proposes authentic leadership as a relevant way of conceptualizing educational leadership processes. It is a way of thinking about ethical and effective leadership that is grounded in professional practices and orientations that have meaning for school administrators.

Ethics and Values

Whether or not values and ethics are consciously employed as guides to decision making by individuals, they remain in general an important influence on the cognitive processes of individuals and groups of individuals. Values can be formally defined as conceptions of the desirable with motivating force characteristic of individuals, groups, organizations, and societies that influence choices made from available resources and means (Hodgkinson, 1978). Begley (2006) describes the influence of values within individuals as the internal psychological reflections of more distilled levels of motivation (e.g. a concern for personal interests, consequences, or consensus) that become tangible to an observer in the form of attitudes, speech, and actions. Thus, values in their various forms, including ethics, can be thought of as conscious or unconscious influences on attitudes, actions, and speech. However, it is important to note that valuation processes can involve more than ethics. Values can take different forms and can be best categorized according to their motivational grounding. Ethics, as a particular form of values, as opposed to the study of Ethics as a scholarly discipline, are normative social ideals or codes of conduct usually grounded in the cultural experience of particular societies. In that sense they are a sort of *uber* form of social consensus. For example, many societies have core ethics equivalent to the American notions of democracy, freedom of speech, and the priority of individual rights. Those of us steeped in the traditions of such classic Western philosophical thought can easily make the mistake of assuming that our most cherished ethical postures, such as democracy, are universal. However, they seldom are, especially as interpreted from culture to culture. Ethics in their purest forms tend to be expressed in a relatively context-stripped form that conveys only the essence of the normative behavior. Indeed, in some forms and social applications they are treated as absolute values. This inclination to view ethics as some sort of absolute value is sometimes inappropriately enabled by evidence of consensus across cultures on certain ethics like respect for human rights, honesty, and democracy. And, indeed there are probably some ethics of the human condition that approach a condition of universal relevance. However, the devil is literally in the details when it comes to ethical postures. The interpretation of meaning associated with an ethic can vary greatly from society to society. Simply pondering the contrasting notions of what constitutes democracy in countries like Sweden, the United States, and China illustrates this point. Except perhaps in the most culturally homogeneous of contexts, using ethical postures as a basis for making social choices requires the inclusion of a dialogic component. This is because of our increasingly culturally diverse societies and a more globalized world. This is not to argue against the relevance and importance of ethics to leadership actions. It is more a caveat to their proper use.

There is another issue when it comes to ethics and their relevance to educational decision-making processes. Human behavior involves a range of motivational bases, only a few of which can be associated with ethical postures. These other motivational bases can range from self-interest to a concern for rationalized positions grounded in consensus or consequences, in addition to the transrational groundings of ethical postures (Begley, 2006; Hodgkinson, 1978). The point is that because ethical postures are usually associated with ideal states, they do not necessarily accommodate the full range of motivations for human behavior. This circumstance is critically important to individuals in leadership positions seeking to understand their own motivational bases as well as those of others. It hardly needs to be said that not all individuals encountered in organizational settings act in ethical ways. Ethics based postures are highly relevant for guiding appropriate responses to complex organizational situations, but they may not be sufficient in themselves for a comprehensive analysis and understanding of human motivations. There is some evidence for this assertion.

As argued earlier, in order to lead effectively, individuals in any leadership role need to understand human nature and the motivations of individuals in particular. Leadership is essentially focused on people and relationships. In the practical professional context of educational administration, school leaders need more than just normative ideology, as relevant as that may be to educational situations. They require frameworks and ways of thinking that will encompass the full range of human motivations and valuation processes encountered in school settings. As indicated above, these can range from the more primitive forms of self-interest all the way to the most altruistic and inspiring transrational values of saints and heroes. To understand and accommodate the full range of human motivations, which are understood to be an important influence on the adoption of particular values (Begley, 2006), one must think in terms of *values* and *valuation processes* where ethics (as opposed to the field of inquiry called Ethics) are one category or component within a broader spectrum of value types. Furthermore, a full appreciation of ethics should include more than just a concern for the high ground of ethics-motivated action. The study of ethics should be as much about the life-long personal struggle to be ethical, about failures to be ethical, the inconsistencies of ethical postures, the masquerading of self-interest and personal preference as ethical action, and the dilemmas which occur in everyday and professional life when one ethic trumps another.

Foundational Approaches to the Study of Ethics

Scholars, just as much as educational practitioners, tend to come to a conversation about values with perspectives reflecting the quite distinct social contexts of their societies. These scholars also approach the study of valuation processes and ethics from a variety of foundational perspectives. For example, Starratt's (1994) work is grounded in philosophy, whereas Stefkovich (2006; Shapiro & Stefkovich, 2001, 2005; Stefkovich & Shapiro, 2003) is influenced by a legal perspective. Gross and Shapiro (2004) reflect a social justice orientation in their work. Langlois' (2004) orientations are applied ethics and moral theory. Begley's (2004) orientations are on the cognitive processes of administrators engaged in problem solving. Other seminal sources on the subject, from which many of these more recent perspectives derive, include: Hodgkinson's (1978, 1991, 1996) extensive writings on the philosophy of administration; Evers' (Evers & Lakomski, 1991) Australian pragmatist discourse on brain theory, coherence, and the formation of ethical knowledge; and Willower's (1994, 1999) Deweyian naturalistic notions of valuation processes and reflective practice. Recognizing the foundational roots of a values perspective or ethical framework is a first step to establishing a shared vocabulary that will facilitate dialogue across disciplines and establish consensus on key concepts. This in turn can increase capacity among scholars for critical reflection on the theory and frameworks they rely upon, and perhaps even generate new insights of benefit to the whole field. Conversely, in the more practical context of teaching about ethics, decision making, and moral literacy in general, it is essential that instructors as well as learners know and understand the epistemological and foundational roots of the frameworks and literature used to structure their courses. Those interested in a more detailed discussion of the epistemological roots of the values and ethics literature are invited to look at Langlois' and Begley's mapping out of existing literature and research on moral leadership in Begley (2006).

Where Do Ethics Fit into Educational Decision Making?

Values, ethics, and valuation processes relate to leadership and educational decision-making processes in several important ways. Perhaps the most fundamental way in which values relate to leadership is as an influence on the cognitive processes of individuals and groups of individuals. It is important, perhaps essential, for persons in leadership roles to understand how values reflect underlying human motivations and shape the subsequent attitudes, speech, and actions of personnel (Begley, 2006; Hodgkinson, 1978; Kohlberg & Turiel, 1971). Begley's conception of authentic forms of leadership (2006) emphasizes this capacity as something that begins with self-knowledge and then becomes extended to sensitivity to the perspectives of others. In that context it is argued that leaders should know their own values and ethical predispositions, as well as be sensitive to the value orientations of others. Branson (2006) has developed a very effective instructional strategy called the deeply structured reflection process that can be used as a support for developing this kind of knowledge and self-awareness. It involves the identification by individuals of critical incidents that have contributed to their personal or professional formation. Through deconstruction of, and reflection on, personal narratives of critical incidents, individuals develop an awareness of how their motivations, values, and attitudes are derived and become predictive indicators of their actions in response to situations they will encounter in the future.

Consistent with this line of thinking, Begley (2006) proposes that genuine forms of leadership begin with the understanding and thoughtful interpretation of observed or experienced valuation processes by individuals. This implies the appropriateness of a focus on the perceptions of individuals in the context of school leadership situations. Although organizational theories, the policy arena, and other macro perspectives are relevant as elements of the context in which a school leader works, they are not a primary locus of concern.

A second way in which valuation processes relate to leadership practices is as a guide to action, particularly as supports to making decisions and resolving ethical dilemmas. Ethics and valuation models are highly relevant to school leadership as rubrics, benchmarks, socially justified standards of practice, and templates for moral action. These may be used by the individual leader or in more collective ways by groups of people. Langlois (2004), to name one scholar, has conducted much research on the ethical dilemma analysis processes of principals and superintendents. A typical application for ethics in this administrative context is as a personal guide to action, particularly as supports to resolving ethical dilemmas. A number of other scholars have also conducted research and published in this area. These include Begley and Johansson (1998), Stefkovich (2006), and Branson (2006). These scholars have each developed well-documented processes for the analysis of dilemma situations and development of ethical responses. One of these processes is outlined and discussed in some detail at the conclusion of this chapter and presented as a resource in support of ethical decision making by educational leaders.

However, there is a third and more strategic and collective application for ethics. It is common in a school or school district setting for ethical postures to be adopted with a strategic organizational intent—for example, as a focus for building consensus around a shared social or organizational objective. To illustrate, a school district superintendent might choose "ethic of community" (Furman, 2003) as a rallying meta-value to focus the energies of personnel on collective action. Or, ethical notions such as "due process" (Strike et al., 1998) or "social justice" (Shapiro & Stefkovich, 2005) might be used as the objective for focusing the reform of school district processes in support of students with special needs. These more collective and strategic applications of ethics may very well be the more common manifestation of this value type in the administration of schools and school districts, at the government level, as well as in the corporate sector. In this sense leaders literally use ethics as leadership tools to support actions taken, model ideal practice, and/or promote particular kinds of organizational or societal activity. However, as will be argued, these strategic adoptions of ethical postures may or may not be ethical.

Using Ethics Versus Being Ethical

As stated at the outset, research findings (e.g. Begley & Johansson, 1998) confirm that the relevance of principles or ethics to administrative situations seems to be prompted in the minds of school administrators by particular circumstances. These circumstances include: situations where an ethical posture is socially appropriate (e.g. the role of the arts); situations where consensus is perceived as difficult or impossible to achieve (e.g. an issue involving ethnic bias); or situations when high stakes and urgency require decisive action (e.g. student safety). There is also some evidence to suggest that school leaders use ethics in strategic applications as ways to develop group consensus, and a basis for promoting compliance with minimum need for justifying proof of effects (Langlois, 2004). These are all examples of *ethically sound*—meaning socially justifiable—applications of ethics to situations. However, one has only to survey the newspapers or work in an organization or live in a community for a few years to readily detect situations where ethics based postures can be unethical and socially unjust. Ethical postures may be *unethical* under a number of circumstances. For example: when a cultural ethic is imposed on others, when an ethic is used to justify otherwise reprehensible action, an ethical posture veils a less defensible value, or when an ethic is used to trump a basic human right. The implication is that using ethical postures is not always *ethical* action. Such is the nature of ethics when they are adopted as guides to action.

Transrational values (Hodgkinson, 1978, 1991, 1996) of any sort, and ethics and principles in particular, are rather vulnerable to multiple interpretations in application from one social context to another. For example, when unexamined values are applied in arbitrary ways, they can be anything but ethical. The essential, and often absent, component that makes adherence to a value genuinely ethical is dialogue. For these reasons unexamined ethics applied in instrumental ways, or values accepted at face value without prior deliberation of meaning, represent a particular category of social or collective values of a transrational nature that may not be consistent with moral leadership processes. It should be apparent that in order to cultivate the ability to distinguish the difference between using ethics and being ethical, we need the capacity to discriminate actual intentions within ourselves and among others. This is not an argument for moral relativism, nor is it value absolutism, it is an argument for critical thinking and moral literacy.

Valuation Processes of Individuals

Begley (2001, 2004) has previously published descriptions of the conceptual framework that serves as a foundation for the preceding assertions and the discussion of professional applications associated with ethical decision making that follows. However, for the sake of those new to the literature and application of values and ethics perspectives to leadership situations, it may be useful to review these key concepts.

In order to understand the relationship between motivation and values, and between values and administrative action, it is helpful to conceptually situate values within the context of one person's being using a simple onion figure. Figure 2.1 (Begley, 2003) is an adaptation of a graphic originally proposed by Hodgkinson (1978, 1991, 1996).

Beginning from the outside, the first ring represents the observable actions and speech of the individual. Leaders working in professional settings, as well as people in general, intuitively rely on the clues provided by the actions and attitudes of others to derive predictive insights into the nature of the values others hold. This is a sound strategy, but it has the same limits to its reliability in day-to-day life as it does in a research context. Political leaders, principals, teachers, parents, and children regularly demonstrate through their speech and actions that their observable actions may or may not be accurate indicators of their underlying values. Individuals often articulate or posture certain values while actually being committed to quite different values. In both the research and the leadership context, the implication is clear. Validity and

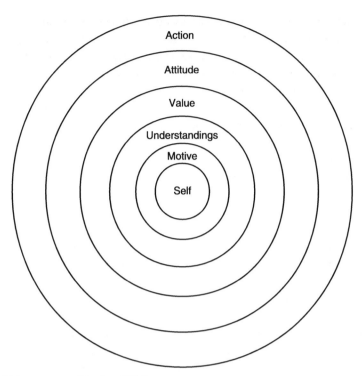

Figure 2.1 Values syntax (Begley, 2004).

reliability of interpretation is best enhanced by sustained periods of observation and multiple measures.

The next ring or layer of the figure represents attitudes. Attitudes can be thought of as the membrane between values and the observable actions or speech of an individual, or the permeable boundary of personality that acts as the interface between the psychological and physical world. They are the predisposition to act specifically as a result of values or value systems acquired previously and elsewhere (Begley, 2001). For example, educators' attitudes towards students encountered in their professional setting may change when they become parents with children of their own. Conversely, when we look across a career, we can see that the values of an individual in one role as a teacher, principal, or professor can readily spill over as attitudes into other social roles. The strength of this extended influence can be residual in nature, a significant spillover of effect, or intrude to such an extent that it overrides or neutralizes the influence of a second value or value system. Hodgkinson (1991) also tells us that attitudes can often be detected in the body language of posture, gait, or unconscious muscular tensions. These are the outward and visible signs of inner and invisible inclinations.

The next layer represents the actual values held or manifested by an individual. For example, an individual might prefer a glass of beer to a glass of red wine. Another might prefer a chat with friends in the staff lounge to reading the newspaper. Some-one may prefer working independently over working in a group. Others may favor a monarchial system of government over a republican system. In an educational context, a principal might gravitate towards relatively controlled approaches to delegating authority over more open styles of distributed leadership. A teacher might prefer computer-mediated instruction to workbook exercises, or instruction individualized to students' needs as opposed to a teacher-centered curriculum. The important thing to keep in mind is that identifying these values is one thing, while knowing why they are held is quite another. Making that latter judgment requires going deeper into the onion.

Between the values layer and motivational base layer of the figure is a category that can be labeled "available knowledge" or "understandings." The kinds of knowledge referenced here are acquired through life experiences, professional training, and reflection, and provide a linkage and context between the motivational bases and the specific values adopted by the individual. The contention here is that, as a result of experience, training and/or reflection, an individual responds to basic motivations by adopting particular value positions that will support the fulfillment of that basic motivation in a specific way. These responses are manifested through actions or speech selected by the individual to achieve the valued objective. Of course, people vary in terms of the skills and sophistication they can bring to bear on achieving their objectives. This is generally applicable to all aspects of human enterprise. Consider how an experienced school administrator, consensually motivated as a professional to achieve a complex set of educational objectives, might employ a carefully orchestrated collaborative school improvement project to achieve those educational objectives. By contrast, a less experienced administrator, with the same desire to build consensus among the faculty, but responding to different knowledge or the absence thereof, might naively decide a memo is all that is required to achieve the same objective.

The motivational base layer of the onion figure provides the key to understanding the nature and function of values as influences on leadership. This is the motivating force dimension behind the adoption of a particular value which, working out through the layers of the figure, shapes attitudes and potentially influences subsequent actions. Hodgkinson (1978, 1991, 1996), proposes that there are four basic motivational bases. These are: *personal preference* or self-interest; an inclination towards *consensus*; an inclination towards or concern for *consequences*; and an inclination towards transrational *ethics or principles*. These four motivational bases are relatively broad and arbitrary distinctions. In application, individuals can manifest a predisposition towards one motivational base over another, or adopt more than one motivational base when responding to a given situation. Research, conducted in several countries, on the valuation processes of school administrators (Begley & Johansson, 1998) suggests that the normative motivational bases for administrative decision making are the rational domains of consequences and consensus. Self-interest is infrequently acknowledged as a motivation, predictably because professional activity is publicly accountable. Ethics and principles tend to be articulated relatively infrequently as motivational influences on the cognitive processing of individuals. Leaders do, however, regularly employ ethics as strategic supports to a collective leadership process. The distinction being made here is between processes where leaders *use ethics* for strategic purposes as opposed to necessarily *being ethical*.

The final layer at the centre of the figure is the *self*—the biological self as well as the existential or transcendent self. The following section addresses the formation of the self.

Arenas of Leadership: Sources of Influence, Values and Conflicts

In recent decades, school leaders have learned how important it is to lead and manage with proper reference to the broader environmental context of their community. The influences on leadership, decision making, and education in general can be thought of as coming from multiple social sources. Some of these influences can take on the status of values when they are perceived as conceptions of the desirable with motivating force (Hodgkinson, 1991). Unfortunately, our personal values as well of those of the profession, organization, community, and society are not necessarily consistent or compatible with each other. As a result, these influences and values derived from the various arenas of our environment can generate inconsistencies and conflicts. A second onion figure (see Figure 2.2) is used to illustrate these distinctions. These are the interactive environments within which valuation processes and administration occur. They are also the source of personal, professional, and social values, as well as the source of many of the conflicts people encounter in life.

Within the figure, the individual is represented within the center ring and extending through all the rings. His or her character is the outcome of many transient influences as well as relatively more enduring values acquired from multiple arenas.

The second ring from the center represents the arena of groups, and other collective entities including family, peers, friends, and acquaintances. The third ring, profession, represents a more formal arena of administration that is closely related to the second ring, but is given special emphasis here because of its relevance to the professional context that is the focus of this chapter.

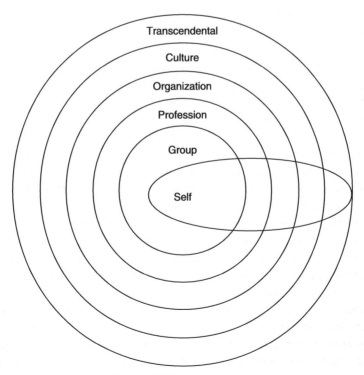

Figure 2.2 Arenas of influence (Begley, 2004).

The fourth ring represents the arena traditionally of most concern to academics and practitioners in the field of educational administration, the organization. Much of the literature of educational administration and most of the corporate literature are grounded within the organizational perspective, adopting it as a primary reference point for administrative activity.

Moving further outwards in the figure, one encounters the arenas representing the greater community, society, and culture. Within recent decades, school administrators have learned that it is necessary to pay a lot more attention to the community as a relevant administrative arena and source of influence on school leadership (Leithwood, Begley, & Cousins, 1992). The increasing diversity of our societies and a general trend towards globalization has highlighted society and culture as relevant arenas of administrative activity.

A final, seventh ring is included to accommodate notions of the transcendental— God, faith, spirituality, even extrasensory perception. Spirituality is of considerable importance to many individuals, and has begun to attract the attention of more scholars as an important influence on educational leadership. Even administrators who do not subscribe to a spiritual dimension as a source of influence in their own daily lives are well advised to keep this arena in mind, if only because at least some individuals associated with their professional role do. A leader who wants to understand the motivations of those they are supposed to lead will be sensitive to all potentially significant categories of influence.

How School Leaders Respond to Moral Dilemmas

The achievement of consensus on educational issues among even traditional educational stakeholders has become more difficult in many communities. School administrators increasingly encounter dilemmas or value conflict situations where consensus cannot be achieved, rendering obsolete the traditional rational notions of problem *solving*. Administrators must now often be satisfied with *responding* to a situation since there may be no solution possible that will satisfy all. Such value dilemmas can occur within a single arena of administration or among two or more arenas. The most difficult dilemmas occur when one ethic literally trumps another.

A pilot study conducted by the author during 2004 examined principals' perceptions of and responses to the moral dilemmas encountered in the professional context of their roles (Begley, 2005). The data were collected from a sample of principals from Ontario, Canada, and Pennsylvania, USA using a survey instrument and follow-up interviews. The data were interpreted through a values framework (Begley, 2006) that is the outcome of an interdisciplinary integration of administrative theory about valuation processes with information processing theory derived from the field of cognitive psychology. An overview of the findings from this project provides insights into how school leaders respond to the ethical dilemmas encountered in their professional work.

Theme or Context of Dilemmas

The dilemmas identified by the principals in this study could be readily grouped according to a number of themes or topics. A surprising number of the dilemmas focused on various forms of educational system policies that were alternately perceived as overly punitive, procedurally rigid, and/or negatively influencing a principal's professional autonomy or expertise and discretion. Another common theme was the principals' overarching desire to do what they perceived to be in the best interests of students. Other themes included: conflicts with parents or other community members, dealing with abusive or incompetent professional staff, and risking career or job in the defense of personal moral beliefs.

Sources of Dilemma

Begley's (2004) graphic portrayal of the arenas or domains (see Figure 2.2) of administration was employed as a guide to determining the source or sources of the dilemmas presented by the participants. Many of the dilemmas reported by the participants could be readily connected to conflicts between organizational policies (e.g., zero tolerance policies, required reporting of alleged abuse) that reduced the professional discretion of the administrator to make decisions in the best interest of students or the school. The most difficult of the situations occurs when the policies are perceived as inappropriately punitive or when the student in question had no intention to break a rule or violate policy. Several participants also reported dilemmas that clearly revealed conflicts between personal moral positions and those of the profession, school district or community (i.e., persistent racial discrimination by administrative colleagues).

Inter-personal / Intra-personal Dilemmas

The notion of arenas as a guide for identifying the source of the dilemmas was also useful for assessing whether the dilemmas were inter-personal or intra-personal; that is, whether the dilemma explicitly involved more than one person or was an essentially internal struggle experienced by one person. In a surprising number of cases, most of the cases actually, clear evidence suggests that the dilemmas were intra-personal. School administrators seem much inclined to sort out the dilemmas on their own, without seeking the opinions and support of others. For the school administrators participating in this study, the dilemmas of practice seem to be private and internal mental processes. Only one principal made reference to actively involving other staff or colleagues in the moral deliberation of the dilemmas encountered in the school.

Guiding Meta Values

Prior work by the author has regularly proposed accountability as a dominant meta-value employed by school administrators in their assessment and interpretation of situations. This apparently strong inclination and quite consistent pattern of response across cultures has also been described as a natural inclination for school administrators to gravitate towards the rational motivational bases of consequences and consensus, again because of their preoccupation with accountability issues. This phenomenon has also been used to explain in part why school administrators often avoid ethics as an explicit guide to decision making, in preference of more rationally defensible decision processes grounded in consequences or consensus.

The data collected in support of this study about administrative responses to dilemmas both confirm and challenge the pre-eminence of accountability as a meta-value for school principals. Many of the dilemmas submitted by the participants do indeed make explicit and/or implicit reference to accountability as an overriding concern. However, there is another equally strong and frequently articulated meta-value that becomes apparent as an outcome of these dilemmas; that is, "doing what is best for kids" or "the best interests of students." As much as accountability may be a primary influence on the general decision-making processes of school administrators, when situations are perceived by administrators to be dilemmas, there appears to be a strong inclination to adopt "students' best interests" as the meta-value of choice.

Strategies for Interpretation

The strategies employed by the participants to interpret and respond to the dilemmas of practice they perceived conform fairly well to the findings of research conducted by Roche (1999) based on the practices of principals in Queensland, Australia. He found that school administrators routinely confront moral and ethical dilemmas that demand a response. His inquiry focused on how school administrators actually respond to moral and ethical dilemmas, the most difficult value conflicts they encounter. He identified four primary ways in which principals respond to moral dilemmas. The press for accountability appears to heavily influence such processes. Listed in order of frequency of use by the administrators in Roche's study, the strategies principals used in response to the professional dilemmas they encounter are: avoidance, suspended morality, creative insubordination, and taking a personal moral stand. Avoidance (reinterpreting the situation so it no longer involves an ethical dimension) is the most frequently employed response among the administrators in the Roche (1999) study. Suspended morality, the second most common strategy, illustrates the ability of administrators to set aside some of their personal value orientations, and consciously respond to situations from a professional or organizational perspective. Campbell (2003) identifies the same phenomena as common administrative practice and condemns it as immoral when student needs are subordinated to organizational imperatives. The third category of response identified by Roche is creative insubordination. As a strategy it is an opposite response to suspended morality. In this case organizational dictates are set aside, or creative approaches to compliance are found, that favor more humane concerns. The taking of a personal moral stand was the least frequently employed response, usually adopted only when the administrator assessed a high likelihood of successfully challenging the competing demands of the profession, organization or society.

There is evidence of all four of Roche's identified strategies being used by the respondents in the current study. Appeals to policy as a basis for responding equate with the avoidance strategy. Many of the dilemmas submitted by the principals conveyed the angst encountered when they felt compelled to suspend their own morality in favor of a professional or organizational position. A few of the reported dilemmas reveal the intent of the principal to take a public moral stand.

Ethical Decision-making Strategies

The balance of the chapter explores several strategies that educational leaders may apply to support ethical decision making and problem solving in their professional practice.

Multi-ethics Analyses as Guides to Problem Solving

As appealing and practical as theories, models, frameworks, and procedural guides may be to people working in professional settings, they must be employed as initial organizers, and not as prescriptions or recipes. Worded another way, the complexity of social and administrative situations makes it attractive for school leaders to employ processes to aid their interpretation and structuring of situations, but this must be done in socially and culturally sensitive ways. For example, Shapiro and Stefkovich (2005) espouse the application of a multi-ethical analytical approach to the interpretation of ethical dilemmas as a way to improve or ensure the quality of decision making. The key ethical orientations suggested by these scholars include the ethic of justice, the ethic of critique, the ethic of care, and a hybrid multi-dimensional model, the ethic of profession. Strike (2003; Strike et al., 1998) is well known for his work grounded in the ethic of justice with its familiar dualistic tension between maximizing benefits and respecting individual rights. Bates (1980) and Giroux and Purpel (1983) are good arch-types for an ethic of critique orientation. Noddings' (1984) writing is a good representation of the ethic of care orientation, as are the work of Beck (1994) and Gilligan (1982). And finally, Starratt (2004) and Shapiro and Stefkovich (2005) are proponents of a multi-dimensional model that subsumes the ethics care, critique, and justice into one ethic of profession.

Although Shapiro and Stefkovich propose the use of multiple ethical lenses as a basis for responding to the dilemmas of school leadership, they stop short of proposing any particular sequence for applying those ethics. Their research suggests that individuals vary in their preferred ethical postures and are satisfied with espousing that administrators adopt a multi-ethical analysis of problems and situations. For example, a school principal responding to an ethical dilemma might prefer, in the sense of a *personal* inclination that is the outcome of their social formation, to gravitate towards the application of an ethic of care. In contrast, Begley (2006), with his foundational roots grounded in administrative problem-solving research, argues that in the *professional* context of school leadership, where the individual is essentially an agent of society and accountable to the community for actions taken in the execution of his or her duties, there is probably an implied sequence for the appropriate application of these classic Western ethical lenses. A professionally appropriate sequence for the application of ethical lenses in a school leadership situation might be: ethic of critique, followed by the ethic of care, and then ethic of justice. Beginning with the ethic of critique is necessary in order to name and understand as much as possible the alternate perspectives applicable to a situation, especially those of minorities and individuals otherwise without voice or representation. To do otherwise is to risk gravitation to the preferred cultural orientations of the leader or the mainstream orientations of a given cultural group. The ethic of care naturally follows next in the sequence as a way to keep the focus of the process on people and their best interests rather than on organizations or policies. Using the ethic of care, one can also assess the capacity and responsibility of stakeholders to a situation in a humane way. Finally, once the ethics of critique and care have been used to carefully interpret a situation, the ethic of justice can be applied as a basis for deciding on actions that will maximize benefits for all while respecting the rights of individuals.

This is not to suggest a dogmatic adherence to a prescriptive sequence of application for these classic ethics of Western philosophy. In all cases, the sequencing and application of ethical perspectives needs to be very fluid and dynamic as an initial organizer, not a recipe, and as a stimulus for reflection or dialogue, not a prescription. However, the application of any lens to a situation, including ethics, begins the process of highlighting some information as relevant and diminishing or veiling the relevance of other information. School leaders accountable to their communities must take care to interpret situations in a sensitive way.

The Value Audit Process: A Resource

In an effort to help school leaders develop their capacity to make ethically sound and professionally effective decisions, Begley has developed several versions of a value audit guide to be used as a resource in support of their ethical decision-making processes (see Appendix). Originally based on a series of value audit questions proposed by Hodgkinson (1991), this resource document has gone through several evolutions and refinements as a result of being used with a succession of groups of school leaders in several countries over several years. An examination of the version included here as the Appendix will reveal that it incorporates many of the key concepts discussed in this chapter, including: a sequenced application of the ethics of critique, care, and justice; a bias towards careful interpretation before moving to action; and the four motivational bases of valuation by individuals. Begley has used this activity with some success as a component of graduate level courses and also as a workshop activity in support of the professional development of principals in several countries.

Notes

Portions of this chapter are based on material taken from two previously published journal articles with the permission of the publishers. These are: Begley, P.T., & Stefkovich, J. (2007), Integrating values and ethics into postsecondary teaching for leadership development: Principles, concepts, and strategies, *Journal of Educational Administration*, *45*(4), 398–412; and Begley, P.T. (2006), Self-knowledge, capacity and sensitivity: Prerequisites to authentic leadership by school principals, *Journal of Educational Administration*, *44*(6), 570–589.

References

Bates, R. (1980). Educational administration, the science of sociology and the management of knowledge. *Educational Administration Quarterly*, *16*(2), 1–20.

Beck, L. G. (1994). *Reclaiming educational administration as a caring profession.* New York: Teachers College Press.

Begley, P. T. (2001). In pursuit of authentic school leadership practices. *International Journal of Leadership in Education*, *4*(4), 353–366.

Begley, P. T. (2003). In pursuit of authentic school leadership practices. In P. T. Begley & O. Johansson (Eds.), *The ethical dimensions of school leadership* (pp. 1–12). Dordrecht, Netherlands: Kluwer Academic Press.

Begley, P. T. (2004). Understanding valuation processes: Exploring the linkage between motivation and action. *International Studies in Educational Administration*, *32*(2), 4–17.

Begley, P. T. (2005, April). *The dilemmas of leadership: Perspectives on the moral literacy of principals from Ontario and Pennsylvania.* Paper delivered at the annual meeting of the American Educational Research Association, Montreal, Quebec.

Begley, P. T. (2006). Self-knowledge, capacity and sensitivity: Prerequisites to authentic leadership by school principals. *Journal of Educational Administration*, *44*(6), 570–589.

Begley, P. T., & Johansson, O. (1998). The values of school administration: Preferences, ethics and conflicts. *The Journal of School Leadership*, *8*(4), 399–422.

Branson, C. (2006). Effects of structured self-reflection on the development of authentic leadership practices among Queensland primary school principals. *Educational Management Administration and Leadership*, *35*(2), 227–248.

Campbell, E. (2003). Let right be done: Trying to put ethical standards into practice. In P. T. Begley & O. Johansson (Eds.), *The ethical dimensions of school leadership* (pp. 107–125). Dordrecht, NL: Kluwer Academic Press.

Duignan, P., & Bhindi, N. (1997). Authentic leadership: An emerging perspective. *Journal of Educational Administration*, *35*(3), 195–209.

Evers, C. W., & Lakomski, G. (1991). *Knowing educational administration.* Toronto, Canada: Pergamon Press.

Furman, G. (2003). Moral leadership and the ethic of community. *Values and Ethics in Educational Administration*, *2*(1), 1–8.

Gilligan, C. (1982). *In a different voice.* Cambridge, MA: Harvard University Press.

Giroux, H. A., & Purpel, D. (Eds.) (1983). *The hidden curriculum and moral education: Deception or discovery?* Berkeley, CA: McCutchan Publishing.

Gross, S., & Shapiro, J. (2004). Using multiple ethical paradigms and turbulence theory in response to administrative dilemmas. *International Studies in Educational Administration*, *32*(2), 47–62.

Hodgkinson, C. (1978). *Towards a philosophy of administration.* Oxford, UK: Basil Blackwell.

Hodgkinson, C. (1991). *Educational leadership: The moral art.* Albany, NY: SUNY Press.

Hodgkinson, C. (1996). *Administrative philosophy.* Oxford, UK: Elsevier-Pergamon.

Kohlberg, L., & Turiel, E. (1971). Moral development and moral education. In G. Lesser (Ed.), *Psychology and educational practice* (pp. 530–550). New York: Scott Foresman.

Langlois, L. (2004). Making the tough calls: Complex decision-making in light of ethical considerations. *International Studies in Educational Administration*, *32*(2), 78–93.

Leithwood, K. A., & Steinbach, R. (1995). *Expert problem solving.* Albany, NY: SUNY Press.

Leithwood, K. A., Begley, P. T., & Cousins, J. B. (1992). *Developing expert leadership for future schools.* London: Falmer Press.

Noddings, N. (1984). *Caring: A feminine approach to ethics and moral education.* Berkeley, CA: University of California Press.

Roche, K. (1999). Moral and ethical dilemmas in Catholic school settings. In P. T. Begley (Ed.), *Values and educational leadership* (pp. 255–272). Albany, NY: SUNY Press.

Shapiro, J., & Stefkovich, J. A. (2001). *Ethical leadership and decision making in education.* Mahwah, NJ: Lawrence Erlbaum Associates.

Shapiro, J., & Stefkovich, J. A. (2005). *Ethical leadership and decision making in education* (2nd ed.). Mahwah, NJ: Lawrence Erlbaum Associates.

Starratt, R. J. (1994). *Building an ethical school.* London: Falmer Press.

Starratt, R. J. (2004). *Ethical leadership.* San Francisco: Jossey-Bass.

Stefkovich, J. A. (2006). *Best interests of the student: Applying ethical constructs to legal cases in education.* Mahwah, NJ: Lawrence Erlbaum Associates.

Stefkovich, J., & Begley, P. T. (2007). Conceptualizing ethical school leadership and defining the best interests of students. *Educational Management and Leadership, 35*(2), 205–226.

Stefkovich, J. A., & O'Brien, G. M. (2004). Best interests of the student: An ethical model. *Journal of Educational Administration, 42*(2), 197–214.

Stefkovich, J., & Shapiro, J. (2003). Deconstructing communities: Educational leaders and their ethical decision-making processes. In P. T. Begley & O. Johansson (Eds.), *The ethical dimensions of school leadership* (pp. 89–106). Dordrecht: Kluwer Academic Press.

Strike, K. A. (2003). Community, coherence, and inclusiveness. In P. T. Begley & O. Johansson (Eds.), *The ethical dimensions of school leadership* (pp. 69–87). Dordrecht: Kluwer Academic Press.

Strike, K. A., Haller, E. J., & Soltis, J. F. (1998). *The ethics of school administration* (2nd ed.). NewYork: Teachers College Press.

Taylor, C. (1991). *The ethics of authenticity.* Cambridge, MA: Harvard University Press.

Willower, D. J. (1994). *Educational administration: Inquiry, values, practice.* Lancaster, PA: Technomics.

Willower, D. J. (1999). Values and valuation: A naturalistic inquiry. In P. T. Begley (Ed.), *Values and educational leadership* (pp. 121–138). Albany, NY: SUNY Press.

Appendix: *Value Audit Guideline* (Paul Begley, 2005)

These questions may be helpful as guides, to be used by individuals or groups, interested in analyzing and responding ethically to critical incidents or dilemmas of practice encountered in school leadership situations.

Step 1: Interpretation of the Problem (ethic of critique)

- Who are the ***stakeholders?*** Are any unrecognized or without voice?
- What ***arenas of practice*** (self, profession, organization, community, culture) are relevant?
- Does the conflict exist ***within an arena or between two or more?*** (e.g., personal vs. organizational)
- Can the ***values in conflict*** be named?
- How much **turbulence** are the values in conflict creating? (Degree of risk for structural damage to people, organizations, or community.)

Step 2: Towards a Humane Response (ethic of care)

- What ***motivations and degrees of commitment*** are apparent among the stake-holders?
  Four levels of motivation:
  — concerned with self, personal preference, habitual, comfort
     (subrational values grounded in preference)
  — concerned with desired outcomes, avoidance of undesirable
     (rational values grounded in consequences)
  — concerned with perceptions of others, consultation, expert opinion
     (rational values grounded in consensus)
  — concerned with ethical postures, first principles, will or faith
     (transrational, no need for rational justification)
- Is the conflict ***inter-personal*** (among individuals) or ***intra-personal*** (within an individual)?
- What are the ***human needs***, as opposed to organizational or philosophical standards?

Step 3: Ethical Action (ethic of justice)

- What actions or response would ***maximize benefits*** for all stakeholders?
- What actions or response would ***respect individual rights***?
- Are desired "***ends***" or purposes *interfering with the selection of a "**means**" or solution?*
- If an **ethical dilemma** exists (a choice between equally unsatisfactory alterna-tives), how will you resolve it? (Avoidance, suspended morality, creative insubordination, taking a moral stand.)

3

Legal Dimensions of Using Employee and Student Data to Make Decisions

R. Lance Potter and Jacqueline A. Stefkovich
Pennsylvania State University

In this day and age, data flood school districts and may include anything from student test scores and student and teacher demographic data to teacher performance evaluations, personnel salary and benefits data, other school expenditure data, student and personnel files, and curriculum. Decisions affecting students and employees are often supported, if not based on, information drawn from these various sources. Kowalski, Lasley, and Mahoney (2008) point out that making objective and analytical decisions based on informed choice is both a disposition and a skill, which ultimately achieves more effective results. We contend that, in this increasingly litigious society, making decisions in light of legal requirements, restrictions, and interpretations is also a necessity.

Whether decisions involve employees or students, school leaders must bear in mind that various aspects of the law can influence their decisions. If school district decision makers are not cognizant of the legal environment affecting education, they may make decisions they should not make or they may be afraid to make decisions they are legally permitted to make. Both types of decision can have a negative impact on the operation of schools and the learning atmosphere for students.

Recognizing the power of such informed decisions, this chapter considers the legal aspects of using data in three key areas: employee and student data for purposes of policy implementation, personnel decisions, and student-related dissemination and decisions. After a brief overview of the legal system and its relationship to data-driven decisions, the remainder of this chapter will focus on these three areas.

The Legal System

In its simplest form, as related to educational decision making, the law typically presents itself at either the federal or state level. Federal law is generally based on the United States Constitution or on laws passed by Congress. As to the latter, No Child Left Behind is a prime example of such a law. State law is generally based on state constitutions and statutes passed by state legislatures as well as on common law, which derives from past practice. All of these laws are subject to interpretation by courts, both federal and state, which resolve legal controversies.

This chapter is designed to serve as a primer for school leaders wishing to move to a more data-based decision-making model. While it is impossible in this short time to enumerate everything a school leader should know about the law, we hope this information provides a basis upon which school leaders may move forward with some confidence in using school and district data to inform their decisions.

Using Data for Policy Implementation

At its broadest level, school districts may employ data to satisfy legal requirements, to inform policy making and, in essence, to make good policy decisions. As early as 1954, in *Brown v. Board of Education*, the Supreme Court realized the importance of using social science data in determining jurisprudence. Here, the Court cited several sources of psychological data, including the well-known doll studies, to help inform their decision that separate was inherently unequal. While the use of such data proved to be controversial, courts have come to rely on data in a variety of educational settings.

Use of data in educational policy making is greatly influenced by both federal statutes and judicial opinions. Statutes such as the No Child Left Behind Act (NCLB, 2002) create a legal regimen that necessitates action by schools in order to secure and retain federal funding. The use of data is integral to satisfying NCLB's statutory requirements.

The No Child Left Behind Act

Traditionally, education policy decisions have been influenced mostly at the state or local level in large part because the vast majority of funding for education comes from these levels and because the U.S. Constitution does not provide the national government a role in education. The national government still played a part in K-12 education as seen in special education policy, which is driven by the Individuals with Disabilities Education Act (IDEA), and Title I programs for economically disadvantaged students. In addition, the federal court system has been used several times for legal challenges of education policy based on U.S. constitutional or national statutory directives.

In recent years, however, the national government has taken unprecedented active interest in education as exhibited by NCLB (2002) and its accompanying regulations. By now, most educators are well aware of the Act's goal that all students in public education will achieve proficiency levels by certain timelines, and the controversies surrounding the funding for and implementation of the requirements of this Act. In this context, NCLB is perhaps the most profound example of the legal dimensions of using employee and student data to make decisions.

In school board and faculty meetings taking place across the country, educators worry about achieving adequate yearly progress (AYP) in the several categories mandated by the Act. Student data must now be gathered regarding attendance, graduation rates, and standardized test scores. These data must be disaggregated to identify the relative performance of boys and girls, different ethnic groups, English language learners, special education students, migrant students, and economically disadvantaged students. Teachers must also be highly qualified to teach their subject matter (NCLB, 2002).

The data gathering and reporting requirements resulting from NCLB give rise to additional administrative burdens on school districts in a time of increased scrutiny and fiscal restraint. Fear of the sanctions that come from failing to achieve AYP drives schools to focus on raising test scores of low achievers. This in turn affects policy and curriculum decisions, and financial as well as personnel resource allocation. Thus, NCLB creates legal requirements that have altered the educational landscape and made an impact on the creation and use of student and employee data. While any detailed discussion of the entire NCLB Act far exceeds the limited scope of this chapter, it is helpful to highlight some of the aspects of NCLB that most directly implicate the use of employee and student data.

Highly Qualified Teachers   NCLB requires that all school personnel teaching core academic subjects earn highly qualified status. For schools to be eligible for Title I funding, core subject teachers must possess at least a bachelor's degree, state teaching certification, and demonstrate competency in the subject area taught (NCLB, 2002). In addition to academic requirements, a teaching competency examination is required for new teachers (Rossow & Tate, 2003). Flexibility was added in 2005 regarding the highly qualified teacher (HQT) requirements for rural, secondary science teachers, and multi-subject teachers. States may now develop strategies for these teachers to demonstrate they are highly qualified in the subjects they teach by either adding time for the process or allowing for alternate methods for teachers to demonstrate they meet HQT standards (New No Child Left Behind Flexibility, 2005).

Keeping up with the HQT regulations and teachers' HQT status adds a layer of data collection for school districts. A teacher's HQT status in one or more subject areas could very well affect hiring and retention decisions.

Disclosure of Assessment Outcomes   Disclosure of assessment outcomes serves as a key dimension to NCLB that concerns students. Title I, part A of the Act requires schools to adopt measures to ensure effective communication of information to parents. Assessment outcomes and school improvement actions must be articulated and disseminated in a manner that is "understandable" and "practicable"(Torres & Stefkovich, 2005). In addition to the requirement that states issue outcomes in a prompt manner, assessment results must be presented in a report format that is "descriptive, interpretative, and diagnostic" and allows school officials to comprehend and use data to address students' academic needs and to modify instruction (Torres & Stefkovich, 2005). However, schools must take care that while complying with the requirements of NCLB, they do not violate the requirements of the Family Educational Rights and Privacy Act (FERPA), a federal law that is discussed in more detail later in this chapter.

Targeted Assistance   Under NCLB, schools may allocate funds directly to students with the greatest academic needs. Eligibility is determined by failure to meet expectations on statewide assessment, demonstration of a high probability for failure, or through performance levels deemed less than proficient according to local assessments. This requires record keeping on the individual student level and school level, as schools with large at-risk populations are eligible for additional funding through a variety of sources (Torres & Stefkovich, 2005).

Targeted assistance programming must entail an ongoing review process, which regularly determines when intervention and assistance are required and/or whether the situation warrants extended time before or after school, during the summer, and/or nontraditional school year formats (Torres & Stefkovich, 2005).

Unlike the efforts to comply with NCLB, in many instances the legal ramifications of policy decisions are often not revealed until after a policy has been established and its implementation offends those affected by it. Ultimately, some of these disputes end up in court and provide guidance for others so they may avoid similar difficulties. It is perhaps instructive to examine a 2007 Supreme Court case involving two districts' attempts to use data based on race as a factor in determining the student composition of their schools.

Parents Involved in Community Schools v. Seattle Public School District No. 1

Parents Involved in Community Schools v. Seattle Public School District No. 1, (2007) concerns two school districts that relied upon an individual student race data in assigning students to particular schools so that the racial balance at each school would fall within a predetermined range based on the racial composition of the school district as a whole. The Supreme Court struck down both plans as being violations to Title VI of the Civil Rights Act, which prohibits discrimination based on race. The lesson that school leaders can take from *Parents Involved* is that while student demographic data may now be more available than they have been in the past, one must take care with how those data are put to use.

The Seattle Public School District No. 1 used race as a factor in deciding which of the city's 10 public high schools its students could attend. The district desired to maintain a racially diverse balance in its high schools so it developed a policy for deciding who would gain admittance to the more coveted schools. High school students could apply to any high school in the district. After taking into account whether a student already had a sibling attending the desired school, the district used race as a tiebreaker followed by geographic proximity. If a school's racial diversity did not fit within district guidelines, a student from an underrepresented race would have preference ahead of a student from the overrepresented race. Parents Involved in Community Schools filed suit in the federal district court alleging that Seattle's use of race in assignments violated the Equal Protection Clause of the Fourteenth Amendment, Title VI of the Civil Rights Act of 1964, and the state of Washington's Civil Rights Act. Both the district court and the Court of Appeals upheld the district's plan and Parents Involved appealed to the Supreme Court.

The Supreme Court also considered a similar program in Kentucky in *Parents Involved*. Jefferson County Public School District encompasses the metropolitan area of Louisville, Kentucky. The school district is racially mixed with approximately 34% African American students and almost all of the remaining 66% White. Non-magnet schools in the district were placed in geographic clusters and students could apply to attend any school in their cluster. In order to maintain racial diversity within each school, Jefferson County developed a policy providing for a certain racial balance. If a school's racial balance fell outside the parameters of the guidelines, new students of the overrepresented race would be assigned to a different school in the cluster. A parent of a new student assigned to an undesirable school sued the district.

The Supreme Court noted that there was no legal need to desegregate in either district. Seattle had never had legal segregation and Jefferson County had satisfied its obligation to desegregate in 2000. The Supreme Court stated that while maintaining racial diversity is a worthy goal, it is not a "compelling interest" such as remedying past intentional discrimination. The districts' plans were not sufficiently narrowly tailored to meet their objectives and were therefore declared unconstitutional. One of the several things the Court found objectionable was that neither district had considered other factors that contribute to overall student body diversity as was the case in *Grutter v. Bollinger* (2003) where race was but one of many factors considered in law school admission decisions. Another problem the Court had with the plans was that districts only distinguished between Whites and non-Whites. In Seattle, at least, there were significant populations of Asians, African Americans, and Hispanics.

Both districts' policies took into consideration available student data such as location, race, and siblings. Neither, however, sufficiently considered the present legal context. While the respective school boards believed they were doing the right thing by using student racial data to promote diversity in the school enrollments throughout their districts, other more compelling legal considerations ultimately prevented them from doing so.

Using Data for Personnel Decisions

Personnel decisions are largely governed by state statutes, regulations and contract law which prescribe appropriate procedures to follow in making such decisions. In this section we concentrate largely on the issue of evaluating teachers so that determinations regarding continued employment can be made and justified in accordance with the law. The use of data in the form of performance evaluations and a record of negative incidents play an important role in such decisions.

Teacher Evaluation

Teachers, both tenured and probationary, are periodically evaluated. Probationary teachers typically are evaluated more often as they work toward tenure. Evaluations are used for two functions: assessing the teaching process for purposes of improving teacher performance, and evaluating outcomes for purposes of building a record for potential discipline or dismissal of a problem teacher (Rossow & Tate, 2003).

To perform the evaluation function in an orderly and evenhanded manner school districts need to have a teacher evaluation policy and follow it. Such policies are usually required by state statutes, which specify the necessary elements of any policy. A district's policy must have clearly defined standards of performance and be written in understandable language. The failure of a district to have an evaluation policy may lead to a suspicion that school officials are acting in an arbitrary manner in order to discriminate against teachers (Rossow & Tate, 2003). A teacher prevailed against a school district when it did not have an evaluation policy in place in violation of state law. The teacher's contract was not renewed even though the board did not follow the mandated procedures required to take such action. As a result, the court ordered the teacher to be reinstated (*Farmer v. Kelleys Island Board of Education*, 1994).

Evaluation Procedure   The evaluation policy of a school district must contain procedures that conform to the protections provided by the Fourteenth Amendment of the U.S. Constitution and state statutes. The Fourteenth Amendment protects tenured teachers from dismissal unless they have been afforded "due process." For evaluations, due process minimally requires adequate notice to the teacher of the criteria that will be used in the evaluation, and an opportunity to remediate the deficiencies cited in the evaluation. Prior to dismissals tenured teachers (and in some cases probationary teachers) are entitled to notice of the dismissal, the reasons for it, and a hearing where the teacher can hear the "charges" and have a chance to respond to them (Rossow & Tate, 2003).

Evaluation Criteria   While teacher performance in the classroom makes up the largest part of the evaluation process, other factors beyond the classroom walls may be taken into consideration in making decisions regarding discipline or dismissal. Examples of these factors include relationships with other teachers, administrators and parents, standing in the community, outside employment, and even personal behavior (Rossow & Tate, 2003). Typically, the types of behavior that can lead to discipline or dismissal are regulated by state statute and fall into several broad categories. These categories usually consist of:

   (a) incompetence, generally involving a teacher's failure to control the behavior of his or her class, or failure to effectively deliver instruction;
   (b) immorality, which can include behavior in and out of school such as drug use, inappropriate sexual conduct or moral turpitude, and criminal behavior; and
   (c) insubordination, the willful failure of teachers to follow the rules, policies or directives of their principals or superintendents.

In order to show that a teacher has violated one of these grounds, a district must have proof. It is the sufficiency of the evidence the school district has gathered to support its decision that often determines the outcome of the matter (Rossow & Tate, 2003).

Teacher incompetence is a common ground for terminating teachers. It usually requires multiple evaluations over a period of time, and the most extensive documentation of all the causes for dismissal. Probationary teachers often do not get their contracts renewed for various reasons, but they are not a major source of litigation because in most states, school districts need little or no justification for not renewing their contracts. Most court cases derive from attempts to remove tenured teachers. While the process may be arduous, school districts are often successful in removing incompetent teachers, in part because of the deference courts give to the school boards' decisions (Rossow & Tate, 2003). While proving teacher incompetence usually requires the showing of multiple incidents over time, teachers can be dismissed over single incidents that fall into the other grounds.

In building a record for dismissal, objective criteria are preferable to subjective factors and should be incorporated into the evaluation of each teacher. Objective criteria require the recording of an observation while subjective factors require some form of discretionary judgment. What is most important is whether the behavior is reasonably related to the job and can be observed (Rossow & Tate, 2003). As *Layman v. Perry Local School District Board of Education* (1998) demonstrates, the use of two subjective items in the report against a dismissed teacher was acceptable when the report also contained 20 objective items. Likewise, in *Bellairs v. Beaverton School District* (2006) the court found that a teacher's dismissal was based on evidence of a series of incidents collected over four years, appropriate legal principles, and substantial reason. On the other hand, in *Shepard v. Fairland Local School District Board of Education* (2000) a dismissed teacher prevailed when she showed that the criteria used in her evaluations were insufficient because they did not provide specific criticisms or recommendations for improvement.

Impact of Different Aspects of the Law on Personnel Decisions

The basics of teacher evaluation just presented incorporate several aspects of the law including contract law, state statutes, and the Fourteenth Amendment Due Process clause. Other laws can also influence personnel decisions made by school districts. There are federal anti-discrimination laws such as the Civil Rights Act of 1964 that prohibit discrimination on the basis of race, ethnicity, gender or religion. There is the Americans with Disabilities Act prohibiting discrimination on the basis of one's disability. There are state collective bargaining laws if the workforce is unionized. Overarching all of these aspects of the law is constitutional law, which pertaining to teachers may concern First Amendment rights of free speech and religion. Further complicating matters is the fact that these areas of law frequently overlap in any given situation.

School decision makers must consider how their use or failure to use available data can implicate a variety of legal issues. What follows are two cases where school districts attempted to dismiss a teacher. In *Macy v. Hopkins County Board of Education* (2007), the district was successful but in *Settlegoode v. Portland Public Schools* (2004), the district was not. These cases arguably turn on the district's use of data and its understanding of other areas of law that can influence the court's decision.

In *Settlegoode* the school district relied on negative evaluations of Settlegoode's teaching performance to justify not renewing her contract. Normally, such reliance is adequate but in *Settlegoode*, First Amendment concerns ultimately carried more weight. In *Macy*, the school district overcame the teacher's claim that she was dismissed in violation of the Americans with Disabilities Act with ample evidence of inappropriate behavior.

Settlegoode v. Portland Public Schools   *Settlegoode* pits contract law against constitutional law. Settlegoode complained about her students' treatment and educational program, which were protected by Section 504 of the Rehabilitation, Comprehensive Services, and Developmental Disabilities Act of 1978. This raised a matter of public concern which made her speech protected by the First Amendment. The court in this case allowed a jury to decide what it thought the reason was for the district choosing not to renew Settlegoode's contract; her poor evaluation at the end of the year or retaliation for speaking out in support of her students. The jury made its decision in favor of Settlegoode and the Court of Appeals stood by it.

Pamella Settlegoode was hired as an adaptive physical education teacher to work with students with physical disabilities in several schools in Portland, Oregon. Settlegoode began to advocate for better conditions and treatment for her students within several months after starting teaching. She tried to talk to her immediate supervisor several times with no success about the problems she was having finding places to teach her students and that equipment was often lacking, inadequate, or unsafe. Near the end of the school year she wrote a 10-page letter to the district's director of special education expressing her frustrations with both the treatment of her students and her supervisor's disregard of her concerns.

Before writing the letter, Settlegoode's performance evaluations had been mostly positive. She was praised as having well-planned appropriate lessons of high interest. Evaluations also stated that she was supportive and respectful of her students and "working to develop her skills in writing IEP goals and objectives which are measurable" (*Settlegoode*, 2004, p. 508). After writing the letter, Settlegoode's evaluations were much more negative and she no longer met the minimum standards of performance in several areas including writing IEPs and classroom management. As a probationary teacher, Settlegoode was not entitled to continued employment after her first year of teaching. Eventually, she was not recommended for renewal and the school board followed the recommendation without investigation. Settlegoode then filed suit and after a trial, a jury found for Settlegoode on all claims and awarded her over $900,000 in damages. The school district appealed, but the 9th Circuit Court of Appeals upheld the verdict.

The district's greatest mistake was probably its poor treatment of students with disabilities, students protected by federal law. Its next mistake was a seemingly casual disregard of Settlegoode's complaints. Perhaps Settlegoode's supervisors did not take her complaints seriously because of her probationary status. Typically, in such cases reasons are not even needed for not renewing a contract.

One key to Settlegoode's case is that she was not initially complaining about her own treatment, rather the treatment of her students. The nature of her complaints amounted to a matter of public concern which then implicated First Amendment protections for Settlegoode's right of free speech. Once her free speech rights were recognized by the court, the issue became more complex. Then the district had to show that it "would have taken the same action even in the absence of the protected conduct" (*Settlegoode*, 2004, p. 512). The jury decided that the failure of the school district to renew Settlegoode's contract was in retaliation for expressing her free speech.

The school district failed to make appropriate use of data. It did not appear from the court opinion that the district had a protocol in place for monitoring its students to see that they were receiving the appropriate services as required by law. Nor does it appear that there was a protocol for addressing complaints by teachers. Settlegoode's supervisors responded that writing letters was not appropriate but they did not point out the proper procedures to initiate necessary change. The only data consulted prior to the nonrenewal decision were Settlegoode's evaluations by her supervisor, which suspiciously went from good to bad after Settlegoode wrote her first letter. The court noted that there was no evidence supporting the negative evaluations other than the word of the supervisor who was also the target of some of Settlegoode's complaints. Finally, there was no independent investigation by the school district to verify the version of events as reported by the supervisors.[1]

Macy v. Hopkins County School Board of Education   A teacher claimed she was fired because she was disabled. The school district successfully claimed that the teacher was dismissed for threatening students and making inappropriate remarks about the students and their families. The teacher had experienced a head injury several years in the past that impaired her ability to behave rationally in stressful situations. She argued that her actions were a result of her disability. The court found that the district could fire her even if her actions were a result of her disability because a teacher who was not disabled could be fired for the same behavior. The district was able to support the charge of threatening the students, as Macy was convicted on criminal charges relating to the event. The district also had evidence of over 20 other incidents of misconduct (*Macy*, 2007). The school district in this case was protected, in part, because of its well-documented record of the incident and previous incidents over time.

Reduction in Force

Sometimes school districts are forced to dismiss teachers who have done nothing wrong in the face of budget cuts or enrollment declines. State law governs the procedures school districts must follow when a reduction in force (RIF) is necessary, but districts must be aware of federal law as well. Generally, a tenured teacher may not be laid off ahead of a non-tenured teacher if the tenured teacher is properly licensed.

In *Taxman v. Board of Education of Piscataway* (1996) an unusual scenario developed when the school board chose to reduce the teaching staff in the business department at the high school by one. Following New Jersey law and procedures, the dismissal decision came down to Sharon Taxman, who is White, and Debra Williams, who is African American. Both were hired on the same day 9 years prior to the RIF decision and both teachers had favorable evaluations and in all other aspects were considered "tied." Since Williams was the only minority teacher in the business department, the school board chose to apply the district's affirmative action policy to break the tie between Williams and Taxman. Therefore, Taxman was laid off. The board's president justified this decision by arguing that the board wanted a culturally diverse staff as it was to the educational advantage of students to come into contact with people of different cultures and backgrounds. Taxman sued, claiming the district had violated Title VII of the Civil Rights Act, which prohibits an employer to discriminate based on race.

The Court of Appeals ruled in favor of Taxman and against the school board. While the court applauded the goal of racial diversity, it found that Title VII only allows employers to make decisions based on race when attempting to remedy past discrimination or a manifest imbalance in the employment of minorities. While Williams was the only African American in the business department at the high school, African Americans were not underrepresented among teachers in the district or at the high school. The policy unnecessarily trammeled the interests of the non-minority employees as it could be used to grant racial preferences. In *Taxman*, therefore, the board used racial data and laudable goals to make an employment decision that satisfied state procedural requirements but violated federal civil rights law.

Using Student Data Appropriately

School administrators, teachers, and other school personnel, such as counselors and special services staff, often use student data as they make decisions, both about individual students and groups of students. In doing so, it is important to be familiar with both federal and state laws and regulations that pertain to the use and confidentiality of such information.

The Family Educational Rights and Privacy Act

From a federal perspective, sharing data related to student records, which is the bulk of information on students, falls under the Family Educational Rights and Privacy Act. Also known as the Buckley Amendment and commonly referred to by its acronym, FERPA, this federal law ensures students and their parents certain rights relative to student records. The general rule, subject to several exceptions, is that parents are granted access to their children's educational records and schools may not divulge student educational records to others without the consent of the parents or students aged 18 or older (FERPA, 2000).

This law was first enacted as part of the Educational Amendments of 1974, which extended the Elementary and Secondary Education Act of 1965. Congress has amended FERPA seven times, with the most recent amendments occurring in 2000 (Daggett, 2007; Daggett & Huefner, 2001). In essence, FERPA requires compliance on the part of all educational agencies or institutions that receive federal funding. If a school district or any other educational organization receiving federal funding violates FERPA, then it could lose their funding.

Parent and Student Access   Rights granted under FERPA do not apply to the students themselves unless they are 18 years old or enrolled in a postsecondary institution. Thus, students under the age of 18 are not explicitly given these rights; however, they can and do extend to students of 18 and over (referred to in the law as "eligible students") and minor students' parents, guardians, or persons acting in the place of a natural parent.

The law defines educational records as "records, files, documents, and other materials" that "contain information directly related to a student" and are "maintained by an educational agency or institution or by a person acting for such agency or institution" (FERPA, 2000). Student discipline records are included in FERPA but certain records may still be shared with any teacher or school official with a legitimate interest in a student's behavior if the student's conduct "posed a significant risk to the safety or well-being of that student, other students, or other members of the school community" (FERPA, 2000).

The United States government's Family Policy Compliance Office explains that parents or eligible students may "inspect and review" students' educational records. They may also request the school to correct records "which they [parents or eligible students] believe to be inaccurate or misleading." If the school disagrees and refuses to make these changes, those persons reviewing the records may be afforded a formal hearing. If no changes are made after the formal hearing, the parent or eligible student has the right to place a written statement in the file telling why he or she contested the record (FPCO, 2007).

Access of Others   FERPA also limits the access of others to a student's educational record. In these instances, records cannot be released to a third party without the parent's or eligible student's written permission. Exceptions to this rule include: teachers and school officials with legitimate educational interest; schools where the students are transferring; officials with duties related to auditing or evaluation; financial aid officers; organizations conducting studies "for or on behalf of the school"; accrediting agencies; judicial orders or subpoenas; emergencies relevant to health or safety; and in accordance with state law, juvenile justice authorities. Schools must keep a record of many of these disclosures and those who receive student records are also obligated not to redisclose such records except as permitted by FERPA (FERPA, 2000).

It is sometimes difficult to determine where the line stands between educational records protected by FERPA and other materials that are not. The Supreme Court helped refine the definition when it unanimously decided that papers graded by other students in class are not student records under FERPA (*Owasso I.S.D. v. Falvo*, 2002). In *Falvo* a parent objected to the common practice of students exchanging assignments and tests and grading them in class as the teacher explains the correct answers to the entire class. The Supreme Court held that though student papers do contain information directly related to the student, they are not records under FERPA because an educational agency or institution does not maintain them (*Falvo*, 2002, p. 433).

Student papers are not maintained as contemplated by the statute, since students only handle the papers while the teacher calls out the answers. To decide otherwise would require adherence to burdensome notice, recording and hearing procedures for schools and teachers that Congress could not have intended. The Court also noted the educational value of going over an assignment as a class, since it gives teachers a chance to reinforce the lesson and discover whether the students have understood the material (*Falvo*, 2002).

Directory Information   Schools may make available "directory" information to outside sources without parental consent. However, the school must tell parents and eligible students of their intentions to disclose as well as provide "reasonable" time for these individuals to request non-disclosure. Directory information may include "a student's name, address, telephone number, date and place of birth, honors and awards, and dates of attendance" (Family Policy Compliance Office, 2007). Each year, the school must notify parents and eligible students of their rights under FERPA in a manner at the discretion of each school. The most common ways of notification include a letter, inclusion in a student handbook or PTA bulletin, or an article in the local newspaper (FPCO, 2007).

Remedies   One potentially confusing aspect of FERPA is that it does not afford private citizens a private right to legal action (*Gonzaga v. Doe*, 2002). This means parents and eligible students cannot sue for damages for violations of FERPA. Therefore, parents' primary remedy for violations of FERPA pertaining to their child is to complain to the United States Department of Education through the Family Policy Compliance Office (Daggett & Huefner, 2001). The office then investigates whether a violation has taken place and works with the offending party to remedy the problem.

The lack of a private right of action under FERPA does not mean that parents are without remedy, however, as most states have statutes that also protect student data and provide a private right of action. In fact, state privacy laws may be a greater cause for caution than federal laws (Stuart, 2005). Stuart warns that school districts that are just complying with federal privacy laws may not have enough protection from litigation as many states have stricter laws and regulations, especially about releasing student information to third parties, than does FERPA.

One recent example of a successful action against a school district occurred when a Minnesota family sued Minneapolis Public Schools for violation of the Minnesota Government Data Practices Act (MGDPA). Two students found copies of a special education summary report about the plaintiff's son blowing in the wind in a school parking lot and were showing that information to others in the school and calling the child "dumb," "stupid," and "retarded." A state appeals court upheld the jury verdict for the parents finding that the MGDPA required school districts to establish appropriate security safeguards for all records containing student data (*Scott v. Minneapolis Public Schools*, 2006).

Other Acceptable Use of Student Data   In addition to exceptions for the release of individual records mentioned above, FERPA and states generally allow the use of student data when they are part of a set of student data and the individual students cannot be identified. A typical example of this is the reporting of state test scores for

NCLB purposes. NCLB requires disaggregated reports of a range of demographic categories but lets states set a minimum number of students for each category. Part of the purpose of this requirement is to prevent a small number of students in any category from skewing adequate yearly progress (AYP) efforts. Another reason is to prevent easy identification of students when there are only a few who fit in demographic categories.

Student data may also be used to develop programs for the benefit of students as a whole. In New Jersey, local social service agencies enlisted the help of the school district to administer a survey to middle and high school students asking about such things as their community and school involvement, relationships, sexuality, stress and depression, drug and alcohol use, sexual matters, and suicide attempts. The survey was supposed to be anonymous and voluntary and the results were to be utilized to determine how to use the town's programs and resources more effectively. The U.S. Court of Appeals found that while a jury could have inferred that the survey was really involuntary, the survey was anonymous. Any personal information was adequately safeguarded and any disclosure occurred only in a way that did not permit individual identification. Furthermore, as the survey was an attempt to understand and prevent social problems confronting youth, the Court found that the goal of the survey was laudable and pursued with the best interests of the students in mind (*C.N. v. Ridgewood Board of Education*, 2005).

Individuals with Disabilities Education Act

Students receiving special education services are another potential area that can cause school leaders legal trouble. Data collection and its use in decision making can influence the outcome of these disputes. The Individuals with Disabilities Education Act (IDEA, 2004) is the federal law that primarily controls this area of education. Its accompanying regulations, state statutes that supplement IDEA and their regulations, create a morass of rules and procedures that must be followed when deciding and implementing the appropriate educational program for a student with special needs. The use of data is very important in the creation of the individual education program (IEP) of special education students. As such, the information gathered before, during, and after the development of each IEP is heavily regulated and protected. Consequently, IDEA requires much more care over student records than FERPA as states are mandated by law to give special education students greater privacy rights than general education students (Stuart, 2005). Parents have access rights to the records and must be given consent prior to disclosure of the records to a party other than those participating in the educational program of the student. Also, a school must have a designated person to safeguard the confidentiality of special education student files and keep track of who has access to the files (IDEA, 2004).

In addition to record keeping, IDEA and its regulations require procedures for virtually every step of the special education process from testing for the need of services to appealing the adequacy of the provision of services. A thorough description of these procedures is beyond the purpose of this chapter but school leaders should be aware of the importance of following procedural requirements. Failure to do so can cost a school district a great deal more time and money than compliance would have taken originally. By the same token, careful adherence to procedures and the gathering and proper use of appropriate evidence and materials throughout the special education process can protect school districts if legal action is taken against them. There are countless cases involving special education, but two examples may prove instructive.

In one such case, parents were unhappy over the implementation of their child's IEP. E.C., a child with multiple disabilities, was supposed to receive three 45-minute speech and language therapy sessions a week on three different days but did not receive therapy on the exact days and often not for the whole 45 minutes. In an appeal of an administrative hearing, the court found that the therapy sessions were shortened due to the student's fatigue and fading attentiveness. The therapist's schedule made it impossible to be in the school at the exact times originally scheduled but she added sessions to make up for her absence on the scheduled day. The court held that the shortcomings in meeting the exact words of the IEP did not constitute a failure to provide a free appropriate public education (*Catalan v. District of Columbia*, 2007).

Another common action by parents is to move their student to a private school and try to have the school district pay for it. In these instances, it is the responsibility of the school district to show that the IEP for a student is sufficient to provide a free appropriate public education in the public school. In a Massachusetts case, parents of a student requiring an IEP unilaterally placed their child in a private school. The court found that the parents had notified the school district of the intended move in a timely manner and the hearing officer found that the IEP did not adequately address the child's specific disabilities. The school district was therefore required to pay the tuition at the private school (*North Reading School Committee v. Bureau of Special Education Appeals of Massachusetts*, 2007). These types of decisions do not always favor the parent. Therefore, it is critical that school districts create an IEP based on appropriate data to support their position.

Conclusion

As federal initiatives such as NCLB have come to drive education policy, data-driven decision making has risen in prominence. More than ever, educational leaders must develop and use information systems for making important decisions in hopes of improving education and raising student achievement scores (Kowalski, Lasley, & Mahoney, 2008). Along with NCLB, other federal and state laws, constitutional protections, and court decisions must be considered when making decisions, even those based on data.

In this chapter, we have taken a glance at how law relates to the constitutional and statutory civil rights of both teachers and students. These laws and other federal statutes protecting teachers and students with disabilities and the privacy of students, influence both policy and personnel decisions. State laws protecting students' privacy and governing the protocol, procedures, and proof required in teacher discipline and dismissal decisions further encumber the decision-making process.

The use of data to drive decision making takes place in a complex and multi-faceted legal environment. Data are used to provide the basis and support for personnel decisions, student IEP formation, and policy, curriculum, and resource allocation decisions driven by NCLB and other laws. These data, however, must be created, managed, and used in compliance with the law. The cost of litigation is high and the wise educational leader who considers these legal dimensions before making new policies and during the decision-making process will be better situated to avoid or successfully face any legal challenges to those policies and decisions. In sum, whether decisions are in response to educational policy making and implementation, personnel decisions, or addressing student needs, using data to make objective, analytical, and informed decisions has important legal implications that should not and cannot be ignored.

Note

1. Two subsequent cases *Garcetti v. Ceballos*, 126 S.Ct. 1951 (2006) and *Weintraub v. Board of Education*, 489 F. Supp. 2d 209 (E.D. N.Y. 2007) call into question whether complaints like Settlegoode's made in a work context would still be protected speech.

References

Bellairs v. Beaverton School District, 136 P.3d 93 (Or. App. 2006).

Brown v. Board of Education of Topeka, 347 U.S. 483 (1954).

Catalan v. District of Columbia, 478 F. Supp. 2d 73 (D.D.C. 2007).

Civil Rights Act, 42 U.S.C. §2000 et seq. (1964).

C.N. v. Ridgewood Board of Education, 430 F.3d 159 (3rd Cir. 2005).

Daggett, L. M. (2007, November). *FERPA update 2007*. Paper presented at the Education Law Association 53rd Annual Conference, San Diego, CA.

Daggett, L. M., & Huefner, D. S. (2001). Recognizing schools' legitimate educational interests: Rethinking FERPA's approach to the confidentiality of student discipline and classroom records. *The American University Law Review, 51*, 1.

Family Educational Rights and Privacy Act, 20 U.S.C. §1232g, 34 C.F.R. Part 99 (2000).

Family Policy Compliance Office (2007). *Family Educational Rights and Privacy Act (FERPA)*. Retrieved December 16, 2007, from http://www.ed.gov/policy/gen/guid/fpco/ferpa/index.html

Farmer v. Kelleys Island Board of Education, 69 Ohio St. 3d 156, 630 N.E. 2d 721 (1994).

Gonzaga v. Doe, 536 U.S. 273 (2002).

Grutter v. Bollinger, 539 U.S. 306 (2003).

Individuals with Disabilities Education Act, 20 U.S.C. §1400 et seq., 34 C.F.R. Parts 300 and 301 (2004).

Kowalski, T. J., Lasley, T. J., & Mahoney, J. W. (2008). *Data-driven decisions and school leadership*. Boston: Pearson Education, Inc.

Layman v. Perry Local School District Board of Education, 94 Ohio St. 1410, 759 N.E. 2d 787 (2001).

Macy v. Hopkins County Board of Education, 484 F.3d 357 (6th Cir.), *cert. denied* 128 S.Ct. 201 (2007).

New No Child Left Behind flexibility: Highly qualified teachers (2005, November 29). Retrieved September 13, 2007, from http://www.ed.gov/nclb/methods/teachers/hqtflexibility.html

No Child Left Behind Act, 20 U.S.C. §6301 (2002).

North Reading School Committee v. Bureau of Special Education Appeals of Massachusetts, 480 F. Supp. 2d 479 (D. Mass, 2007).

Owasso Independent School District v. Falvo, 534 U.S. 426 (2002).

Parents Involved in Community Schools v. Seattle Public School District No. 1, 127 S.Ct. 2738 (2007).

Rossow, L. F., & Tate, J. O. (2003). *The law of teacher evaluation* (2nd ed.). Dayton, OH: Education Law Association.

Scott v. Minneapolis Public Schools, Special Dist. No. 1, 2006 WL 997721 (Minn. Ct. App. 2006).

Settlegoode v. Portland Public Schools, 371 F.3d 503 (9th Cir.), *cert. denied* 543 U.S. 979 (2004).

Shepard v. Fairland Local School District Board of Education, 2000 WL 1717551 (Ohio Ct. App. 2000).

Stuart, S. P. (2005). A local distinction: State education privacy laws for public school children. *West Virginia Law Review, 108,* 361.

Taxman v. Board of Education for the Township of Piscataway, 91 F.3d 1547 (3rd Cir. 1996), *cert. granted* 521 U.S. 1117, *cert. dismissed* 522 U.S. 1010 (1997).

Torres, M. S. & Stefkovich, J. A. (2005). The No Child Left Behind Act. In K. E. Lane, M. J. Connelly, J. F. Mead, M. Gooden, & S. Eckes (Eds.), *The principal's legal handbook* (3rd ed., pp. 365–381). Dayton, OH: Education Law Association.

4

The Role of Private Firms in Data-Based Decision Making

Patricia Burch and Tracy Hayes
University of Wisconsin-Madison

Since the adoption of the No Child Left Behind Act (NCLB), the 2001 reauthorization of the Elementary and Secondary Education Act (ESEA), the work of schools has been focused increasingly on the collection of data and the use of the data in informing policy decisions (U.S. Department of Education, 2001). Although significant numbers of large, urban districts are purchasing testing goods and services (as suggested by the survey data reported in a subsequent section of this chapter) there is virtually no scholarly research on their use or impact. There are case studies provided by vendors themselves, which are available on their Web sites, but most of these do not appear to be based on systematic, rigorous research. There is a nascent and insightful scholarship conducted by a handful of academics seeking to understand *how* these systems are being used (Halverson, Pritchett, Grigg, & Thomas, 2005; Mandinach, Rivas, Light, & Heinze, 2006). However, these studies are isolated examples.

This chapter aims to contribute to research on the implementation and effects of the current press for data-based decision making through analysis of both the role of private firms as suppliers of the goods and services being purchased to meet the mandates of NCLB and the recent trend toward the adoption of testing technology. We present empirical evidence of widespread district purchase of testing technology since the adoption of NCLB, the cost of services, and patterns in usage. The emphasis of NCLB on test score data has triggered some interesting and potentially useful innovations in the testing market, in particular improvements and needed overhaul in the design of tests themselves. However, on balance, the kinds of goods and services being designed by firms in response to adequate yearly progress (AYP) mandates represent a very partial and potentially costly solution to a deeper set of problems linked to long-standing structural inequalities and institutionalized district practices.

Research Methods

To begin to map the policy landscape of testing technology from the perspective of public agencies and customers, we collected survey data from 28 of the 30 largest school districts in the United States. We drew our sample from the 2003–2004 survey of the 100 largest school districts as conducted by the National Center for Education Statistics (NCES, 2006). These were the 30 largest districts in the country as measured by student enrollment in the 2003–2004 school years.

The survey data provided broad patterns in district usage, but provided little in the way of contextualized knowledge of how local political, economic, and social histories interact with and shape the implementation of testing technology. To investigate more micro-level contextualized influences, we selected three communities, each of which contracted with a firm that provided assessment solutions, and we conducted case studies in these communities. These case studies included interviews with district administrators, school staff, and firm employees. Based on this combined analysis, we conclude with a discussion of potential benefits and risks in the trends described and offer several suggestions for further developing depth of understanding around these issues and informing action.

NCLB placed heavy emphasis on expanding the scale of testing in K-12 schools, both through mandates regarding the frequency of testing (once a year), the scope of testing (students in all public schools, including English Language Learners and Special Education students), and even the format of tests. With regard to the latter, it required that states design and administer tests in English to students attending public schools in the United States for three years or more. NCLB also introduced a highly detailed set of regulations about how the data should be analyzed, reported, and disseminated (by subgroup, within a certain time frame, and via new reporting formats, to parents).

Benchmark Assessment Systems as a Strategy for Complying with NCLB

Although NCLB provided detailed guidance to local and state governments around testing, devising ways to pay for the tests and their administration remained the responsibility of local and state education agencies. In response to the mandates of NCLB, communities have purchased benchmark assessment systems. We use the term benchmark assessment systems to describe the services and products that districts and states employ to gauge student performance on standardized tests system-wide prior to the annual state level summative exams that are used to measure AYP under NCLB. The cost structure of benchmark assessment systems is different from the textbook and testing purchases of the past. Rather than actually purchasing a device as in the case of a textbook, typically districts lease the system for one to three years. The basic contract is for the database shell—the application that allows the district to store test results and generate and disaggregate data. The district will sign up for a software license and an initial year of support and services to implement the system. Firms typically charge about 20% of the license for the support services which include telephone support and updates for the product. These costs, as described later in the chapter, appear to range from $5 to $15 annually per student. In addition to the basic contract, districts may decide to purchase additional supplementary components such as professional development, kits for customizing analysis of data in ways that are aligned with state or local policies, and software for generating different kinds of reports.

As current subscribers, districts may receive free software updates from the con-tractor as they become available. However, these updates tend to be automatic, and every district with a contract with the firm receives them. New software typically is loaded onto the district server whether the district desires it or not. When districts lease the software, issues of ownership over data can also become more blurred. In the past, assessment data (in paper form) would be housed in the district offices—typically under the jurisdiction and lock and key of offices with titles such as Research and Evaluation. In the current structure, data can be housed on a server managed and operated by external providers. Firms that sell assessment software offer these services at an additional charge. The security of these data is the responsi-bility of the firm, although the confidentiality of the data is governed in part by local and federal policy.

The cost structure of the system has implications for public access and ownership of the data. When districts purchase textbooks, they may not have control over the design of the content; yet through the contract, they acquire a physical asset—the textbook itself, which they keep even if they decide to adopt a different textbook series from a different publisher. In contrast, when they contract with private firms of testing software, districts do not own the software that is used for managing the requirements of NCLB and its instructional goals. They borrow it. They essentially lease the shell or software program that allows them to manipulate the test score data. If they terminate the contract, they no longer have access to the shell and may not have access to the data.

Preliminary Trends in District Purchases and Usage

To begin to investigate local perspectives and responses to industry developments, district officials in 30 large urban school systems were surveyed. Survey questions were designed to map the extent to which large, urban school districts are purchasing benchmark assessment systems in order to meet the mandates of NCLB and to begin to identify where the pressure for these purchases originates. The sample was limited to all 30 school districts (excluding Puerto Rico and Hawaii, which are state-run organizations) with a student population greater than 94,000 according to the NCES report, *Characteristics of the Largest 100 Public Elementary and Secondary School Districts in the United States, 2003–2004.* As reflected in Table 4.1, we received a response from at least one official in 93.33% of the 30 school districts surveyed. Out of a total of 148 people across those districts, 54 (36.54%) responded. The people most likely to respond were those in the role groups of Technology (32.69%) and Research, Assessment, and Accountability (32.69%), although we also received responses from those in Title I Administration (15.38%), Budget and Finance (13.46%), and Curriculum and Instruction (9.25%). There are several primary patterns suggested by the survey data.

Table 4.1 District survey: Characteristics of sample.

Response rate (districts)	93.33%
Response rate (individual respondents)	36.54%
Percent of responding districts by region	
South/Southeast	53.57%
Northeast	21.42%
West	14.29%
Midwest	10.71%
Percent of individual respondents by role group	
Technology	32.69%
Research, Assessment, and Accountability	32.69%
Title I/Supplemental Educational Services	15.38%
Budget and Finance	13.46%
Curriculum and Instruction	9.25%

Widespread Use of Benchmark Assessment Systems

Large urban school districts are purchasing testing technology and doing so in part to meet the mandates of NCLB. Over 82% of the responding districts indicated that their district currently invested in the testing technology commonly known as a benchmark assessment system that was intended to allow them to administer periodic assessments and score, disaggregate and report the results to stakeholders in the district. Sixty-nine percent (69.57%) of these districts stated that they had purchased their system since the passage of NCLB. Five districts (21.74%) purchased their systems before NCLB. Two districts (8.7%) were unaware of when the system was purchased.

While NCLB is an important factor, district officials reported that the pressure to purchase these systems is coming from multiple directions. This includes pressure from school boards and superintendents (73.91%) and state mandates (52.17%). A much smaller percentage identified the pressure to purchase the system as emanating from pressures *within* lower levels of the system including other district staff (13.04%), school administrators (8.69%), and teachers (21.74%).

Improving instruction across grade levels appeared to be a prominent objective for purchasing the system; simplifying accountability reporting was not. By and large, the two most frequently mentioned goals were improving instruction (47.83%) and predicting student progress (17.39%). Employees from several of the districts gave differing responses, but all of those responses were the same as the two mentioned above. No district or individual respondent selected simplifying accountability reporting as a primary goal for the system.

These systems are typically implemented across all grade levels at most schools within each district. Eighty-two percent of districts which have a system report that it is in place at all levels: elementary, middle, and high school. Only one district indicated that the system had been installed in only the elementary and middle grades. In addition, nearly two-thirds of districts had installed the system at 76 to 100% of their schools.

Officials from five districts gave answers which varied from their co-workers when indicating what percentage of their schools had installed the system. This may indicate an ongoing, phased rollout of the system. Indeed, when asked to choose an adjective to describe the speed of system implementation, employees from 26.09% of districts all selected "phased." The discrepancy in answers between some colleagues also points to minimal involvement in implementation by employees of certain departments. This conclusion is further supported by the fact that a discrepancy in answers also occurred between officials in 39.10% of our districts when they were asked about implementation speed.

Many Suppliers; No Apparent Monopoly Yet

Interestingly, although many of the large vendors of this technology claim to be working with hundreds of school districts (Burch, in press), they were a very small presence among this group of large, urban districts. The most frequently mentioned products were Edusoft, a product of Riverside Publishing (a Houghton Mifflin subsidiary), and The Princeton Review, which is a public company specializing in standardized test preparation and K-12 solutions. However, Edusoft is currently in place in only three out of the 23 districts with systems, and Princeton Review was mentioned by only four districts. Additionally, 50 to 75% of those districts who mentioned either Edusoft or Princeton Review also indicated other systems. About 10.53% of officials indicated that the district's prior relationship with the provider was the main reason for their district's choice of provider. Therefore, although familiarity with a provider appeared to have no effect on a district's decision to buy a benchmark assessment system in the first place, it did give some of the major players a slight advantage over others once the district had made the choice to buy.

Cost of Systems

District officials across role groups appeared to have limited information about the costs of the systems. However, as reflected in Figure 4.1, of the 15 districts that were able to answer this question, all of them paid under $15 per student per year, and the majority (80%) paid under $10 per student per year. If these estimates were to apply to all the districts in the sample, the base cost of a system (without add-ons) per student per year would vary within the approximate ranges of $200,000 to $500,000 for the smallest district, and $1.4 million to $4 million for the largest.

The full costs of these services and products may be much higher given that 24 of the 28 districts reported purchasing additional components from vendors and that in interviews executives described setting up software licenses in ways that required customers to make additional purchases over time as part of the contract. Over 43% of districts purchased services marketed as helping them customize assessments, while 30.43% of districts reported that they purchased additional question item banks. Over 20% of districts bought professional development and over 25% bought a service contract. Only four districts did not buy any additional components, either

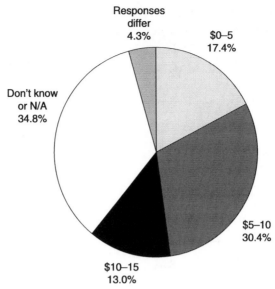

Figure 4.1 Cost of assessment systems.

Note: Based on responses from 23 districts.

because they were still investigating options or because they built their own systems and therefore did not have to "purchase."

Relative to district spending as a whole, the amount of money being spent on these systems is small. In our sample, the range of per-pupil spending falls between $6,000 and $11,000 per student per year. Thus, given the cost per student estimated above, benchmark systems represent approximately 1% of what districts spend on students every year. The more fundamental issue, which requires additional research, concerns the indirect and hidden costs to districts for these purchases, as suggested from our case study data. This includes the significant costs involved in the development and administration of the Request for Proposal process, and the training and capacity building of firms that may have little experience in school districts or in the education market generally.

There appears to be a lack of connection between the policy impetus for buying the system and the funds used for the purchase. Even though external forces (policy pressures emanating from outside of the district) are identified by districts as driving purchases, districts are relying heavily on district general funds in order to cover the cost of the systems. In the survey, 60.87% reported drawing on district general funds. However, only six (26.08%) districts listed funds from ESEA as having helped to pay for their system, and a mere 13.04% drew on state funds (see Figure 4.2).

Varying Perceptions of Usage

In the survey, we also asked district officials for their assessment of the percentage of teachers, school administrators, and district officials who they believed were active users of the benchmark assessment systems (see Figures 4.3 and 4.4). Perceptions of

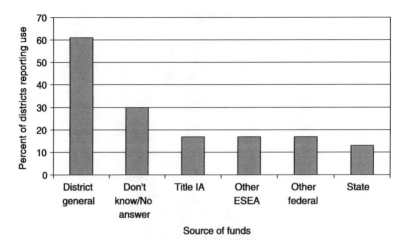

Figure 4.2 Funding streams for purchase and implementation of assessment systems.

Note: Based on responses from 23 districts. Respondents could choose multiple sources of funding.

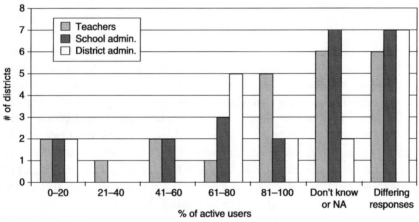

Figure 4.3 District perceptions of active use of the benchmark assessment system among teachers, school administrators, and district administrators.

Note: Based on responses from 23 districts.

active use differed dramatically both between and within role groups. The majority of respondents felt that less than 80% of district administrators were active users. As a group, respondents were much more likely to identify higher numbers of active users among both school administrators and teachers. A full 27% of respondents had no idea how many employees in any role group were active users of the system. When disaggregated by district instead of by official, the responses also show that perceptions differ not only between districts, but within them. Within very few districts were respondents in agreement over what percentage of teachers, school administrators, and district administrators were active users of the system. All respondents within 30.43% of districts had no idea how many school and district administrators were active users, and respondents within another 30.43% of districts disagreed with one another as to the percentages. There was only slightly less uncertainty when it

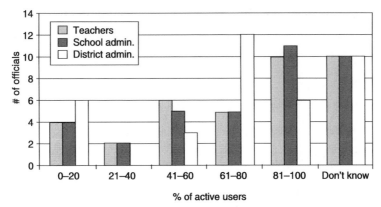

Figure 4.4 Officials' perceptions of the percentage of "active users" among teachers, school administrators, and district administrators.

Note: Based on responses from 37 officials across 23 districts.

came to perceptions of teacher usage. The primary conclusion that the data on usage support is that there is often not one prevailing perception of teacher, school administrator or district usage within or across districts.

These preliminary patterns raise several potential trends around the purchase of benchmark assessment systems in the move toward data-based decision making. We briefly identify these trends before exploring them in greater depth in the case studies that follow. First, the survey provides further evidence of the role of NCLB as a supporting factor in the selling of K-12 assessment services and goods. The data from the survey suggest that the pressure to buy is coming from multiple levels of the system, not just federal mandates. The pressures include superintendent/school board (72%), state mandates (50%) and NCLB (40%). These patterns appear to contradict or at least add nuance to assertions that districts' decisions to contract emanate from or are based primarily on internal needs or capacity. Here, as in other aspects of the education market, the pressure to contract is inextricably linked to the external policy environment (Burch, 2006).

Second, the survey data suggest evidence of loose coupling between district practice and private firms' policy intents. When applied to education, loose coupling generally refers to the gap between policy goals and administrative practices. Here, we are suggesting that loose coupling can also occur between private firms representing policy goals and the interests and practices of public agencies. While the marketing materials of firms emphasize economic principles of cost cutting, time efficiency, and ease of reporting, district officials intend the systems for a different set of purposes. They aim to use them to improve instruction and refer infrequently to the firms' stated objectives of streamlining reporting.

Third, those officials responsible for overseeing the implementation of these systems appear to possess either conflicting or limited knowledge about critical aspects of the systems. The systems are designed for use across multiple district departments and yet officials within districts appear to have limited and contradictory information about usage and cost. This trend is important because districts may actually need more support than they are getting in implementing the systems. In addition, if district officials cannot agree on usage figures, how can they judge whether the implementation has been successful or whether the system has managed to help them improve instruction?

Benchmark Assessment Systems in Local Context

We next consider the locally situated meanings and significance of the trends through three case studies of district practice. The first district, which we call Beachside, was a very large, decentralized urban school district with over 200,000 students. The second district, which we call Carbondale, was a much smaller urban school district with a student enrollment in the range of 40,000 to 50,000 students. The third district, which we call Chesterville, also was urban. It fell between Beachside and Carbondale in terms of student enrollment, with just over 100,000 students. During the school year in which data were collected, Carbondale was not yet in program improvement. In contrast, Beachside and Chesterville have both been in need of improvement since the 2004 to 2005 school years.

In each district, we conducted extended interviews with several district officials across different departments from January 2007 to August 2007. Data collection in each site included repeated semi-structured interviews with district officials and extensive document review. In one district (Carbondale) we supplemented interviews and document review with shadowing of district officials and observations of school level usage of benchmark assessment systems. In our primary case (Carbondale), we interviewed three staff members in the Department of Curriculum and Instruction, two staff in the Office of Technology and Instruction, and the Director of Assessment and Accountability. In Beachside, we interviewed the Director of Technology Instruction, the Director of Evaluation and Research and the Director of Curriculum and Instruction. In Chesterville, we spoke with the current Chief Academic Officer and Executive Director of Technology Instruction, and the former Director of Middle School Programs.

Each case focuses on the district level functions and challenges emerging in districts under pressure to make test score targets under NCLB. We start with a vignette of the implementation of Test Whiz in our primary case Carbondale and then compare this, through a narrative of broader brush strokes, to the implementation of Test Whiz in Beachside and Chesterville. All three case studies illustrate how power differentials within district organizations are activated by the purchase of these systems and the complex issues around equity and access that these "solutions" engender. Here, as in other forms of top-down policy, context still matters. Whether these systems are used and how they are adapted is contingent on local situations including the strength of unions and the size of the district.

Carbondale School District

The school district of the city of Carbondale enrolls approximately 40,000 to 50,000 students and is located in the western United States. Approximately 6,000 to 7,000 of the students in the district are ELL students and 4,000 have Individualized Education

Plans. Close to half the students enrolled in Carbondale identify as Hispanic or Latino. Approximately 30% of students enrolled are African American, and 10% are Asian. Over half of the residents in the city of Carbondale itself are White, 40% are Hispanic and Latino and 8% are African American. Approximately 16% of Carbondale's population lives below the poverty line. The school district was placed under court ordered desegregation in the mid-1960s. Most of the city's poverty and crime are concentrated in one area of the city—which is also largely African American and Latino. This neighborhood also has the highest unemployment rate in the district and lowest educational rate as measured in terms of number of adults over 18 with high school diplomas.

Sharon K has been a K-12 Mathematics Instructional Specialist in Carbondale since 1998. In her words, this meant that she was responsible "for all things mathematics" in the district, from overseeing textbook adoption every seven years, to organizing staff development for teachers across grade levels, to analyzing math scores for the district. Prior to her current position, she worked as a product development manager and before that as an elementary school principal. She was one of three African Americans working in the district at the level of professional—Master's degree and higher. She was raised "poor and Black" in central city Los Angeles and moved to Carbondale to attend college and obtain her teaching certification. She has lived there ever since.

Access to Data   In 2002, the district purchased a benchmark assessment system called Test Whiz. According to Sharon and others interviewed in the district, Test Whiz offered the district many advantages in terms of facilitating district management of large amounts of data. Before Test Whiz, teachers would score common assessments by hand. Staff would then get together at each school and with pencil and paper attempt to identify problem areas. There was little capacity for item analysis based on skill strands and little capacity for the district to develop a picture of student performance districtwide. Sharon found Test Whiz to be a useful tool for analyzing the added value of her own work and that of her staff and making more informed decisions about where to invest resources. On occasion, she would analyze the test scores of students in schools and classrooms in which her staff had done intensive staff development. In other instances, Sharon used Test Whiz to analyze the efficacy and equity of particular items on district level assessments. She would then use these data to assess students' difficulty with those items on a districtwide basis in relation to other items, as another gauge for where to focus staff development.

Further, Sharon and others in the district reported that Test Whiz had helped decentralize access to data within the district. Specifically, it made data more available to staff in Curriculum and Instruction, rather than being the exclusive domain of staff in Research and Accountability. Before the district began using Test Whiz, if Sharon was interested in comparing the performance of certain schools to others in the district (for example, schools with higher proportions of White students to schools with higher proportions of ELL and African American students) she would have to go through the Office of Research and Accountability—the four-person department that occupied a small room on the second floor of the district offices. It could be weeks or even months before Sharon could expect an answer. With Test Whiz, there was less paper and Sharon could simply conduct the analyses herself.

Raising Attention to Equity Issues at District Level   Perhaps the thing that Sharon liked most about Test Whiz had less to do with Test Whiz and more to do with NCLB. While the district had a long history of collecting data—and like most districts, had an entire department devoted to this purpose—it rarely did anything with the data, according to Sharon. The data might show that there were significant differences in the academic performance of subgroups in the district by race or socioeconomic status, but from Sharon's perspective, the district rarely felt compelled to do anything about the gaps. The data were available (although time-consuming to obtain) but even after being analyzed "they just sat there." Sharon referred to her district's approach to data before NCLB and Test Whiz as "living on the average." It paid attention to the kids in the middle and ignored the sharp differentials between the scores of children at the high and low ends of the scale. In a district which one of the few African American district employees characterized as largely indifferent to the needs of students of color, Test Whiz made available to the district for the first time periodic (rather than annual) data of student performance by race and income level.

In other ways Test Whiz seemed to Sharon and others to be disconnected from the core issues of equity and access in the district. One core issue involved teachers' low expectations of students of color and students living in poverty. Throughout her years in the district, Sharon had become increasingly convinced that ELL and African American students in the district were not being given the same opportunities to learn challenging content in spite of state standards and in spite of the fact that the district was no longer under a court desegregation order. Specifically, early in her career, while teaching at a low-income, high-ELL, high-minority school, she had been at first surprised at the amount of improvement her students would make and then eventually realized after consulting with the students' teachers from past years that they had not been held to grade level expectations before, but had been given a watered down curriculum. Later, as a curriculum staff developer, she recalled walking through the campus of a school that had consistently low test scores for ELL and African American students and while visiting the classrooms, "seeing that not a single classroom in the school was teaching on grade level and that students of color and ELL students were assigned to what was quietly referred to as 'non-regular classes.'"

For individuals like Sharon, who know the district and have committed their lives to it, the achievement gap stems primarily from lack of parity in students' opportunities to learn rather than inefficient district organization or lack of good data. This point hit home for Sharon last year while working with the group of schools that had not made proficiency under NCLB and were therefore deemed in need of improvement. In the course of Sharon's work with the schools it became clear to her that teachers in the second and third grades were not teaching fractions in ways defined by grade level standards. Analysis of test scores (powered by Test Whiz) had revealed low levels of proficiency in math for second- and third-grade students in the school, particularly as compared to the performance of second and third graders in a neighboring school that had a much smaller proportion of students from a low socio-economic bracket. The teachers interpreted the results to mean that the material was too hard for the students. When Sharon discussed the issue with the teachers, they told her they felt that their students (the majority of whom were Black, Latino and very poor) could not handle the content defined by grade level standards. In response, they had adjusted the curricula and adopted their own vision of what it meant to teach fractions at grade level standards for their students.

Thus, tools such as Test Whiz can assist in the goal of more democratic schooling by helping districts disaggregate data by subgroup. However, particularly in districts such as Carbondale, with long legacies of institutional racism, benchmark assessment systems appear to have little effect on deeply entrenched race- and class-based biases about who can achieve. In a policy climate where the rhetoric is heavy on "leaving no child behind," benchmark assessment systems hold out the promise of helping all children have access to challenging content and to achieve. However, as in the case of any other externally designed "reform," benchmark assessment systems are implemented into existing routines and systems of practice. This includes both systems of practice that may *enable* deep change in instruction as well as routines and deeply entrenched stereotypes that impede equal access and opportunity to challenging curriculum.

Beachside School District

Beachside is a much larger school district than Carbondale (over 200,000 students as opposed to 45,000 students). The City of Beachside is a large, densely populated area. It is a very diverse city in which 49% of residents are White, 10% are Black, 11% are Asian, 49% identify as Hispanic, and 27% identify as other ethnicities. Beachside School District serves one of the largest and most diverse populations of students in the country. The characteristics of this student population stand in marked contrast to those of the residents: 73% of Beachside students are Hispanic (not White or Black), 11% are Black, only 9% are White, and just over 6% are Asian, Pacific Islander, or Filipino. Almost 82% of Beachside schools are Title I eligible, and 64.4% of Beachside students participate in schoolwide Title I programs.

Although it has consistently increased the percentage of proficiency among students in most subgroups over the past four years, the district has still struggled to meet the mandates of NCLB, and in fact has never made AYP itself. Additionally, while some subgroups have met the criteria for AYP year after year, no subgroup is anywhere near 100% proficient in either language arts or mathematics. It is a highly decentralized district, separated into regions, with subject area coordinators designated for each region.

Beachside started experimenting with benchmark assessments in 2000, when the district adopted a curriculum for elementary reading that was offered through the state and included periodic assessments. This curriculum represented the first time that the district had adopted standardized tests that were to be used across all elementary schools. As one Beachside official notes, "prior to that, mostly, schools were using teacher-developed materials, or test prep, or end-of-chapter tests, but nothing was done in a systematic way to collect data." The assessments were given and then hand-scored by teachers. To enable the data from the assessments to really be of use to teachers and principals, a district employee developed a basic spreadsheet program into which the test data could be inputted. It eventually developed into a system that was connected to the district's student information system and would indicate in reports the teachers could print out which students were progressing as expected, which students were starting to struggle, and which were at a critical point of need.

In mid-2001, a new superintendent arrived at the district with a very strong view of where it should be headed. His theory of action was geared toward implementing a standards-based curriculum, improving instruction through professional development, school-site coaching for teachers, strong positive leadership, and periodic assessments. It was therefore time to expand the benchmark assessment system to include more grade levels and subject areas. Unfortunately, the district's developer, who by that time had gone out on his own, did not have the capacity to do it. The district had also been warned in an audit against building too many of its own structures from scratch because it could cost more time and money than buying products from outside vendors. So instead, they contracted with Test Whiz to design and write a series of benchmark assessments for multiple grade levels. The following year, Beachside later re-contracted with Test Whiz for three years of additional service at a fixed cost, with an annual option to renew.

The terms of the contract were discussed and agreed to by both sides beforehand. However, according to district officials, neither Test Whiz nor the vendor that succeeded Test Whiz was prepared for the size and complexity of the district. As reported by one district official, "The system was unusable for more than a year. They [vendor] were not prepared for the complexity of our district." Beachside district staff had to spend an extraordinary amount of time teaching Test Whiz about the district and helping the company adapt its products to the district's unique needs; for example, the fact that the district had year-round schools. After three years, the district signed a new contract with a new vendor. According to several administrators, the district then had to spend a whole year backtracking. As one individual commented, "We had to start all over with the new company."

In its bid for a renewed contract, Test Whiz had banked on the district paying a much higher price. The new price estimate was 50% greater than what the district had been paying ($6,000,000 versus $9,000,000). In addition, while Test Whiz had grown to know Beachside well, there were still aspects of the system that were not working. Specifically, under Test Whiz, teachers were responsible for scanning the test score data themselves, but the equipment that the district had purchased was not up to the demands of the system, and Beachside's strong teachers' union strenuously objected to this use of teachers' time. Furthermore, as in the case of Carbondale, the individuals we spoke with viewed the system as deeply disconnected from the deeper set of changes required if the achievement gap was to be addressed in any significant way. The Chief Instructional Officer in Beachside put it this way:

> Changing instruction is the hard work. Putting periodic assessments into the system is a snap compared to the larger issue of helping people understand how to use this [sic] data and how to create the conditions for teachers to help teachers be reflective about their practice. That's professional development in itself. It's conversations about removing barriers, it's about the

principal being present and observing their [sic] teachers. It is examining the quality of a grade level meeting and pressing on that quality. It's not letting people off the hook simply because they gave the test but getting them to look at the data. No, that is the hard work before us.

As in the case of Carbondale, Beachside officials also referenced the role of racist and class-based stereotypes, and a district culture "where it has been OK to look at data through the lens that it is the kids have the problem" rather than looking critically at district and school level policies and practices.

The implementation of the formative assessment system also depends on the strength of the union in the district and its involvement in the process. In Beachside, union officials appeared to have considerable input into the planning and use of formative assessment systems; specifically, when the assessments would be given, and whether teachers or the vendor would be responsible for scanning answer sheets. The union was adamantly opposed to an approach where teachers scanned the test scores themselves. Although the district had little sense beforehand that there might be an uproar, the strength of the union is likely one reason why Beachside was eventually forced to establish a contract with a vendor that provided scanning services rather than relying on teachers for this work. Part of what won the second vendor the contract was its solution to this issue, which involved having FedEx pick up answer sheets from each school and return them to a central location for scanning and uploading to the system.

The Beachside case further reveals the complex web of district policy and practice that intersect with the technological tools being introduced by private firms in the context of NCLB. As in the case of Carbondale, district officials in Beachside viewed contracts with firms like Test Whiz as one slice of what necessarily must be a larger set of system changes that involved professional development, collaboration and (over time, in part because of pressure from the union) respect for teachers' primary responsibility for classroom instruction. In Beachside as in Carbondale, effective implementation of the system required substantive learning and change on the part of the firm itself. The ability of firms to learn and adapt to diverse district contexts helps frame and define district level usage of the system and ultimately, its interactions with teachers around the system. At the same time, district context must play a large part in determining whether to lease a product off-the-shelf from an established firm, or to enter into partnership with a developer to build a system from scratch. This is illustrated by the decision made by our third case, Chesterville School District, which decided to create a system in-house tailored to its specific needs.

Chesterville School District

The Chesterville School District is a large, urban district with over 100,000 students. Along with the community that surrounds it, Chesterville has undergone sustained growth in recent years; doubling in student population since 1990. Unlike in Carbondale and Beachside, the majority of the students in the district are White. The percentage of Chesterville students enrolled in Title I programs also stands in marked contrast to both Carbondale and Beachside, although it has jumped dramatically with the increase in population. Much like Beachside, Chesterville has never made

AYP. Indeed, the percentage of schools making AYP within Chesterville has dropped steadily and dramatically over the past four years, from a high of nearly 75% in school year 2003 to 2004 to the current low of roughly 40% in year 2006 to 2007.

For years prior to 2001, Chesterville was what some researchers call "data rich and information poor" (Dufour, Eaker, & Dufour, 2005; Halverson et al., 2005). For example, in the elementary schools, teachers created detailed, handwritten profile cards for each student, on which they collected information about that child's performance in mathematics and literacy. However, as one official noted, "other than spreading all these cards out on the living room floor, there was really no way of grouping children to make informed instructional decisions." Each level of schooling was also at a different point with regard to the collection of data. While the elementary schools had their profile cards, the middle schools were referred to by some as "assessment-free zones" in which no formative data whatsoever were collected.

An initiative called Project SUCCESS was introduced to low-performing elementary and middle schools within the district beginning in school year 2001 to 2002. Project SUCCESS bills itself as a comprehensive school improvement program with seven components, one of which is "evaluation and outcomes." Chesterville implemented new curriculum and periodic assessments as part of the initiative. Project SUCCESS did not come with a benchmark assessment system, and as a result, the district hired a developer to produce a basic program to track the scores from the tests. The tests were all taken by hand and had to be run through a Scantron machine to be scored, and then the data had to be transferred to the database program and manually manipulated. Thus, there was a very slow turnaround of information, and the technology was in use only by schools that were struggling. By the start of the 2003 school year, only three out of 27 middle schools were participating in Project SUCCESS.

It was at this point that the Director of Middle School Programs decided that she needed a way to track and improve performance in her middle schools across the board, and seized upon the already existing Project SUCCESS assessments as a good way to start. However, she also wanted a more complex database system that would allow the tests to be taken online and an updated, improved capability for analysis and additional reports.

She began to investigate off-the-shelf assessment systems, but what she found was either prohibitively expensive or did not allow for the district's existing Project SUCCESS assessments to be used. Additionally, she needed something that would allow for the evolution of her program, and as another official noted, "if you were dealing with a commercial product, they would never change it. You'd have to adapt what you did to the commercial product." So instead, Chesterville officials began a discussion with the programmer who had built the program used to record scores for the Project SUCCESS schools, and asked if he could expand its capabilities and make the assessments available online to all students, and not just to those in struggling schools. Not only was he able to expand it, but the work he did cost much less than any estimates Chesterville had received from off-the-shelf vendors. Although Chesterville still leased the system from the developer, two of the officials we spoke to estimated that the system now known as Gold Star costs them under $5 per student per year.

Over the past three years, local demand for Gold Star skyrocketed. The system itself has evolved through the suggestions of teachers and central office staff members, who began to request adjustments and additions that would make it easier for them to manipulate and understand the data they collected through the assessments. Staff from all levels of the district also participated in expanding the range of assessments that was available, both by writing items and by participating in the item review process. It is now a comprehensive benchmark assessment system, similar to off-the-shelf products, yet customized to Chesterville's specifications. The system is widely used in elementary and middle schools, and has begun to expand into the high schools.

Although Gold Star is similar to Test Whiz in many ways, Chesterville's experience is distinct from that of Beachside and Carbondale. Officials spoke very positively of the responsiveness of the developer, of Gold Star itself, and of the changes in practice the system had helped to facilitate. For example, although there were initial technical problems with Gold Star, they were fixed very quickly after a simple series of visits the programmer made to schools using the system. Further, in speaking of the effects of the system, one official noted that it had actually helped teachers to break down some of their existing stereotypes. Because of the immediate availability of data, and the ability to see individual item analysis, teachers began to realize that kids who had been previously assumed to be of "low ability" were actually doing much better on some objectives than kids assumed to be of "higher ability." The system helped teachers not only change perceptions, but also understand how to build up support for students in crucial areas.

Chesterville's positive experience with Gold Star might be attributed to the fact that the impetus for the system was somewhat organic and came from the ground up rather than externally. Further, the fact that Gold Star was built and not bought off-the-shelf allowed for input from a much wider variety of school level stakeholders, and may have contributed to less initial resistance toward the system and a quicker adoption.

However, it would be a mistake to assume that building a system is the right choice for every district, or even for the other two in this study. Chesterville's unique structure and context allowed for this option in ways that neither Beachside's nor Carbondale's would have. For instance, with Beachside's strong and active union playing a major role in all teacher-related business it is unlikely that building a system would have been as quick or easy for its officials. The district might have had to formally negotiate the building of the system in a way that Chesterville, which has no teachers' union, did not. Similarly, in Carbondale, a district which had not struggled as much with its AYP goals, the local demand for data might not have been as urgent as it was in Chesterville, a district whose AYP performance had worsened every year since that standard's initiation.

Additional evidence to support the idea that customization is not always best can be found in the cost structure of the systems in Beachside and Chesterville. Both districts paid an annual licensing fee for the use of their systems which was based on the number of students and teachers, and which officials in both districts said fell in the range of $0 to $5 per student annually. Beachside's system came with a long list of different report formats that were available to teachers and administrators, which would reveal different things about the data. Chesterville, on the other hand, had to pay an additional fee for each new report officials wanted. Thus, rather than being available at a fixed price, the annual cost of Chesterville's system varied based on the changes the district made to it each year. In a district the size of Beachside, a fluctuating annual cost may not have been worth the level of customization it offered, especially if it meant sacrificing other benefits of choosing a large, established vendor—such as the unique scoring system Beachside's second provider ultimately offered. Ultimately, the decision of whether to build or buy a system appears to have no obvious or consistent answer, and again must depend on an analysis of each district's structure and available resources.

Benchmark Assessment Systems in the Era of NCLB

The events in these three districts cannot be assumed to generalize to all districts, but they do suggest some problems in the underlying assumptions of NCLB. First, sanctions and mandates may create the incentive for districts to test more frequently, to include special education students in the testing, and to look at data. However, on their own, they do not provide answers on how districts should address these problems, nor do they provide any real indicators of why these problems exist in the district in the first place.

Second, the best-designed, most efficient assessment services and devices are being introduced into social contexts where the people in charge of the system and the people using the system have deeply rooted expectations and stereotypes of what children can achieve. Even when the new technology is installed democratically so that every school has a log-in, even when the tool itself is keyed to local goals in its alignment to standards, even when the technology "works" and allows districts to manage data in a way that they never have before, the overall problem of uneven outcomes and expectations will remain unchanged. In a district like Carbondale where Test Whiz had been implemented across many schools, there were still students left behind, students whose teachers were excused from looking critically at their own practice, on the basis of assumptions about what students placed in special needs classrooms could achieve.

Third, once the decision has been made to use a benchmark assessment system, there is no easy or standard way to determine whether the most cost effective and productive choice would be to construct a system from scratch or lease one off-the-shelf. While constructing a system may win over stakeholders and lead to increased equity and changed perceptions of students as it did in Chesterville, it may also be impossible given the political constraints and the resources of the district in question. A district may spend millions of dollars implementing a system only to realize that there is a seemingly insurmountable roadblock standing in the way of full adoption.

In summary, the stories that unfolded in the three districts suggest the need for considerable caution on the part of districts racing to install benchmark assessment systems in order to meet the mandates of NCLB. For the testing industry, this is a very exciting time as the mandates of NCLB and other policy pressures create incentives for local purchases. The problem is *not* that private firms are involved in the design and delivery of testing and measurement services. These firms do bring to the table expertise that districts may lack. For example, they can assist in the development of tests that more accurately measure what students know and can do. Yet at the same time, these firms are currently not assisting districts in evaluating the full implications of their decisions, and are not engaged in assessing whether their product is really the right choice for each particular district. If a district is not able to muster the resources or make the changes required of practice at all levels, it runs the risk of allowing the assessment system to become a mechanism for unnecessary summative exams. Finally, as a strategy for helping schools and districts develop a more fine-grained and nuanced picture of their performance, draw appropriate conclusions from the data and use the data to revise district strategy, benchmark assessment systems hold considerable promise. Thoughtful attention by districts of the appropriate role of for-profit firms in developing and managing these systems is important. This should include consideration of the importance of developing internal district capacity, sustaining the work over time, and employing the data in the service of urgent equity issues.

Note

Portions of this chapter also appear in Burch, P. and Hayes, T. (2007) and Hayes, T. (2007). Burch is an Assistant Professor in the Department of Educational Policy Studies at the University of Wisconsin-Madison. At the time of writing, Hayes was a graduate student in the Department of Educational Policy Studies.

References

Burch, P. (2006). The new educational privatization: Educational contracting and high stakes accountability. *Teachers College Record, 108*(12), 2582–2610.

Burch, P. (in press). *Hidden markets: The new education privatization.* New York: Routledge.

Burch, P., & Hayes, T. (2007). *Accountability for sale: Testing, markets and NCLB.* Madison, WI: Center for Education Research.

Dufour, R., Eaker, R., & Dufour, R. (2005). Recurring themes of professional learning communities and the assumptions they challenge. In R. Dufour, R. Eaker, & R. Dufour (Eds.), *On common ground: The power of professional learning communities* (pp. 7–29). Bloomington, IN: Solution Tree.

Halverson, R., Prichett, R., Grigg, J., & Thomas, C. (2005). *The new instructional leadership: Creating data-driven instructional systems in schools* (WCER Working Paper No. 2005–10). Madison, WI: Center for Education Research.

Hayes, T. (2007). *Sea change: The proliferation of benchmark assessment systems in U.S. school districts.* Unpublished Master's thesis, University of Wisconsin, Madison.

Mandinach, E., Rivas, L., Light, D., & Heinze, C. (2006, April). *The impact of data-driven decision making tools on educational practice: A systems analysis of six school districts.* Paper presented at the annual meeting of the American Educational Research Association, San Francisco, CA.

National Center for Education Statistics (2006). *Characteristics of the 100 largest public elementary and secondary school districts in the United States: 2003–2004* (NCES Rep. No. 2006–329). Washington, DC: Author. Retrieved December 19, 2006, from http://nces.ed.gov/pubsearch/pubsinfo.asp?pubid=2006329.

U.S. Department of Education (2001). *NCLB overview.* Retrieved June 15, 2007, from http://www.ed.gov/nclb/overview/intro/execsumm.html.

5

The No Child Left Behind Act
Making Decisions Without Data or Other Reality Checks

Timothy R. Konold and James M. Kauffman
University of Virginia

Making Decisions Without Data or Other Reality Checks

A very strange thing happens to many people's thinking when education is the topic: they do not make use of reality checks, including knowledge of basic mathematics and fundamental statistical concepts, critical thinking, and data. They seem to assume that education operates in an alternate universe in which realities do not apply at all or may safely be assumed to be trivial or irrelevant to the task of teaching students. They seem not to make logical connections between words and their referents, not to employ basic concepts, not to demand reliable data, and not to engage in logical inductive or deductive thinking, all of which they rightfully expect of school children. Yet their discourse about education is taken seriously, and the result is what one would expect: failure. Given this level of discourse about education, it is no surprise to find the conclusion that "our so-called system of education is far less well planned and executed than our system of highways and of mail delivery" (Shattuck, 1999, p. 34). The actual improvement of education awaits the application by everyone whose discussion is taken seriously of data-based, reality-based thinking skills (Kauffman, 2002).

We realize that life is full of absurdities, but we think that rhetoric about education should not be among them. When someone suggests that all children will be able to perform at ___ (>0) level, that all children will succeed, that all students will be proficient, or that no child will be left behind, he or she is contributing to unhelpful silly talk about schools and schooling. Some individuals may argue that the No Child Left Behind Act (NCLB) at least focuses attention on education and motivates educators to work harder to make sure that all students achieve what they can. But NCLB is a prime example of absurd education policy that is divorced from data and reality checks about the meaning of data. (We assume that the basic provisions of NCLB are described in other chapters in this volume.)

Policies like NCLB, though conceptually flawed, may produce some benefits for some students, perhaps even for many. In fact, just about any policy enacted with good intentions, regardless of how conceptually vacuous, will benefit *some* students. However, policies like NCLB—based on irrational premises and ignoring important realities—are not only doomed to collapse, but in the longer term hurt the cause of education more than they help. We are not the only ones to note the irrationality of

NCLB and the blithe avoidance of realities by those who enacted it. "Oxymoron" is an accurate descriptor of the universal proficiency demanded by NCLB (Rothstein, Jacobsen, & Wilder, 2006).

Unfortunately, NCLB is not the only poorly conceived education policy. It is only a convenient and popular example. Senseless statements about education and policies to match them are common but incompatible with education's goals. "Especially in the case of education, which at its most fundamental level is helping people make sense of things, senseless rhetoric runs against the grain of what one is trying to accomplish" (Kauffman, 2002, p. 284). *Senseless rhetoric* describes much of what has been written and said about education by many educators, captains of industry, politicians, newspaper columnists, and others. Rhetoric may safely be judged senseless when it ignores any reality.

Most people realize that when they ignore data and other realities they are courting disaster. In fact, when someone ignores realities most observers conclude that he or she is mentally ill or at least is engaging in very dangerous behavior. We try to teach our progeny and our students about realities so that they do not harm themselves or others. If they ignore realities, we apply restrictions and warn them about the dangers of assuming that reality does not affect them. We want our children and our students to talk and act as if they are in a real world in which some things are universally, unalterably true, whether anyone likes it or not and where the reliability of data is important.

However, too often educators and others seem to assume that data and other realities are distractions, unimportant or avoidable in their proposals to reshape, restructure, or improve education. Their assumption may be based on one or more false premise. Sometimes, it is based on the philosophical proposition that what we consider realities are socially constructed by one's culture, and therefore not universal. Sometimes it reflects ignorance, misunderstanding, or presumed political finesse. Sometimes it is expressed as a desire to "think outside the box," as if the "box" of realities is an artificial constraint that needlessly inhibits creative thinking. It may sometimes reflect extreme frustration in trying to change education policy, such that an unrealistic policy may be supported as the best one can hope for—at least a beginning of change in the right direction. Or it may reflect the assumption that moral decisions can be made in the absence of reliable evidence or the misrepresentation of data to fit one's purposes (see Brantlinger, 2006; Gallagher, 2004; Gartner & Lipsky, 1989; Kohn, 1999, for examples of evading or denying realities while calling for reform). But regardless of *why* anyone thinks and talks as if realities do not exist in education or that data can be interpreted willy-nilly for one's benefit, this gambit has adverse consequences.

Also too often, any statement about education or any call for reform, regardless of its failure to conform to the real world, goes unchallenged. Some seem to assume that every statement or suggestion about education should be taken seriously. The consequences of this assumption are dire: actual improvement of education is stymied while possibilities that are only imaginary are pursued. Long ago, we learned that some things (e.g., turning lead to gold) are flatly impossible. For many things, proof is demanded in the scientific tradition before someone is allowed to market an idea or product. Nevertheless, as a society we have not only allowed but supported and sometimes even enshrined in law preposterous propositions about education. Silly talk—pretense—has too often been allowed to share a place at the table with serious talk about education. This produces babble, not constructive conversation.

In many ways, education *is* rocket science—complex, difficult to understand, and disastrous when one seemingly small detail is forgotten or one fundamental reality is overlooked. Space shuttle disasters occurred because little realities were neglected; getting things mostly right but making one critical assumption incorrectly can result in disaster. Getting things mostly right in education is not good enough either. In education, we too often forget or ignore realities that may be considered inconvenient but that bring about an inevitable policy failure when they are assumed to be trivial.

Education as an enterprise is supposedly designed to help students separate fact from fiction and deal productively with the confusing world in which we live. Teaching based on the premise that fact cannot be distinguished from fiction will always be derelict. So will talk of education that does not frankly acknowledge realities—and reject as frivolous—the fictions to which people cling implicitly when their thoughts and actions reflect ignorance of or disregard for realities.

Most people understand how projects in the physical or social sciences are doomed ultimately to failure by ignorance of or disregard for realities. For example, no one is allowed to construct and sell airplanes if he or she has ignored any reality of gravity or aerodynamics in the process. No view of criminality that ignores the necessity of negative consequences for criminal behavior is taken seriously. Talk of education that does not recognize important realities should not be accepted, simply because any proposal for reform, legislation, or regulation that does not start from the premise that realities must be incorporated into the plan is doomed to failure. Reality-evading proposals may be appealing to the masses, may be sold to the unsuspecting, and may seem initially to be successful. Ultimately, they crash and burn, as does any reality-evading proposal in the natural sciences. NCLB is a case in point of education policy doomed to failure because it ignores realities. It is decidedly not even logical or reality-based, much less evidence-based.

NCLB, Measurement, and Distributions

The improvement of education depends on attention to more realities than those involving measurement (see Kauffman & Konold, 2007), but the realities on which we focus in this chapter involve what we know about distributions of data. In particular, we discuss the necessity of measurement and of attending to all of the mathematical realities of statistical distributions.

Indispensability of Measurement

Measurement is essential to any science. Without measurement, no scientific venture can be seen as legitimate, much less succeed. In education, we must have measurement to know how our students are doing. Otherwise, we have no way of judging whether teaching is having any effects on our students. Teaching without wanting to know how students are doing as a result of our teaching is what Sasso (2001) calls "willful ignorance."

Although teaching may have its highly individualistic features, it is also based on—and only evaluated legitimately by—methods that have a scientific base in reliable data. The call for scientifically validated methods of teaching is not misguided. However, one cannot reasonably call for scientifically validated methods of instruction and then ignore data on which science is based. The fact that educators, politicians, or others have sometimes embraced the notion of scientifically validated instruction while ignoring realities (e.g., data on which scientific principles are based), merely illustrates the way in which discussions of education and proposals for its reform can go awry.

Some may oppose measurement, including classification and ranking, yet deny that accountability implies measurement (e.g., "Obviously, I am not eschewing accountability for what we do. I am breaking the particular equation of accountability = measuring/ranking," Heshusius, 2004b, p. 295). But people can write explicitly self-contradictory statements, make a claim and then refute it in the next sentence, make explicit statements that are the opposite of what is implied in another of their statements, and write or speak gibberish that others of similar bent defend as understandable or even describe as insightful (see Kauffman, 2002; Kauffman & Sasso, 2006a, 2006b; Mostert, Kavale & Kauffman, 2008).

Measurement in Education Requires Testing

Any type of test is a way of checking to see whether students have acquired particular skills. Tests may be essays, performances, portfolios, or those types most often criticized—multiple item, more objectively scored tests that may be true/false statements, fill-ins, or multiple choice. Tests are sometimes misused or abused. More often, they are simply misunderstood. The most dangerous misunderstanding is that testing can be avoided. Those who criticize NCLB because it requires standardized testing are on the wrong track (see Kohn (2000, 2001) for examples of criticizing standardized testing). NCLB is misguided policy, not because it requires standardized testing but because it is based on misunderstanding of the statistical properties of tests and on warped interpretations of the meanings of test scores.

All types of tests have advantages and disadvantages. None is perfect, but some are very good at giving us important information. Of all tests, we must inquire about what is being assessed, how the knowledge or skill of interest is being measured, who comprises the comparison group, and what the obtained score means. Tests may be criticized on any of these grounds—that they measure the wrong thing or something trivial; that they are of questionable reliability or validity; that they result in inappropriate or invidious comparisons; or that the obtained score is meaningless or misleading. Standardized tests have been the objects of scorn primarily because critics do not understand what they are designed to do and why they are important. Standardized tests have also been criticized because the results have often been used inappropriately. But workers, not their tools, should be held accountable for shoddy work.

Test developers and measurement specialists are well aware of the limits of tests. Tests serve as tools, but as the Standards for Educational and Psychological Testing of the American Educational Research Association and American Psychological Association (1999) remind us, decisions about individuals or groups should not be made on the basis of a single measure. Recently, editors of several measurement journals crafted a joint letter to various NCLB policy makers highlighting the dangers of making high-stake decisions on the basis of a single measure. Among the points made were the facts that a single measure does not have the psychometric quality to serve as the sole basis for making high stakes decisions, and that such decisions should be based on multiple *sources* of evidence that are reflective of student achievement (Fitzpatrick, 2007).

Aside from education, most people understand the importance of testing. Most believe it is important that products be tested before they are marketed. And most desire services from professionals who have passed tests of their knowledge and skill. Testing is required for quality control. Quality control in education is needed, but children are not products that can be manufactured to a uniform tolerance. Other aspects of the measurement of human beings preclude treating children as if they can be discarded if they do not measure up to a given criterion, not the least of which is the reality that measurement of human beings always results in what Gould (1996) refers to as a "full house"—a full distribution (in the present discussion, of test scores or other performances), any part of which is ignored only at the cost of denying reality.

Measurement is Required for Identifying Failure and Success

The words *failure* and *success* are nonsensical in the absence of measurement. Failure and success for an individual are always defined by that student's performing or not performing some expected task or by a student's reaching or not reaching a given criterion. To suppose that failure is impossible or that a student will be judged successful regardless of performance is to deny the meaning of the terms. Certainly, saying that all fish are large is nonsensical; saying that all those that do not pass through a net are large may make sense. Likewise, to say that all children are successful (or successful at ___) is nonsensical, although all who can demonstrate a certain level of proficiency in a particular activity may be judged successful.

One legacy of bad thinking about education is the assumption that failure at one thing means failure in general. The solution to this problem is not to try to pretend that failure can be avoided for all students but to recognize that failure by a given measure signifies only failure on what was measured. True, we "make" failure by our measurement, and we cannot do otherwise unless we are to draw no lines or set no expectations for accomplishment for any purpose or for any age. Any measurement that produces only successes is bogus—it does not reflect the real world. Nevertheless, failure by one criterion does not imply failure by every criterion.

Measurement is Necessary for Accountability

Regardless of whether measurement is a very subjective judgment of a more objective judgment such as a certain score on a standardized test, measurement is required if educators are going to be held accountable. In fact, accountability in the absence of measurement is a non-sequitur—it does not follow, and indeed cannot follow, that accountability has been demonstrated in the absence of measurement of either student performance or teacher behavior. Those who call for accountability and moral judgment but condemn testing and measurement (e.g., Heshusius, 2004a, 2004b) are not describing something that comports with the actual world of accountability—except that a person may be empowered to judge that someone has or has not been "accountable" or "successful" by undisclosed criteria, a tactic of misanthropes.

Measurement Allows Us to Identify and Work on Gaps

Most educators and observers of education are aware of gaps in achievement, knowledge, or performance (regardless of what term one uses to describe evidence of learning) among individuals' abilities and among various groups (which may be categories defined by ethnicity, gender, age, class, or disability).

Educators may wish to widen the gap between the means for those who are gifted and those who are not, but we want to narrow or close most gaps between the means of groups. Without measurement, it is impossible even to make the case that gaps exist, and it is impossible also to know whether gaps are widening or narrowing. Thus, any suggestion that achievement gaps, disability, or diversity can be identified without measurement (e.g., Heshusius, 2004a, 2004b) is nonsense, as is denial that measurement always reveals differences that may be interpreted as gaps. Some gaps may be impossible to close by any legitimate means, but others can and should be narrowed or closed altogether.

One of the problems with NCLB is that it ignores realities about the nature of gaps and what is required to close gaps of various kinds. It does not seem to recognize that

(a) there is a mean of means (i.e., that means, as well as scores for individuals, have a distribution),

(b) some of the variance in achievement scores is due to factors other than teaching,

(c) the mathematical properties of continuous distributions apply in all cases, and

(d) besides mean differences, other differences in distributions reveal important gaps.

The failure of NCLB to recognize realities regarding all of the various gaps in distributions of achievement scores is a fatal flaw—as certain to result in disastrous consequences as the failure of the National Aeronautics and Space Administration to take into consideration the effects of cold temperatures on booster rockets' O-rings and the damage done by foam insulation striking surfaces at high velocity.

NCLB's Lack of Attention to the Realities of Individual Differences and Distributions

Supporters of NCLB argue that schools have not been successful in educating all students. In fact, the rationale for NCLB is that schools do not "work" or are "failures" (see Popham (2004) for descriptions of how NCLB defines "failing" schools; criticism of public schools as failures and calls for reform so that they "work" has a long history, as Cuban (1990) recounts). Saying that schools are "failing" begs the question of what we should expect to see if schools or any of the programs offered therein are "working" (Kauffman, 1990). Would children's test score distributions be different, and if so how? Would measures of central tendency (e.g., mean, median) be higher? Would we expect to see all students obtaining the same score on these measures with little or no tolerance for any variation in expected student outcomes? Is it really possible to raise the central tendency of test scores and at the same time reduce the variation in scores? These questions are central to resolving whether the goals of NCLB are attainable even if public schools are really good.

Individual differences are a reality. People differ on so many factors (e.g., interests, attitudes, motivation) that it is difficult to identify *in*variant characteristics. Student achievement is no exception. To illustrate, standardized achievement tests are typically normed so that the mean of the raw score distribution is set at 100, and the standard deviation is 15. For decades, the resulting scores have been shown to be approximately normally distributed when tests are administered to large populations of students. The reality of such distributions is that 50% of the students measured will have scores below the mean, and 50% will have scores above the mean. In fact, 68% of the students will have scores that range in value from 85 to 115, or a 30 point standard score difference; and 95% of the tested population will have scores ranging in value from 70 to 130, or a 60 point standard score difference. Children show individual achievement differences, and these differences were pervasive even before we started measuring them.

Some individual differences are important for instruction, but others are not (Kauffman, Conroy, Gardner, & Oswald, in press). The most important differences for instruction are differences in prior achievement (Engelmann, 1997). Some students are simply better equipped to accumulate knowledge at a faster rate than are others, and the uniform application of programs across students of different ability levels does little to help groups on either side (of the central tendency) of the achievement continuum—though it may serve to reduce the existing variability in student achievement. These ideas are in contrast with NCLB initiatives that assume a one-size-fits-all model (Lawrence, 2006). Moreover, individual student variation is likely to be masked by the currently adopted school level aggregates for classification (i.e., AYP vs. non-AYP) of accountability based on a single school-wide measure. For example, in a recent analysis of schools meeting AYP, benchmarks were found to be comprised of both below-average students demonstrating very little progress and above-average students showing material gains. Other schools, however, also meeting AYP benchmarks, were found to contain below-average students making positive gains with above-average students showing little progress (Choi, Seltzer, Herman, & Yamashiro, 2007).

Because of the punitive consequences of NCLB for schools that do not "measure up," administrators feel threatened by the looming prospect of losing resources when struggling students fail to reach proficiency. As a result, greater emphasis is placed on those struggling students who are relatively close to but below the expected standard, with fewer resources being made available for gifted education (Winerip, 2006) or those with cognitive limitations who obviously will not meet the standard. In the end, this may well result in distributions of achievements that show smaller differences between children at opposite ends of the achievement scale. However, these are not the gaps that we wish to narrow. This unfortunate consequence will also contribute to leaving students behind in a more important sense than their being lower than a population mean (i.e., leaving them far below their potential). That is, students holding the greatest academic potential for success in achieving domestic and international advances are likely to be "left behind" in that they are unchallenged and do not achieve what they could (Gentry, 2006; Goodkin, 2005).

Most Educational Variables are Continuous in Nature

Some educational measurement consists only of categories (e.g., male–female; did/did not meet a performance criterion) or ranks (e.g., first in class, second-to-last to finish). However, most measurements of educational performance (e.g., most standardized achievement tests) produce a score distribution that lies atop a continuous distribution of outcomes. As Kauffman (2002) and Kauffman and Hallahan (2005) point out, continuous distributions are those in which what is measured varies from a little to a lot with fine gradations or increments being possible. There are no natural, inherent, or obvious breaks in a continuous distribution. Height and weight are examples of continuous distributions, as is rate or speed.

Whenever human performance (as well as many other physical attributes of humans and many things in the material world) is measured, the results of measurement produce a discrete distribution. This occurs because, regardless of the degree of precision inherent in the measurement tool (tenths, hundredths, thousandths), there will be a break in the scale when moving from one of these measured points to another. Often, however, the data resemble what has come to be known as a "normal" distribution, in that a graph of the scores approximates the symmetry of a bell by modeling the underlying continuous scale that is inherent to the variable being measured (hence, "bell-shaped curve" or "bell curve"). Not all distributions or curves are "normal" or symmetrical; some are lopsided or skewed. Nevertheless, all continuous distributions have immutable properties.

The immutable properties of continuous distributions are referred to by psychometricians as "moments," of which there are four: central tendency, variability, skewness, and kurtosis. These are well-established realities in spite of attempts to cast them as mere human inventions (see Gallagher, 2006) or to ignore their implications for closing gaps in performance (see Kauffman, 2005). These distributions and immutable qualities apply to all groups—including all groups of averages for schools, districts, states, nations, and subgroups of students. They are as real and as useful as many other human inventions, including houses, arithmetic, roads, laws, and languages. Moreover, criteria that may be used to categorize individuals (e.g., did or did not meet a criterion for reading ability—in short, all "criterion-referenced" tests and judgments of grade-level performance) are actually derived from the measurement of continuous distributions of performance; the criterion is based on a continuous distribution.

Philosophical objections and observations that the smoothed curve depicting a continuous distribution is actually drawn from a histogram (a bar graph) or that the first such curve was drawn from estimates of measurement error (Gallagher, 2006) do not mean that continuous distributions are not real. Assuming that continuous distributions can be ignored, changed, or violated at will because they are educational or psychological invites disaster.

The only way to consider no student or group (or no school, district, or state) "behind" or "low-performing" is to make questionable comparisons or comparisons that at least partially obscure the truth for the unsuspecting observer. For example, one can compare a given score or average to a distribution obtained long ago. Although it may be the case that we could have education so good that fewer than 25% of students score below the 25th percentile on a test given 25 years ago (or even on a more recently administered test), it is impossible to have fewer than 25% of students scoring below the 25th percentile on the test their group has taken for the purpose of describing the distribution. Thus, questions about the comparison group and the comparison distribution are always pertinent. But of even greater importance for the present discussion is the fact that there will be—always, every single time—a distribution, including a portion below average, a bottom quartile, a lowest score, and, if Gould's (1996) full house is considered, those whose disabilities are profound and whose scores are zero. NCLB blithely disregards this reality and is, consequently, doomed to disgrace as education policy.

No Measurement is Error-Free

Regardless of the type of measurement employed (whether categorical, ranking, or continuous; whether personal judgment of performance or a standardized multiple-choice test), it is not absolute or perfect. This is true also in the physical world; our measurements, even the most precise ones in physics, have a margin of error. Thus, measurements are always estimates, although some are more reliable, more valid, more precise, or more accurate (i.e., less variable) than are others.

Generally speaking, the less the margin of error, the more desirable the measurement. Those seeking to improve a particular field of study are always desirous of more precise and less variable measures. It is wise to recognize two realities about the measurements we use in education: (a) they are often highly useful and (b) they have a margin of error. The fact that educational measurement contains error is not justification for ignoring or refusing to use it. Error just needs to be recognized and taken into account in educational decisions based on measurement. Measurements that are known to have a margin of error (e.g., speedometers, thermometers, test scores of various kinds) are nonetheless useful. Margins of error, possible sources of error, and judgments based on measurement must simply be recognized for the realities that they are. Measurement may be essential, but it does not preclude judgment. Yet in many assessments of progress related to NCLB, there is no reporting of the standard error of measure, so readers have no way of judging whether the reported differences in means are chance variations or statistically significant changes.

Yearly Measurement is Useless for Preventing Failure

Yearly measurement, like that demanded by NCLB for assessing progress, has its place in telling us how groups and individuals are doing compared to a standard. However, such measurement is useless for avoiding failure. Prevention of failure requires anticipating it or at least catching it in its incipient stages, not pointing it out long after the fact (see Kauffman, 2002, 2003, 2004). The kind of testing demanded by NCLB can tell us that something went wrong (or right), but it cannot tell us precisely *what* went right or wrong or even *when* it occurred, and it is always too late to avert disaster for an individual. The kind of measurement that is useful for averting prolonged failure is curriculum-based—frequent, if not daily, assessment by the teacher of a student's progress in the curriculum.

Moreover, no one has invented a measurement device that is reliable and valid, yet produces no variance in what is measured (probably such a device cannot be invented, as it contradicts what we know about the achievement construct we are measuring). And when a designated group of students is measured, it is simply a reality that there will be a lower or bottom part of the distribution, including those who are lowest or last, some of whom will be judged to have failed. This is why setting a universal standard for performance, as suggested by NCLB, is unrealistic—unless *universal* is taken to mean *all who do not fail*, in which case it is clearly nonsensical.

In addition, policy makers in NCLB seem to assume that proficiency holds the same meaning across tests and states (Fuller, Wright, Gesicki, & Kang, 2007). The reality, however, is that definitions of AYP differ from state to state because states use tests of different difficulty, different standards of proficiency, and measurements of different curricula. Thus, making realistic assessments of achievement gains as a nation is difficult at best. The flexibility afforded to states in setting their own performance standards distorts a common understanding of "proficiency." For example, King (2007) reported that 89% of fourth-grade students passed the 2005 state-sponsored reading test in Mississippi. By contrast, Massachusetts could only claim a reading pass rate of 50% among their fourth graders in the same year. These results would likely suggest that students in Mississippi were receiving better instruction—that is, until one considers how these groups performed on the National Assessment of Educational Progress (NAEP). Results on this common, across-state, measure indicated reading pass rates of 18% and 44% in favor of Massachusetts fourth graders. In general, analyses of NAEP data reveal material state-to-state levels of variation in terms of progress trends, but within-state trajectories of growth are fairly stable across different grades and content areas (Schafer, Liu, & Wang, 2007).

Statistical Data Other than the Mean are Critically Important

Perhaps the most disappointing thing about NCLB and many of its discussants is failure to consider statistical concepts other than central tendency. Gaps between groups in performance are apparently conceptualized only as differences in means; *the achievement gap* is an apparent reference to the difference in test score means for African Americans and Caucasians, although many gaps of many kinds could be discussed.

Typically, mean scores for groups are the target of concern, likely reflecting a failure to consider the best index of central tendency. The failure to consider variance and the nature of the dispersion of scores—standard deviation, standard error, kurtosis, and skew, for example—are more serious concerns. Means can lead people to make silly and invidious comparisons of groups when variance is ignored (see Gladwell, 1997). Moreover, statistically significant mean differences between groups can be of no practical significance when very large samples are compared, and significant mean differences may occur in the absence of any significant differences among groups in very high or very low performers.

Although researchers have applied sound methodological tools that capture student and school-level variations to the investigation of student growth (Choi et al., 2007; Schafer et al., 2007), virtually all discussion of NCLB in the popular press ignores these statistical realities and takes an extraordinarily simplistic view of critical issues about measurement of educational performance—so simplistic that it insults the intelligence of many who read or hear it. An issue of considerable importance in evaluating the effects of education is the dispersion of scores—the shape and nature of the distribution of scores. For example, would we see increased variance as an indication of progress or regression? Moreover, in evaluating the differences between means, the absolute difference between them is meaningless without knowledge of the variances of the samples (or populations) being compared. Yes, for the most part, academic discussion of growth or progress related to NCLB ignores or makes marginal use of estimates of variance (e.g., "A vote for 'No Child'," 2007; Fuller et al., 2007). We are not suggesting that educational researchers such as Fuller et al. (2007) or government officials are incapable of understanding distributions and their importance, but the fact remains that most of the discourse about NCLB has not included statistical concepts other than mean differences. In fact, issues of statistical distribution were totally ignored by both a 2007 *Washington Post* editorial ("Save School Standards," 2007) and every letter writer in the September 10 issue of that newspaper, including the U.S. Secretary of Education and the President of the National Education Association.

Regardless of the origin of the intellectually impoverished view of education reflected by NCLB and most of the discussion of it and its effects, the level of discourse about this law has not been raised by legislative debate, administrative argument, or even by most academic dialogue. In our opinion, it is time for people in academic and administrative roles to insist that the level of discourse be more firmly grounded in the realities of data, including the mathematical realities of score distributions that give data their meaning. This includes those at the highest levels of government as well as those in other roles that affect educational policy.

Advocacy for reauthorization of NCLB, perhaps with a few changes making it ostensibly better, appears to be widespread and bipartisan. The *Washington Post* (2007a) reported support for NCLB from both Representative George Miller and Senator Edward Kennedy and found encouraging the suggestion that state standards be toughened. Another editorial ("Save School Standards," 2007) offered similar support for not "letting schools off the hook" in attempts to "water down" NCLB. Unfortunately, suggestions that NCLB holds schools accountable in a rational way and that state standards should be toughened require either (a) misrepresenting reality or (b) living with a higher rate of failure. Statistical realities may be ignored by members of Congress or anyone else, but that does not make these realities disappear. It only ensures the collapse of the policy based on false assumptions and disaster for those caught in the wreckage, which in the case of NCLB are the children and educators crushed by the ruins.

Implications for Policy Makers and Practitioners

As Gallagher (2007) has noted, educational policy casts long shadows—it influences services, personnel preparation, and research. Policy is not a trivial matter for the practitioner. It affects what teachers are expected to do and what and how they teach, and a given policy is likely to affect educational practice for a generation or more. Thus, it is incumbent upon policy makers and those who advise them to acknowledge all realities, as ignoring any given reality will neutralize policy initiatives, no matter how well intended and no matter whether grounded in reality in most respects.

NCLB is an example of a well-intentioned policy that ignores realities about groups and gaps in educational performance, and it is therefore headed for eventual ignominy (Johns, 2003; Kauffman, 2004, 2005). It ignores the many realities involving distributions of test scores, the reasons for success and failure, and the nature of the differences among groups. The fact that the law was passed with overwhelming and bipartisan support does not make it rational or defensible. Votes may indicate the political palatability of a policy, but they do not make a policy that ignores realities viable. That is, votes do not change all of the realities of the world, only the political reality that they represent.

The implications of this discussion for policy makers and practitioners are simple and straightforward:

- Before you enact or support a policy, make sure that it is firmly and thoroughly grounded in realities about the world of education.
- Resist all attempts, for whatever reasons, to enact or support a policy that you know skirts any reality.
- Do not succumb to the temptation to engage in rhetoric that does not conform to every known reality about education.
- Demand of advisors the kind of data and thinking that will convince reasonable skeptics of the policy's workability.
- Demand consideration of all statistical information, not merely those indices that reflect central tendency.

Some practitioners do not acknowledge realities, partly because their teachers or their policy makers (or both) do not. They have been convinced that realities can be ignored without disastrous consequences. Most practitioners do know fantasy from reality about education. Nevertheless, not all are equipped to articulate all of their quibbles with NCLB. Moreover, many practitioners acquiesce in efforts to implement policies that they know are unworkable because they believe that refusing to go along with pretense will cost them their employment. It is much more difficult to guess why many of those whose employment is not threatened by dissent also acquiesce in the charade of NCLB.

We are not under the illusion that policy must be shown to be flawless before it can be supported. However, supporting a policy *known* to be conceptually faulty is in our opinion unethical. Finding flaws not known to exist at the time a policy is enacted and fixing them are inevitable aspects of policy development. Gillon (2000) pointed out how policies often have unintended consequences, and we do not believe that people can be held responsible for the unpredictable effects of their behavior. Nevertheless, it is also the case that in our society when a person knows (or should know) the negative consequences of an action but performs that action anyway, we consider that person negligent or malicious. Our society does not countenance constructing and marketing goods that are known to be defective. Neither do we fail to hold people responsible for negative outcomes when those people knew or should have known that their actions would harm others. For example, we accept the fact that it is malicious to manufacture and sell vehicles that people know or should have known are unsafe. Our courts generally excuse people from responsibility for the unknowable, but not from the known or knowable. Neither our colleagues in education nor those in politics are free of responsibility when they embrace policies with known deficiencies. We find it incomprehensible that people of average or better intelligence produce or defend education policies like NCLB that so clearly ignore important realities. In most civil endeavors other than education, criminal penalties are exacted or people are found insane for pretending that fundamental realities do not exist. The education of our children is too important to be approached with sloppy thinking, and the consequences of bad thinking about education should be no less serious than the consequences of bad thinking about planes, trains, automobiles, and other things that are important to us.

Conclusion

The improvement of education demands the acknowledgement of basic realities. These realities are things that happen regardless of anyone's wishes or statements; they are features of the world that humans may have discovered and described (or "constructed" through their language), but they will not change because of philosophical preferences or denials. Any philosophy, pronouncement, or policy based on the pretense that these realities do not exist or will not be encountered is doomed to eventual failure, regardless of its social acceptability, emotional appeal, or apparent initial success.

Most people in our society seem to understand that any project in the material world launched with even a single flawed assumption regarding physical realities will come to naught and may result in very negative consequences. Educators and other people in our society must understand that something similar occurs in the world of education—that any educational project, reform, or policy launched with a flawed assumption regarding reality or a side-stepping of reality is headed for inevitable failure. Rhetoric about education that does not account for basic realities must be labeled the siren call that it is and be resoundingly rejected. NCLB need not be honored. In fact, it should be recognized as another example of silly talk about education.

Written or spoken proposals that ignore realities should prompt imitation of the statement of the late Senator Daniel Patrick Moynihan regarding proposed changes to the Aid For Dependent Children program: "Are there no serious persons in the administration who can say, 'Stop, stop right now? No, we won't have this?' " (Moynihan, 1995, p. A31). Of many reforms and proposals, more people need to say, "Stop! Stop right now! We won't have this!" Frustration with the powers that be is not a sufficient excuse to treat seriously ideas that are not fully grounded in reality (Kauffman, 2002, 2005). Neither is the suggestion that a proposal is known to be partly or mostly right and therefore worthy of support. Only one assumption not grounded in reality is sufficient to render a project or proposal inoperable or disastrous. NCLB is no exception.

Note

Portions of this chapter were previously published by the authors as an article in the journal *Exceptionality*, Vol. 15, No. 2, pp. 75–96 (also accessible at www.informaworld.com).

References

A vote for "No Child": Welcome support in the House for the law that brought accountability to public education [Editorial] (2007). *Washington Post*, p. A12.

American Educational Research Association, American Psychological Association, and National Council on Measurement in Education (1999). *Standards for educational and psychological testing.* Washington, DC: American Educational Research Association.

Brantlinger, E. A. (Ed.) (2006). *Who benefits from special education? Remediating (fixing) other people's children.* Mahwah, NJ: Lawrence Erlbaum Associates.

Choi, K., Seltzer, M., Herman, J., & Yamashiro, K. (2007). Children left behind in AYP and non-AYP schools: Using student progress and the distribution of student gains to validate AYP. *Educational Measurement: Issues and Practice, 26*(3), 21–32.

Cuban, L. (1990). Reforming again, again, and again. *Educational Researcher, 19*(1), 3–13.

Engelmann, S. (1997). Theory of mastery and acceleration. In J. W. Lloyd, E. J. Kameenui, & D. Chard (Eds.), *Issues in educating students with disabilities* (pp. 177–195). Mahwah, NJ: Lawrence Erlbaum Associates.

Fitzpatrick, A. R. (2007). NCME members write Congress on NCLB. *National Council on Measurement in Education, 15*(3), 5–7.

Fuller, B., Wright, J., Gesicki, K., & Kang, E. (2007). Gauging growth: How to judge No Child Left Behind? *Educational Researcher, 36*, 268–278.

Gallagher, D. J. (Ed.) (2004). *Challenging orthodoxy in special education: Dissenting voices.* Denver, CO: Love.

Gallagher, D. J. (2006). If not absolute objectivity, then what? A reply to Kauffman and Sasso. *Exceptionality, 14*, 91–107.

Gallagher, J. J. (2007). *Driving change in special education.* Baltimore: Paul H. Brookes.

Gartner, A., & Lipsky, D. K. (1989). *The yoke of special education: How to break it.* Rochester, NY: National Center on Education and the Economy.

Gentry, M. (2006). No Child Left Behind: Neglecting excellence. *Roeper Review, 29,* 24–27.

Gillon, S. M. (2000). *That's not what we meant to do: Reform and its unintended consequences in twentieth-century America.* New York: Norton.

Gladwell, M. (1997, May 19). The sports taboo: Why Blacks are like boys and Whites are like girls. *The New Yorker,* 50–55.

Goodkin, S. (2005, December 27). Leave no gifted child behind. *Washington Post,* p. A25.

Gould, S. J. (1996). *Full house: The spread of excellence from Plato to Darwin.* New York: Three Rivers Press.

Heshusius, L. (2004a). From creative discontent toward epistemological freedom in special education: Reflections on a 25-year journey. In D. J. Gallagher (Ed.), *Challenging orthodoxy in special education: Dissenting voices* (pp. 169–230). Denver, CO: Love.

Heshusius, L. (2004b). Special education knowledges: The inevitable struggle with the "self." In D. J. Gallagher (Ed.), *Challenging orthodoxy in special education: Dissenting voices* (pp. 283–309). Denver, CO: Love.

Johns, B. H. (2003). NCLB and IDEA: Never the twain should meet. *Learning Disabilities: A Multidisciplinary Journal, 12*(3), 89–91.

Kauffman, J. M. (1990, April). *What happens when special education works: The sociopolitical context of special education research in the 1990s.* Invited address, Special Education Special Interest Group, annual meeting of the American Educational Research Association, Boston.

Kauffman, J. M. (2002). *Education deform: Bright people sometimes say stupid things about education.* Lanham, MD: Scarecrow Press.

Kauffman, J. M. (2003). Appearances, stigma, and prevention. *Remedial and Special Education, 24,* 195–198.

Kauffman, J. M. (2004). The president's commission and the devaluation of special education. *Education and Treatment of Children, 27,* 307–324.

Kauffman, J. M. (2005). Waving to Ray Charles: Missing the meaning of disability. *Phi Delta Kappan, 86,* 520–521, 524.

Kauffman, J. M., Conroy, M., Gardner, R., & Oswald, D. (in press). Cultural sensitivity in the application of behavior principles to education. *Education and Treatment of Children.*

Kauffman, J. M., & Hallahan, D. P. (2005). *Special education: What it is and why we need it.* Boston: Allyn & Bacon.

Kauffman, J. M., & Konold, T. R. (2007). Making sense in education: Pretense (including NCLB) and realities in rhetoric and policy about schools and schooling. *Exceptionality, 15,* 75–96.

Kauffman, J. M., & Sasso, G. M. (2006a). Certainty, doubt, and the reduction of uncertainty: A rejoinder. *Exceptionality, 14,* 109–120.

Kauffman, J. M., & Sasso, G. M. (2006b). Toward ending cultural and cognitive relativism in special education. *Exceptionality, 14,* 65–90.

King, L. (2007, June 6). Data suggest states satisfy no child law by expecting less of students. *USA Today.* Retrieved June 21, 2007, from: http://www.usatoday.com/news/education/2007-06-06-schools-main_N.htm.

Kohn, A. (1999). *The schools our children deserve: Moving beyond traditional classrooms and "tougher standards."* Boston, MA: Houghton Mifflin.

Kohn, A. (2000). *The case against standardized testing: Raising the scores, ruining the schools.* Westport, CT: Heinemann.

Kohn, A. (2001). Fighting the tests: A practical guide to rescuing our schools. *Phi Delta Kappan, 82,* 349–357.

Lawrence, M. (2006, April 7). *The impact of no child left behind.* Presidential invited speech to the American Educational Research Association, San Francisco.

Mostert, M. P., Kavale, K. A., & Kauffman, J. M. (Eds.) (2008). *Challenging the refusal of reasoning in special education.* Denver, CO: Love.

Moynihan, D. P. (1995, September 21). "I cannot understand how this could be happening." *The Washington Post,* p. A31.

Popham, J. W. (2004). *America's "failing" schools: How parents and teachers can cope with No Child Left Behind.* New York: Routledge Falmer.

Rothstein, R., Jacobsen, R., & Wilder, T. (2006, November). *"Proficiency for all"—An oxymoron.* Paper presented at a symposium on "Examining America's Commitment to Closing Achievement Gaps: NCLB and its Alternatives," New York: Teachers College, Columbia University.

Sasso, G. M. (2001). The retreat from inquiry and knowledge in special education. *The Journal of Special Education, 34,* 178–193.

Save School Standards: Congress should resist attempts to water down the No Child Left Behind Law [Editorial] (2007). *Washington Post,* p. A14.

Schafer, W. D., Liu, M., & Wang, H. (2007). Content and grade trends in state assessment and NAEP. *Practical Research and Evaluation, 12*(9), 1–25.

Shattuck, R. (1999). *Candor & perversion: Literature, education, and the arts.* New York: Norton.

Winerip, M. (2006, April 5). No child left behind? Ask the gifted. *The New York Times,* p. B7.

Part II: Building Support for Data-Based Decisions

6

Preparing Educators to Effectively Use Student Data Systems

Jeffrey C. Wayman and Vincent Cho
University of Texas-Austin

Introduction

The use of educational data to make decisions and foster improvement is increasing dramatically. Federal and state accountability mandates have created a strong market for formal achievement testing, both in terms of state achievement tests and benchmarking assessments that help predict performance on these tests. Many schools and districts are looking beyond accountability to find ways of using these and other student data to assess learning and improve educational practice.

As a result, a growing research base has provided knowledge about the effective use of student learning data for educational improvement. Data use has been shown to increase the conversations that educators have with each other, with students, and with parents about education (Brunner et al., 2005; Halverson, Grigg, Prichett, & Thomas, 2005; Massell, 2001; Wayman & Stringfield, 2006). Collaboration, long a difficult task for educators, has been shown to work well when centered around data use (Chen, Heritage, & Lee, 2005; Wayman, Midgley, & Stringfield, 2006; Wayman & Stringfield, 2006; Young, 2006). Teachers report data uses that improve practice, such as adjusting instruction, grouping students, and better understanding learning needs (Brunner et al., 2005; Chen et al., 2005; Datnow, Park, & Wohlstetter, 2007; Lachat & Smith, 2005; Wayman & Stringfield, 2006; Young, 2006).

While much research touts the benefits of data use, such use has historically been a difficult undertaking. Educational data were often stored in ways that rendered them inaccessible to most educators, so using educational data usually involved an unrealistic amount of time and effort (Stringfield, Reynolds, & Schaffer, 2001). This situation has eased recently, with the advent of user-friendly computer systems that deliver data to educators in rapid fashion (Wayman, 2007; Wayman, Stringfield, & Yakimowski, 2004). Wayman (2007) suggested that it is impossible for a school or district to realize full efficiency from a data initiative without the support of such technology.

Data systems are a necessary component of effective data use but they are not sufficient—there are many considerations in preparing educators to use such a system. In this chapter, we provide a discussion of important issues facing districts that are implementing data systems and preparing educators to use them.

Tenets of an Effective Data Initiative

Effective educational data use is about integration. District-wide, data users at every level must be using data toward a common purpose; therefore, an effective data initiative should be considered a systemic initiative. To this end, an effective initiative must be directly related to teaching and learning. This precept is the lens through which every data activity must be seen (Wayman, Cho, & Johnston, 2007).

Guided by this principle, it is important that data use be aligned throughout the district and that a systemic vision or outline for data use exists (Datnow et al., 2007; Halverson et al., 2005; Wayman et al., 2007). Wayman et al. (2007) outlined a data initiative that was cast in terms of a "data informed district," where data are used to support education at every level. In a data informed district, clear understandings exist regarding how education will be conducted, what is meant by learning, and how data will be used to understand and support these. Individuals and entities through-out the district understand the different ways they connect and align to this vision, how their work affects and supports the district and each other, and how various forms of data support their work. Educators at every level are engaged in data use to improve their practice, including district administrators, central office workers, counselors, principals, teachers, and many more.

Building-level educators are particularly critical to the health of a data initiative. Data use lives and dies in the principal's office, and nearly every piece of research on school data use has discussed the role of the principal in some form (e.g., Chen et al., 2005; Datnow et al., 2007; Lachat & Smith, 2005; Wayman, 2005; Wayman & Stringfield, 2006; Wayman et al., 2007; Young, 2006). These studies have shown principals serving as instructional leaders, as administrators who provide time and structure for faculty data use, and as effective data users themselves. Unfortunately, research also suggests that this picture of principals may be optimistic because prin-cipals are often unprepared to use data, lead faculty in using data, or sometimes lack support from their districts (Wayman et al., 2007).

At the building level, teachers are also an important set of data users. While research has suggested that teachers may be initially resistant to data use (Ingram, Louis, & Schroeder, 2004), they will engage in data use when properly supported and when they recognize value in the data (Chen et al., 2005; Lachat & Smith, 2005; Wayman & Stringfield, 2006; Young, 2006). In discussing the importance of involving teachers, Wayman (2005) suggested that one of the most important supports is the presence of user-friendly data systems that provide rapid, efficient access to student data.

A Brief Overview of Computer Data Systems

An increasing number of computer systems are being marketed for the purpose of delivering student data to educators (Mieles & Foley, 2005; Wayman, 2007; Wayman et al., 2004). While, these systems provide many different functions, no data system performs every function a district may want. Instead, data systems typically perform specific functions and districts join various individual systems to form one overall system. Increasingly, commercial vendors are looking to provide solutions that combine features from varied areas, but district personnel are still well served to understand the various functions and limitations of each type of system.

Wayman (2005) described three common types of data systems that deliver student data to educators:

(a) student information systems (SIS) that provide real-time accounting of daily school function (e.g., attendance, schedules);

(b) assessment systems that rapidly organize and analyze frequent benchmark assessments; and

(c) data warehousing systems that provide access to historical data of all types and link disparate databases.

Wayman (2007) additionally described "instructional management systems" as a different type of system that offers connections between student data and supports such as curriculum resources, learning standards, intra-staff communication, and home–school linkages.

Empirical research has demonstrated the value that educators are finding in such systems. For example, hands-on work with data systems can help educators see benefits of data use that they may not grasp in the abstract (Chen et al., 2005). By offering access to a breadth of student data, these systems help educators see data uses beyond simply examining state achievement test data (Chen et al., 2005; Lachat & Smith, 2005; Wayman & Stringfield, 2006). Data systems can also bring issues of at-risk students closer to educators because of the individual student detail offered by these systems (Chen et al., 2005; Lachat & Smith, 2005; Wayman, Conoly, Gasko, & Stringfield, in press; Wayman & Stringfield, 2006). Further, data systems offer unprecedented scope and detail regarding student learning histories; research has shown the utility of student learning histories for teachers (Brunner et al., 2005; Chen et al., 2005; Lachat & Smith, 2005; Wayman & Stringfield, 2006), even in the presence of more recent data sources (Wayman & Stringfield, 2006).

Two other benefits of data systems seem evident, although they are not yet empirically supported. First, data and evidence are often used for political purposes (Coburn, Honig, & Stein, in press) and this often fosters mistrust of data among teachers (Ingram et al., 2004). Data systems should help improve this situation by allowing all district educators to independently use a breadth of data to inform their own decisions. Second, while calls are being made for the use of multiple measures in assessing student learning (Herman & Gribbons, 2001; Wassermann, 2001; Wayman & Stringfield, 2006), others have worried that an overabundance of student data would make it impossible for educators to realize maximum benefit (Massell, 2001). Data systems offer a solution to these concerns by managing multiple measures in a usable fashion.

Preparing Educators to Use Data Systems

Data systems are a necessary component of effective data use but they are not sufficient. Although data systems are powerful, indispensable tools for using data, they are like any tool: without proper training, knowledge, and support, they serve a less effective function. Therefore, it is important that individuals planning for data system use endeavor to prepare, teach, and support users at every turn. This is true not just initially, but ongoing—as with the data systems themselves, users will evolve in their capacities and abilities. More globally, the data system should be a critical component of a focus on making a district-wide data initiative useful and sustainable.

There are many considerations in preparing educators to use such a system, and we will use this chapter to discuss many of these issues. In doing so, we offer sections on necessary groundwork for system use, aims of system use, professional development, collaboration, and institutional structures that support system use. We will finish with a brief discussion of issues to consider beyond preparation and initial use.

Groundwork for System Use

Before using the data system, there are a few foundational prerequisites that districts and schools must consider. In this section, we discuss preparations from three areas: (1) "calibration" conversations that establish an aligned vision for data use, (2) system preparation, and (3) system rollout.

Calibration

Prior to selecting and implementing a student data system, it is critical for educators throughout the district to have conversations that establish an aligned, common vision for education and how data use will support this vision. Termed *calibration* (Wayman et al., 2007; Wayman et al., 2006), this process engages educators in important dialogue about the educational process, using questions such as: What do we mean by teaching and learning? How will teaching be conducted under these definitions? How will we assess student learning so we know it when we see it? How will we react to the results? A more detailed description of calibration and recommendations for establishing a formal calibration process can be found in Wayman et al. (2007).

Components of calibration conversations that involve data use will be much richer if they are preceded by a detailed district evaluation of data use—without such an evaluation, it is difficult to decide how student learning should be assessed and to articulate processes for adjusting practice. Consequently, we strongly recommend that any district looking to implement a data initiative and system should first conduct a thorough, district-wide evaluation of available data, data practices, and support capacities. Wayman et al. (2007) provide findings and recommendations resulting from one such evaluation.

System Preparation

The process of selecting and preparing a system for use is a complicated one. Districts that place high importance on this process are usually rewarded with smoother implementation and more effective use.

Correctly choosing the type of system that fits the district context is an important process. Research has described many issues that should be considered in choosing a system, such as the types of modules or functions to be included, whether to build or buy a system, data storage and cleaning, and many more (Mieles & Foley, 2005; Wayman, 2007; Wayman et al., 2004). The calibration process provides a helpful base from which to choose a system because a calibration-based district has clearly identified data uses and goals and is thus able to tailor a system to district needs. Unfortunately, our anecdotal observation is to the contrary: most districts choose a system, then base their data uses on system capacities.

Data preparation and identification is an important task. District, school, and classroom data are typically stored using a variety of systems and methods, so it is important that district personnel conduct a thorough audit to identify every type of data used in the district and take measures to eliminate overlap and redundancy. Once a data system is acquired, data must be loaded and cleaned (examined for accuracy and quality). District personnel should budget plenty of time and resources for data cleaning; a considerable amount of work is required to prepare data and educators may be surprised by how incomplete and inaccurate their data actually are (Chen et al., 2005; Lachat & Smith, 2005; Wayman et al., 2004).

System Rollout

We believe the initial implementation of a data system is critical to the long-term success of the data initiative because users who are immediately able to make practical use of the system are more likely to advance in their later use of the system. Consequently, we do not recommend that all functions of the system be rolled out at the same time. Rather, we advocate that the system is introduced in small, immediately useful pieces, offering the easiest and most useful functions first. Besides easing users into the often unfamiliar process of using a data system, this approach reduces the time from acquisition to initial rollout because it does not demand the entire system be immediately functional. Wayman and Conoly (2006) and Wayman et al. (2004) have provided more detailed discussion of rollout issues.

Prior to rolling out the system, it is advantageous to prepare users for system use so they encounter as shallow a learning curve as possible. Besides training on the system itself, this preparation should also help users understand effective use of the data elements included in the initial rollout. An example of this process was given in Wayman et al. (2007); their district-wide evaluation of data use identified two sets of formal assessments that were most popularly used. The resulting recommendations suggested the district not just focus initial system implementation on these two assessments, but prior to rollout, provide thorough professional development on the proper use of these assessments. Such a strategy should enable district educators to efficiently access the data systems and apply the results to their everyday practice right from the start.

Aims of System Use

District personnel should clearly articulate how the system should be used to best fit district needs. Clearly, all system use should be connected to student learning and educational improvement, and it is important that this vision is clearly described relevant to the various roles represented in the district. Consequently, the details and shape of this vision are very context-dependent and should be refined during the calibration and system identification process. Although details will be determined by the local context, two important generalities will apply to all contexts: (1) system use will be more efficient if uses focus on small-scale, workable problems, and (2) system use should fit directly with educator work.

Identify Workable Problems

Educators at different district levels will have different uses for the data system. For example, teachers will use the system differently than principals, who will use the system differently than central office administrators, and so on. From the boardroom to the classroom, we recommend focusing on problems that are small in scope, short in term, and immediately useful and relevant to the educator. These recommendations are not unlike those that researchers advocate in effecting more general organizational change (e.g., Fullan, 1999).

Results from the calibration process will help identify workable problems at every level; in addition, research has highlighted a number of different kinds of workable problems that could be applicable to many district contexts. For instance, teachers and principals often review prior year test scores and other historic information on their incoming students at the beginning of a school year (Brunner et al., 2005; Chen et al., 2005; Lachat & Smith, 2005; Wayman & Stringfield, 2006). In an effort to rapidly inform practice, teachers may also use a data system to process frequent, formative assessments (Chen et al., 2005; Wayman & Stringfield, 2006). Administrators at both the school and district level may use a data system to determine instructional program priorities (Brunner et al., 2005; Wayman & Stringfield, 2006), but it is important to keep these decisions aligned with the priorities articulated in the calibration process.

Fit System Use to Educator Work

Educators are often skeptical of data use and data systems because such initiatives often add to their already full workdays (Ingram et al., 2004; Valli & Buese, 2007; Wayman et al., 2004). Consequently, we believe that system use will become widespread if the uses fit directly into the fabric of educator work. More specifically, we recommend that system uses should be initially focused on components that either reduce work or improve efficiency.

Research provides some examples of such use. Collaboration is often forwarded as sound educational practice, but has typically entailed an undue amount of work (Wayman et al., 2006). Wayman and Stringfield (2006) described one school that used its data system to post and share instructional strategies for individual students as a result of data examination; prior to system implementation, educators had found this collaborative task to be difficult. Lachat and Smith (2005) found that collaborative teacher inquiry with a data system was more effective when school leaders modeled inquiry. Chen et al. (2005) reported educators using a data system to efficiently examine state test results.

Data systems can help make administrative work more efficient while improving individual student outcomes. Wayman et al. (in press) outlined how district administrators used a data system to examine weekly the progress of each student in special education. The same study highlighted how a principal, concerned that test scores for one particular ethnic group would result in a lower school rating, used the data system to track and provide special help to each individual student in that group for an entire year. In both cases, administrators in the Wayman et al. (in press) study agreed that the work required to address these problems would have been unmanageable without a data system.

Wayman et al. (2007) provided an example where system use was less widespread because of poor system integration with educational work. In their study, a teacher described the incredible amount of work placed upon him by a new data system. Because of poor system alignment, this teacher was maintaining parallel grading processes: he kept his gradebook as he had done for many years, but was also maintaining the system-specific gradebook required by the district. Teachers in this school reported that they used the system as little as possible because it represented extra work.

Professional Development

In this section, we describe some approaches to professional development that can help educators become proficient in using data systems in everyday practice. The data use research base contains little rigorous study of which professional development practices are best suited for various types of data use. However, we are able to provide guidelines that will help districts in implementing a data initiative and system.

Ultimately, professional development, like data systems themselves, should improve and shorten an educator's day (Wayman et al., 2007; Wayman & Stringfield, 2006). Professional development for data use should encompass all educators and be fundamentally tied to educational practice (Massell, 2001). District personnel should also endeavor to provide professional development that is immediately, specifically, and practically relevant to each educator, regardless of his or her district role. In the following sections, we use these guidelines to discuss professional development for introducing a data system and ongoing professional development.

Introducing the System

Professional development should be offered *prior to* data system implementation. Such pre-emptive professional development helps build awareness throughout the district for the initiative's goals, direction, and expectations (Wayman et al., 2007). It can also provide a foundation for data literacy and clear understandings regarding the purposes, distinctions between, and uses of assessments (Knapp, Swinnerton, Copland, & Monpas-Huber, 2006; Perie, Marion, & Gong, 2007; Supovitz & Klein, 2003).

The possible focuses of pre-emptive professional development are numerous and will depend on the local context. Generally, district personnel should look to make these trainings specific and relevant, concentrating on components that provide the most value and immediate impact when the system is introduced (Wayman et al., 2007). The calibration process will help define which topics best suit each context; hopefully, this process will have been thorough enough to identify the initial aims of data and system use.

As the system is introduced, it is critical that ample professional development be provided regarding the system itself—the data system should be central to the data initiative and user incompetence would be crippling to the initiative (Wayman et al., 2004, 2007). Most commercial vendors offer some training as part of their agreement, but districts should plan to provide deeper and ongoing training on the use of the system. Wayman and Conoly (2006) provided one example of system training, describing a district's train-the-trainer approach that resulted in preparation for each district educator.

Ongoing Professional Development

A comprehensive professional development plan should support elements from the entire cycle of educator decision making, from access, to interpretation, to taking action and using feedback. This lens, coupled with knowledge that the backgrounds and needs of district educators are as varied as the educators themselves, suggests that preparation offerings should be widely varied and offered at regular, frequent intervals. Educators should be provided whatever they need to continue to develop proficiency as data and data system users.

District personnel have many options in crafting how professional development is offered and organized, and we recommend that an appropriate variety be integrated into the plan. For instance, training can be offered at the district level, with one example being uniform, district-wide training in data system use (Wayman & Conoly, 2006). Development may also be offered at the building level, such as a faculty-wide session offered by a principal, district personnel, or outside experts (Darilek, & Barney, Kerr, Marsh, Ikemoto, 2006; Wayman & Stringfield, 2006). Specific training may be offered for groups of educators with similar needs, such as central office groups or grade-level teacher teams; such training is often effective when coupled with collaboration initiatives (Lachat & Smith, 2005; Wayman et al., 2006). Although one-on-one arrangements or data coaching can be challenging to implement successfully, some districts may choose to implement this strategy (Symonds, 2003; Wayman et al., 2007). Third-party help has also been used, with varying results (Kerr et al., 2006; Supovitz & Klein, 2003).

Space limitations preclude us from detailed discussion of the various topics that may be addressed in professional development sessions, but district personnel should generally ensure that professional development be relevant to educators' roles. For instance, professional development topics for teachers might focus on accessing data, making meaning of data, and using them to adjust classroom practice (Wayman et al., 2007; Young, 2006). Principals and other instructional leaders will not only need to know how to use data themselves, but how to prepare others and implement effective leadership structures that promote system use (Datnow et al., 2007; Wayman et al., 2007; Wayman & Stringfield, 2006; Young, 2006). In addition, as practices advance, educators may find that they are faced with unexpected or conflicting data (Coburn et al., in press; Knapp et al., 2006; Massell, 2001; Supovitz & Klein, 2003); this presents the opportunity to teach educators how to manage, or even embrace, the tension between these data as grounds for fruitful investigation.

Finally, we note the importance of tailoring ongoing professional development to the data system. Some aspects of training may depend on a data system's manner of presentation, flexibility, strengths, and content. Knapp et al. (2006) noted that data system capacities and offerings usually affect what educators come to define as problems, or select as areas of focus. This underlines the importance of choosing a system that is tailored to specific district needs and adaptable to new developments in how educators think about and use student data. Tailoring professional development in this way should result in a better integrated data system, data initiative, and improved professional development.

Collaboration

Although researchers often tout the benefits of collaboration, propagating collaboration among faculty in schools can sometimes prove to be a difficult and challenging task. Collaborating around data can help remedy this situation, bringing focus, a sense of purpose and a common language to collaborative efforts (Wayman et al., 2006). Further, the data–collaboration relationship is reciprocal: data initiatives are more likely to be successful if educators are allowed to work collaboratively, and data use itself can foster that collaboration (Chen et al., 2005; Lachat & Smith, 2005; Wayman, 2005; Wayman et al., 2006; Wayman & Stringfield, 2006).

Data systems can be great facilitators of collaboration, providing data in an accurate, timely, and user-friendly way (Wayman et al., 2004). In this way, data systems can reduce the frequent roadblocks shown to slow collaboration around data, thus allowing educators to work together in developing initiatives and resolving clearly articulated problems (Chen et al., 2005; Lachat & Smith, 2005; Wayman, 2005; Wayman et al., 2006; Young, 2006). In many ways, an investment in a quality data system is an investment in a school's overall capacity to combine efforts toward school improvement.

In this section, we discuss how to leverage collaboration and the use of student data systems. We first describe the centering of collaboration around a student data system, then offer some examples of collaborative arrangements and how they may be used to support data use.

Center Collaboration on the Data System

Since data provide a foundation for sustaining collaboration, it is useful to establish collaboration around the use of a student data system. Addressing collaboration in this manner provides a scaffold for educator learning—educators are not only learning how to use a data system, they are learning new ways of thinking about their craft and developing new professional relationships.

As with the data system and data initiative, we recommend implementing collaboration around the system in small, organic doses (Wayman et al., 2006, 2007). Doing so allows the nature of collaboration to build around the culture of data use relative to the specific context. Further, since data systems offer more clear and timely points for discussion than may have been previously available, the systems become part of a larger overall process of change and reform.

Varied Forms of Collaboration

Collaboration among school members can come in many forms; we supply a few examples for ways in which their work together may be centered on a data system and data use. Accordingly, these examples are a springboard for thinking about how existing and emerging collaborative relationships may be developed, strengthened, or formalized.

Teachers are likely to find it meaningful to work together by grade, by subject, or by other groupings. Halverson et al. (2005) discussed "data retreats" and methods for offering time to reflect upon data as a group. Supovitz and Klein (2003) described the benefits and challenges faculties can face as they use data to set long-term and intermediary goals. Symonds (2003) described how teachers can work together in attending to unique student needs, especially those of low-performing students. Structured meetings also afforded teachers the opportunity to share instructional strategies, develop long-term school-wide plans, and address issues of race and equity. Many of these issues have been ignored without the support of data systems (Lachat & Smith, 2005; Wayman et al., in press).

School administrators' roles can vary greatly, serving to underline the importance of their collaboration with teachers, other administrators, and central office personnel. Administrators are in a unique position to shape how and the extent to which teachers use data collaboratively (Young, 2006), and teachers respond positively when administrators personally make an effort to collaborate with teachers regarding data use (Supovitz & Klein, 2003; Wayman & Stringfield, 2006). Further, administrators can work with others to make informed decisions regarding curriculum and assessment, student services, budgeting, personnel, and community outreach (Halverson et al., 2005). Data systems can help facilitate these relationships; a counterexample was shown by Wayman et al. (2007), who described the isolation that occurred at various administrative levels eager to collaborate about data, but unable to leverage the technology to do it.

District administrators may find it useful, if sometimes challenging, to collaborate between departments or by connecting to individuals at the building level. Coburn et al. (in press) described the organizational and political challenges central offices face in using data collaboratively. Wayman et al. (2007) found the absence of a quality data system can also suppress the capacity of central office to operate in a well-integrated manner. Such fragmentation can shape central office members' patterns of interaction, further influencing how and with whom they share understandings, and in turn influence how data are used (Coburn et al., in press). In contrast, Wayman et al. (2006) described how a data system made possible central office collaboration about special education issues and Wayman et al. (2007) described how a data system would support extant—but difficult—collaborations between central office departments and other district areas.

Institutional Structures

While the issues discussed to this point are critical for successful use of a data system, none will efficiently support system use unless the district implements various structures to ensure that system use goes smoothly. In this section we will discuss four structures that will enhance the use of data and a data system: (1) system access, (2) time to engage in data use, (3) principal leadership, and (4) "go-to" individuals to support others.

System Access

One important function of data systems is to provide easy access to data (Chen et al., 2005; Wayman, 2007; Wayman et al., 2004). Full access has been shown to enhance and broaden teacher data use (Chen et al., 2005; Wayman & Stringfield, 2006) and lack of technological access has been cited as a hindrance to effective data use (Halverson et al., 2005; Supovitz & Klein, 2003).

Even in the presence of fully efficient data systems, some educators do not access data directly, but instead rely on other individuals (Lachat & Smith, 2005). Further, some leaders are wary of providing access to data for all educators (Young, 2006). We believe these situations can stifle effective use of a data system. We argue that data systems are most effective when each educator has full access to their permitted data, and we advocate that structures be built to ensure such access.

With full system access, users (e.g., teachers, support staff, principals, central office administrators) are given personal login information that allows them 24-hour access to data and system functions they are legally allowed to access. Merely structuring opportunity for access, however, is not enough to ensure full access. Structures must also be put in place that encourage and permit users to take advantage of this access. These structures are discussed in the following sections.

Time

Allowing educators time to examine data is cited throughout the literature as a critical support for effective data use and to efficiently use data systems (e.g., Ingram et al., 2004; Lachat & Smith, 2005; Wayman, 2005; Wayman & Stringfield, 2006). Young (2006), Massell (2001), and others have observed schools providing large portions of time in periodic intervals, and while the educators in these schools found this time to be an effective support, other researchers (Chen et al., 2005; Wayman & Stringfield, 2006) have described the utility of time set aside at more frequent intervals. It is our position that educators must use the data system on a daily basis in order to fully integrate it into the fabric of their workdays.

Consequently, we suggest that school and district leaders should endeavor to set aside multiple opportunities per week for the examination of educational data. This may involve daily set-aside time such as planning periods; less formal time per week may be structured if educators are properly encouraged and supported to use data daily on their own. Structuring time to use data and data systems, rather than specifying use as an extra mandate, sends a clear message that data use is valued, expected, and supported.

Many examples are available in research to describe how schools or districts have structured time for using data. These include the use of common planning time (Massell, 2001; Wayman et al., 2006), specifically dedicating time for collaboration (Lachat & Smith, 2005; Wayman & Stringfield, 2006), and creating teacher groupings such as subject- or grade-level teams (Chen et al., 2005; Wayman & Stringfield, 2006).

Principal Leadership

The literature is clear that principals play an integral role in the health of any data initiative (Copland, 2003; Lachat & Smith, 2005; Wayman & Stringfield, 2006; Young, 2006); research also describes ineffective data initiatives that are characterized by poor principal leadership (Wayman et al., 2007; Young, 2006). Recognizing the importance of principal leadership, we suggest that district leaders work with principals and other building leaders to establish clear structures describing how principals should lead faculties in using data and data systems, along with supports for carrying this out.

In some cases, these specifications may demand a restructuring of the principal's role or job description. In doing so, district leaders will have to carefully consider the drains of these new responsibilities on principals' time, along with strategies to support principals who are unprepared to use data or to lead faculties in using data. District personnel may additionally find it necessary to shift some responsibilities to other building support staff, as seen in the recommendations offered by Wayman et al. (2007).

Another principal leadership structure shown to be facilitative of data use is shared leadership (Copland, 2003; Lachat & Smith, 2005). In sharing leadership, principals designate and help develop faculty members (e.g., teachers or coaches) to guide other faculty members in effectively using data, through such activities as leading teams or providing expertise. Certain aspects of shared leadership may be formally structured for faculty leaders, such as creating specific positions, providing stipends, or supplying further training. Copland (2003) describes how other aspects of shared leadership may be intentionally less formal, allowing faculty leaders to develop as the data initiative develops.

Go-to Individuals

Related to the concept of shared leadership is the development of "go-to" individuals who regularly provide advice and support in the effective use of data and data systems. Research suggests these individuals may play numerous formal and informal roles, such as support for data cleaning (Chen et al., 2005), support for system use (Lachat & Smith, 2005; Wayman et al., 2004), and support for data interpretation (Lachat & Smith, 2005; Massell, 2001; Wayman et al., 2007; Young, 2006).

It is likely that these individuals will surface on an informal basis in every school. Additionally, many schools or districts formally establish such a position (Lachat & Smith, 2005; Massell, 2001) or formally shift the responsibilities of existing coach or facilitator positions (Wayman et al., 2007; Young, 2006). If districts choose to formally establish such positions or responsibilities, we believe it is critical that their duties be very clearly outlined and formal provisions be established for building and maintaining the data skills of the individuals filling these roles.

Although the data use literature is generally supportive of a formally structured role for supporting effective data use (e.g., coach, facilitator), we believe the literature is not robust regarding the positive effects of these positions on data use. Wayman et al. (2007) and Young (2006) described coaches present in both weak and strong data-using schools, and most research does not go into adequate detail regarding the tasks, actions, and training of these individuals. Further, the presence of "go-to" individuals has been shown to create bottlenecks that stifle independent data use (Lachat & Smith, 2005; Wayman et al., 2004). Consequently, we caution against heavy reliance on these formal positions. We are optimistic about the shared leadership that "go-to" individuals can provide and we believe that coaches or facilitators can be good support for using data systems. However, we also recognize that recruiting, training, and maintaining these positions may be a very difficult task.

Beyond Preparation

We have described some critical issues about preparing educators to effectively use data systems. Throughout this discussion, there has been an undercurrent that preparation is only the start: in fact, the use of data systems for school improvement is an ongoing, transformative process. Beyond initial preparation, district educators should look for ways to grow the data initiative and data system in ways that improve education in the local context. In this section, we discuss three issues that should be addressed: linking data to instruction, increasing capacity for using data, and expanding the data system.

Linking Data to Instruction

Wayman et al. (2007) described how many teachers in one district were avidly and frequently examining student data, but these same teachers were unable to thoroughly describe how they used these data to adjust their practice. This highlights an unfortunate paradox: increasingly, the literature describes how educator data use and data system use is growing, but this literature devotes far less detail to describing how practice is increasing. We believe this inconsistency suggests that accessing and examining data is one thing, but reflecting and deciding on how this information should inform practice is another, more difficult task.

Beyond preparation for system use, we suggest that educators closely monitor the status of practice in their district and provide support to this end. When data are used to help inform decisions and improve practice, a data system is a cost-effective, efficient investment. Absent the improvement of educational practice, however, a data system is an expensive waste of school resources.

Increasing Data Use Capacity

The implementation and growing of a data initiative never stops. In fact, the only constant will be change. As educators, schools, and districts learn how to best use data in their context, new needs will arise. Consequently, district personnel should have in place a long-range plan to build each user's capacity for effective data use. Many ways for building future capacity have been described above, such as implementing structures and support, fostering collaboration, and offering relevant professional development.

Knowing exactly how to engage these practices to increase capacity can be a difficult task. To ease this process, we recommend planned, ongoing evaluation of district data use. Each school year, evaluation should be conducted about the types of data being used by district educators, frequency of use, unmet needs, and how the system hinders or facilitates these. The calibration process should also be revisited each year, allowing the learning provided by data use to shape district goals and vision. It is also important that district personnel maintain contact with new developments in data use, through examination of research, monitoring other districts, and relationships with experts.

Expanding the Data System

In addition to increasing user capacity, the district must consistently look to increase data system capacity. New technologies and user abilities are being developed daily, so the intelligent expansion of a data system is a critical component to growing a district data initiative.

Such expansion may take the shape of additional modules that are needed to respond to increased user ability. System expansion may also include the implementation of new technology that was not available when the original system was built. If a district has been diligent in choosing the right system for its needs, the system should allow for these types of expansion.

Conclusion

Data systems provide critical and effective support that help educators examine student data for the purpose of educational improvement. Without the proper technology, though, even the most capable and interested educators will find it difficult to examine data in an efficient, fruitful manner.

The mere presence of these data systems does not ensure effective data use. Besides the obvious financial investment, data systems also require a substantial district investment in terms of vision, support, and structure. In this chapter, we have discussed several issues that are particularly important in preparing educators to use these systems effectively. We view these issues as integrated and inextricable: attending to one but ignoring others will result in less effective implementation. We believe district officials who attend to all of these issues will realize a great return on their investment.

Still, there is much to be learned about the effective application of data systems. While knowledge in this area has increased exponentially in just the last few years, we consider the greatest lesson to be the need for more learning. Consequently, we view the recommendations set forth in this chapter as a starting point. As research becomes fuller, deeper, and more detailed, new research will be conducted that strengthens these recommendations, resulting in a sound set of scalable practices that foster educational improvement.

References

Brunner, C., Fasca, C., Heinze, J., Honey, M., Light, D., Mandinach, E., & Wexler, D. (2005). Linking data and learning: The Grow Network study. *Journal of Education for Students Placed At Risk, 10*(3), 241–267.

Chen, E., Heritage, M., & Lee, J. (2005). Identifying and monitoring students' learning needs with technology. *Journal of Education for Students Placed At Risk, 10*(3), 309–332.

Coburn, C. E., Honig, M. I., & Stein, M. K. (in press). What is the evidence on districts' use of evidence? In J. Bransford, L. Gomez, D. Lam, & N. Vye (Eds.), *Research and practice: Towards a reconciliation.* Cambridge, MA: Harvard Educational Press.

Copland, M. A. (2003). Leadership of inquiry: Building and sustaining capacity for school improvement. *Educational Evaluation and Policy Analysis, 25*, 375–395.

Datnow, A., Park, V., & Wohlstetter, P. (2007). *Achieving with data: How high-performing school systems use data to improve instruction for elementary students.* Los Angeles: University of Southern California, Rossier School of Education, Center on Educational Governance.

Fullan, M. (1999). *Change forces: The sequel.* London: Falmer.

Halverson, R., Grigg, G., Prichett, R., & Thomas, C. (2005, September). *The new instructional leadership: Creating data-driven instructional systems in schools.* Retrieved January 11, 2008, from http://www.wcer.wisc.edu/publications/workingPapers/Working_Paper_No_2005_9.pdf

Herman, J. L., & Gribbons, B. (2001, February). *Lessons learned in using data to support school inquiry and continuous improvement: Final report to the Stuart Foundation* (CSE Technical Report No. 535). Los Angeles, CA: Center for the Study of Evaluation (CSE), University of California, Los Angeles.

Ingram, D., Louis, K. S., & Schroeder, R. G. (2004). Accountability policies and teacher decision making: Barriers to the use of data to improve practice. *Teachers College Record, 106*, 1258–1287.

Kerr, K. A., Marsh, J. A., Ikemoto, G. S., Darilek, H., & Barney, H. (2006). Strategies to promote data use for instructional improvement: Actions, outcomes, and lessons from three urban districts. *American Journal of Education, 112*(4), 496–520.

Knapp, M. S., Swinnerton, J. A., Copland, M. A., & Monpas-Huber, J. (2006). *Data-informed leadership in education.* Seattle, WA: Center for the Study of Teaching and Policy, University of Washington.

Lachat, M. A., & Smith, S. (2005). Practices that support data use in urban high schools. *Journal of Education for Students Placed At Risk, 10*(3), 333–349.

Massell, D. (2001). The theory and practice of using data to build capacity: State and local strategies and their effects. In S. H. Fuhrman (Ed.), *From the capitol to the classroom: Standards-based reform in the states* (pp. 148–169). Chicago: University of Chicago Press.

Mieles, T., & Foley, E. (2005). *Data warehousing: Preliminary findings from a study of implementing districts.* Philadelphia: Annenberg Institute for School Reform.

Perie, M., Marion, S., & Gong, B. (2007). *A framework for considering interim assessments.* Dover, NH: National Center for the Improvement of Educational Assessment.

Stringfield, S., Reynolds, D., & Schaffer, E. (2001, January). *Fifth-year results from the High Reliability Schools project.* Symposium conducted at the annual meeting of the International Congress for School Effectiveness and Improvement, Toronto, Ontario, Canada.

Supovitz, J. A., & Klein, V. (2003). *Mapping a course for improved student learning: How innovative schools systematically use student performance data to guide improvement.* Philadelphia: Consortium for Policy Research in Education.

Symonds, K. W. (2003). *After the test: How schools are using data to close the achievement gap.* San Francisco: Bay Area School Reform Collaborative.

Valli, L., & Buese, D. (2007). The changing roles of teachers in an era of high-stakes accountability. *American Educational Research Journal, 44*(3), 519–558.

Wassermann, S. (2001). Quantum theory, the uncertainty principle, and the alchemy of standardized testing. *Phi Delta Kappan, 83*(1), 28–40.

Wayman, J. C. (2005). Involving teachers in data-driven decision-making: Using computer data systems to support teacher inquiry and reflection. *Journal of Education for Students Placed At Risk, 10*(3), 295–308.

Wayman, J. C. (2007). Student data systems for school improvement: The state of the field. In *TCEA Educational Technology Research Symposium: Vol. 1* (pp. 156–162). Lancaster, PA: ProActive.

Wayman, J. C., & Conoly, K. (2006). Managing curriculum: Rapid implementation of a districtwide data initiative. *ERS Spectrum, 24*(2), 4–8.

Wayman, J. C., & Stringfield, S. (2006). Technology-supported involvement of entire faculties in examination of student data for instructional improvement. *American Journal of Education, 112*(4), 549–571.

Wayman, J. C., Cho, V., & Johnston, M. T. (2007). *The data-informed district: A district-wide evaluation of data use in the Natrona County School District.* Retrieved January 11, 2008, from http://edadmin.edb.utexas.edu/datause

Wayman, J. C., Conoly, K., Gasko, J., & Stringfield, S. (in press). Supporting equity inquiry with student data systems. In E. B. Mandinach & M. Honey (Eds.), *Linking data and learning.* New York: Teachers College Press.

Wayman, J. C., Midgley, S., & Stringfield, S. (2006). Leadership for data-based decision-making: Collaborative data teams. In A. Danzig, K. Borman, B. Jones, & B. Wright (Eds.), *New models of professional development for learner centered leadership* (pp. 189–206). Mahwah, NJ: Erlbaum.

Wayman, J. C., Stringfield, S., & Yakimowski, M. (2004). *Software enabling school improvement through analysis of student data.* Retrieved January 11, 2008, from http://www.csos.jhu.edu/crespar/techReports/Report67.pdf

Young, V. M. (2006). Teachers' use of data: Loose coupling, agenda setting, and team norms. *American Journal of Education, 112*(4), 521–548.

7

Accessing and Analyzing National Databases

Terrell Lamont Strayhorn
University of Tennessee

Introduction

There has been a plethora of published studies in education. Yet, despite the advancements of virtually every single line of inquiry in educational research from student achievement to access, faculty promotion to institutional finance, each study has a number of limitations and each design brings with it both virtues and dangers. While some studies are limited due to the lack of statistical controls for potentially confounding factors, others are limited by the number of respondents to the study's survey or the extent to which the study's findings are generalizable to other populations. To address some of these issues, federal, state, and other research organizations such as the National Center for Education Statistics (NCES) and National Science Foundation (NSF) have developed a number of large-scale databases, consisting of nationally representative samples, which can be used in secondary data analysis.

In this chapter, the use of large national databases in educational research at the K-12 and postsecondary level is discussed. Drawing on the existing literature, studies that employ national databases to examine a myriad of experiences and outcomes across all constituent groups including students and faculty/teachers are examined. Special attention is given to the opportunities that secondary analysis provides, the challenges associated with analyzing large-scale databases, and the supports available to secondary data analysts. Before readers can mine the idea of secondary data analysis for what it is worth—that is, the opportunities, challenges, and supports associated with this form of research—a general understanding of national databases and secondary analysis is warranted.

Secondary Data Analysis in Education

Secondary data analysis is a widely accepted form of educational research and K-12 and higher education analysts have used it extensively. For example, Crosnoe (2005) explored the experiences and outcomes of children from Mexican immigrant families using a national sample of 14,912 American kindergarteners who participated in the Early Childhood Longitudinal Study-Kindergarten Cohort (ECLS-K) sponsored by the National Center for Education Statistics within the U.S. Department of Education. He conducted multilevel analyses and found that "children from Mexican immigrant families were overrepresented in schools with a wide variety of problematic characteristics, even when family background differences were taken into account" (p. 269). Other K-12 researchers have employed nationally representative samples drawn from the *National Education Longitudinal Study of 1988* (NELS:88/ 2000) to estimate the effects of working part-time in high school (Marsh & Kleitman, 2005; Singh & Mehmet, 2000; Steinberg, Fegley, & Dornbusch, 1993); opportunity to learn (Braun, Wang, Jenkins, & Weinbaum, 2006); and school and family contexts (Strayhorn, in press-b) on important educational outcomes such as student achievement.

Using large-scale national databases to study issues germane to postsecondary education has a long history as well. For instance, Carter (2001) used *Beginning Postsecondary Students Longitudinal Study* (BPS:90/92) data to examine the degree aspirations of Black and White college students. Zhang (2005) analyzed data drawn from the *Baccalaureate and Beyond Longitudinal Study* (B&B:93/97) to "examine the effect of college quality, among other academic and non-academic factors, on educational continuation for college graduates" (p. 314). But, even earlier researchers used large national databases to study dropouts of higher education (Munro, 1981) and attrition at 2- and 4-year colleges (Williamson & Creamer, 1988).

Focusing on another constituent group in higher education, Perna (2001) conducted hierarchical multinomial logit analyses on data from the *National Study of Postsecondary Faculty* (NSOPF:93) to determine if family responsibilities are related to the employment status of women and men junior faculty. NSOPF is the largest national survey of faculty members; it has been used extensively in prior research on postsecondary instructors (Bellas & Toutkoushian, 1999; Kirshstein, Matheson, & Jing, 1997; Rosser, 2004; Strayhorn & Saddler, 2007).

Even sociologists of education whose principal interests center on socioeconomic disparities, the academic profession, and educational organizations as a system characterized by an institutional division of labor (Clark, 1973; Clark & Trow, 1966) have analyzed data from secondary databases (Constantine, 1995; Mau & Kopischke, 2001). In a previous study data from the *Baccalaureate and Beyond Longitudinal Study of 1993* (B&B:93/97) were used to estimate the influence of "attending a historically Black college or university (HBCU)" on three labor market outcomes of recent African American college graduates: annual earnings, occupational status, and job satisfaction (Strayhorn, in press-a). Drawing on data from the same source, analyses were conducted on 11,192 individuals, representing approximately 1 million students nationwide, to estimate the effect of background, pre-college, and college experiences on the achievement disparities between first- and continuing-generation college students (Strayhorn, 2006a).

While our knowledge of national databases in education has burgeoned in the past few decades, researchers have focused their attention on presenting the *results* of secondary data analyses rather than the *mechanisms* through which national databases are accessed and analyzed. Such mechanisms are sometimes implied but rarely made explicit. Some book chapters point to the plethora of secondary data sources that is available in the public domain (Carter, 2003). Other researchers provide highly technical guidance about how to analyze large-scale national databases appropriately using adjusted sample sizes, panel weights, and design effects (Galloway, 2004; Thomas & Heck, 2001), to name a few. Yet, far less is known about how to access and analyze national databases, particularly those provided by federal organizations like the U.S. Department of Education, and what national databases provide in terms of opportunities and challenges. It is out of this context that the need for the present chapter grew.

Conceptual Framework

When I was in seminary at the Samuel Dewitt Proctor School of Theology at Virginia Union University, I studied with the late Rev. Dr. Myles Jones who taught homiletics or the art of preaching. He introduced me to the concept of an "organizing observation," which he generally referred to as "the OO." An organizing observation generally fit the following template, "There are times when . . . [something occurs]; when such conditions exist, we must . . . [do something]." When preparing to write this chapter, I reflected on the masterful teaching of Dr. Jones and found his idea of "the OO" particularly relevant to my approach in this chapter. Indeed, *there are times when* we, as educational researchers, want to enhance the generalizability of our findings; when such conditions exist, we must consider the important role that national databases play in advancing lines of inquiry within the social sciences (Carter, 2003). Indeed, there are other "conditions" under which the use of a national database is justified if not absolutely necessary. Based on this theoretical construct, part of the present chapter is devoted to identifying opportunities for using large-scale, nationally representative data in research.

To organize my thoughts about accessing and analyzing data drawn from nationally representative samples, I settled upon Sanford's (Sanford, 1966; Sanford & Adelson, 1962) notion of *challenge and support*. I found this conceptual framework useful as it provided constructs for talking about the issues involved in the process of securing and using secondary data in educational research. Also, Sanford's ideas are related, at least in part, to the "OO" described above. That is, I considered the antithesis of "challenge" which is generally believed to be "opportunity."

Drawing on these underlying concepts, the present chapter is organized into three main sections: opportunities, challenges, and supports. The final section presents an extended example of how researchers might employ a national database in higher education research. The balance of the chapter turns to potential research questions that can be investigated using large-scale national data.

Opportunities

This section focuses on the seemingly limitless opportunities provided by using national databases in educational research. In a way, it serves as an introduction to the sections that follow, which emphasize the challenges and supports associated with secondary analysis of large-scale survey data in social sciences and education.

Variety of Databases

First, the sheer number of national databases available represents a state of affairs that is opulent with opportunity for research purposes. Not only are there many providers of national databases such as the National Center for Education Statistics (NCES) within the U.S. Department of Education, National Science Foundation (NSF), Educational Testing Service (ETS), and Higher Education Research Institute (HERI), but each of these organizations provides access to a wide range of national databases that can support different sorts of research questions. For instance, quite often researchers want to measure the impact of educational policies on student outcomes; one might use National Postsecondary Student Aid Survey (NPSAS) data which are perfectly suited for exploring questions like: What percent of African American, low-income students received Pell grants before and after recent reauthorization of the Higher Education Act? Galloway (2004) proffered a useful five-category typology of research questions that are supported by large-scale national surveys— those measuring the relationship among variables, those testing the significance of group differences, those involving the prediction of group membership, those exploring the underlying structure of data, and those involving the time course of events. Researchers are encouraged to match their techniques to their questions, their questions to their database.

Yet, not all databases are made equal; there are important characteristics that distinguish national databases. For instance, some databases are appropriately titled population studies while others consist of nationally representative samples. Population, "census," or universe studies include information for every element (i.e., student, institution, etc.) in the larger group. IPEDS and Survey of Earned Doctorates (SED) are good examples of population studies. The SED is an annual census of all research doctorates awarded by U.S. degree-granting institutions. The database includes information on individuals in all fields, not just science and engineering. On the other hand, most national databases consist of nationally representative samples drawn from the population using complex, stratified sampling designs. *Baccalaureate and Beyond Longitudinal Study* (B&B), *High School and Beyond* (HSB), *Education Longitudinal Study* (ELS), *National Education Longitudinal Study* (NELS), *National Study of Postsecondary Faculty* (NSOPF), *Survey of Doctorate Recipients* (SDR) and *Cooperative Institutional Research Program* (CIRP) are good examples of nationally representative samples.

National databases may also differ in their purpose and intended use. For example, the NCES provides access to a wide range of databases that serve significantly different purposes, contain remarkably different samples, and can be used to answer qualitatively different research questions. The following list describes the nature and purpose of several databases available through federal agencies and national research centers:

1. *National Education Longitudinal Study* (NELS): The NELS:1988/2000 tracks 24,599 individuals, who represent the national population of eighth graders in 1988, up to eight years after high school graduation. NELS consists of over 6,000 variables and includes surveys from students, teachers, parents, and

administrators in a series of data collection waves (Curtin, Ingels, Wu, & Heuer, 2002). NELS is one of the most widely used databases in educational research. Researchers have studied the effects of motivation and academic engagement on math and science achievement (Singh, Granville, & Dika, 2002), race and academic disidentification (Osborne, 1997), and the effects of social capital on students' transition to selective colleges (Kim & Schneider, 2005) using NELS data.

2. *Baccalaureate and Beyond Longitudinal Study* (B&B): The B&B study follows baccalaureate degree completers over time to provide information on work experiences after college and post-BA outcomes such as postgraduate educational experiences, earnings, occupation, and job satisfaction to name a few. This database is particularly useful for studying the long-term effects of college on student outcomes. In prior studies, B&B data have been used to examine the decision to enroll in college (Perna, 2004), the impact of undergraduate college selectivity on enrollment in graduate school (Zhang, 2005), and graduate student persistence (Strayhorn, 2005).

3. *Education Longitudinal Study of 2002* (ELS): According to the NCES website, ELS is "designed to monitor the transition of a national sample of young people as they progress from tenth grade through high school and on to postsecondary education and/or the world of work" (National Center for Education Statistics, n.d.). The database is ideal for studying critical transitions from high school to college, pathways to postsecondary education, the role parents play in their child's success, and the influence of course-taking patterns on subsequent achievement. Given its relative newness, the ELS database has not been used extensively in education research; researchers have used ELS data to study the initial college experiences of high school seniors (Bozick & Lauff, 2007).

4. *College Student Experiences Questionnaire* (CSEQ): The CSEQ consists of 191 items designed to measure the quality and quantity of students' involvement in college activities and their use of college facilities. Other items measure students' sociodemographic characteristics, educational aspirations, and perceived development across an array of learning domains including critical thinking, self-awareness, and appreciation of diversity (Pace, 1990). More than 500 colleges and universities in the United States have used the questionnaire. In previous studies, CSEQ data have been used to understand the effect of involvement for employed students (Lundberg & Schreiner, 2004); faculty–student interactions and college grades (Anaya & Cole, 2001); and the impact of collegiate experiences on self-assessed skills (Grayson, 1999). There is an adapted version of the CSEQ primarily designed for students at two-year community colleges called the Community College Student Experiences Questionnaire (CCSEQ). For more information, consult the primary author (Friedlander, Murrell, & MacDougall, 1993; Friedlander, Pace, & Lehman, 1990).

5. *Cooperative Institutional Research Program* (CIRP): The CIRP is the oldest and largest empirical study in higher education focusing on entering college students. Initiated in 1966 by Alexander Astin, the survey provides useful

information on entering students' academic preparation for college, high school activities, academic major, values, and demographic characteristics, to name a few. This database is particularly useful for studying the predisposition of high school students to college, self-reported competencies, and how college affects student learning and development. Previous researchers have used CIRP data to study student leadership development (Kezar & Moriarty, 2000), faculty–student interactions (Cole, 1999), and citizenship and spirituality (Sax, 2004).

Table 7.1 presents a list of several national databases by level of education; while this list does not include all databases that are available to secondary analysts, it includes those that are most commonly used.

Table 7.1 National databases in education, by level of schooling.

Early childhood/elementary	Secondary	Postsecondary and beyond
Early Childhood Longitudinal Study (ECLS) +	Education Longitudinal Study of 2002 (ELS) +	Baccalaureate and Beyond Longitudinal Study (B&B) +
National Household Education Survey +	National Household Education Survey +	Beginning Postsecondary Students Longitudinal Study (BPS) +
Crime and Safety Surveys +	Crime and Safety Surveys +	Integrated Postsecondary Education System (IPEDS) +
	National Education Longitudinal Study of 1988 (NELS) +	National Education Longitudinal Study of 1988 (NELS) +
	High School and Beyond Longitudinal Study (HSB) +	High School and Beyond Longitudinal Study (HSB) +
	National Longitudinal Study of the High School Class of 1972 (NLS: 72) +	National Longitudinal Study of the High School Class of 1972 (NLS: 72) +
		National Postsecondary Student Aid Study (NPSAS) +
		National Study of Postsecondary Faculty (NSOPF) +
		National Survey of Student Engagement (NSSE) *
		College Student Experiences Questionnaire (CSEQ) *
		Survey of Earned Doctorates (SED) #
		Recent College Graduates Survey (RCG) #
		Cooperative Institutional Research Program (CIRP) *

(+) provided by the National Center for Education Statistics.
(#) provided by the National Science Foundation.
(*) provided by an independent research center.

Maximizing Generalizability

Results produced by large-scale secondary data analyses are inferentially robust. And, more often than not, national databases are used for the expressed purpose of drawing generalizations about behaviors, trends, or patterns in the broader population of "units of analysis" (i.e., institutions, students, faculty/staff) in higher education. This is accomplished in a number of ways. First, national databases such as those provided by NCES and NSF consist of entire populations or large samples. For example, the Integrated Postsecondary Education Data System (IPEDS) is a population study that contains *every* single element in the broader group (i.e., postsecondary institutions). IPEDS, also known as the postsecondary institution universe survey, contains information on 6,600 institutions plus 80 administrative units. As another example, *High School and Beyond* (HSB) is a longitudinal study of 28,000 high school seniors in the United States. Studies based on such samples are more representative of the broader population than any sample that individual researchers can generate without enormous resources and time.

Nevertheless, gains in generalizability come at the expense of specificity to some degree. In other words, findings based on nationally representative samples are more representative of the broader population (i.e., students, teachers, women) but may not reflect subtle nuances that exist for a particular school, a specific classroom, "exceptional" individuals, or a campus that has established a new program or service that aids students' adjustment to college. In such instances, locally designed surveys may be a more appropriate strategy for assessing the impact of educational practices on specific outcomes (Strayhorn, 2006b).

There is at least one other way in which nationally representative analyses require analysts to give up a degree of specificity. When using primary data sources (e.g., locally designed surveys, commercial questionnaires administered to individuals directly), researchers have more control over the way in which variables are measured. For instance, in a study of first-year college student experiences at a single institution, items were developed for measuring students' satisfaction with college and sense of belonging (Strayhorn & Blakewood, 2007, 2008). Satisfaction was assessed in multiple areas including students' satisfaction with campus life, individual support services (e.g., academic advising, cultural centers, etc.), and their relationships with faculty members to name a few. Also, satisfaction with college was assessed generally using multiple items; an example of this scale is, "I am satisfied now with my college experience at [said institution]." This allowed my collaborators and myself to tap various facets of student satisfaction in a highly specific way at a single institution.

To test whether the determinants of first-year student satisfaction at "said university" are similar to those found in the broader population of college-going students, multivariate analyses were conducted on a nationally representative sample of students who participated in the 2004–2005 administration of the College Student Experiences Questionnaire (CSEQ) sponsored by the Center for Postsecondary Research at Indiana University. To access data, a research proposal was sent to the Center for Postsecondary Research along with the paperwork required to request a slice of CSEQ data (for more information, see the Center's website). Specifically, a large, random sample of students who matched certain criteria (e.g., race, institutional type, etc.) was obtained. To analyze these data, measures were identified in the database that were appropriate for operationalizing student satisfaction and sense of belonging. However, my choice of "proxies" for these two constructs was constrained by decisions made by those who created the CSEQ (Pace, 1990). According to the codebook and related sources (Gonyea, Kish, Kuh, Muthiah, & Thomas, 2003), several items on the CSEQ have psychometric qualities that are consistent with student satisfaction with college; an example of this scale is, "how well do you like college?" While there is considerable agreement among researchers about the use of these items in satisfaction studies (Hollins, 2003; Kuh & Hu, 2001; Strayhorn & Terrell, 2007) and the *generalizability* of findings based on national samples (Thomas & Heck, 2001), it is plausible that CSEQ items have a marginal relationship (lack *specificity*) with the constructs they are purported to measure. Using CSEQ data to increase the reliability of my estimates also required me to surrender a degree of precision in measuring constructs like satisfaction; while important to this discussion, such trade-offs are inevitable in secondary data analyses and do not necessarily limit the usefulness of studies based on large-scale survey samples.

Combining Data Sources

The development and use of national databases in education afford researchers the opportunity to combine information from multiple sources to create powerfully robust datasets for secondary analysis. To be sure, this presents an unparalleled occasion to calculate highly reliable parameter estimates that might otherwise require decades of data collection, inordinate amounts of time, millions of dollars in survey design and storage, and an unfathomable number of hours for participants in responding to surveys, questionnaires, and interviews which most institutional review boards would consider unnecessarily stressful, if not inhumane.

To avoid such "costs," many national databases either (a) draw information from previously existing sources or (b) include an identifier that can be used to merge information from multiple sources into a single dataset. To illustrate the former, National Postsecondary Student Aid Study (NPSAS) serves as the base-year on which several other NCES databases are built. Using NPSAS:93 as the base year, the B&B:1993/2003 follows baccalaureate (BA) degree completers up to 10 years after college graduation (Wine, Cominole, Wheeless, Dudley, & Franklin, 2006). That is, from the NPSAS:93 sampling criteria, 16,316 baccalaureate degree recipients were identified and surveyed in the base year (1993), the first-year follow-up (B&B:93/94), the second follow-up (B&B:93/97), and the third follow-up (B&B:93/03). The resulting database provides information on how students and their families pay for college (NPSAS) as well as their post-BA experiences (B&B). Similarly, the *Beginning Postsecondary Students* (BPS) *Longitudinal Study* collects information on the undergraduate experiences of students who responded to the NPSAS initially (Wine et al., 2002).

Finally, developers of national databases may often include an "identifying" variable that can be used to combine multiple datasets and to connect various units of analysis. For instance, several NCES databases consisting of stratified samples (i.e., students within schools) include identifiers for the individual and the institution that allow analysts to combine student- and institution-level data for multilevel analyses. The *Baccalaureate and Beyond Longitudinal Study* (B&B:1993/2003) includes information at the student level ranging from demographic variables such as age, race, and gender to academic factors such as undergraduate grade point average (GPA), academic major, and degree goals (Green et al., 1996). Institution-level data can be merged into the B&B from extant data sources like IPEDS and Barron's *Profiles of American Colleges* using the institution's name or IPEDS code (usually labeled "unitID"). For example, Zhang (2005) created an integrated B&B database by extracting information on institutional control from IPEDS and college selectivity from various editions of the *Barron's Guide*. In a previous paper, measures were derived of institutional control, selectivity, and campus type (i.e., historically Black or not) from IPEDS data and merged with B&B:1993/1997 information to create an expanded panel study (Strayhorn, in press-a).

It is important to note, however, that identifying information is included in "restricted datasets" only and not those available in the public domain. Analysts must secure a license to access restricted databases; this issue is addressed in the next section. However, research centers like the Higher Education Research Institute (HERI) at the University of California, Los Angeles, and the Center for Postsecondary Research at Indiana University have their own application process for analysts who desire to use their data. Readers are encouraged to contact individual agencies for information about their application process.

Challenges

Indeed, secondary analysis of data from nationally representative samples provides a number of unique opportunities for advancing lines of scholarly inquiry. However, secondary analysis of national data is rife with a number of challenges as well. Generally, these challenges can be organized into two areas: challenges associated with accessing and analyzing databases.

Accessing Databases

Restricted Use Licenses   As previously mentioned, identifying information (i.e., student- and institution-level identifiers, continuous data on earnings, etc.) is included in restricted datasets only and not those available in the public domain. For this reason, analysts must secure a license to access restricted use databases. For NCES and NSF databases, the process can be simplified into five steps:

(1) access license application forms (NCES now uses an online application process);
(2) submit a research proposal that identifies the database requested, its intended purpose, and the researcher's intended use including research questions, hypotheses, analytic plan, and outcomes or products that might emanate from such analyses;

(3) submit a license agreement signed by the principal investigator (PI) or project officer and a senior official with authority to bind the organization to the terms of the license;

(4) submit signed affidavits of nondisclosure for everyone involved in the research project (e.g., PI, research assistants, collaborators), each bearing the seal of a notary public; and

(5) a detailed security plan signed by the individuals listed in #3 plus a system security officer.

It is important to note that federal organizations like NCES and NSF grant restricted use licenses to organizations (i.e., research centers, educational institutions, etc.) not individuals. In other words, individuals apply on behalf of their institution. This is clarified in the license agreement statement described above.

Cost   Another challenge associated with gaining access to national databases is cost. Cost is fees that must be paid either to receive a copy of the database on compact disc or for the time and effort of staff at the "data granting" organization to prepare the dataset for secondary use. In some instances, staff not only prepare the dataset but also analyze the data and provide external researchers with the necessary tables, graphs, and output. Rates for compiling data on specific schools, individuals, or scales can range from $100 per hour and up. For instance, a simple random sample of 8,000 individuals was purchased, in a previous study, for approximately $1,500. Those interested in conducting secondary data analysis would do well to secure grant funds to subsidize such costs. The American Education Research Association (AERA) awards up to $20,000 to individual researchers who conduct studies using large-scale survey data provided by the NCES and NSF. For more information, go to AERA's grants program online.

Analyzing Databases

Missing Data   Secondary analysis of national databases is often complicated by the amount of missing cases or missing data (Graham & Hoffer, 2000; Little & Rubin, 1987). As a general rule, cases, for which data are missing completely at random, tend to be dropped from analyses. However, if patterns are observed in the "missingness" of data (e.g., family income and student aid amounts are missing for many more minorities than majority students), analysts must take steps to account for missing information. There are at least three commonly used solutions to this problem:

(1) dropping missing observations for analyses,

(2) imputing the sample mean in place of the missing information known as the *zero-order correction* procedure, and

(3) predicting or forecasting the missing information on Y_1 (e.g., family income) by estimating other models based on non-missing variables (e.g., gender, race, parent's education) that are correlated with Y_1.

If missing information on the dependent variable, analysts have no option but to drop the case from all analyses.

Complex Sampling Designs   In most cases, nationally representative data were collected using complex sampling designs. That is, most large-scale survey data were collected using stratified, multistage, cluster sampling techniques or "sample designs that involve nesting observations at one level within higher-order units at another level" (e.g., students within schools, families within neighborhoods, faculty within institutions, etc.). Nested strategies are further complicated by the oversampling of *certain* individuals in *certain* situations that need to be included in sufficient numbers for the purposes of analysis. A good example of this is the B&B database that employed a stratified multistage sampling design and oversampled for education majors. Without proper adjustments, estimates of variances and standard errors derived from such data would be at least biased and at worst incorrect, leading to inaccurate statistical conclusions or Type I errors (Muthen & Satorra, 1995).

Most datasets, especially those provided by the NCES, provide a set of sample weights to adjust for unequal probabilities of selection due to the sampling design. A detailed discussion of various types of weights goes beyond the limits of this discussion (Thomas & Heck, 2001), but it is important to note that different weights (e.g., raw versus relative) affect differently standard errors and sample sizes, upon which most statistical conclusions are drawn. Thus, applying the appropriate relative weight to national databases using complex sampling designs is a critical adjustment.

It is important for readers to note, however, that considerable debate exists (and persists) about how to remedy potential problems associated with secondary data analysis (Thomas, Heck, & Bauer, 2005). Most scholars agree that decisions about dealing with complex samples should be based on the conceptualization of one's study. For instance, researchers must apply appropriate sample weights to account for the unequal probability of selection when using National Study of Postsecondary Faculty (NSOPF) data to study gender equity in terms of salary among tenured full-time professors. However, if the study was designed to measure differences in compensation among faculty members employed at two-year and four-year institutions, researchers would do well to (a) estimate the model using specialized software (e.g., SUDAAN, WesVar, AM) that takes into account the complex sampling design, (b) apply appropriate sample weights to adjust for unequal selection rates, and (c) adjust estimated standard errors upward using the design effect (DEFF) to account for the intracluster homogeneity of variance. Again, the decision should be based on the study's design and purpose, and researchers are encouraged to link databases to questions, questions to techniques, and designs to adjustment decisions.

Supports

Despite the challenges listed above, a number of supports are available to assist secondary data analysts in their work with large-scale national databases.

Codebooks and Surveys   To analyze secondary databases, one must know which questions to ask and why, how to interpret or make meaning of the data addressing those questions, the limitations of the instruments and methods selected, how data were collected including sampling designs and design effects, and how to best report findings to those concerned. To this end, most developers of large-scale secondary data sources produce copies of the actual instrument and codebooks that explain how items were worded, response options for each item, and the meaning of each response category (e.g., 1 = *female;* 5 = *very often,* etc.). Technical reports also provide information on data collection procedures (i.e., paper survey, computer-assisted telephone interview) and design effects that should be considered when analyzing and reporting findings based on national data. NCES provides electronic copies of its methodological reports and codebooks on the center's website (http://nces.ed.gov).

Data Analysis Software   Technological advances in terms of data analysis software also support the work of secondary analysts. Standard statistical packages (e.g., SPSS and SAS) can be used to conduct single-level studies on national data. Advanced software packages also exist that specialize in adjusting for complex sampling designs, accounting for multi-level clustering (i.e., faculty within institutions), and applying pre-determined design effects (DEFF). These packages range from expensive, sophisticated programs like SUDAAN, WesVar, PCCARP, and HLM (Raudenbush & Bryk, 2002) to free programs like *AM* v.0.06 provided by the American Institutes for Research. All of these programs make it relatively easy to apply sample weights (e.g., WEIGHTBY function in SPSS) and impute sample means for missing cases. Finally, users may also use NCES' *Data Analysis System Online* (DAS) to create descriptive tables or calculate correlation matrices.

Theory   Analyzing national databases often requires the researcher to operationalize various constructs, or complex abstractions, using multiple items from the dataset. Theory is a powerful support or tool for making sense of such "complex abstractions." In other words, theory, by definition, presents a plausible explanation for observed phenomena and may provide clues for measuring variables that are difficult to observe or quantify otherwise such as motivation, self-concept, or self-esteem to name a few.

Indeed, there are a number of theories that can prove useful when measuring independent and dependent factors in educational research. For instance, research studies, based on nationally representative samples, might be grounded in theoretical underpinnings related to cognitive-structural, psychosocial, attribution, and college impact theories. This list is not exhaustive; rather it provides a starting place for those who need assistance with identifying theories that might be employed in large-scale national analyses. Examples of published research studies, grounded in theory, that use national databases abound (Perna, 2001, 2004; Stage & Rushin, 1993; Strayhorn, 2006a, 2006c).

In this way, theory serves as a guide to support secondary data analysts in their work with large-scale surveys that employ complex sampling designs and yield information on thousands of items that, in isolation, may hold little meaning (e.g., "I feel good about myself at times") but taken together may measure important theoretical constructions (e.g., self-concept, self-esteem, identity, etc.).

Workshops/Training Seminars   There are workshops and training seminars available for those who are concerned about analyzing data from nationally representative samples. Several of these are provided by the U.S. Department of Education such as "Using ELS:2002 and NELS:88 for Research and Policy" (http://iesed.gov/whatsnew/conferences).

Professional associations in education sponsor a number of training seminars as well. The Association of Institutional Research sponsors a summer data policy institute, with support from NCES and NSF, to train researchers on the use of federal databases in educational research. Also, the American Educational Research Association provides pre-conference workshops on analyzing secondary data, in advance of its annual meeting, for a fee (ranging from $85–$150). In 2007, I served as director of such a pre-conference course that enrolled approximately 50 participants. Participants represented a range of experiences from doctoral students and faculty members in K-12 and higher education, to institutional researchers and researchers from national organizations such as the American Council on Education. Readers are encouraged to consider these professional development options as many are designed to offer hands-on experience in analyzing secondary data under the guidance of expert users of large-scale national data.

Relevant Readings   Finally, in consonance with my professional identity as a graduate faculty member, the set of readings, handbooks, and articles found in this chapter's list of references are recommended for interested persons. This list is not designed to be exhaustive but rather a mere illustration of the kinds of supports available to novice and advanced secondary analysts. Indeed, there is more to be read, including the present chapter, and most good readings end with more stuff to read. Thus, readers are encouraged to "go where the path leads" until you feel equipped with enough information to design a study carefully and to analyze secondary data appropriately.

An Extended Illustration

A Chinese proverb reads, "Example carries more weight than preaching." This wisdom is relevant to using national databases for research purposes. However, a modifier is warranted—a "good" example carries much weight. The chapter's author created the anecdote presented below with this goal in mind—to provide a good, albeit brief, illustration of how large-scale national datasets can be employed in research studies.

> Fred Panera is the advisor of Latino-American students at the University of Knox. For several years, he has expressed concerns about the relatively low representation of Latino students on campus and the limited number of opportunities available in which Latino students can be involved. After reading through a recent article in the *Chronicle* about low co-curricular involvement rates among Latino males and the important role that summer bridge programs play in the socialization and success of minorities in college, he logged three questions in the back of his day planner:

(1) What affect do summer bridge programs have on Latino student success in college?
(2) What affect does campus involvement have on Latino student success in college?
(3) Do these effects differ between men and women?

After reading published works on student involvement, summer bridge programs, and Latino students in college, Panera learned that first-year Latino students faced unique challenges related to student success. He decides to explore his questions by way of research. With few staff to assign to this project and limited resources to collect data, Panera decides to use pre-existing data to probe his concerns. Using his reflection as a guide, the following questions were adopted for the study:

(1) What affect do precollege programs have on *first-year* Latino student success in college?
(2) What affect does campus involvement have on *first-year* Latino student success in college?
(3) Do these effects differ between men and women?

After talking with Dr. Edwards, a faculty member in the college of education about his interests, Fred is encouraged to consider the *Beginning Postsecondary Students Longitudinal Study* (BPS:1996/2001) which tracks first-time entering collegians up to six years after enrolling initially. He applies for a restricted use license through the NCES website, identifying himself and Dr. Edwards as principal investigators. After receiving the data, Panera struggles to identify suitable proxies for his variables of interest. Returning to the literature that he read earlier, he decided to draw upon extant theories to develop "working" or operational definitions for success outcomes (i.e., institutional selectivity, first-year grades, first-year retention) and campus involvement (i.e., individual items from the social integration subscale in BPS). Since BPS does not include information on actual participation in a TRIO program, the team modified their focus on *being eligible* to participate in TRIO programs; this reflects the issue of specificity to which I alluded earlier in the chapter.

Given the stratified, multi-stage complex sampling design employed in BPS, Dr. Edwards chooses the appropriate sample weight from the database. As a prior user of federal databases, he is comfortable calculating the relative weight by dividing the raw weight (provided in BPS) by its mean: $w_i/\bar{w}$. Using the survey design effect (DEFF) published in the methodology report, Dr. Edwards calculates the design effect adjusted weight by dividing the relative weight by the DEFF. Using the "WEIGHTBY" function in SPSS, they conduct regression analyses on a nationally representative sample of Latino students—regressing first-year GPA (SEGPAY1) on measures of involvement in clubs and organizations (CMCLUBS, CMINTRAM) and whether the respondent was eligible to participate in a pre-college outreach or TRIO program (e.g., Upward Bound).

To test for differences within group, they created interaction terms between "gender" and their independent variables. These cross-product variables were entered in the next step of the equation. Increased variance explained at the $p < 0.01$ level suggests the presence of conditional effects. The researchers decided to use a more rigorous threshold of statistical significance (0.01 versus 0.05) in accordance with recommendations provided by Thomas, Heck, and Bauer (2005); using a more conservative critical alpha value is one of their "corrective strategies" for adjusting for design effects. Reports were presented in tabular and written form to administrators on campus. For instance, using information found in Table 7.2, they presented evidence to student affairs staff members of the benefits that campus involvement provides to students, especially Latino students. In their study, Latino students who were involved in campus clubs and activities earned higher first-year GPAs than those who were not involved in clubs and organizations. That is, the predicted first-year GPA of uninvolved students was 2.22 while the predicted GPA of involved students ranged from 2.26 to 2.29. With this information in mind, the group considered barriers to Latino students' involvement in campus clubs and organizing including the limited number of ethnic and multicultural student organizations on campus (e.g., Latino Student Union) and the virtual absence of Latino faculty and staff members who might serve as advisors and mentors to such students.

Future Research Using National Databases

Future research based on national databases might pursue a number of promising directions. Similar to the example above, future researchers might use BPS data to study the college experiences of students who qualify for federal TRIO programs (e.g., low-income, first-generation minorities). Data from the Survey of Earned Doctorates can be used to study comparatively the educational pathways of Asian scientists in engineering and the social sciences. Recent data from ELS:2002 can be used to study science course taking in high school, opportunity to learn math skills, and even the college choices of students grounded in prevailing theory about the college decision-making process (Hossler & Gallagher, 1987).

Darling-Hammond (2007) noted that "for students of color, the [educational] pipeline leaks more profusely at every juncture" (p. 318). To test the validity of this statement or perhaps more appropriately to provide evidence of the "leaking pipeline," future research might use longitudinal databases like the ELS, NELS, or BPS to measure the proportion of minority students who move, or fail to move, across critical junctures between middle school and high school, high school and college,

Table 7.2 First-year GPA regressed on campus involvement variables, BPS:1996/2001.

Variable	B	SE	t
Intercept	222.20	11.84	18.77
Clubs			
Sometimes	6.70	3.94	1.70*
Often	3.45	6.63	0.52*
Never (reference)			
Intramural sports			
Sometimes	4.31	6.38	0.68
Often	−18.08	4.70	−3.85*
Never (reference)			

$R = 0.18$, $R^2 = 0.03$.
* $p < 0.01$.

college and graduate school. To further this line of inquiry, future studies may also be designed to model the way in which various factors at multiple levels (i.e., individual, family, school) coalesce to affect future educational opportunities. An example of this kind of study might employ NELS data and Bronfenbrenner's (1979) theory to explore the question: Are parental expectations, teachers' perceptions, and students' aspirations related to degree attainment for African American collegians after controlling for differences in human capital and prior academic achievement?

Conclusion

This chapter extends our understanding about the nature of national databases in education, the opportunities that secondary data analysis provides, and the challenges and supports associated with accessing and analyzing national databases. While many research questions linger, research in education has benefited greatly from the availability of relatively high-quality data through large-scale national databases. Using this chapter as a guide, researchers, educators, and policy makers can easily access and appropriately analyze national databases for decision making in education.

References

Anaya, G., & Cole, D. (2001). Latina/o student achievement: Exploring the influence of student–faculty interactions on college grades. *Journal of College Student Development, 42*(1), 3–14.

Bellas, M. L., & Toutkoushian, R. K. (1999). Faculty time allocations and research productivity: Gender, race and family effects. *Review of Higher Education, 22*, 367–390.

Bozick, R., & Lauff, E. (2007). *Education Longitudinal Study of 2002 (ELS:2002): A first look at the initial postsecondary experiences of the high school sophomore class of 2002.* Washington, DC: National Center for Education Statistics, U.S. Department of Education.

Braun, H. I., Wang, A., Jenkins, F., & Weinbaum, E. (2006). The Black–White achievement gap: Do state policies matter? [Electronic version]. *Educational Policy Analysis Archives, 14*(8).

Bronfenbrenner, U. (1979). *The ecology of human development.* Cambridge, MA: Harvard University Press.

Carter, D. F. (2001). *A dream deferred? Examining the degree aspirations of African American and White college students.* New York: RoutledgeFalmer.

Carter, D. F. (2003). Secondary analysis of data. In F. K. Stage & K. Manning (Eds.), *Research in the college context: Approaches and methods* (pp. 153–167). New York: Brunner-Routledge.

Clark, B. R. (1973). Development of the sociology of higher education. *Sociology of Education, 46*, 2–14.

Clark, R., & Trow, M. (1966). The organizational context. In T. M. Newcomb & E. K. Wilson (Eds.), *College peer groups: Problems and prospects for research.* Hawthorne, NY: Aldine de Gruyter.

Cole, D. G. (1999). *Faculty–student interactions of African American and White college students at predominantly White institutions.* Unpublished doctoral dissertation, Indiana University, Bloomington.

Constantine, J. M. (1995). The effects of attending historically Black colleges and universities on future wages of Black students. *Industrial and Labor Relations Review, 48*(3), 531–546.

Crosnoe, R. (2005). Double disadvantage or signs of resilience? The elementary school contexts of children from Mexican immigrant familes. *American Educational Research Journal, 42*(2), 269–303.

Curtin, T., Ingels, S., Wu, S., & Heuer, R. E. (2002). *NELS 1988/2000: Base year to fourth follow-up data user's manual.* Washington, DC: National Center for Education Statistics.

Darling-Hammond, L. (2007). The flat earth and education: How America's commitment to equity will determine our future. *Educational Researcher, 36*(6), 318–334.

Friedlander, J., Murrell, P. H., & MacDougall, P. R. (1993). The community college student experiences questionnaire. In T. W. Banta (Ed.), *Making a difference: Outcomes of a decade of assessment in higher education* (pp. 196–210). San Francisco: Jossey-Bass.

Friedlander, J., Pace, C. R., & Lehman, P. W. (1990). *Community college student experiences questionnaire.* Los Angeles: University of California, Center for the Study of Evaluation.

Galloway, F. J. (2004). *A methodological primer for conducting quantitative research in postsecondary education at Lumina Foundation for Education.* Retrieved November 27, 2004, from www.luminafoundation.org/research/researchersgalloway.pdf

Gonyea, R. M., Kish, K. A., Kuh, G. D., Muthiah, R. N., & Thomas, A. D. (2003). *College student experiences questionnaire: Norms for the fourth edition.* Bloomington, IN: Indiana University Center for Postsecondary Research, Policy, and Planning.

Graham, J. W., & Hoffer, S. M. (2000). Multiple imputation in multivariate research. In T. D. Little, K. U. Schnable, & J. Baumert (Eds.), *Modeling longitudinal and multilevel data: Practical issues, applied approaches, and specific examples* (pp. 201–218). Mahwah, NJ: Erlbaum.

Grayson, J. P. (1999). The impact of university experiences on self-assessed skills. *Journal of College Student Development, 40,* 687–699.

Green, P. J., Meyers, S. L., Giese, P., Law, J., Speizer, H. M., & Tardino, V. S. (1996). *Baccalaureate and beyond longitudinal study: 1993/94 First follow-up methodology report* (NCES Report No. 96–149). Washington, DC: U.S. Government Printing Office.

Hollins, T. N. (2003). *Participation in an extended orientation course and its relationship with student involvement, student satisfaction, academic performance, and student retention.* Unpublished doctoral dissertation, Florida State University, Tallahassee.

Hossler, D., & Gallagher, K. S. (1987). Studying student college choice: A three-phase model and the implications for policymakers. *College and University, 62,* 207–221.

Kezar, A., & Moriarty, D. (2000). Expanding our understanding of student leadership development: A study exploring gender and ethnic identity. *Journal of College Student Development, 41*(1), 55–69.

Kim, D. H., & Schneider, B. (2005). Social capital in action: Alignment of parental support in adolescents' transition to postsecondary education. *Social Forces, 84*(2), 1181–1206.

Kirshstein, R. J., Matheson, N., & Jing, Z. (1997). *Instructional faculty and staff in higher education institutions: Fall 1987 and Fall 1992* (NCES Report No. 97–447). Washington, DC: U.S. Department of Education, National Center for Education Statistics.

Kuh, G. D., & Hu, S. (2001). The effects of student–faculty interaction in the 1990s. *Review of Higher Education, 24,* 309–332.

Little, R. J. A., & Rubin, D. B. (1987). *Statistical analysis with missing data.* New York: J. Wiley & Sons.

Lundberg, C. A., & Schreiner, L. A. (2004). Quality and frequency of faculty–student interaction as predictors of learning: An analysis by student race/ethnicity. *Journal of College Student Development, 45*(5), 549–565.

Marsh, H. W., & Kleitman, S. (2005). Consequences of employment during high school: Character building, subversion of academic goals, or a threshold? *American Educational Research Journal, 42*(2), 331–369.

Mau, W., & Kopischke, A. (2001). Job search methods, job search outcomes, and job satisfaction of college graduates: A comparison of race and sex. *Journal of Employment Counseling, 38,* 141–149.

Munro, B. (1981). Dropouts from higher education: Path analysis of a national sample. *American Educational Research Journal, 18*(2), 133–141.

Muthen, B. O., & Satorra, A. (1995). Complex sample data in structural equation modeling. In P. Marsden (Ed.), *Sociological methodology* (pp. 267–316). Washington, DC: American Sociological Association.

National Center for Education Statistics (n.d.). *Education longitudinal study of 2002.* Retrieved January 2, 2008, from http://nces.ed.gov/surveys/els2002

Osborne, J. W. (1997). Race and academic disidentification. *Journal of Educational Psychology, 89*(4), 728–735.

Pace, C. R. (1990). *College student experiences questionnaire* (3rd ed.). Los Angeles: University of California, Center for the Study of Evaluation, Graduate School of Education.

Perna, L. W. (2001). The relationship between family responsibilities and employment status among college and university faculty. *Journal of Higher Education, 72*(5), 584–611.

Perna, L. W. (2004). Understanding the decision to enroll in graduate school: Sex and racial/ethnic group differences. *Journal of Higher Education, 75*(5), 487–527.

Raudenbush, S. W., & Bryk, A. S. (2002). *Hierarchical linear models: Applications and data analysis methods* (2nd ed.). Thousand Oaks, CA: Sage Publications.

Rosser, V. J. (2004). Faculty members' intentions to leave: A national study on their worklife and satisfaction. *Research in Higher Education, 45*(3), 285–309.

Sanford, N. (1966). *Self and society: Social change and individual development.* New York: Atherton.

Sanford, N., & Adelson, J. (1962). *The American college: A psychological and social interpretation of higher learning.* New York: Wiley.

Sax, L. (2004). Citizenship and spirituality among college students: What have we learned and where are we headed? *Journal of College and Character* 2. Retrieved December 29, 2004, from http://www.collegevalues.org/articles.cfm?a=1&id=1023

Singh, K., & Mehmet, O. (2000). Effect of part-time work on high school mathematics and science course taking. *Journal of Educational Research, 94,* 67–74.

Singh, K., Granville, M., & Dika, S. (2002). Mathematics and science achievement: Effects of motivation, interest, and academic engagement. *Journal of Educational Research, 95*(6), 323–332.

Stage, F. K., & Rushin, P. W. (1993). A combined model of student predisposition to college and persistence in college. *Journal of College Student Development, 34,* 276–281.

Steinberg, L., Fegley, S., & Dornbusch, S. M. (1993). Negative impacts of part-time work on adolescent adjustment: Evidence from a longitudinal study. *Developmental Psychology, 29,* 171–180.

Strayhorn, T. L. (2005). More than money matters: An integrated model of graduate student persistence. *Dissertation Abstracts International, 66*(2), 519A. (ATT No. 3164184)

Strayhorn, T. L. (2006a). Factors influencing the academic achievement of first-generation college students. *NASPA Journal, 43*(4), 82–111.

Strayhorn, T. L. (2006b). *Frameworks for assessing learning and development outcomes.* Washington, DC: Council for the Advancement of Standards in Higher Education (CAS).

Strayhorn, T. L. (2006c). Influence of gender, race, and socioeconomic status on college choice: A National Longitudinal Survey of Freshmen (NLSF) investigation. *NASAP Journal, 9*(1), 100–117.

Strayhorn, T. L. (in press-a). Influences on labor market outcomes of African American college graduates: A national study. *Journal of Higher Education.*

Strayhorn, T. L. (in press-b). The invisible man: Factors affecting the retention of low-income African American males. *NASAP Journal.*

Strayhorn, T. L., & Blakewood, A. M. (2007, June). *Studying the wonder year: A university-wide first year assessment.* Paper presented at the National Association of Student Personnel Administrators International Assessment and Retention Conference, St. Louis, MO.

Strayhorn, T. L., & Blakewood, A. M. (2008, February). *Using empirical data to improve first-year seminars.* Paper presented at the 27th Annual Conference on The First-Year Experience & Students in Transition, San Francisco, CA.

Strayhorn, T. L., & Saddler, T. N. (2007, April). *Factors influencing employment satisfaction for African American faculty members.* Paper presented at the annual meeting of the American Educational Research Association, Chicago, IL.

Strayhorn, T. L., & Terrell, M. C. (2007). Mentoring and satisfaction with college for Black students. *Negro Educational Review, 58*(1–2), 69–83.

Thomas, S. L., & Heck, R. H. (2001). Analysis of large-scale secondary data in higher education research: Potential perils associated with complex sampling designs. *Research in Higher Education, 42*(5), 517–540.

Thomas, S. L., Heck, R. H., & Bauer, K. W. (2005). Weighting and adjusting for design effects in secondary data analyses. In P. D. Umbach (Ed.), *Survey research: Emerging issues* (pp. 51–72). San Francisco: Jossey-Bass.

Williamson, D. R., & Creamer, D. G. (1988). Student attrition in 2- and 4-year colleges: Application of a theoretical model. *Journal of College Student Development, 29,* 210–217.

Wine, J. S., Cominole, M. B., Wheeless, S. C., Dudley, K. M., & Franklin, J. W. (2006). *1993/03 Baccalaureate and beyond longitudinal study (B&B:93/03) methodology report* (NCES Report No. 2006–166). Washington, DC: National Center for Education Statistics.

Wine, J. S., Heuer, R. E., Wheeless, S. C., Francis, T. L., Franklin, J. W., & Dudley, K. M. (2002). *Beginning postsecondary students longitudinal study: 1996–2001 (BPS:96/01) methodology report* (NCES Report No. 2002–171). Washington, DC: U.S. Department of Education, Office of Educational Research and Improvement.

Zhang, L. (2005). Advance to graduate education: The effect of college quality and undergraduate majors. *Review of Higher Education, 28*(3), 313–338.

8

Developing and Nurturing Resources for Effective Data-Driven Decision Making

Anthony G. Picciano
Hunter College

> A vibrant professional culture depends on a group of practitioners who have the freedom to continuously reinvent themselves via their research and knowledge production.
>
> (Kincheloe, 2003, p. 19)

Introduction

During the past 50 years, humankind has experienced what many have called the computer or the information age, an era marked by the use of digital technology to collect, sort, manipulate, and report data. James Duderstadt, President *Emeritus* and University Professor of Science and Engineering at the University of Michigan, observed that educated people and their ideas, facilitated and augmented by information technology, have become key to our social well-being and a driving force for great change in all social institutions (Duderstadt, 1997). Corporations, government agencies, and schools have devoted significant resources to the computer-information age through the development, expansion, and improvement of their computer-based information systems.

For the past decade, the computer-information age has been evolving into the age of knowledge. Drucker, world-renowned writer and consultant, has called knowledge, rather than capital or labor, the only meaningful economic resource of the post-capitalist society. He believes one of the most important roles of management is to ensure the application of knowledge, and the application of knowledge to knowledge (Drucker, 1993). Success and progress will depend upon the ability of institutional leaders to harness information about what is happening within an organization and convert it into knowledge while monitoring the forces that influence the organization from the outside. In this chapter, the development and nurturing of information resources is examined as the foundation for establishing effective data-driven decision making in a school or school district. Specifically, the hardware, software and, most importantly, the people components of data-driven decision making are examined as the foundational components of every successful information system development and implementation.

Information Infrastructure

Webster's Third New International Dictionary defines infrastructure as the underlying foundation or basic framework of an organization or system. The term can be applied to a host of entities, such as energy, water, or communications, that undergird an organization—state, city, corporation, medical center, or school district—and its operations. Conceptually an organization's infrastructure might include a central source such as an energy power station, water supply, communications center or school district information system that distributes resources through a series of nodes. The flow (see Figure 8.1) is frequently top-down from the source (e.g., school district office) to the nodes (e.g., individual schools and administrative departments). In the case of information systems and the distribution of data throughout an organization, the emergence of digital communications and the Internet/World Wide Web has changed the conceptual framework of the infrastructure. While central sources for communications and data processing activities still exist, a more appropriate diagram (see Figure 8.2) of an organization's information infrastructure shows a hub-based network in which resources are shared across all nodes rather than moving back and forth or from the top-down between the central source and the nodes within the organization. Fundamental to this model is the ability of nodes to share resources with other nodes without necessarily going back to the source. This model is particularly important when developing the information infrastructure for data-driven decision making in a school district. All those involved in decision making are able to share activities, strategies, and data with one another. While technical assistance, support, and databases may be provided centrally at the district level, ultimately the success of the data-driven decision-making process will rest on the ability of individuals in the schools to effect changes in classrooms and offices. It

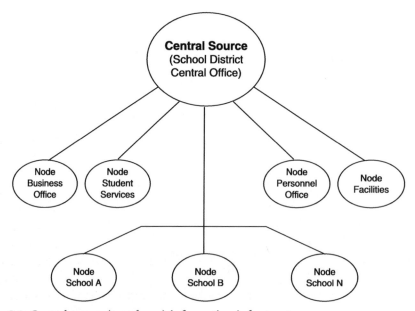

Figure 8.1 Central source (top-down) information infrastructure.

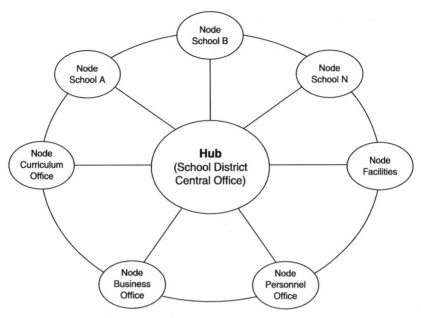

Figure 8.2 Hub-based information infrastructure.

is highly desirable, if not critical, for administrators and teachers in the schools
to share their knowledge, expertise, and experiences with others across the district.
This framework for sharing information resources across the school district is the
foundation that will empower shareholders and enable them to realize the potential
of data-driven decision-making activities in their schools. When conceptualizing
infrastructure, the tendency is to think about the physical elements of the system.
This is not the case with data-driven decision making where it is most beneficial
to think of the infrastructure as composed of hardware, software and especially
people—their expertise, experience, and knowledge.

Hardware for Effective Data Management and Access—Networks

During the past several decades, educators have seen data communications systems
and networks develop in size, sophistication, and the ability to communicate over
distances. In the late 1970s and 1980s, schools began to install their first local area
networks, or LANs. By the mid-1990s, the vast majority of the 15,000-plus school
districts in the country had established one or more LANs (Quality Education
Data, 1995). The use of LANs in computer laboratories, libraries, and administrative offices has now become commonplace. In larger school districts, wide area
networks (WANs) are also in evidence connecting computers and LANs that are
dispersed throughout the district sometimes miles apart. In a WAN configuration, a
large computer network serves to integrate the activities of smaller computer networks. Using a district-wide WAN, a student in one school, for example, can
determine whether a library in another school has a particular book, an assistant
principal can examine the transcript of a student who has just transferred from

another school, or a district business manager can monitor the daily expenditures of several schools.

The data communications technology (e.g., cables, telephone lines, satellite transmission) that enables a computer in one school to communicate with a computer in another school is essentially the same whether the schools are many miles apart or in close proximity. Once a WAN has been established, the distance between sites becomes immaterial. In the late 1980s, this concept flourished as computers in school districts began to communicate with computers on networks outside the school district. A student looking for a particular book might use a computer in a school's library to locate the book at a local public library or a local college library. A superintendent using a computer in a school district office might transfer data on student demographics to a computer located in a state education office.

In the 1990s, data communications technologies continued to advance to the point where a computer on one network could easily communicate with a computer on another network thousands of miles away. Now, the grants officer in a local school district office in Juneau, Alaska, can examine a database of funded programs on a computer network maintained by the United States Department of Education in Washington, DC. A state education department administrator in Albany, New York, can e-mail a new curriculum proposal to all 800 school district superintendents on a state-wide education network. A social studies teacher in Tulsa, Oklahoma, developing a module in cultural studies, can access a database of curricular materials maintained by the National Geographic Society.

With the expansion of data communications' capabilities over the past two decades, networks have expanded to cover greater distances and to link with many more networks. Increasingly, this data traffic, occurring on thousands of networks throughout the country and the world, is passing over a common universal network we call the Internet. As of 2003, 97% of all schools in the United States were connected to the Internet (Park & Staresina, 2004). To support data-driven decision making, the school district's fundamental hardware configuration comprises computer workstations distributed on a high-speed digital network which is fully compatible with the Internet. Each node in the school district's network may be a school or office with its own mini-network capable of intercommunication with any other node in the district as well as with networks outside of the district.

Once a network is in place, the next question is "where should the computer workstations be located?" The answer to this question is everywhere. The Internet was established as a ubiquitous resource; users are able to connect to it from anyplace. Administrators have computer workstations in their offices, teachers in their classrooms, parents and students in their homes. As early as 1989, the NEA recommended that a computer be installed on the desk of every teacher (National Education Association, 1989). The emergence of portable electronic devices, namely laptop computers and personal data assistants (PDAs), allows connectivity to the network from anyplace there is a telephone connection or a clear satellite signal. While all school districts have not yet provided computers to all of their teachers and staff, this is the direction in which Internet-based technology is heading. The long-range plan for developing data-driven decision making calls for providing access to information resources to just about everybody in a school district. Principals, teachers, and administrative staff should have ready access to information about students, budgets, and personnel. Furthermore, these resources need to be available so as to allow access from anyplace (office, classroom, home) that a desktop, laptop, or other portable electronic device can connect to the Internet.

The implementation of an extensive data communications system to support the development of information resources needed for data-driven decision making may appear daunting; however, the vast majority of school districts have already begun to make this investment. It is critical that the leaders in these districts nurture and maintain these systems to keep up with current communications technologies. If we consider other enterprises where access to information is important, we can easily understand the need for this ongoing investment in our schools. When we go to a bank, we expect to see tellers accessing information about our accounts via computer workstations. We make deposits and expect ready access to our funds at ATM machines located anywhere, including shopping malls and supermarkets. In today's world, what would we think if the teller at our local bank accepted our funds and wrote the transaction in a notebook? Our children are more important than our bank accounts; the most efficient methods must also be employed for making decisions about their "educational transactions."

A final comment about the power of networks. Networks are not just simply the latest technological advancement designed to move data more efficiently throughout an organization. They can have profound effects on how people work with one another. Watts (2003) and Birabasi (2002) have studied the effects of networks on various people-intensive processes. What they have found is that networks enable individual behavior to aggregate into collective behavior. Something special happens when individual entities (nodes, components, people) are able to interact to form larger wholes (networks, systems, communities). Furthermore, the "interaction effect" or collective behavior may result in a far more productive environment than individuals acting by themselves: one individual working with another individual does not simply comprise two individuals but a third, more powerful collaborating entity which can extend the benefits beyond two. Modern data communications networks now make it possible for many individuals to share and work with one another, and their collective behavior can be most effective in supporting complex processes including data-driven decision making.

Software for Data Management and Analysis

The Database Management System

Database management is the underlying software system for developing and support-ing a school district's information resources. The terminology used for describing databases has been inconsistent over the years, and certain terms mean different things to different people. Identifying and defining some of these terms may be helpful. The general definition of a database is a collection of files in which data can be created, updated, and accessed. However, a more modern definition of a database requires that the data files be interrelated or integrated so that data can be accessed easily across all files and redundancy of the data be kept to a minimum. The basic concept of databases involves managing the data in an increasingly more complex hierarchy. The members of this hierarchy, from least to most complex, are the *character*, the *data element*, the *data record*, the *data file*, and the *database*. When integrated, the members of this hierarchy form a school district's information system. The software that controls, integrates, and provides reports from this information system is the database management software system.

Figure 8.3 illustrates the major administrative database applications that comprise a school district's information system. Each application area has a unique role in contributing to the overall information resources of a school. The student applications tend to be the most complex because of the amount of data that needs to be collected. In addition, student data in these applications are volatile and subject to frequent change. Applications such as attendance reporting and scheduling require extensive data collection efforts and careful coordination. Student applications are important because certain areas such as achievement and performance come under a good deal of scrutiny, from both inside and outside the school. Administrators need ready access to information such as retention, attrition, graduation rates, and test scores. Student enrollment data are also usually critical for various state and local funding formulae, and accurate data on students in attendance become a necessity for various reporting purposes.

Curriculum and course applications are vital for a school's internal academic operations. Curriculum meetings and discussions are, in many schools, the center-pieces of academic planning. Administrators and teachers collect extensive amounts of data to develop new courses and modify existing ones. Data on student perform-ance tied to curriculum and course enrollment become critical for such planning.

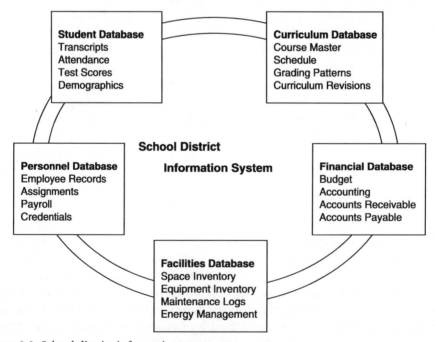

Figure 8.3 School district information system.

A good curriculum and course database is also necessary for developing a student scheduling application, one of the most time-consuming activities when done manually or without sufficient technological support.

Personnel and financial applications are frequently the first database systems to be implemented. In public schools, they may tie into other local governmental agencies for applications such as payroll, accounting, and purchasing controlled at the municipal or county levels. For any administrator, the management of a budget is a critical responsibility. Access to up-to-date and accurate information on budgets and finances is a necessity and affects all of a school's operations. Personnel files are important complements to the financial data files for purposes of managing a budget, because the major costs in most school operations are personnel items such as salaries and fringe benefits.

Facilities are generally the last of the database applications to be implemented. Facilities data are not as critical or volatile and do not need to be as tightly integrated. However, applications such as space utilization, equipment inventory, and supplies inventory should not be ignored because they contribute to overall effectiveness and efficiency.

The database management system software is common to all of the applications in Figure 8.3 and serves as an integration mechanism. It also allows a school district to warehouse or maintain data longitudinally (over time). This becomes most critical in analyzing student progress from semester to semester and year to year. By developing such a system, schools greatly enhance administrative cohesiveness because offices become more dependent on one another by virtue of sharing common data files. A single system also significantly improves the consistency of information and eliminates issues involving the accuracy of one office's data versus another's.

Data Reporting and Analysis

One of the most important features of database software is the ability to generate reports. A query language is generally provided that enables users to access data in many different ways. Query languages were the precursors to search engines that have been popularized on the Internet and World Wide Web. However, the power of query languages is that they can be customized to access data stored in a specific database system. For this reason, query languages are very efficient in providing specific information, creating reports and establishing temporary data files for subsequent analysis. Designed for non-technical staff, they can give users excellent access to data while eliminating dependence upon others to perform the task. Query languages also allow teachers and administrators to go beyond static standardized reports that have a set format and cannot be manipulated and altered. They can be used to create subsets of the database that can be analyzed and reanalyzed delving deeply into a particular issue regarding a particular group of records. For instance, a committee of mathematics teachers could create a subset of the test scores of all the students in fourth grade in order to analyze and reanalyze performance compared to student demographics and characteristics. If they need additional information, they simply do another query on the data subset. This method of inquiry is far more sophisticated and effective than examining a static (either on paper or on a display screen) report. This analysis and reanalysis is referred to as data mining, a common term used in data-driven decision-making activities that refers to searching or "digging into" a data file for information in order to understand better a particular phenomenon.

One of the most commonly used tools for analyzing data is the electronic spreadsheet, including programs such Microsoft Excel and Quattro Pro. Used for applications that require frequent analysis and manipulation of numbers such as budget, accounting, enrollment projections, and test scores, electronic spreadsheet software is essentially an electronic grid or matrix of rows and columns. It replaces the accounting tablet as a tool for organizing numbers into appropriate boxes or cells, and it performs automatically the arithmetic operations that formerly were performed manually or with calculators. It also provides graphics capabilities for producing bar graphs, pie charts, and line graphs which are very effective in doing longitudinal and trend analyses. When integrated with query languages, spreadsheets become indispensable for financial analyses when preparing budgets, projecting expenditures, and determining personnel costs.

A complementary and a more powerful tool for data-driven decision making is the statistical software package such as the Statistical Package for the Social Sciences (SPSS) or the Statistical Analysis System (SAS). These packages can perform most of the data analysis routines that Excel and other spreadsheet programs do and in addition can much more easily perform statistical routines such as contingency tables (cross-tabulations), frequency distributions, and correlations. While spreadsheet software is a good starting point for doing basic data analysis, statistical packages such as SPSS can take the analysis much further. The latest version of SPSS has been converted to a spreadsheet-like format so that users familiar with software such as Excel can more easily learn SPSS.

A final comment on data analysis software tools is that they are critical in analyzing, manipulating, and presenting data and are most effective when integrated with database management systems. The benefits of these tools are best realized if they have good data sources such as a school district database from which the aggregate data are drawn and are shared among all stakeholders in data-driven decision-making activities. As mentioned previously, critical to the effectiveness of these tools is the concept of mining (analyzing and reanalyzing) a dataset rather than reading numbers from a static paper report.

People, Decision Making and the Social Nature of Information

Building Communities

A good deal of literature exists on the importance of collaboration in decision making. Authors such as Senge (1990; learning organizations) and Wenger (1999; communities of practice) see collaboration as crucial for organizations to grow and thrive. In a sense, organizations are transformed into organic entities that learn and advance;

advance and learn. Sergiovanni and Starratt (1998) redefined educational administration as reliant on "organic management" that makes the promotion of the community the "centerpiece" of supervision. Each of these authors has promoted concepts that elevate school management above the bureaucratic, top-down, do-it-this-way style of administration to another level of collaborative, we-are-in-this-together activity. In more recent years, a link has been made between collaboration and information sharing especially with regard to complex decision processes and the use of data as the fulcrum upon which communities develop. Seeley Brown and Duguid (2002), in their work entitled *The Social Life of Information,* call for a better understanding of the contribution that communities and people make to complex decision processes and a realization that the data, information systems, and technology only take the process so far. This concept is essentially an extension of the Nobel prize-winning work of Simon (1945, 1957, 1960, 1979, 1982), on the "limits of rationality" or "bounded rationality" which posited that rational decision-making processes are "limited" and people with their expertise, intuition, and experience are critical to effective decision making.

Increasingly, dialogue and social interaction in decision making are being seen as critical to effective management and administration. Elmore and others have expressed concern that teachers in particular have not been encouraged to engage in dialogue, nor are they often given the time or support to allow such activity (Elmore, 2004; Wilhelm, 2007). Wilhelm (2007, p. 19) begs the question: "Why are meaningful inquiry and exploratory dialogue so rare in American schools, despite the fact that leading researchers agree that it is essential to student learning?" While hardware and software are the vehicles for delivering accurate and timely information, there is still great concern that integrating these with the people element is lacking in many schools. Most of these people are school-based and include administrators who know their schools and constituents; teachers who know their students and curricula; and staff who know their operations and services. All of them need to be trained and brought together to use the information resources that will help them make informed decisions.

People Development

A good training program first starts with the design of the technology resources (hardware, software, data) to be used by those involved with data-driven decision-making activities. While it is true that the development of extensive information resources using current technology is complex, the complexity of the design need not be passed on to the end-users. On the contrary, modern technology design emphasizes the importance of providing user-friendly interfaces to information resources. Information systems that require many levels of inquiry in order to download basic information, World Wide Web interfaces that are overly cluttered, or database software that lacks a friendly query language are systems that will be difficult for end-users.

Secondly, training workshops and classes must be readily available either in person or online. The nature of these sessions will depend upon the level of technological expertise that exists within the staff. If technology and sophisticated information systems are new to a school district, then the staff training and development will be extensive. However, technology is constantly evolving so that even sophisticated technology users will need to refresh and update their knowledge and skills on a regular basis. Learning to use an information system and its resources for data-driven decision making will require specialized staff development activities not limited to the use of technology. Additional training in other areas such as curricula, standards, testing, and the fundamentals of quantitative analysis might also be necessary.

Thirdly, every good staff development training program is ongoing; one-time workshops are only modestly successful. If data-driven decision making is to be integrated into the administrative fabric of a school or district, then ongoing training will be needed to keep skills honed and to allow entry to the process by new teachers and staff. Furthermore, given that so much educational activity is influenced and guided by multiple levels of government, decision making must regularly adjust to the newest regulation, standard, or directive. Participants in decision-making activities will need to be kept up-to-date if they are to be effective.

Lastly, data-driven decision making requires enhanced leadership skills on the part of district supervisors, principals, and other administrative staff. School leaders must be capable of setting a climate that allows for a "we" process that includes teachers and staff rather than a "me" process. Teachers and staff will need to feel comfortable and that they are not the objects of data-driven exercises wherein their skills and abilities are constantly questioned. Given the current emphasis on accountability and standards, teachers have become a focus of attention in the success or failure of our children. Teachers and other staff are indeed critical to the educational enterprise; they should be treated, assigned, and developed with skill and competence. Price (2004) in an article entitled, "New age principals," that appeared in *Education Week*, expressed concern that:

> Both current principals, and those entering the principalship for the first time, find that they are ill-prepared to manage an infrastructure that supports instruction and has as its constant focus the technical core of teaching and learning.
>
> (p. 36)

He recommended that all principals, new and old, develop four key skills to create and manage the type of infrastructure needed to support instructional improvement:

1. ability to manage information
2. ability to analyze and use data to determine areas in need of improvement
3. ability to align and monitor curriculum to meet needs
4. ability to build a professional community of learners (stakeholders) committed to instructional improvement.

While all four of these skills are important, the last is the most critical and undergirds all the others.

The Data Analyst

As school districts begin to invest in data-driven decision processes, the need for someone with technical expertise in data analysis becomes more apparent. The data analyst possesses a number of skills, especially familiarity with information systems and fundamental statistical analysis, and serves as an important resource person for others (administrators, teachers, parents) in using data effectively. The data analyst also performs a coordinating function by providing data in a timely manner so that they coincide with a district's or school's planning activities. Minimally, as data-driven decision-making activities evolve, districts will have one person performing this function on a full-time basis. Large districts will have more than one person, depending upon size. In addition, individual schools will have someone performing this function perhaps on a part-time basis, while large schools, especially middle and high schools, will likely have a full-time person.

The need for a data analyst has grown considerably as data are used more frequently in shaping instructional activities. In other areas where data are critical for decision making such as budget and finance, it is more likely that the staff assigned to these areas will have had some formal training in information systems management and business statistics or quantitative analysis. In addition, generally a small cadre of business personnel work with data files on a daily basis and are comfortable "mining" these files to support decision-making activities. Instructional decision making, however, requires sharing data on students, testing, and other performance indicators with teachers and parents who are going to be less familiar with data analysis. The data analyst can be very helpful in designing standard reports that are produced on a cyclical basis and that serve as common resources in the discussion and planning of instructional activities. In addition, with some training and assistance, teachers will use the standard report to begin the process of mining the data as group and individual judgments about instruction evolve. The support of a data analyst with expertise in information processing and quantitative methods will facilitate their analysis and judgments.

Another way in which a data analyst can be helpful is in monitoring the external environment. While much of data-driven decision making is internal to a district or school, scanning the external environment for resources or data-related mandates and compliance issues can be helpful if not critical. Front-line administrators have difficulty finding the time to do this effectively while a data analyst may be able to do this quite easily.

Finally, data-driven decision making for instruction also assumes that the community, especially parents, will be invited to become involved in the process or at least to share in its results. To involve the community, reports will have to be easily understood by the broader population. Having a knowledgeable data analyst design, explain, and answer questions about these reports will contribute to the success of the activity and garner support from the community.

Evaluation and Nurturing the Process

The relationship between modern information systems and decision making has been evolving for many years. While the term "data-driven decision" has gained popularity in K-12 education during the past 10 or 15 years and especially since No Child Left Behind in 2001, it has been used and studied conceptually in other organizations for decades. Mason (1969) and later Craven (1975) studied "information decision systems" that established the importance of information to the decision process in private industry and public agencies. One important aspect of their approach (see Figure 8.4) is the evaluation of the decision-making process. Evaluation requires stakeholders (administrators, teachers, staff) to review how well the process worked and to reflect on the effectiveness of the decisions and courses of action taken. Unfortunately, the evaluation step is not always taken or is sometimes done very informally with little feedback into future decision-making activities. What Mason, Craven and others recommended is that evaluation be formalized as part of the decision process and that the outcomes of the evaluation be used as input or "lessons learned" into future decision processing. In this approach, evaluation is never punitive but is used positively and formatively to help improve and nurture the process for the next decision-making cycle. Issues typically examined in an evaluation involve stakeholder access to accurate and timely data, knowledge of stakeholders and their readiness to engage in decision making, and a clear delineation of the outcomes of the decision. However the evaluation is configured, stakeholders will do well to reflect on and determine what worked well in their decision making and to learn from those elements that did not work as well. It is in this manner that schools become less bureaucratic institutions and more organic communities that grow to the best they can for their students.

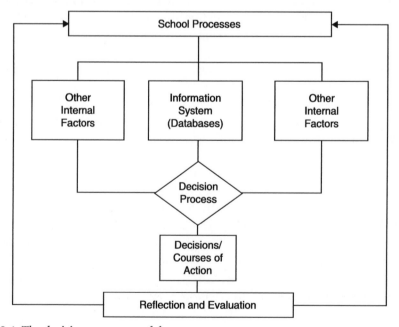

Figure 8.4 The decision process model.

This last point ties back to the work of Senge, Wenger, and Sergiovanni and Starratt mentioned earlier in this chapter. Education leaders and policy makers interested in promulgating effective decision-making processes in their schools need to develop communities in which all stakeholders see themselves as moving forward toward a common goal. Data-driven decision-making processes can help in this movement forward. In addition to operational aspects such as current hardware technology, user-friendly software that provides accurate and timely data, and informed and knowledgeable people, data-driven decision making needs enlightened leadership to integrate these into a dynamic process that utilizes as well as fosters a sense of community. The enlightened leader sets in motion group decision processes that trumpet "we are in this together" rather than "you better be careful if this does not work out." Embracing evaluation as a positive and healthy activity that nurtures and helps grow the school community works best. In sum, data-driven decision making is a technology-based process that requires the human touch in order to reach its potential as an effective tool in moving the education of our children forward.

References

Birabasi, A. L. (2002). *Linked: The new science of networks.* Cambridge, MA: Perseus Publishing.

Craven, E. C. (1975). Information decision systems in higher education: A conceptual approach. *Journal of Higher Education, 46*(2), 125–139.

Drucker, P. F. (1993). *Post-capitalist society.* New York: HarperCollins.

Duderstadt, J. J. (1997). The future of the university in an age of knowledge. *Journal of Asynchronous Learning Networks, 1*(1), 78–88. Retrieved September 23, 2007, from http://www.aln.org/publications/jaln/v1n2/v1n2_duderstadt.asp

Elmore, R. (2004). *School reform: From the inside out.* Cambridge, MA: Harvard Education Press.

Kincheloe, J. (2003). *Teachers as researchers: Qualitative inquiry as a path to empowerment* (2nd ed.). London: Routledge-Falmer.

Mason, R. O. (1969). *Basic concepts for designing management information systems* (AIR Research Paper No. 8).

National Education Association (1989, July). *Report of the NEA special committee on educational technology.* Paper presented at the 127th annual meeting of the National Education Association, Washington, DC.

Park, J., & Staresina, L. (2004, May 6). Tracking U.S. trends. *Education Week,* 64–67.

Price, W.J. (2004, January 7). New age principals. *Education Week, 23*(16), 36–37.

Quality Education Data (1995). *Education market guide.* Denver, CO: Author.

Seeley Brown, J., & Duguid, P. (2002). *The social life of information.* Boston: Harvard Business School Press.

Senge, P. M. (1990). *The fifth discipline: The art and practice of the learning organization.* New York: Doubleday-Currency.

Sergiovanni, T. J., & Starratt, R. J. (1998). *Supervision: A redefinition* (6th ed.). Boston: McGraw-Hill.

Simon, H. A. (1945). *Administrative behavior.* New York: Macmillan.

Simon, H. A. (1957). *Administrative behavior* (2nd ed.). New York: Macmillan.

Simon, H. A. (1960). *The new science of management decision.* New York: Harper & Row.

Simon, H. A. (1979). Rational decision making in business organizations. *American Economic Review, 69,* 493–513.

Simon, H. A. (1982). *Models of bounded rationality.* Cambridge, MA: MIT Press.

Watts, D. (2003). *Six degrees: The science of a connected age.* New York: W.W. Norton and Company.

Webster's third new international dictionary of the English language (1986). Springfield: MA: Merriam-Webster Publishers.

Wenger, E. (1999). *Communities of practice: Learning, meaning, and identity.* Cambridge, UK: Cambridge University Press.

Wilhelm, J. (2007). *Engaging readers and writers with inquiry.* New York: Scholastic.

9

Preparing Educators to Use Curriculum-Based Measurement

Robin S. Codding

University of Massachusetts Boston

and

James E. Connell, Jr.

Temple University

Introduction

Academic assessment is multi-faceted and can be used to make various kinds of decisions including: (a) referral, (b) screening, (c) classification, (d) instructional planning, (e) monitoring student progress, and (f) program evaluation (Salvia & Ysseldyke, 2001). Not all forms of assessment can be used to address each of these decisions; therefore, it is critical the measurement tool used matches the pending instructional decision. Curriculum-based Measurement (CBM) was initially created to fill a gap within academic assessment; specifically to generate a tool that was simple, easy to use, and was an accurate indicator of skill proficiency that could be used to monitor student progress (Deno, 1985; Wayman, Wallace, Wiley, Ticha, & Espin, 2007). The most unique feature of CBM compared to other types of assessment is the sensitivity to small changes in student learning, making these tools particularly effective for that purpose. Perhaps one of the most important research findings is that instructional quality and student achievement increase when teachers use CBM to monitor students' performance (Fuchs, Fuchs, Hamlett, & Ferguson, 1992). CBM is also fluency based; that is, these measures are intended to evaluate performance within a brief, pre-determined amount of time (Fuchs & Fuchs, 2004). Evidence has shown that CBM is also useful for making decisions related to screening and instructional planning.

Direct Academic Assessment

CBM is a form of direct academic assessment of basic skills. Direct assessment refers to the direct evaluation of student performance on materials that students are expected to learn; thus, the content of the assessment is derived from curricular objectives (Shapiro, 2004). There are many models subsumed under the umbrella of direct assessment including criterion-referenced curriculum-based assessment

(CBA-CR; Blankenship, 1985), curriculum-based assessment for instructional design (CBA-ID; Gickling & Havertape, 1981), curriculum-based evaluation (CBE; Howell & Nolet, 1999), and CBM (e.g., Deno, 1985; Shinn, 1989). All of these models share the common notion that assessment should test what is taught (Shapiro, 2004). Other essential features of direct academic assessment are that measurements (a) be repeated over time, (b) include valid indicators of critical outcomes of instruction, and (c) inform instructional decisions (Fuchs & Deno, 1994). Research has indicated that these measurements need not be derived from the specific instructional curriculum used in a particular district (Bradley-Klug, Shapiro, Lutz, & DuPaul, 1998; Fuchs & Deno, 1994; Wayman et al., 2007). Consequently, several applications of curriculum-based assessment (CBA) and CBM are available such as Dynamic Indicators of Basic Early Literacy Skills (DIBELS), AIMSwebfi (www.aimsweb.com), and STEEP (www.isteep.com). Readers are encouraged to consult an Office of Special Education Programs sponsored website, entitled National Center on Student Progress Monitoring, which describes and evaluates commercially available CBM/A tools (www.studentprogress.org/chart/chart.asp).

Each form of direct assessment can be categorized as either general outcome or subskill-mastery models (Fuchs & Deno, 1991; Shapiro, 2004). The goal of the general outcome model (GOM) is to assess long-term growth across expected year-end objectives. This is done using standardized measures, for which difficulty level is controlled, that represent "brief, timed samples of performance" (Shapiro, 2004, p. 18). A limitation of this model is that it is not designed to inform specific instructional changes on short-term curricular objectives. However, because GOMs provide indicators of progress toward year-end performance goals, teachers can modify instruction accordingly (Fuchs & Fuchs, 2004). A form of direct assessment that falls into this category is CBM (Shinn, 1989). The content of CBM reflects indicators of student learning often described as "vital signs" that have been demonstrated as valid and reliable through over 20 years of research. That is, each CBM score serves as a gauge of overall competence in the associated academic area (Fuchs & Fuchs, 2004; Shinn, 1989).

Subskill-mastery models address the aforementioned limitations by determining whether students are meeting short-term objectives. Measurements differ as they are based on skill hierarchies and thus a new form of measurement (i.e., probe) is administered in correspondence with each new objective instructed. Furthermore, mastery criteria are identified for each subskill area (Shapiro, 2004). Therefore, these measurements provide more specific details that permit educators to fine-tune delivery of instruction as necessary. CBA-CR (Blankenship, 1985), CBA-ID (Gickling & Havertape, 1981), and CBE (Howell & Nolet, 1999) can be subsumed under the subskill mastery model.

The most effective way to make data-based decisions using direct forms of academic assessment is to combine the use of general outcome and subskill mastery models (e.g., Shapiro, 2004). In this way both long-term and short-term curricular objectives can be monitored. For most students, examining CBM (general outcome) performance is sufficient. However, for students not responding to instruction, conducting a skills analysis consistent with CBA procedures may also be required. Therefore, for the purpose of this chapter we will describe the use of CBM (Deno, 1985) and subskill mastery models of CBA, such as CBA-ID (Gickling & Havertape, 1981) and CBE (Howell & Nolet, 1999), at the elementary level (Grades 1 to 5). We will begin our discussion by describing the following: (a) CBM/A types, (b) administration and scoring procedures, and (c) technical adequacy across reading, mathematics, and writing. Subsequently, instructional decision making will be described for these academic areas and focus on using these tools for screening, progress monitoring, and instructional planning.

Using CBM/A-Reading to Make Instructional Decisions

Types of CBM/A Reading Assessment

There are three general areas of direct assessment in reading: (a) CBM-R, (b) CBM-Maze, and (c) early literacy. These measures address reading fluency, basic comprehension, and beginning literacy skills (e.g., letter-naming fluency, phoneme segmentation), respectively. Because the focus of this chapter is on primary grades (i.e., Grades 1 through 5) the ensuing section will not include discussion of early literacy CBM. Administration of CBM-R requires that one (screening) or three (progress monitoring) passages be provided to students using the appropriate grade-level material (Ardoin et al., 2004; Shinn, 1989). Students read the passage(s) aloud for one minute, while the examiner follows along marking errors. For the purpose of error analysis, examiners might also record the types of mistakes made. Scores are computed by subtracting the number of errors from the total number of words read to yield the number of words read correctly per minute (WRCM; Shinn, 1989). When three passages are administered the median WRCM should be used (see Table 9.1 for administration and scoring procedures).

Test-retest, alternative form, and interobserver agreement indicate strong reliability evidence for CBM-Reading (CBM-R), also described as Oral Reading Fluency (ORF; Marston, 1989). Validity coefficients with published measures of reading range from moderate to strong. A recent review of research (Wayman et al., 2007) confirmed earlier findings by demonstrating that a strong relationship exists between CBM-R and reading proficiency across primary grades. CBM-R was also found to be a better indicator of reading comprehension than other common measures. Additionally, several studies found that CBM-R was strongly correlated with state reading tests. This review also indicated that CBM-R may not be the best choice for beginning or secondary readers. CBM-Maze and early literacy measures may be more useful for middle school and kindergarten students, respectively. Less research has evaluated psychometric properties of subskill mastery models of reading CBA; however, preliminary research on CBA-ID yielded good reliability evidence (Burns, Tucker, Frame, Foley, & Hauser, 2000).

CBM-Maze is a multiple-choice closed passage comprehension measure. Unlike CBM-R, administration of CBM-Maze can be conducted in a group and requires that one, three-minute passage be provided to students. Every seventh word in the passage is replaced with a choice of three words representing the correct choice, a near distracter (i.e., a word of the same type) and a far distracter (i.e., randomly selected).

Table 9.1 General administration and scoring procedures for CBM/A measures.

CBM/A measure	No. administered	Minutes	Scores
CBM-R	3 (1)*	1 Minute	WRCM (Total Words–Errors)
			WRIM (Words Incorrect)
CBM-Maze	1	3 Minutes	Correct Choices
CBA-M (Single Skill)	1	2–5 Minutes	CD (Digits Counted as Correct)
			DCPM (Total Digits–Errors/2)
			DIPM (Digits Incorrect/2)
CBM-M (Multiple Skill)	3	2–5 Minutes	CD (Digits Counted as Correct)
			DCPM (Total Digits–Errors/2)
			DIPM (Digits Incorrect/2)
CBM-WW	1	3 Minutes	WW (Total Words Written)
CBM-CWS	1	3 Minutes	CWS (Correct Writing Sequences)
CBM-WSC	1	3 Minutes	WSC (Words Spelled Correct)

* (1) passage may be used for universal screening (Ardoin et al., 2004). CBA-M = Curriculum-Based Assessment Mathematics; CBM-M = Curriculum-Based Measurement Mathematics; WRCM = words read correctly per minute; WRIM = words read incorrectly per minute; DCPM = digits correct per minute; DIPM = digits incorrect per minute. These are basic guidelines (Gansle et al., 2006; Shinn, 1989; Shinn & Shinn, 2002), although depending on application used these procedures may vary slightly.

Students are instructed to circle the correct answer and scores are computed by counting the number of correct word choices (Shinn & Shinn, 2002). Findings for CBM-Maze indicate that this measure has adequate reliability and validity across Grades 2 through 8 and growth rates were more consistent than CBM-R (Wayman et al., 2007).

Screening Using CBM: Reading Benchmark Assessments

Within the framework of multi-tiered models of instruction, CBM-R and CBM-Maze can be used as indicators of all students' reading proficiency. In this way, CBM is used to screen for students at risk; that is, students who may need academic interventions in addition to instruction in the grade-level curriculum. Universal screening occurs three times yearly (fall, winter, and spring), and is often referred to as benchmark assessments. Theoretically, it is anticipated that approximately 20% of students will need support in addition to the core instruction, presuming that instruction is conducted using scientifically validated curricula (Batchse et al., 2006).

Schoolwide data at each grade level can be examined according to percentiles and averages obtained from national normative samples, such as provided by AIMSwebfi, or can be examined at the local level (Shinn, 1989). Generally, students falling below the 25th percentile are considered to be at risk (Fuchs, 2003) and those students performing below the 16th percentile have been described as likely to have a valid special education referral (VanDerHeyden, Witt, & Naquin, 2003). Two basic decisions are made using CBM-R or CBM-Maze data at this level. First, students above the 25th percentile are confirmed to be responsive to core instruction (Fuchs, 2003). Second, students below the 25th percentile are considered to be potentially at risk. Once the at-risk students are identified, then another set of decisions needs to be made; will at-risk students: (a) be monitored weekly or bi-weekly for four to eight weeks (Hintze, 2007; Shapiro, 2004), or (b) receive additional instructional support? It is possible that some at-risk students may be monitored while others require instructional interventions. For example, a school building-level team may decide to provide additional reading interventions to students below the 16th percentile (option b; VanDerHeyden et al., 2003) while monitoring all at-risk students below the 25th percentile (option a). Educators might also combine the CBM results with other data collected such as previous performance on state assessments or other standardized measures (e.g., Iowa Tests of Basic Skills; Hoover, Hieronymus, Frisbie, & Dunbar, 1993) to determine which students should receive additional instructional support.

Although initial decisions are made after the fall CBM-R or CBM-Maze data are collected, screening in the winter and spring allows educators to determine whether students previously identified as responding to core instruction continue to perform well. That is, some students who performed well during the fall screening may read in the at-risk range according to the winter benchmarks. Therefore, the same sets of decisions made after examining the fall data should also be made after CBM data are collected in the winter and spring.

Progress Monitoring and Instructional Planning Using CBM/A-Reading

Monitoring At-Risk Students Not Receiving Additional Academic Support For students that are determined to be at risk following the initial benchmark assessment, reading progress in response to the core curriculum should be monitored weekly or bi-weekly using the same CBM procedures described earlier but using alternate reading passages (Hintze, 2007). That is, a new passage is administered each week. Student performance should be graphed, which could be done by using Microsoft Excelfi or other data management systems (e.g., isteep, AIMSwebfi, Monitoring Basic Skills Progress; Fuchs, Hamlett, & Fuchs, 1997), and evaluated for improvement. Improvement is determined by looking at the level of performance (e.g., did performance reach or exceed the criterion?) as well as the slope of progress (i.e., is performance increasing?). Measurement of performance level *along with growth*, as described here, uses a dual discrepancy approach to decision making (Fuchs, 2003).

The level of performance can be determined by identifying whether the student reached the 25th percentile at the end of eight weeks using local or national norms or examining whether the student has reached a criterion-referenced benchmark, such as reading 40 words correctly per minute (WRCM) in first-grade material (Fuchs, 2003; Good, Simmons, & Kame'enui, 2001). In order to evaluate growth, a realistic but ambitious goal needs to be established and therefore it is necessary to know how much growth should be expected (Fuchs, Fuchs, Hamlett, Walz, & Germann, 1993). If these data have not been collected by the local school district, then data from Fuchs et al. (1993) can be used (Table 9.2 provides criteria and growth data for CBM across academic areas). For example, a third-grade student reading 60 WRCM on the third

Table 9.2 Common benchmarks and growth rates.

Measure	Grade	Benchmark	Growth[a]
CBM-R	1	60 WRCM[b]	2.00–3.00 Words/Week
	2	60 WRCM	1.50–2.00 Words/Week
	3	100 WRCM	1.00–1.50 Words/Week
	4	100 WRCM	0.85–1.10 Words/Week
	5	100 WRCM	0.50–0.80 Words/Week
CBM-Maze	1–5	—	0.39, 0.84 Replacements
CBA/M-M	1–3	20 DCPM[c]	0.30 Digits/Week
	4	40 DCPM	0.70 Digits/Week
	5	40 DCPM	0.75 Digits/Week
CBM-W	1	15 WW[d]	—
	2	28 WW	—
	3	37 WW	—
	4	41 WW	—
	5	49 WW	—

Note: Benchmark numbers for reading and mathematics represent the mastery-level criterion. CBA/M-M growth rates are based on multiple-skill probes. These criteria are from the following sources: [a]Fuchs et al. (1993), [b]Fuchs & Deno (1982), [c]Deno & Mirkin (1977), and [d]Mirkin et al. (1981).

grade fall CBM benchmark is performing below the 25th percentile (Fuchs, 2003; Fuchs & Deno, 1982). According to Fuchs et al. (1993), third-graders should gain between 1 and 1.5 words read (aloud) per week. In order to establish the student's goal, the average learning rate (i.e., 1.0 or 1.5 WRCM) is multiplied by the number of weeks the student will be monitored (eight weeks) and this number is added to the current reading score ([1.0 WRCM × 8 weeks] + 60 WRCM = 68 WRCM). In this example, it would be expected that the student read 68 WRCM by the end of eight weeks. This goal can be plotted on a graph and becomes the aim line for the student (see Figure 9.1, Panel 1). These same procedures can be followed using CBM-Maze. Unlike CBM-R, expected growth may not be different depending on grade level. Preliminary data suggest that targets for weekly improvement may be .39 and .84 words correct for realistic and ambitious goals, respectively (Fuchs et al., 1993). For example, if a third-grade student obtained a score of 7 at the fall benchmark, then the ambitious goal at the end of eight weeks may be 14 ([0.84 × 8 weeks] + 7 = 13.72).

A goal can also be established by expecting a student to reach the 25th percentile for the fall or winter benchmark criterion by the end of the monitoring period (Shapiro, 2004). Continuing with this example, the student would be expected to read between 65 and 70 WRCM (Hasbrouck & Tindal, 1992). This might be particularly useful when monitoring at-risk students not yet receiving supplemental reading support. If a student reaches the expected goal by the end of the monitoring period or is making adequate progress toward this goal, then the student is responding to the core curriculum. If, however, a student is not reaching the expected level of performance and is not progressing, additional reading support may be necessary.

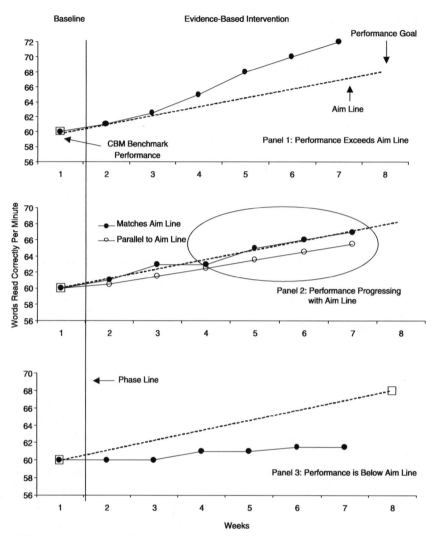

Figure 9.1 Instructional decisions when CBM performance exceeds, meets, or is below the aim line (goal).

Monitoring At-Risk Students Receiving Additional Academic Support   When students are not performing as expected in the core curriculum according to the earlier described decision rules, two levels of academic support may be identified. The first may be within small groups using empirically supported supplemental reading interventions. The second may be individualized reading support, often provided when response to small group interventions is unsuccessful (Batsche et al., 2006). For these students it is important to have more information regarding specific reading weaknesses so that appropriate intervention planning can occur. This can be done by analyzing the CBM data to determine what kind of reading problem appears to be evident or by using a subskill mastery model of CBA (e.g., CBE).

A first step may be to determine whether students have reading fluency, decoding, or comprehension problems. This can be done by examining the WRCM and the errors made. Specifically, if a student is making two or fewer errors when reading grade-level material but WRCM are falling below the 25th percentile, s/he may be exhibiting reading fluency problems (Daly, Witt, Martens, & Dool, 1997; Gravois & Gickling, 2002). For students who exhibit low WRCM and are reading with many errors, decoding may be problematic. Finally, in order to identify comprehension problems it might be useful to examine performance on CBM-Maze or generate five to eight open-ended questions (literal and inferential) to be answered following administration of a CBM-R probe (Shapiro, 2004). Students with comprehension difficulties may exhibit low fluency on CBM-R and low scores on CBM-Maze. Corresponding small group interventions should match student areas of need.

A second step may be to conduct a survey-level assessment (SLA) to determine the grade-level material that provides the appropriate instructional match (Howell & Nolet, 1999; Shapiro, 2004). In this process material that was mastered and that which is too difficult (frustrational) for students to read is identified. In order to conduct the SLA, examiners need to obtain CBA passages from various grade levels. The SLA begins with material (i.e., CBA probe) that corresponds with a student's grade of record. Consistent with CBA procedures, three passages are presented and the median score is computed. Additionally, a miscue analysis should be conducted during which types of errors, such as omissions, substitutions, transpositions, and hesitations (three-second pause), are recorded. Next, the median WRCM and errors are compared to placement criteria. These criteria could be generated from local or national normative data such that below the 25th percentile would represent the frustrational level, performance between the 25th and 50th percentile would represent the instructional level, and above the 75th percentile would represent mastery (Shapiro, 2004). Fuchs and Deno (1982) also provide placement criteria. If a student's performance falls in the frustrational range on grade-level material, then passages from the previous grade should be administered and compared to the placement criteria. This process continues until the appropriate instructional, mastery, and frustrational levels are identified. SLA permits the analysis of specific skill development so that individualized reading interventions can be generated in which students have the opportunity to read material at their instructional level using strategies that address individual error patterns.

Short-term goals for these students should be established as described above and evaluated to determine if the type and the intensity (e.g., number of minutes or sessions per week) of support is leading to reading improvements. Growth is measured by comparing the actual student performance with the aim line that was generated from the goal. Instructional decisions can be made accordingly using simple decision rules (Fuchs & Fuchs, 2007; Hintze, 2007). First, when looking at these data visually, the most recent four data points should be isolated to determine whether they are going up (increasing), going down (decreasing) or are variable. Second, it is determined whether performance: (a) matches the aim line, (b) exceeds the aim line, or (c) is below the aim line and unlikely to reach goal. If performance *matches* the aim line (see Figure 9.1, Panel 2) then the current intervention procedures should be continued until the goal is reached (Hintze, 2007). Once the goal has been achieved and if the goal reflects an adequate level of progress (e.g., 30th percentile of winter CBM benchmark in grade-level material), then supplemental reading support may be reduced. Similarly, if progress is parallel to the aim line, a decision may be made to wait and see if performance will improve at the expected rates. If the most recent four data points *exceed* the aim line (see Figure 9.1, Panel 1), the goal should be increased. Finally, if these data do not illustrate progression toward the established goal (see Figure 9.1, Panel 3), then a change in the intervention procedures may be warranted (Fuchs & Fuchs, 2007). Once the intervention is changed, a solid vertical line (phase line) would be added to the graph so that performance under both interventions can be evaluated. In each of these circumstances progress should continue to be monitored (at least weekly) and evaluated.

Using CBM/A-Mathematics to Make Instructional Decisions

Types of CBM-Mathematics Assessment

There are three general areas that comprise CBM-M: (a) computation/operations, (b) applications/problem solving, and (c) early numeracy. The most frequently researched form of CBM-M assessment is computation, including single skill and multiple skill operations demonstrating concurrent validity (Connell, 2005; Foegen, Jiban, & Deno, 2007; Skiba, Magnuson, Martson, & Erickson, 1986), reliability (Fuchs, Fuchs, & Hamlett, 1990; Tindal, German, & Deno, 1983), and progress monitoring of performance indicators (Fuchs, Fuchs, Hamlett, & Stecker, 1991). Applications-type assessments (e.g., word problems, algebra, data analysis, measurement, geometry, and patterns) have less supporting data, though the research has found that these measures are reliable (Fuchs et al., 1994) and valid indicators of student performance on standardized assessments (Connell, 2005; Fuchs et al., 1994). Additionally, the applications assessments have high face validity with teachers (Connell, 2005). Correspondence with state assessments range from moderate to strong for computation and applications/problem-solving measures across primary and middle school grades (Shapiro, Keller, Lutz, Santoro, & Hintze, 2006). Finally, and important to note for the remaining discussion, research demonstrates that the constructs representing applications and computation problems, though separate, *are related* (Thurber, Shinn, & Smolkowski, 2002). To date, no studies were identified that investigated early numeracy or application problems in a response-to-intervention framework, where benchmark scores and growth rates were provided. Therefore, the remainder of this section will be limited to computation assessments.

Screening Using CBM: Computation Benchmark Assessments

Within the GOM, the *primary* CBM-M datum is described as the "performance indicator" of overall math proficiency. The performance indicator is a measure of individual student performance on all skills targeted for instruction across the year (Fuchs et al., 1990). School districts across the nation are presently developing "benchmark assessments." And, whether developed in schools by district personnel or outsourced to test development agencies (e.g., Educational Testing Service), the purpose of these benchmark assessments is to acquire a performance indicator in a specific content area (e.g., mathematics, literacy) for each student assessed. It is expected that with this performance indicator, teachers will differentiate instruction to meet each student's instructional needs.

Like CBM-R, universal screening in mathematics occurs three times per year, fall, winter and spring, and can be group or individually administered (VanDerHeyden et al., 2003; Witt, Daly, & Noell, 2000). As stated above, computation assessments are used because they are reliable and valid measures of overall mathematics performance, are easy to administer, are brief, can be used diagnostically, and can be used to monitor progress. The administration procedure is as follows. First, assessments are developed that represent, in equal number, the types of skills students are expected to learn across the year. There are typically 25 to 30 problems on a page. For example, a third-grade performance indicator assessment might include five multi-digit addition with regrouping and five multi-digit addition without regrouping, five multi-digit subtraction with borrowing and five multi-digit subtraction without borrowing, and five multiplication facts to 9, totaling 25 computation problems (Hosp, Hosp, & Howell, 2007). If group administered, assessments are placed face down on each student's desk. Students are instructed that the sheet contains several types of math facts (e.g., addition, subtraction, and multiplication). Next, students are told they have two minutes (three to five minutes for more complex skills) to complete as many problems as they can, and attend to the operation. Then, students are told to begin the assessment and the timer is started. After two minutes, students are told to stop and the assessments are collected. Assessments are scored by counting the number of correct digits per two-minute assessment. Correct digits (CD) are determined by counting the number of CD in the answer to the problem (attending to place value). Each correct digit is given one point. Points are tallied and the total number of points (i.e., CD) is the student's score for that assessment. Once the data are collected and analyzed, school teams are able to evaluate if the core curriculum is effective for most students by comparing the assessment scores to the local or national norms (Burns, VanDerHeyden, & Jiban, 2005; Deno & Mirkin, 1977).

Performance indicators are effective screening tools because they allow for individual basic skills to be assessed. In other words, by assessing the skills students are expected to learn across the year, educators can determine which skills have yet to be acquired for which students. Thus the performance indicator can be used diagnostically. For example, if a student's assessment data illustrate that multi-digit addition without regrouping has been established (i.e., all digits attempted are correct), but multi-digit addition with regrouping has not been acquired (i.e., no correct digits), then educators can determine, by making data-based decisions, if more intensive intervention is required on the missing skill(s).

Progress Monitoring and Instructional Planning Using CBM/A-M

Monitoring At-Risk Students Not Receiving Additional Academic Support   Progress monitoring is recommended for students identified as at risk (below the 25th percentile) following universal screening. Progress monitoring includes weekly or bi-weekly (Hosp et al., 2007) re-administration of the performance indicator assessment used in universal screening for up to eight weeks. Graphing the data by pencil or with a computer-based graphing application allows for visual analysis of performance over time (i.e., slope). Following the dual-discrepancy model, level and rate of growth are evaluated. If the at-risk student reaches or exceeds the 25th percentile (i.e., level) after the monitoring period, then the student is no longer considered at risk. If the rate of growth matches or exceeds those performing above the 25th percentile, then progress monitoring continues until the student reaches the expected level of performance (i.e., local norm or criterion-referenced benchmark score). If the level of performance does not reach the local or national norms by the end of the eight weeks and the slope is less than the local or national growth rates, then intervention is needed.

Monitoring At-Risk Students Receiving Additional Academic Support Skills-based measures (SBM) are assessments used to screen and monitor one mathematics basic skill (i.e., addition, subtraction, multiplication, and division). Thus, the *secondary* datum is the CBA skills analysis (Fuchs et al., 1990). A skills analysis is a process whereby performance on any one skill is analyzed to determine skill proficiency, monitor progress, and guide instruction. Following the example above, all classroom students are reassessed on multi-digit addition with regrouping to determine if the skill deficit is a result of ineffective curriculum and/or instruction. If the SBM universal screening data illustrate that only a few students have not acquired this skill, then intervention and progress monitoring is initiated for these students in small group format using evidence-based interventions (Ardoin, Witt, Connell, & Koenig, 2005). For each student, the SBM universal screening performance level serves as the baseline data point from which projected slope is calculated. For example, if John's SBM assessment score was 15 CD/two minutes, then 15 would be the baseline data point. A realistic goal across eight weeks of intervention would be an increase of .3 CD per week (Fuchs et al., 1993) from 15 CD to 17.4 CD per two minute assessment. An ambitious goal would be an increase of .5 CD per week from 15 to 19 CD per week after eight weeks of intervention. The projected realistic and ambitious slope data would be presented on a graph such as that illustrated in Figure 9.1, Panel 1. It is recommended that progress monitoring occur at least weekly and preferably, twice weekly (Hosp et al., 2007). Finally, the student's performance level on the SBM (multi-digit addition with regrouping) is recorded on the same graph as the projected slope for direct visual comparison.

Using CBM-Writing to Make Instructional Decisions

Types of CBM-Writing Assessments

CBM-writing (CBM-W) has remained consistent over the years in terms of the administration procedures for elementary and secondary students (Deno, Mirkin, & Marston 1980; Shinn, 1989). The assessment tool consists of a story starter (also called an incomplete stimulus prompt, or sentence fragment) as described by

Gansle, VanDerHeyden, Noell, Resetar, and Williams (2006). First, students are given a story starter on lined paper and instructed to think about what they will write for the next minute. After one minute has passed, students are instructed to construct a story from the opening sentence provided. Finally, students are told they have three minutes[1] to write, the timer is started and when the timer stops, the writing samples are collected. This procedure can be administered individually for progress monitoring or in group format for screening.

Scoring CBM-W assessments has been less consistent through the years as researchers have evaluated procedures that are reliable and valid indexes of student writing performance across and within grade level(s). The results of those studies indicate that as writing instruction and expectations increase as the grade level increases, more complex scoring methods are then required. Therefore, a brief description of the scoring methods will follow as will a selected sample of reliability and validity studies. For a thorough review of the CBM-W research, see McMaster and Espin (2007).

A number of scoring procedures have been evaluated for the three-minute writing sample. Fluency-based CBM-W measures (i.e., a three-minute assessment as described above) have found total words written (WW), words spelled correctly (WSC), and correct word sequences (CWS) to have adequate reliability coefficients with criterion measures such as the Test of Written Language (Hammill & Larsen, 1978) and the Stanford Achievement Test (Deno, Marston, & Mirkin, 1982; Gansle, Noell, VanDerHeyden, Naquin, & Slider, 2002; Madden, Gardner, Rudman, Karlsen, & Merwin, 1978). Other scoring procedures such as correct letter sequences, correct minus incorrect word sequences, and percentage of legible words also have adequate reliability coefficients, but are less researched. Much of the extant literature identifies WW and WSC (for primary grades) and WSC and CWS (for secondary grades) as reliable and valid indicators of overall writing performance. Finally, when using the Stanford-9 measures of written expression as the criterion measure, CBM-W scoring procedures including WW, WSC and CWS were found to be valid and reliable indicators of student writing performance. The Six Trait model (used in many schools throughout the United States) was not an adequate predictor of written expression when the criterion measure was the Stanford-9 written language subtests (Gansle et al., 2006). Finally, teachers' holistic ratings of students' written expression indicate less support for WW, and more support for WSC and CWS (Parker, Tindal, & Hasbrouck, 1991). However, as a universal screener, teams will need to consider the time it takes to score WSC and CWS (see Hosp et al. (2007) for explicit scoring instructions).

Screening Using CBM: Writing Benchmark Assessments

As a universal screening tool, Parker et al. (1991, Study 1) found WW, WSC, and CWS to be suitable scoring procedures for second- through fourth-grade students, though WSC was considered the most viable scoring procedure across all the grades and has moderate correlations with teachers' holistic ratings of student writing performance. Parker et al. (1991, Study 2) found that CWS was a sufficient predictor of writing when correlated with holistic ratings of student writing performance for students in Grades 6 through 11.

Little research is available identifying percentiles for *at risk* and *in need of additional support*. AIMSWebfi and Hosp et al. (2007) do provide percentiles for CWS for Grades 1 through 8. Teams will need to decide if students below the 25th percentile will receive additional support, be monitored across a specified amount of time (e.g., eight weeks), or if a more diagnostic process is required. For example, school teams could use the 25th percentile and below on WW as the lower limit for the school/ district at-risk category. Students' written expression assessments below the 25th percentile could then undergo a more diagnostic scoring procedure such as WSC and CWS. Next, students falling below the 25th percentile when using WSC and CWS scoring procedures would require additional instructional support, and those above the 25th percentile of CWS fall into the at-risk group for progress monitoring.

Progress Monitoring and Instructional Planning Using CBM-W

Monitoring At-Risk Students Not Receiving Additional Academic Support Following the example provided above, students not receiving additional academic support are monitored for progress over an eight- to ten-week period for growth. Sensitivity to growth has been demonstrated using WW and WSC measures in first through sixth grade. One to two writing samples per week over the next eight to ten weeks (Marston, 1982; Shinn, 1981) allow enough time for adequate instruction to occur and related performance to reflect growth. The goal is to establish that students will respond to instruction, as demonstrated by an increase in performance across the time monitored from at risk to above the 25th percentile in CWS. If students do not respond to instruction, additional academic support is needed.

Monitoring At-Risk Students Receiving Additional Academic Support When students do not respond to the general education curriculum in writing, then more intensive writing instruction is required. Again, progress monitoring should occur one to two times per week across the length of the intervention. Secondary and tertiary interventions can occur in small groups or as individual instruction. As stated above, WW and WSC measures have demonstrated sensitivity to instruction (Marston, 1982; Shinn, 1981) and therefore should be used as progress monitoring measures. However, CWS is the more complex measure and therefore the goal is to move the student from below the 25th percentile on this measure to above the 25th percentile (whether using local or national norms). Eight to ten weeks of intervention can include as little as 20 minutes and up to one hour of additional instruction per day, depending on the student support needed (e.g., some support, intensive support).

Incorporating CBM/A into IEP Objectives

CBM/A information may also be incorporated into the Individualized Educational Program (IEP) for students identified as having specific reading, mathematics,

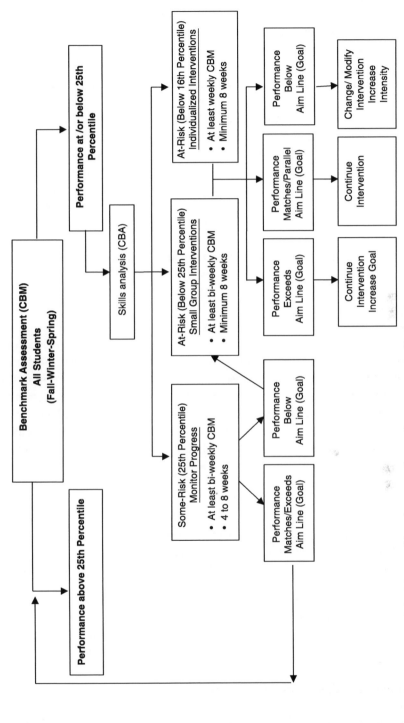

Figure 9.2 Instructional decision making for screening and progress monitoring.

or writing disabilities, or for those students in need of intensive individualized academic support after failing to respond to less intensive evidence-based treatments. CBM/A provides academic goals in the form of observable, measurable, and objective behaviors and criteria (Codding, Skowron, & Pace, 2005; Shinn, 1989). CBM data (fall benchmark), or as determined by the CBA skills analysis (i.e., SLA or SBM), would be listed under the current performance section of the IEP. Using CBM-R as an example, the IEP may read: Given three randomly selected third-grade reading passages from <insert reference to an appropriate curriculum or application>, Molly read aloud a median of 60 WRCM with two errors. The annual goal would reflect the year-end expected level of progress, such as the 50th percentile on the spring CBM benchmark assessment. The objectives to achieve the annual goal would be generated using the procedures described earlier (incorporating average learning rates according to local norms or Fuchs et al., 1993). For example, the first objective may be written as: In 12 weeks, when given three randomly selected third-grade reading passages from <insert reference to an appropriate curriculum or application>, Molly will read aloud a median of 72 WRCM minute with two errors. This goal was determined by multiplying the average learning rate (1.0) by the number of weeks for the objective (12) and adding the product to the fall CBM benchmark (60 WRCM).

Summary

Increased accountability requirements and adoption of response-to-intervention frameworks require that educators utilize measures that are sensitive to small gains in student performance, which also correspond with and inform short-term and year-end curricular objectives. CBM and CBA are particularly suitable for this purpose and the school environment given that these measures are time and resource efficient. The diagram in Figure 9.2 provides an overview of the ways in which CBM and CBA can be used for screening, instructional planning, and monitoring progress.

Note

1. Writing time ranged from one to five minutes in Deno et al. (1980) with the strongest validity coefficients for writing times of three to five minutes with Test of Written Language.

References

Ardoin, S. J., Witt, J. C., Connell, J. E., & Koenig, J. L. (2005). Application of a three-tiered response to intervention model for instructional planning, decision making and the identification of children in need of services. *Journal of Psychoeducational Assessment, 23*, 362–380.

Ardoin, S. P., Witt, J. C., Suldo, S. M., Connell, J. E., Koenig, J. L., Resetar, J. L., et al. (2004). Examining the incremental benefits of administering a maze and three versus one curriculum-based measurement reading probes when conducting universal screening. *School Psychology Review, 33*, 218–233.

Batchse, G., Elliott, J., Graden, J. L., Grimes, J., Kovaleski, J. F., Prasse, D., et al. (2006). *Response to intervention: Policy considerations and implementation.* Alexandria, VA: National Association of State Directors of Special Education, Inc.

Blankenship, C. S. (1985). Using curriculum-based assessment data to make instructional management decisions. *Exceptional Children, 42,* 233–238.

Bradley-Klug, K. L., Shapiro, E. S., Lutz, G. J., & DuPaul, G. J. (1998). Evaluation of oral reading rate as a curriculum-based measure within literature-based curriculum. *Journal of School Psychology, 36,* 183–197.

Burns, M. K., VanDerHeyden, A. M., & Jiban, C. L. (2005). Assessing the instructional level for mathematics: A comparison of methods. *School Psychology Review, 35,* 401–418.

Burns, M. K., Tucker, J. A., Frame, J., Foley, S., & Hauser, A. (2000). Interscorer, alternate-form, internal consistency, and test-retest reliability of Gickling's model of curriculum-based assessment for reading. *Journal of Psychoeducational Assessment, 18,* 353–360.

Codding, R. S., Skowron, J., & Pace, G. M. (2005). Making data-based decisions: Training teachers to use assessment data to create instructional objectives. *Behavioral Interventions, 20,* 165–176.

Connell, J. E. (2005). Constructing a math applications, curriculum-based assessment: An analysis of the relationship between applications problems, computation problems and criterion-referenced assessments (Doctoral dissertation, Louisiana State University and Agriculture & Mechanical College, 2005). *Dissertation Abstracts International,* 3933.

Daly, E. J., Witt, J. C., Martens, B. K., & Dool, E. J. (1997). A model for conducting a functional analysis of academic performance problems. *School Psychology Review, 26,* 554–574.

Deno, S. L. (1985). Curriculum-based measurement: The emerging alternative. *Exceptional Children, 52,* 219–232.

Deno, S. L., & Mirkin, P. K. (1977). *Data-based program modification: A manual.* Reston, VA: Council for Exceptional Children.

Deno, S. L., Martson, D., & Mirkin, P. (1982). Valid measurement procedures for continuous evaluation of written expression. *Exceptional Children Special Education and Pediatrics: A New Relationship, 48,* 368–371.

Deno, S. L., Mirkin, P. K., & Marston, D. (1980). *Relationships among simple measures of written expression and performance on standardized achievement tests* (Research Report No. 22). Minneapolis: Institute for Research in Learning Disabilities, University of Minnesota.

Foegen, A., Jiban, C., & Deno, S. (2007). Progress monitoring measures in mathematics: A review of the literature. *Journal of Special Education, 41,* 121–139.

Fuchs, L. S. (2003). Assessing intervention responsiveness: Conceptual and technical issues. *Learning Disabilities Research & Practice, 18,* 172–186.

Fuchs, L. S., & Deno, S. L. (1982). *Developing goals and objectives for educational programs* [Teaching guide]. Minneapolis: Institute for Research in Learning Disabilities, University of Minnesota.

Fuchs, L. S., & Deno, S. L. (1991). Paradigmatic distinctions between instructionally relevant measurement models. *Exceptional Children, 57,* 488–500.

Fuchs, L. S. & Deno, S. L. (1994). Must instructionally useful performance assessment be based in the curriculum? *Exceptional Children, 61,* 15–21.

Fuchs, L. S., & Fuchs, D. (2004). Determining adequate yearly progress from kindergarten through grade 6 with curriculum-based measurement. *Assessment for Effective Intervention, 29,* 25–37.

Fuchs, L. S., & Fuchs, D. (2007). *Using curriculum-based measurement for progress monitoring in math.* Retrieved November 19, 2007, from http://www.studentprogress.org/summer_institute/2007/math/Mathmanual_10–4.pdf

Fuchs, L. S., Fuchs, D., & Hamlett, C. L. (1990). The role of skills analysis in curriculum-based measurement in math. *School Psychology Review, 19,* 6–22.

Fuchs, L. S., Hamlett, C. L., & Fuchs, D. (1997). *Monitoring basic skills progress: Basic reading* (2nd ed.) [Computer software manual]. Austin, TX: PRO-ED.

Fuchs, L. S., Fuchs, D., Hamlett, C. L., & Ferguson, C. (1992). Effects of expert system consultation within curriculum-based measurement, using a reading maze task. *Exceptional Children, 58,* 436–450.

Fuchs, L. S., Fuchs, D., Hamlett, C. L., & Stecker, P. M. (1991). Effects of curriculum-based measurement and consultation on teacher planning and student achievement in mathematics operations. *American Educational Research Journal, 28,* 617–641.

Fuchs, L. S., Fuchs, D., Hamlett, C. L., Walz, L., & Germann, G. (1993). Formative evaluation of academic progress: How much growth can we expect? *School Psychology Review, 22,* 27–48.

Fuchs, L. S., Fuchs, D., Hamlett, C. L., Thompson, A., Roberts, P. H., Jubek, P., & Stecker, P. M. (1994). Technical features of a mathematics concepts and applications curriculum-based measurement system. *Diagnostique, 19,* 23–49.

Gansle, K. A., Noell, G. H., VanDerHeyden, A. M., Naquin, G. M., & Slider, N. J. (2002). Moving beyond total words written: The reliability, criterion validity, and time cost of alternate measures for curriculum-based measurement in writing. *School Psychology Review, 31,* 477–497.

Gansle, K. A., VanDerHeyden, A. M., Noell, G. H., Resetar, J. L., & Williams, K. L. (2006). The technical adequacy of curriculum-based and rating-based measures of written expression for elementary school students. *School Psychology Review, 35,* 435–450.

Gickling E. E., & Havertape, J. (1981). *Curriculum-based assessment.* Minneapolis, MN: National School Psychology Inservice Training Network.

Good, R. H., Simmons, D. C., & Kame'enui, E. J. (2001). The importance and decision-making utility of a continuum of fluency-based indicators of foundational reading skill for third grade high-stakes outcomes. *Scientific Studies of Reading, 5*, 257–288.

Gravois, T. A., & Gickling, E. E. (2002). Best practices in curriculum-based assessment. In A. Thomas & J. Grimes (Eds.), *Best practices in school psychology IV* (pp. 885–898). Washington, DC: National Association of School Psychologists.

Hammill, D. D., & Larsen, S. C. (1978). *Test of written language.* Austin, TX: PRO-ED.

Hasbrouck, J. E., & Tindal, G. (1992). Curriculum-based oral reading fluency norms for students in grades 2 through 5. *Teaching Exceptional Children, 24*, 41–44.

Hintze, J. (2007). *Using student progress monitoring in a response to intervention model.* Retrieved November 19, 2007, from http://www.studentprogress.org/library/Webinars.asp#RTI

Hoover, H. D., Hieronymus, A. N., Frisbie, D. A., & Dunbar, S. B. (1993). *Iowa test of basic skills.* Itasca, IL: Riverside Publishing.

Hosp, M. K., Hosp, J. L., & Howell, K. W. (2007). *The ABCs of CBM: A practical guide to curriculum-based measurement.* New York: Guilford Press.

Howell, K. W., & Nolet, V. (1999). *Curriculum-based evaluation: Teaching and decision making* (3rd ed.). Belmont, CA: Wadsworth.

Madden, R., Gardner, E. F., Rudman, H. C., Karlsen, B., & Merwin, J. C. (1978). *Stanford achievement test.* New York: Harcourt Brace Jovanovich.

Marston, D. B. (1982). *The technical adequacy of direct, repeated measurement of academic skills in low-achieving elementary students.* Unpublished doctoral dissertation, University of Minnesota, Minneapolis.

Marston, D. B. (1989). A curriculum-based measurement approach to assessing academic performance: What it is and why do it. In M. R. Shinn (Ed.), *Curriculum-based measurement: Assessing special children* (pp. 18–78). New York: Guilford Press.

McMaster, K., & Espin, C. (2007). Technical features of curriculum-based measurement in writing. *Journal of Special Education, 41*, 68–84.

Mirkin, P. D., Deno, S. L., Fuchs, L. S., Wesson, C., Tidal, G., Marston, D., & Kuehnle, K. (1981). *Procedures to develop and monitor progress on IEP goals.* Minneapolis: Institute for Research in Learning Disabilities, University of Minnesota.

Parker, R. I., Tindal, G., & Hasbrouck, J. (1991). Countable indices of writing quality: Their suitability for screening-eligibility decisions. *Exceptionality, 2*, 1–17.

Salvia, J. A., & Ysseldyke, J. E. (2001). *Assessment in special and remedial education* (8th ed.). Boston: Houghton Mifflin.

Shapiro, E. S. (2004). *Academic skills problems: Direct assessment and intervention* (3rd ed.). New York: Guilford Press.

Shapiro, E. S., Keller, M. A., Lutz, J. G., Santoro, L. E., & Hintze, J. M. (2006). Curriculum-based measures and performance on state assessment and standardized tests: Reading and math performance in Pennsylvania. *Journal of Psychoeducational Assessment, 24*, 19–35.

Shinn, M. R. (1981). *A comparison of psychometric and functional differences between students labeled learning disabled and low-achieving.* Unpublished doctoral dissertation, University of Minnesota, Minneapolis.

Shinn, M. R. (Ed.) (1989). *Curriculum-based measurement: Assessing special children.* New York: Guilford Press.

Shinn, M. R., & Shinn, M. M. (2002). *AIMSwebfi training workbook: Administration and scoring of reading maze for use in general outcome measurement.* Eden Prairie, MN: Edformation, Inc.

Skiba, R., Magnusson, D., Marston, D., & Erickson, K. (1986). *The assessment of mathematics performance in special education: Achievement tests, proficiency tests or formative evaluation?* Minneapolis, MN: Special Services, Minneapolis Public Schools.

Thurber, R. S., Shinn, M., & Smolkowski, K. (2002). What is measured in mathematics tests? Construct validity of curriculum-based mathematics measures. *School Psychology Review, 31*, 498–513.

Tindal, G., German, G., & Deno, S. L. (1983). *Descriptive research on the Pine County Norms: A compilation of findings* (Research Report No. 132). Minneapolis: Institute for Research in Learning Disabilities, University of Minnesota.

VanDerHeyden, A. M., Witt, J. C., & Naquin, G. (2003). Development and validation of a process for screening referrals to special education. *School Psychology Review, 32*, 204–227.

Wayman, M. M., Wallace, T., Wiley, H. I., Ticha, R., & Espin, C. A. (2007). Literature synthesis on curriculum-based measurement in reading. *Journal of Special Education, 41*, 85–120.

Witt, J. C., Daly, E. J., III, & Noell, G. H. (2000). *Functional assessments: A step-by step guide to solving academic and behavior problems.* Longmont, CO: Sopris West.

10

Principal Leadership, Data, and School Improvement

Michael A. Copland, Michael S. Knapp, and Juli A. Swinnerton
University of Washington

Educational leaders operate in an increasingly data-rich environment, where they are expected to make decisions that require sophisticated knowledge, skills, and practices with the use of data. Routinely, today's educational leaders grapple with what it means to draw data into decision-making processes in ways that are more systematic, relevant, and sufficiently nuanced to carry the weight of important decisions. This chapter puts forward conceptual and practical definitions of what we will call "data-informed educational leadership," illustrating ways in which data collection and use play out in intentional efforts to improve teaching and learning.[1] We focus particularly on how these ideas play out in the work of school and district leadership, where data practices are embedded most directly in ongoing efforts to improve teaching and learning in schools.

As we write, the data dialogue has entered a new era in which educational leaders' engagement in data-based problem solving is benefiting from new tools and trends not previously known. Building on a robust evaluation movement in the 1960s and 1970s, a variety of techniques and strategies are now available for systematically evaluating the implementation, effects, and effectiveness of educational programs, policies, or initiatives. Underlying standards-based reform has been growing attention to outcomes and results, with a corresponding lessening of interest in inputs. Moreover, the associated accountability movement has become a fact of educators' lives, steadily ratcheting up the demand for an evidence base concerning educational programs' effectiveness since the late 1980s. Finally, the rapid sophistication of technologies for handling digital information makes the prospects for educational decisions rooted in relevant evidence more realistic, yet simultaneously more costly and complex.

In this context, deep data analysis focused on student learning is becoming increasingly a routine means for informing teachers' and administrators' daily work. The growing attention to questions of what counts as data, sophistication in understanding data, and technologies for manipulating data open up important possibilities for educational leaders.

This chapter pursues three integrated agendas. First, we synthesize and interpret research that informs the field's understanding of data-informed leadership in schools and school districts. We rely largely on published accounts in the research literature and also descriptive material concerning current or emerging practices.

The ideas concern the availability, quality, and use of data in the work of school and school district leaders related to the improvement of teaching and learning.

Second, we offer an inquiry-focused framework that provides a set of lenses for understanding change work, and in particular, how data enter into change processes. In this effort, we establish processes or cycles of inquiry as the foundation for data-informed decision making in schools and school districts. We endeavor to ground these ideas operationally through an illustration of how they might play out in a school engaged in data-informed change work.

Finally, we use the ideas from the first two sections to focus on intentional efforts at data-informed leadership, in one linked school-district case vignette. In particular, we highlight the theory of action at work within this context, and examine the role that data play in school (and district) improvement efforts. We find this particular case compelling because of the context of the district's specific and intentional data-informed efforts to link technology, curriculum, assessment, and professional development in powerful ways to support the work of school leaders in improving teaching and learning. Our case discussion daylights a number of the current issues facing school and district leaders across the country as they wrestle with how to understand and use data productively in service of improving learning.

Data-Informed Educational Leadership

To explain the central construct in our argument we must first lay out what we are treating as "data" and identify what kinds of data might be regularly available to school leaders in the course of their work. We also need to distinguish data-informed educational leadership from the more common conceptions of "data-driven leadership" and "data-based decision making" and locate it in the decision-making infrastructure that districts and schools create.

What Counts as Data?

To explore what the concept of data-informed leadership might entail, we need first to clarify what we mean by "data," and for what purpose leaders might be using them. Here, we limit our attention to data implicated in what is arguably the central function of educational leaders—to guide, direct, assess, and support teaching and learning. Accordingly, for purposes of this chapter, we concentrate on data as information that:

(1) Represents the content or conduct of instruction or its effects on student learning and the student experience, as well as the factors and conditions that most immediately affect these matters.

(2) Is, or could be, used in leadership actions aimed directly at the improvement of instruction, learning, and the student experience, or the organizational conditions that support instructional improvement.

A wide range of data, both quantitative and qualitative, falls within this boundary. While leaders and their audiences may often use data that can be quantified or averaged, such as grades, graduation rates, teachers' experience levels or qualifications, and scores on state assessments there is clear evidence that many forms of qualitative evidence (e.g., capturing the qualities of student work, teachers' perceptions, or various features of classroom-based assessment) have as important a role in improving teaching and learning as their quantitative counterparts. As the boundary definition makes clear, we are particularly interested in data that pertain most directly to the improvement of teaching and learning.

Given a focus on learning, leaders' ability to bring data to bear on it is shaped in large measure by the actual data they can find or generate with a reasonable investment of time and resources. Some of these data reside in information systems created through state policies and investments—such as those that have created "data warehouses," management information systems, or reporting systems. Other sources are more likely to be "homegrown," derived from the school or district leaders' own efforts to put together data that have meaning and usefulness in the local situation, or from research, media accounts, or other efforts to represent what is going on in schools (Weiss, 1995).

Table 10.1, adapted from Bernhardt's (1998) work, provides an overview of the kinds of data (demographic, perceptions, student learning, school processes) educators may use as they engage in data-informed decision making, especially in "information-rich" environments.

From these raw materials, leaders may conduct various kinds of inquiries, including simple indicator systems that offer "warnings and hints" about performance (e.g., trends in the achievement gap, student attendance, teacher retention, and funding equity (Celio & Harvey, 2005)).

Moreover, we also acknowledge that data are not the same as evidence. Put another way, data by themselves are not evidence of anything, until users of the data bring concepts, criteria, theories of action, and interpretive frames of reference to the task

Table 10.1 Types of data available to educational leaders in information-rich environments.

Data category	Sample data points
Student demographic	Enrollment, attendance, dropout rate, ethnicity, gender, grade level (by school, or district)
Perceptions	Perceptions of learning environment, values and beliefs, attitudes, observations . . . (e.g., held by a school's teachers, district-wide educators, or the local community)
Student learning	Standardized tests, norm/criterion-referenced tests, teacher observations, authentic assessments
School processes	Descriptions of programs, instructional strategies, classroom practices
Teacher characteristics, behavior, and professional learning	Teacher assignment (grade, subject area, students served), qualifications, retention, participation in professional development

(Adapted from Bernhardt, 1998)

of making sense of the data. In this regard, flooding leadership practice with data is unlikely to bring about much improvement, and could even get in the way, absent time and attention to the central issue of sense making.

Data-Informed Educational Leadership Defined

In the current context of accountability and school reform, data-driven decision making is increasingly seen as an essential part of the educational leader's repertoire, yet more is at stake—and more is possible—than this term, or even the term data-based decision making may imply. Leaders' productive work with data implies more than laying out test scores, noting areas of weakness, and mounting remedies that address patterns in the data. We suggest the scope of such work is better described as *data-informed educational leadership*—a term that broadens the scope of thinking and action in two productive ways.

First, a shift to data-informed leadership escapes the sometime deterministic implication of data "driving" action. Tempting though it may be to imagine educational leaders' actions single-mindedly "driven" by "bottom-line numbers," complex educational problems require greater depth of understanding. While they can be fully knowledgeable of available data when taking action, wise leaders also bring to their work core values and insights into those aspects of practice for which there is not yet good data, and may never be. Weiss (1995) reminds us that no matter how systematic and comprehensive the data gathering, several other factors are always likely to influence decision making, including interests, ideologies, and institutional context.

Second, the concept presumes that data are useful for more in the practice of leadership than the making of decisions, per se. Given the inherent ambiguity and multiple meanings of much data in educational settings, data may prompt questions and deliberation more than they point to specific decision options (Coburn & Talbert, 2006; Honig & Coburn, 2005). For example, certain data points (e.g., disaggregated state math test scores) may provide an awareness of a given situation (e.g., performance gap between seventh-grade boys and girls), but the data do not necessarily indicate how educators should address the issue at hand. In this example, assessment data certainly *inform* conversation about possible actions, but they do not necessarily "drive" decisions or provide information about how best to address the issue of low performance.

Finally, we suggest leaders' expertise with data—what may be referred to as their "data literacy" (Earl & Katz, 2002)—defines how much and what they are able to do with data. The challenge is more than a technical one limited to the assembling and manipulation of information, but rather extends to what Fullan (2001) calls "knowledge building," the capacity to extract and share useful meaning from organizational experience. Data literacy presumes more than trial-and-error experience with data, but rather an accumulating facility with the interpretation of data, not to mention familiarity with data sources and creativity in assembling relevant data quickly and efficiently. As implied by work on cultures of inquiry (Copland, 2003), members of a school, district, or other educational organization can become more "literate" in the use of data and committed to this feature of their collective practice. For purposes of this chapter, we focus in on leadership practices of those in schools and classrooms (e.g., principals, department heads, teacher leaders, teachers, and others who take part in instructionally related inquiry), and in district central offices (school board members, superintendents, directors, and other staff who are involved in decision making focused on instructional improvement). Leaders at each of these levels are potentially engaged in data-informed leadership, broadly construed; hence, our discussion concerns the ways that data are or are not part of their daily practice.

Data can serve a range of purposes in the leaders' toolkit, as Table 10.2 suggests (e.g., Bernhardt, 1998; Holcomb, 1999). Each implies different ways of representing what the data say and communicating them to the intended audiences.

As the Table 10.2 entries suggest, not all of these leadership actions imply specific decisions, but rather imply a range of actions (including the investigation of new questions). Such public availability of data has multiple implications for leaders as they interact with those both internal and external to their schools and districts, among them the continuing questions about the effectiveness of their ongoing efforts to improve teaching and learning.

Table 10.2 A range of ways that educational leaders use data.

Type of leadership activity (with and for internal or external audiences)	How data are used and what kinds of data are implied
Diagnosing or clarifying teaching and learning problems (primarily internal to the decision-making group).	Seeking to know whether, or to what extent, student learning matches those overarching expectations (standards) established at the top of the system, leaders seek out information that reflects one measure of student learning in particular content areas.
Weighing alternative courses of action (primarily internal).	Leaders use data to evaluate existing programs or curriculum approaches, and (where they have relevant data) judge their potential in comparison with alternative programs.
Justifying chosen courses of action (primarily external).	Data (e.g., concerning learner characteristics, learning outcomes, comparative program benefits, school closure decisions) are used selectively to "make a compelling case" for programs or courses of action that may or may not have been chosen on the basis of the data.
Complying with external requests for information (external).	Leaders are careful to generate information requested by external agencies, authorities, or groups providing funding—for example, descriptions of how different learner groups are served, evaluations of services to these groups.
Informing daily practice (internal).	Data of various kinds are used by administrators and teachers to guide daily practice. The data are often informal, gathered in mid-stream, and in a form that can be immediately interpreted and used by the practitioner for refining teaching and learning.
Managing meaning, culture, and motivation (internal).	Data help leaders understand and guide the cultural aspects of the professional workplace, by representing to staff what the organization is accomplishing, how people feel about their work, what matters in the work, and what professional learning needs exist.

Finally, data-informed leadership for school improvement assumes an infrastructure that supports and cultivates this kind of activity. A number of larger system dimensions bear on questions of infrastructure, but given our focus on school and district leaders, the role of the school district is particularly important. District considerations of infrastructure that support data-informed leadership include:

- *Offering sources of data or help with assembling or interpreting data* (which may involve responding to school needs for particular kinds of information, etc.).
- *Embedding new technologies that assist with data collection and interpretation* (such as computer-based attendance, discipline records, or grading systems that enable access and make analysis more efficient).
- *Creating occasions for inquiry* (as when an influx of new immigrant children raises questions about appropriate educational programs or school assignment).
- *Setting expectations for reliance on data in school planning and decision making* (as in mandates for the inclusion of certain kinds of evidence in the School Improvement Plan).
- *Creating accountability structures for data-informed leadership linked to overarching district initiatives* (such as expectations for principals to engage in learning walks in classrooms to observe in particular content areas that are the focus of district curriculum work, etc.).

Conceptual Framework

The capacity for data-informed leadership—embodied in leaders' values, expertise, theories of action, and availability of data—sets the stage for particular leadership activities that bring systematic information into consideration by leaders and others. Specifically, educational leaders who are so inclined engage, along with others, in cycles of data-informed inquiry and action. This may mean being open to going beyond the initial boundaries of a given question or problem, and reframing the issues in ways to help the organization and its inhabitants to "see" different possibilities.

Building Organizational Cultures that Enable and Motivate Data-Informed Leadership

Data are only useful to the extent that leaders and those who work with them ask questions that can be answered with the data. Schools, districts, and other educational settings vary in the degree to which they make data a prominent feature of deliberation about the myriad issues that confront these organizations on a daily basis. The literature is beginning to offer a number of examples of educational organizations in which participants accept—even hunger for—data, as they plan and implement their respective programs. Such instances appear in descriptions of "reforming districts" (McLaughlin & Talbert, 2002); schools engaged in "cycles of inquiry" (Copland, 2003); schools in the midst of school improvement planning or "self-reflective renewal" (Portin, Beck, Knapp, & Murphy, 2003; Streifer, 2002); and schools enacting, or responding to, accountability systems (Lemons, Luschei, & Siskin, 2003; Spillane et al., 2002).

In these cases, leaders have taken deliberate steps to *build a culture that supports inquiry* into the pressing problems facing the organization. Such a culture is supported by the stance leaders take as learners themselves, not having all the "answers," which sets an example for others that engenders trust and reduces the perceived risk from asking and answering questions about practice and performance (Copland, 2003), and ultimately can support collective learning (Scribner, Cockrell, Cockrell, & Valentine, 1999).

A central part of the culture of inquiry is that it characterizes the organization, not just a few key players; many players are participants in it, often implying that data-informed leadership is *distributed*, as are other aspects of the exercise of leadership. In line with recent formulations of the idea of distributed leadership (e.g., Elmore, 2000; Spillane, 2006), leaders who find ways to stimulate and sustain inquiry into problems of practice confronting a school, district, or state system invite others to share in the framing, conduct, and interpretation of the inquiry, and the subsequent actions based on it. The participants often become co-leaders and over time they develop shared norms and expertise in data-informed problem solving.

Such activities emphasize expert over hierarchical authority, an essential attribute of distributed leadership arrangements (Bennett, Wise, Woods, & Harvey, 2003). Such arrangements also recognize that the knowledge and skills necessary to shape or exercise data-informed leadership may be located within a professional community of practice more than in a particular individual (Wenger, 1998). That said, leadership informed by data may not be shared equally among participants, as research on committee deliberations about math performance in a school indicates. When committee members held different beliefs about what the data "Said," it was the leader with positional power whose framing of the problem predominated (e.g., are we facing a curriculum problem or a professional development problem?) and whose beliefs largely informed the final decisions for action (Coburn, 2006).

Engaging in Cycles of Data-Informed Inquiry and Action

Cultures of inquiry support—and, in turn, develop from—repeated attempts to use data to support work on key problems facing the school or school district. At least five discrete phases of activity, schematically represented in Figure 10.1, define this kind of "inquiry in action," work that connects data to learning improvement.

- *Focusing and reframing problems for inquiry.* Leaders focus attention on problems of practice and frame them in terms that invite inquiry. Work that highlights problem-framing ability (Cuban, 1990) and capacity to *reframe* problems from multiple vantage points or perspectives (Bolman & Deal, 1997; Copland, 2003) captures what leaders do, or can do, to set inquiry in motion, thereby giving context for the use of data. This emphasis on framing and

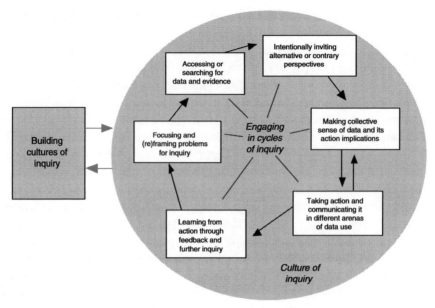

Figure 10.1 Culture and cycles of inquiry.

reframing means that leaders pay careful attention to, and continuously engage in grappling with how to identify and understand what count as problems of practice that should ground their work and the work of others in the collective. They hold on to the present framing of problems to anchor their present work but also remain prepared to let go of current frames as conditions (people, tools, time trajectories) change. Most importantly, for framing purposes here, they engage in an ongoing search for relevant data to guide this work.

- *Accessing or searching for data and evidence.* Leaders and their collaborators generate or search for data using available inquiry tools, sources, and strategies, as delineated in various works on "organizational learning" (e.g., Honig, in press; Huber, 1991), or simply access data that are already available.

- *Intentional invitation of alternative (or contrary) perspectives.* Inquiry-based leadership is open to critical feedback from others, and understands that the reframing of problems and/or change strategies is enhanced by the intentional invitation of alternative perspectives, including those which are contrary to, or in direct conflict with, the current overriding decision direction. This notion emphasizes the importance of leaders taking time to deliberately open their doors (and minds) to alternative ways of framing problems and of creating formal and informal structures to facilitate this engagement around problem framing.

- *Making sense of data and implications for action.* With data in hand, leaders create occasions for *making collective sense of the data* and probing the data for possible action implications. Here, drawing on underlying frameworks concerning sense making in organizations (Coburn & Talbert, 2006; Weick, 1995), recent work has begun to outline how leaders approach the sense-making task

(Spillane, Reiser, & Reimer, 2002). The leap from data to action is not simple, however. Scholarship that captures patterns of actual data use in school districts, for example, notes how ambiguous the data often are, a fact that can curtail their perceived usefulness, but can also stimulate deliberation about ways to serve student needs better (Honig & Coburn, 2005). In addition, individuals' conceptions of what counts as evidence, how evidence should be used, and how research informs practice varies across systems, is often informed by where an individual sits within an organization (Coburn & Talbert, 2006). Thus, the same data may likely be interpreted differently and suggest different courses of action depending on who is engaged in decision making.

- *Taking action and communicating it in different arenas of data use.* Informed by the sense they make of the data, and by other matters not intrinsic to the data (e.g., the politics of the situation, basic values, reporting demands), leaders take action and communicate what the data say to relevant audiences. Some actions take place out of the public eye, but others are intimately connected to the relation between leaders and relevant audiences (Witherspoon, 1997). A central part of the leaders' work is "making it public" in ways that are respectful and politically astute (Holcomb, 1999).

- *Learning from action through feedback and further inquiry.* Scholarship by cognitive scientists on short-term "quasi-repetitive feedback cycles" supports the notion that regular feedback can be a powerful influence on learning, and by implication, the learning of leaders' who receive such input (Schwartz, Bransford, & Sears, 2005). Not surprisingly, syntheses of work on effective educational leadership draw attention to the role feedback can play as an influence on leaders' and others' learning (e.g., Hattie, as cited in Marzano, Waters, & McNulty, 2005).

Presented this way, leaders' attempts to make use of data within cycles of inquiry may appear logical, rational, and orderly. In actual practice, these cycles are likely to be "messier," and they are likely to differ considerably depending on the participants' experience and comfort with inquiry, as in research that has identified schools exhibiting "novice," "intermediate," and "advanced" cultures of inquiry (Copland, 2003) as well as where data users reside in relation to the organization (Coburn & Talbert, 2006). But the underlying impulse is the same, regardless of the sophistication with data use: to raise questions about practice and to develop insights into these problems by considering what can be learned from data about practice.

Operationalizing Data-Informed, Inquiry-Based Leadership in a School

A hypothetical example illustrates how these ideas play out in more concrete, operational terms. Imagine a school engaged in efforts to overcome inequitable patterns in student achievement data that persist over time; year after year the school's achievement data reveal that, with regard to particular assessments, second language learners were underperforming the rest of the school's population. A school community that took seriously the process of working through cycles of inquiry would recognize that defining the problem was an all-important first step; they would understand that the data did not constitute the "problem" but rather were reflective of something underneath the numbers that needed to be explored in greater depth. In particular, they would avoid assigning blame to kids, or families, or teachers, or prevailing community norms, and turn instead to ask openly—what is the cause of this persistent inequity? What might the problem be?

Deeper consideration of the problem would ensue. The school operating in the mode of inquiry would avoid adopting quick solutions based on limited or superficial understanding of the problem(s) represented by the disparities in data. Rather, they would devote time and energy to deep consideration of the underlying problem dimensions, attempting to discern the root causes of the disparities, and why the trends persisted over time. They would consider a variety of alternative sources of information that might help deepen their understanding of the problem to be addressed; they might, for example, consider what second language students were saying about their experience at the school, or how families of second language learners perceive their connection with the school. Teachers might engage in dialogue about learning among themselves, working to make assumptions held by members of the school community about students, about teaching, about families they served more explicit. In these efforts they might unearth conflicts and reframe more fundamental problems to resolve regarding school members' perceptions or beliefs about which students can achieve, gaps or concerns in particular aspects of their collective instructional practice, or varying perspectives about whose interests were being served by the school. Importantly, they would take critical account of what efforts (programs, practices, etc.) the school had already instituted that were intended to help solve the situation, and try to learn from what resulted in those earlier efforts in ways that could guide their deeper understanding of the problem(s) to be solved. Efforts at problem framing and reframing like these run counter to prevailing norms that encourage schools to "jump on the bandwagon" of new reforms, without first understanding the problem for which new reforms may be solutions.

Armed with a deeper, clearer understanding of the problem(s) to be addressed, the school community could become much more intentional and specific about the choice of particular strategies or solutions. If, for example, it became clear that the fundamental challenge had something to do with lower achievement expectations for second language learners held by some teachers, a new curriculum or new set of pedagogical strategies would be unlikely to help close the disparities in achievement. Rather the school would necessarily need to tackle the deeper work on changing teachers' beliefs and attitudes, and devise strategies that would work on helping teachers to hold all students to high expectations. Importantly, a theory of action hailing from this kind of critical inquiry would provide a rationale for why the particular choice of strategies and solutions would be likely to address the underlying problem(s) that was uncovered.

Finally, school personnel would engage in continual efforts to learn from outcomes, to assess progress in at least two dimensions. First, they would pay attention to whether or not the problem they started to work on was the "right" problem, or if efforts at change helped to develop an even deeper understanding and a new problem frame. A new problem frame would call for a reconsideration of their theory of action, and possibly different strategies specific to the new understanding of the problem. Second, they would pay attention to whether the solutions they put in place, supported by the theory of action, actually worked the way they had anticipated. If progress of the kind they anticipated was not evident, they would seek to understand why, and make concerted efforts to learn from the efforts they had made initially, that could guide new rounds of decision making.

A school working this way would recognize that problems underneath inequitable achievement for second language learners are complex and unlikely to respond without ongoing and persistent learning and reinvention. Educators engaged in critical inquiry are always attending to new challenges on the horizon, and looking honestly at the progress in their practice, learning from efforts to make productive change.

Given this conceptual and operational backdrop, we turn now to a brief case vignette of a school and its school district to consider how these ideas play out in one example of what might be termed data-informed leadership.

Data-Informed Leadership in Context: The Bodewell (WA) School District

The Bodewell (WA) School District (pseudonym) is recognized regionally and nationally as a "high performing" system, pursuing a rigorous, college preparatory education for every student. For nearly a decade, the district has realized strong and steady growth in various measures of student achievement. Under Superintendent Mike Rodgers' (pseudonym) leadership, state test scores have risen steadily across all grades tested, and, in recent years, Bodewell high schools are consistently ranked among those with the greatest student participation in Advanced Placement courses in the country. However, data analysis now reveals a "plateauing effect" in key indicators. Over the past three years, for example, the district has stalled at about 80% of students taking at least one Advanced Placement course, and last year saw a slight decline in student performance on state assessments in mathematics across grade levels.

In what follows, we focus on the case of this specific school district's efforts at data-informed leadership. We begin with a brief illustration of the current work playing out on the ground, in one elementary school in the district—Alexander Elementary—in which the building principal and teachers are working to improve teaching and learning in connection to the district's goals and strategies. From here, we move out to the system, to highlight the district goals for students, and the theory of action at work within this context, and explicate ways data play in the learning-focused efforts that the superintendent, central office administrators, and building leaders have made to move the district toward identified goals, and in considerations of next steps.

Alexander Elementary

Of the 16 elementary schools in the Bodewell district, five receive Title One funding from the federal government to support disadvantaged students. We turn attention first to one of those elementary schools, Alexander, to explore ways in which the efforts of the district to embed data collection, analysis, and use in increasingly powerful ways in service of student learning are playing out in schools.

Alexander principal Kathleen Washington does not soft pedal the learning issues the school faces. "There is an achievement gap at Alexander Elementary School, particularly for students of poverty and color," she notes, before detailing efforts the Alexander faculty have pursued intensively to close the identified learning gaps among students at the school. Alexander's approach involves a variety of strategies and interventions revolving around a restructuring of the school's Title One program, which was the subject of data collection and scrutiny in 2002–2003. The work, in many ways, embodies the district's stated directions, focused on increasing student achievement, by grade level, toward specified district literacy benchmarks, with an eye on all students ready for high levels of curriculum at the secondary level.

Through an analysis of data on outcomes for students receiving Title One services, conducted by the school's leadership team, personnel realized that students were entering Title One programs at Alexander and staying there—some never exiting to mainstream classes despite two, three or even four years of special intervention. Based on the data dialogue, Alexander staff determined the model was not working and, with Washington's leadership, changed the delivery of remedial services from "pull out" to in-class support using teacher facilitators. Since the change, Alexander's professional development, including that of principal Washington, has centered around learning how to improve literacy learning for both students and teachers.

Identifying a Clear Problem for Focus   During 2002–2003, Washington's focus on data analysis and conversation with faculty began to shift collective attention on the achievement gap between poor students and students of color, and their more advantaged counterparts. The district's infrastructure designed for supporting school-level data analysis and use was rapidly developing, and Alexander's leadership took advantage of the opportunity to go deeper with their understanding of which students were achieving. While only 55–60% of Alexander students were achieving at expected levels on standardized assessments overall, the vast majority of the 40–45% that were not achieving were students of color, students living in poverty, or in some cases students whose profile included both characteristics. As a result of dialogues resulting from this data analysis, the school embarked on the journey of realizing all students achieving at high standards.

A School-Level Theory of Action   Washington led her teachers, drawing on research and their own experiences, in an effort rooted in the fundamental belief that students are successful when they have outstanding teachers, who are well versed in instructional strategies and can meet a variety of needs within one classroom. Washington and the Alexander staff also worked from an understanding that more students are successful when the cognitive demand in a classroom is high, and when the climate of the school supports high academic achievement. Washington's working theory of action was that improving the quality of the classroom experience, through intentional professional development, and numerous opportunities for observation, interaction, and conversation with and among teachers, would ensure that by any measure, students at Alexander will be more successful.

In addition to a focused set of professional development activities, the Alexander staff has begun to develop an organizational culture of teaming in which analysis of classroom-level data plays a central role. Teachers work with each other in grade-level groupings, cross-grade groupings, and in other intensive work with district technology/curriculum specialists, and developers who provide ongoing, job-embedded support for improvements in literacy instruction, employing frequent, common assessments of student learning as the means for dialogue and learning. Principal Washington notes:

> The entire (school) team is focused on meeting the specific reading goals for our kids. Grade-level teams meet every week with a facilitator, discussing student progress and strategies. Teachers routinely observe each other teaching, giving feedback and ideas. . . . Our (district) technology/curriculum specialist is in the building one day per week, in classrooms, focusing on those teachers that struggle with implementation. She teaches, models, and provides support. . . . We have moved from what I would describe as a closed culture (i.e., "I'll teach my students, and you teach yours"), to a much more open one. The rooms are open, our practice is open, our results are open, and we routinely share and receive feedback on our progress. Teachers, in contrast to the old model, are doing a significant amount of discussing, examining, speculating, both about students' progress and their own practice.

Evidence suggests that the processes around deep and ongoing data gathering and analysis are influencing at least some of the Alexander teachers to challenge their beliefs and expectations about students, and the role they play in promoting learning. By way of example, the Alexander staff recently tested out an assumption that was prevalent in the school—that transient students, those who drifted into the school over the course of their elementary experience, were performing far below those who had been in residence at the school for their entire elementary experience, and, in the process, contributing to lower state test scores. Data analysis revealed, in fact, that the opposite was true. Students present at the school since kindergarten were underperforming their more transient counterparts. The finding caused this teacher to deeply question her assumptions about students, and her personal role in helping all students learn, stating:

> When we looked at the data, we were blown away. What we had assumed for so long as being a primary problem for our kids—their transience—was, in fact, not their problem at all. It challenged me to revisit how I think and act in the classroom, and made me realize that I'm implicated in ways I'd failed to consider before.

Assessing Progress Thus Far   While it is arguably difficult to link specific professional development efforts at the school to quantifiable improvements in learning for students, some indicators appear promising. Evidence suggests, for example, that, consistent with district direction, teachers are using assessments linked to the curriculum to track progress in greater detail than ever, and that this process is informing teacher dialogue and instructional strategies for individual students. This detail further illustrates how the data dialogue is changing the work at Alexander. Washington illustrates:

As an example, a first-grade teacher reported that 84% of ALL her students are testing at or above a Level 16 (the target). She has two more students who are at a Level 14 and may be at 16 by June 21. The one other child is on an extensive IEP and will not test past a Level 8. Comparatively, last year's first-grade class had only 61% of the students at or above a Level 16 (interview, 2004).

Bodewell District Goals and the Theory of Action

Working productively with data to inform leadership actions requires ongoing efforts to clarify the intended outcomes, as well as the means or strategies rooted in an explicit rationale, that aim to move the organization in a productive direction. In Bodewell's case, as illustrated by the snapshot provided above of Alexander School, the desired outcomes are both lofty and clear.

In achieving such outcomes, the district's support is of utmost importance, and in Bodewell a coherent theory of action for improving student learning has evolved under Superintendent Rodgers' leadership that centers around three key elements: curriculum, professional learning, and student support.

Curriculum at the Center   Initially, Rodgers worked from an intuitive sense that specification of curriculum, across content areas, and spanning the K-12 spectrum, was essential to move the district toward the goal of graduating all college-ready students. He notes:

> Because learning targets are ambiguous and inconsistent, American kids typically march from kindergarten through 12th grade repeating content and skills more times than necessary and, at the same time, skipping large chunks of important things they should be learning. No wonder it is so unusual for all students to end their K-12 education at advanced levels. It is indeed impossible under (typical) conditions.

Early district efforts in curriculum began with the purchase of existing curricular solutions in science, and later evolved to have district teachers engaged in developing curriculum and associated classroom-level assessments that are now common across schools and grade levels.

Most recently, a sophisticated technology infrastructure has enabled the district to digitize curricular materials and assessments and make them accessible online, an effort which will eventually encompass the entire curriculum in core content areas. The technology initiative, in addition to making curriculum readily available down to the level of individual unit and lesson plans, is also structured to invite ongoing, interactive teacher development of exemplar lessons that can be made available to every teacher in the system through the district's curriculum "share point" website, accessible to all. In this sense, the Bodewell curriculum effort is not static, but continuing to evolve based on teachers' use and experimentation with it over time.

Leadership challenges remain as to how to encourage and promote interaction around the curriculum. Clearly, as the Alexander Elementary discussion highlights, data collection, analysis, and use will continue to play an ever more important role in leading the work. During annual leadership institutes for all district administrators and coaches, Rodgers challenges principals, assistant principals, coaches, and district administrators to connect the curriculum efforts to the goals they created for students, and to rely on data skills to determine what comes next.

Connected Data-Informed District Professional Learning Opportunities   Alongside curriculum specification, development, and leadership, the district has pursued an ongoing robust professional development agenda for teachers, integrally linked to the curriculum, in an effort to deepen and extend pedagogical content knowledge and skills. Professional development efforts have both been informed by ongoing analysis of student data, and designed to build teachers' and administrators' "data skills."

For example, recent professional development focused on connections between technology and curriculum is a high priority in Bodewell, including efforts to help teachers learn to use the district's developing "data warehouse." Efforts focus on helping teachers learn data analysis operations, and to develop ways to conduct meaningful research connected to particular curricular efforts in content areas. Strategies involve layers of different activity, providing choices for teachers, including curriculum workshops, lesson study, individual coaching and/or assistance from technology/curriculum coaches, peer observation and peer coaching (including incentives to support this activity), and high numbers of classroom observations by administrators.

Data-Informed Supports for Students   Finally, in addition to curriculum and linked professional development for district teachers and leaders, Bodewell has pursued a third component focused on providing additional support for struggling students to enable them to learn the specified curriculum. Rodgers and other leaders in the system recognized that raising expectations for what would be taught and learned in the curriculum across the district would challenge students in new ways, and require thoughtful efforts to add supports for struggling students to be able to learn the material.

Toward this end, the district has developed classes at key junctures that offer support in key content areas, in many cases allowing teachers to "pre-teach" material to struggling students, and set them up with greater opportunity for success in their other "regular" courses. Rodgers places a high priority on providing what he calls "successful academic support," noting:

> Bodewell's academic support system is effective only to the extent that it enables students to master the curriculum. . . . Students typically predicted not to become college graduates—the ones most likely to need extra support—are the very ones who will benefit the most from being free from pre-college classes on their entry to college.

The district is working to provide interventions for students who need extra support in the earliest grades, as well as "catching up" those who are already in the system, but may have fallen behind. The efforts include systemic assessments administered as early as kindergarten to identify students who need help, and provision of more time before, during, and after school in support classes, as well as summer experiences designed to provide an academic boost. With the student support initiatives, Rodgers brings the conversation back to data and evidence, asking questions that are aimed at determining program effectiveness in the area of student support. He notes:

We may have the right elements in place, but are we using them to their full advantage? Are assessments effective diagnostic tools? Are they given frequently enough to identify problems early? Are programs that provide extra time targeted enough in their goals for content and skill development? Are these programs used by the right students? How closely aligned are Title One, ESL and Special Education to the mainstream curriculum? How well trained are teachers in these areas in the delivery of our district curriculum?

Despite this systemic approach to curriculum, professional development, and student support that extends to the earliest grade levels, the superintendent expresses the realization that the district has progressed as far as it can given the current level of knowledge and skills of its educators. He notes, "What Ron Edmonds said years ago simply isn't true—we don't have all the knowledge and skills we need to ensure every student's success. I'm saying, I've been at this work for a long time, and I don't know how to teach all kids in a way that will guarantee their success." The district sits poised on the edge of moving to the next level of accomplishment, but the way from here is not clear. Rodgers asks, "How can the district promote experimentation, and harness new forms of data and data use to break through the ceiling?"

Case Discussion

The case example sheds light on how Bodewell leaders, and, in particular, Super-intendent Rodgers and Principal Washington, are deepening data-informed efforts to enable the district to achieve better results for students, developing new data sources, analyses and uses in service of realizing greater progress toward their specific goals for students. The case highlights the district's specific and intentional efforts to link technology, curriculum and assessment, professional development, and student support in powerful ways, and the role data of various kinds play in those efforts at the school level. The following discussion of the Bodewell case applies key framework ideas introduced earlier to bring to light promising aspects of the work underway there, and to raise questions about the road ahead.

Stepping back from the specifics of the Bodewell case, three lenses on data-informed leadership related to key ideas introduced earlier seem particularly relevant in considering the case. These include:

(1) efforts to define elements of data-informed leadership in context;
(2) cultures and cycles of inquiry at the district and the school; and
(3) considerations of district infrastructure that inform and support school-level activity.

Defining Data-Informed Leadership in Context

At both school and district level, leaders have established a clear focus for data use by staff; they have developed a theory of action emphasizing curricular coherence across grades and schools that offers a reference point for data-informed leadership; and they are developing a basic level of data literacy, while recognizing that there is more they can learn.

Focus for Data-Informed Leadership   Leaders are in a position to define the focus for the data they might generate and use, reflecting their own leadership priorities and their response to events such as that call for data and evidence. The district has developed efforts to increase accountability for principals to use data in developing plans and tracking progress. State assessments play a minor, but supporting role in this; more important are data from common classroom assessments that shape teaching decisions more immediately.

Coherence Through a Curricular Theory of Action   To the extent that the perspectives of those at the top of the organization in Bodewell reflect understandings that permeate the rest of the district, there is relative clarity about what the district is being designed to accomplish (all students rigorously prepared for college), and about the means for how that will be accomplished (a curricular theory of action). The theory outlines how the presence of a shared curriculum enables teachers at the same grade level, regardless of their school affiliation to engage in dialogue about their work, and build shared assessments that can provide more systemic understanding of progress in key content areas coherently across the entire system. Coherence is created through linkages to robust professional development opportunities tied to curricular efforts, and student support structures and programs targeting key student learning needs.

Leaders' Development of Data Literacy   As noted earlier, numerous scholars (e.g., Dembosky, Pane, Barney, & Christina, 2006; Earl & Fullan, 2003; Wayman & Stringfield, 2006) cite the importance of building educators' expertise in using data to inform action. The case suggests some evidence that Bodewell educators' ability to interpret and apply data is growing, and that they are on the road to becoming "data-literate" (Earl & Katz, 2002, p. 1013). Yet, as comments from both Rodgers and Washington suggest, becoming data-literate in Bodewell likely means developing new capacities for using data effectively that are not yet imagined.

Cultures and Cycles of Inquiry

The cases illustrate what it might look like when district and school leaders have encouraged a culture of inquiry and how a system of collective learning by teachers might ensue, as participants across the district share what they are doing in their practice.

Efforts to Develop and Sustain Cultures of Inquiry Across the System   Some evidence suggests that Bodewell is developing an organizational culture that encourages inquiry into problems of practice. Such cultures develop over time through repeated activity by many individuals, but data-oriented leadership, such as that displayed by Superintendent Rodgers, is often a "driving force" behind data use

(Supovitz & Klein, 2003). Clear from the case description is that some Bodewell leaders, and in particular Superintendent Rodgers, have embraced the idea that the only way to continued improvements is to turn the district into a learning community, where experimentation with new ideas and forms, and ongoing analysis of results of those experiments, becomes the norm for teachers' work, rather than the heroic exception. Whether or not this will come to pass ultimately is part of the question of how to promote continuous progress and break through the ceiling that appears to have capped learning outcomes at around the 80% mark.

Unleashing the Power in Collective Teacher Learning The picture Rodgers paints of a teacher community is compelling—intimately linked, one to another, over the Internet, working to continually develop the range and depth of the district's curriculum, and using those same web-based structures to enable the sharing of knowledge about what works, both inside and outside the district.

Considerations of Infrastructure

The case clarifies the role data infrastructure can play in enabling data-informed leadership to take place. Furthermore, access to data through technology and associated assistance makes it possible for teachers to connect to the tools and means for addressing the problems of practice they face.

Deep Data Infrastructure and Access for Schools and Classrooms Bodewell has taken steps to rapidly improve data infrastructures (i.e., merging silo systems), and leadership is mandating the analysis and use of data to inform instructional improvement. The district has also engaged in strategic partnerships to enhance support for the analysis and use of data, in service of building a stronger instructional program. Rodgers, probably correctly, sees the need for ever deeper data structures that enable teachers to gain even more clarity about the specific needs students bring, and learn from their ongoing efforts to improve learning.

Access to Resources for Improving Teaching Bodewell's technology initiatives include both "people" expertise and hardware/software. Human resources include district technology/curriculum coaches—a new role in the system designed to help teachers work from data on issues that are present in student learning. Smart boards are in the multi-year plan to remodel all the district's schools, and are included as part of a package of best available technology infrastructure in those schools, to enable teachers to archive and access data related to the curriculum for teaching and assessment purposes.

Conclusion

The concept of data-informed leadership embraces a realm of practice central to the improvement of learning in schools and the educational prospects for the full range of students served by these schools. For those who have just begun to see data as a resource to practice, the framework offered here suggests a vocabulary for thinking about and experimenting with the possibilities, For other leaders, like those in Bodewell, who have already become comfortable practicing data-informed leadership, the framework points to areas that need further exploration and hints at new dimensions of practice that are only just beginning to be imagined. For researchers who wish to understand the roles data can play in leadership and school improvement, the framework highlights activities, assumptions, and dimensions of practice that deserve careful scrutiny.

Together, practitioners and scholars who engage in data-informed practice or who study it will help the field to evolve richer, grounded conceptions of *data literacy* in the leadership of schools and districts. Specifically, they will help the field get beyond the notion that data literacy consists only of the ability to read data tables and interpret simple statistics—rather, it includes facility in collective inquiry into practice while in the midst of the urgencies of practice.

While they do so, practitioners and scholars engaged in data-informed leadership will help us all resist current calls, intensified by the current accountability context, to use student performance data single-mindedly to *drive* decisions. Rather, our hope is to reframe the conversation to emphasize inquiry about student performance *informing* decisions through collective examination of practice *with* data, in iterative cycles. The ultimate questions—and answers—do not sit inside student performance data themselves but rather in the search for new ways of framing seemingly intractable problems. This search will produce new understandings of what is possible and desirable for students' education.

Note

1. Earlier versions of this chapter's argument appear in Knapp, Copland, & Swinnerton (2007), and in a report commissioned by The Wallace Foundation (Knapp, Swinnerton, Copland, & Monpas-Huber, 2006).

References

Bennett, N., Wise, C., Woods, P., & Harvey, J. (2003). *Distributed leadership*. Oxford, UK: National College for School Leadership.

Bernhardt, V. L. (1998). *Data analysis for comprehensive schoolwide improvement*. Larchmont, NY: Eye on Education.

Bolman, L., & Deal, T. E. (1997). *Reframing organizations: Artistry, choice, & leadership* (2nd ed.). San Francisco: Jossey-Bass.

Celio, M. B., & Harvey, J. (2005). *Buried treasure: Developing a management guide from mountains of school data*. Seattle, WA: Center on Reinventing Public Education.

Coburn, C. E. (2006, April). *District evidence use: An analysis of instructional decision making*. Paper presented at the annual meeting of the American Educational Research Association, San Francisco.

Coburn, C. E., & Talbert, J. E. (2006). Conceptions of evidence use in school districts: Mapping the terrain. *American Journal of Education, 112*(4), 469–495.

Copland, M. A. (2003). The bay area school collaborative: Building the capacity to lead. In J. Murphy & A. Datnow (Eds.), *Leadership lessons from comprehensive school reform* (pp. 159–184). Thousand Oaks, CA: Corwin Press.

Cuban, L. (1990). *Problem-finding: Problem-based learning project*. Stanford, CA: Stanford University School of Education.

Dembosky, J., Pane, J., Barney, H., & Christina, R. (2006). *Data driven decision-making in southwestern Pennsylvania school districts* (Working paper). Washington, DC: Rand Corporation. Retrieved October 1, 2007, from http://www.rand.org/pubs/working_papers/2006/RAND_WR326.pdf

Earl, L., & Fullan, M. (2003). Using data in leadership for learning. *Cambridge Journal of Education, 33*(3), 383–394.

Earl, L., & Katz, S. (2002). Leading schools in a data-rich world. In K. Leithwood & P. Hallinger (Eds.), *Second international handbook of educational leadership and administration* (pp.1003–1022). Dordrecht, Netherlands: Kluwer Academic Publishers.

Elmore, R. (2000). *Building a new structure for school leadership.* New York: The Albert Shanker Institute.

Fullan, M. (2001). *Leading in a culture of change.* San Francisco: Jossey-Bass.

Holcomb, E. (1999). *Getting excited about data: How to combine people, passion and proof.* Thousand Oaks, CA: Corwin Press.

Honig, M. (in press). District central office administration as learning: How socio-cultural and organizational learning theories elaborate district-central-office participation in teaching and learning improvement efforts. *American Journal of Education.*

Honig, M., & Coburn, C. E. (2005). When districts use evidence for instructional improvement: What do we know and where do we go from here? *Urban Voices in Education, 6,* 22–26.

Huber, G. P. (1991). Organizational learning: The contributing processes and the literatures. *Organization Science, 2*(1), pp. 88–115.

Knapp, M. S., Copland, M. A., & Swinnerton, J. A. (2007). Understanding the promise and dynamics of data-informed leadership. In P. Moss (Ed.), *Data and evidence—Yearbook of the National Society for the Study of Education, Volume I.* Chicago: National Society for the Study of Education.

Knapp, M. S., Swinnerton, J. A., Copland, M. S., & Monpas-Huber, J. (2006). *Data-informed leadership in education.* Seattle, WA: Center for the Study of Teaching & Policy, University of Washington.

Lemons, R., Luschei, T. F., & Siskin, L. S. (2003). Leadership and the demands of standards-based accountability. In M. Carnoy, R. Elmore, & L. S. Siskin (Eds.), *The new accountability: High schools and high-stakes testing* (pp. 99–127). New York: Routledge-Falmer.

Marzano, R. J., Waters, T., & McNulty, B. A. (2005). *School leadership that works.* Alexandria, VA: Association for Supervision & Curriculum Development.

McLaughlin, M., & Talbert, J. (2002). *Bay area school reform collaborative: Phase one (1996–2001) evaluation.* Stanford, CA: Stanford University, Center for Research on the Context of Teaching.

Portin, B., Beck, L., Knapp, M. S., & Murphy, J. (2003). The school and self-reflective renewal: Taking stock and moving on. In B. Portin, L. Beck, M. Knapp, & J. Murphy (Eds.), *Self-reflective renewal in schools: Local lessons from a national initiative* (pp. 179–199). Westport, CT: Greenwood Publishing Group.

Schwartz, D. L., Bransford, J., & Sears, D. (2005). Efficiency and innovation in transfer. In J. Mestre (Ed.), *Transfer of learning from a modern multidisciplinary perspective* (pp. 1–51). Greenwich, CT: Information Age Publishing.

Scribner, J. P., Cockrell, K. S., Cockrell, D. H., & Valentine, J. W. (1999). Creating professional communities in school through organizational learning: An evaluation of a school improvement process. *Educational Administration Quarterly, 35*(1), 130–160.

Spillane, J. P. (2006). *Distributed leadership.* San Francisco: Jossey-Bass.

Spillane, J. P., Reiser, B. J., & Reimer, T. (2002). Policy implementation and cognition: Reframing and refocusing implementation research. *Review of Educational Research, 72,* 387–431.

Spillane, J. P., Diamond, J. B., Burch, P., Hallett, T., Jita, L., & Zoltners, J. (2002). Managing in the middle: School leaders and the enactment of accountability policy. *Educational Policy, 16,* 731–762.

Streifer, P. A. (2002). *Using data to make better educational decisions.* Lanham, MD: Scarecrow Press.

Supovitz, J., & Klein, V. (2003). *Mapping a course for improved student learning: How innovative schools use student performance data to guide improvement.* Philadelphia: Consortium for Policy Research in Education.

Wayman, J. C., & Stringfield, S. (2006). Technology-supported involvement of entire faculties in examination of student data for instructional improvement. *American Journal of Education, 112*(4), 549–571.

Weick, K. E. (1995). *Sensemaking in organizations.* Thousand Oaks, CA: Sage.

Weiss, C. (1995). Nothing as practical as good theory: Exploring theory-based evaluation for comprehensive community-based initiatives for children and families. In J. Connell, A. Kubisch, L. Schorr, & C. Weiss (Eds.), *New approaches to evaluating community initiatives* (pp. 65–92). Washington, DC: The Aspen Institute.

Wenger, E. (1998). *Communities of practice: Learning, meaning, and identity.* Cambridge, UK: Cambridge University Press.

Witherspoon, P. D. (1997). *Communicating leadership: An organizational perspective.* Boston: Allyn & Bacon.

11

Building Data-Driven District Systems
Examples from Three Award-Winning Urban Systems

Heather Zavadsky
University of Texas System

When the No Child Left Behind Act (NCLB) of 2001 required increasing achievement for all student groups, districts and schools suddenly needed to learn how to assess student performance to identify specific areas for intervention and acceleration. Slow incremental improvement was no longer acceptable under the potential sanctions of NCLB; districts had to efficiently and effectively raise improvement for all schools, student groups, and grade levels. To address that need and take it to the necessary scale, a district would have to create a well-aligned system in which teachers, principals, and central office administrators comfortably use data on a daily basis to inform decisions on all aspects of learning. The few districts that are on the right path to creating those systems have done three things:

1. created easily accessible systems and tools that include multiple measures that address numerous aspects of the educational process;
2. used those systems and tools to create and constantly monitor system alignment and progress; and
3. instituted data-use within all levels of their system.

Building such systems requires a careful and strategic process to overcome numerous barriers characteristic of data transparency, including mistrust and fear of data; failure of system actors to react to data constructively; lack of data interpretation skills; lack of user-friendly accessible data systems; and failure to clearly identify and discuss desired goals and outcomes at the teacher, classroom, school, and district levels.

This chapter presents the concept of systemic data-use through case studies describing three award-winning urban districts that built a culture of data-use throughout every level of their system to improve student achievement. The first section provides an overview of research on data-use in districts and schools, the second section describes the methodology behind this study and presents three separate district case studies, and the final section discusses the overlapping case study themes and suggests important elements to consider for building systemic data-use in districts.

Data-Use in Districts and Schools

Practitioners and researchers agree that the data requirements within NCLB have prompted a beneficial demand for school systems to have not only more data, but data disaggregated by student groups. The requirements also sparked more public interest and attention to district/school performance data, creating a greater interest in data systems and data-use in districts and schools. Research on data-use in education systems increased greatly between 2003 and 2007, illustrating movement from isolated practices in isolated schools to growing examples of entire districts that are well-aligned performance-driven systems.

Many case studies focused on the beginnings of systemic data-use in individual schools. In their comparison of data-use in two similar schools, Heritage and Chen (2005) illustrate the effective practices of a school that engaged numerous stakeholders in an ongoing process of setting goals, collecting and analyzing data, setting priorities, and developing strategies. In contrast, the comparison school was less effective with its cursory annual year-end data review. Agreeing that effective data-use requires a well-aligned process that also includes numerous supports, Lachat and Smith (2004) conclude that school-wide data-driven decision making requires three elements: access to high-quality data; leadership structures that support data-use; and processes that support collaborative inquiry. Obstacles to effective data-use found in their five study schools included limited technical knowledge for data collection, lack of data storage capacity, and lack of structured time for collaborative data analysis.

Earlier case studies also addressed systemic data-use at the district level, mainly as a means to provide the necessary data systems, tools, and support for widespread use in schools. Ramnarine (2004) describes how the Saint Paul Public School District worked with a vendor to develop a customized, easily accessible data management system that was also compatible with its student information system. After a year's implementation, teachers went from having little or no student achievement data to having real-time student achievement data tied to demographic data on their current students. Renzuli (2005) describes a similar data system development process in the School District of Philadelphia, resulting in the capability to produce timely accessible data to teachers and administrators along with information on curriculum, learning resources, and some analytical tools. Agreeing that powerful information systems provide important real-time data and promote data transparency, Golden (2005) describes how the Pennsylvania Department of Education took the concept to scale through its statewide information system devised to help districts track student progress over time and across districts.

The presence of an accessible information system does not of itself create data-based decision making. Such a system requires a strategic approach at all levels that utilizes and aligns the appropriate tools, leadership, and communication structures. Rudy and Conrad (2004) discuss the importance of supporting and sustaining data-use at the district level through ongoing professional development for leaders and teachers and by securing buy-in from central office and school leaders. Regarding the issue of system alignment, Supovitz and Klein (2003) discuss the importance of using multiple assessments but caution that assessments should be aligned to each other on the district, school, and classroom levels to better connect planning and instruction.

Agreeing that data-use should occur within all district levels, Kerr, Marsh, Ikemoto, Darilek, and Barney (2006) discuss barriers that districts must address to successfully connect the system levels, including distrust of data validity, lack of district-wide flexibility to respond to data, and lack of staff capacity to use data.

Two recent case studies address all the above-mentioned aspects of data-use: district and school culture, types of data used, data management systems, data-use practices, structures and supports, and creating system alignment. Using their own framework, Wayman, Cho, and Johnston (2007) analyzed the extent to which a particular district was "data-informed," describing successful data-use practices and suggesting areas for improvement. Addressing similar elements of data-use, Datnow, Park, and Wohlstetter (2007) describe how four high-performing districts and charter systems carefully and strategically developed the right culture, system, tools, and practices for comfortable data-use at all system levels. Two of their selected districts, Garden Grove and Aldine, were Broad Prize finalists, and one is discussed in this paper.

While these studies have moved the notion of data-use from a singular focus on data systems and practices to the concept of well-aligned performance-based systems, there is a need for more concrete examples of how successful data-driven systems are created, evolve, and are sustained over time. This study provides three such concrete examples.

Case Studies of Three School Districts

This study analyzes the evolution of systemic data-use in districts that have successfully increased student achievement. The researcher served as the project manager for the Broad Prize for Urban Education between 2003 and 2006 for the National Center for Educational Accountability (NCEA), who managed the Prize from 2002 to 2006. The Broad Prize for Urban Education, funded by Eli and Edythe Broad of The Broad Foundation, is an annual award honoring urban school districts that demonstrate the greatest overall performance and improvement in student achievement while reducing achievement gaps among poor and minority students. Using data collected through the Broad Prize process, this study focused on Broad Prize finalists that had particularly strong, well-aligned data and accountability systems. The study is primarily qualitative and utilizes a case study format.

The three selected sites, Aldine Independent School District (Texas), Boston Public Schools (Boston), and Norfolk Public Schools (Virginia), were repeat Broad Prize finalists prior to 2006, and had at least two separate site visits covering a two-year time-span. Two of the districts, Norfolk and Boston, were Broad Prize winners in 2005 and 2006 respectively. Broad finalists are selected using statistical measures for modeling performance and improvement over a four-year period to eliminate making a finalist selection based on one-time performance increases. The actual process for selecting a finalist involves a multi-dimensional year-long process that includes: data collection on all eligible urban districts in the U.S.; finalist selection by a review board comprised of educational researchers and experts; site visits to each of the five finalists; and selection of the winner by a prestigious jury comprised of civic leaders (see http://www.broadprize.org/ for further details).

Data for this study came from the interviews and the documents collected on Broad Prize finalist site visits. For the site visits, teams of five members consisting of superintendents, principals, professors, the NCEA Broad project manager, and an additional NCEA researcher were trained to conduct a uniform site visit process across the finalist districts. During each visit, the team spent one day interviewing central office leaders; one day interviewing administrators and teachers at one district-selected elementary, middle, and high school; and one day conducting four separate focus groups of randomly selected new and experienced principals and teachers. In addition to interviews, the research team gathered district and school documents to further describe and support the practices being studied. Finally, one teacher team meeting was convened at each selected school to observe the structure and content of collaborative meetings.

The case studies focus on each district's data collection and data systems as well as their data-use and how they implemented their systems throughout their different organizational levels. Case study details vary depending on the number of site visits and quality of interviews attached to each district. Each case study is discussed separately.

Aldine Independent School District

Located in Texas just north of Houston, Aldine Independent School District is the 73rd largest school district in the nation. The district has 66 schools, 3,616 teachers, and 56,292 students. Seen as a minority district, Aldine ISD has 33% African American students, 58% Hispanic students, and 7% White students, with 76% of its students eligible for Free and Reduced Price School Lunch and 25% designated as English Language Learners (NCES, Common Core of Data, 2004).

Aldine gained attention in Texas over the past five to seven years as a district that embraced the accountability movement early and showed success with a challenging population before the implementation of the No Child Left Behind Act. Highlights contributing to their two-time nomination as a Broad Prize finalist show that Aldine has:

- Met their Adequate Yearly Progress (AYP) targets in 2004 for 100% of all schools.
- Consistently performed higher among demographically similar districts between 2001 and 2004.
- Narrowed the external gap (the gap between the district's disadvantaged group and the state's advantaged group) for all groups in reading and for low-income and Hispanic students in math.

District personnel attribute many of their successes to early efforts to clearly define what all students must know and be able to do at all grade levels, and to a consistent focus on the same goals and priorities over time, making changes only as a result of further refinement. Once teaching and learning was defined, the district worked to fully align all of their practices by providing tools to all system levels to monitor progress towards desired outcomes; and by providing effective interventions at the first sign of trouble. For Aldine, data are at the heart of all of these practices.

Of the five finalists in 2005, Aldine displayed the tightest coordination among the district, school, and classroom levels through its benchmark and common assessments, student performance management system, Balanced Scorecard, and constant monitoring practices. Central office administrators asserted that data "provides the road map" to (1) identify strengths and weaknesses of curriculum and instruction; (2) monitor alignment of written curriculum, classroom instruction, and student assessment; and (3) monitor progress from the district, campus, teacher, and student levels. Led by the philosophy that they should leave nothing to chance, Aldine has a rich data collection and monitoring system that includes formative and summative assessments, a multi-level scorecard, a structured walk-through process, and a powerful data management system that ties all the pieces together.

Data Collection and Data Use

Assessments

One of Aldine's most impressive features is the frequency with which the district monitors student progress on an ongoing basis. District-mandated and district-developed benchmark assessments are given every nine weeks in all core areas. In addition to district-level assessments, schools have developed Common Assessments that are given as frequently as every two to three weeks in all grades and core subjects. Frequent feedback from these assessments helps teachers and principals identify weak instructional objectives early, regroup students for short-term intensive interventions, and provide disaggregated assessment information to teachers to plan future instruction both across same grades and vertically from lower to higher grades. When describing how benchmark results are used, one district leader commented, "We work with teachers and principals not from the standpoint of what are you doing, but what you think your data says and why do you think it is happening?"

As one might imagine, teachers did not instantly embrace benchmarks when they were first introduced. A district leader described the first implementation of the benchmarks as "interesting," because the teachers who did not follow the curriculum had terrible results. For example, in biology, teachers who loved genetics did not teach the full curriculum and their kids missed most of the other items. He described the process as "a real wake-up call to the teachers."

When the site visit team visited the district in 2005, the benchmarks had been in place for approximately three years. Surprisingly, both district leaders and teachers reported that their successful increases in student achievement yielded increased buy-in for the quarterly and common assessments and the curriculum pacing guides. Highlighting the importance of their constant feedback system, one principal commented, "It's the frequency of monitoring that prevents the gaps from getting so wide that you cannot deal with them. We keep the data real-time and we use it for immediate interventions."

In addition to principals, teacher interviews yielded numerous favorable comments about the benchmarks as being an instructional tool rather than a "gotcha." Several described using benchmark assessment results to reflect individually or within teacher teams on how instruction could be improved. One group of teachers explained:

> Our data drives our instruction and helps us revisit and revise our curriculum. If we see there is an area where our first-graders are not achieving, we rethink it—Is it taught too early? Is it taught too late? How do we adjust our curriculum and/or instruction to make up for that?

Data System

The common and benchmark assessments are used in Aldine's custom-designed data management system called TRIAND. Serving as a "one-stop data shop," TRIAND allows teachers to access student scores on summative and formative assessments, student profiles, records, and transcripts. Additionally, TRIAND provides the curriculum scope and sequence, lesson plans, and resource materials for teachers. TRIAND also allows users to query state and local assessments immediately with a powerful disaggregation and item analysis tool. To maximize effectiveness, Aldine mandates that every teacher upload their classroom data into this system with the help of Scantron machines that eliminate the need to enter data by hand.

Monitoring

In addition to analyzing performance data, Aldine frequently monitors classroom activities through observations and walk-throughs. Teachers are routinely observed by principals, department chairs, and their peers who have been trained to use a structured rubric to record walk-through observations and conduct follow-up conferences. Area superintendents and program chairs also spend time in schools and classrooms monitoring instruction. The classroom observation sheet collects focuses on four domains: (1) student participation in learning; (2) learner-centered instruction; (3) evaluation and feedback on students' progress; and (4) management of student discipline, instructional strategies, time, and materials. The sheet also includes a chart for rating effective teaching strategies according to Bloom's Taxonomy.[1] One secondary principal interviewed said each of her teachers received walk-throughs and feedback at least four times a year.

While a few teachers mentioned feeling nervous at times when being observed, most of them characterized the process as providing instructional support. One teacher stated that her principal often gave her good ideas after walk-throughs, and she, in turn, shared those ideas with her peers. A new teacher stated that she was "being evaluated by everyone" from her alternative certification supervisor to team leaders and assistant principals. She commented that she liked "the constant monitoring because it helps me correct any mistakes, helping me not to repeat them all year long."

Accountability System

Aldine's data collection and analysis tools are folded into an overall monitoring process that functions like a feedback loop. The formative and summative assessments and walk-throughs are all used to develop district, department, campus, and subject- or grade-level Action Plans. Each Action Plan delineates goals, objectives, specific tasks, measures of success, monetary resources, and timelines. The Action Plans are monitored by Scorecards (discussed below) that are tied to each level of an Action Plan.

Based on the Baldrige Model for Performance Excellence,[2] the Scorecards measure the success levels within the Action Plans. The Scorecards, distributed quarterly, are standard from campus to campus with the exception of elementary schools, which follow a six-week schedule versus the nine-week schedule in secondary schools. Area superintendents work with schools on a quarterly basis to collect data for their Scorecards. These data include student assessments, staff development feedback, attendance, and other information. The central office leaders compile the various school Scorecards on a given level to produce a vertical Scorecard.

Central office leaders explained the Scorecard process as "coming right back to objectives, action plans, and the goals we have set." The goals relate back to the district improvement plan to evaluate overall district performance. Once compiled, the vertical Scorecard goes to the district. Campuses compare their results with other campuses and review the goals and compare their data. Core subject department chairs share Scorecard results with teachers, who meet in groups to monitor the different objectives within the Scorecards.

One district leader characterized the process as, "monitoring as you go, and at the lowest level, doing more frequent monitoring." This process has helped various district stakeholders "keep up with what's happening" and address concerns early. When asked what district practice most greatly affected her school's performance, this leader pointed to the Scorecards and action planning process. She said,

> Originally, we worked very much on the math, reading, and composition and didn't focus enough on science and social studies. We realized through analyzing the data we needed to work on this. What also helped was having the benchmarks broken down into weekly increments, which helped pace the teachers and track what they should cover each day. That has been a significant improvement.

Systemic Implementation

Teachers and administrators alike highlighted the importance of having information early to focus on prevention rather than intervention. Illustrating this theory of action, one principal stated, "We're a very focused and proactive district. We are looking ahead and are not reactionary. We anticipate trends and make adjustments as needed." Another principal described the process of building a culture of regular data-use as starting from the top, engaging in staff development, and moving the process down to schools through the vertical feeder pattern teams. To gain system-wide trust, she stated,

> You need to have the buy in from the people you are working with. You need to convince them that there needs to be change . . . we worked very hard on getting our students to perform as well as the children from middle-class school systems. That was a big change.

Agreeing with her, another principal asserted that principals support each other through the process, which is made possible by the district's approach to data and accountability as "very non-threatening, very open, and very willing to share from within." An appreciation for information was very prevalent at all levels of the district and was a prominent topic throughout the site visit.

Boston Public Schools

Boston Public Schools, one of the few high-poverty, high-minority districts in Massachusetts, is the 67th largest school district in the nation. The district has 144 schools, 3,926 teachers, and 60,150 students. A very diverse district, Boston has 46% African American students, 30% Hispanic students, and 14% White students, with 73% of its students eligible for Free and Reduced Price School Lunch and 19% designated as English language learners (NCES, Common Core of Data, 2004).

With its size, history of racial tension, and political difficulties both within the culture of the city and with the teachers' union, Boston has many challenges. Despite these challenges, Boston has maintained relatively high levels of student achievement, which is why they have been a finalist every year since the inception of the Broad Prize in 2002 and why they won in 2006. Highlights of its performance contributing to their recent win show that Boston has:

- Consistently outperformed other Massachusetts districts with similar low-income populations in six out of six areas (reading and math at the elementary, middle, and high school levels) in the Broad Prize methodology from 2002 to 2005.
- Demonstrated greater improvement by African American students than similar districts in the state in five out of six areas (math at the elementary, middle, and high school levels, and reading at the middle and high school levels).
- Improved fourth- and eighth-grade reading and math scores at a faster rate than other large American cities on average on the 2005 National Assessment of Educational Progress (NAEP) Trial Urban District Assessment (TUDA).

Boston attributes its successes to a long, steady process of pulling its diverse system into one stable, aligned system. Tom Payzant, Boston's recently retired superintendent who served the district for 11 years, discusses his long-term priority for Boston as improving a "system of schools beyond more than just a few good ones." He characterizes that process as a "K-12" issue involving a whole-school improvement process—where "the whole is greater than the sum of its parts." Dr. Payzant's key focuses for the district have been standards-based leadership and instruction; the provision of clear expectations and curriculum; support systems for teachers connected to learning standards; and strong accountability measures.

The Broad site visits to Boston, spanning five years, have yielded a gradual increase in systemic data-use in the district and schools. Boston's powerful data management system and numerous structured monitoring procedures help keep the system well apprised of its strengths and weaknesses. Interviews during the recent 2006 visit contained more references to data, with principals asserting that teachers were moving beyond superficial use of data to really "digging into the data" to understand student performance. One comment repeated several times by different district leaders and teachers was "the data show everything. You can no longer hide."

Data Collection and Data-Use

Assessments

The district requires quarterly assessments in all subjects and grade levels and provides mid- and end-of-year open response assessments. At grades 3, 6, and 9, students are retained unless they have mastered the standards assessed in the district reading and mathematics benchmarks by the end of summer school. Benchmarks are reviewed every four to eight weeks.

Teachers review results from both formative and summative assessments in grade-level meetings. Instructional coaches from the district also attend teacher meetings to help develop additional instructional interventions based on the data. Individual teachers report using data to assess whether students are mastering the skills being taught. One teacher described how teachers use data in her school:

> Our school is really heavy on looking at data. We looked at the MCAS results and noticed the questions the kids bombed on. We developed a curriculum map so we could ramp up our kids so that none of them would be retained. We figured this out through our teacher team meetings and that has been very powerful. Anyone can look at our curriculum map and figure out where we are going.

Data System

Boston Public Schools developed MyBPS in 2003 as a means to communicate information and make data useful to administrators and teachers. The secure web-based system contains student performance information on formative and summative assessments, as well as report cards, tips on how to use and interpret the data, links to state standards and learning objectives tied to assessment questions, and copies of students' writing compositions and scores. Interactive graphs displaying student performance data linked to specific questions on the state assessment are also available.

Through MyBPS, users can query the data to answer questions such as "How did my students perform on the English Language Arts multiple choice questions?" or "What was the distribution of student responses on a specific test item?" One administrator commented,

> It's remarkable! You can sort your own class by different subgroups and people who work across the school can look at it. We can see how the district data brings us all back to the school plan. Instead of requiring every teacher to be a data analyst, the tool does it, allowing teachers to focus on learning objectives.

Teachers in the district also spoke favorably of the usefulness of the system. One teacher offered the following example of how data are used in her school:

> We look at a lot of the formative assessments and we are able to see the weak areas. For example, we know that the students did not do well on nonfiction pieces, so that's one of our focuses. We also wanted to make sure that the students could become independent learners and thinkers. Now we are trying to use assessments in our classrooms with the students to show them, "This is where you are," and question them about why they chose certain responses on particular tests.

Similar examples of teachers using data to drive instruction were abundant throughout the district.

Boston is continually working to improve the usefulness of MyBPS by connecting data from other sources to data currently available on the system. District leaders mentioned future plans to make it possible to query the formative assessments and to add student indicators to more closely track secondary school students. The additional student data will be called "MyBPS Indicators." MyBPS Indicators will include non-academic data such as student absences, suspensions, and dropouts. Their purpose will be to help high schools use real-time data to identify and track students at risk of dropping out. Central officer leaders feel that information is necessary, as they believe schools are often surprised at the end of the year to find out which students had dropped out or displayed poor attendance. With the new system, a high school principal will be able to click on the particular indicators to review academic and non-academic data simultaneously to identify potential problems early.

Monitoring

The district conducts curriculum implementation reviews of the middle and high schools that are similar to "mini accreditation visits." Deputy superintendents observe one department at a time to give feedback to every teacher on their classroom instruction. These visits also review how well campus administrators support and monitor instruction. Additionally, school instruction and performance are monitored through "cluster walk-throughs," with a cluster being defined as a feeder pattern. Principals in each cluster decide at the beginning of the year which schools to target for walk-throughs. These walk-throughs are also used as a means to share best practice instructional strategies across schools and to view model programs. District leaders feel the walk-through process has been valuable to them because they are "uncovering concerns much earlier than before, and in much greater quantity."

Accountability System

All district activities center on the unifying goal of Focus on Children II, a five-year plan "to accelerate the continuous improvement of teaching and learning to enable all students to meet high standards." The two main goals are to move students beyond the minimal to the proficient level and to close achievement gaps between different ethnic and income student groups. To monitor school progress towards the goals in Focus for Children II, school performance is monitored several times a year through the Whole School Improvement Plan (WSIP). The WSIP is a document created by each school which identifies several goals each year that are tied to the district's overall goals. The plans are monitored by assistant and deputy super-intendents who spend the majority of their time working directly with schools. The plans are displayed in MyBPS to connect schools and district leaders to each other and add transparency to school performance. In 2006, the WSIPs were updated to include implementation benchmarks for the curriculum and outcome benchmarks tied to academic goals.

Systemic Implementation

Responses from the focus groups with principals and teachers confirmed that most school personnel are comfortable with Boston's data and monitoring systems. Almost every principal and teacher interviewed seemed enthusiastic and comfortable with using data to guide daily decisions. Nicely illustrating the spirit in which data are used and their growing prevalence, one principal commented,

> We monitor performance in many different and exciting ways with whatever data are available. The conversation trickles on down to the deputies who are in the buildings more frequently, and they have conversations with the principals about the data. The conversations are very specific and focus on ownership rather than blame. "What haven't I done as a teacher? Where am I missing? As a teacher, I have a gap." It's not "Children have the gap," but "I have a gap."

Clearly Boston is using data to encourage accountability for the adults in the system rather than viewing all problems as student-driven.

Norfolk Public Schools

Norfolk Public Schools, a three-time Broad Prize finalist and the 2005 winner, is a moderate-sized district with 36,724 students, 58 schools, and 3,363 teachers. The diverse student body consists of 68% African American students, 3% Hispanic students, 27% White students, and 2% Asian American students, with 60% of students eligible for Free or Reduced Price School Lunch (NCES, Common Core of Data, 2004). Norfolk's results demonstrate higher levels of achievement than demographically similar districts in Virginia. Highlights contributing to the district's nominations for and becoming winner of the Broad Prize include:

- Met its adequate yearly progress (AYP) targets in 2004 for 76% of schools.
- Increased the number of elementary students who reached proficiency in reading by 14% in the past four years, and increased the number of middle school students who reached reading proficiency by 12%.
- Increased the number of elementary students who reached proficiency in math by 14% in the past four years, and increased the number of middle school students who reached proficiency in math by 23%.
- Reduced achievement gaps in elementary reading for Hispanic students (by 11%) and middle school math for African American students (by 10%).

The accomplishments of this diverse district with highly mobile Navy families are impressive. When now-retired superintendent John Simpson came to Norfolk in 1998, he thought the district's student performance was "abysmal." Believing that the few pockets of successful schools could be replicated, he strove to duplicate their successes by working with his team to reproduce their practices. This process entailed re-centralizing instructional programs and practices (reducing 54 reading programs to one, for example) and building a cohesive culture through consistent messaging, clear communication to all system levels, and by using a "laser-like focus" on student achievement. Although the district focused somewhat on data before Dr. Simpson's arrival, they strengthened its academic focus and accountability practices with the help of Doug Reeves and his Center for Performance Assessment.

Data Systems and Data-Use

Assessments

The district requires quarterly benchmark assessments at all levels. In 2005, 90% of NPS schools had developed common assessments given at least every month. To help with data collection, many schools have the capability to electronically score their test sheets on site to receive immediate feedback on student achievement. Additionally, the district provides schools with a detailed item analysis per classroom.

District leaders feel the quarterly assessments have been crucial for improving instruction in the district. As one administrator described it,

> There's immediate feedback for the teachers and for the students. The item analysis reports in particular have been very powerful because the teachers use them with their students to discuss the thinking behind student responses. Students can reason through the answers they choose, whether or not they were correct or incorrect answers. This is a huge change.

The benchmark assessments were frequently referenced in school interviews. One department chairman explained that in his school, they review the results to analyze whether missed questions are likely attributed to instruction or to the test itself. He found the process helpful for adjusting instruction and creating alignment within grade levels and subjects. Teachers also voiced appreciation for the cross-school alignment created by the curriculum pacing guides, benchmarks, and common assessments. Explaining the importance of having "everyone teaching the same thing," one teacher said, "It is really neat, because when a student transfers in mid-year, we are working in the same book that was being used at another school."

Instructional alignment across classrooms occurs frequently as teachers meet in "data teams" on a regular basis to review data, make common plans, and adjust instruction. An observation of a high school data team meeting during the 2005 site visit found teachers in a grade-level team meeting reviewing benchmark item analysis results to determine mastery of specific learning objectives. Unhappy with the results, the team decided to review their lesson plans on the weak objectives to understand why students had not learned what the teachers had taught. The teachers also decided to review the lesson plans of teachers who scored higher on those objectives to see if they could glean successful techniques for their own lessons. During the entire meeting the teachers appeared quite comfortable with and accustomed to reviewing data together to boost their instructional practices, with the common and singular goal of improving student achievement.

Data Systems

The district manages its data through two Web-based data systems; one is a data warehouse that allows queries to be run on longitudinal data, and the other is called Assessor, which houses the district's quarterly benchmark assessments. Giving teachers almost immediate results, the quarterly assessments are in the same format as the state assessments, and are scanned into Assessor immediately.

Both data systems give district leaders, principals, and teachers immediate reports displayed graphically. The systems' goal is to provide "24/7" data access to teachers, with results available within one to three days of testing. One interesting comment made by a central office leader was the importance of a subtle detail like adding different colors to the data charts to improve data interpretation for teachers and principals.

Monitoring

Similar to Aldine, Norfolk developed a structured walk-through process to monitor school activities, share ideas, and provide feedback on program implementation and performance. To build a more trusting environment, then-superintendent Dr. Simpson promised the schools that walk-through results would not be tied to teacher evaluations and would not be shared beyond the principals' immediate supervisors. Once comfortable with the process after the first year, teachers and principals were anxious to share walk-through results with central office leaders. Capitalizing on the trust built through the walk-through process, the practice has expanded vertically to include elementary teams visiting high schools and vice versa, with best practice documents being created as an end-product.

Accountability System

One important tool for capturing and communicating data across the system is the district's three-tiered Comprehensive Accountability System (CAS). The CAS is used to hold all levels of the district accountable, including the district, school feeder pattern, school, and classroom levels. Data are compared longitudinally over five years to monitor improvement. Tier I indicators include state- and district-level data, Tier II focuses on school-level data, and Tier III provides a qualitative narrative that describes the context of each school's accountability results. District leaders view the CAS as an important tool for sharing and improving district practices. In addition to creating alignment between the district and school plans, school leaders also see the CAS as a mechanism for gaining district support. One new principal commented,

> The support system is unique and very tight. I was impressed that, once we developed our accountability plans, central office came to us lending support. You don't have to seek it out. If they see something, they give us a call and ask "Is there anything I can do for you?" [The plan] helps us to speak with one voice. It's really critical having the same language.

School performance is also monitored by executive directors and content specialists who review the same campus reports, looking at targets and benchmarks for gap closures. After the review, these administrators meet with principals on a regular basis to look at their data and discuss adjustments. The executive directors also have ongoing discussions about assessment data. As an example, the executive directors make sure that any students with a low third-grade reading score have the appropriate intervention and resources.

Systemic Implementation

Conversations about using data as a positive means to inform instruction and district practices were common throughout the interviews in Norfolk. When asked what practices have had the most impact on improving student performance, the superintendent stated that they used a systemic approach, describing it as "coming at the elephant" from different angles by communicating clear goals and expectations on the classroom, school, feeder pattern, and district levels. Highlighting the importance of measuring the outcomes of those expectations, one principal identified their most important reform as, "Data-driven decision making and accountability. There's no other answer to that. There IS a magic bullet: data-driven decision making."

Other leaders cited Doug Reeves and his Center for Performance Assessment as key to helping the district refine its accountability system through training and tools that enabled staff at all levels to use data as a part of the district's daily culture. Data not only served as a mechanism for driving decisions, but also created common dialogue and set processes for the district, schools, and classrooms. One principal described how Reeves helped him organize his school in vertical data teams. While the public review of data was at first unnerving to his teachers, in the end, he said, they voiced appreciation for the process. "Doug always said the data will provide the buy-in!" said the principal. Several central office administrators agreed that Reeves was a key element in building their accountability system because he "presents a very logical, easy-to-understand researched-based message."

Discussion

All past and present Broad Prize finalists use data to drive instruction and other decision-making processes—possibly one reason why they have been successful in raising student achievement and closing gaps.

Aldine Independent School District, Boston Public Schools, and Norfolk Public Schools have been Broad Prize finalists more than once, and have shown marked increase in student achievement over time while reducing ethnic and income achievement gaps. These three districts have thoughtfully built well-connected systems that prompt daily use of data as a transparent practice from the central office to individual classrooms. Each of these districts began its "road to Broad" upon discovery that its student achievement needed to improve drastically to prepare students for college and skilled careers. Understanding that its goals depended on creating much more cohesion between classrooms, schools, feeder patterns, and the district, each of the three districts began systemic alignment by clearly defining what was to be taught and learned in every grade and level. The major tools used to manage and monitor consistent and correct implementation of curriculum and instruction were various forms of data and monitoring systems.

Data as a Diagnostic Tool

These three districts are driven by the philosophy that engaging in early and frequent intervention can promote student success and prevent unchecked development of larger individual or systemic problems. Through the use of real-time data, teachers, principals, and district leaders can target areas of weakness early instead of waiting until the end of the year "to find out students didn't get it." Many interviewees pointed to their benchmark, quarterly, and common assessments as a key to their success in raising student achievement. Paired with curriculum pacing guides that clearly articulated what teachers should cover in a prescribed time period (but not in a prescribed manner, one should note), benchmark assessments help teachers understand if students are mastering instructional sequences appropriately to move on to the next level. Although these assessments are often district-developed, they are created with the input of teachers.

Teachers, principals, and district staff members said that frequent real-time data helped them identify areas where individual students or groups of students were struggling. Identifying instructional needs and developing appropriate interventions happens often through groups of teachers getting together in data teams or weekly collaborative meetings to analyze results and plan future instruction. Meeting over data not only helps teachers plan and improve instruction, but also serves as an important vehicle for aligning instruction across both horizontal and vertical grade levels. Frequent team meetings are made possible through the availability of common planning time for teachers.

Data as a Monitoring Tool

In addition to implementing frequent assessments and data reviews, all three districts also have overarching systemic tools and processes for monitoring school performance and connecting school and district goals. These tools are implemented and reviewed several times a year and include both summative and formative assessment data. Each of the tools has different features and formats to manage goal-planning processes and strategies. Aldine uses a Baldridge-based Scorecard that includes formative, summative, and walk-through results that directly feed into Action Plans. Scorecards have been implemented at the classroom, grade, feeder-pattern, and district levels. Boston's Whole School Improvement Plan includes formative and summative assessment data tied to school goals that feed into the district's goals. Norfolk's Comprehensive Accountability Plan includes three tiers that contain summative and formative performance data as well as a narrative that analyzes the different data points within the schools' context. All of these monitoring systems are public within the district through a local intranet or through a district website to connect different system levels and create an open accountability environment.

Data are also gathered on overall school and classroom performance through structured walk-through processes. All three districts implement a walk-through process that includes training the walk-through teams and using a rubric to document activities and evaluate targets, which in most cases is classroom instruction. In Norfolk and Aldine, the district leaders took particular care in building a trusting environment prior to implementing the walk-through process. They assured schools and teachers that walk-through data would not be used for formal evaluations and would not go directly to central office, and that the walk-throughs would always be treated as opportunities to offer support, share practices, and align activities across the K-12 system. Once teachers and principals found that the process was used solely to improve instruction, they felt comfortable and open about having outsiders visit their classrooms.

Data Management Systems

Aldine, Boston, and Norfolk developed powerful data management systems to collect and analyze data. The most important feature of these systems is the ability for district leaders, principals, and teachers to access and query data easily and on an ongoing basis. The data management systems in all three districts provide summative state assessment results and formative benchmark, quarterly and common assessments results. The differences in the data management systems vary only slightly, with Boston having the most interactive and inclusive tools, including data training modules, links to lesson plans, and interactive graphs connecting performance results to specific questions.

Additionally, all three districts provide or plan to provide student demographic data within the same data management system so that student progress and course placement can be easily monitored. Norfolk houses its summative and formative assessment data within two different data tools, and this is one of the most obvious differences among these districts' systems. Impressively, all three districts have invested the time necessary for creating and updating their systems to ensure they are easily accessible and user-friendly. Each district gradually introduced the data management systems to the users, providing training to central office leaders, principals, and teachers, resulting in successful high-volume use.

Systemic Implementation and Culture Building

Creating an atmosphere that is comfortable with frequent, if not daily, scrutiny of student, teacher, and administrator performance requires care and consideration. Multiple interviews conducted in Aldine, Boston, and Norfolk supported the belief that data were truly used as "a flashlight rather than a hammer" for improving student achievement. Statements like "We looked at the data and just didn't get it right, so we worked together to find a better way" were frequent, and we heard those statements at all levels of these three districts.

Accustomed to witnessing the pressure of data management systems trickle down from the superintendent to teachers, we were surprised at how comfortable and excited teachers and principals were in analyzing and discussing data results openly and honestly. Several leaders in Norfolk and Boston referred to the process as acknowledging and addressing "the brutal facts" that are revealed through the use of tools to disaggregate data by various programs and student groups. In addition to practices around data, it seemed that all the practices within these districts, including goal setting, curriculum development, and professional development selection involved multiple stakeholders functioning within a "customer-service" framework.

Conclusion

The data-use commonalities among these three districts include frequent student performance data collection through various types of formative and summative assessments; diagnostic and monitoring tools that provide ongoing feedback on performance at all system levels; a comprehensive data management system that is easy to access and use; and development of a culture that uses data to guide instructional decisions rather than for punishment. Other practices supporting data-use included training and supports for principals and teachers to use data, and opportunities for leaders, principals, and teachers to meet for the purpose of analyzing and discussing data results. The end result is that teachers meet frequently—often daily—in all three districts to analyze data, plan instruction, and share best practices. The ensuing dialogue around data has proven to be important, as it has led to problem-solving and finding ways to improve and align instruction and instructional supports.

The "best practice" uses of data as illustrated by the three featured Broad Prize finalists are valuable for two reasons. First, they demonstrate how higher performing school systems have focused on the most strategic and effective ways for improving student learning by using data as a guide. All three districts assert that data have been an important catalyst for increasing student achievement and narrowing achievement gaps. Second, they demonstrate that a culture of trust can coexist with the frequent use of data, given the right supports and structures. When district leaders, school administrators, teachers, and even students open a dialogue about data, these systems begin to inspire personal and collective accountability to the same goal: student success.

Notes

1. Bloom's Taxonomy identifies six types of knowledge: knowledge, comprehension, application, analysis, synthesis, and evaluation. Bloom was an educational expert who believed that learning involves, or should involve, moving from simple to more complex kinds of thinking.
2. The Baldrige Model for Performance Excellence is a process of continuous improvement that has been used in business. Named after former Secretary of Commerce Malcolm Baldrige, the Baldrige criteria are a blueprint for developing quality business practices. In 1998, the Malcolm Baldrige National Quality Award was expanded into healthcare and education and an education application of Baldrige was developed called BiE (Baldrige in Education). The criteria are built upon a set of core values and concepts that include visionary leadership, customer-driven excellence, valuing employees and partners, management by fact, and a focus on results and creating value.

References

Datnow, A., Park, V., & Wohlstetter, P. (2007). *Achieving with data: How high-performing school systems use data to improve instruction for elementary students.* Los Angeles, University of Southern California, Rossier School of Education, Center on Educational Governance.

Golden, M. (2005). Making strides with educational data. *T.H.E. Journal, 32*(12), 38–40.

Heritage, M., & Chen, E. (2005). Why data skills matter in school improvement. *Phi Delta Kappan, 86*(9), 707–710.

Kerr, K. A., Marsh, J. A., Ikemoto, G. S., Darilek, H., & Barney, H. (2006). Strategies to promote data use for instructional improvement: Actions, outcomes, and lessons from three urban districts. *American Journal of Education, 112*(4), 496–520.

Lachat, M. A., & Smith, S. (2004). *Data-use in urban high schools.* Providence, RI: The Education Alliance at Brown University.

Ramnarine, S. (2004). Impacting student achievement through data-driven decision-making. *MultiMedia & Internet@Schools, 11*(4), 33–35.

Renzulli, P. (2005). Testing the limits of one-stop data access. *T.H.E. Journal, 32*(12), 45–46.

Rudy, D. W., & Conrad, W. H. (2004). Breaking down the data. *American School Board Journal, 191*(2), 39–41.

Supovitz, J., & Klein, (2003). *Mapping a course for improved student learning: How innovative schools systemically use student performance data to guide improvement.* Philadelphia, University of Pennsylvania, Graduate School of Education, Consortium for Policy Research in Education.

Wayman, J. C., Cho, V. & Johnston, M. T. (2007). *The data-informed district: A district-wide evaluation of data use in the Natrona County School District.* Austin: The University of Texas at Austin.

12

School System Strategies for Supporting Data Use

Amanda Datnow and Vicki Park
University of Southern California

Introduction

> Imagine an afternoon when a teacher can sit down at a computer desktop and quickly sort through reams of data she'll use to plan lessons for the next day. . . . She'll compare every student's achievement against state standards to decide which students need review and which ones are ready to move on. . . . That technological capability can only be found in the rare classroom today, but some experts say that such a data-rich approach to instruction will soon be common place.
>
> (Hoff, 2006, p. 12)

As part of a study of data-driven decision making, we were fortunate to visit schools and districts where such practices are indeed becoming commonplace. In this chapter, we capture the work of four school systems that were identified as leaders in data-driven decision making. As we show in our case studies of these school systems, the gathering and examining of data is merely a starting point to developing a culture and system of continuous improvement that places student learning at the heart of its efforts. Our study reveals that there is not one way to be a performance-driven system. All of these schools and school systems approached data-driven decision making differently—and all achieved successes in the process. At the same time, the school systems we studied had many features in common that seem to support the effective use of data. In this chapter, we highlight the choices and tradeoffs made by these schools and school systems.

Background

With the advent of the No Child Left Behind Act (NCLB), the push for increased accountability and improved student achievement in American public schools has never been greater. Prominent educational researchers have long decried education as a field in which practitioners make decisions based on intuition, gut instinct, or fads (Slavin, 2002). Supporters of data-driven decision-making practices argue that effective data use enables school systems to learn more about their schools, pinpoint successes and challenges, identify areas of improvement, and help evaluate the effectiveness of programs and practices (Mason, 2002). In fact, the theory of action underlying NCLB requires that educators have the will and expertise to analyze, interpret, and use data so that they can make informed decisions in all areas of education, ranging from professional development to student learning.

Previous research, though largely without comparison groups, suggests that data-driven decision making has the potential to increase student performance (Alwin, 2002; Doyle, 2003; Johnson, 1999, 2000; Lafee, 2002; McIntire, 2002; Peterson, 2007). When school-level educators become knowledgeable about data use, they can more effectively review their existing capacities, identify weaknesses, and better chart plans for improvement (Earl & Katz, 2006). A recent national study of the impact of NCLB found that districts are indeed allocating resources to increase the use of student achievement data as a way to inform instruction in schools identified as needing improvement (Center on Education Policy, 2004; see also Borja, 2006). Student achievement data can be used for various purposes, including evaluating progress toward state and district standards, monitoring student performance and improvement, determining where assessments converge and diverge, and judging the efficacy of local curriculum and instructional practices (Crommey, 2000).

However, data need to be actively used to improve instruction in schools, and individual schools often lack the capacity to implement what research suggests (Diamond & Spillane, 2004; Ingram, Louis, & Schroeder, 2004; Marsh et al., 2005; Mason, 2000; Petrides & Nodine, 2005; Wohlstetter, Van Kirk, Robertson, & Mohrman, 1997). To address this problem, districts have invested in management information systems and professional development to develop expertise and capacity at the school level (see, for example, Borja, 2006). Some districts have also contracted with external agencies and consultants to assist in their capacity-building efforts district-wide (Jacobson, 2007; Marsh et al., 2005).

Similarly, in the charter school arena, education service providers, including education management organizations (EMOs) and charter management organizations (CMOs), have also sought to build capacity in schools and districts (Colby, Smith, & Shelton, 2005). Several expressly utilize data-driven decision making as one of their key pillars. For example, a case study of an Edison school found that the EMO helped to cultivate a culture of data use and data-driven practice through its curriculum, assessment, and organizational structure (Sutherland, 2004).

In spite of system-level investments to build capacity and expertise for data-driven decision making, many studies conclude that teachers are not actively using data to guide planning and instructional decisions (Earl & Katz, 2006). Teachers need not only the capacity to use data, but also the empowerment and the will to do so. Thus, how can data-driven decision-making plans be most effectively executed at the system level? This chapter addresses this question.

Research Methods

During the 2006–2007 school year, we conducted a qualitative case study of four school systems to capture the details of data-driven instructional decision making. The study was supported by a grant from NewSchools Venture Fund, with funding from the Gates and Hewlett Foundations. Our study included two mid-size urban school districts and two nonprofit charter management organizations. Our rationale for including both regular public school districts and charter management organizations in this study was based upon research suggesting that both types of school systems are engaging in innovative practices in data-driven decision making. These particular school systems were chosen on the basis of being leaders in using performance results in general—and data in particular—for instructional decision making, which seems to have led to improved student achievement over time (see Datnow, Park, & Wohlstetter, 2007).

In collaboration with NewSchools, we chose four school systems from a list of over 25 school systems that had been recommended as fitting our criteria. We narrowed down the list of possible sites after reviewing system websites, speaking with experts in the field, and conducting phone interviews with system leaders. While acknowledging the successes they had experienced in becoming more data-driven, all system leaders were also careful to note that their work was "in progress." Our study included the four school systems described in Table 12.1.

These school systems have obvious differences in size, history, and mission. Garden Grove and Aldine are mid-size urban public school districts that have been in operation for many years. Both have histories of steadily improving student achievement over the past decade. Aspire and Achievement First are relatively new organizations, the former having been founded in 1998, and the latter in 2003. They are both networks of charter schools that operate "home offices" that function similarly to school districts' central offices, providing oversight in accounting, curriculum, governance, and organization. All four school systems are composed primarily of schools in urban locations or those serving large numbers of low-income students and students of color.

We studied two schools in each of the four school systems, with a focus on practices in the elementary Grades (K-8). These schools were recommended to us by system personnel because of their high level of engagement in data-driven decision making. Our study included six elementary schools, one middle school, and one high school serving ninth graders only. Table 12.2 gives a detailed demographic picture of the individual schools and the systems themselves.

Table 12.1 Overview of system sample.

System	No. of schools	Location	Type
Garden Grove Unified School District	70	CA	Regular public school district
Aldine Independent School District	63	TX	Regular public school district
Achievement First Public Schools	6	NY; CT	Nonprofit charter management organization
Aspire Public Schools	14	CA	Nonprofit charter management organization

Table 12.2 Characteristics of schools and systems.

| | Grades | Size | Race/ethnicity | | | | | Free-lunch status | LEP status | |
			% Afr. Am.	% Asian or Pac. Isl.	% Latino	% White	% Nat. Amer.	% Eligible	% ELL	Location
California										
Garden Grove		49,574	1	31	53	15	<1	60	47	
School A	K-6	571	<1	72	11	17	<1	33	25	Urban
School B	K-3, 4-6	1,223	1	25	67	7	<1	73	56	Urban
Aspire		3,600								
School A	K-8	405	15	0	72	0	0	88	66	Urban
School B	K-5	351	9	13	37	35	<1	34	30	Suburban
Connecticut										
Achievement First	K-8	1,539								
School A	5-8	270	64	<1	33	2	0	84	10	Urban
School B	K-3	218	75	<1	22	2	0	77	5	Urban
Texas										
Aldine	PK-12	57,931	32	2	61	6	<1	78	27	
School A	K-4	609	15	2	81	4	0	86	66	Urban fringe
School B	9	898	20	2	73	5	0	78	12	Urban fringe

Note: All data reported are for 2005–2006. Figures have been rounded to the nearest percent.

Our site visits to the school systems and schools took place between March and May 2006. We interviewed two to three administrators from the home or central office, including the superintendent, assistant superintendent (in three of the four systems) or chief academic officer, and the director of research and/or assessment. At each school, we interviewed the principal, often an assistant principal, and a minimum of five teachers across grade levels. We also interviewed lead teachers where possible. We conducted approximately 70 interviews across the four school systems and schools. At each school, we also conducted informal observations of the school, classrooms and relevant meetings. Finally, we gathered a plethora of documents at the school and system levels that were pertinent to our study.

All interviews were taped and transcribed verbatim at the conclusion of the site visits. Interview transcripts were then coded with the aid of HyperResearch, a qualitative data analysis software package. We initially coded the data according to an early conceptual framework we had developed about the role of the system in supporting school-level data-driven decision making. The coded data were then used to develop detailed case reports on each system in the study. These case reports were organized according to a common outline, thus facilitating cross-site analysis.

Findings

Our findings are organized around the key strategies that we identified systems using to support data-driven decision making. These include:

(1) Building a foundation for data-driven decision making;
(2) Establishing a culture of data use and continuous improvement;
(3) Investing in an information management system;
(4) Selecting the right data;
(5) Building school capacity for data-driven decision making; and
(6) Analyzing and acting on data to improve performance.

Each of these is discussed below.

Building a Foundation for Data-Driven Decision Making

Before implementing strategies for data-driven decision making, these school systems invested time and resources in building a solid foundation for system-wide improvement efforts. Integral to this process was establishing specific, measurable goals at the system, school, classroom, and individual student levels. Once such goals were established, school system leaders concentrated on developing and monitoring the implementation of a system-wide curriculum. A coherent curriculum got educators on the "same page" and moving in the same direction, which was essential in helping them gather, organize, discuss, and act on data about student achievement.

Setting Student Achievement Goals   The four public school systems we studied approached goal-setting in a number of different ways; however, all melded the need to meet larger accountability demands with goals tailored to the needs of their own students and schools. For most school systems, taking the time and space to develop specific goals geared toward their needs ended up being a pivotal aspect of using data purposefully. Setting up system goals enabled school leaders to grapple with and reflect on their history, their current progress, and future plans. Thus, goal-setting was a critical step to beginning the process of continuous improvement.

All of the school systems we studied set goals that were both strongly influenced by, and tightly interwoven with state and federal accountability systems. As one principal in Aldine stated, "Accountability is a strong force for change. It truly is the change agent." While goal-setting was generally led by administrative teams in the central or home office, often principals, teachers, and other key school-level stakeholders were involved in the process.

In concert with system-wide goals, schools also formulated goals specific to the needs of their students and communities. Often, schools would establish school-wide goals, then grade-level goals, classroom goals, and in some cases individual student goals. Again, the emphasis seemed to be on making goals meaningful in the local context.

Additionally, school staff developed goals pertaining not only to student progress but also to their own professional responsibilities and learning. For example, one principal in Garden Grove met regularly with teachers to establish goals regarding student data. These goal-setting conferences helped to guide each teacher's instructional and professional development plan for the year. Both CMOs required teachers to create annual professional growth plans. For instance, one school in Achievement First expected teachers to establish goals in three areas: student learning, personal/professional, and community. Ultimately, both at the system and school levels, goals were tied to improving learning and instruction.

Developing and Monitoring a System-Wide Curriculum   Data-driven decision making was greatly facilitated when clear, grade-by-grade curricula were adopted system-wide, when high-quality materials were aligned to the curriculum, and when pacing guides clearly described the breadth and depth of content to be taught. Both districts, Garden Grove and Aldine, had put into place system-wide curriculum, accompanied by a pacing plan and instructional materials. Implementation of the curriculum was closely monitored for several years before data-driven decision making came to the forefront of their policy agendas. For example, Aldine developed a pacing plan in 1997 and framed it as "you're going to follow it, and it's non-negotiable." The plan followed the state standards and was divided into six-week periods. At the same time, the district curriculum had flexibility built into it. As a district administrator shared, "the text does not drive the curriculum, and you're not going to walk in and find everybody using the same things in the book at the same time." A teacher reinforced this perspective and noted, "the district gives us lesson plans, but they don't tell us how to teach them."

The CMOs, on the other hand, were more recently moving toward requiring that a consistent, system-wide curriculum be used across schools. Interestingly, it was the analysis of data that led them to become more invested in this. For example, the Aspire system decided to focus on the "literary response and analysis" strand of the standards after scores on the California Standards Test (CST)—the state's standardized assessment—indicated that this was an organization-wide weakness.

The existence and implementation of a system-wide curriculum facilitated data-driven decision making in these school systems, as it allowed all teachers to be "on the same page" in their discussions regarding data about student learning. On the other hand, the tradeoff was that teachers at the local level had less autonomy. However, it seems that a balance can be struck, with a district pacing plan that allows some flexibility to account for the needs of individual students, classrooms, or teachers. Several educators pointed out that allowing flexibility to use different instructional strategies is a necessary component in fostering data use.

Establishing a Culture of Data Use and Continuous Improvement

Establishing a culture of data use was also a critical component of each system's efforts. Leaders within the school systems created explicit norms and expectations regarding data use, and principals followed through at the school level by reinforcing system expectations. Through their efforts to build data-driven cultures, school systems also attempted to foster mutual accountability between schools and the central office, which helped to build a commitment to continuous improvement.

System Efforts to Foster the Culture of Data Use   System leaders found it was essential to create explicit expectations for data use among all principals and teachers. System leaders were keenly aware of the importance of hiring staff that would support their belief in data-driven decision making. In some ways, the CMOs had a distinct advantage here. Because they were starting schools "from scratch," they could hire teachers and principals who bought into their expectation of data-driven decision making. During the interview process, teachers were probed on their comfort with, and openness toward using data. Many of the teachers hired in Aspire and Achievement First schools were new to the profession and have thus incorporated data-driven decision making from the beginning.

The school districts, Aldine and Garden Grove, obviously had to cultivate an interest in data-driven decision making with a wider variety of teachers, many of whom had been in the system for some time. They are working to create an atmosphere around data that would gain buy-in from different staff members, as the superintendent in Garden Grove explained, "by making data non-threatening." She added, "Just like for doctors, lab reports are not a bad thing." Instead of blaming a teacher or a school for poor performance on the tests, district leaders focused on examining the data. Gaps evidenced by tests were addressed in a manner that invited help from the district.

School Efforts to Foster the Culture of Data Use   In alignment with the system, school site leaders also took up the task of fostering a culture of data use. Principals became adept at conveying the district's message about how to approach data. One principal told her staff that data serve as a resource for asking questions and making improvements. She shared that when a teacher expresses sentiments such as, "this is so depressing, I worked so hard, and these are my scores," she responded with, "Don't go there. Don't look at it that way. What we need to do then is to say, okay, what can we do differently next time?"

All in all, teachers came to view data as absolutely relevant and necessary. One teacher exclaimed, "I don't know what I ever did without it." Teachers commented that data are helpful in ensuring that teachers are not acting by instincts or "shooting darts blindfolded." Furthermore, a sixth-grade teacher mentioned that data "open your eyes more" because they help teachers realize that teaching does not always lead to learning. In some cases, the presence and focus on data seems to help cause a shift in thinking about the utility of data.

Often, school leaders set expectations for how meetings regarding data would be conducted. They took time to cover such issues as how to behave in meetings, what materials teachers and principals were expected to bring to meetings, what not to bring (e.g., papers to grade), and how to compile data binders. While these types of concerns seem very basic, educators indicated that these discussions helped set the tone for accountability among the staff members and ensured that meetings were purposeful.

Investing in an Information Management System

Merely having data does not ensure that data-driven decision making will take place. In order to conduct meaningful analysis and to use data to create effective action plans, each of the school systems had to grapple with organizing data in an accessible format and presenting them in a comprehensible manner. Therefore, they had to figure out how to organize, prioritize, and manage data.

A User-Friendly Data Management System Investing in a user-friendly data management system is among the most important actions a school system can take in becoming more data-driven. Three of the four school systems in this study had data management software systems that allowed them easily to run reports that display student results on interim and state assessments, and sometimes on other assessments as well. Timely and useful reports of student achievement data on benchmarks and other assessments were all integral parts of an effective data management system, particularly for teachers and school site leaders. The most useful reports at the school level were those that quickly identified the students who needed extra help, and specified in which particular areas or on which learning standards help was needed.

Each of the school systems found that its needs for a more complex data system grew as their use of data increased. In fact, some system leaders acknowledged that early in their efforts, simple software programs such as Microsoft Excel served their needs, whereas later, as they began to ask more complex questions about the data, more sophisticated systems were required.

System leaders in Garden Grove and Aldine both explained that they worked in partnership with external providers in building their own data systems, which have since been marketed to other districts. Aldine uses a system called Triand and Garden Grove uses a system called Data Director. Aspire used Edusoft, a system which it purchased "off the shelf" rather than having software customized for its needs. Achievement First was in the process of negotiating with an external provider, Acsys, to build a data management system to meet its specific needs.

Utilizing Personnel to Assist in Data Management and Use   The four school systems studied offered differing levels of support by personnel to assist in data management and use. In all cases, there was an individual at the district or home office who directed data management efforts. This person performed the critical role of supporting both the system and the schools in obtaining the data and reports necessary to make decisions. Interestingly, rather than being statisticians or researchers, these individuals all shared the background of having worked in schools, often as a principal and teacher, or had worked in a school support capacity. This appears to be a change from the past, when many districts and other school organizations were staffed with individuals who had detailed statistical knowledge, but less experience in how to translate the data into valuable information for schools.

These school systems varied in the amount of support provided at the school level. However, most schools had at least one designated person who assisted with data management and use. In Achievement First schools, principals were instructed and expected to support teachers in data use. They actually ran the analyses of interim assessments themselves. In Aldine, each school site had a designated assessment coordinator and a technology specialist.

Informally, leadership team members and other teachers at school sites became "data experts." Across all of the school systems, teachers named one or two teachers to whom they specifically turned to assist them with using the data system with things like inputting results, analyzing results, and creating reports. Many of these teachers took the initiative to learn how to gather and analyze data—ultimately for the purpose of sharing their knowledge with the rest of the staff. In Aspire schools, lead teachers took informal roles to assist in data use. Garden Grove also trained teams of teachers from each school to serve as leaders regarding data-driven decision making. They also had teachers on special assignment working at the district level on issues related to data use, and two full-time district staff dedicated to assisting schools in this effort.

Selecting the Right Data

All four of these school systems grappled with selecting the right data that would best inform the work of teachers and administrators. While student assessment data were an integral part of the data-driven decision-making process, school systems drew upon many different types of information—student achievement data, instructional practice data, and goal implementation data—to help guide improvement efforts.

A Diverse Array of Student Learning and Instructional Practice Data   Educators across all four school systems stressed the importance of collecting and basing decisions upon multiple sources of data. One teacher remarked, "I think it is important to make sure that you know what you're measuring and you know the limitations of your data collection." Aldine delineated between "trailing vs. leading" data, an indication of how different types of data are used and for what purposes. The assistant superintendent described "trailing" data as "older data . . . it's done" (e.g., state test scores) that would not lead to teachers changing their instruction immediately. "Leading" data are assessments that are administered more frequently, such as the district benchmark tests, which help teachers assess what standards need to be retaught in the short term. Aldine used trailing data to write the action plan, and leading data to revise the action plan and to monitor progress toward goals. In addition to state tests and benchmark assessments, educators also used curriculum-embedded tests, teacher-created quizzes, and scoring guides. Student achievement results, usually emphasizing interim and state assessments, were the main data used to monitor student learning; however, student behavior and discipline data were also considered to be important elements in improving learning and instruction.

System-Wide Interim Assessments Aligned to Standards   The regular administration of benchmark (or interim) assessments was a key feature of these performance-driven school systems: the tests served as guideposts for future instruction and indicated whether or not students had mastered and retained standards. In some cases, the same benchmark assessment was administered at approximately the same time across all of a system's schools. This enabled comparisons across schools and allowed teachers to collaborate on data analysis and action planning. Other school systems allowed schools to decide when to administer the benchmarks, though this allowed only for within-school planning and not for comparisons or planning across schools.

Locating or creating interim assessments that are well aligned with the local curriculum and with state standards was a challenge in all of the school systems we studied. However, most have now settled on assessments with which they are fairly satisfied, at least at the elementary level. Garden Grove developed its benchmark assessments through a combination of curriculum embedded and external assessments with the help of outside consultants. In Aldine, benchmark assessments were originally designed by the district but are now supplemented by the state's Regional Service Center. According to the superintendent, district benchmarks have been shared free of charge and have "traveled all over the state." In Aldine, the district is also trying to align student grades with the district benchmark and state assessments. The superintendent noted that, "It gets very embarrassing for a principal to have to explain to parents, your child has made all As and Bs, but he can't pass this test." The four school systems studied administered benchmark assessments frequently, somewhere between three times a year to as often as every six weeks.

The four systems understood that assessment data needed to be timely if they were to be useful for improving instruction. However, each school system had its own unique way of scoring the assessments and various turnaround times for doing so. In Garden Grove, assessments were collected by testing clerks at the school immediately after they were administered; the clerks then took the tests to the district office, scanned them, and had the data uploaded into Data Director within two days. Achievement First was the only school system that required teachers to score the tests themselves and enter the data into a Microsoft Excel template. The template was then given to the principal, who compiled class- and school-level reports. The results were used to plan classroom instruction for the next six weeks, leading up to the next interim assessment. Achievement First was in the process of developing a customized, automated system that would be used to score, store, and analyze benchmark assessment data.

Using Implementation Data and Other Sources of Information   At the system level, all the CMOs and districts also gathered and used other types of data related to improving overall system performance. Data regarding the implementation of action plans, curriculum programs, and goal progress were all used to pinpoint areas needing improvement. Assessing implementation helped these school systems fine-tune their next courses of action.

Data were constantly used to examine instructional practices and to determine an intervention focus (e.g., student, teacher, or standard). Beyond formal evaluation methods, teachers and administrators at one school also gathered informal observational data. For example, a teacher at one Aldine school noticed that across practice state tests, one student's reading score would fluctuate from 30% to 75%. The teacher flagged those results, observed the student taking the next test, and realized that some of the test-taking strategies she had been practicing with her students were actually slowing this student down.

At one Aspire school, the leadership team began tape-recording its data discussions to improve these conversations and to monitor group progress. The leadership team discussed what they would want to see, what was actually observed when the video was reviewed, and how they could better facilitate the meetings. Garden Grove used "Action Walks" to assess the implementation of programs.

Building School Capacity for Data-Driven Decision Making

The school systems we studied worked hard to build capacity by empowering educators to use data to inform instruction at the school level. The key strategies they undertook to empower educators were investing in professional development, providing support for staff in how to use data and modeling data discussions, and structuring time for teacher collaboration.

Professional Development on Data Use   Professional development regarding data management systems and data use was an important strategy for building people's capacity in all four school systems. The monitoring of student performance and analysis of data were framed not as auxiliary duties or distractions, but rather as central tools for improving instructional practices and learning. Therefore, a great deal of professional conversation and meeting time focused on student data.

All of the school systems provided ongoing professional development support to principals in the area of data-driven decision making, as well as more generally. Much of this support was provided by central office staff. The training typically took place in conjunction with the adoption of a data system or a set of new practices, and training was also made available to all new teachers at the beginning of the school year. For example, new teachers in Achievement First schools received one day of training in data use, which involved grading a mock interim assessment, conducting data analysis, and then participating in a mock conversation with the principal about their six-week instructional plan. Across all four school systems, ongoing training was also available to anyone who asked for it. Garden Grove even had a tutorial on its data management system posted on the district's website.

The CMOs tended to provide most of the professional development training in-house, whereas the districts did a combination of in-house and outsourced trainings. Aldine district staff had worked extensively with an external consultant and researcher named Larry Lezotte, who focused on effective schools and on how to use data to identify the root causes of problems and challenges in raising student achievement. Garden Grove worked with external educational organizations to help teachers learn about goal-setting and using their data management system.

Whereas teachers in the CMOs appeared to receive more direct professional development from their central office staff, in the districts, principals and lead teachers tended to be the main source of building professional capacity for the teaching staff. The districts seemed to focus on developing site-level capacity by using district or external resources sparingly to train a small number of school staff, then expected those staff members to train their colleagues. In most of these school systems, direct aid was provided to struggling teachers. In fact, leaders often believed that it was incumbent upon them to support and instruct staff members who were uncomfortable accessing or utilizing data. Administrators might hand out copies of the electronic information until individuals became more adept at using the system. In some cases, the leadership team facilitated the use of data by breaking down data by grade level or by classroom as needed. Lead teachers and coaches might also conduct the analysis for teachers and then visit a teacher's classroom to model a lesson. In sum, district and school leaders not only modeled high expectations and professional accountability, but also took responsibility to build data-driven decision-making capacity directly within their schools.

Along with gaining more buy-in, helping staff members to use data appropriately and thoughtfully remained an ongoing effort. Expressing a sentiment echoed by several teachers across these school systems, one teacher in Aldine remarked that gathering and disaggregating data was not the problem, but having training on what to do with the data and how to read it more carefully would be welcomed. When asked about what schools should avoid, a teacher stated, "Don't just throw the data out there and expect the teachers to be able to pick them up and run with it." Principals from district schools indicated that they needed to develop the skills and capacity to have "quality conversations" around data.

Building teacher capacity for effective data use seemed to go hand-in-hand with building instructional knowledge and skills. Some teachers expressed frustration about assessing so frequently; they constantly asked, "How am I supposed to teach differently?" Although the use of data could pinpoint areas for improvement and areas of strength, data alone could not help improve student learning. Without professional development to build instructional knowledge for reteaching, differentiating instruction, and scaffolding students, teachers did not have the tools to utilize data to make improvements.

Time for Within-School Collaboration   The school systems we studied also supported their schools by establishing time for teachers to learn from one another. One administrator observed that the key to making data relevant was developing working relationships between staff, because "without collaboration and collegiality, data is impossible." Teachers relied heavily on one another for support, new instructional strategies, and discussions about data. In fact, participants across all systems and levels we spoke with stressed the importance of having built-in collaboration time; this was seen as a crucial factor in developing mutual trust between educators and for sharing knowledge to improve practice. A common sentiment was that "you can't do it alone"; in fact, "we do it together" was a common refrain across many of our conversations with teachers.

Most of the school systems devoted frequent and substantial time to reviewing data and planning accordingly. Aldine and Aspire not only had weekly structured data discussion times, but teachers also had daily instructional planning time within grade levels or partner teams. The ways in which schools structured time around data discussions was probably the most important scaffolding for continuous improvement. Most schools had early dismissal for students in order to provide two to three hours of uninterrupted time for data discussions. At Aspire, teachers also had daily preparation time (50 minutes every day for fourth/fifth-grade teachers). As noted by the principal, "it's better to have well-planned instruction than just have [kids] in the room." Additionally, there was built-in time for discussions around data and instruction. At least once a month, two meetings were devoted to team data discussions. Another meeting was set up for similar discussion between instructional coaches and teams. The last meeting of the month was used by the principal, leadership team, and coaches to look at data together to decide which teachers needed instructional support or which students needed intervention.

All of the school systems recognized that data-driven decision making was enhanced when educators shared data not only within schools, but also across them. These interschool networks helped to strengthen connections and spread innovation across sites. While most data discussions still occurred at the school level or between an individual school and the central office, the districts and CMOs we studied were attempting to structure data discussion across schools.

Analyzing and Acting on Data   In addition to building capacity and creating structures to foster data-driven decision making, school system leaders developed tools and processes to help principals, teachers, and other staff members to act on data. All four school systems provided immediate feedback to schools on student achievement and progress toward meeting their goals. The systems also created explicit data analysis protocols and goal-monitoring reports for administrators, teachers, and in some cases for students as well.

Tools to Help Teachers Discuss and Act on Data   The school systems found that they had to develop tools in order to ensure that discussions about classroom-level data occurred and that actions were taken as a result of these conversations. All of the school systems developed some type of discussion template that typically began with a discussion of basic trends and then delved into more detail regarding strengths, weaknesses, grade-level trends, and ethnic, gender, and language subgroup trends. These discussions were then generally followed by brainstorming on strategies and action plans. These discussions typically took place after the results from benchmark assessments had been analyzed and often arose even more frequently.

In three of the four school systems we studied, such discussions occurred primarily among teams of teachers, often facilitated by a lead teacher. For example, Aspire instituted a "cycle of inquiry" process. Although details of the process differed slightly from school to school, all Aspire schools engaged in structured data discussions around student achievement and instructional data. Most schools conducted the cycle in a meeting held every three weeks. Groups met in either multi-age-level or subject area teams to examine data from benchmark assessments and develop action plans focusing on instructional strategies. At one school, every two weeks on Wednesday afternoons, grade-level teams gathered to discuss data in a meeting facilitated by the grade-level lead teacher. Teachers were asked to prepare ahead of time by filling out data summary sheets. They were also required to bring in an assessment (e.g., pre- and post-test, benchmark, or unit test). They typically shared what worked well, areas of struggles, and their action plans.

Tools for Monitoring Progress Toward Goals   In most of these school systems, every school's progress toward goals was monitored, reviewed, and assessed regularly. Both Aspire and Garden Grove produced reports detailing each school's progress toward achieving the school system's goals; these reports included student achievement data, enrollment patterns, and areas where growth was needed. In Aldine, the district required that each school submit a "Scorecard" every six weeks that reported measures of student achievement by subject, data on student behavior and discipline, and data on parent engagement. For each area, the report included both the actual scores and the variance from the target scores. After scorecards were compiled by administrators and teachers at the site level, they were reported to area superintendents.

Aldine schools were also required to have action plans at the system and campus levels. Each campus had an action plan that detailed its goals and uses of data as evidence of progress. Each grade level and department—and in some cases, individual teachers—were also expected to develop action plans. One assistant principal referred to the action plan as "a living, working document" that was constantly revised and updated based on data that were gathered and examined by the school site.

Tools for Engaging Students in Data Discussions   Most of the school systems were moving toward engaging students in goal-setting and in discussions about data. In particular, teachers seemed to be leading the way in fostering student-level discussions by developing data analysis tools to guide them. At Aldine, departments of teachers created several tools such as the Student Analysis Sheet, which included item analysis and student reflection questions, such as, "What was your target score? On a scale of 1–5 how much effort did you put in? What skills do you need to work on? What will you do to improve those skills?"

Aspire also developed tools to encourage student use of data. In one Aspire school, all of the teachers with whom we spoke mentioned analyzing assessments with their students. Some teachers graphed their class results for student discussions. One teacher used the class results of one benchmark assessment to conduct a math lesson on median and mode. Another teacher made bi-weekly graphs of math, reading, and writing benchmark scores, showing the class average and the names of students who performed above the goal of 85% proficient.

Overall, the schools were becoming increasingly adept at getting students involved in using data to help improve their own achievement. It is important to note that the purpose of this was not to blame the students or "pass the buck," but rather to help students become more engaged in and accountable for their own learning.

Conclusion and Implications

Our goal in this chapter was to identify the key strategies used by school systems that were leaders in using data for instructional decision making and improving student achievement. We found that the general actions taken by the four school systems in our study—each having a unique history, context, and mission—were actually quite similar. However, when one delves more deeply into their processes for data-driven decision making, we found that each system and school approached the process a little differently, in ways that made sense to them given the goals they were trying to achieve. Each system also built upon different strengths, as well as liabilities.

Although all four of the school systems made great strides in the area of data-driven decision making, they identified areas for further development. Managing and prioritizing data continued to be a challenge. All four also identified the need to expand the types of data collected and used for school improvement efforts. System and school leaders also acknowledged that helping staff members to use data thought-fully was an ongoing effort. In other words, sustaining a culture of continuous improvement through the use of data-driven decision making requires a continual investment in data management resources, including both human and social capital.

In addition, the study reported in this chapter helps to lay the groundwork for future investigations of the role of the central or home office in supporting data-driven decision making. The findings of this study convince us that school system leaders play a critical role in supporting schools in using data, and there is still much to learn about their work in this area. First, we suspect that the process of data-driven decision making in elementary and secondary schools will be different. We are currently undertaking a new study that focuses on secondary school data use.

Second, we believe it is important to examine further how school systems grapple with educators who are resistant to using data. The schools we focused on in this study were those in which most educators were excited about using data, but all system leaders acknowledged that there were other schools that were less enthusiastic. Third, we think it is important to gather more information on how school systems garner board, community, and union support for data-driven decision making. By virtue of their unique histories, the districts and CMOs we studied did not face major challenges in these areas; however, we suspect a lot could be gained by examining school systems with more difficult political circumstances.

Finally, we believe that further research is sorely needed on how teachers use data to differentiate instruction. This study indicated that teachers are indeed differentiating instruction in response to data that show which students need additional support and in which areas; however, we did not have sufficient opportunity to gather data on the details of this process. A study that focused on the differentiated instructional techniques that arise out of data-driven decision making would be useful.

References

Alwin, L. (2002). The will and the way of data use. *School Administrator, 59*(11), 11.

Borja, R. R. (2006). District initiative. The information edge: Using data to accelerate achievement. *Education Week, 25*(35), 24–41.

Center on Education Policy (2004). *From the capital to the classroom: Year 2 of the No Child Left Behind Act.* Washington, DC: Author.

Colby, S., Smith, K., & Shelton, J. (2005). *Expanding the supply of high quality public schools.* San Francisco: The Bridgespan Group.

Crommey, A. (2000). *Using student assessment data: What can we learn from schools?* Oak Brook, IL: North Central Regional Educational Laboratory.

Datnow, A., Park, V., & Wohlstetter, P. (2007). *Achieving with data: How high performing elementary school systems use data to improve instruction for elementary school students.* Retrieved March, 15, 2007, from http://www.usc.edu/dept/education/cegov/achieving_data.pdf

Diamond, J. B., & Spillane, J. P. (2004). High-stakes accountability in urban elementary schools: Challenging or reproducing inequality? *Teachers College Record, 106*(6), 1145–1176.

Doyle, D. P. (2003). Data-driven decision making: Is it the mantra of the month or does it have staying power? *T.H.E. Journal, 30*(10), 19–21.

Earl, L., & Katz, S. (2006). *Leading schools in a data rich world.* Thousand Oaks, CA: Corwin Press.

Hoff, D. J. (2006). Delving into data. *Education Week, 25*(5), 12–14, 20–22.

Ingram, D., Louis, K. S., & Schroeder, R. G. (2004). Accountability policies and teacher decision making: Barriers to the use of data to improve practice. *Teachers College Record, 106*(6), 1258–1287.

Jacobson, L. (2007). Districts make strides with common vision. *Education Week, 26*(21), 28–30.

Johnson, J. H. (1999). Educators as researchers. *Schools in the Middle, 9*(1), 38–41.

Johnson, J. H. (2000). Data-driven school improvement. *Journal of School Improvement, 1*(1), 16–19.

Lafee, S. (2002). Data-driven districts. *School Administrator, 59*(11), 6–7, 9–10, 12, 14–15.

Marsh, J., Kerr, K. A., Ikemoto, G. S., Darilek, H., Suttorp, M., Zimmer, R., & Barney, H. (2005). The role of districts in fostering instructional improvement: Factors affecting data use. *RAND Education, 72*, 1–15.

Mason, S. (2002, April). *Turning data into knowledge: Lessons from six Milwaukee public schools.* Paper presented at the annual meeting of the American Educational Research Association, New Orleans, LA.

McIntire, T. (2002). The administrator's guide to data-driven decision making. *Technology and Learning, 22*(11), 18–33.

Peterson, J. L. (2007, winter). Learning facts: The brave new world of data-informed instruction. *Education Next, 1*, 36–42.

Petrides, L., & Nodine, T. (2005). *Anatomy of school system improvement: Performance-driven practices in urban school district.* San Francisco: NewSchools Venture Fund.

Slavin, R. E. (2002). Evidence-based education policies: Transforming educational practice and research. *Educational Researcher, 31*(7), 15–21.

Sutherland, S. (2004). Creating a culture of data use for continuous improvement: A case study of an Edison Project school. *American Journal of Evaluation, 25*(3), 277–293.

Wohlstetter, P., Van Kirk, A. N., Robertson, P. J., & Mohrman, S. A. (1997). *Organizing for successful school-based management.* Alexandria, VA: Association for Supervision and Curriculum Development.

13

Research on Teachers Using Data to Make Decisions[1]

James Raths, Stephanie A. Kotch, and Christine Carrino Gorowara
University of Delaware

What is Data-Driven Decision Making?

Upon undertaking this review of research on teachers' use of data-driven decision making, we first endeavored to define data-driven decision making. We began this process by determining what would *not* constitute data-driven decision making.

This is a challenging exercise, in that it is difficult to imagine any professional not responsive to some kind of feedback. Here is an apparently clear-cut non-example of the concept, "data-driven decision making."

> *A teacher who is guided by a syllabus and teaches Topic A on September 12, and Topic P on November 22, just as the syllabus directs.*

One might, for argument's sake, take the position that the syllabus is evidence or it was created based on data of some sort, but this position does not reflect what the advocates of data-based decision making mean by teachers using "data." Our sense of the process, reinforced by our reading countless pages of literature, is that teachers who take frequent measures of how well their students are progressing in the acquisition of instructional goals, and in response to what the evidence tells them, adjust their instruction and are engaged in "data-driven decision making." It is important to note, as note 1 explains, that evidence can be collected at the school level or the district level for purposes of implementing changes in policies or practices. Our focus is on teachers using data relevant to their own teaching, their own classrooms, and their own students.

To engage in data-driven decision making, there is no need that the data be relevant to standardized tests. We found an example of a teacher using data described in the *Milwaukee Sentinel* (Hetzner, 2007) and this account surely represents data-based decision making even though the evidence is not concerned with scores on a standardized test.

A teacher observed a student in her class who refused to do her school work. The teacher paired the student with another student who would make the reluctant student feel safe and observed the results. As a result of these observations, including a close study of body language, the teacher adjusted her plan to help the student's performances.

Why is Data-Driven Decision Making Receiving so much Attention Recently?

Several articles noted that NCLB-mandated accountability serves as a driver for data-driven decision making (Bernhardt, 2004; Bloomfield & Cooper, 2003; Johnson, 2004; Trimble, 2003; Wayman, 2005). School leaders in most districts are under pressure to have their schools do well on high stakes annual assessments. The consequences of failing to have sufficient numbers of students passing the state tests can be job threatening. Teachers are advised, under this high stakes regimen, to attend to evidence of student learning to optimize the chances that sufficient numbers of students will pass the state tests. Again, this process is seen as "evidence-based teaching" (see Fuchs et al., 1999, p. 610).

What are Some Examples of Research on the Effectiveness of Data-Driven Decision Making?

It seems odd to ask whether those who advocate that teachers engage in data-driven decision making have evidence to support their recommended approaches to teaching. As Wayman (2005) put it, "few would argue that creating more information for educators to use is a negative" (p. 236).

A useful summary of research into data-driven decision making would probably not compare scientific procedures with random, intuitive, commonsense approaches to teaching. On the other hand, teachers who use data-driven decision making, or at least a grounded, idiosyncratic version of it, to work with pupils who are facing a high stakes accountability test, might believe that any successes they saw—reflected in rising test scores—were attributable to the fact that the evidence-based procedures were being used. Assume for a moment that these teachers had no control groups, or any other way of sorting out rival explanations for the rise in test scores. With such problems notwithstanding, a case study of their experiences with data-driven decision making could be written. The case study would report pre-scores and post-scores and assert or imply that the observed gains were due to the teaching processes described as data-driven decision making. We found quite a few studies in this genre. Samples of these case studies are summarized here.

Hansen, Gentry, and Dalley (2003) described a case involving Dixon Middle School in Provo, Utah. Teachers and administrators used state assessment data to identify areas of deficiency, and they used data about the school context to determine how to address these deficiencies, using a collaborative model that built on their experience with quality circles. Hansen et al. noted that the teachers and administrators concluded that:

> measurement and data-utilization were effective because they helped educators determine the effectiveness of activities, tasks, and programs; generated possible solutions to problems and issues within the school; encouraged the charting of future directions and decisions; and provided feedback and progress checks as a strategic planning source to monitor, adjust, redirect, and readjust things that occur.
>
> (p. 40)

Ramnarine (2004) illustrated features of a district-wide database system in St. Paul, Minnesota, through which teachers could access standardized test scores as they became available, and create pre-defined as well as user-defined reports about the scores with the ability to analyze the data according to a number of descriptors. Teachers and other school personnel responded very positively to the timeliness of and easy access to the data, and the district identified a number of results they attributed to the use of this system, including culture changes in the expectations about having access to timely and accurate test score data and using data to plan instruction.

Decker (2003) documented the improvement plan for Lead Mine Elementary School in Raleigh, North Carolina, which centered upon the state end-of-grade tests: the curriculum was aligned to the test; teachers and other school personnel mapped out the curriculum sequence over the course of the school year; benchmark tests measured students' understanding of the curriculum four times a year; and students used course system software several times each week to provide differentiated development of curricular goals. Decker credited this improvement plan with the school's citation by the state for exemplary growth two years in a row.

Often data-driven decision making is described as a collaborative process. We found articles that cited research about the effectiveness of the collaborative process, then used this research as support for data-driven decision making, although these two constructs were not satisfactorily decoupled (Hansen et al., 2003; Trimble, 2003).

What Are Some Potential Research Studies in the Area of Data-Driven Decision Making?

Wayman (2005, p. 237) asserted that the research base associated with data use "lacks rigor and many oft-cited references are short studies or opinion pieces." Our recent search of the literature supported his judgment in this matter. What would research look like that informed the field about data-driven decision making? At this point we are suggesting seven generic sorts of research efforts that could be undertaken in this area.

Research on Teacher Skills in Using Evidence

One might assume that data-driven decision making requires certain skills or understandings on the part of teachers—and that some teachers, because of their enhanced levels of skill, make use of evidence more effectively than do other teachers. We have not found a study which investigates the existence of variance in skills associated with using evidence to guide teaching decisions. If we had, it might look like this: A sample of teachers could be given some evidence of student learning for a group of students and asked to plan a lesson responsive to the evidence. A finding of the study might be that some teachers are more effective in interpreting evidence of student learning than other teachers.

Research on Teacher Uses of Evidence

If it were observed that some teachers consistently produced better plans based on evidence than others, researchers might inquire into the factors that account for the observed difference. Are the better planners brighter, more experienced, or do they hold more sophisticated understandings of evidence? This line of research could generate important ideas for training teachers in the process of evidence-based decision making. We did not find research studies that addressed this problem.

Research on Teacher Training in the Uses of Evidence

Another approach would be to train teachers to use evidence in making instructional plans. One group of teachers could receive the training and another group, perhaps those waiting for a chance to receive training, could be a control group. Teachers in both groups could be presented with evidence for a group of students and asked to suggest "next steps." The findings might show that trained teachers produce plans that are likely to be more effective than those who were untrained. Researchers of course could look beyond planning decisions, and focus instead on the performances of students who studied with trained teachers and untrained teachers. We did find several studies of this nature, which are summarized in a later section.

The Fuchs et al. study (1999) mirrored the last paragraph above fairly precisely. Thirty-two teachers from a southeastern urban school district were randomly assigned either to a performance assessment treatment group or to a control group. The control group continued to teach in their usual manner; the performance assessment group (PA) learned about performance assessment, met to assess performance assessments, and discussed among themselves what some next steps were for students based on the assessments. The PA treatment group worked together for several months prior to a summative assessment. Overall, the PA treatment was more effective than the control treatment in terms of signs of increased levels of problem solving—the goal of both the intervention and the control groups. The effect sizes ranged from .76 to 1.15. The intervention was more successful with the students who were at or above grade level, than for the students who were initially below grade level. Effect sizes for these students ranged from .09 to .50.

Research on Teachers' Decision-making Styles

There may be many ways of responding to data. Some writers who seek to study less analytic approaches to interpreting data speak of "naturalistic decision making" (Clemen, 2001, p. 359). This approach to interpreting data models itself on studies of "experts" who decide on courses of action with great effect. It would be possible to compare the products of planning decisions and/or the impacts on students of implementing the plans put forward by "naturalistic decision makers" and those who are more "analytic" in their approaches. The merits of such a study would depend on the definitions, both connotative and operational, that guided its procedures. We were not able to locate such a study in our literature search.

Research on the Transfer of Teacher Skills

As teachers develop dispositions to use evidence to make decisions about their instructional practices, researchers might ask if their dispositions transfer to other situations, namely to interpret data *other* than test scores of youngsters in the context of a high stakes accountability program. For example, schools could collect attendance data, evidence of absenteeism, ratings of student satisfactions with schools, records of truancy, or the dollar cost of damages inflicted on school property by vandals. As these figures vary, teachers might offer recommendations for school policies and practices. The research question would ask: Are teachers who are efficient using evidence of student learning on tests also effective using other kinds of data? We did not find a study similar to this one.

Research on the Forms of Data

Surely, there are data and there are data. A researcher can ask, "In what forms and in what amounts can teachers make use of the evidence available to them?" "Do teachers find item analyses helpful?" "Are means and standard deviations sufficient for making decisions?" "Do the data need to be disaggregated in some way to be useful to teachers?" Researchers could randomly assign teachers to various data forms and ask them to interpret the evidence and to plan instructional changes. This line of research could help isolate the characteristics of evidence that are optimally helpful for teachers. We did not find a study that investigated the nature of the evidence made available to teachers.

Research on the Role of Decision Making in the Teaching Process

Researchers have long been aware of the role decision making plays in teaching. Jackson (1968) estimated that teachers may make as many as 1,000 decisions each day in planning and implementing lessons in the classroom. Shavelson (1973) called decision making "the basic teaching skill." The complexity of decision making can be reduced by identifying and applying "rules." An example of a rule would be the following: "In selecting words for use in a vocabulary study, choose words that are critical to the text and not solely on the basis that the students do not know the words" (Downes, 2004). Researchers could seek out rules that could guide teachers' decisions in planning for instruction. We did not find examples of research studies into rules that influenced or guided teachers' decisions related to instruction.

Wayman's (2005) introduction to a special issue of the *Journal of Education for Students Placed at Risk* identified an even dozen questions that he judged merited study. Many of his questions focus on the school as the unit of analysis and not the teacher, but they are certainly important and worthwhile questions.

What are Some Flaws in the Research Focused on Data-Driven Decision Making?

Our search of the literature yielded a number of studies that used the school building or the district as the unit of analysis rather than the classroom. As such, these studies were outside of our chapter's focus. However, the studies were instructive to researchers interested in addressing questions about teachers' use of evidence. We observed the following general flaws in those studies.

Many if not most of the studies used "teacher self-report" to describe the processes utilized in the decision-making process or in estimating the impact of the process on student learning. It is important in studies of teacher decision making to make use of assessments independent of the teachers' perceptions or at least in conjunction with them.

Most studies we read suffered from a problem identified in the research literature as "multiple treatment interference." Rarely was the independent variable solely data-driven decision making. Instead, the treatment included data, collaboration, training, and consultant help. When gains were observed in the study, it was difficult to isolate what factor contributed to the gains.

Almost always, interventions that were called data-based decision making were instituted when a school was in some sort of crisis as a result of low scores on a high stakes examination. This nexus between weak performances and the adoption of something new and promising is understandable. However, the connection raises a threat to the findings of any study that eschews using a control group, namely regression. When initial scores are low, any intervention is likely to be associated with increased scores, whether it is effective or not. It is important in many of the designs we reviewed to introduce control groups.

Finally, there is the notion of "reactive arrangements," also known as the Hawthorne Effect. Almost all the case studies we read about using data to improve instruction and student learning included a great deal of enthusiasm on the part of the main participants. Such enthusiasm may be hard to transplant to other sites or even to other times at the target site. Again, control groups can help discredit this research design problem.

What are Some Optimum Conditions for Using Data-Driven Decision Making?

As we read through the case studies, the few experiments, and the advocacy state-ments by people championing the current high stakes accountability movement in the United States, we learned that there was a great deal of consensus concerning the optimum conditions for using evidence to guide teaching toward state tests. We identify these optimum conditions and describe them, citing the sources from which they were gleaned. It is clear that the specific, individual conditions are not independent. That is, the condition that teachers have sufficient time to examine data is related to the condition of teachers collaborating with colleagues. Time is a common factor. However, we thought it important to summarize the themes we identified in the literature. The various themes are linked to specific references in the narrative that follows and in Table 13.1.

School climate must "honor" the uses of evidence in making teaching decisions
(Ellingsen, 2007; Lachat & Smith, 2005; Murnane & Sharkey, 2004; Wayman & Stringfield, 2006; Young, 2006)

Many of the identified optimum conditions are interwoven but our sources acknowledged several characteristics which epitomize school climate conducive to supporting teachers in analyzing, interpreting, and most importantly using data to benefit student learning.

Young (2006) used the term "agenda setting" to describe the school leadership role in communicating teachers' use of data by establishing a rationale, expectations, time, and learning opportunities. Young (2006, p. 544) concluded that school leaders "need to embed teaching and learning and their improvement in the heart of data-related activities ... or risk data analyses as compliance activity divorced from teachers'

Table 13.1 Display of support for selected optimum conditions.

	School climate	Sensitive measures	Timely access to evidence	Buy-in by teachers	Teacher skills	Conceptual interpretation of evidence	Time for teachers in school day	Team work
1						*		
2		*						
3	*					*	*	
4				*				
5								*
6				*	*		*	*
7		*	*	*	*		*	
8	*		*		*		*	*
9		*				*		
10	*	*	*			*	*	
11								*
12		*						
13			*	*	*		*	
14						*		
15			*				*	
16				*			*	
17	*		*	*	*		*	
18	*					*	*	*

Note: Numbers in the first column refer to citations numbered in the bibliography. The column headings represent the eight "optimum conditions" we identified in the literature. School climate, alignment of evidence with teaching objectives, timeliness of evidence, teacher buy-in to the process, teacher skills, conceptual approaches to interpreting data, time for teachers to work with data, and teaming (collaboration).

classroom actions." In addition, strong school leadership should model data usage in meaningful and manageable ways. Lachat and Smith (2005) found that the commitment to data use for continuous improvement needs to be championed by school leaders. Successful instructional leaders know that they cannot mandate an environment that values data usage (Ellingsen, 2007). School leaders have a responsibility to develop and nurture a culture of data-driven inquiry and co-responsibility among their faculty. Murnane and Sharkey (2004, p. 4) found that a school cultural condition necessary for success is adopting "the idea that the achievement of all students is the responsibility of the whole teaching staff and that success depends on continued learning." It is extremely important to remember that district administrative support and commitment are keys to success (Murnane & Sharkey, 2004).

Evidence should be "curriculum sensitive" and should align with the teacher's instructional objectives

(Coburn & Talbert, 2006; Kerr, Marsh, Marsh, Ikemoto, & Barney, 2006; Marzano, 2003, Murnane & Sharkey, 2004; Popham, 2007)

Teachers find more validity in assessment results if they are closely aligned to their classroom teaching. Marzano (2003, p. 56) reported that "using measures of student learning that are not sensitive to the actual learning occurring in the classrooms is the first mistake." Teachers find more validity in assessment results if they are closely aligned to their classroom teaching (Coburn & Talbert, 2006). Even though high stakes assessments are aligned with the standards and we assume that teachers are planning instruction around the standards, many teachers view the data as old news (Kerr et al., 2006). Lessons learned by research encourage districts and states to utilize benchmark or interim assessments that are closely aligned to the standards (Murnane & Sharkey, 2004). Popham (2007) alerted the field to the pitfalls of using tests that are insensitive to the quality of instruction. In his view, insensitive tests undermine the fundamental assumptions of accountability. His article proposed ways of assessing tests for their instructional sensitivity.

Teachers need to have access to evidence close to the time it is collected

(Kerr et al., 2006; Lachat & Smith, 2005; Murnane & Sharkey, 2004; Reeves & Burt, 2006; Supovitz & Klein, 2003; Wayman & Stringfield, 2006)

Once teachers are provided time to work with data, they want data that are meaningful to them. Yet, the high stakes testing schedule of assessing students in late winter or at best early spring frustrates classroom teachers. They find the state data not as useful as current classroom data in trying to make instructional decisions. School administrators also find the inability to receive data in a timely fashion to be a barrier to effective use (Reeves & Burt, 2006). In most instances, once the data are received from the state, the school year is ending or has ended. The teachers find these data less relevant (Kerr et al., 2006). Research indicates that teachers want assessment results returned quickly and in a user-friendly format (Murnane & Sharkey, 2004;

Supovitz & Klein, 2003; Wayman & Stringfield, 2006). A recommendation advanced by Kerr et al. (2006, p. 515) is for districts to implement "assessment and data analysis strategies that include multiple types of data collected at regular intervals to allow for a timely, balanced, and meaningful review of data." For example, Lachat and Smith (2005) found that data were used effectively when teachers received the data in a timely fashion which allowed them to plan immediate intervention strategies.

Teachers need to "buy-in" and have faith that the process is worthwhile, and that data will not be used punitively
(Ingram, Louis, & Schroeder, 2004; Kerr et al., 2006; Reeves & Burt, 2006; Trimble, 2003; Wayman & Stringfield, 2006)

As part of the school culture, school leaders need to help teachers develop confidence in the data and the process by which decisions will be made. Teachers will respond in varying degrees depending upon their perceptions of data use (Ingram et al., 2004). These perceptions can be addressed by allowing teachers to vent negative feelings, and by assuring them that tests are diagnostic and results will not be used punitively (Trimble, 2003). Engaging in evidence-based decision making can be a positive process in which teachers feel supported by the data (Wayman & Stringfield, 2006). For example, Kerr et al. (2006) found that principals and teachers viewed data in a constructive manner when they were consistently engaged in making evidence-based instructional decisions. In this case teachers were supported in a positive school culture that promoted the use of data. Wayman and Stringfield (2006) referred to "non threatening triangulation of data" in which multiple measures are utilized in a positive manner to inform instruction.

Often, stakeholders are at odds as to which data are meaningful (Coburn & Talbert, 2006; Ingram et al., 2004; Kerr et al., 2006; Reeves & Burt, 2006). Variations of conceptions of valid evidence seem to be based on individual roles within the school system. "Individuals with different work roles have substantively different data needs" (Coburn & Talbert, 2006, p. 491). Recognition of the diverse perceptions is a much needed step to build a collaborative culture and buy-in.

Teachers need to acquire new skills and improved understandings about evidence and/or understandings about assessment and how to respond to assessment results
(Guskey, 2003; Ingram et al., 2004; Kerr et al., 2006; Lachat & Smith, 2005; Reeves & Burt, 2006; Wayman & Stringfield, 2006)

Ingram et al. (2004) found that teachers are not "data-phobic" but rather lack the experience of working with data. Some teachers are unprepared or unfamiliar with data practices to fully utilize evidence available to them (Wayman & Stringfield, 2006). Guskey (2003) noted that teachers receive little training in assessment design or analysis, and that fewer than half the states require competence in assessment for licensure. Consequently, many teachers regard assessment only as a tool for assigning grades at the end of a unit, rather than as a means of improving instruction and student learning.

The problem is not only with teachers. District officials may also lack the skills needed to analyze data (Kerr et al., 2006; Reeves & Burt, 2006). It is difficult to create a school culture rich in inquiry when the basic skills or knowledge is lacking. It seems to be crucial that all stakeholders develop data-analysis skills. Professional development for principals and teachers must be sustained, job-embedded, focused on understanding data, and using data to inform practice (Reeves & Burt, 2006).

Kerr et al. (2006) recommended administrative support for teachers "in analyzing and interpreting data, as well as identifying strategies to address diagnosed problems" (p. 515). In a case study, Lachat and Smith (2005) found success with data coaches. The data coaches supported the administration and teachers in their quest to analyze data, interpret data, question data, and arrive at informed decisions. The data coaches assisted principals and teachers in developing the needed skills to effectively utilize data.

Teachers should utilize a conceptual approach to interpret the data
(Clemen, 2001; Ellingsen, 2007; Marzano, 2003; Murnane & Sharkey, 2004; Schmoker & Wilson, 1995; Young, 2006)

Data do not speak for themselves in spite of the common notion that they do. Teachers need tools for interpreting data. Researchers working in the field of decision analysis attempt to provide models to guide practitioners' decision making (Clemen, 2001). Data are only useful if they can be used to arrive at credible explanations of observed variations (Marzano, 2003). With newly developed skills and a better understanding of analyzing and interpreting data, teachers need to process their thinking about data in a conceptual manner. Once the data are aggregated or disaggregated, the initial step is to look for patterns. The next critical step is for educators to brainstorm possible explanations and develop strategies for identifying the most plausible explanation (Murnane & Sharkey, 2004). The explanatory process is the most neglected and in need of educators' time (Ellingsen, 2007; Murnane & Sharkey, 2004), and the tendency is to jump from data patterns to quick fixes (Ellingsen, 2007; Schmoker & Wilson, 1995) without examining possible causes. A school or district needs a systemic and conceptual plan for first interpreting data and using the data. The teachers then need to be supported within this system through agenda setting and school norms (Young, 2006).

Teachers need time in the school day to interpret evidence and to plan instruction based on the evidence
(Ellingsen, 2007; Ingram et al., 2004; Kerr et al., 2006; Lachat & Smith, 2005; Murnane & Sharkey, 2004; Reeves & Burt, 2006; Supovitz & Klein, 2003; Trimble, 2003; Wayman & Stringfield, 2006; Young, 2006)

An obstacle cited in much of the research is the lack of time provided for teachers to effectively use data to drive instruction. Ellingsen (2007) reminded the field that the greatest gift school leaders can provide to their faculty is time. The challenges of No Child Left Behind have spurred the evolution of educators' roles and responsibilities. Educational reformists and school administrators need to rethink the teachers' role, set time priorities for data examination, and structure collaborative activities (Ingram et al., 2004; Young, 2006). Murnane and Sharkey (2004) recommended that time should be provided within the school day. Reeves and Burt (2006, p. 70) also concurred that the teachers' "workday and responsibilities need restructuring" if we expect effective utilization of data to improve instruction. Lachat and Smith (2005) stressed the expectation within the school culture for teachers to regularly engage in collaborative examination of student data. Though the research is limited on suggesting ways to restructure the roles and responsibilities, many researchers describe methods in which school leaders have provided time to their faculty: Ellingsen (2007) observed modified school days as the most prevalent method in providing teachers time to work with data; Young (2006) described teacher collaboration time during full-day grade-level meetings throughout the year and/or frequent team meetings; and Trimble (2003) noted that collaboration can take place during daily common planning periods. Principals try to work creatively within the system to utilize planning time, faculty meetings, grade-level meetings, as well as professional development days (Kerr et al., 2006; Wayman & Stringfield, 2006). Supovitz and Klein (2003, p. 37) identified "more time" as a factor for "schools that seek to use data more effectively."

Evidence should be interpreted collaboratively and instructional decisions should be arrived at in conjunction with colleagues
(Hansen, Gentry, & Dalley, 2003; Ingram et al., 2004; Lachat & Smith, 2005; Murname, Sharkey, & Boudett, 2005; Wayman & Stringfield, 2006; Young, 2006)

In the spirit of creating a school culture that nurtures data-driven inquiry and decision making, research finds success in collaboration. Teachers are more likely to engage in data analysis as a group (Ingram et al., 2004). Lachat and Smith (2005) found that the modeling of collaborative data inquiry by school leaders was a positive influence on schoolwide data utilization, while Wayman and Stringfield (2006) reported that teachers noted an increase in professional interactions when working with data; teachers began to feel a sense of "common language" in professional discussions. Young (2006) recommended that time should be provided for joint analysis of data, but also heeds warning that collaboration is only a single piece of the larger picture—several other optimum factors contribute to effective data use by teachers such as school/district capacity and agenda setting. Hansen et al. (2003) cautioned that the norms of the group must support learning—members must be willing to share and cooperate with each other, ask questions of one another, and challenge the status quo at times.

How can Teachers be Prepared to Use Data-Driven Decision Making?

Hiebert, Morris, Berk, and Jansen (2007) proposed a framework for teachers to learn from evidence about their own instruction, built on the following four skills:

1. Specify the learning goal(s) for the instructional episode: What are students supposed to learn?
2. Conduct empirical observations of teaching and learning: What did students learn?
3. Construct hypotheses about the effects of teaching on students' learning: How did teaching help [or not] students learn?
4. Use analysis to propose improvements in teaching: How could teaching more effectively help students learn?

This framework is supported in part by studies documenting the success of schoolwide efforts to use analysis of teachers' instruction to improve student learning. The effectiveness of this framework, of course, depends on the skills of the teachers implementing it. Several researchers have begun to examine ways of developing these skills.

Van Es and Sherin (2002) noted that teacher training tends to focus on helping teachers learn to *act*, but not to *interpret*. They studied the effects of using a software package known as Video Analysis Support Tool (VAST) designed to scaffold teachers' analysis of student thinking, the teacher's role, and classroom discourse in the context of their own videotaped lessons. The authors compared teachers who used VAST to those who did not. They found that lesson analysis essays written by VAST users were organized increasingly around noteworthy teaching events rather than chronology, that they included more evidence to support their analyses, and that they incorporated more interpretations about student thinking, the teacher's role, and classroom discourse. Control group participants gained in these areas as well, but at lesser rates and levels of growth.

Santagata, Zannoni, and Stigler (in press) also used a video software package, LessonLab's Visibility software, this time to train preservice teachers with videotaped lessons from the TIMSS project. Masters-level teacher education students in Italy participated in a course which featured guided analysis of the lessons, focusing on parts of the lesson and learning goals, students' thinking and learning, and alternative teaching strategies. As in the Van Es and Sherin study, participants moved from simple descriptions in the pre-test to cause-and-effect analyses in the post-test.

Morris (2006) compared two different cuing conditions on preservice teachers' ability to collect evidence about students' learning and to use that evidence to analyze and revise instruction. Participants were asked to view a fifth-grade mathematics lesson and to form hypotheses about variations in the children's learning, and finally to cite evidence that supported their hypotheses. One group of participants, identified as CL (Children's Learning), were not cued one way or the other as to whether the lesson was successful, while the other group, identified as SP (Sources of Problems), were cued with the information that several children had difficulty with the homework following the lesson. Once the participants had made and supported their hypotheses, they were asked how they would change the lesson, and to give reasons for their changes. Morris found that although both groups of preservice teachers had very elementary skills in identifying evidence about student learning, with many describing teacher statements as "evidence" of what students had learned (e.g., "The children understand that the height and base are not always in the same places on a triangle because the teacher said that a triangle's height must always form a right angle with the base," Morris, 2006, p. 487), the SP participants were much more likely to cite evidence that referred to students learning than were their CL counterparts. Furthermore, SP participants were more likely to suggest improvements to the lesson that provided opportunities for students to develop their understanding of the mathematical concepts and relationships covered in the lesson.

Fuchs et al. (1999) studied the effects of training teachers to use the results of performance assessments by comparing two groups of eight randomly assigned mathematics teachers each. One group (PA condition) attended an initial training workshop, administered three performance assessments over several months, and met with colleagues after giving each performance assessment to score the assessments and share ideas for providing students with feedback and instruction, with instructional support from the researchers. The other group (no-PA condition) did none of these things. Outcomes for both teachers and students were measured. Following the intervention, PA teachers were able to construct performance assessments in which they incorporated more appropriate features, were able to cite more instructional strategies in response to performance assessment results, and planned instruction more closely aligned with reform goals, as compared to their no-PA colleagues. In addition, above-grade-level students and grade-level students in the PA classrooms made significant gains (with above-grade-level students making gains across more problem types), while their no-PA counterparts made no similar gains.

What are Some Limitations of Data-Driven Decision Making in Education?

The literature highlights a number of limitations associated with the data-driven decision-making process. As Marzano (2003) pointed out, the data collected may identify concepts, topics, or skills that need reteaching, but the evidence does not speak to how the reteaching should be done. Some state accountability processes include suggestions to teachers as to what interventions are called for, but those suggestions are hardly "data-based" or the results of scientific inquiry. Marzano (2003) characterized this problem as "having no explanatory model to interpret the data" (p. 57). He chose to illustrate his point with his own findings about "what works in schools," but his suggestions for a model almost surely do not give direction to teachers who find that a significant number of students in his class do not know how to subtract fractions or read Roman numerals or translate Centigrade readings into Fahrenheit readings. As Biesta (2007) commented, "research cannot supply us with rules for action but only with hypotheses for intelligent problem solving" (p. 20).

When teachers find, after studying the evidence, that some students need help in a particular area, there are *not* a lot of research-based interventions available to them

(Duffy & Roehler, 1982). Teachers can group students for instruction—with those who are having difficulty with skill A in one group, and those having trouble with skill B in another group. There is little direction as to what to do next. Reteaching is not a highly studied process. In a recent meta-analysis on teacher research, grouping had an effect size of .10, while differentiation/adaptive instruction had an effect size of .22. The latter is larger, but still in the low end of the scale as interventions go (Siedel & Shavelson, 2007). The advocates of data-driven decision making rarely address this issue in their writings.

Another limitation to the process is related to the acceptance of the state content standards as important goals for students in our schools. Biesta (2007) cautioned that data cannot tell us whether our ends are desirable. Meanwhile, teachers and administrators are urged to accept, without inquiry, the state curriculum mandates as the gold standard, and to work to pass assessments that measure progress toward the state standards. How important are the standards to students in our schools? How well do the assessments measure students' grasp of the content? No one seems to know or even to pose the question.

The model of data-driven decision making does not account for the mutual efforts of teacher and student in the education process, but instead treats education as if it occurs solely through causal professional action. It is as though the advocates of evidence-based decision making understand that teachers "learn" their students.

Note

1. Our review was limited in scope to classroom teachers using evidence to shape their decisions.

References

Bernhardt, V. (2004). Continuous improvement: It takes more than test scores. *Leadership, 34*(2), 16–19.
Biesta, G. (2007). Why "what works" won't work: Evidence-based practice and the democratic deficit in educational research. *Educational Theory, 57*(1), 1–22.
Bloomfield, D., & Cooper, B. (2003). Making sense of NCLB. *T.H.E. Journal, 30*(10), 6–9.
Clemen, R. T. (2001). Naturalistic decision making and decision analysis. *Journal of Behavioral Decision Making, 14,* 359–361.
Coburn, C. E., & Talbert, J. E. (2006). Conceptions of evidence use in school districts: Mapping the terrain. *American Journal of Education, 112*(4), 469–495.
Decker, G. (2003). Using data to drive student achievement in the classroom and on high-stakes tests. *T.H.E. Journal, 30*(6), 44–45.
Downes, D. M. (2004). *Choices and challenges: Decision making in the classroom.* Unpublished executive position paper, Newark: University of Delaware.
Duffy, G. G., & Roehler, L. R. (1982). The illusion of instruction. *Reading Research Quarterly, 17,* 438–443.
Ellingsen, J. (2007). Data unwrapped. *Leadership, 37*(1), 22–23.
Fuchs, L. S., Fuchs, D., Karns, K., Hamlett, C. L., & Katzaroff, M. (1999). Mathematics performance assessment in the classroom: Effects on teacher planning and student problem solving. *American Educational Research Journal, 36,* 609–646.
Guskey, T. (2003). Using data to improve student achievement. *Educational Leadership, 60*(5), 6–11.
Hansen, J. M., Gentry, R., & Dalley, T. (2003). Mindful change in a data-driven school. *Principal Leadership, 3*(6), 37–41.
Hetzner, A. (2007). Data building better teachers. *Milwaukee Journal-Sentinel.* Retrieved November 13, 2007, from http://www.jsonline.com/story/index.aspx?id=683861

Hiebert, J., Morris, A., Berk, D., & Jansen, A. (2007). Preparing teachers to learn from teaching. *Journal of Teacher Education, 58*(1), 47–61.

Ingram, D., Louis, K. S., & Schroeder, R. G. (2004). Accountability policies and teacher decision making: Barriers to the use of data to improve practice. *Teachers College Record, 106,* 1258–1287.

Jackson, P. W. (1968). *Life in classrooms.* New York: Holt, Rinehart, & Winston.

Johnson, D. (2004). A data mining primer and implications for school library media specialists. *Knowledge Quest, 32*(5), 32–35.

Kerr, K. A., Marsh, J. A., Ikemoto, G. S., Darilek, H., & Barney, H. (2006). Strategies to promote data use for instructional improvement: Actions, outcomes, and lessons from three urban districts. *American Journal of Education, 112,* 496–520.

Lachat, M. A., & Smith, S. (2005). Practices that support data use in urban schools. *Journal of Education for Students Placed at Risk, 10,* 333–349.

Marzano, R. (2003). Using data: Two wrongs and a right. *Educational Leadership, 60*(5), 56–60.

Morris, A. (2006). Assessing pre-service teachers' skills for analyzing teaching. *Journal of Mathematics Teacher Education, 9,* 471–505.

Murname, R. J., & Sharkey, N. S. (2004). *Learning from student assessment results: Lessons from New York state.* Cambridge, MA: Harvard University Graduate School of Education.

Murname, R. J., Sharkey, N. S., & Boudett, K. P. (2005). Using student-assessment results to improve instruction: Lessons from a workshop. *Journal of Education for Students Placed at Risk, 10,* 269–280.

Popham, W. J. (2007). Instructional insensitivity of tests: Accountability's dire drawback. *Phi Delta Kappan, 89*(2), 146–150, 155.

Ramnarine, S. (2004). Impacting student achievement through data-driven decision making. *Multimedia & Internet@Schools, 11*(4), 33–35.

Reeves, P. L., & Burt, W. L. (2006). Challenges in data-based decision making: Voices from principals. *Educational Horizons, 85*(1), 65–71.

Santagata, R., Zannoni, C., & Stigler, J. W. (in press). The role of lesson analysis in pre-service teacher education: An empirical investigation of teacher learning from a virtual video-based field experience. *Journal of Mathematics Teacher Education, 10*(2), 123–140.

Schmoker, M., & Wilson, R. B. (1995). Results: The key to renewal. *Educational Leadership, 52*(7), 62–63.

Shavelson, R. J. (1973). *The basic teaching skill: Decision making.* Stanford, CA: Stanford University School of Education Center for R&D in Teaching.

Siedel, T., & Shavelson, R. J. (2007). Teaching effectiveness research in the past decade: The role of theory and research design in disentangling meta-analysis results. *Review of Educational Research, 77,* 454–499.

Supovitz, J., & Klein, V. (2003). *Mapping a course for improved student learning: How innovative schools systematically use student performance data to guide improvement.* Philadelphia: Consortium for Policy Research in Education.

Trimble, S. (2003). Between reform and improvement in the classroom. *Principal Leadership, 4*(1), 35–39.

Van Es, E. A., & Sherin, M. G. (2002). Learning to notice: Scaffolding new teachers' interpretations of classroom interactions. *Journal of Technology and Teacher Education, 10,* 571–576.

Wayman, J. C. (2005). Guest editor's introduction. *Journal of Education for Students Placed at Risk, 10,* 235–239.

Wayman, J. C., & Stringfield, S. (2006). Technology-supported involvement of entire faculties in examination of student data for instructional improvement. *American Journal of Education, 112*(4), 549–570.

Young, V. M. (2006). Teachers' use of data: Loose coupling, agenda setting, and team norms. *American Journal of Education, 112,* 521–548.

14

Research and Evaluation on Data-Based Decisions in Education

Gregory J. Marchant and Sharon E. Paulson
Ball State University

The purpose of this chapter is to identify the characteristics of good research that can be applied to educational decision making and the subsequent evaluations of those decisions. For years, research has been evaluation's uppity brother, having strict rules and requirements for asking and answering empirical questions in educational settings; whereas evaluation could be as informal as asking, "Well, how did you like it?" In turn, researchers and evaluators might argue that data-based decision making is even less rigorous than evaluation. Although important educational decisions are being made using data-based evidence, the results of the decisions are inconclusive unless research principles are used in making the decision and empirical evaluations are conducted to see if the desired outcomes have been attained. As these educational decisions and evaluations turn increasingly to objective data and research method-ologies, they begin looking more like their rigid brother. In this chapter, we argue that, given the right tools, data-based decision making can be as reliable and valid as good evaluation and research. In fact, using the right tools and approaches, data-based decision making is indeed an alternative form of evaluation and research.

Data-Based Decision Making and Educational Evaluation

Data-based decision making has grown out of the need to eliminate guesswork in developing curriculum, creating programs, or changing instructional practice. Educational policies, including those driven by No Child Left Behind (NCLB), now mandate that data be collected in almost every educational arena to determine the success of schools, teachers, and students. Schools and school districts have built massive databases of test scores, drop-out rates, school attendance, disciplinary actions, and financial expenditures. By using these data, teachers and administrators can make decisions regarding curriculum, instruction, and programming that will improve the success of their schools and their students. There are a number of definitive sources on how to use data to make decisions (e.g., Kowalski, Lasley, & Mahoney, 2008), including this book; it is not the purpose of this chapter to repeat those methods. However, both the data and the decisions must be derived using sound research principles. In turn, once a decision is made, one needs to determine whether or not the outcome of interest has been realized. Data-based decision making cannot stop with the decision (and its implementation); the decision must then be evaluated to ensure its effectiveness. Indeed, those who have written extensively on data-based decision making have argued that the basis for educational decisions must be grounded in educational evaluation (Kowalski et al., 2008).

Driven in the 1960s by policy requirements to evaluate educational programs, educational evaluation initially meant *measurement*, not unlike what is done today to produce the very educational data of which we speak. Popham (1993) argued, however, that measurement is *status appraisal*, whereas evaluation is *quality appraisal*. Evaluation goes beyond simply collecting the data (measurement) and includes appraising their worth. *Evaluation is the process of delineating, obtaining, and providing useful information for judging decision alternatives* (Stufflebeam et al., 1971). Over the past 20 or more years, numerous methods and models of educational evaluation have emerged, but ultimately the goal of all evaluation is to determine whether or not some measurable outcome was attained. Although evaluation can be as simple as asking, "Did the participants like it?" (where *it* is curriculum, instruction, program, or other decisional process), the most common form of evaluation currently used to assess educational practice is *outcome-based evaluation* that answers the question, "Did it work?" (Popham, 1993; Schalock, 2001). More recently, *theory-based evaluation* which answers the question, "Why did it work (or not work)?" has been added to the repertoire of evaluation techniques in education (Rogers, Hacsi, Petrosino, & Huebner, 2000; Weiss, 1997). Both of these types of evaluation require strict research principles including asking the right questions, planning a valid research design using reliable and valid measurement, analyzing the results statistically, and drawing appropriate conclusions.

In the sections to follow, we will explore the concepts and methods of conducting empirical research to serve as a lens for viewing data-based decision making in education. Topics include asking the right questions, reviewing the existing literature, developing a purpose to guide methodology, using valid procedures and measurement, analyzing results, and drawing appropriate conclusions. Educators should be mindful of these techniques at all points of the decision-making process: when collecting the data, when using the data to make decisions, and when evaluating the decisional outcomes. To demonstrate these research principles, we will use several examples of data-based decisions that we have encountered in our own research and evaluation efforts.

The Question and its Purpose

For years there has been an emphasis on the importance of the research question to any study. It is the question that specifies the topic of the study, defines the outcomes of interest, and directs the research methods. Obviously, these are key elements in any data-based decision as well. For example, school district A is concerned with high school dropout rates and with pass rates on the state standardized achievement test. It is likely that these data have been collected and the district wants to use these data to make decisions; in particular, to decide what can be done to reduce drop-out rates and to increase pass rates on achievement tests. Similarly, teacher B has concerns over her students' grades: what can I do to help my students get higher grades (with the assumption that higher grades is a reflection of greater learning)? Neither district A nor teacher B is going to randomly make changes to curriculum and instruction to see whether drop-out rates, pass rates, or grades change over time. To address these concerns, the school district or the teacher needs to formulate specific, well-crafted questions. Principles of research propose several types of research questions that might be used to address such concerns (Meltzoff, 1998).

- *Questions of description*: These questions address the characteristics of the data. For example, what are the characteristics of students who drop out of school; or what are the qualities of students who make higher grades?
- *Relationship questions*: These questions address whether or not a relationship exists between two factors. Do pass rates on standardized achievement tests relate to drop-out rates? Is student attendance related to grades?
- *Causality questions*: These questions address the factors that influence the outcome of interest. For example, does the school mentoring program affect drop-out rates; or does peer-tutoring increase students' test scores?
- *Interaction questions*: These questions take into account the specific circumstances under which an outcome or relations among factors exist. Does the school mentoring program lower drop-out rates more for students with higher grades than for those with lower grades?

Formulating the specific question(s) to be asked requires a great deal of insight into the issues related to the question(s) and the context of the data. Research articles in education start out with a literature review for just this reason, to establish the background (Boote & Beile, 2005). Likewise, those in decision-making positions need to know the literature related to the questions they are formulating. Despite what some might think, some pretty definitive research results already exist concerning many educational policies and practices. For example, take the question, "Does retaining students who do not pass the state standardized test improve their long-term achievement?" The research on retention has already determined that the answer to that question is "no," decision made (Jimerson & Kaufman, 2003). "Does retaining students who do not pass the state standardized test increase drop-out rates?" That answer is "yes"; again, decision made (Jimerson & Kaufman, 2003). We already know that student retention is not good practice, so making the decision to utilize it would be poor policy. Already knowing that, a school district might focus its questions on other interventions that could be developed and tested for students not passing *the* test.

In addition to acquiring a knowledge base concerning research findings and the educational context, decision makers need to establish the ultimate purpose behind their question(s). Good research creates consistency among the questions to be addressed, the purpose of the questions, and the methods used to collect the data (Newman, Ridenour, Newman, & DeMarco, 2003). The purpose behind a decision is of paramount concern; otherwise the whole data-based process could be completed without informing any actual decision.

Different types of purposes have been identified for research that would apply to data-based decision making (Newman et al., 2003). For example, data are often collected to examine a school or district's power or organizational structure, priorities, practices, or policies. In addition, school data might be used to measure outcomes or the consequences of certain practices. Data can be used to examine the past, or to generate or test new ideas. Sometimes data are used to understand complex situations and/or to add to the knowledge base. Data can also be used to predict events based on past information, or to inform constituents about present conditions. The key is to know why the data are being collected or considered, so that what is being asked of the data is appropriate.

Figure 14.1 is commonly presented to consider the issue "Which line is longer, AB or CD, or are they the same?" A similar but much more complex question is often posed in educational contexts: Which program is more effective? Program A, Program B, or are they equally effective? There are at least two ways to answer both of these questions. One way is to look at the perceptions and opinions of those involved, and the other is to use some formal, objective method of measurement.

So, what is the purpose of the data to be collected? Is it to be used to present the differences in people's perceptions of the length of the lines, or is some actual measure of length required? About half of the people asked believe that line CD is longer than line AB with most others thinking they are the same length. When measured, the lines are in fact the same length. The first purpose, to discover people's perceptions, might provide insight into human beliefs; whereas the second purpose is to find the actual relation between the lengths of the two lines: two different questions, two different purposes, two different answers. Similarly, questions asked by decision makers in education often involve issues of perception versus some other outcome or measurement. Is the concern whether constituents value or like a policy or program, or whether that policy results in some other measurable outcome? For example, surveys generally find that parents would like to be able to choose the school their children attend; however, there is little evidence that school choice results in higher achievement (Lubienski, 2007; Zimmer et al., 2007).

Now take, for example, the teacher trying to decide how to increase students' grades in the classroom. The teacher with two sections of the same course wanted to test whether or not reciprocal learning (students teaching each other) is more effective than lecture. To do so, he alternated methods between the two classes twice and gave a test after each lesson. He also gave a survey asking which method the students preferred. The results indicated that the achievement was the same across the two

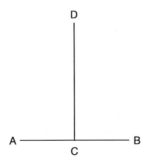

Figure 14.1

teaching methods, but the students greatly preferred the reciprocal learning approach. Being an advocate for reciprocal learning, the teacher was disappointed that the reciprocal learning groups did not achieve more than the lectured groups. He thought that the *purpose* of his study was to establish the superiority of the more innovative approach based on achievement. If that were the case, he should have involved a number of instructors and only collected test results. However, because he was the only instructor involved, had the reciprocal learning groups scored higher, it would only have meant that the students could teach each other better than *he* could. Although the instructor considered the student preference data secondary and almost inconsequential compared to the achievement data, collecting the data meant there was another purpose to his study. He wanted to know what the students preferred. Therefore, within the context of the limited scope of just his instruction, he learned that he could use a teaching approach that he advocated and that his students preferred with no decrease in achievement.

Validity and Getting at the Truth

The second major research concept that is important to any data-based decision is validity. In paradigms of logic, validity is the *truth* of a statement. In research, validity is the most important aspect of the study. In a sense, it is the *truth* of the study. If the results are valid, they represent the truth, and not some alternative explanation. There are those who believe that it is possible to get data and statistics to support any position available. However, there is an inherent truth in any data set and the results gleaned from it. That truth may provide a clear direction to guide decision making, or that truth may be obscured or inconclusive because of flaws in the research design. These flaws are threats to the validity of research and distractions from the truth. Many of these problems have been spelled out in the literature on research methods (Cook & Campbell, 1979).

Selection

By far the biggest threat to the truth in education is the selection of the participants included in the data. In true experimental research, participants are randomly selected from a larger population and randomly assigned to treatment groups. The idea is that any differences inherent in the participants will not be over- or under-represented in the sample or any subgroups (those getting or not getting a treatment or intervention). However, random selection and assignment are almost nonexistent in real educational environments.

The samples of students and teachers that researchers get to study are often the same sets available to administrators (or less so). These samples are not random nor are they comparable. For example, we have found that more than 50% of the differences among elementary schools in pass rates on standardized tests can be attributed to the race and income of the students (Marchant, Ordonez, & Paulson, 2008). Any effort to attribute school differences to special programs or to faculty must be examined in light of the demographic characteristics of the students. Similarly, when the College Board releases the list of SAT test scores averaged for each state, newspapers report front-page stories indicating the rise or fall in the rankings of their states suggesting that this has something to do with the quality of a state's schools. Unfortunately, the differences among states have little to do with the quality of the states' educational programs. The truth is that over 90% of the differences among states can be tied to two variables: the percent of Black test takers in each state and more importantly the education level of the test takers' parents (Marchant & Paulson, 2001). The overall percent of high school students taking the test for each state really does not matter (although the College Board claims this is a major factor). Therefore, state averaged SAT scores do not provide valid data for making decisions regarding effective state-level educational policies because of the selection differences among states.

Selection problems can occur at any level: state, district, school, or classroom. At the classroom level, most students are randomly assigned to teachers at each grade level. However, boys at an urban elementary school might need "a positive male role model," so these boys, who also tend to be lower achieving, are assigned to the few male teachers in the building. A review of annual achievement data finds the male teachers' classes are not achieving as high as other classes in the school. Are these male teachers less effective? Of course not, but when students with demographic characteristics known to be associated with lower test scores are disproportionately present in a classroom, school, district, or state, it follows that average scores at those levels will be affected.

The word "volunteer" associated with any data should be a red flag. Simply put, those who volunteer are often different from those who do not. Therefore, any comparisons between volunteers and non-volunteers are likely to reflect this difference, not any program the volunteers are involved in. Due to instructional freedom, teachers' unions, and simple courtesy, teachers usually are not forced to try certain programs or practices. It is not unusual for a publisher or a researcher to be introduced at a faculty meeting looking for volunteers to try a particular program or approach. Often that program requires time for training and possibly classroom observations of the teachers who volunteer. The data at the end of the study show that the teachers who volunteered, who were probably more dedicated and more confident, had students with higher achievement; but did the special program have anything to do with the achievement? We simply cannot know.

Maturation

Another confounding event, particularly in education data, is maturation of the students. A few years ago we were involved in a meta-evaluation of a popular Title I math program for an urban school district (Paulson & Marchant, 2001; Paulson, Marchant, & Rothlisberg, 1999). The program employed special instructors to teach elementary students algebra using group involvement techniques. The program was received positively by both students (there were no tests) and teachers (they had an hour a day off). An evaluation of the program (which doubled students' math time) showed positive effects on state achievement tests in math. However, looking at the achievement broken down by grade level provided some insight. Our review of the program found little or no advantage for students at the lower grade levels; however, when students reached fifth grade and the program's algebra content matched the curriculum and was developmentally appropriate for the students, the extra math time mattered and the students excelled. Therefore, the achievement seemed less a result of the special nature of the costly program, but more a function of time-on-task as the students matured.

Testing

Our national obsession with testing requires close attention to a couple of problems associated with testing. The simple act of taking a test can improve a student's performance on subsequent tests; familiarity with the content and format of tests is likely to help a student on future tests regardless of instruction or intervention. Any special program that includes the use of a test similar to the outcome measure is likely to yield higher performance regardless of the nature of the rest of the program. Therefore, any gains in performance attributed to No Child Left Behind that mandate annual testing must be tempered with the fact that scores should increase even if "real learning" does not.

Mortality

We conducted a study, exploring whether having a high school graduation exam was related to states' SAT scores, that could have fallen victim to two threats to its validity: increased testing and mortality (Marchant & Paulson, 2005). Mortality occurs when members of a data set leave or they are removed from the data in a non-random fashion (mortality is almost never random), and this change in the data then influences the outcome of the study. In this study, we speculated that high schools that required a graduation exam would have a curriculum that is more focused on the exam content and less involved in the type of reasoning skills measured by the SAT, subsequently resulting in lower SAT scores. However, we were concerned that the states that required a high school graduation exam would have students who were more familiar with testing, thereby effectively increasing their SAT scores. In addition, states with graduation exams have lower graduation rates (Amrein & Berliner, 2002; Jacob, 2001; Marchant & Paulson, 2005), so lower performing students would not be taking the SAT; again, effectively raising a state's average SAT scores. Consequently, even if the presence of graduation exams had a negative impact on reasoning skills, the threats to validity would diminish such findings. Surprisingly, our analyses found that the graduation exams were related to lower SAT scores despite the confounding effects of testing and mortality. Had we not been aware of these possible threats, however, we may not have found the truth.

Instrumentation

Another threat to a study's validity involves measurement. In the process of collecting data, any change in the instrument (e.g., version of a survey or test, criteria or cutoff scores, or method of record keeping) may result in changes in scores over time that could be incorrectly attributed to another cause (e.g., student learning or quality of teaching). As state departments of education began to understand the requirements and procedures for demonstrating adequate yearly progress (AYP) for No Child Left Behind, they realized that the percentage of students passing the state achievement test was the functional criterion for avoiding negative consequences. Therefore, some states worked to lower their cutoff scores (Cavanagh, 2005). Simply looking at changes in pass rates in these states would suggest that learning had increased because more students were now passing the test, perhaps because of the implementation of NCLB. Obviously, such a conclusion would not be valid.

On the classroom level, teachers also collect data to inform their instruction. Increasingly, teachers are using pre-tests before their instruction to determine what students have learned from a lesson. To determine what students have learned from a pre-test to a post-test, the two instruments need to be similar: comparable in both content and difficulty. However, teachers sometimes make their pre-test relatively easy because the students have not been taught the material; then the post-test covers the more difficult new material. It is quite possible that students will do better on the easier pre-test than the more difficult post-test. Someone analyzing the data is left with the conclusion that the students became more ignorant because of instruction, when in reality no comparison can be made because of the threat to validity called instrumentation.

Regression to the Mean

Regression to the mean may help a remedial reading teacher (personal experience), but it can cause problems when teachers do not understand its threat to the validity of their classroom data. There is an established trend in testing that individual scores tend to gravitate toward the mean of a group of scores; so the students who score inordinately high on the first administration of a test are likely to score lower (closer to the mean) on a subsequent testing. Similarly, the students who score very low on a reading test are likely to have improved scores on the next test (score closer to the mean) even if the instruction was not particularly effective. Although this effect is usually small, it can be significant and create problems for data interpretation. Gifted programs that appear to be stagnant in achievement may actually be performing quite well, just as remedial programs may display false improvement. In large data sets with normal distributions, these effects tend to offset each other over time; therefore, although local school district scores may go up or down slightly, the overall scores for the state remain relatively stable.

In sum, research has identified many of the potential flaws in data that can get in the way of accurate analyses and well-informed decisions. There is a poignant saying in statistical analysis of data, "Garbage in, garbage out." If there is a problem with the data before they are analyzed, the results and conclusions in turn will be flawed. Using data at any level, classroom, school, or statewide, to make potentially important educational decisions requires a keen awareness of these potential threats.

Results, Analyses, and Statistics

Research is designed to describe, to look for relations among factors, or to look for differences among groups. The same is true for data-based decisions. Sometimes what is needed is just a deeper understanding of a situation; sometimes there is a need to know whether two or more events are related in some way, maybe such that some outcome can be predicted (like drop-outs); other times the issue concerns determining differences among two or more groups, perhaps between those using a special program and those who are not. In any case, once you know the purpose of the study, you can formulate specific questions that can guide the data you collect, how you collect them, and finally how you analyze them.

Analyzing data is probably one of the most difficult aspects of good research-based decision making. Often teachers, administrators, or other educators do not have the training to conduct appropriate statistical analyses on their data. For this reason, they produce simple statistics like means or frequencies, and such analyses rarely represent much by themselves. Data-based decision makers should seek the expertise to conduct meaningful analyses. This is the one aspect of data-based decision making that might require a good relationship with a local college or university. Academics in higher education can either provide the training or the consultation that will make any data-based decisions more effective. Although this section is not meant to provide the information that one would need to analyze data effectively, it will describe the techniques and terminology used in statistical analyses that can inform decision makers, whether they are merely reading the literature or deciding what types of analyses might be appropriate for the questions and purposes being examined.

Questions of Description

Descriptive research does just that (and only that); it describes what happened, without seeking to establish a cause or to determine group differences. It simply describes through qualitative narratives or quantitative means and distributions a unique situation or an unanticipated event. Statistics in a descriptive study are usually not very complicated: means and standard deviations. A mean is the arithmetic average: the scores (any quantitative measure) added up and divided by the number of scores. A standard deviation is the average distance from the mean for all of the scores. If most of the scores are close to the mean, the standard deviation is small. If there are large differences among the scores so that the range is great and the scores are spread out, the standard deviation is large. In some situations the distribution and standard deviation are as important as the mean in understanding data. For example, a group of students have a low mean and a small standard deviation on a test. An intervention is employed that raises the mean, but it greatly increases the standard deviation. Such results suggest that the intervention really helped some students a lot, but did not help others nearly as much. If you looked at the mean without considering the variation, you might assume that all students improved because of the intervention; a conclusion that might lead to less than adequate decisions in the future. Furthermore, to provide meaningful information for decision making, more complex questions and analyses are required.

Relationship Questions

To answer questions regarding relations among factors, correlation analyses are most common. A simple relationship can be addressed using a simple correlation (known as Pearson r); but questions addressing the relations among multiple factors would require multiple regression analyses. A multiple regression in simple terms is just a multiple correlation; the statistical analysis establishes how several factors are related to one outcome. To revisit some of our earlier questions: what factors are related to higher standardized test scores or lower drop-out rates? A multiple regression would report whether the factors are related to the outcome and which factors are more important to the relationship. It is crucial to remember, however, that correlation does not mean causation. To actually test whether or not an outcome was caused by some program or intervention, a more controlled design is required. In the case of most educational decisions that might be made at the classroom, school, or district level (testing a curriculum or program, for example), the most common way to answer the question of causation is to assess change over time or to compare groups (e.g., the group with the intervention to one without).

Causation Questions Using Change Scores or Group Differences

To show change, some type of pre-test or pre-measure is needed. As mentioned, the pre-measure needs to be the same in content and difficulty as the post-measure. Identical measures can be problematic due to familiarity to the specific instrument. The change between a pre-measure and a post-measure can be statistically tested to assess whether or not the change was large enough to be significant (i.e., that it was not due simply to chance). The simple statistic used to test the difference between two sets of scores is a t-test. Simply subtracting the pre-measure from the post-measure yields a change score that can be used in this analysis.

Similar to change scores, these same types of analyses can be used to analyze differences among groups. When an intervention or treatment (e.g., instructional technique or program) is examined for a group, that group is referred to as the experimental or treatment group. The group that does not receive the treatment is called the control group. Having a control group that is comparable to the treatment group is critical to determining the effectiveness of any treatment. Unfortunately, obtaining control groups can be a politically tricky endeavor. If there is a special population eligible for a program, it just makes sense to place all of these students (or the most needy of the students) in the program. However, if all of the eligible students receive the intervention, then comparisons on a range of outcomes including achievement between very needy students and not so needy students are likely to underestimate the effectiveness of the program. For example, a group of students, who are behind one grade level and progressing at about half a grade level each year, are placed in a special program where they progress three fourths of a grade level in a year. Such a change in achievement may represent substantial improvement for these students and indicate a successful program. Unfortunately, threats to validity, like selection and maturation, make it difficult to know whether the program itself was responsible for the change (maybe the students just matured during the course of the intervention and made greater gains because of normative changes in skill). A comparable control group who did not receive the treatment would show whether or not the change occurs naturally, in which case it would occur in the control group too, or whether the change occurred because of the intervention, in which case the control group would not show improvement over the same period of time. However, if this needy treatment group with .75 grade-level improvement is compared to a control group of regular classroom children who demonstrate their normal growth of one whole grade-level achievement, one might incorrectly conclude that the needy students would have achieved more had they not received the special program. Fortunately, there are statistical techniques to control for these pre-existing differences between experimental and control groups, but they are never as good as having a control group formed by randomly assigning students to either the treatment group or the control group. In educational settings, however, random assignment is usually neither politically nor ethically likely.

The more sophisticated analysis of variance (ANOVA) is needed to make comparisons among multiple groups (e.g., does school climate differ across four elementary schools in a given school district?) or to make comparisons among multiple factors that might differ between groups (e.g., does school climate differ by grade level and by school?). The ANOVA is similar to running multiple *t*-tests (just like a multiple regression is similar to running multiple correlations). The advantage of ANOVAs (and a troubling and confusing thing as well) is that the results for the group interactions are known as well. In this way, an administrator knows which schools and which grade levels reported a better school climate (these are known as main effects), but the administrator may also learn that fourth and fifth grades at two of the four schools have a significantly better school climate than the rest of the classes. This may provide much better direction for decisions than either of the main effects alone.

Interaction Questions

Most decisions in education are complicated, such that simple answers are either not enough or simply wrong. Interactions exist among most factors that might be measured in educational settings. It is not unusual for analyses to be conducted without concern for interactions (this is called a Type 6 Error; Newman, Marchant, & Ridenour, 1993). In the earlier ANOVA example regarding school climate, it is possible that both or neither main effect (grade level and school) was significant. Only knowing the main effects might have suggested that school climate was always better at upper-grade levels across all schools or that school climate was always better at two particular schools across all grade levels; or it could have indicated that none of the grade levels or schools were better than the others. Examination of the interaction would show that only two grades at two schools had a higher school climate. Perhaps the factor that is affecting school climate in two of the elementary schools is that the schools have designated content specialist teachers for the upper two grade levels. Knowing the true nature of the differences among schools and grade levels will lead to more accurate decisions for intervention or programming.

Another benefit of ANOVA, that is shared with multiple regression, is the ability to include covariates, usually to statistically control for differences among groups. The function of a covariate is to partition out the effect of a confounding variable that might threaten the validity of the study, so that other factors may be examined more accurately. In our study that explored the relations between graduation exams and SAT scores (Marchant & Paulson, 2005), one of the research questions was: Do states that require graduation exams have lower SAT scores? Going into the study, there was a confounding problem because over 90% of the differences among states have been associated with the education level of the test takers' parents and the percent of minority test takers in the states. Because these characteristics are not randomly distributed among states, it is possible that demographic variables like these could influence the results. Therefore, when the statistical analyses were performed, demographic variables were included as covariates to control for pre-existing differences among states. Although this approach is by far inferior to random assignment, it does reduce the effect that the known factors can have on the outcome.

Finally, it is important to mention that although good data are more important than more data, more data are good, and generally the more times something is measured the better. Multiple measurements before an intervention help to determine whether a trend existed that carries on through the treatment. In other words, what appeared to be an effect of an intervention could merely be the continuation of a trend. More important is the continuation of any effect after intervention. After an inservice, teachers feel very positively about a particular practice, but have they increased that practice a week later? If so, are they still using the particular practice a year later? There has been a great deal of research on Head Start and similar programs with most of it reaching the conclusion that immediate effects of these programs are decidedly positive; however, if there is no continued support for these students, the benefits diminish and disappear (Barnett & Hustedt, 2005). Therefore, regardless of the design and analysis, the purpose of the study should suggest the need for short-term and/or long-term results.

Interpreting and Misinterpreting Results

In conducting sound research, there is one final principle: drawing accurate conclusions. Any data-based decision that has heeded the preceding principles of research and evaluation will yield accurate conclusions from the results of whatever questions were being addressed. Even if those making decisions are not collecting the data or conducting the research, it is important that they know what they are looking for and not accept results blindly. Knowing what to look for in data and research allows decisions to be made correctly, or as importantly, provides insight into when to reject the data or the conclusions others have drawn.

Earlier the concept of validity was described in the context of arguments in logic as the truth. Assuming there were no serious factual or procedural errors, there are still threats to the truth. The context in which data are presented can inappropriately influence their acceptance, either positively or negatively. Not all data or research are from reliable sources, but not all questionable sources should be dismissed. Bias, real and perceived, is a threat to correctly identifying valid information for decision making.

Schools, school districts, and the state and federal governments collect much of their education data by involving academics from local colleges and universities. Moreover, many of the analyses of educational data are run in academic settings, although the federal government does some of its own research, and state departments of education issue many of their own reports. Most of what local schools and governmental agencies report are descriptive studies. Test scores or other indicators of achievement may be reported as going up or down, but there is seldom any type of sophisticated statistical analyses of what the data mean. This information is often released as reports and/or released to the media. Unfortunately, there are no reviews of the reports or their conclusions before the results are disseminated. Therefore the truth of what is presented is usually the interpretation of the results by the media. Test scores or other indicators change slightly (oftentimes due to chance) and suddenly public concerns are raised over the quality of education in a particular school, district, or state.

In contrast, research completed in colleges and universities (often funded by government agencies or private foundations) is usually presented at research conferences and published in professional journals. Before being accepted for presentation or publication, the studies must undergo blind review (authors and institutions are not identified) to establish the quality of the research, and other researchers critique the study to identify validity problems. Although professional organizations may accept half or more of the studies they review for their conferences, some journals of empirical research publish fewer than 5% of the manuscripts they receive for review. Any research that has undergone the scrutiny of academics or other research professionals is more likely to be a valid indicator of the state of educational practice.

One of the concerns of reviewers of empirical research is bias: Did the researchers ignore threats to validity and/or come to conclusions that likely misrepresent the truth because they were guided by a desire to obtain a particular result? The review process is an important step in safeguarding the public and other professionals from this type of misinformation. In contrast, when reports are directly issued and/or released to the press, they sidestep the review process. Fortunately, school and government reports that are more descriptive do not tend to present causal inferences or analyses that are open to much misinterpretation. Media sources are more likely to be guilty of presenting interpretations that inaccurately reflect what is being reported.

More recently, there has been a proliferation of think-tanks aligned with conservative policy agendas that issue research reports directly to the media. Although the think-tanks claim to be nonpartisan, their funding sources are not, and the research is often critical of public education practices and supportive of privatization efforts like vouchers and charter schools. This research has usually not withstood the review process of other empirical research endeavors, so their findings might need to be considered in that light. In an effort to provide academically sound reviews of this type of research, the Think-Tank Review Project (http://epsl.asu.edu/epru/thinktankreview.htm) was created as a collaboration between the Education Policy Research Unit at Arizona State University and the Education and the Public Interest Center at the University of Colorado. The reviews of this research have identified problems that range from slight errors in interpretation to fatal flaws in research methods and gross misstatements of facts. The Project also annually presents The Bunkum Awards that "highlight nonsensical, confusing, and disingenuous education reports produced by think tanks" that "have most egregiously undermined informed discussion and sound policy making" (Education Policy Research Unit, 2006). For example, the 2006 runner-up for the award "collected data, analyzed [the data], and then presented conclusions that their own data and analyses flatly contradicted" (Welner & Molnar, 2007).

Our review of the Title I math program previously mentioned found that student maturation influenced the results. This thorough evaluation of an existing evaluation is called a meta-evaluation. For this particular program quite a few evaluations had been conducted to assess the program's effectiveness, most by a former school administrator who became associated with the project. All of these evaluations were very positive about the impact of the project on math and even English achievement (that in itself raised questions for us: why would a program specific to algebra improve English skills?). There were only a couple of evaluations available from other sources, both of which were negative and resulted in the school districts involved dropping the program. The conclusion of our meta-evaluation of the program in a large midwestern urban school district was inconclusive in that the data presented in the evaluations did not clearly substantiate their positive conclusions (Paulson, Marchant, & Rothlisberg 1999).

Consumers of research and educational decision makers need to be careful not to blindly accept or reject data-based information. This is true of publicized accounts in the media, as well as more local reporting of data. Fallacies can undermine the correct interpretation of data and lead to misinterpretations that cause either incorrect acceptance or rejection of information. Fallacies are errors in reasoning that, if better understood, are easier to avoid (see Table 14.1, adapted from Labossiere, 1995). As with any information, decision makers need to consider their sources. However, they need to be knowledgeable enough of research principles to judge the data, research, and conclusions independent of the sources.

Future Directions

In the past, the types of research questions addressed by academic researchers and school administrators have been somewhat different. Academia was interested in investigating psychological concepts, theoretical models of learning, and general teaching approaches (like cooperative learning). School districts, on the other hand,

Table 14.1 Thirteen fallacies and examples that can detract from data for decision making.

Fallacy	Example statement
Characteristics of the person	"Of course you found our students do better in reading than math, you're an English teacher."
Previous position	"During our last negotiations you thought the health care provisions were fine, so how can you say there is a problem now?"
Position of authority	"I don't care about the problems you claim to have found with the program, Dr. Smith says it leads to more achievement."
Appeal to a belief	"Everyone knows that the schools in this country are failing, so they must be bad."
Common practice/tradition	"We have always used basal readers, why are you trying to change things?"
Appeal to emotion	"The students and the teachers all love Project C, so it must be doing great things."
Appeal to novelty	"This new math curriculum is fresh off the press, it is going to be great."
Appeal to ridicule	"Those who can't do, teach; now they even want more money for supplies, right!"
Burden of proof	"You have not proven that cooperative learning works, so we're going back to lecturing."
Confusing cause and effect	"We tend to have lower expectations for poor low achieving students. So, those poor students do not achieve as much because of the low expectations."
Hasty generalization	"Ms. Artbunkle's class didn't benefit from the extra tutoring, so why waste money on it for the other classes?"
Misleading vividness	"Of course violent crime is up in schools, don't you remember hearing about the awful shooting in that school last month?"
Straw man	"You want to reduce emphasis on standardized testing. Fine, let's just eliminate all accountability for schools."

wanted information about their specific schools and specific programs. Although there was some overlap between the two areas of inquiry, schools were put off by much of the statistics and research jargon. Similarly, researchers wanted answers to the big questions and did not like being limited to a context that would make it difficult to generalize their findings.

Recently there has been a convergence of perspectives. Among decision makers in education, there is a growing acceptance of methods once considered the domain of educational researchers, as educators are realizing that getting to the truth is the important next step to having data support their decisions. Approaches once considered obstacles, such as control groups and statistical analysis, are now accepted as important tools for making sound decisions; and being able to demonstrate results in an objective, justifiable way is now the currency of funding and programmatic decisions. Likewise, educational researchers are acknowledging the importance of context and recognizing the function of exploring specific programs that operationalize their concepts (Ball & Forzani, 2007). Although much theoretical research still exists, studies regarding bigger concepts in carefully controlled laboratory settings are very few. The bottom line now for most research is: Can this study improve school learning or inform educational policy? And the answer to that question does not stop with statistical significance, either.

Even the statistics presented in educational research have become more applied. The most popular statistical test of significance, based on the number of participants in the study and variability on the measures, indicates the likelihood that relations among variables or differences among groups is due to chance. With a large sample size, very small differences or relationships could be statistically significant, but are they relatively important? For example, in a study of effects of high stakes testing on state math achievement (Marchant, Paulson, & Shunk, 2006), both demographic differences among students and high stakes testing indicators across states were significant indicators of state math achievement. However, the demographic differences across states accounted for 78% of the variance, whereas differences in high stakes testing indicators accounted for only 3% (NAEP Math). Both were statistically significant, but relatively speaking, how important were the high stakes testing indicators?

Consequently, the statistic now used more commonly to reflect the relative impact of a factor is called an "effect size." One indicator of effect size uses a standardized form of means and standard deviations to assess the relative difference between two groups on some outcome. In this case, the mean for the control group is set at zero with a standard deviation of one (similar to z-scores) and the effect size tells where the mean for the experimental group would be on that scale if the factor of interest were present (e.g., some program or teaching method). In a popular article from 1984, Bloom reviewed the effect sizes generated from all of the research on effective teaching from the 1970s and 1980s in an effort to find methods of group instruction as effective as one-to-one instruction. One-to-one instruction had been found to have an effect size of two. This meant that compared to traditional instruction, an equivalent group of students receiving one-to-one instruction would achieve with a mean two standard deviations above the mean of the group receiving traditional instruction (this is a huge difference). This translates to about 98% of the one-to-one instruction group scoring above the mean of the traditional instruction group (welcome to Lake Wobegon where all the kids are above average).

Effect size is an extremely useful tool for those making data-based decisions, especially in conducting cost-benefit analyses in schools. In education, costs and benefits seldom use the same unit of measure; whereas costs can usually be measured in money or time, benefits are often a measure like student achievement or graduation rate. Effect size allows one to conceptualize the size of a benefit. If there are few costs associated with a programmatic benefit in school achievement, the decision is easy. If there is a major cost and little benefit determined by a small effect size, the decision is also easy. It is when costs and benefits are both considerable that decisions become more difficult. Although effect size does not put costs and benefits on the same scale, it is an effort by educational researchers to give decision makers a common gauge for considering outcomes.

The discussion of cost-benefit analysis points out the difficulty that educators face in data-based decision making that does not exist in the business world. This is important to elucidate because there are always those trying to impose a "business model" on education and educational decision making. As in medicine, the ultimate outcome of the process of education results in the quality of life of people. It is difficult to answer questions like: How much is a program worth that is likely to keep 10 students a year from dropping out? A school could calculate the funding it loses from a student dropping out, but that is not the point of education. There is a societal and humanitarian imperative that goes beyond dollars and cents. How much is it worth for a disadvantaged child to achieve a complete grade level in one year versus something less? How much is that worth to the child? To the parents? To society?

The decisions faced by educators are some of the most difficult of any profession. The outcomes are sometimes abstract, long-term, and difficult to gauge. Simple information may be useful, but it can also be wrong. Although the immediate concern must be the education of students, teachers and parents and the general public all have a vested interest in the education process. Turning guesswork into data-based decision making is a step in the right direction, while finding the truth in the data and the results by adopting educational research procedures is another step. Decision making in education will never be a perfect science or be able to function under a strict business model but making the best decision possible has always been the goal, and data bases and research methodology are changing what is possible in a very positive way.

References

Amrein, A. L., & Berliner, D. C. (2002). *An analysis of some unintended and negative consequences of high stakes testing* (Research document). Tempe, AZ: Education Policy Research Unit, Education Policy Studies Laboratory. Retrieved January 15, 2008, from http://epsl.asu.edu/epru/documents/EPSL-0211–125-EPRU.pdf

Ball, D. L., & Forzani, F. M. (2007). What makes educational research "educational?" *Educational Researcher, 36*, 529–540.

Barnett, W. S., & Hustedt, J. T. (2005). Head Start's lasting benefits. *Infants and Young Children, 18*, 16–24.

Bloom, B. S. (1984). The 2 sigma problem: The search for methods of group instruction as effective as one-to-one tutoring. *Educational Researcher, 13*(6), 4–16.

Boote, D. N., & Beile, P. (2005). Scholars before researchers: On the centrality of the dissertation literature review in research preparation. *Educational Researcher, 34*, 3–15.

Cavanagh, S. (2005). Illinois board lowers bar on English-learners' test. *Education Week, 24*, 25.

Cook, T. D., & Campbell, D. T. (1979). *Quasi-experimentation.* Boston: Houghton-Mifflin.

Education Policy Research Unit (2006). *Bunkum awards in education.* Retrieved October 4, 2007, from the Arizona State University Education Policy Studies Laboratory website: http://espl.asu.edu/epru/epru_2006_bunkum.htm

Jacob, B. A. (2001). Getting tough? The impact of high school graduation exams. *Educational Evaluation and Policy Analysis, 23*(2), 99–121.

Jimerson, S. R., & Kaufman, A. M. (2003). Reading, writing, and retention: A primer on grade retention research. *The Reading Teacher, 56*, 622–635.

Kowalski, T. J., Lasley, T. J., & Mahoney, J. W. (2008). *Data-driven decisions and school leadership: Best practices for school improvement.* Boston: Pearson.

Labossiere, M. C. (1995). *Fallacy tutorial pro 3.0, A Macintosh tutorial.* Retrieved December 25, 2007, from The Nizkor Project website: http://www.nizkor.org/features/fallacies/

Lubienski, C. (2007). Charter schools, academic achievement and NCLB. *Journal of School Choice, 1*(3) 55–62.

Marchant, G. J., & Paulson, S. E. (2001). State comparisons of SAT Scores: Who's your test taker? *NASSP Bulletin, 85*(627), 62–74.

Marchant, G. J., & Paulson, S. E. (2005). The relationship of high school graduation exams to graduation rates and SAT scores. *Education Policy Analysis Archives, 13*(6). Retrieved October 26, 2007, from http://epaa.asu.edu/epaa/v13n6/

Marchant, G. J., Ordonez, O. M. M., & Paulson, S. E. (2008, August). *Contributions of race, income, and cognitive ability to school level achievement.* Paper to be presented at the American Psychological Association, Boston.

Marchant, G. J., Paulson, S. E., & Shunk, A. (2006). Relationships between high-stakes testing policies and student achievement after controlling for demographic factors in aggregated data. *Educational Policy Analysis Archives, 14*(30). Retrieved October 26, 2007, from http://epaa.asu.edu/epaa/v14n30/

Meltzoff, J. (1998). *Critical thinking about research: Psychology and related fields.* Washington, DC: American Psychological Association.

Newman, I., Marchant, G. J., & Ridenour, T. (1993, April). *Type VI errors in path analysis: Testing for interactions.* Paper presented at the American Educational Research Association, Altanta, GA (ERIC Document Reproduction Service No. ED 362 529).

Newman, I., Ridenour, C., Newman, C., & DeMarco, G., Jr. (2003). A typology of research purposes and its relationship to mixed methods. In A. Tashakkori & C. Teddie (Eds.), *Handbook of mixed methods in social and behavioral research* (pp. 167–188). Thousand Oaks, CA: Sage.

Paulson, S. E., & Marchant, G. J. (2001, April). *Does Project SEED improve math achievement and self-concept?* Paper presented at the annual meeting of the American Educational Research Association, Seattle, WA.

Paulson, S. E., Marchant, G. J., & Rothlisberg, B. A. (1999). *Review of Project SEED* (unpublished evaluation). Muncie, IN: Educational Program Evaluation Center, Ball State University.

Popham, W. J. (1993). *Educational evaluation* (3rd ed.). Englewood Cliffs, NJ: Prentice-Hall.

Rogers, P. J., Hacsi, T. A., Petrosino, A., & Huebner, T. A. (Eds.) (2000). Program theory evaluation: Practice, promise, and problems. *New Directions for Evaluation, 87,* 5–13.

Schalock, R. L. (2001). *Outcome-based evaluation* (2nd ed.). New York: Kluwer.

Stufflebeam, D. L., Foley, W. J., Gephart, W. J., Hammond, L. R., Merriman, H. O., & Provus, M. M. (1971). *Educational evaluation and decision-making in education.* Itasca, IL: Peacock.

Weiss, C. H. (1997). Theory-based evaluation: Past, present, and future. *New Directions for Evaluation, 76,* 41–53.

Welner, K. G., & Molnar, A. (2007, February 28). Truthiness in education [Commentary]. *Education Week, 26*(5). Retrieved January 2, 2008, from http://epsl.asu.edu/epru/articles/EPSL-0702–407-OWI.pdf

Zimmer, R., Gill, B., Razquin, P., Booker, K., Lockwood, J. R., Vernez, G. et al. (2007). *State and local implementation of the No Child Left Behind Act: Volume I—Title I school choice, supplemental educational services, and student achievement,* Retrieved December 15, 2007, from the Department of Education website: http://www.ed.gov/rsch-stat/eval/choice/implementation/achievementanalysis.doc

Part III: Data-Based Applications

15

Using Data to Make Critical Choices

Thomas J. Lasley II
University of Dayton

The use of data to make decisions is not new. Historically, practicing professionals (lawyers, doctors) have used data to make decisions to benefit the clients they serve. Similarly, scholars (academics) have always been devoted to the use of data and information in ways that further professional understandings and expand the professional literature. More recently educational professionals (teachers and school administrators) have been using varied databases to shape educational practices in order to understand and enhance student and school performance.

What is changing, and changing rapidly for all educators in general and classroom practitioners in particular is the access to and use of data. The No Child Left Behind world, whether good or bad in terms of its demands on student achievement, is clearly influencing how teachers think about and use data.

This chapter focuses on the use of varied databases to make program and instructional decisions. Such decision making can be deceptively complex. How does a teacher sort through the masses of available data and information in order to make a thoughtful decision? And, once a decision has been made, how do teachers implement those decisions? This chapter focuses on questions around the use of data by teachers and the relative success of teachers in using data in educationally efficacious ways. More specifically, why do some teachers become "high performers" in using data to make decisions about classroom practices while others, seemingly, evidence low performance? What steps are taken by high performers to ensure that the decisions they do make are effective in achieving defined outcomes?

The decision-making process starts with understanding the context and the data being used. An aphorism in philosophy suggests, if you grant someone the first premise, anything can be proven. In essence, where one starts will influence the conclusions that are reached. For decision making the consequences seem clear. If teachers limit (or circumscribe) the data being used, they should not be surprised by the conclusions that they subsequently reach.

Data Sources and Interpretation

A simple Internet query on almost any topic will yield pages of information and facts that potentially can be used to make decisions about practices, problems or issues.

The practices or problems may be highly conceptual and theoretical, with scholarly implications, or largely practical in nature, with direct applications to one's personal life (e.g., how to purchase a car online) or a teacher's classroom practice (e.g., vivid pictorial accounts of a famous battle).

Scholars in almost all disciplinary fields use data to reach conclusions or produce recommendations that in turn become the foundations for public policy. Inevitably, those conclusions and recommendations are shaped by the ideological biases or intellectual dispositions of those interpreting the data. Though this chapter will not focus on how personal subjectivity influences the policy or practice decisions an individual makes, it is critical to understand that the world view any scholar or professional practitioner possesses influences the conclusions ultimately reached. As an example, many social reformers concerned with socioeconomic inequities between Blacks and Whites have argued that the civil rights legislation and Great Society programs of the 1960s are the reasons why Blacks in America have become more socioeconomically competitive. In 1940, 87% of all Black families lived in poverty; in 1970, that figure was 30%, and with the "help" of affirmative action programs, so the social reform argument goes, that figure dropped even further (Sowell, 2005). The conclusion seems logical: The social reform programs of the 1960s impacted positively the socioeconomic circumstances of Blacks and, as a consequence, persons of color became more economically competitive. Many used those data about poverty and the associated conclusions to argue for more social reform-type programs because they believed certain social policies needed to be instituted by the federal government given the data that were available to policy makers.

Sowell (2005), however, "mined" some of the same data and reached a different conclusion. Indeed, Sowell observed that "the poverty rate among blacks had been nearly cut in half [*before*] either the civil rights revolution or the Great Society programs began in the 1960s" (p. 24). Sowell's "answer" for the poverty rate drop was education and access to it. Sowell writes:

> Similarly, despite a widespread tendency to see the rise of blacks out of poverty as due to the civil rights movement and government social programs of the 1960s, in reality the rise of blacks out of poverty was greater in the two decades *preceding* 1960 than in the decades that followed. Education was a major factor in this as well. As of 1940, non-white males averaged just 5.4 years of schooling, compared to 8.7 for white males. Over the next two decades, the absolute amount of education increased for both—and the gap between them narrowed. In 1940, the difference in schooling between black and white young adult males, aged 25 to 29, was four years but, by 1960, that had shrunk to less than two years. Because this was an era of massive black migration out of the South, this quantitative narrowing of the gap in schooling may well have been accompanied by a qualitative improvement, as many blacks left behind the low-quality schools in the Jim Crow South. (p. 241)

Clearly, one problem in using data to make decisions is decision-maker objectivity. Just as it is a hopeless task to attempt to eliminate biases from the research process itself, it is also virtually impossible to eradicate the ideological and dispositional biases of any individual who is reading research for the purpose of making a decision (Kaplan, 1964). The less inclined the decision maker is to understand and explore personal values and biases, the less likely it is that the decisions reached will be efficacious. The key is to make explicit what those biases are and to fully understand the conceptual or empirical basis that underpins the research product.

But, even when decision-maker values and biases do not play a significant role in policy and practice decisions, access to good data can still make decision making difficult for professionals and more significantly for the clients being served. Educators are just beginning to deal with this reality. Educational practices have been ideologically driven for decades. Few teachers or researchers could prove that their methods were "best practices" for students, so they simply argued for others to embrace advocated approaches based on theoretical arguments and selected anecdotal evidence. The method de jure was often a result of what conference or professional meeting a teacher or principal had just attended, not on sound evidence about what educational practice really worked. Educators are not the only ones who have struggled with knowing how to access and use good data to ground sound practice, and they are not the only professionals who have had to ascertain if practices "advertised" as best for clients truly represented that in reality. To illustrate this fact, consider Gawande's (2004) description of cystic fibrosis (CF) medical practices.

In particular, Gawande (2004) describes the plight of two parents, Honor and Don Page, who have a child with CF. The Pages, like all parents, wanted the best treatment possible for their child and began a search for appropriate medical care. They were making a critical life and death decision: What hospital or team of doctors could extend the life of their child? Using the information that they as parents had available, the Pages selected Cincinnati Children's Hospital, which, putatively, was known as one of the most respected CF facilities in the country.

The reality, as Gawande (2004) suggests, was something quite different from what the Pages concluded:

> The one thing that the [Cincinnati] clinicians failed to tell them [the Pages], however, was that Cincinnati Children's was not, as the Pages supposed, among the country's best centers for children with cystic fibrosis. According to data from that year, it was, at best, an average program. This was no small matter. In 1997, patients at an average center were living to be just over thirty years old; patients at the top center typically lived to be forty-six. By some measures, Cincinnati was well below average. The best predictor of a CF patient's life expectancy is his or her lung function. At Cincinnati, lung function for patients under the age of twelve—children like Annie [the Pages' daughter]—was in the bottom twenty-five per cent of the country's CF patients. And the doctors there knew it. (p. 2)

The Pages' biases did not mitigate the quality of the decision they were making; rather, they simply lacked key data (in this case, patient lung function statistics) necessary to determine where they could receive the best care for their child. Patient lung function data would have pointed the Pages to seek treatment at the truly exceptional Minneapolis Cystic Fibrosis Center, Fairview-University Children's Hospital, whose programs in 1997 were adding up to 16 years of life for patients. Not an insignificant time period for anyone, but especially so for young people with CF who at best might live to their mid-40s.

Interestingly, when Gawande visited the best CF center in the country, the Minneapolis Cystic Fibrosis Center, he uncovered a significant variable in the data-driven decision-making process. Physicians there were using data and information that extended beyond extant research *and* informed professional judgments to reach conclusions about professional practice. Gawande implicitly concludes that an over-reliance on one CF data source (e.g., the research that currently exists) and an unwillingness to continually explore a problem results all too frequently in an ineffectual decision. The Minneapolis Cystic Fibrosis Center's high success rate could be traced back to the efforts of an aging, indefatigable doctor, Warren Warwick, who argued for "an expiration date" on research findings and who evidenced aggressiveness, ingenuity, and intuitiveness in solving CF problems. Despite his years of successful experience as a clinician, Warwick was not ideologically bound to one way of treating CF patients or interpreting data. His approach was to employ continual data collection to intentionally move beyond the traditional evidence base accessed by most physicians. By expanding the type of data he collected, Warwick better equipped himself to make the best decisions on behalf of his CF clients.

In summary, good CF treatment data-based decisions were being made under three conditions, and those same three conditions pertain to decision making by teachers and administrators:

1. The decision maker (teacher) possesses a clear awareness of personal biases.
2. The decision maker (teacher) has access to good data, understands the appropriate "timeliness" of such data for problems of practice, and has a reasonable amount of time to examine data sources.
3. The decision maker (teacher) is never satisfied with the data that currently exist and assiduously and thoughtfully looks for other types of qualitative and quantitative data to support decisions made on behalf of clients (students).

The Data-Driven Decision-Making Bell Curve

In every profession there is a performance bell curve representing a few top performers, a relatively larger number of average performers, and then a smaller (hopefully) group of under-performers. Though everyone likes to believe that his or her doctor or lawyer or school teacher is in the top performance category, the reality is that many clients ultimately select professionals who are simply average—less skilled than the best diagnosticians and decision makers in the field. The differences between average and best may appear subtle, but the end results in critical services like heart surgery or elementary reading instruction can have life-altering implications. Gawande observes:

> In ordinary hernia operations, the chances of recurrence are one in ten for surgeons at the unhappy end of the spectrum, one in twenty for those in the middle majority, and under one in five hundred for a handful. A Scottish study of patients with treatable colon cancer found that the ten-year survival rate ranged from a high of sixty-three per cent to a low of twenty-per cent, depending on the surgeon. For heart bypass patients, even at hospitals with a good volume of experience, risk-adjusted death rates in New York vary from five per cent to under one per cent—and only a very few hospitals are down near the one-per-cent mortality rate. (p. 2)

Educators are just beginning to understand the qualitative difference that the best teachers can make in classrooms. Coleman et al. (1966) asserted that schools contributed in minimal ways to student achievement; the real influence on student achievement was the family. This orientation persisted through the mid-1990s, with proponents arguing that parents (and parental socioeconomic status) were the primary determiners of student performance. Teachers were considered secondary in terms of enhancing student academic growth. With the value-added research of the past decade, that priority ordering has changed. Educators now proceed from the understanding that effective teachers can "trump" parents in terms of fostering and influencing student academic learning. Nye, Konstantopoulos, and Hedges (2004) reported that:

> These findings would suggest that the difference in achievement gains between having a 25th percentile teacher (a not so effective teacher) and a 75th percentile teacher (an effective teacher) is over one-third of a standard deviation (0.35) in reading and almost half a standard deviation (0.48) in mathematics. Similarly, the difference in achievement gains between having a 50th percentile teacher (an average teacher) and a 90th percentile teacher (a very effective teacher) is about one-third of a standard deviation (0.33) in reading and somewhat smaller than half a standard deviation (0.46) in mathematics. . . . These effects are certainly large enough effects to have policy significance. (p. 253)

Nye and colleagues confirm what many other value-added researchers document: better teachers make a bigger academic difference. In essence, their work confirms the existence of a performance bell curve for schools and for teachers just as is found in other professions. And, as in other fields, where an educator lands on that bell curve depends in part on how effectively he or she makes decisions using data.

Professional Decision-Making Performance Levels

One of the critical dynamics is *how* professionals use data to make decisions. At each level of performance, is it possible to see what is or is not occurring that separates excellence from mediocrity? For the purposes of this chapter, only two groups, high performers and low performers, will be considered relative to their uses of data to make decisions about practice. (See Table 15.1.)

Characteristics (Low Performers)	*Characteristics (High Performers)*
Use learning patterns for *some* students to generalize principles of instruction for *all* students	Understand that patterns for some students are not mandates for all learners
Seek "one way" of approaching students even when conflicting data are evidenced	Understand "exceptions" and can appreciate how to use opposing ideas to deal with exceptions
Use personal biases in ways that limit instructional options	Never allow biases to limit the options they explore
Possess a narrow view of what constitutes "data"	Look for data everywhere from a variety of formal and informal sources
Unwilling to try new teaching methods that are unfamiliar and feel uncomfortable	Willing to try new teaching methods, even if they are unfamiliar or initially uncomfortable

Table 15.1 Low and high performers data-based decision-maker bell curve.

High performers use data with an openness to significant data anomalies. That is, they know what they believe but are not bound by it, and they look for relevant data but understand that "patterns in findings" do not mandate action. Exceptions to the norm are matters of personal and professional interest. High performers understand how to use data in ways that match client or situational needs. They may be ideological, but they are still able to see and interpret exceptions in ways that serve the best interests of the clients (or students) they serve.

Collins (2001) captures this characteristic best: The high performers "lead with questions, not answers" (p. 74). Those questions drive them in insatiable ways to find answers to complex problems of practice. True: high performers have biases. Equally true: they never allow those biases to keep them from searching for or using data that might cause professional discomfort. Collins describes the disposition toward inquisitiveness of great leaders (and decision makers) by describing from business the behaviors of Alan Wurtzel (creator of Circuit City):

> When Alan Wurtzel started the long traverse from near bankruptcy to these stellar results, he began with a remarkable answer to the question of where to take the company: *I don't know.* Unlike [other] leaders, Wurtzel resisted the urge to walk in with "the answer." Instead, once he put the right people on the bus, he began not with answers, but with *questions.* (p. 74)

Interestingly, teachers who are high performers evidence this same drive to get things right and to do so in ways that ensure success for all students. Haberman (1995) called these high performers "star teachers." Their "star power" was reflected in how they treated the teaching act as a problem-solving activity that caused them to look for answers with persistence and creativity.

Haberman's "stars" know that no one answer is sufficient because no two children are alike. In Haberman's words: "[Stars] not only listen, they hear. They not only hear, they seek to understand. They regard listening to children, parents, or anyone involved in the school community as a potential source of useful information" (p. 93).

The high-performing star teachers look for information everywhere as they structure the classroom environment. They want to know test scores, but they understand that such scores (whether from standardized or teacher-made tests) are only part of the educational practice equation. The pedagogical stars, those who are able to make thoughtful and effective decisions, are individuals who know that data are, quite simply, everywhere. They look at multiple sources (both formal and informal) as they make instructional decisions, and they do so in ways that foster emotionally and academically healthy classrooms.

Low performers frequently do not use or do not have access to data about the systems within which they work. Other low performers do have access to data, but they use them without regard to context factors. Many low or under-performers simply do not want the facts or data to confuse what they perceive as the answer. Consider this example from the corporate world. Collins (2001) describes the tendency in the decision making of Roy Ash (CEO of Addressograph), who possessed a plan for growth but failed to consider all the different types of data that would allow him to gauge its effectiveness. Collins notes:

Ash set forth a vision to dominate the likes of IBM, Xerox, and Kodak in the emerging field of office automation—a bold plan for a company that had previously only dominated the envelope-address-duplication business. There is nothing wrong with a bold vision, but Ash became so wedded to his quixotic quest that, according to *Business Week*, he refused to confront the mounting evidence that his plan was doomed to fail and might take down the rest of the company with it. He insisted on milking cash from profitable arenas, eroding the core business while throwing money after a gambit that had little chance of success.

Later, after Ash was thrown out of office and the company had filed for bankruptcy (from which it did later emerge), he still refused to confront reality, saying: "We lost some battles, but we were winning the war." But Addressograph was not even close to winning the war, and people throughout the company knew it at the time. Yet the truth went unheard until it was too late. In fact, many of Addressograph's key people bailed out of the company, dispirited by their inability to get top management to deal with the facts. (pp. 70–71)

Low-performing teachers evidence the "Ash" tendency. For whatever reasons, they are unable (or unwilling) to appreciate the complexity of the classroom environment. Some fail to understand the different ways in which children and young people learn; others are steadfastly singular in how they teach content. All children, regardless of their socioeconomic context, are mistakenly assumed to learn content one way, and many low performing teachers justify that "one way" as being well grounded on the extant research (e.g., direct instruction).

Those low performers fail to appreciate the intuitive aspects of the decision-making process. Because they possess "the answers," they are blind to all the other facts confronting them about the students they teach. That blindness has significant social and academic consequences, most importantly students who fail to reach their potential by dropping out of school, either physically or psychologically.

The blindness to multiple data sources may be even more pronounced in many urban school districts where an acute focus exists on alignment issues (standards with instruction, instruction with assessment) and where teachers often find themselves "encouraged" to use highly scripted approaches to content delivery. Hess (2005) and others argue eloquently for aligning the systems within urban schools to ensure enhanced student opportunities for success. They point to examples of where alignment has occurred, such as San Diego City Schools, and describe the imperative of "common strategies" in order for students to truly reach their potential. Though low performing schools (and teachers) may benefit from enhanced uniformity and alignment, it is imperative that reformers do not lose sight of the fact that the drive for consistency must never compromise teachers' focus on bringing together the art and science of teaching. Such a compromise will deaden the learning environment of the school (Kozol, 2005).

The ability to appropriately blend the art and science of teaching separates the high performers from their low-performing colleagues. Low performers tend to rely too exclusively on their intuition or too narrowly on one real or imagined scientifically based approach. Marzano (2007) captures the essence of this balancing act for making decisions in the classroom:

In short, research will never be able to identify instructional strategies that work with every student in every class. The best research can do is tell us which strategies have a good chance (i.e., high probability) of working well with students. Individual classroom teachers must determine which strategies to employ with the right students at the right time. (p. 5)

Steps in the Decision-Making Process

If, then, high-performing teachers and principals use data and draw those data from multiple external and personal sources, what process do they (or should they) follow in arriving at best practice answers? The steps outlined below are not a prescription for dealing with the multiple routine decisions that are made daily by classroom practitioners. Instead, they should be considered as a process that can be used in addressing more serious problems of practice such as determining the most effective reading approach to use with a particular student or crafting educational practices that will specifically address school drop-out problems.

Step 1: Articulate the Problem or Question   Without a clear sense of what a problem is, it is quite literally impossible to move through the decision-making process in a thoughtful manner. Teachers and administrators need to begin by isolating the core problem to be solved *and* identifying the associated questions that need to be answered. For example:

   Problem: An achievement gap exists between White and Black students at the middle grade levels in X urban school district.
   Questions:

1. What is the magnitude of the achievement gap for the different schools within the district?
2. Do any "pockets of excellence" appear within the district? In other words, are some schools and teachers effectively reducing the gap?
3. What types of professional development might be instituted to address the achievement gap problem? What practices have worked in other districts to reduce the gap, and how can those methods be adapted to meet local needs?

Notice that in answering the questions the decision maker is doing more than simply collecting a list of practices used by other school districts. The focus is on what practices appear to be working in other districts to reduce the achievement gap and on how best to transport successful practices from another district to one's own situation.

Step 2: Identify What "Model" Will be Used to Answer the Questions and Address the Problem   Some problems require reliance on more limited amounts of data because they are relatively simple or they require an almost immediate response. Others are more complex and entail (and provide for) the involvement of more personnel and access to more varied data. Ikemoto and Marsh (2007) describe four different types of database usage models:

   Basic: Involves limited database usage and a relatively simple decision-making process (e.g., a single teacher or administrator decides what is best given a particular circumstance).

   Analysis-focused: Involves limited database usage but requires a much more complex set of dynamics to make the decision (e.g., may involve a team of individuals who must reach agreement of what approach to use). According to Ikemoto and Marsh (2007), the decisions emerging from analysis-focused approaches "were less likely to take advantage of expert knowledge, empirical evidence, and sophisticated analysis techniques to interpret and explain the data" (p. 114). In essence, those making the decision rely on one type of data (e.g., test data) to make decisions even though they might be very inclusive of experts and others in terms of acting on the data.

Data-focused: Involves the use of complex databases, but the decisions reached tend to be time specific (i.e., occur at one point in time). Those who use this approach tend not to access expert opinion or to draw on the available empirical research. They tend to access lots of data but, regrettably, engage in a simpler, less sophisticated analysis of the data utilized.

Inquiry-focused: By far the most time-intensive and in-depth approach, the inquiry-focused model brings together a wide variety of stakeholders who, through both formal and informal meetings, draw on "multiple types and sources of data, [engage] in a collective effort to examine evidence, and [consider] expertise as part of an ongoing process of improvement" (Ikemoto & Marsh, 2007, p. 119).

Ikemoto and Marsh (2007) assert that the type of model used is typically dictated by factors such as accessibility (i.e., are multiple data sources actually available?) and staff capacity (i.e., do faculty members possess the requisite expertise to either interpret the data they have access to or to formulate and answer the questions that are essential for enhanced practice?). In their words, with inquiry-focused decision making "educators drew on multiple types and sources of data, engaged in a collective effort to examine evidence, and considered expertise as part of an on-going process of improvement" (p. 119).

In essence, teachers and administrators need to be able to identify salient problems, identify relevant questions vis-à-vis those problems, and then use an appropriate decision-making model. Though, in the ideal, inquiry-focused models would appear most desirable, in reality they may often be untenable because they require too much time or faculty expertise (see, for example, Jerald, 2008).

Basic decision-making models often evolve solely out of immediate practical considerations (e.g., what is possible given obvious extant resources or the time available to make a decision). Unfortunately, reliance on such approaches may also result in faulty or undesirable practices. When too few data sources are accessed, when data sources are misinterpreted, or when findings are not adequately vetted by knowledgeable persons, the conclusions reached are either spurious or intervention steps that may not be appropriately implemented. Smith (2008) notes:

> In the past three years, the idea of using data to help improve instruction has caught on like wildfire in the United States. Unfortunately, many schools and districts do not appreciate the complexity of the process: Teachers must have effective and easy-to-use measurement instruments, they must have the knowledge to interpret the instruments, and then they must understand how to alter their instruction to respond to the diagnostic information the instruments provide. In many districts, none of the steps is successfully implemented. (p. 379)

Data-Based Decision Making: Mitigating Factors to Taking the Steps

Teachers and administrators are making decisions each and every day. They are forced by their respective roles to be decision makers. As discussed previously, however, the quality of the decision making varies according to the person, the particular situational context, and the decision-making process (or model) used. But what can educators do about that variation in effectiveness? If it is imperative that teachers and administrators become high-performing decision makers for their students to achieve their learning potential, what conditions or circumstances mitigate decision-making effectiveness? In essence, what factors negatively influence or impede the quality of the decisions being made in schools and by teachers in classrooms?

Factor 1

Teachers possess limited technical skill in using and interpreting data. Until recently, the demands placed on educators to use data to make decisions were limited, or at least they were not formalized and explicit. Clearly, the No Child Left Behind (NCLB) legislation in 2002, whether right or wrong in terms of its expectations, has placed more emphasis on using data to make decisions about efficacious educational practices.

Regrettably, far too many teachers and administrators have far too little preparation for interpreting the test results (and other data) they now have available (Jerald, 2008). Reeves and Burt (2006) note that practicing educators are often well aware of their deficiencies in data analysis: "Principals expressed concern about their own lack of training and understanding of how to use data. Several admitted having fears about mathematics and data analysis" (p. 67).

As a result, many educators over-rely on the basic decision-making model (i.e., one person using limited data to make a decision) because they do not trust themselves (or perhaps others) to engage in more sophisticated types of analysis. They simply do not believe that their academic preparation provided them with the skills necessary to conduct more sophisticated analysis or that their innate abilities predispose them to examine complex databases in ways that will result in enhanced practice. Further, they may not know how to access or use the type of expertise needed in order to more thoughtfully examine multiple data sources. If teachers and school administrators are going to be expected to analyze complex databases and "cross-tabulate information to work for telling patterns" (Jerald, 2008, p. 68), they need the preparation to engage effectively and confidently in such analysis.

Factor 2

Teachers are provided with too little time to make thoughtful decisions. Today's complex school environments increasingly require teachers and administrators to accommodate a wide variety of student needs with little time and too few resources to discern how to make requisite educational accommodations. Rubenfeld, Newstrom, and Duff (1994) observe: "This need to respond rapidly to competitive pressures is often exacerbated by resource limitations and frequent staffing alignments, which together may have the effect of discouraging careful and thorough analysis" (p. 20).

True, readily available software (such as Excel and Statistical Analysis System or SAS) offers the potential for powerful and efficient data analysis. Equally true, teachers and administrators need training and practice time to really understand how to use this software for their specific data analysis needs. When educators possess volumes of data but lack the requisite professional development opportunities and time for professional reflection to learn how to benefit from them, they are positioned for frustration and failure. Rubenfeld et al. conclude: "technological advances may [even] have a negative effect since they can provide so much data and information that the decision maker may be overwhelmed and find it difficult to determine which are actually most germane" (p. 21).

Factor 3

Teachers are provided with too much disaggregated and untimely data. The NCLB legislation has fostered increased testing mania in P-12 schools, resulting in data overload for teachers and administrators. Complicating matters, teachers and administrators are often unable to discern the critical *need to know information from the* less relevant *nice to know* information. The excessive amounts of raw data coupled with the frustrations of how to piece together those data to better structure the learning environment are frustrating and even crippling for many educators. Reeves and Burt (2006) describe this phenomenon using the words of one data-overloaded principal: "We have so many pieces—I know that each piece has its own job, but it's overwhelming—to get it all and make sense" (p. 69).

The combination of too much data and too little time for analysis may be one reason that educators tend toward the use of basic decision-making models (Ikemoto & Marsh, 2007). Complex data analysis and inquiry-focused decision making takes time, requires resources, and necessitates a level of collaboration that seems out of reach to far too many classroom educators.

Data-Based Decision Making: Essential Factors

Helping teachers and administrators become effective data-based decision makers requires more than the initial step of addressing the mitigating factors (i.e., providing more time for data analysis, more professional development, and focusing the data collection processes). Even if more time is provided and enhanced data analysis skills are acquired, the full capacity for high-performance data-based decision making requires two additional, essential ingredients: an appreciation of the inquiry process and empowerment to act on acquired knowledge. These two ingredients move educators beyond being minimally involved consumers of data to a level where they champion effective data-based decision making for improved student outcomes and fight for the necessary resources to do so. As Smith (2008) notes:

> One of the more promising approaches to improving instruction involves the use of system-atic and frequent data to inform teachers and students about how well students are learn-ing the material and strategies they are expected to be learning. Substantially improving student performance—bringing almost all students to *challenging* standards of achievement, whether at the 2nd grade or community college level—appears to require that teachers have the data, skills, and opportunities necessary for continuously improving their instruction. As many researchers argue, systems of formative assessment, where teachers regularly identify and respond to students' changing needs, can lead to very substantial gains in student performance. (p. 379)

For those student gains to be realized, teacher inquiry is imperative. The inquiry process is important because, quite simply, we still know far too little about the instructional process. The absence of defined, empirically based instructional proto-cols means that all teachers must be inquirers. Research findings with direct and specific applications to classroom settings remain limited (Jalongo, 2006). Until we know with more certainty what constitutes best practices for the particular students being taught, it is imperative that each teacher be focused on identifying, in context and using the data available, what practices are most efficacious.

There is a certain idiosyncratic and highly contextual nature to the teaching pro-cess. Two teachers might take the same data, engage in very complex analyses of that data, but reach different conclusions on how to teach required content. Students adjust to those differences, but what may be altered differentially is the amount of learning. That is, students with reading Teacher X may grow 1.3 years and with Teacher Y .8 years. Growth occurs for the students with both teachers, but the amount of growth is the dependent variable. Teachers who are inquirers look for such outcomes (and for whether there are patterns in the learning outcomes) and then engage in additional inquiry to identify methods to enhance student performance through subsequent instructional interventions.

Earlier in this chapter, Gawande's bell curve of CF doctors was used to illustrate high and low professional (medical) performers. Gawande identifies one weak per-forming hospital (Cincinnati Children's) but then illustrates how, through the inquiry process, it began to systemically transform the quality of its service delivery. Being a low performer should always be a temporary phenomenon. Once data illustrate a performance level, the conscientious teacher, administrator, or doctor can (and should) begin to search for better answers regarding how to serve clients or students.

Empowerment to act on acquired knowledge is essential, as is a willingness to consider change. The empowerment imperative means that teachers and adminis-trators who are equipped with newly acquired knowledge may have to act in ways that are counter to personal dispositions. The gifted lecturer may be uncomfortable moving toward more student-centered inquiry or the "new math" advocate may feel "compromised" when a search for how best to teach urban, high-poverty third graders leads him or her to the selective use of direct instruction methods.

"Low performers" are individuals bound by what they already know and uncom-fortable with new information that might change how they interact with students.

"High performers" on the instructional bell curve, are those consistently engaged in researching best practices and personally willing to act on that newly acquired knowledge in ways that benefit the students they are teaching.

The Context for Using Data

Using data in meaningful and significant ways means that teachers and administrators have access to good, usable data. That assumption is far from valid for many practicing educators. In many instances, data availability is simply not a reality. In other situations essential data are not available in a timely fashion. I conclude this chapter with a discussion of both of these circumstances.

The No Child Left Behind legislation has generated a national testing mania, and though critics and advocates debate heatedly the efficacy of the law, relatively independent and non-ideological think-tanks have concluded that NCLB has had a positive impact on student performance. Student achievement appears to have increased in math and reading since enactment of the legislation in 2002, and in a majority of states with adequate data (9 of 13 states), gains in test scores have been greater after NCLB than before its implementation (Center on Education Policy, 2007). That is the good news! (See, for example, Table 15.1.) The bad news is that far

Table 15.1 Comparison of trends on state middle school math tests and NAEP Grade 8 math tests.

Change on State Test	Gain on NAEP	NAEP Flat	Decline on NAEP	Total
Moderate to large gain	16 states CA, DE, FL, GA, KS, IA, MA, MS, NE, NJ, OR, PA, SD, TN, VA, WA	7 states AL, HI, ID, IN, MI, NY, RI	9 states CO, IA, KY, MD, ME, NH, UT, WV, WY	32
Slight gain	3 states IL, NV, SC	1 state NC	2 states MO, OK	6
Slight decline	1 state WI		1 state CT	2
Moderate to large decline				
Insufficient years for trend	6 states AR, AZ, MT, NM, TX, VT	2 states ND, OH	2 states AK, MN	10
Total	26	10	14	50

Note: Thirty-two states have demonstrated moderate to large gains on state middle school (usually Grade 8) math tests since 2002. Of these, 16 states also showed gains on NAEP Grade 8 math tests between 2003 and 2005, while 7 states had flat results on NAEP, and 9 states showed declines.

This figure compares trends in the percentage of students scoring proficient on state middle school (usually Grade 8) math tests since 2002 with trends in the percentage scoring basic on NAEP Grade 8 math tests between 2003 and 2005.

Source: Has student achievement increased since No Child Left Behind? (2007) Washington, DC: Center on Education Policy.

too many teachers are still not taking advantage of test data in ways that really benefit student learning.

One reason is the excessive lag time between the point of test administration and the time when results are received, with the consequence that teachers simply are not using data in instructionally effective ways. Kozol (2005) describes this circumstance as he depicts the differential educational experiences provided to Black and White students in America's urban schools. His rhetoric about schooling in urban America is harsh, and at times debatable, but his observation about schools' inability (through most standardized tests) to provide alacritous access to essential data about student learning needs is unquestioned. Kozol writes:

> The usual administrative rationale for giving tests like these [standardized tests] to children in their elementary years is that the test results will help to show their teachers where the children's weaknesses may lie, so that they can redirect the focus of their work in order to address these weaknesses. In practice, however, this is not the way things generally work, because of the long lapse in time between the taking of these tests and the receipt of scores.
> Principals and teachers in some schools have told me that the scores on standardized exams, which are administered most frequently between late winter and the early spring, are not received until the final weeks of June and, in some cases, not until the summer. "I get no help from this at all," a teacher in one Massachusetts district told me. "By the time the scores come back, they're not my students anymore, unless they fail—and then maybe I'll see them in my class again the next September." In some states, test results are given to the teachers far more quickly, and in a number of districts, including New York City, "interim assessments" have been introduced so that teachers can derive some benefit from these exams close to the time at which the children take them; but this is not the pattern in most sections of the nation. (pp. 115–116)

Being able to make good use of data means that teachers must have more immediate access to the type of testing data that will help them discern what their students know and do not know. Fortunately, some testing companies (such as the Northwest Evaluation Association or NWEA) are finding ways to deliver tests more effectively, to provide test results more rapidly, and to gauge student academic groups in more instructionally and curriculum-sensitive (aligned local and state expectations) ways (Springer, 2008). Internet-enabled testing systems such as NWEA clearly represent the future, but for many students that future possibility is more remote than real. The consequence being that far too many teachers continue to administer tests without concomitantly using test results (since those results are not available to them in a timely fashion) to determine instructional interventions.

Even those who do have access to student data, however, often find that the data systems are simply not in place to ensure a comprehensive understanding of each student's academic status and potential. For example, many states are still not able to provide growth data on students, which means that teachers are still judged too heavily on the intellectual capital students bring to school as opposed to the intellectual and academic gains fostered by each teacher at a school. Ensuring that students realize fully what schools can provide will necessitate the creation in all states of a seamless P-16 data collection and management system.

The development of enhanced data management systems is the result of more emphasis on using data to make critical instructional decisions. Such decisions at the classroom level became increasingly difficult due to the highly mobile environment found in American schools and given the absence of comprehensive data management systems at the state level. As students migrate across schools and districts, providing appropriate educational growth measures to a student's new school is impossible if appropriate background data on each child are not available. Those statewide data management systems must also be sophisticated enough to accommodate the growing numbers of P-12 students who are home-schooled and/or taking coursework online. In essence, states will have to develop and implement student information systems that "track students over time as well as collect the student demographic data essential for disaggregating test scores by subgroups" (Sunderman, 2008, p. 129).

At minimum, Ewell (2007) identifies the following data elements that must be a part of any data management system: a unique student identifier for each learner (an identifier should not just be the student's social security number); an appropriate demographic description for each student; the competency descriptors (to include how the competency was assessed); and, for postsecondary students, descriptors for the different educational delivery methods (e.g., distance learning) that a student has had during his or her P-16 experiences.

Unless teachers have timely data (i.e., immediate access to appropriate test data) and a means of monitoring and securing such data throughout and across a student's educational history, the ability of teachers to use data in ways that enhance their decision making and foster student learning will be compromised. Clearly, individual teachers and school districts have always maintained student files. What is now required are centralized data management systems in all 50 states that provide teachers with access to information about students and that document what students have achieved in learning experiences in multiple educational contexts.

Summary

Good teachers have always used data to make decisions. In the past, that meant relying on subjective assessments (soft data) about student performance and careful examination of student performance on a variety of formative and summative tests. Good teachers in the future will do the same thing: they will use both informal personal observations of student performance and formal assessments (teacher-made and standardized tests) to make instructional judgments. The difference will be (should be) how readily they can access more formal data sources to enhance and explore the informal assessments that they make daily.

They will (and should) use both because even with good data, accessed quickly, they may know what students have learned, but not necessarily why such learning occurred, nor how to achieve similar results for all students (Ewell, 2007). In essence, using data to make decisions will continue to be part art, part science. The good news is that the science has the potential to inform the art in ways that have simply never been possible in the past. And, as a consequence, student learning for all should be fostered in ways that have never been achievable because teachers either have not been given adequate data or have not known how to interpret such data when they were available.

References

Center on Education Policy (2007). *Has student achievement increased since No Child Left Behind?* Washington, DC: Author.

Coleman, J. S., Campbell, E. Q., Hobson, C. J., McPartland, J., Mood, A. M., Weinfeld, P. D., et al. (1966). *Equality of educational opportunity.* Washington, DC: Department of Health, Education and Welfare, Office of Education.

Collins, J. (2001) *Good to great.* New York: HarperCollins.

Ewell, P. T. (2007). Seamless data systems to promote student progression. In N. Hoffman, J. Vargas, A. Venezia, & M. S. Miller (Eds.), *Minding the gap* (pp. 239–248). Cambridge, MA: Harvard University Press.

Gawande, A. (2004, December 6). The bell curve. *The New Yorker.* Retrieved October 24, 2007, from http://www.newyorker.com/archive/2004/12/06/041206fa_fact

Haberman, M. (1995). *Star teachers of children in poverty.* West Lafayette, IN: Kappan Delta Pi.

Hess, F. M. (2005). *Urban school reform: Lessons from San Diego.* Cambridge, MA: Harvard University Press.

Ikemoto, G. S., & Marsh, J. A. (2007). Cutting through the "data-driven" mantra: Different conceptions of data driven decision making. *Yearbook of the National Society for the Study of Education 106*(1), 105–131.

Jalongo, M. R. (2006) [Editorial]. Reconsidering data-driven decision making—A personal journey and advice for teachers. *Early Childhood Education Journal, 34*(2), 99–101.

Jerald, C. (2008). Planning that matters: Helping schools engage in collaborative, strategic problem solving. In J. H. Munro (Ed.), *Educational leadership* (pp. 62–71). Boston: McGraw-Hill.

Kaplan, A. (1964). *The conduct of inquiry.* Scranton, PA: Chandler Publishing Company.

Kozol, J. (2005). *The shame of the nation.* New York: Crown Publishers.

Marzano, R. J. (2007). *The art and science of teaching.* Alexandria, VA: Association for Supervision and Curriculum Development.

Nye, B., Konstantopoulos, S., & Hedges, L.V. (2004). How large are teacher effects? *Educational Evaluation and Policy Analysis, 26*(3), 237–257.

Reeves, P. L., & Burt, W. L. (2006). Challenges in data-based decision making: Voices from principals. *Educational Horizons, 85*(1), 65–71.

Rubenfeld, S. A., Newstrom, J. W., & Duff, T. B. (1994). Caveat emptor: Avoiding pitfalls in data-based decision making. *Review of Business, 16*(2), 20–23.

Smith, M. S. (2008). What's next? Our gains have been substantial, promising, but not enough. In J. H. Munro (Ed.), *Educational leadership* (pp. 375–380). Boston: McGraw-Hill.

Sowell, T. (2005). *Black rednecks and White liberals.* San Francisco: Encounter Books.

Springer, M. G. (2008). Accountability incentives: Do schools practice educational triage? *Education Next, 8*(1), 75–79.

Sunderman, G. L. (2008). *Holding NCLB accountable: Achieving accountability, equity and school reform.* Thousand Oaks, CA: Sage.

16

Formative versus Summative Assessments as Measures of Student Learning

Robert J. Marzano
Mid-continent Research Lab for Education and Learning

One can make a case that No Child Left Behind (NCLB) raised the emphasis on assessing and reporting student academic achievement to new levels. Guilfoyle (2006) chronicles the history of NCLB and its heavy reliance on testing. She notes: "The original law provided funding to school districts to help low-income students. Today, NCLB holds Title I schools that receive . . . federal money accountable by requiring them to meet proficiency targets on annual assessments" (p. 8). Guilfoyle (2006) describes the position of the U.S. Department of Education as follows:

> The law requires tests in reading and math for students annually in grades 3–8 and once in high school. In 2005–2006, 23 states that had not yet fully implemented NCLB needed to administer 11.4 million new tests in reading and math. Science testing began in 2007—one test in each of three grade spans must be administered (3–5, 6–9, and 10–12)—the number of tests that states need to administer annually to comply with NCLB is expected to rise to 68 million. (p. 8)

Assessment systems currently in use to fulfill the requirements of NCLB might best be described as "status oriented" in that they reflect the percentage of students who are at specific levels of achievement. Presumably the reason for using a status orientation is to provide no excuse for failure; regardless of the background characteristics of students, regardless of when students enter a particular school, all are expected to succeed. Theoretically, following the basic sentiment of NCLB, a district or school should have or at least approach 100% of students passing every state test at every grade level.

Typically a status approach utilizes summative assessments. McMillan (2007) describes summative assessment as "conducted mainly to monitor and record student achievement and . . . used for school accountability" (p. 1). While the logic behind a summatively based, status approach might be understandable, it is unfair as a method of determining the effectiveness of a district or school for a number of reasons. First, many districts and schools have highly transient populations. Consequently a district or a school that has a transiency rate of 50% is compared to a district or school that has a transiency rate of 5%. Quite obviously the districts and schools with the lower transiency rate will have had more time to work with students than the districts and schools with a rate of 50%. Relative standing in terms of percent of students at or above a specific criterion score on a summative assessment might be more a function of the stability of the student population than it is the effectiveness of the district and school.

Second, districts and schools have student populations with very different demographics and those demographic differences are strongly related to differences in student achievement (Hedges & Nowell, 1998, 1999; Jacobsen, Olsen, Rice, Sweetland, & Ralph, 2001; Ladewig, 2006). Again a status orientation makes no allowances for differences in student demographics across districts and schools.

Third, summatively based approaches can drain resources from the classroom. Zellmer, Frontier, and Pheifer (2006) analyzed the effects of NCLB reporting requirements on district resources in Wisconsin. They begin their treatment in the following way:

> How do the testing mandates of No Child Left Behind (NCLB) affect schools and students? Last November, while bipartisan politics and philosophical debates continued, 435,000 Wisconsin students sat down for an average of six and one-half hours each and took the expanded Wisconsin Knowledge and Concepts Exam (WKCE) required for NCLB accountability. As the dialogue about the 2007 reauthorization of the Elementary and Secondary Education Act (ESEA) unfolds this fall in the United States, it is imperative that we look beyond the rhetoric and consider the effect of NCLB testing on students and schools. (p. 43)

They explain that the tests require 4.75 to 8.66 hours of administration time annually for each student. This amounted to 1.4 million hours of testing in Wisconsin schools in 2004–2005. They note that when NCLB testing is fully implemented, 2.9 hours of test administration will be required. When special populations are considered, the impact of NCLB testing is even more dramatic. Specifically because teachers are involved in test administration special education students lose 8.5, 7.7, and 6.3 days of instruction at the elementary, middle school, and high school levels respectively. Title I students lose 8.6, 7.9, and 6.3 days at elementary, middle school, and high school. English language learners lose 7.4 days of instruction at elementary, middle school, and high school. Finally, cost of test administration paints an even bleaker picture. State tests cost an average of $33.91 per student. Extrapolating this cost across the 435,000 students in Wisconsin, they estimate that Wisconsin spent $14,700,000 on NCLB-related testing. Similar conclusions have been reported by Cizek (2007). Specifically, he notes that estimates of the cost of testing under NCLB range between $271 million and $757 million for the years 2002 through 2008.

Fourth, status systems that are based on large-scale summative assessments are not designed to be used to help individual students. Abrams (2007) reminds us: "It is important to note that the law [NCLB] only prescribes how schools—not students— should be held accountable" (p. 82). Cizek (2007) further makes the point that large-scale summative assessments are not designed to provide feedback on specific aspects of knowledge and skill within a subject area. He explains that the total score reliability across 40 items for the mathematics portion of the fourth-grade state test in a large midwestern state is .87—certainly an acceptable level of reliability. That test reports pupils' subarea performance using the National Council of Teachers of Mathematics categories: algebra, data analysis and probability, estimation and mental computation, geometry, measurement, number and number relations, patterns, relations, and functions, and problem-solving strategies. Unfortunately the reliabilities for these subscale scores range from .33 to .57. Perhaps even more striking is the reliability of difference scores between those scales. Cizek provides the example of the reliability for the difference score between algebra and measurements. It is .015. He notes:

> it still might be that the dependability of conclusions about differences in subarea performance is nearly zero. In many cases, a teacher who flipped a coin to decide whether to provide the pupil with focused intervention in algebra (heads) or measurement (tails) would be making that decision about as accurately as the teacher who relied on an examination of subscore differences for the two areas. (p. 104)

For the reasons above as well as others, Barton (2006) has called for an accountability system built on a value-added or growth model:

> If we had an accountability system that truly measured student gain—sometimes called *growth* or *value added*—we could use whether students in any year have gained enough in that school year to show adequate progress. The end goal should not be achieving set scores by 2014. The goal should be reaching a standard for *how much* growth we expect during a school year in any particular subject. (p. 30)

The Role of Formative Assessments

The potential power of a value added or growth model is supported by a considerable amount of research on formative assessment. To illustrate, as a result of analyzing more than 250 studies British researchers Black and Wiliam (1998) report the following conclusions regarding formative assessments:

> The research reported here shows conclusively that formative assessment does improve learning. The gains in achievement appear to be quite considerable, and as noted earlier, amongst the largest ever reported for educational interventions. As an illustration of just how big these gains are, an effect size of 0.7, if it could be achieved on a nationwide scale, would be equivalent to raising the mathematics attainment score of an "average" country like England, New Zealand or the United States into the "top five" after the Pacific rim countries of Singapore, Korea, Japan and Hong Kong. (p. 61)

A value-added approach that is based on formative assessments appears to address many of the shortcomings of a summatively based, status approach. First, it addresses the issue of different transiency rates in that a school could estimate the unique effect it had on a student's learning regardless of when a student entered school. Even if a student were in school for a few months only, the student's knowledge gain could be estimated.

Second, a formatively based, value-added system also addresses the issue of different demographics. A school with a majority of students from higher income homes will most likely have a greater proportion of students at or above a specified level of proficiency than a school with a majority of students from low income families. This situation notwithstanding, the knowledge gain in the low income school might be greater than that in the higher income school.

Third, a formatively based, value-added system might even address some of the resource problems of a status system. This is because it relies on classroom-level assessments that do not detract from instructional time as do the high stakes state-level tests that are characteristic of status approaches. Assessment data can be gleaned as a regular part of the instructional process as opposed to taking time away from instruction as do state-level tests.

Fourth, a formatively based, value-added system addresses the characteristic inability of large-scale status systems to provide guidance regarding instructional practices for individual students. To this end Marzano and Haystead (in press) have recommended that state standards documents be reconstituted into parsimonious "measurement topics" that form the basis for formative assessment. For example, they suggest the list of measurement topics in mathematics depicted in Figure 16.1.

While it seems evident that a formatively based, value-added system is superior to a summatively based, status system, just how to implement the former is not evident. Some districts and schools use "off-the-shelf" formative assessments developed by standardized test makers. In his article entitled "Phony formative assessments: Buyer beware," Popham (2006) harshly criticizes the unquestioning use of commercially prepared formative assessments. He notes that:

> As news of Black and Wiliam's conclusions gradually spread into faculty lounges, test pub-lishers suddenly began to relabel many of their tests as "formative." This name-switching sales ploy was spurred on by the growing perception among educators that formative assessments could improve their students' test scores and help their schools dodge the many accountability bullets being aimed their way. (p. 86)

He further explains that the impressive results regarding formative assessment relate to classroom assessments—those designed and administered by classroom teachers during their daily interactions with teachers—not to external benchmark assessments. In effect, any external assessment that is not intimately tied to the

---

Numbers and Operations:
  1. Number Sense and Number Systems
  2. Basic Addition and Subtraction
  3. Basic Multiplication and Division
  4. Operations, Computation, and Estimation
Algebra:
  5. Basic Patterns
  6. Functions and Equations
  7. Algebraic Representations and Mathematical Models
Geometry:
  8. Lines, Angles, and Geometric Objects
  9. Transformations, Congruency, and Similarity
Measurement:
  10. Measurement Systems
  11. Perimeter, Area, and Volume
Data Analysis and Probability:
  12. Data Organization and Interpretation
  13. Probability

Figure 16.1 Sample measurement topics.

Source: Adapted from Marzano and Haystead (in press).

classroom by definition violates the tenets of formative assessment. Shepard (2006) makes the same criticism of external formative assessments:

> The research-based concept of formative assessment, closely grounded in classroom instructional processes, has been taken over—hijacked—by commercial test publishers and is used instead to refer to formal testing systems called "benchmark" or "interim assessment systems."
>
> (as cited in Popham, 2006, p. 86)

A similar criticism might be leveled at district-made formative assessments. Specifically, they violate one basic tenet of formative assessment which is that they must allow for both formal and informal judgments of student achievement. As McMillan (2007) explains:

> [Benchmark] assessments, which are typically provided by the district or commercial test publishers, are administered on a regular basis to compare student achievement to "benchmarks" that indicate where student performance should be in relation to what is needed to do well on end-of-year high stakes tests. . . . Although the term *benchmark* is often used interchangeably with *formative* in the commercial testing market, there are important differences. Benchmark assessments are formal, structured tests that typically do not provide the level of detail needed for appropriate instructional correctives. (pp. 2–3)

Clearly, then, a formatively based, value-added system cannot be populated exclusively by district- or school-designed assessments nor can it be populated by commercially prepared assessments. They simply do not satisfy the defining features of formative assessment. What, then, is necessary to develop a comprehensive system of formative assessments?

In their meta-analytic review of research on assessment, Black and Wiliam (1998) defined formative assessment in the following way: "all those activities undertaken by teachers and/or by students which provide information to be used as feedback to modify the teaching and learning activities in which they are engaged" (pp. 7–8). Wiliam and Leahy (2007) describe formative assessment as follows:

> the qualifier *formative* will refer not to an assessment or even to the purpose of an assessment, but rather to the function it actually serves. An assessment is formative to the extent that information from the assessment is fed back within the system and actually used to improve the performance of the system in some way (i.e., that the assessment *forms* the direction of the improvement). (p. 31)

At face value these sentiments seem to characterize formative assessment as involving a wide array of formal and informal techniques for designing and interpreting assessments. This places the classroom teacher clearly at the center of effective formative assessment. Unfortunately, many teacher-designed assessments are not adequate to the task of formative assessment. This is because of the century-old practice of using the 100-point scale.

The Problem with Points

Clearly the most common way teachers design assessments is to use a point or percentage approach. Bock (1997) traces the point system to World War I and the Army Alpha Test. The test required a quick and efficient scoring system that could be applied to multiple-choice items scored as correct or incorrect. Correct items were assigned one point; incorrect items were assigned no points. The summary score on the test was easily computed by forming the ratio of the number of correct items divided by the total number of items and multiplying by 100 to obtain a percentage score.

While the point system has a long history in K-12 education, opinions from experts, common sense, and research indicate that it simply does not work well in a formative approach. Thorndike (1904) commented indirectly on the lack of utility in the point system in the following way:

> If one attempts to measure even so simple a thing as spelling, one is hampered by the fact that there exist no units in which to measure. One may arbitrarily make up a list of words and observe ability by the number spelled correctly. But if one examines such a list one is struck by the inequality of the units. All results based on the equality of any one word with another are necessarily inaccurate. (p. 7)

By inference assigning points to something seemingly as straightforward as spelling words is still highly subjective. If spelling the word *cat* correctly receives one point, how many points are assigned to the word *octopus*?

More recently, Thissen and Wainer (2001) commented on the use of points for large-scale assessments:

> In classroom examinations, combinations of selected-response and constructed-response items have often been scored by arbitrary assignment of a certain number of points for each, but that procedure may not be acceptable for a large-scale testing program, in which scoring may be subject to extensive public scrutiny, professional standards of precision are expected to be met (p. 2).

The problem with points is illustrated in a study by Marzano (2002). In that study five teachers were asked to score the tests of ten students. Prior to scoring those tests each teacher was asked to assign points to each item representing the relative importance of the items. Because of the differential weighing of items students received vastly different scores from the five teachers. For example, one student received a total score of 50 from one teacher and a score of 91 from another teacher.

In short, the practice of differential weighting of items for teacher-designed assessments creates a situation in which a student can receive high scores on one test regarding a specific topic and receive low scores on a subsequent test even though the student has learned during the interim. Weighting easy items higher in the first test than in the second test would create this apparent contradiction—a student has learned but his or her scores have gone down. In short, when teachers design assessments using the 100-point scale, each scale for each assessment will likely be very different due to differential weighting of items.

Moving Away from Points

Conceptually one might say that the solution to the problem of points is a scale that remains constant across all formative assessments. In large-scale assessments this issue is addressed using latent trait or Item Response Theory (IRT) models. Such models postulate a continuum of latent scores (somewhat related to the classical test theory concept of true score) and then mathematically estimate each student's score on the latent continuum. Theoretically, if uni-dimensional, parallel assessments were administered, students' progress on the latent continuum could be computed and tracked. This is the essence of formative assessment—demonstrating progress over time. However, Hattie (1984, 1985) has noted that the ideal of uni-dimensional parallel tests is rarely if ever attained. This conclusion notwithstanding, IRT models are designed to allow for multiple parallel assessments. Thissen and Orlando (2001) explain that

> because the probability of a correct response is a function of the ratio of the proficiency of the person to the difficulty of the item, the item parameters cancel for the ratios of probability-correct for two persons, leaving an *item-free* comparison of their proficiencies. Thus the model makes *objective* or *item-free* statements about the relative likelihood that two persons will respond correctly to an item or a set of items, without any reference to the items themselves. (p. 75)

In an earlier statement Thissen and Orlando note:

> This aspect of IRT means that comparable scores may be computed for examinees who did not answer the same questions, without intermediate equating steps. As a result, an extremely large number of alternate forms of a test may be used. (p. 73)

While it is theoretically possible to use IRT models to construct a wide array of parallel tests to be used as classroom formative assessments, such a task would take an enormous amount of time and resources. To illustrate, consider the 13 measurement topics for mathematics depicted in Figure 16.1. Multiple IRT-based assessments would have to be designed for each topic at each grade level. Even if such assessments could be designed they would not address the need for informal formative assessments that teachers might construct and administer on an ad hoc basis. This seems to be a staple of effective formative assessment. Recall Black and Wiliam's (1998) comment that formative assessment involves a wide variety of activities undertaken by teachers and/or by students which provide feedback to modify the teaching and learning activities.

Another shortcoming of formative assessments based on IRT models is that they provide no information that could guide teachers and students regarding how to improve teaching and learning. Again, this is a staple of formative assessment. While the scores generated by an IRT model line up nicely in terms of a mathematical continuum they are meaningless in terms of specific components of knowledge. One can assume that a student with a latent trait score of 2.5 knows more than a student with a latent trait score of 1.5. However, little can be said about what type of knowledge is possessed by one student versus another. Therefore little can be said about how a student might improve.

A more flexible option to designing IRT-based formative assessments is to articulate a continuum of knowledge as opposed to assuming a latent continuum. At first blush, this seems incompatible with current test theory since a basic assumption underlying both classical test theory and latent trait theory is that the underlying continuum of knowledge need not or cannot be articulated. As Thissen and Orlando (2001) note: "Item response theory is concerned with the measurement of such hypothetical constructs as *ability* and *proficiency*. Because such constructs have no concrete reality, their measurement is by analogy with some directly observable variable" (p. 78). Fortunately, for the purposes of formative assessment, the last decade of the twentieth century witnessed a movement that was designed in part to identify the components of continuums of knowledge within specific subject areas. That movement is the standards movement. Discussing the movement's impact, Glaser and Linn (1993) explain:

> In the recounting of our nation's drive toward educational reform, the last decade of this century will undoubtedly be identified as the time when a concentrated press for national educational standards emerged. The press for standards was evidenced by the efforts of federal and state legislators, presidential and gubernatorial candidates, teachers and subject-matter specialists, councils, governmental agencies, and private foundations. (p. xiii)

Glaser and Linn made their comments at the end of the twentieth century. There is no indication that the standards movement has lost any momentum at the beginning of the twenty-first century. Indeed, over a dozen national standards documents have been created and transformed into state-level standards documents in virtually every state in the union. In effect, the standards movement has provided an unprecedented opportunity to enhance measurement theory in that it provides guidance as to how to construct continuums of knowledge within various subject areas. With continuums of knowledge articulated for a given subject area formal and informal formative assessments could be designed that reference those explicit continuums.

Articulating a Continuum of Knowledge

It is probably impractical to articulate a complete continuum of knowledge within a given subject area. However, in a series of works Marzano (2006; Marzano & Haystead, in press) has offered the scale in Figure 16.2 as a tool for articulating partial continuums of knowledge.

The lowest score value on the scale in Figure 16.2 is a 0.0 representing no knowledge of a given topic—even with help the student demonstrates no understanding or skill relative to the topic. A score of 1.0 indicates that *with help* the student shows partial knowledge of the simpler details and processes as well as the more complex ideas and processes. To be assigned a score of 2.0 the student independently demonstrates understanding of and skill at the simpler details and processes but not the more complex ideas and processes. A score of 3.0 indicates that the student demonstrates understanding of and skill at all the content—simple and complex—*that was explicitly taught in class*. Finally, a score of 4.0 indicates that the student demonstrates inferences and applications that *go beyond what was taught in class*.

Using the scale depicted in Figure 16.2, subject-specific measurement topics at

Score 4.0: In addition to Score 3.0 performance, in-depth inferences and applications that go beyond what was taught.

Score 3.5: In addition to Score 3.0 performance, partial success at inferences and applications that go beyond what was taught.

Score 3.0: No major errors or omissions regarding any of the information and/or processes (simple or complex) that were explicitly taught.

Score 2.5: No major errors or omissions regarding the simpler details and processes and partial knowledge of the more complex ideas and processes.

Score 2.0: No major errors or omissions regarding the simpler details and processes but major errors or omissions regarding the more complex ideas and processes.

Score 1.5: Partial knowledge of the simpler details and processes but major errors or omissions regarding the more complex ideas and processes.

Score 1.0: With help, a partial understanding of some of the simpler details and processes and some of the more complex ideas and processes.

Score 0.5: With help, a partial understanding of some of the simpler details and processes but not the more complex ideas and processes.

Score 0.0: Even with help, no understanding or skill demonstrated.

Figure 16.2 A scale designed for articulating a partial continuum.

every grade level can be written in scale format. To illustrate this, consider Figure 16.3 from Marzano and Haystead (in press).

Figure 16.3 depicts the measurement topic of "atmospheric processes and the water cycle" at the eighth-grade level. Similar scales would be designed for multiple topics in grades kindergarten through high school. Using these scales teachers would design and score formative assessments. That is, teachers would construct score 2.0 items, score 3.0 items, and score 4.0 items. Together, these items would constitute a single formative assessment on a particular topic. Assessments would be scored using the same logic articulated in Figures 16.2 and 16.3. If a student answered all score 2.0 items correctly she would receive a score of 2.0; if the student answered all score 2.0 items correctly and received partial credit on score 3.0 items she would receive a score of 2.5 and so on.

Designing and scoring formative assessments as described above is in keeping with the Fuchs and Fuchs (1986) finding that scoring assessment according to an explicit rule has an effect size of .91. That is, the scales depicted in Figures 16.2 and 16.3 are explicit rules for scoring that can be communicated directly to students, thus providing students with explicit guidance regarding how to improve. Marzano (2002) has found that the reliability of scoring assessments using this system is about three times greater than the reliability of teachers designing and scoring assessments using a 100-point scale.

Tracking Student Progress on Formal and Informal Assessments

With a system of measurement topics in place like that in Figure 16.1 and their accompanying scales like those in Figure 16.3, teachers can design formal and

	Atmospheric Processes and the Water Cycle	
	Grade 8	
Score 4.0	In addition to score 3.0, in-depth inferences and applications that go beyond what was taught, such as: • how climatic patterns differ between regions • how people living today impact Earth's atmosphere	
	Score 3.5	In addition to score 3.0 performance, in-depth inferences and applications with partial success.
Score 3.0	While engaged in tasks that address atmospheric processes and the water cycle, the student demonstrates an understanding of important information such as: • how water cycle processes impact climatic patterns (temperature, wind, clouds) • the effects of temperature and pressure in different layers of Earth's atmosphere (troposphere, stratosphere, mesosphere, thermosphere) **The student exhibits no major errors or omissions.**	
	Score 2.5	No major errors or omissions regarding the score 2.0 elements and partial knowledge of the score 3.0 elements.
Score 2.0	No major errors or omissions regarding the simpler details and processes such as: • recognizing and recalling specific terminology, such as: — climate/climatic pattern — troposphere — stratosphere — mesosphere — thermosphere • recognizing and recalling isolated details, such as: — precipitation can cause temperature to change — the atmosphere of the Earth is divided into five layers **However, the student exhibits major errors or omissions with score 3.0 elements.**	
	Score 1.5	Partial knowledge of the score 2.0 elements but major errors or omissions regarding the score 3.0 elements.
Score 1.0	With help, a partial understanding of some of the score 2.0 elements and some of the score 3.0 elements.	
	Score 0.5	With help, a partial understanding of some of the score 2.0 but not the score 3.0 elements.
Score 0.0	Even with help, no understanding or skill demonstrated.	

Figure 16.3 Science: Atmospheric processes and the water cycle (Grade 8).

Source: Adapted from Marzano & Haystead (in press).

informal formative assessments and track students' progress. Within such a system assessments could employ traditional formats such as forced choice and constructed response items. Marzano (2006) has observed that score 2.0 items tend to employ forced-choice formats, whereas score 3.0 and 4.0 items tend to employ constructed response formats. Assessment formats could also be quite nontraditional. For example, the scales in Figures 16.2 and 16.3 allow teachers to use a discussion with a particular student as a form of assessment. The teacher would ask questions of the student making sure that score 2.0, score 3.0, and score 4.0 questions were included in the discussion. A final score would be assigned to the informal oral examination again using pattern of responses across item types. Valencia, Stallman, Commeyras, Pearson, and Hartman (1991) have found that discussions like this provide three times the information about a student's knowledge of academic content as assessments that employ forced-choice and constructed response formats. As Valencia and colleagues note: "On average, 66 percent of the typically relevant ideas students gave during interviews were not tested on any of the . . . [other] measures" (p. 226). This is a rather startling finding from an assessment perspective. It implies that more traditional classroom assessment formats like forced-choice items and essays might not allow students to truly show what they know about a given topic. One of Valencia et al.'s final conclusions was that "a comprehensive view of a person's topical knowledge may well require multiple measures, each of which contributes unique information to the picture" (p. 230).

A system of formal and informal assessments allows a teacher to generate multiple scores for students on measurement topics. Multiple scores allow for a tracking system like that depicted in Figure 16.4.

The first column in Figure 16.4 represents an assessment given by the teacher on October 5. This student received a score of 1.5 on that assessment. The second column represents the assessment on October 12. This student received a score of 2.0 on that assessment and so on. Having each student keep track of his or her scores on learning goals in this fashion provides him or her with a visual tracking of his or her progress. It also allows for powerful discussions between teacher and students. The teacher can discuss progress with each student regarding each learning goal. Also, in a tracking system like this the student and teacher are better able to communicate with parents regarding progress in specific areas of information and skill. Of course, one of the most powerful aspects of tracking as depicted in Figure 16.4 is that it allows for value-added interpretations; students see their progress over time. In a value system

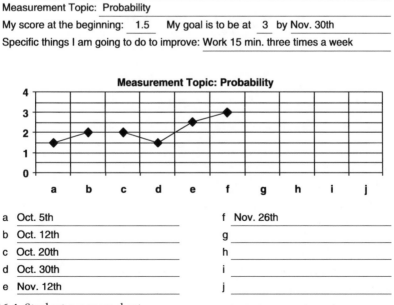

Figure 16.4 Student progress chart.

Source: Adapted from Marzano (2006).

virtually every student will "succeed" in the sense that each student will increase his or her knowledge relative to specific learning goals. One student might have started with a score of 2.0 on a specific learning goal and then increased to a score of 3.5; another student might have started with a 1.0 and increased to a 2.5—both have learned. "Knowledge gain," then, is the currency of student success in an assessment system that is formative in nature. Focusing on knowledge gain also provides a legitimate way to recognize and celebrate success. Covington (1992) has noted that reporting knowledge gain has the potential of stimulating intrinsic motivation for virtually every student.

Summary and Conclusions

This chapter has provided a case for the superiority of formative assessments as measures of student learning. While NLCB has created an emphasis on assessment, a status-oriented, summatively based approach has been the default value. For a variety of reasons a formatively based, value-added approach is superior. By definition formal and informal assessments are needed for a comprehensive system of formative assessments. Unfortunately, use of the 100-point scale has proved to be insufficient to the task of effective formative assessment. A scale was provided that allows for a partial articulation of the specific continuums of knowledge within subject areas. This scale allows teachers to design and score formal and informal formative assessments so that learning can be tracked and knowledge gain quantified and celebrated.

References

Abrams, L. M. (2007). Implications of high-stakes testing for the use of formative classroom assessment. In J. H. McMillan (Ed.), *Formative classroom assessment: Theory into practice* (pp. 79–98). New York: Teachers College Press.

Barton, P. E. (2006). Needed: Higher standards for accountability. *Educational Leadership, 64*(3), 28–31.

Black, P., & Wiliam, D. (1998). Assessment and classroom learning. *Assessment in Education, 5*(1), 7–75.

Bock, R. D. (1997). A brief history of item response theory. *Educational Measurement, Issue and Practice, 16*(4), 21–33.

Cizek, G. J. (2007). Formative classroom and large-scale assessment: Implications for future research and development. In J. H. McMillan (Ed.), *Formative classroom assessment: Theory into practice* (pp. 99–115). New York: Teachers College Press.

Covington, M. V. (1992). *Making the grade: A self-worth perspective on motivation and school reform.* New York: Cambridge University Press.

Fuchs, L. S., & Fuchs, D. (1986). Effects of systematic formative evaluation: A meta analysis. *Exceptional Children, 53*(3), 199–208.

Glaser, R., & Linn, R. (1993). Foreword. In L. Shepard, R. Glaser, R. Linn, & G. Bohrnstedt (Eds.), *Setting performance standards for student achievement: A report of the National Academy of Education Panel on the evaluation of the NAEP trial state assessment: An evaluation of the 1992 achievement levels* (pp. xiii–xiv). Stanford, CA: National Academy of Education, Stanford University.

Guilfoyle, C. (2006). NCLB: Is there life beyond testing? *Educational Leadership, 64*(3), 8–13.

Hattie, J. (1984). An empirical study of various indices for determining unidimensionality. *Multivariate Behavioral Research, 19,* 49–78.

Hattie, J. (1985). Methodology review: Assessing the unidimensionality of tests and items. *Applied Psychological Measurement, 9*(2), 139–164.

Hedges, L. V., & Nowell, A. (1998). Black–White test score convergence since 1965. In C. Jencks & M. Phillips (Eds.), *The Black–White test score gap* (pp. 149–181). Washington, DC: Brookings Institution Press.

Hedges, L. V., & Nowell, A. (1999). Changes in the Black–White gap in test scores. *Sociology of Education, 72,* 111–135.

Jacobsen, J., Olsen, C., Rice, J. K., Sweetland, S., & Ralph, J. (2001). *Educational achievement and Black–White inequality.* Washington, DC: National Center for Educational Statistics, Department of Education.

Ladewig, B. G. (2006). *The minority achievement gap in New York State suburban schools since the implementation of NCLB.* Unpublished doctoral dissertation, University of Rochester.

Marzano, R. J. (2002). A comparison of selected methods of scoring classroom assessments. *Applied Measurement in Education, 15*(3), 249–268.

Marzano, R. J. (2006). *Classroom assessment and grading that work.* Alexandria, VA: Association for Supervision and Curriculum Development.

Marzano, R. J., & Haystead, M. W. (in press). *Making standards useful in the classroom.* Alexandria, VA: Association for Supervision and Curriculum Development.

McMillan, J. H. (2007). Formative assessment: The key to improving student achievement. In J. H. McMillan (Ed.), *Formative classroom assessment: Theory into practice* (pp. 1–7). New York: Teachers College Press.

Popham, W. J. (2006). Phony formative assessments: Buyer beware. *Educational Leadership, 64*(3), 86–87.

Shepard, L. (2006, June). Panelist presentation delivered at the National Large-Scale Assessment Conference sponsored by the Council of Chief State School Officers, San Francisco, CA.

Thissen, D., & Orlando, M. (2001). Item response theory for items scored in two categories. In D. Thissen & H. Wainer (Eds.), *Test scoring* (pp. 73–140). Mahwah, NJ: Erlbaum.

Thissen, D., & Wainer, H. (2001). On overview of *Test Scoring.* In D. Thissen & H. Wainer (Eds.), *Test scoring* (pp. 1–19), Mahwah, NJ: Erlbaum.

Thorndike, E. L. (1904). *An introduction to the theory of mental and social measurement.* New York: Teachers College Press.

Valencia, S. W., Stallman, A. C., Commeyras, M., Pearson, P. D., & Hartman, D. K. (1991). Four measures of topical knowledge: A study of construct validity. *Reading Research Quarterly, 26*(3), 204–233.

Wiliam, D., & Leahy, S. (2007). A theoretical foundation for formative assessment. In J. H. McMillan (Ed.), *Formative classroom assessment: Theory into practice* (pp. 29–42). New York: Teachers College Press.

Zellmer, M. B., Frontier, A., & Pheifer, D. (2006). What are NCLB's instructional costs? *Educational Leadership, 64*(3), 43–46.

17

Using Evidence to Support Administrative Decisions

Jane Hemsley-Brown
University of Surrey, United Kingdom

The gap between the researcher's world and the practitioner's world has long been recognized: research literature is generally not part of a practitioner's library (Huberman, 1990). One of the effects of this is that actions by decision makers and practitioners are unlikely to be informed by research, and dissemination of research information and knowledge is problematic (Hillage, Pearson, & Tamkin, 1998). The need for practitioners to utilize the findings from research as a basis for decision making is not just an issue for schools, but is a compelling idea for the workplace as a whole (Davies & Nutley, 2002; Gruber & Niles, 1973; Huberman, 1990; Kelemen & Bansal, 2002; Percy-Smith, 2005; Sutton, 2004; Walter, Nutley, & Davies, 2003a, 2003b; Weiss, 1979). Many studies have explored how and why new ideas and practices are adopted (Sturdy, 2004) in an attempt to discover how practitioners and managers could be encouraged to use research to support their decision making (Hemsley-Brown, 2004) and to increase the performance of schools (Hemsley-Brown & Sharp, 2003). The increasing interest in utilizing research findings for improving schools and providing evidence for management decision making is an important response to the rapid pace of change, the availability of electronic data, and the considerable pressure to improve increasingly complex organizations. Successful and continuous improvement depends less on who has the information and increasingly on those able to make the best use of that information (Hemsley-Brown, 2004; Moorman, Zaltman, & Deshpande, 1992). However, much of the knowledge generated by research fails to impact on a practitioner audience and although some research focuses on facilitating the utilization of research, much research effort has been devoted to explaining and justifying the gaps—the research–practice gap (Bero et al., 1998; Boostrom, Hansen, & Jackson, 1993; Huff & Huff, 2001; Johnson, 2000; Kelemen & Bansal, 2002; Klein, 1995).

Use of Research

Research may not solve specific problems or make decisions, but research can provide information for managers and practitioners to use to reduce risk in the decision-making process (Oulton, 1995). Management research is also an applied discipline—the ideas, solutions and insights have application in the real world if they are shared with practitioners (Tranfield & Starkey, 1998). The benefits of utilizing research for decision making are well known in theory, but considerable effort also goes toward documenting the reasons why this is not happening in practice (Huberman, 1990; Kelemen & Bansal, 2002; Louis, 1996; Percy-Smith, 2005; Sutton, 2004; Walter et al., 2003a; Zaltman & Moorman, 1988). A key problem is that the academic style of research is significantly different from the style preferred by practitioners, and due to poor dissemination channels and lack of communication between researchers and practitioners, potential user-managers often remain unaware of research findings (Kelemen & Bansal, 2002).

Research into school principals' perceptions of research use (Biddle & Saha, 2000; Saha, Biddle, & Anderson, 1995) does show that principals judge research knowledge to be valuable; they consider themselves to be regular, thoughtful users of research and believe it is relevant to decision making. Principals are skeptical though, and they think that research findings may be flawed or presented in a biased way largely because differences in the way research knowledge is constructed in social sciences often leads to researchers being challenged about their findings—particularly in relation to the context, generalizability, and validity of the research (Hemsley-Brown & Sharp, 2003). In contrast, studies also reveal that few teachers turn to research literature to expand professional knowledge, solve problems, or to meet the requirements of their job (Shkedi, 1998). Research literature is not accessed by teachers because they perceive it to be irrelevant, unhelpful and too theoretical. They claim they lack the time, do not trust the findings, and cannot understand the language or make sense of the statistics (Hemsley-Brown & Sharp, 2003; Shkedi, 1998). The reasons why research is generally not being utilized, therefore, are complex and whilst addressing some of the barriers might facilitate greater research use, some of the gaps between researchers and users need to be better understood.

The Research–Practice Gap

Studies of the researcher–practitioner gap (Bero et al., 1998; Boostrom et al., 1993; Huff & Huff, 2001; Kelemen & Bansal, 2002; Klein, 1995; Leseure, Bauer, Birdi, Neely, & Denyer, 2004) attempt to address the problem in a number of ways but principally they focus on trying to explain the reasons for the gap—there is less evidence of successful attempts to close that gap and ways of addressing these barriers are still unclear and unproven (Hemsley-Brown, 2004; Hemsley-Brown & Sharp, 2003).

Researchers are often accused of doing research largely in a vacuum, unnoticed and unheeded by anyone, and this can result in a perceptual gap between research and practice which creates tension between researchers and the users of research—the practitioners involved in making decisions (Ferlie, Hartley, & Martin, 2003). There are three dimensions of the research–practice gap which seem to provide a barrier to effective research utilization:

1. The mode of research, or the research itself, and how research is categorized
2. The process of dissemination or transfer of research knowledge
3. The context in which the research knowledge is utilized: for example, is

research knowledge utilized by individuals, or by individuals with organizational support, or by organizations?

Research utilization is important for a number of reasons: first, researchers need to identify successful strategies to ensure that the knowledge is successfully disseminated to users; and in that context it is important to work toward not only exploring, but bridging these gaps by identifying successful facilitation strategies and by focusing on both organizations and individual users. Recommendations for facilitating research utilization focus on organizational issues such as: school structure and culture; collaborative approaches (Walter et al., 2003b); and partnerships and networking (Hemsley-Brown, 2004; Hemsley-Brown, Cunningham, Morton, & Sharp, 2002; Hemsley-Brown & Sharp, 2003).

But what do we mean by "use" and "utilization"? The different meanings of the terms associated with research use and research utilization, and modes of research, in addition to exploring fundamental terminology (e.g., the nature of knowledge) need to be clarified.

Usefulness and Utilization

Managers and researchers tend to differ widely on the factors they believe to be most important in making research useful (Deshpande & Zaltman, 1984). The problem of use has long been a concern in the field of management and a key distinction seems to be between instrumental and conceptual uses of knowledge (Deshpande & Zaltman, 1982). Instrumental use implies direct application of knowledge to solve a specific problem or to make a particular decision. Instrumental use of knowledge requires changes in behavior or practice (Huberman, 1990). Conceptual use of knowledge on the other hand refers to information utilized for enlightenment or intrinsic interest rather than any action a decision maker might take (Deshpande & Zaltman, 1982). These different interpretations of the word use require different forms of research information, and engagement with information.

Research *utilization* (most often used in healthcare research) is "the purposeful application of research findings"—although this definition fails to reveal any clear differences between the term use and utilization (Montgomery, 2005, p. 86). The National Center for the Dissemination of Disability Research (1996) questioned the notion of dissemination as a linear, mechanical process—implied by the term *use*—and argues that research *utilization* is more than mere *use*; it is a two-way process—that is, a partnership—that includes support for change.

Modes of Research

Research utilization studies focus on explaining and justifying the researcher–practitioner gap, by categorizing research and setting out the differences in aims, processes, and outcomes of different categories of research. Research has frequently been defined and categorized as *Mode 1* and *Mode 2* research (Huff & Huff, 2001; Tranfield

& Starkey, 1998). Because research is categorized in this way it partly explains the research and practice gap and provides a way forward in closing this gap.

Mode 1 research is the "unfettered pursuit of knowledge" (Huff & Huff, 2001, p. S51) and follows a traditional model of research whereby the knowledge produced is the result of academic curiosity and resides in universities, guarded by elite gate-keepers (Tranfield & Starkey, 1998). The conventional criticism of academically driven management research is one of over-domination by academic criteria and isolated from a wider set of interested stakeholders (Ferlie et al., 2003; Tranfield & Starkey, 1998). This form of research, therefore, is about conceptual use, and is not intended for a practitioner audience and perhaps it is not surprising that managers are not utilizing the findings. We cannot build a bridge to close the research–practice gap by focusing on dissemination of Mode 1 research.

Mode 2 research output is instrumental, aims to provide more immediate solutions to management problems (Ferlie et al., 2003), and has a more practical focus for bridging the gap. However, this is also a problem because Mode 2 research output treats knowledge as a "storehouse of facts" where "knowledge appears beyond the reach of critical interrogation except at the level of immediate application" (Dehler, Welsh, & Lewis, 2001, p. 504), and yet to some extent this is the kind of knowledge practitioners seek. A study of research utilization that specifically concentrated on the way teachers use research findings in Michigan, USA (Zeuli, 1994), aimed to find out how teachers read and respond to educational research. Teachers in the study argue that research should exclusively identify strategies and techniques that could have a *direct* impact on their teaching, and they judge a study's merits on the basis of whether the findings can be translated into procedures that work (Hemsley-Brown & Sharp, 2003).

Research knowledge is rarely produced simply with the aim of applying that knowledge directly to management contexts. When managers themselves problematize an issue they become active knowledge producers instead of passive recipients (Dehler et al., 2001) which suggests that the notion of researchers as producers of knowledge and managers as recipients or users of knowledge is a naive and simplistic one: the context in which dissemination takes place is considered to have an impact on whether research is utilized. Research cannot simply be generated by researchers, and utilized by practitioners.

The Process and Dissemination of Research

Considerable speculation and discussion focuses on the factors or barriers which prevent managers from making use of research results (Deshpande & Zaltman, 1982, 1984; Moorman et al., 1992; Zaltman & Moorman, 1988), especially in the public sector and the management of schools (Hemsley-Brown, 2004; Hemsley-Brown & Sharp, 2003). The context of the research process accounts for a number of barriers to research utilization and these factors are broadly separated into three categories: access and dissemination; style and relevance; and trust and mistrust, which incorporate two overlapping themes, the context of the research process and the dissemination of the findings.

Access and Dissemination

With little consideration for the mode or type of research, poor access and weak dissemination channels are often identified as key barriers to research utilization (Walter et al., 2003b). Lack of access to research is a key barrier to its use, although it is not always clear whether access relates to intellectual access, or physical (or virtual) access to research, or both (Hemsley-Brown, 2004; Hemsley-Brown & Sharp, 2002, 2003; Kelemen & Bansal, 2002; Walter et al., 2003b). Because management research is written in an alienating style for most practitioners and is published only in academic, rather than practitioner journals, this has a serious impact on research use by managers (Kelemen & Bansal, 2002).

These comments also seem to imply that some of the responsibility for facilitating research utilization rests with the researchers themselves—should academic researchers be involved in dissemination to users? Should researchers aim to influence management practice through the research they carry out? These recommendations fail to acknowledge the clearly different audiences for different modes of research; fail to recognize the lack of incentives; and fail to note that researchers may be focusing on dissemination channels which carry significantly more status than a user audience. Recommendations for improving access to research findings include the requirement to translate relevant research for use by managers, and to focus and localize the findings to meet specific needs (Castle, 1988; Walter et al., 2003b). Increasing use of computer technology and the Internet can also support this process (Walter et al., 2003b).

Poor dissmentation channels are therefore often identifed as key barriers to research use (Kelemen & Bansal, 2002), although it is not clear who should be responsible for dissemination to manager-practitioners. Although these accusations may be true, the audiences for academic publications and those who are interested in practical implications may be quite different target groups. Academic publications are not targeted at practitioners.

Style and Relevance

Research impact is affected by how finely tuned it is to meeting managers' needs (Hemsley-Brown, 2004; Hemsley-Brown & Sharp, 2003; Kelemen & Bansal, 2002) and the relevance of research to decision making is also a barrier to research use (Castle, 1988; Cousins & Simon, 1991; Deshpande & Zaltman, 1984; Edwards, 2000; Tranfield & Starkey, 1998; Zaltman & Moorman, 1988). The style in which academic research is written is significantly different from the style preferred by practitioners, so should researchers ensure that topics are relevant and of interest to decision makers; specify the implications; and be more precise and realistic about claims? (Castle, 1988; Cousins & Simon, 1991; Deshpande & Zaltman, 1984; Edwards, 2000; Tranfield & Starkey, 1998; Zaltman & Moorman, 1988).

Practitioner-managers are often unable to decode academic research because it is written for other academics, with different aims, and in a style that alienates many practitioners (Kelemen & Bansal, 2002). There are of course incentives and advantages for researchers in using a more esoteric style because "by writing in code we decrease the likelihood that our ideas will ever be used by managers" (Sutton, 2004, pp. 28–29) and "research shows that being difficult to understand or even completely incomprehensible can increase prestige" (Sutton, 2004, p. 29). No surprise then, that research findings are rarely used by managers and practitioners. Successful initiatives in research utilization are those that target specific barriers to change: the context and relevance of the research to potential users needs to be a priority (Walter et al., 2003b) and the sources need to be both Mode 2 and relevant Mode 1 research.

Trust and Mistrust

Furthermore, there is also skepticism among practitioners about the credibility of academic research conducted almost entirely in universities, and this results in a lack of trust in what practitioners view as essentially practical knowledge (Sutton, 2004). However, these conclusions rarely acknowledge different categories and modes of research: this is a good description of Mode 1 research, which is not aimed at practitioners.

.Therefore, there seems to be a mistrust of research and a concern about the quality and design of research studies (Boostrom et al., 1993; Moorman et al., 1992; Zaltman & Moorman, 1988). What seems to be lacking is the development of mutual understanding between practitioners, managers, and researchers which might potentially increase users' trust of the research provider. Strategies to build greater trust between managers and researchers could contribute to improved research utilization, but this trust can only be built through working in collaboration and partnership.

The Context of Research Utilization

Following the identification of barriers to the use of research and to research utilization, authors frequently make recommendations for facilitating research use. The relevance of the source information was a key factor in the utility of research findings, and respondents (principals and district staff) are more likely to use research when the findings meet their information needs. The perceived sophistication (how finely tuned it is to match local needs), value, relevance, and timeliness of the information has a positive impact on its use (Cousins & Leithwood, 1993; Hemsley-Brown & Sharp, 2003). More practical suggestions for facilitating research utilization include:

1. making information readily available
2. enabling teachers to devote time to reading research
3. using outside consultants
4. providing evidence of the benefits of using research
5. ensuring that research has practical application.

School improvement is an organizational change process; schools are social systems and knowledge is socially constructed; therefore, social learning needs to take place in order for research utilization to occur. In order to promote social learning school improvement information should be shared and practitioners should be involved in the design, delivery, and follow-up activities associated with school improvement (Cousins & Leithwood, 1993; Hemsley-Brown & Sharp, 2003).

A common recommendation for improving research use, therefore, relates to the culture, structure and collegiality of the school—promotion of a collegial atmosphere between researchers and teachers and developing a collaborative culture (Hemsley-Brown & Sharp, 2003). For this reason, the recommendations for improving research utilization in all sectors including schools predominantly focus on the organization (Corwin & Louis, 1982): organizational structure and researcher–manager interaction (Deshpande & Zaltman, 1982). Organization culture, particularly a collaborative organizational culture, networking, and partnerships are the most frequent recommendations, although research to demonstrate the effectiveness of these strategies is hard to find (Hemsley-Brown, 2004; Hemsley-Brown & Sharp, 2003; Walter et al., 2003b). A long-term study, carried out in Austin, Texas (Hipp & Huffman, 2007), from 1995–2000 confirms that the development of a collegial relationship as part of a professional learning community for school principals, other school leaders, staff, and school office staff enabled the school to build the capacity and supportive conditions to share in the learning process. The authors argue that schools and districts were struggling with initiating and implementing reform measures, and there is a need to convince colleagues that decisions should be made based on *real data*. This successful initiative involved: shared and supportive leadership; shared values and vision; collective learning and application; shared personal practice; and supportive conditions (Hipp & Huffman, 2007).

The recommendations and good practice in facilitating research use focus mainly on organizational issues, school or organizational culture and collaborative approaches—despite the barriers, which are often individual. These recommendations are based on the argument that research utilization requires social learning to take place, and social learning is facilitated most effectively in a collaborative culture.

Individual or Organizational?

The barriers are associated with the aims, process and outcomes, usefulness, and types of research; and individual barriers have been identified as those associated with access and dissemination, style and relevance, and trust and mistrust. But can collaboration and partnership address individual barriers, and problems of mistrust and the mode of research? Many authors assume that research is utilized by individuals, and by individuals within organizations, but others assume research is utilized by organizations. One of the main barriers to knowledge use in schools in the U.S., according to Louis (1996), is at the organizational level rather than the individual level; frequently the culture of the school does not encourage management learning through the use of research (Hemsley-Brown & Sharp, 2003). In contrast, however, Simon (as cited by Van der Sluis & Poell, 2002) claims that all learning is *individual* learning and that an organization can only learn in two ways: by the learning of its members, and by embracing new members who have prior knowledge. So can research utilization only take place through individuals, or can this be achieved through organizations? The notion of organizational learning "proves particularly slippery in the interface between the individual learning and organizational learning" (Popper & Lipshitz, 2004, p. 37). To a great extent the work conducted thus far on research utilization is focused on individual barriers to learning but organizational factors such as structure and culture, collaborative approaches and organizational learning play a key role in promoting research use.

Structure and Culture

Factors associated with organizational culture and structure are also consistently perceived as strong barriers to research use; more decentralized and less formalized organizations are more likely to make greater (and perhaps better) use of research than centralized and formal organizations (Deshpande & Zaltman, 1982). A large organization which is highly centralized may have difficulty in implementing results from research. For purposes of implementing research a highly centralized school system may need to decentralize decision making at least during the implementation phase (Deshpande & Zaltman, 1982). This approach favors devolved decision making at national, local, school, or even departmental level. The benefit of strong and visible leadership is also highlighted, and seems to provide motivation, authority and enthusiasm for using research, particularly at higher levels in an organization—that is, at management decision-making level (Walter et al., 2003b).

Many of the factors which facilitate research use generally demand an organizational culture that supports learning (management learning) and the key to research utilization is organizational learning. In order to facilitate research utilization a new culture needs to be created within the school—a culture that focuses on, and values organizational learning as well as individual learning. Most authors who write about organizational learning agree that both the individuals and the organization learn (Örtenblad, 2002).

Organizational Learning

Organizational learning is "a process in which an organization's members actively use data to guide behavior in such a way as to promote the ongoing adaptation of the organization" (Edmondson & Moingeon, 2004, p. 28). For schools, organizational learning is a process of continuous school improvement through the use of data and research—utilization of research and data. By promoting a culture of organizational learning the findings from relevant research might be more readily used by managers of schools for organizational change and adaptation. Research utilization approached in this way is part of knowledge- and evidence-informed practice: a co-creation of knowledge approach. Organizational learning is a process of acting, assessing, and acting again—an ongoing cycle of reflection and action that cannot be taken for granted (Edmondson & Moingeon, 2004).

If research utilization is facilitated through organization learning and learning organizations, then perhaps a transformation will need to take place followed by a demand for research intelligence to meet that need. Once organizations transform themselves into learning organizations, then there might be greater demand for research intelligence, which could then be met by research and researchers. This cultural shift needs to take place in schools before there is sufficient demand for research intelligence. Incentives are the key: sufficient incentives for academics to collaborate in providing relevant knowledge, and sufficient incentives on both sides of the partnership. Policy makers in most countries believe that with proper incentives schools can be encouraged or required to become better consumers of research results. Popular documents funded by a variety of agencies in the U.S. aim to pave the way toward better understanding of the connection between research knowledge and good school practice. However, that knowledge is political and political contexts are critical to understanding knowledge use.

The focus of research use needs to shift from a personal level to an organizational level: it is simplistic to blame individual practitioners for their failure to access or use research (Hemsley-Brown, 2004). A two-way relationship between practitioners in organizations and academics in universities is one approach—they each need to continue to learn from one another and share in developments and ideas, to achieve utilization of research. Mode 1 research does not have a monopoly over new ideas, and there can be a reciprocal situation where ideas are developed by practitioners themselves: research utilization works best in settings of collaboration and mutual support (Hemsley-Brown, 2004; Hemsley-Brown & Sharp, 2003).

Collaboration

A collaborative organizational culture that values learning and values the insight that research provides is a key recommendation for improved research utilization (Hemsley-Brown & Sharp, 2003; Walter et al., 2003b). There are eight broad categories which reflect the mechanisms which drive research impact in different interventions: dissemination, education, social influence, collaboration, incentives, reinforcement, facilitation, and multifaceted initiatives (Walter et al., 2003b). So there is not a magic answer, and no single factor facilitates research use—a multiple-methods approach is needed to improve the use of research for decision making. The development of communication networks, links between researchers and practitioners, and greater involvement of practitioners in the research process are also strategies which improve research impact, but with the possible exception of Huberman (1990) the research evidence to demonstrate the success of these approaches is still hard to find (Hemsley-Brown & Sharp, 2003). One of the many benefits of collaborative approaches to research use is that this approach generates a sense of ownership and enthusiasm for new knowledge, which considerably increases the likelihood of utilizing knowledge (Hemsley-Brown, 2004; Hemsley-Brown & Sharp, 2003; Walter et al., 2003b).

Conclusion

First, research on the barriers to research utilization seems to be unclear about which type of research users should have access to, and it would be a mistake to assume that all research in education management is intended to be "useful" to practitioners. This is partly because of differences in the aims of research in the two contexts, which necessarily create a gap between the two worlds. Research on the barriers to the use of research to support decision making focuses on research "use," rather that "utilization": utilization implies that users would have some involvement in the process of generating research knowledge, but "use" implies that the research can be applied more directly. The relationship between educational research and practice is not a linear relationship, although it is all too easy to assume it is. The notion of research use suggests a clear, identifiable, measurable and direct relationship, but a multi-layered, unpredictable, interacting process of engagement between the researcher and the educator is much more realistic (Department of Education, Training and Youth Affairs, 2000; Hemsley-Brown & Sharp, 2003).

Second, there are three aspects of the research–practice gap in terms of research utilization: the research itself or the mode of the research; the process of dissemination; and the context of dissemination. Knowledge is local and specific, especially utilitarian knowledge, and knowledge created elsewhere needs to be compatible with existing belief structures so that it becomes legitimized and has utility within the local setting (Louis, 1996). All three aspects of the research–user gap need to be addressed before appropriate management research can be utilized to facilitate improvement in schools. These recommendations are summarized in Table 17.1, alongside the barriers (Hemsley-Brown, 2004; Hemsley-Brown & Sharp, 2003).

Third, much research conducted by academics has been accused of failing to focus on the needs of user-practitioners—but to some extent this is because of the way research is categorized, and because of the different demands of funding bodies, and the targets which need to be met by researchers themselves and the organizations they represent. Funding bodies as well as the researchers themselves drive the process and the expected outcomes. Research-based knowledge, particularly when the agenda is set by the curiosity of the researcher, is necessarily "imprecise, inconclusive, complex and contingent" (Nutley & Davies, 2000, p. 35). The metaphor of "blue skies" research—often used to describe such research—gives the impression of research which has no constraints, such as finance, utility or application (Calvert, 2002). Users, on the other hand, may use knowledge only when it gives clear guidance and is presented in simple terms which can be directly applied (Nutley & Davies, 2000). Users seem to be less concerned with the process of conducting research and the pursuit of knowledge for its own sake, but rather more focused on the *outcomes* or the potential use of the research in practice (Huff & Huff, 2001; Kelemen & Bansal, 2002).

Therefore, the gap between researchers' perceptions of research and users' perceptions of research can be partly explained by their different perceptions of the aims of research, and whether the focus is on process or outcomes. Closing the gap may not be feasible; indeed, explaining and justifying the reasons for the gap has been the most frequent approach to addressing this issue. It is unsurprising that pure research,

Table 17.1 Summary of factors which hinder and facilitate research utilization.

Factors which hinder research utilization	*Factors which are claimed to facilitate research utilization*
The research itself and the mode of the research	*The research should be:*
• Categorization of research into Mode 1 and Mode 2 (Tranfield & Starkey, 1998), Mode 3 model proposed (Ferlie et al., 2003). • Research is inaccessible (Bracey, 1989; Walter et al., 2003b), both intellectually and practically, and is not useful (Deshpande & Zaltman, 1984) or relevant (Kelemen & Bansal, 2002) to user-managers.	• Accessible and relevant (Kelemen & Bansal, 2000); localized or focused, and meet the needs of users (Castle, 1988; Deshpande & Zaltman, 1984; Hemsley-Brown, 2004; Hemsley-Brown & Sharp, 2003; Zaltman, & Moorman, 1989). Research must be translated (Walter et al., 2003b). • Statistical information should be interpreted (Hemsley-Brown, 2004; Hemsley-Brown & Sharp, 2003); and greater use should be made of computer technology (Duncan, 1993).
The process of the dissemination of research	*The individual users should be:*
• Poor access and weak dissemination channels (Walter et al., 2003b); being difficult to understand or even completely incomprehensible can increase prestige (Sutton, 2004). Skepticism among practitioners about the credibility of some academic research	• Targeted and users should be given the opportunity to feel ownership (Hemsley-Brown, 2004; Hemsley-Brown & Sharp, 2003; Walter et al., 2003b). • Enthusiastic—Individual enthusiasts can help carry the process of research impact. They are vital to "sell" new ideas and practices. Personal contact is most effective (Walter et al., 2003b).
The context of research utilization	*Organizations should seek to support and facilitate:*
• A highly competitive environment contributes to this mistrust of research	• Collaboration, partnership and involvement; sharing and networking (Hemsley-Brown, 2004; Hemsley-Brown & Sharp, 2003; Wenger, 1998; Wenger, McDermott, & Snyder, 2002); closer links between researchers and practitioners (Huberman, 1990) and reduce the element of surprise (Deshpande & Zaltman, 1982). • Strong and visible leadership (Walter et al., 2003a) particularly at higher levels, helps provide motivation, authority and organizational integration (Walter et al., 2003b). • Support, education and training (Hemsley-Brown, 2004; Parahoo, 2000; Parahoo, Barr, & McCaughan, 2000). Ongoing support for those implementing changes increases the chance of success. Financial, technical and emotional support; sufficient incentives and dedicated project coordinators have been keys to the success of several initiatives (Walter et al., 2003b).

blue skies research, or Mode 1 research are not easily accessible, understandable, or used by non-academics, since the aims of this mode of research are not based on utility, usability, or application by practitioners.

The Mode 2 research approach or a problem-solving model might be more appropriate in terms of providing usable research findings for practitioner-managers, but the demand for this kind of research needs to be stimulated through the creation of appropriate funding streams and through the development of learning organizations which demand such research intelligence. There should perhaps be more of a two-way relationship between practitioners in organizations and academics in universities—they need to continue to learn from one another and share in developments and ideas: a co-creation of knowledge approach. Good links established prior to and during a research study contribute toward a more energetic approach to dissemination of the findings from research (Huberman, 1990). A utilitarian approach based on Mode 2 research or a problem-solving approach cannot exist in isolation and ignore the complexities and conflicts raised by curiosity-driven research such as Mode 1 research; but nonetheless it is Mode 2 research that is most readily applied by practitioners for management decision making. Such an approach can be naive and superficial, however, unless it is combined with Mode 1 research. As a possible solution, authors have suggested developing Mode 3 research which combines the best of both Modes 1 and 2, to facilitate greater research utilization (Ferlie et al., 2003).

If research utilization is facilitated through organizational learning and learning organizations then a transformation needs to take place before managers start to demand research intelligence. This cultural shift can only take place if sufficient incentives (e.g., status, recognition, and effectiveness, as well as financial incentives) are made available on both sides of a partnership to enable academics to become involved in collaborative research utilization. There is a need to work toward creating, developing, and supporting learning organizations and moving toward greater research utilization. When this becomes a reality, then perhaps there will be an increasing demand for research intelligence to support this climate, and researchers and practitioners can work more closely together to close the research–practice gap.

References

Bero, L., Grilli, R., Grimshaw, J., Harvey, E., Oxman, D., & Thomson, M. (1998). Getting research funding into practice. Closing the gap between research and practice. An overview of systematic reviews of interventions to promote the implementation of research findings. *British Medical Journal, 317*, 465–468.

Biddle, B. J., & Saha, L. J. (2000, April). *Research knowledge use and school principals.* Paper presented at the annual meeting of the American Educational Research Association, New Orleans, LA.

Boostrom, R., Hansen, D., & Jackson, P. (1993). Coming together and staying apart: How a group of teachers and researchers sought to bridge the "research/practice gap." *Teachers' College Record, 95*, 35–44.

Bracey, G. (1989). Why so much education research is irrelevant, imitative and ignored. *American School Board Journal, 176*(2), 2–22.

Calvert, J. (2002). *Goodbye blue skies: The concept of basic research and its role in a changing funding environment.* Unpublished doctoral dissertation, University of Sussex, UK.

Castle, S. (1988, April). *Empowerment through knowledge: Linking research and practice for school reform.* Paper presented at the annual meeting of the American Educational Research Association, New Orleans, LA.

Corwin, R. G., & Louis, K. S. (1982). Organizational barriers to the utilization of research. *Administrative Science Quarterly, 27*, 623–640.

Cousins, J., & Leithwood, K. (1993). Enhancing knowledge utilization as a strategy for school improvement. *Knowledge Creation Diffusion Utilization, 14,* 305–333.

Cousins, J., & Simon, M. (1991). The nature and impact of policy-induced partnerships between research and practice communities. *Educational Evaluation and Policy Analysis, 18,* 199–218.

Davies, H. T. O., & Nutley, S. M. (2002). *Evidence-based policy and practice: Moving from rhetoric to reality* (Discussion Paper). Retrieved November 1, 2007, from http://www.ruru.ac.uk/PDFs/Rhetoric%20to%20reality%20NF.pdf

Dehler, G., Welsh, A., & Lewis, M. (2001). Critical pedagogy in the "new paradigm." *Management Learning, 32,* 493–511.

Department of Education, Training and Youth Affairs (2000). *The impact of educational research: Research evaluation program report by the Department of Education, Training and Youth Affairs.* Canberra: Australian Government Publishing Service.

Deshpande, R., & Zaltman, G. (1982). Factors affecting the use of market research information: A path analysis. *Journal of Marketing Research, 14,* 14–31.

Deshpande, R., & Zaltman, G. (1984). A comparison of factors affecting researcher and manager perceptions of market research use. *Journal of Marketing Research, 21,* 32–38.

Duncan, G. T. (1993). Management research methodology: Prospects and links to practice. *International Journal of Organizational Analysis, 1,* 255–272.

Edmondson, A., & Moingeon, B. (2004). From organizational learning to the learning organization. In C. Grey & E. Antonacopoulou (Eds.), *Essential readings in management learning* (pp. 21–36). London: Sage Publications.

Edwards, T. (2000). All the evidence shows . . .: Reasonable expectations of educational research. *Oxford Review of Education, 26,* 299–311.

Ferlie, E., Hartley, J., & Martin, S. (2003). Changing public service organizations: Current perspectives and future prospects. *British Journal of Management, 14,* S1–S14.

Gruber, W., & Niles, J. (1973). Research and experience in management. *Business Horizons, 16*(4), 15–24.

Hemsley-Brown, J. (2004). Facilitating research utilization: A cross sector review of the research evidence. *International Journal of Public Sector Management, 17,* 534–552.

Hemsley-Brown, J., & Sharp, C. (2002, September). *The use of research by practitioners in education: Has medicine got it cracked?* Paper presented to the British Education Research Association Conference, University of Exeter, Devon, UK.

Hemsley-Brown, J., & Sharp, C. (2003). The use of research to improve professional practice: A systematic review of the literature. *Oxford Review of Education, 29,* 449–470.

Hemsley-Brown, J., Cunningham, M., Morton, R., & Sharp, C. (2002). *Education decision making under scrutiny: The impact of local government modernization.* Slough, UK: NFER/LGA.

Hillage, J., Pearson, R., & Tamkin, P. (1998). *Hillage Report: Excellence in research on schools* (Research Report RR74). Department for Education and Employment. London: Institute for Employment Studies.

Hipp, K. A., & Huffman, J. B. (2007). Using assessment tools as frames for dialogue to create and sustain professional learning communities: Divergence, depths and dilemmas. In L. Stoll & K. S. Louis (Eds.), *Professional learning communities* (pp. 119–131). Maidenhead, UK: McGraw Hill Open University Press.

Huberman, M. (1990). Linkage between researchers and practitioners: A qualitative study. *American Educational Research Journal, 27,* 363–391.

Huff, A. S., & Huff, J. O. (2001). Re-focusing the business school agenda. *British Journal of Management, 12* (Suppl. 1), S49–S54.

Johnson, G. (2000). Strategy through a cultural lens. *Management Learning, 31,* 403–426.

Kelemen, M., & Bansal, P. (2002). The conventions of management research and their relevance to management practice. *British Journal of Management, 13,* 97–108.

Klein, L. (1995). Making use of research: Have we forgotten how? *People Management, 1*(17), 17.

Leseure, M., Bauer, J., Birdi, K., Neely, A., & Denyer, D. (2004). Adoption of promising practices: A systematic review of the evidence. *International Journal of Management Reviews, 5/6,* 169–190.

Louis, K. S. (1996). Reconnecting knowledge utilization and school improvement: Two steps forward, one step back. In A. Hargreaves, M. Fullan, & D. Hopkins (Eds.), *International handbook of educational change* (pp. 1074–1095). Boston: Klewer.

Montgomery, K. S. (2005). Utilization of research via the Internet. *Journal of SPN, 7,* 86–88.

Moorman, C., Zaltman, G., & Deshpande, R. (1992). Relationships between providers and users of marketing research: The dynamics of trust within and between organizations. *Journal of Marketing Research, 29,* 314–328.

National Center for the Dissemination of Disability Research (1996). *A review of the literature on dissemination and knowledge utilization.* Retrieved May 12, 2002, from http://www.ncddr.org/kt/products/reviews/du/

Nutley, S. M., & Davies, H. T. O. (2000). Making a reality of evidence-based-practice: Some lessons from the diffusion of innovations. *Public Money and Management, 20*(4), 35–42.

Örtenblad, A. (2002). A typology of the idea of learning organization. *Management Learning, 33,* 213–230.

Oulton, T. (1995). Management research for information. *Management Decision, 33*(5), 63–67.

Parahoo, K. (2000). Barriers to, and facilitators of, research utilisation among nurses in Northern Ireland. *Journal of Advanced Nursing, 31*, 89–98.

Parahoo, K., Barr, O., & McCaughan, E. (2000) Research utilisation and attitudes towards research among learning disability nurses in Northern Ireland. *Journal of Advanced Nursing, 31*(3), 607–613.

Percy-Smith, J. (2005). *Promoting change through research: The impact of research in local government.* York, UK: The Joseph Rowntree Foundation.

Popper, M., & Lipshitz, R. (2004). Organizational learning: Mechanisms, culture and feasibility. In C. Grey & E. Antonacopoulou (Eds.), *Essential readings in management learning* (pp. 37–52). London: Sage Publications.

Saha, L., Biddle, B., & Anderson, D. (1995). Attitudes towards education research knowledge and policymaking among American and Australian school principals. *International Journal of Educational Research, 23*, 113–126.

Shkedi, A. (1998). Teachers' attitudes towards research: A challenge for qualitative researchers. *International Journal of Qualitative Studies in Education, 11*, 559–577.

Sturdy, A. (2004). The adoption of management ideas and practices. *Management Learning, 35*, 155–179.

Sutton, R. I. (2004). Prospecting for valuable evidence: Why scholarly research can be a goldmine for managers. *Strategy and Leadership, 32*(1), 27–33.

Tranfield, D., & Starkey, K. (1998). The nature, social organization and promotion of management research: Towards policy. *British Journal of Management, 9*, 341–353.

Van der Sluis, L., & Poell, R. (2002). Learning opportunities and learning behavior: A study among MBAs in their early career stage. *Management Learning, 33*, 291–311.

Walter, I., Nutley, S. M., & Davies, H. T. O. (2003a). *Developing taxonomy of interventions used to increase the impact of research* (Discussion Paper 3). Retrieved January 31, 2008, from http://www.ruru.ac.uk/PDFs/Taxonomy%20development%20paper%202007103.pdf

Walter, I., Nutley, S. M., & Davies, H. T. O. (2003b). *Research impact: A cross sector review literature review.* Retrieved January 31, 2008, from http://www.ruru.ac.uk/PDFs/LSDA%20literature%20review%final.pdf

Weiss, C. H. (1979). The many meanings of research utilization. *Public Administration Review, 39*, 426–431.

Wenger, E. (1998). *Communities of practice: learning, meaning and identity.* Cambridge, UK: Cambridge University Press.

Wenger, E., McDermott, R., & Snyder, W. M. (2002). *Cultivating communities of practice: A guide to managing knowledge.* Boston: Harvard Business School Press.

Zaltman, G., & Moorman, C. (1988). The importance of personal trust in the use of research. *Journal of Advertising Research, 28*(5), 16–24.

Zeuli, J. (1994). How do teachers understand research when they read it? *Teaching and Teacher Education, 10*, 39–55.

18

Swimming in the Depths
Educators' Ongoing Effective Use of Data to Guide Decision Making

Leanne R. Bettesworth, Julie Alonzo
University of Oregon

and

Luke Duesbery
San Diego State University

Educators are awash with data. Classroom teachers calculate student grades using the data they collect: attendance, participation points, test scores, and homework completion. School administrators track different data in their daily work: discipline referrals, average daily attendance, school budgets, and expenses related to extracurricular programs. At the district level, data are more departmentalized: with the Personnel Department calculating salaries, benefits packages, and retirement accounts; those in Instruction tracking expenditures on curricular materials and professional development, and Special Services keeping tabs on students receiving additional assistance, completing annual reports to document compliance with a variety of laws. With all these data, one might expect to find educators confident in their data acumen. Sadly, the opposite is more likely to be the case. As a public spotlight is focused on AYP-based school performance data, teachers and administrators all too often are caught floundering in the depths, as waves of data threaten to drown them.

Our work with school leaders (building and district administrators, as well as teachers studying for their administrative licenses) has highlighted three main findings.

1. The educators we have worked with have little training in the meaningful use of data beyond the scope of a single classroom. Although they are familiar with the use of total scores and percentiles to calculate grades, their knowledge does not extend beyond these rudimentary skills.
2. Basic statistics offer meaningful insights to educators who understand how to use them. Simple concepts such as measures of central tendency and variance, standard error, domain sampling, and rank can help educators make more informed decisions.

3. Introduction to these measurement concepts is not sufficient. For educators to move beyond basic familiarity to actual comfort in using data to guide instructional decision making requires a transformation in their approach to schooling. This transformation requires ongoing mentoring and forced practice to move into educators' working knowledge.

In this chapter, we first locate our studies in the research literature on data-based decision making before introducing the dual theoretical lenses through which we view the adoption of new practice: cognitive dissonance (Festinger, 1957) and self-efficacy (Bandura, 1982, 1993, 1997). We then describe our findings from two studies documenting educators' increased ability to use data to make instructional decisions before concluding with suggestions based on our research for those who work in this area. It is our hope that this chapter will provide some guidance to others involved in the effort to help educators gain the skills they need to be able to swim rather than drown in the sea of data in which they work.

The Focus on Data in School Improvement

The Center for Research on Evaluation, Standards, and Student Testing (CRESST; Mitchell, Lee, & Herman, 2000) suggests that

> Data-based decision-making and use of data for continuous improvement are the operating concepts of the day. School leaders are expected to chart the effectiveness of their strategies and use complex and often conflicting state, district, and local assessments to monitor and ensure progress. These new expectations, that schools monitor their efforts to enable *all* students to achieve, assume that school leaders are ready and able to use data to understand where students are academically and why, and to establish improvement plans that are targeted, responsive, and adaptive. (p. 22)

However, research literature on data-driven decision making to guide instructional practices is still limited. Early research in this area was conducted in the 1980s (Popham, Cruse, Rankin, Sandifer, & Williams, 1985), but as a whole, this area of research did not gain momentum at the classroom or school level because complex, easy to access data systems were not readily available and were not being used in school systems until recently. Today, however, more school systems and states have the capacity to collect, analyze, and share data with all stakeholders in an efficient and timely manner (Ackley, 2001; Thorn, 2002). This trend has been further accelerated by legislated requirements of No Child Left Behind (NCLB; U.S. Department of Education, 2001) to use data to improve school performance (Hamilton, Stecher, & Klein, 2002).

In the 2002 publication, *Leading Learning Communities: Standards for What Principals Should Know and Be Able to Do*, the National Association of Elementary School Principals (NAESP) included among its six performance standards for principals: "Use multiple sources of data as diagnostic tools to assess, identify, and apply instructional improvement" (p. 2). Five strategies accompanying the standard on data use encourage principals to consider a variety of data sources to measure performance; analyze data using a variety of strategies; use data as tools to identify barriers to success, design strategies for improvement and to plan daily instruction; benchmark successful schools with similar demographics to identify strategies for improving student achievement; and create a school environment that is comfortable using data. (p. 7)

Principals are expected to use data by first beginning with a "global question" or issue, then breaking down the issue into its component parts for analysis to make reasoned decisions on subsequent steps (Streifer, 2002). Killion and Bellamy (2000) suggest

without analyzing and discussing data, schools are unlikely to identify and solve the problems that need attention, identify appropriate interventions to solve these problems, or know how they are progressing toward achievement of their goals. Data are the fuel of reform. Because data abound, schools must become data savvy. (p. 1)

Jandris (2001) describes data-driven decision making as an integral part of the continuous improvement process guided by quantitative and qualitative data drawn from the classroom, the school, the district, and state sources. For a variety of reasons, however, schools continue to struggle with meaningful use of schoolwide data.

Establishing Data-Driven Decision-Making Practices in Schools

One barrier to implementing a data-driven decision-making culture is the need for parents, teachers, administrators, district leaders, and school boards to know what to do with the data once they are collected (Bernhardt, 1998, 2003; Cromey & Hanson, 2000; Killion & Bellamy, 2000; Lambert, 2003). A further barrier is an integrated, well-conceived systems approach to data-driven decision making. This includes an accessible data storage system, benchmarking, planning, personnel evaluation, and professional development showcasing the interdependency of inputs, processes, and outcomes under scrutiny (Streifer, 2002).

Holcomb (1999) identifies eight key school improvement activities involving staff that increase student achievement, with three relating specifically to data. The activities that focus on data collection, analysis, interpretation, and decision making described by Holcomb are:

(a) identifying significant, meaningful data to compile for the school;
(b) interpreting the data, requesting more data, and identifying areas of concern; and
(c) discussing and analyzing data evidencing progress with implementation and goal attainment.

Holcomb (1999) and Schmoker (2001) both maintain that all instructional staff should be involved in data analysis and goal setting.

The lack of formal training on how to evaluate programs and student data and how to apply assessment information or the new data-mining tools to the school improvement process is a serious challenge, as is the lack of an established, coherent process for using data in ways that support ongoing, continuous systemic improvement in schools (Cromey, 2000; Paige, 2002; Schmoker, 2001; Streifer, 2002). Focused acts of improvement founded in well-conceived data-driven decision-making processes will help superintendents and school board members, as well as their constituents, gain confidence in their school improvement initiatives (Bernhardt, 1998). The key to meaningful use of educational data lies in the verb: *use.* All too often, educators collect data without clear understanding of how to analyze them (Creighton, 2001), a practice which must be confronted directly (Beghetto & Alonzo, 2006).

Professional Development is a Key to Data Use

There may be reasons why schools do not effectively make the most of their data. In some schools and districts, data analysis is not a high priority (Van der Ploeg & Thum, 2004). Some state education departments may put little emphasis on schools gathering data for improved student performance and thus provide little incentive for districts and schools to devote time, money, and staff resources to utilizing data in new ways to increase student performance. School-based educators may fear data analysis; others may not fear data analysis yet may not have received adequate training to gather and disaggregate data or to establish and maintain databases. Although educational reformers suggest that teachers should embrace data as a way to make their jobs easier and more rewarding (Kinder, 2000; Wiggins, 1993), practice often lags far behind theory in the reality of everyday schooling.

The North Central Regional Educational Laboratory (NCREL) suggests that professional development is central to any attempt to improve the way student achievement is assessed in schools. For the greatest effect on continuous school improvement, a school leader or a district evaluator with a solid grounding in the use of data who is familiar with the school vision (Van der Ploeg & Thum, 2004) should conduct this professional development. Professional development can bring rigor to the use of data-driven decision making. Educators do not need advanced degrees in statistics to begin gathering data and analyzing them in ways that benefit their schools and students; they need professional development training focused on the facets of data-driven decision making.

Professional development and role modeling focused solely on effective data-driven decision-making practices, however, is not enough. Training must also include supports targeted at increasing the educators' efficacy around data-driven decision making. Feelings of self-efficacy and cognitive dissonance play a complementary role in getting educators to use skills gained from professional development activities in their classrooms and schools. Successful performance raises self-efficacy, while failures lower self-efficacy (Bandura, 1977, 1997). Cognitive dissonance research suggests the impact of failure is exacerbated even more when people are sure they put forth their best effort to accomplish a task that they believe to be important. The potential negative impact of failure when educators are learning how to use data to inform their instructional decisions implies that educators in professional development situations need opportunities to participate in data-driven initiatives in safe and successful contexts prior to expecting them to use their skills in the real world.

The importance participants place on professional development opportunities focused on data-driven decision making is also key. If consonant feelings toward data use are unattainable, the efforts at training are wasted, as the person will never fully support the practice (Festinger, 1957). It is evident then that educators participating in professional development activities focused on data-driven decision making must believe data are worthwhile. Without this basic belief, it is unlikely that they will persist in their effort to master the skills required to become competent users of school data, impacting the effectiveness of professional development initiatives.

The lack of substantial and relevant professional development has been a barrier to many initiatives. Wayman (2005) asserts this to be a characteristic also found in many data initiatives. Armstrong (2003) supports this claim, suggesting that a crucial characteristic of a data-driven district is professional development, without which no data initiative involving teachers and technology can be sustainable. Professional development alone, however, is not enough. The support of school leadership and their modeling of data use are essential (Lachat & Smith, 2005; Wayman, 2005). Research conducted by Lachat and Smith (2005) stressed that data use is strongly influenced by the leadership practices of the principal. Their findings further suggest that data use is also influenced by the shared leadership of other administrators and teacher leaders in the school.

Cognitive Dissonance, Self-Efficacy, and the Use of Data

Success in data use goes beyond professional development that trains a person to use a few new skills or strategies in their practice. Data initiatives must also address human behavior; a belief system related to data use, and feelings of efficacy toward applying the new skills. Psychologists and educational researchers turn to theories to better understand human behavior. Two theories from the work of cognitive and social psychologists are particularly relevant to our interest in moving educators to use data to guide their instructional decisions: cognitive dissonance and self-efficacy.

Cognitive Dissonance: The Motivator Behind Behavior Change

Cognitive dissonance, a psychological theory first published by Festinger (1957) in *A Theory of Cognitive Dissonance*, refers to discomfort felt because of a discrepancy between what one already knows or believes, and new information or interpretations. Cognitive dissonance occurs when there is a need to make informed instructional decisions, yet at the same time develop or expand our thoughts to accommodate new ideas. Cognitive Dissonance Theory has encouraged many studies focusing on a better understanding of what determines an individual's beliefs, how individuals make decisions based on their beliefs, and what happens when their beliefs are brought into question. This theory deals with pairs of cognitions defined as "any knowledge, opinion, or belief about the environment, about oneself, or about one's behavior" (Festinger, 1957, p. 3).

Of primary concern are those pairs of elements that are relevant to each other. If two cognitions are, in fact, relevant to one another, they are classified as either *consonant* or *dissonant* cognitions (Festinger, 1957). Consonant cognitions occur when elements of knowledge follow from one another without conflict. Dissonant cognitions occur when one element of knowledge is followed by the opposite of the element. It is these dissonant cognitions that are most applicable to our understanding of educators' use of data to guide instructional decision making.

According to Festinger's theory, the existence of dissonant cognitions produces an uncomfortable feeling, which motivates an individual to lessen or to eliminate the dissonance. "The strength of the pressure to reduce the dissonance is a function of the magnitude of the dissonance" (Festinger, 1957, p. 18). The number of dissonant beliefs and the importance associated with each belief are two factors that affect the magnitude of the dissonance and the motivation to work toward consonance. The theory, because it is so broad, is relevant to many different topics, including data-driven decision making (Harmon-Jones & Mills, 1999).

Self-efficacy: A Force that Maintains Momentum for a Change

Self-efficacy, a major construct of Social Cognitive Theory (Bandura, 1982, 1993, 1997), refers to a person's judgment about being able to perform a particular activity. It can be conceptualized as a person's *I can* or *I cannot* belief. Unlike self-esteem, which reflects how individuals feel about their worth or value, self-efficacy reflects how confident people are about performing specific tasks. Because self-efficacy is specific to the task being attempted, high self-efficacy in one area may not coincide with high self-efficacy in another area. And, although self-efficacy indicates how strongly people believe they have the skills to do well, there may well be other factors that keep them from succeeding.

Bandura's theory of self-efficacy has important implications with regard to motivation. Bandura's basic principle is that people are likely to engage in activities to the extent that they perceive themselves to be competent at those activities. With regard to education, this means that learners will be more likely to attempt, to persevere, and to be successful at tasks for which they have a sense of efficacy. When learners fail, the failure may occur because they lack the skills to succeed or because they have the skills but lack the sense of efficacy to use these skills well.

Applying these two psychological theories to educators' use of data, we build from Festinger's (1957) view that educators need to have the motivation to move toward consonance, the desire to use data, and the understanding that it is a necessary component in the decision-making process. To this understanding, we add the patina of efficacy. Bandura (1977, 1993) believed that those using data to inform their instruction must have both the knowledge to perform the tasks and the feelings of efficacy to actually enact those skills. In spite of the endorsements for data-based decision making as a critical school reform initiative, there appears to be inadequate preparation of how to use the data-driven decision-making process effectively and accurately.

Empirical Studies: Bridging the Gap Between Administrators and Data

This chapter, then, addresses the critical questions of how best to address this need. In two studies which built upon each other, we tested the effectiveness of professional development focusing on basic statistics with an emphasis on the use of student performance data to guide instructional decision making. In both studies, we sought to create dissonance in our participants as a mechanism for motivating awareness of a need to change their approach to using data, then built on their knowledge through structured group and individual assignments to increase their sense of efficacy in data manipulation, analysis, and use. The chapter contains information and findings from two studies varied in setting (the first took place in the Pacific Northwest of the United States, the second in western Canada) and participants (the first study involved 31 individual preservice administrators from a range of schools and districts throughout a region enrolled in an administrative licensure program; the second included teams of three from five suburban schools, each comprised of a principal and two lead teachers), but provided complementary results. Because the studies were so closely linked and the findings so congruent, we present them both together in this chapter.

In both cases, we found that participants began with quite rudimentary knowledge of basic statistics and measurement principles and ended with much greater skills in this area. In all cases, educators in our studies both before and after receiving the intervention reported greater knowledge of and comfort with interpreting graphs and charts compiled by others than constructing their own graphs—or selecting relevant data to display graphically. Their efficacy toward data manipulation and use, however, was directly related to the degree to which they had experienced success in analyzing their own school data during the course of the study. We found that the participants who had received the most regular feedback (whether from the instructor in the first study or from organized peer groups in the second study) exhibited the greatest growth in skill as well as efficacy over the course of the study. In fact, this finding from Study 1 led us to select school-based data teams as a critical organizing component of Study 2. We now move to a discussion of the two studies.

Methods

The studies in this chapter both used a pre-test, post-test design. In Study 1, a two-day intervention (workshop on measurement principles, basic statistics, and the use of data to guide instructional decision making) was preceded by a pre-test and followed by two guided assignments and a post-test. There were 31 participants in the treatment group, 16 participants were female, the mean age was 39 ($SD = 9.8$) and participants had an average of 10 years' teaching experience ($SD = 6.5$). Participants were a convenience sample of educational leaders in generally equivalent stages of their careers. At the time of the study, they were all participating in an administrative training program seeking further opportunities for leadership in their district. In the six months between pre- and post-test, three follow-up interviews were conducted with each of four participants, who represented different levels of skill and efficacy, based on performance on the pre-test and a survey to measure efficacy delivered prior to the intervention. Two high-skilled participants (one demonstrating low efficacy for data use, the other high efficacy) and two low-skilled participants (also demonstrating opposite extremes on the efficacy scale) were selected for follow-up interviews.

In Study 2, the two-day intervention was followed by six months of bi-weekly coaching and peer support group meetings. Five teams made up of three people each were involved in both the training and the coaching/peer support groups. Coaching sessions included mini-lessons and scenarios involving data as well as question and answer sessions and collaboration on school data projects with a data expert. Peer support groups were established within school teams and met at the school site: one administrator and two lead teachers from each school participated, representing one elementary school, two middle schools, and two high schools. Principals volunteered themselves and their staff to be part of the study. Each school principal chose the two teachers who would make up their team. There were 15 participants in the second study; seven participants were male. The mean age of the group was 46.2 ($SD = 7.4$) and the average years of teaching experience was 18.4 years ($SD = 8.6$).

The Intervention: Teaching Basic Statistics and Measurement Principles

The intervention was delivered through a three-part seminar using computer-based training modules to teach how to use school data to make informed decisions regarding instructional practices. The modules covered the following three topics: (a) distribution and percentile rank, (b) cut scores and standard error of measurement, and (c) domain and skill sampling. Content for the training modules was based on the type of knowledge and skills identified by Schmoker (2003), Creighton (2001), and Bernhardt (2003) as being of critical importance to educators. Each lesson was accompanied by small pre-tests intended to induce dissonance in participants by presenting the information in a context that illustrated why the knowledge would be useful for school leaders to possess while highlighting their unfamiliarity with the type of knowledge being presented (see Figure 18.1). These small pre-tests were not intended to be used to measure intervention effectiveness but rather to be part of the intervention itself. To measure intervention effectiveness, we used overall pre- and post-tests in conjunction with efficacy surveys, interviews, and focus groups.

Task: From each selection of three **bold** words, choose the word that fits the sentence best.

1. Imagine student scores are arranged in rank order from lowest to highest. Next, the scores are divided into 100 equally sized groups or bands. The lowest score is in the **[1st percentile/0 percentile/1st percentage]**. The highest score is **[the 100th percentile/the 99th percentile/100 percent]**.
2. If you were going to compare two or more sets of data using box-and-whisker plots, first you would need to look at the **[boxes/percentiles/whiskers]** to get an idea whether or not they are located in about the same place. Next compare the **[mean/median/mode]** to find out how the data are separated into two equal parts. Then study the lengths of the boxes to determine whether or not the **[variability/predictability/scattering]** as measured by the quartiles, are about the same. It may be that the data sets are very similar, but with a different spread of data. Check the pattern of **[outliers/skewness/predictability]** in each data set to find the scores furthest from the middle.

Figure 18.1 Examples of module questions designed to create cognitive dissonance in participants.

Measuring the Effectiveness of the Intervention   Overall pre- and post-tests sampled all content presented in the three modules of the training sessions. These three-part tests were organized into three levels of cognitive demand: identification, evaluation, and application. The *identification* section required participants to match data analysis terms with their definitions. The *evaluation* section required participants to read one to two sentence scenarios and then to choose the appropriate type of analysis to use from a given list. Participants also provided a rationale for their data analysis choice. The *application* portion consisted of three scenarios accompanied by data sets (see Figure 18.2). Based on information provided in the scenarios, participants analyzed data and explained their decisions based on their analysis. All three sections sampled participants' content knowledge of distributions, percentile rank, cut scores, standard error of measurement, and domain and skill sampling.

Initial and exit surveys used Likert-type scale questions to address perceptions, confidence, and efficacy in data analysis, interpretation, and decision making. Open-ended questions had respondents describe their current ability and understanding of assessment, data, data collection, data analysis, data interpretation, and data-based decision making. On the exit survey, additional questions asked participants to share their perceived area of greatest growth and their biggest fears about using data-driven decision-making practices in their school.

Case studies (Study 1) or focus groups (Study 2) helped us interpret the quantitative results. In the first study, four of the 31 participants were purposefully selected to participate in the case studies. In Study 2, all participants participated in the focus groups. Interview participants were interviewed three times over a six-month period. In the replication study, we conducted three 20-minute focus groups with each of the five participating groups (September, November, and February). The interview questions evolved from session to session; however, the same questions were asked of each participant. Questions focused on participants' feelings of efficacy and confidence regarding analysis, interpretation, and decision making using data.

Data Analysis   This chapter used three different types of data: a series of test results, surveys, and interviews. Each type of data required its own data analysis procedures. Test results were analyzed using repeated measures analysis of variance (ANOVA). Likert-type survey questions were analyzed by counting the frequency of answers in each response category. Survey results were used to describe the sample and

---

Scenario 1: Central Elementary school is an urban school in the Pacific Northwest with an enrollment of 300 students in grades K-5. The staff members at Central have decided to report the year-end average math scores in each grade. They plan to collect these data annually, to demonstrate growth in these areas each year. Further, the teachers want to find out how their individual students in each grade compare to other students in the school and district.

The principal and her head teacher decide to explore the district math assessment to provide each of the grades with the appropriate information. The fourth grade data are given below.

<note to reader: this scenario is followed by a table of data, an accompanying spreadsheet, and series of tasks requiring application of knowledge>

Figure 18.2 Example of an application scenario prompt presented to participants.

determine subjects' perceived abilities in data-based decision making prior to the intervention and how their perception changed over time. Interview transcripts were analyzed to evaluate the degree to which participants' sense of efficacy, confidence, and comfort level increased as a result of the intervention.

Results

Results in this chapter indicate that the seminar on the use of data increased participants' knowledge of measurement and data analysis as well as their feelings of efficacy toward the use of data to inform instructional decisions at their schools. Our second study, in which we included peer support groups and more structured, peer-mediated learning activities resulted in greater increases in knowledge but perhaps more importantly, given the role of efficacy in people's willingness to persist in using new knowledge, these additional supports also resulted in greater gains in participants' feelings of efficacy toward the use of data in their school settings.

Gains in Test Performance   In Study 1 participants experienced growth in all three areas. On average, participants grew on the identification section, going from a mean of 5.17 ($SD = 2.93$) on the pre-test to a mean of 10.41 ($SD = 3.28$) out of 15 on the post-test. Their gain on the interpretation section was equally noteworthy, moving from a mean of 2.93 ($SD = 2.39$) on the pre-test to a mean of 7.66 ($SD = 3.72$) out of 16 on the post-test. On the third and most challenging section of the tests, participants' learning was even more impressive. On the pre-test, the mean score on the application section of the test was a low 1.14 ($SD = 1.03$) out of 23 possible points. In contrast, participants scored a mean of 4.00 ($SD = 4.65$) on the post-test. Improvement from pre- to post-test was statistically significant on all three sections (Identification, $F(1,28) = 76.58$, $p < .0001$; Analysis, $F(1,28) = 54.29$, $p < .0001$; Application, $F(1,28) = 11.40$, $p < .0001$).

Similarly, in Study 2 participants' growth in performance was dramatic on all three sections of the tests. On average, participants more than doubled their scores from pre- to post-test on the identification section, going from a mean of 5.87 ($SD = 3.46$) on the pre-test to a mean of 12.80 ($SD = 1.86$) out of 15 on the post-test. Scores on the interpretation section grew from a mean of 3 ($SD = 2.45$) on the pre-test to a mean of 11.73 ($SD = 2.66$) out of 16 on the post-test. On the third section participants' learning was most impressive. On the pre-test, the mean score on the application section of the test was only 1.33 ($SD = 1.04$). On the post-test participants scored a mean of 14.00 (SD = 6.18) out of 23, a dramatic increase indeed. Improvement from pre- to post-test was statistically significant on all three sections (Identification, $F(1,14) = 92.67$, $p < .0001$; Analysis, $F(1,14) = 102.06$, $p < .0001$; Application, $F(1,14) = 61.56$, $p < .0001$). Growth in both studies was marked, but was more pronounced in Study 2 in all three sections of the test.

Changes in Self-Reported Efficacy   Survey findings supported test results. Frequency counts on the survey indicated that educators felt they were overwhelmingly better able to apply their knowledge of data analysis and interpretation after the intervention. Participants reported an increase in confidence to analyze, interpret, and make decisions as a result of the training and practice received as part of the intervention. The most significant reported increase in confidence in the first study, from 32% to 64.5%, was found in respondents' confidence in explaining to others why a certain approach to analyzing data was used. In the second study, one of the most significant increases in confidence, from 27% to 87%, was in participants' overall ability to work with student learning data.

In addition, participants in both studies reported an increase in frequency of inter- preting student data. The most significant increase, from 32% to 65% in the first study, occurred when respondents were asked by school personnel to interpret district data. Respondents in the second study also exhibited an increase in interpreting district data; however, the most dramatic increase in interpreting data, from 20% to 87%, was in interpreting school data. Twice the number of respondents in the first study and four times the number of respondents in the second study indicated they were asked to interpret data since participating in the seminar. Counts also demonstrated an increase in feelings of efficacy to interpret and use data between the initial survey and the exit survey. When respondents were asked if they considered themselves as someone who has a lot of experience using student learning data to make instructional decisions, responses in both studies more than doubled from the initial questionnaire to the exit survey. Clearly, test scores and survey responses alike indicate that professional development modules on data analysis and interpretation can result in enhancements of educators' skill and sense of efficacy related to data-based decision making.

Case Studies and Focus Groups Enhance the Overall Interpretation of Improvement   To further understand the quantitative findings in this chapter, case studies and focus groups were conducted following the intervention. In the first study we conducted case studies of four participants over six months. In the second study, during the six months that followed the intervention, focus groups were con- ducted of five teams of educators concurrently as the coaching and peer group meetings occurred. Case studies and focus groups focused on educators' confidence, ability, and willingness to analyze, interpret, and make decisions using data in their respective schools.

Initially, all respondents agreed that the two-day training seminar did increase their ability to analyze assessment data. An elementary participant recounted in her first interview, "as we went through the training, I would say by the second day I felt really confident, like 'Oh, I get this' . . . and I felt confident in how to use it and how to really analyze it and really understand what does it tells, what data tells you." However, participants reported not liking analysis, citing a lack of time and con- fidence, concern over making mistakes, frustration with complex statistical programs such as EXCEL, and challenges posed by limited and/or unreliable data. All respond- ents discussed their personal lack of confidence and avoidance of data analysis. A high school participant with high pre-test scores and higher reports of efficacy explained, "Data analysis is easy, it is math. The real problem, to make, to choose the analysis to do and to, to know the choice was right. Good quality, reliable data better than . . . chapter ending tests is also important."

A further interview session supported the respondents' resistance to analyze data. During this session, participants' reported confidence to analyze data appeared to have lessened since the first focus group two months prior. In fact, the high school participant who had expressed the most confidence in her initial survey and earned the highest pre-test score seemed to be losing ground two months after the intervention. "I think it would be great if there was one person that the district had that was . . . kind of the data person," she explained. "If there was someone that their job was to be the data person, and they could come and sit down with the department and analyze the data for us and make sense out of the numbers, and say, look at it in numbers and just say [this is] where your kids are at, they [are] this far away from the average or from grade level . . . I think that would be a great service." Halfway through the study, although participants had demonstrated the ability to analyze data on several previous occasions, they still lacked confidence in their ability to fill that role in their schools. All participants echoed the sentiments expressed by the high scorer quoted above in wishing that somebody else in their district would analyze their data for them.

Knowing that new skills require repeated practice to master, in the second study we built additional structured opportunities for participants to engage in data analysis as part of their peer data teams. The final interviews were scheduled after all teams had completed assignments related to identifying, gathering, and analyzing data from their school. In this focus group, it was clear that participants' confidence level had increased. A middle school participant from the first study stated, "I'm much more confident; I'm probably at that dangerous level where I know just enough to be dangerous and not enough to really know what I am doing. But I can follow the directions on the training website." This increased confidence, however, did not necessarily translate to independent application. One elementary participant explained that unless she is forced to analyze data, or if she could work with a group of very competent colleagues, she would not voluntarily analyze data. Another elementary participant, like the others interviewed, reported that she would prefer to either collaborate on the analysis portion of data-driven decision making or have someone, more practiced and less likely to make errors, analyze her school data. Most seemed fearful of making errors and not catching them if they were to attempt data analysis on their own.

Despite this concern about analyzing data on their own, participants reported that they felt confident in their ability to interpret data analysis. Further, all participants indicated that they thought it was much easier to interpret a chart or graph than to make sense of raw numerical data reported by the state on student assessments. A middle school participant captured the essence of all interview participants, stating, "By putting stuff in charts, it really is for someone who's not a real data person a much, much easier way to look at it . . . and there's almost no explanation needed." When participants were asked about interpreting graphs and charts, they all suggested that they did not feel they had to be an expert with statistics or data to interpret a graph.

Participants were asked to describe any opportunity they had to interpret data and how they felt about their interpretation skill. An elementary participant stated, "Right now, we collect a lot of data. I see eyes glaze over real quickly when we talk about analysis, but I was really afraid of EXCEL, and I am not afraid of EXCEL [anymore]. I can't make it do a lot for me, but for the kind of stuff I'm doing, like standard error and standard deviation, and mean, median stuff, and graphs, I can do that and I can explain it to my staff so their eyes don't glaze over as quickly."

During the second interview, all participants suggested they were making decisions using data; however, their level of confidence varied. Both a high school participant and an elementary participant suggested that their schools were collecting too much data and were not spending enough time looking at the data or making decisions from them. They also suggested that even if people knew what the data meant, their practices in the school would be unlikely to change. It appeared that the schools, in both cases, were collecting data for the sake of collecting data and that no one was using the data to make instructional decisions. An elementary participant said,

> They're collecting a ton of information about what is being done in the building, where the kids are at in each building, we have been collecting data, since September, in math, reading, science, what materials each building has, what protocols each school uses. All this and we are still not at any decision-making process at this point. We practice at our meetings with you, but this seems to be where the discussion ends. More people need to be able to join in the conversation to make an impact. This is a problem if the school wants to change, make changes to instruction, this is taking too long. I think they're afraid of what to do next so they are just going to keep collecting data.

All participants seemed to be at different stages in their confidence as a result of many different situations in their schools. Amount of data collected, length of time since training, collegial acceptance of data use, and time were issues affecting their confidence.

All participants continue to express their willingness, ability, and confidence to make decisions using instructional data in the final interviews and focus group sessions.

Discussion

The central purpose in this chapter was to examine the impact of training in measurement statistics and follow-up coaching on educators' ability to use data to make instructional decisions. Quantitative measures suggested training was effective, while qualitative measures such as interviews and surveys identified facets that worked, did not work, and helped pinpoint where additional support and practice were needed to enable educators to use data to guide their instructional practices.

Training increased participants' ability to use data to inform decision making. However, all sources of data support the finding that participants had the lowest feelings of efficacy with analysis and were most hesitant to explore their new abilities in this area. Although participants followed instructions to use data and were more confident to work in a collaborative group after the intervention, they were still not confident about analyzing data independently, nor did they feel confident and equipped with the right tools to make decisions that went beyond their immediate classroom or team.

Focus group participants claimed that once data were collected, people did not seem to know what to do next. Festinger (1957) would say this is where cognitive dissonance exists: Educators know to collect data but are uncomfortable with the next steps, and therefore, until something interferes with their current situation, there is no motivation to move forward, toward cognitive consonance, even if educators know they should use data to inform their practice.

Clearly, the training session conducted was useful and applicable to participants; however, educators must get beyond collecting data to actually using their data to inform instruction. Independently, most participants were very hesitant to use data. As individuals, participants did not indicate strong confidence in their analysis skills, nor did they have confidence in the decisions they made from the results of their data analysis. They were quick to cast their decisions aside and revert back to "gut-level" decisions rather than those based on data. Their own school colleagues could easily crumble their confidence simply by asking them to explain why they made a specific decision rather than choose what appeared to be an equally viable alternative.

In groups, participants were much more confident and willing to take risks. They would challenge each other to defend the analysis used or the decision made, particularly if two group members differed on their analysis or final decision. They would explore more than one way to analyze the same data set, or they would use different data sets to confirm a theory or to support a decision. Each of the five groups reported out to either its staff or its parent council as a group, whereas not a single individual demonstrated a willingness to present to peers or parents. A middle school teacher explained, "If I share our data and decisions with staff, and they ask me questions, and I'm not sure of the answer one of my group members will step in and respond and then I can build on their answer if they leave out some details. My team has me covered and I am more confident." To further explain the risks one middle school group took, data from a group of struggling readers were analyzed over a three-month period, then the middle school team took its information to the school board in an effort to seek further support and funding for a reading program. Interestingly, in most groups the participants were quick to defer to the school principal when a final decision was necessary. Three of the five school principals said this left them in a slightly uncomfortable position. However, as they were responsible for all decisions in the school anyway, they felt their decisions supported by data would be much easier to explain and defend should the need arise.

Focus groups indicated that participants in this study felt overwhelmingly successful at interpreting data. All shared their feelings of efficacy and their increased ability to interpret data. Participants also stated that using data displays such as box and whisker plots, charts, and graphs assisted them in interpreting and explaining data. They further conveyed that they would, without hesitation, continue to interpret the types of data and graphic displays in which they were trained. In examining these feelings of success and efficacy toward interpretation of data through the lens of cognitive dissonance and efficacy, an interesting pattern emerges. Festinger (1957) proposed that two cognitions are in question: interpretation and application. Both need to be relevant and somewhat consonant to determine an individual's success. Participants established that they had limited cognitive dissonance and high efficacy in interpreting data, suggesting that they knew data interpretation was important and that they were able to apply the skills successfully. As a result, most participants suggested they would incorporate interpretation into their educational practice.

Bandura recommended that efficacy be increased by providing people with small tasks with which they can be successful, that simultaneously build on a specific competency (1997). Interpretation of data is a skill introduced in elementary mathematics when students are asked to interpret bar graphs or pie charts in relation to problem solving or fractions. A typical American adult has engaged in the interpretation of graphs since elementary school. Therefore, when contemplating data interpretation, participants' efficacy should be high and their dissonance should be low given their exposure and experience with this particular skill.

Streifer (2002) extended this point by advocating that one of the barriers to a data-driven decision-making model is, in fact, an integrated, well-articulated systems approach to the process. This systems approach must build on the strengths and efficacy of educators (Bandura, 1993) and offer collaborative training rather than individual experiences in data use (Wayman, 2005). At the same time, the systems approach needs to ensure that all parts of the decision-making model are addressed and understood so that educators can move from cognitive dissonance toward cognitive consonance and strong feelings of efficacy. A well-articulated system of data use, with supports, would assist participants in effectively using data. It is apparent from this study that training alone will not suffice. Our initial study resulted in improved test scores, indicating greater knowledge, yet no change in participants' efficacy, suggesting limited potential for changing their actual behavior. In Study 2, we increased the supports offered to participants by introducing small school data teams and bi-weekly data team meetings with a data expert. These enhancements to the intervention appeared to improve its overall effectiveness, particularly in the area of efficacy. The ongoing coaching and peer group meetings encouraged people to use data and created a safer environment for participants to take risks and apply their new skills to the task at hand.

Bandura (1977) advises that people need to feel success in order to increase efficacy with data use. Wayman (2005) and Lachat and Smith (2005) highlight collaboration in using data as an idea to increase teacher efficacy, suggesting that data initiatives are more successful if teachers work together. If data use is to cause change in our schools, Killion and Bellamy (2000) note that educators need to discuss data and be able to explain why they make the decisions they do with the data they have. Educators must become savvy in data use if school improvement is to result from data use. Our findings certainly support these assertions, as the more collaborative Study 2 resulted in greater changes in participants' knowledge as well as efficacy, compared to Study 1.

It is important to note, however, that although participants in this study were successful with analysis, interpretation, and decision making on a post-test and discussed their successes with using data in focus groups and coaching sessions, it was less clear if they were able to return to their schools and actually use data to inform their decisions beyond what was done in the coaching sessions. The findings of Lachat and Smith (2005) highlight the importance of teacher collaboration in analyzing data and making decisions set around a clearly defined goal or question. This chapter demonstrates that educators worked collaboratively through the training sessions and throughout the coaching and peer group meetings. Collaborating on data analysis and decision making required participants to engage in conversation. This conversation, while it required extensive time, helped move participants toward cognitive consonance as they articulated their personal views to their team and listened to the perspectives of others.

Suggestions for Future Research

Given the exploratory nature of the studies in this chapter, several suggestions for future research are in order. With regard to the training session, it is certainly warranted to replicate this type of training across different groups of educators so that findings can be further generalized. If training sessions are effective, it is important to determine how much educators' abilities in analysis, interpretation, and decision making increase based on the training. Moreover, long-term application and on-site use of data were not addressed in this chapter, but it is of great interest because of a central belief that improving teachers' ability to analyze, interpret, and use data to make decisions leads to better outcomes in the classroom (Cromey, 2000; Popham, 1999). Examination of teachers' change over time in their use of data to inform their instructional practices, in both ability and efficacy, should be an essential part of similar future research into the application of data-driven decision making.

Conclusion

This chapter describes an effort through two different studies to provide direction and clarification for research in helping educators use data to make informed instructional decisions. Although the findings in this chapter should be viewed as exploratory, they suggest that this type of training and ongoing coaching can influence content knowledge and effectiveness in using data to make informed instructional decisions. In the current climate of educational accountability, further research in the effective and appropriate use of data-driven decision making can help address issues regarding curriculum and instruction effectively.

Improving district and school leaders' ability to develop effective internal accountability systems using data-driven analysis may assist them not only in finding the answers to their school performance questions and creating new knowledge about their schools, but may also assist them in engaging the entire community in a level of detailed, objective, purposeful reflection (Fuhrman, 1999). It is our hope that our findings may serve as an indication of what is possible. Educators can be taught how to gather, analyze, and interpret data from their schools and districts without requiring large allocations of time or resources to the efforts. In the two studies reported here, participants spent a total of 12 hours attending a seminar on measurement principles and data analysis. They then completed additional independent (Study 1) or small group (Study 2) assignments which required them to apply their new learning to their own school data. These extended assignments were particularly effective in enhancing participants' comfort with data analysis when they were completed as part of small collegial teams, providing support along the way.

The findings in this chapter suggest that modest interventions, such as the lessons used in our studies reported here (available free of charge from www. cbmtraining.com) can offer educators a life preserver when it comes to negotiating the waves of data which wash over them in their daily school lives. Basic knowledge of measurement principles and data analysis, especially when coupled with ongoing peer support and coaching, can help school leaders stay afloat even in the most tempestuous seas.

References

Ackley, D. (2001). Data analysis demystified. *Leadership, 31*(2), 28–29, 37–38.

Armstrong, J. (2003). *Next generation models of educational accountability: Accountability*. Education Commission of the States. Retrieved March 11, 2005, from http://www.ecs. org/clearinghouse/39/95/3995.doc

Bandura, A. (1977). Self efficacy: Towards a unifying theory of behavior change. *Psychological Review, 84*, 191–215.

Bandura, A. (1982). Self-efficacy mechanism in human agency. *American Psychologist, 37*, 122–147.

Bandura, A. (1993). Perceived self-efficacy in cognitive development and functioning. *Educational Psychologist, 28*, 117–149.

Bandura, A. (1997). *Self-efficacy: The exercise of control*. New York: W. H. Freeman & Company.

Beghetto, R. A., & Alonzo, J. (2006). Instructional leadership: Supporting the learning process. In S. C. Smith & P. K. Piele (Eds.), *School leadership: Handbook for excellence in student learning* (4th ed., pp. 284–301). Thousand Oaks, CA: Corwin.

Bernhardt, V. L. (1998). *Data analysis for comprehensive schoolwide improvement*. Larchmont, NY: Eye on Education.

Bernhardt, V. L. (2003). No schools left behind. *Educational Leadership, 60*(5), 26–30.

Creighton, T. B. (2001). *Schools and data: The educator's guide for using data to improve decision-making*. Thousand Oaks, CA: Corwin.

Cromey, A. (2000). *Using student assessment data: What can we learn from schools?* Oak Brook, IL: North Central Regional Educational Laboratory.

Cromey, A., & Hanson, M. (2000). *An exploratory analysis of school-based student assessment systems*. North Central Regional Educational Laboratory Evaluation Reports. Retrieved March 29, 2005, from http://www.ncrel.org/policy/pubs/html/data/index.html

Festinger, L. (1957). *A theory of cognitive dissonance*. Evanston, IL: Row, Peterson & Company.

Fuhrman, S. H. (1999). *The new accountability*. Retrieved May 24, 2005, from http://www.cpre.org/Publications/rb27.pdf

Hamilton, L. S., Stecher, B. M., & Klein, S. P. (2002). *Making sense of test-based accountability in education*. Santa Monica, CA: Rand.

Harmon-Jones, E., & Mills, J. (1999). *Cognitive dissonance progress on a pivotal theory in social psychology*. Washington, DC: Braun Brumfield.

Holcomb, E. L. (1999). *Getting excited about data: How to combine people, passion, and proof*. Thousand Oaks, CA: Corwin.

Jandris, T. P. (2001). *Essentials for principals: Data-based decision-making*. Alexandria, VA: National Association of Elementary School Principals.

Killion, J., & Bellamy, G. T. (2000). On the job: Data analysts focus school improvement efforts. *Journal of Staff Development, 21*, 27–31.

Kinder, A. (2000). *D-3M: Helping schools distill data*. Oakbrook, IL: North Central Regional Educational Laboratory.

Lachat, M. A., & Smith, S. (2005). Practices that support data use in urban high schools. *Journal of Education for Students Placed at Risk, 10*, 333–349.

Lambert, L. (2003). *Leadership capacity for lasting school improvement*. Alexandria, VA: Association for Supervision and Curriculum Development.

Mitchell, D., Lee, J., & Herman, J. (2000, October). Computer software systems and using data to support school reform. In M. Honey & C. Shookhoff (Eds.), *The Wingspread Conference on Technology's role in urban school reform, Achieving equity and equality: A summary report* (pp. 22–28). New York: EDC Center for Children and Technology. Retrieved April 14, 2005, from http://www2.edc.org/CCT/admin/publications/ policybriefs/wingspread00.pdf

National Association of Elementary School Principals (2002). *Leading learning communities: Standards for what principals should know and be able to do.* Alexandria, VA: Author.

Paige, R. (2002). An overview of America's education agenda. *Phi Delta Kappan, 83*, 708–713.

Popham, W. J. (1999). Why standardized tests don't measure educational quality. *Educational Leadership, 56*(6), 8–15.

Popham, W. J., Cruse, K. L., Rankin, S. C., Sandifer, P. D., & Williams, R. L. (1985). Measurement-driven instruction. *Phi Delta Kappan, 66*, 628–634.

Schmoker, M. J. (2001). *The results field book: Practical strategies from dramatically improved schools.* Alexandria, VA: Association for Supervision and Curriculum Development.

Schmoker, M. J. (2003). First things first: Demystifying data analysis. *Educational Leadership, 60*(5), 22–24.

Streifer, P. A. (2002). *Using data to make better educational decisions.* Lanham, MD: Scarecrow.

Thorn, C. (2002). *Data use in the classroom: The challenges of implementing data-based decision-making at the school level.* Madison: University of Wisconsin, Wisconsin Center for Education Research.

U.S. Department of Education (2001). *No child left behind.* Washington, DC: Author.

Van der Ploeg, A., & Thum, Y. M. (2004). *Finding additional value in new accountability systems.* Naperville, IL: North Central Regional Educational Laboratory.

Wayman, J. C. (2005). Involving teachers in data-driven decision making: Using computer data systems to support teacher inquiry and reflection. *Journal of Education for Students Placed at Risk, 10*, 295–308.

Wiggins, G. (1993). *Assessing student performance: Exploring the purpose and limits of testing.* San Francisco: Jossey-Bass.

19

Creative Decision-Making Strategies through Technology-Based Curriculum Tools

John Castellani and Deborah Carran

Johns Hopkins University

Introduction

Using data for informed decision making is important for determining how systems should allocate resources and strengthen programs to improve teaching and learning. Schools and organizations are increasingly responsible for documenting and reporting progress and the available data are growing. New federal legislation is encouraging states to enact policies for making all school data publicly available and to use these data to hold districts accountable for all students to learn. Within this current climate of data for informed decision making, there are issues surrounding how current assessment of student achievement is linked with all other data available within schools. In many education environments, there are few questions about data availability. Rather, the issue is with how to understand and use these data to improve student learning and to support the educators to enhance student performance within the curriculum.

The climate for using quantitative data for informed decision making has grown over the past few years and educators are making decisions about instruction based on more standard measurements. However, hard data are not solely responsible for proving success or improving instruction. The intent of this chapter is to demonstrate various ways in which data may be used to support instructional decision making, primarily through exploring curriculum-based measures. For the purposes of this chapter, a curriculum measure is any measure that a teacher uses in his/her classroom to assess student performance and improve instruction. The chapter will also present issues surrounding standards, curriculum, assessment, and the implications for technology. Lastly, the chapter will present knowledge-based reform strategies and issues for supporting a climate for data and school change.

Indicators of School Improvement

What a teacher does in his/her classroom must fit into the broader picture of instruction and assessment. School administrators are responsible for student achievement; however, these results come from performance in classrooms. How to target data at the classroom or individual student level for continuous school improvement is an ongoing process, and requires careful consideration of the many factors that mediate achievement, since the factors used to measure state, district, school, teacher, and student performance are classroom based and classrooms vary. When put in context, there are many variables surrounding classroom instruction that can impact performance, including where the school is located, who attends the school, and educational or other initiatives currently underway within the building. Nationally, school accountability is measured through adequate yearly progress (AYP); however, many other variables can be used to establish whether or not schools are progressing in a broader context.

Consider Figure 19.1. Educational entities, whether schools, districts, or states, are each and every one unique; many are similar but not identical. It is this uniqueness that must be considered when selecting indicators for performance. For example, it is possible to invest a great deal of time trying to figure out whether or not student performance is related to teaching. A suburban school with a one-to-one laptop initiative for all high school students might look very different than a suburban school with a non-technology-based reading initiative. Subsequently, schools with active parents and high standards for learning will respond differently to a school with poor teachers, few resources, and daily attendance and drop-out issues. As a result, no discussion of curriculum and assessment can exist in isolation without considering descriptive data available about the entire school context.

Not until recently have there been consistent measures available to all schools. As a result of the No Child Left Behind Act, states have developed content standards; schools, in turn, have interpreted these standards and developed curriculum, and teachers have responded by integrating these standards into their daily instructional lessons to help students learn content that is consistent across grade levels and subject areas. This effort is to increase student performance on assessments and hold schools accountable for instruction. All of these rich data have helped educators know when to continue, adapt, or change content material, and/or teacher methods. But along with daily curriculum delivery comes the overarching umbrella of the

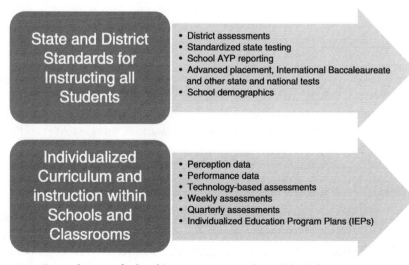

Figure 19.1 General areas of school improvement and possible indicators.

mediating variables, which include setting, demographic characteristics, and climate. This leads to four main questions:

1. How does high-quality teaching and achievement happen within a climate of data-driven decision making?
2. How are both formal and informal assessment measures considered and used?
3. What curriculum-based assessment measures are important for guiding ongoing instruction?
4. What is the role of technology in the assessment process?

These four questions should guide discussions decision makers and stakeholders have regarding school improvement and will be examined in the rest of this chapter.

Data Collected in the Classroom: Assessing Progress

Schools collect vast amounts of data but often fail to use them (Streifer, 2002). This is the real problem; translating the data into usable information. To make data-informed decision making a reality, several steps must be taken. Streifer (2002) points out, "the first building block needed to conduct data-driven decision making is to bring all of our educational data together for easy access and analysis" (p. 3). Tsantis and Castellani (2001) add that it is necessary to build a comprehensive data collection and discovery system that is responsive to individual intricacies in the teaching and learning process. Ease and utility of data collection is only the first step. What follows next, as Streifer states, must be the creation of a concept map that "effectively frame(s) problems . . . [and] breaks the larger problem down into smaller, more manageable components" (p. 4). Framing the problem will help to identify data elements that will be necessary and essential to guide stakeholders in a discussion of data collection and concept mapping.

Table 19.1 identifies the major areas presented in Figure 19.1 and lists the range of data that practitioners and administrators need to consider when thinking about data available to assess progress. In the No Child Left Behind era of accountability, ALL students must be achieving. This includes general and special education students as well as those targeted as English as a Second or Other Language (ESOL). Therefore, educators need to consider all available data when making decisions about instruction because school accountability and student progress are two very different variables to measure. It is possible to have schools making progress and students progressing in the general education curriculum without meeting AYP and passing state achievement tests.

What is evident from Table 19.1 is that data exist whenever students interact with the educational system; from the classroom to the community to central administration to the state educational agency. If a student is involved, some form of assessment will likely occur. But Table 19.1 only lists a thin layer of data. When schools start adding other elements, like integrating content standards into the curriculum, and begin the "drilling down in the data" process, the process of assimilating data elements becomes much more complex.

Table 19.1 Data elements to consider for assessing student progress.

Achievement data	Staff data	School/district data	Demographic and performance data	Student behavior and compliance data
• Curriculum-based measures for reading and math (pre- and post-tests) • Comprehensive test of basic skills • State assessments (reading and math) • State functional tests (used for reading, math, and writing) • Wilson steps (Wilson Reading program steps–internal progress measure) • Benchmark assessments (monthly, used to indicate progress on state learning outcomes) • Quarterly learning contract reports (classroom grades) • Standardized tests of achievement (Woodcock-Johnson Tests of Achievement, III)	• Attendance: staff and students • Credential status (this would be very interesting) • Staff retention • Education level (staff) • Teacher demographics and number of years teaching • Staff evaluation scores • Observation/feedback information	• Reading and math curriculum used for instruction • Teaching models for inclusion • Technology use in school • Capital investment per student • School performance ranking	• Diagnosis codes (and make sure that both primary and secondary disabilities are addressed) • Medical assistance billing data • Medications • Intelligence Quotients (as measures on the WISC IV) • Attendance (student)	• Suspensions, referrals, and other discipline measures besides time out • Focus room (time-out area, measured in both minutes off task and by infraction) • IEP progress reports • Interruptions in service • Parent attendance at IEP (and general parental involvement scale) • Timely evaluations • IEP implemented on time • Inclusion rate • IEP held on time

Twenty-first-Century Curriculum-Based Measures

Teachers consistently apply assessment measures for their students to gauge student learning. This has been accomplished mainly through what teachers know about individual student learning within a subject matter and by testing student knowledge. This traditional approach to teaching method is started when teachers enter teacher certification programs and is reinforced year after year, as teachers continue to learn about how best to teach their content. Teachers move forward with additional content based on intuition which involves observing students' reactions to course content in class, taking into account their questions while learning, and assessing students through informal and formal observations. When applied in a spirit of continual improvement, this type of approach is very qualitative or constructionist in nature and responsive to the dynamic nature of classrooms.

In this era of accountability, however, teachers have been introduced to tools and techniques that can provide quantitative "proof" of how curriculum, teaching, and assessment fit closely together. Current data-driven decision-making approaches have been expanded to include the use of concrete data for more "informed" or easily communicated efforts that lead to results. However, this does not eliminate the daily challenges of teaching nor the ongoing trials of integrating standards into content areas.

In order to respond to these standards, districts and schools have been left to translate these standards into what a daily teaching routine might look like. In some instances, this has resulted in decreased teaching flexibility and a general confusion about teaching (Tsantis & Castellani, 2001). This happens primarily when districts restrict what teachers can teach, the way content should be taught, and the materials available for teaching. Because of increased accountability for end of year tests, teachers need to cover all content sometimes in lieu of responding to the individual nuances of classroom learning. In many cases, though, teachers have come together in learning communities to develop common assessments and "standardize" the way students are being assessed.

Foundations for Knowledge for Collaboration

Information-sharing plans, at the most introductory level, are going to include some form of technology and information. Petrides and Nodine (2003) have identified guiding questions related to school improvement that should be considered in any plan:

- Which programs and services are integral to our mission?
- How could we better meet the needs of our students?
- What student interventions are most effective?
- How can we improve student outcomes?

The plan should focus around what is best for the students and the school as a whole. "The goal is system improvement. This means that a school principal has to be almost as concerned about the success of other schools in the district as he or she is about his/her own school" (Fullan, 2001, p. 12). After the data have been collected, teams of staff members should begin the daunting task of analyzing what they all mean; translating the data into information. Where have patterns appeared and do they mean anything? In order to gain information, "Data becomes information when humans place them in context through interpretation that might seek to highlight, for instance, patterns, causes, or relationships" (Petrides & Nodine, 2003, p. 17). Once the patterns and relationships have been identified, staff may then begin to communicate with the stakeholders about their discoveries. This sharing of information may take place at a School Improvement meeting, team meeting, or faculty meeting. In order for all stakeholders to be properly informed, the collected data will be shared amongst the team. At the meeting the administrative team will begin by presenting the most relevant issues (i.e., graduation/suspension rates, test scores, etc.). Similar to businesses, the meetings should be open for discussion and constructive: "They have valued both the 'giving' and the 'receiving' of knowledge as critical to improvement" (Fullan, 2001, p. 130). In turn, the once collected data have now transformed into information, what the committee does based on that become "knowledge." A key term, Assessment Literacy, is the process of examining student performance data, making sense of the data, developing school improvement plans and monitoring the actions put in place (Fullan, 2001). The teams (staff, administration, board members, parents, and other stakeholders) work together in context to discuss the information they have learned from the data, and then plan the process of knowledge management—how to continue to collect, analyze, and use the data for continuous improvement. The data, like the targets, are not static but continually changing.

The collaboration brings staff members together to further discuss similar concerns or issues and to identify solutions. In addition, peer groups could be formed to observe other classrooms. For example, if a teacher is having difficulty with a few students, the teacher could observe these students in another teacher's class when they are not displaying the same behavioral concerns.

The teacher could then apply those working strategies to his/her classroom to limit the undesired behavior. The technology aspect behind information-sharing groups allows these data to be distributed much more quickly than it is possible with paper. Allowing all groups or teams to view the data quickly and consistently, rather than one group getting the information two weeks past due when the data are no longer valuable. Technology also allows the user to sort and manage the data much more efficiently; graphs can be composed quickly.

Technology, Curriculum, and Multimedia-Based Instruction

While schools are intent on increasing student achievement, teachers must address the changing nature of the student population in their classrooms and prepare them for "twenty-first-century skills" (see Table 19.2).

The current generation of students has the benefit of growing up in a time of wondrous innovation. Technological advances are being introduced at an astonishing pace. Prensky (2001) coined the classification Digital Native to describe the current

Table 19.2 Partnership for twenty-first-century skills.

Core subjects and twenty-first-century themes	Promotion of learning and innovation skills	Enhanced information, media and technology skills	Development of life and career skills
Mathematics	Creativity and innovation skills	Information literacy	Flexibility and adaptability
English, reading or language arts	Critical thinking and problem-solving skills	Media literacy	Initiative and self-direction
Arts	Communication and collaboration skills	ICT literacy	Social and cross-cultural skills
Science			Productivity and accountability
History			Leadership and responsibility
Economics			
Government and civics			

generation of students in the educational setting (i.e., students who have grown up with technology). Teachers must instruct their pupils using the same methods they experience at home every day. The curriculum materials presented to students in school must also change with this "Digital Native" era. The growth of the Internet has provided an extensive list of resources for teachers to utilize in a classroom setting. Connecting computers to the Internet has provided teachers with an inexhaustible well of instructional materials. Text and pictures are no longer the only media sought after by teachers. Streaming technology has given teachers an alternative to provide or supplement instruction. The benefits of using multimedia software are quite profound. First, multimedia resources are providing students with a multisensory experience during a lesson that will help prepare them with abilities for the work force. Next, they provide students with the ability to take ownership of their learning by putting them in control of their experiences. Finally, many of the multimedia experiences are self-paced, so users can learn at their own speed in a differentiated manner. With all of this available at a touch, the question arises: Does the use of multimedia in the classroom motivate digital natives?

Multimedia provides students with a plethora of knowledge in a variety of ways. Eskicioglu and Kopec (2003) define multimedia as multiple forms of media (text, graphics, images, animation, audio, and video) that work together. It is unparalleled in its ability to disseminate information quickly and accurately. Students learn in different ways. A visual learner may benefit from viewing images or videos, while an auditory learner might excel at listening to an audio recording. Multimedia provides a medium that will present information in multiple ways to differentiate the experience for each learning style. Computers are also used for assessment, whether this be history, writing, reading, math, science, or art. Schools are integrating technology through course delivery platforms, as well as individual software programs. Data from these systems are often more readily translated into formats that can be easily disseminated and used.

Students learn concepts and ideas at varying speeds. Teachers must be sensitive to this developmental obstacle. Multimedia tools are often self-paced and allow the users to control the flow of information to their comfort level. With the paradigm shift from teaching to learning, hypermedia offers an excellent way for self-paced and exploratory learning to occur that is more in tune with constructivist methodology. Students can experience the material, rather than sit through it. Active participation allows students to feel they have ownership of their education. On the other hand, teachers no longer take center stage. The classroom becomes student-centered rather than teacher-centered. The teacher's role is being restructured to fit the needs of the students.

Motivation is also a key to student achievement. We would say—the key. Students will not excel if they are not interested in their own personal achievement. Multimedia stimulates a great deal of enthusiasm for its users. Wishart (2000) used multimedia encyclopedia CD-ROMs to analyze student motivation. She found that students were motivated to use the CD-ROMs, because it fostered in them the ability to be in control of their own learning. Once again, students felt a sense of accomplishment by becoming facilitators of their own educational experiences.

Multimedia provides a unique opportunity for students and teachers. Does the use of multimedia in the classroom motivate digital natives? It promotes motivation in students to accomplish tasks set before them. It alters the requirements of the teachers by allowing students to become instructional facilitators rather than lecturers. Self-paced activities allow students to continue on at their own pace and provide differentiation between different learning styles. Teachers must embrace valuable resources like multimedia to change with their student population. So how does a teacher put all of these big ideas together in a form useful for decision making?

Curriculum-Based Example

All Curriculum-Based Assessments (CBAs) and measures, regardless of the type of curricula, are constructed in the same general way (Deno, 1985). First, sample items are selected from the curriculum or constructed to match the curriculum. These items are then ordered by difficulty and combined within a single or multiple test situation. Then, two or more forms of the same test, containing similar items and identical orders of difficulty, are constructed; these are administered on the second and third days of testing. It is more effective if teachers use multiple measures with curriculum-based measures on different forms and/or several occasions, to control for sporadic student response and to ensure that students are processing and using the content over a period of time as opposed to one point in time.

When administering the assessments, the teacher tests the students across several skill levels. This includes measuring for content, specific skills, speed or proficiency, as well as for accuracy. A CBA assessment form is developed to record the student responses. Performance criteria are then established to determine acceptable levels of student performance or mastery. These criteria should be established collaboratively, with the classroom teacher and the consulting teacher (learning specialist) functioning as an assessment team.

Example A seventh-grade math teacher is preparing to develop a curriculum unit that is linked to state standards and incorporates technology. He selects from the Voluntary State Curriculum, and chooses the appropriate topic area and begins to think about instructional delivery. Based on needed content to be learned, the teacher selects the following:

Standard 4.0 Knowledge of Statistics	Topic: A. Data Displays	Assessment
Students will collect, organize, display, analyze, or interpret data to make decisions or predictions.	Organize and display data. Organize and display data using back-to-back stem-and-leaf plots. Organize and display data to make circle graphs.	Assessment limit: Use no more than 20 data points using *whole numbers* (0–99).

In order to develop an assessment that will measure content learned from engaging in this activity, this teacher also needs to consider how an assessment item on the state assessment might be presented. He should also decide how best to assess the overall learning, to complete this specific task; the student would need math and statistic skills (standards), technology skills (curriculum), as well as problem-solving skills (twenty-first-century learning) all integrated into the same curriculum unit (see Figure 19.2).

Teachers can easily pull from their state's Voluntary Curriculum, and select

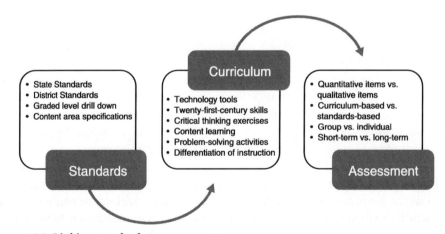

Figure 19.2 Linking standards to assessment.

assessment items that match the state assessment, but they must develop personal lessons and strategies to link these two ends of the process. In this example, the teacher demonstrates how to use a software program such as Excel to input data, correctly uses the appropriate statistics to complete equations, as well as select the appropriate chart, choose the format for the chart based on the problem statement, and then solves the final problem. However, in doing so, teachers need to decide on the skills being assessed. While content standards guide the development of most assessments, alternate skills, like problem solving and the ability to use technology, are just as important to measure. A teacher can use a quantitative test to measure math performance, but can also use technology to allow for multiple methods that students can use to demonstrate mastery over both content and higher level thinking skills. In this case the teacher decides that he will use multiple measures to assess different concepts and do this over time. He can also decide to use a Web-based assessment to more easily and quickly grade student work, as well as keep track of student achievement data in an Excel file. He can start by teaching students basic Excel features, testing kids with quizzes to understand what content is being learned, and then use both formats over time to measure growth in both technology skills and content application. These types of data can then be used as a collaboration tool with other teachers working with similar content to understand how students are responding to instruction. Electronic data are more easily shared within a group, and assessment items developed electronically, or captured through the use of online assessments or within structured questions in software are made consistent much faster.

By using technology tools, teachers can automatically report out on students weekly and/or at least quarterly; however, by the time results are reported it is often too late to alter instructional strategies, implement new models, revise existing curriculum, and adapt and accommodate instruction. The instructional strategies for special education students often include the use of instructional and assistive technologies that have built-in features to collect data, such as Web-based assessment systems, augmentative communication devices with built-in data collection features, and technology based literacy materials that monitor how students are progressing through the software.

Knowledge Management: Schools Responding to a Culture of Data

Knowledge management is a critical and fundamental part of the data-driven decision-making process. Petrides and Nodine (2003) further define Knowledge Management as "a human centered approach and a framework that enables people within an organization to develop a set of practices to collect information and share what they know, leading to action that improves services and outcomes" (pp. 10–11). Utilizing Knowledge Management effectively includes bringing three organization resources together in making educational decisions: people, processes, and technology. This three-component human-centered approach will successfully drive the process of change development needed to move systems in a direction to work more effectively.

Investing in People: Who are the Users?

In making key decisions within a school regarding curriculum-based assessment, a process must include a teamwork-based approach by members of the organization in which a shared decision-making approach is utilized in determining the strategy for assessment. Including users within a school who have multiple levels of experience builds ownership of the evolving change development and provides the opportunity for everyone to inclusively take part in the change process.

Training is critical to this aspect of the change process, and professional learning communities need to be identified, developed, and sustained. Opportunities for professional development should be made available to all users. This may warrant differentiated training classes so that everyone is included. Appropriate collaboration time is also needed to share information among team members. Teachers will want to compare and contrast lessons and assessments, share ideas, and standardize short-term and long-term assessment routines. Users need to obtain a level of comfort to share what they know and to learn what they do not know.

Processes: How Does the Information Reach the Users?

According to Petrides and Nodine (2003), the change process must include multiple levels of information research and sharing that may have an impact on the change development. Process influences can include things such as staff allocation numbers, curriculum changes/developments, scheduling challenges, along with other dominant factors that may impact decision making for school improvement. Processes are those points in the chain of information that should be considered.

In the case of school improvement, utilizing a particular team-based curriculum change model, school leaders address school concerns through collaboration in the development of the school improvement plan. The process is to efficiently utilize time and resources by identifying the concerns that need to be addressed for the school improvement process. By allowing more individuals in the process, the multiple members in each department provide several points of view allowing for more informed decision making. The process used in this model is similar to a "divide and conquer" approach to school improvement.

Technologies: What Tools will be Used?

Utilizing technology in the school improvement process does not mean that new software or hardware is required. Depending on the area of improvement that a school focuses on could include systems already established to monitor success toward the improvement process.

In the question of providing an intervention for new and retained ninth graders, those students that have been targeted for intervention can be grouped and monitored throughout the school year in SASI XP. SASI XP is a student information system by Pearson Education Incorporation which provides software that can track different types of data including attendance, grading, student information, discipline, and scheduling. Through entry of data, including marking period grading, a filtered list of students can be provided based on the teacher's particular area of inquiry. The data can then be exported into a Microsoft Excel file for filtering, sorting, and documentation. By establishing a practice of data collecting and reviewing through an already imbedded technology program allows for a more efficient method of tracking students toward school improvement success.

Conclusion

This chapter has provided some basic principles and guiding questions to launch the improvement process in an educational setting. The key ideas of selecting indicators, instructional tools, and knowledge management have been highlighted. There is more. We believe that there are some other points that should be kept in mind when approaching data-driven decision making:

(a) Technology implementation does not by default improve decision making (Petrides & Nodine, 2003), and
(b) leadership must be established and maintained for the data-assisted decision-making process to work.

Data-driven decision making for schools is an excellent process, readily made available thanks to enhanced technology and public policy mandates, but it is a process that should be approached with a plan. To begin the plan, we have provided some thoughtful recommendations.

School reform is successful and sustainable when administrators, counselors, and teachers share a common vision, build a collaborative culture, and weave changes into the organization of the school (Fullan, 1991). Senge (1990) comments that within learning communities the success or failure of one person influences others' successes or failures. At this point, there is no single model under which a discussion of teaching and learning can be contained. This should be seen as a positive attribute to past efforts in education.

Education is a systemic process that includes many individuals. Cuban (1993), in an historical analysis of teaching from 1890 to 1980, documents changes in educational beliefs and practices over the past 100 years. Cuban's focus is on those "organizational mechanisms that attempt to integrate new ideas into the teacher's instructional repertoire" (p. 87) and the fact that many school-wide strategies for instruction remained the same. Cuban's final analysis reveals that many instructional decision-making procedures in the regular and special education environment are often not solely the responsibility of the classroom teacher. As the number of student variables increases, the intricacies of determining what to teach and the changing landscape of how to learn becomes increasingly complex. As technology grows and is integrated into classrooms, teachers have yet another set of instructional tools. A further effort in school and individual decision-making processes requires our most creative, responsive, and thoughtful attention.

References

Cuban, L. (1993). *How teachers taught: Constancy and change in American classrooms, 1890–1990.* New York: Teachers College Press.

Deno, L. (1985). Curriculum-based measures: The emerging alternative. *Exceptional Children, 52*(3), 219–232.

Eskicioglu, A., & Kopec, D. (2003). The ideal multimedia-enabled classroom: Perspectives from psychology, education, and information science. *Journal of Educational Multimedia and Hypermedia, 12,* 199–221.

Fullan, M. (1991). *The new meaning of educational change* (2nd ed). New York: Teachers College Press.

Fullan, M. (2001). The new meaning of educational change. *School Effectiveness and School Improvement, 2*(4), 336–343.

Partnership for 21st Century Skills (2008). Framework for 21st century learning. Retrieved January 31, 2008, from http://www.21stcenturyskills.org/index.php?option=com_content&task=view&id=254&Itemid=120

Petrides, L. A., & Nodine, T. (2003). *Knowledge management in education: Defining the landscape.* Half Moon Bay, CA: The Institute for the Study of Knowledge Management in Education (ERIC Document Reproduction Service No. ED 477349).

Prensky, M. (2001). Digital natives, digital immigrants, part 1. *On the Horizon, 9*(5), 1–6.

Senge, P. (1990). *The fifth discipline.* New York: Doubleday.

Streifer, P. A. (2002). *Using data to make better educational decisions.* Lanham, MD: The Scarecrow Press.

Tsantis, L., & Castellani, J. D. (2001). Enhancing learning environments through solution based data mining tools: Forecasting for self-perpetuating systemic reform. *Journal of Special Education Technology, 16*(4), 39–52.

Wishart, J. (2000). Students' and teachers' perception of motivation and learning through the use in schools of multimedia encyclopaedias on CD-ROM. *Journal of Educational Multimedia and Hypermedia, 9*(4), 333–347.

20

Aggregating and Analyzing Classroom Achievement Data Supplemental to External Tests

John M. Burger, Brian Perry, and Meghann Eagle

Alberta (Canada) Ministry of Education[1]

Introduction

In this chapter we describe an initiative of the Alberta Department of Education (hereafter referred to as Alberta Education) that involves supplementing the provincial achievement tests administered in Grades 3, 6, and 9 with classroom-based Grade Level of Achievement (GLA) data in Grades 1–9 to better inform the Department's and school jurisdiction's program planning and evaluation capabilities. We describe the GLA data when they are disaggregated relative to various subgroups of the provincial student population and when related to variables such as students' birth month, gender, and student mobility. We also describe the relationship between the provincial achievement test results and the school-based GLA measures in the subjects of Language Arts and mathematics, and how this more comprehensive approach to student assessment can support enhanced school improvement processes.

Two necessary factors permit Alberta Education to access classroom-based student achievement data in a reliable and valid way. First, all students in Alberta are assigned a unique "Alberta Student Number" upon registering in a school in the province, thus permitting the tracking of student variables provincially. Second, all schools in Alberta follow the provincial curricula; hence every student regardless of location is expected to be taught the same learning outcomes as defined in the programs of study documentation produced by the Department.

Grade Level of Achievement (GLA) data reported to Alberta Education are a teacher's judgment of a student's academic progress. GLA is based on the learner outcomes in a subject area of the provincial curriculum after a course for a specific grade level has been completed and reflects the results from the full range of classroom assessments. The comprehensiveness of GLA data underscores the value and importance of collecting and providing value-added analysis of the data.

Prior to the introduction of the collection of GLA data, the provincial education system relied on Provincial Achievement Tests (PATs) in Grades 3, 6, and 9 and Diploma exams (Grade 12) to provide valuable information on how well students are doing. Schools, school authorities, and Alberta Education use this information in their planning to enhance student success, but given the testing intervals, have to wait three years to see the impact of their strategies to improve student success for a specific grade cohort. GLA provides data supplemental to the PAT's on an annual basis in each grade from 1 to 9. As a result, schools, school authorities, and Alberta Education can receive more timely information about how well different populations of students are doing and can be more responsive to the needs of students.

Alberta Education intends the GLA data to have as much utility as possible. In addition to using GLA data for reporting students' progress to parents, the data will be used for program evaluation purposes to support school, authority, and provincial planning. The key purpose of GLA is identifying students who are under achieving, asking why, and providing solutions both individually and systemically.

Implementation of GLA reporting to Alberta Education was grounded in an established Alberta Education (2007c) policy that has, for the past 11 years, required teachers to report GLA clearly to parents.

GLA pilots were run in 2003–2004 and again with a larger set of schools in 2005–2006. Detailed analysis of the outcomes of these pilots, including the reliability and validity of the initial GLA data collection initiatives (Alberta Education, 2005, 2007b), was undertaken and provided empirical support for continuing with the implementation of the GLA initiative.

In this chapter we describe the processes and outcomes associated with the 2006–2007 Grade Level of Achievement (GLA) pilot data collection, data management, and data analysis with the view to providing the reader with some indication of the efficacy of classroom-based achievement data when used to inform program evaluation and planning at multiple levels of the education system.

Four purposes for reporting GLA have been defined in the *Grade Level of Achievement Reporting: Teacher and Administrators Handbook* (Armstrong, Laird, & Mulgrew, 2006), specifically:

- to provide richer information at the system level (both jurisdictional and provincial) to inform effective practices to determine the impact of specific programs (e.g., English as a Second Language, special education) on student learning and to determine processes to further refine these programs;
- as a catalyst within the school's professional learning community to focus on individual student learning needs and interests;
- to determine effective practices and strategies to foster higher levels of student achievement and confidence; and
- to contribute to the data or evidence used to report student achievement to parents/guardians, fulfilling the school's responsibility as outlined in the *Guide to Education: ECS to Grade 12* in the section entitled "Assessment as the Basis for Communicating Individual Student Achievement" (Alberta Education, 2007c).

Limitations

GLA data were submitted in 2006–2007 for students in 60% of the schools in Alberta, well ahead of the planned implementation schedule. The higher than expected participation rate generated a much larger sample of Alberta students than anticipated; however, there is still the potential for sampling bias which must be taken into consideration. Generalizations should be considered in relationship to the estimated confidence intervals detailed in Table 20.2.

GLA 2007 Data Collection

Given that 2006–2007 was still a pilot year, a remarkably low number of data transmission errors occurred during this year's GLA data collection. Of a total of 228,150 student GLA records submitted, there were 5,023 errors received (2.2%), most commonly reflecting incorrectly entered data. The Edulink software and manual (Alberta Education, 2007a) used to support transmission of GLA data to Alberta Education has been upgraded to identify solutions to errors that exist in the data files when they are transmitted to Alberta Education. The *GLA-Edulink Manual* will be revised to require that errors be corrected before the deadline for GLA data submissions. This step is expected to reduce the error rate to 0% in 2007–2008. The individual student records having errors were not included in the 2006–2007 data reported here.

Description of GLA Data

A total of 923 schools from 71 school authorities submitted usable Grade Level of Achievement data, reporting for 220,682 students, 3,380 of whom were not on a graded curriculum, i.e., students' programming was restricted to learning outcomes different from the provincial curriculum. The information fields collected for all students are as follows:

- student name (surname and given name);
- Alberta Student Number; and
- enrolled grade (defined as the grade to which the student was assigned).

GLA data were collected for students on a graded curriculum as defined in the Alberta programs of study, in the following fields where applicable:

- GLA in English Language Arts;
- GLA in French Language Arts (French as the Language of instruction or Immersion);
- GLA in mathematics; and
- Grade English Language Arts introduced (typically ranges from Grades 1–3 for French Language Arts students).

Grade Level of Achievement in 2006–2007 is defined as the grade level expressed as a whole number in relationship to the learning outcomes defined in the program of studies that teachers judged the student to have achieved at the end of the school year. Beginning in the 2007–2008 school year the Ministry has accepted stakeholder input to shift reporting GLA to the Ministry in the format of "at, above or below" grade level.

A GLA handbook (Armstrong et al., 2006) was developed and distributed in the 2005–2006 school year to facilitate pilot school participation in GLA reporting. The handbook can be accessed at http://education.alberta.ca/media/346277/teachadmin handbook.pdf. The GLA handbook encourages teachers to consider GLA assessment in relationship to the full range of formative and summative assessment information available to them over the course of the school year in making a professional judgment of the student's grade level of achievement.

Students not on a graded curriculum also had data submitted. "Not on a graded curriculum" was meant to indicate that the student's program was restricted to learning outcomes that were significantly different from the provincial curriculum defined in the programs of study and was specifically selected to meet the student's special needs as defined in the *Standards for Special Education* (Alberta Learning, 2004). The information collected was teachers' ratings of students' learning outcomes in three areas: communication skills, functional skills, and academic readiness skills.

"Communication skills" refer to the development of expressive and/or receptive communication. This could be verbal communication and/or alternative modes of communication. "Functional skills" refer to skills that would assist the student in developing independence in the home, school, and community. "Academic readiness skills" refer to skills that would prepare the student for learning outcomes in the programs of study.

Alberta Education staff used the Alberta Student Number to append data fields such as Provincial Achievement Test (PAT) results (both raw scores and achievement levels), student age, gender, number of school registrations, any additional special needs codes associated with the student, and initial enrollment date. Individual student identifiers were replaced with a discrete GLA data ID, leaving no personal identifiers in the dataset used in data analysis.

Grade Level of Achievement—Summary of Results

In this section we will consider what GLA data can tell us about how well specific groups of students are doing in school. There were 217,302 students in the 2006–2007 sample who were studying the provincial graded curriculum. The students are roughly evenly distributed by enrolled grade with approximately 11% of the students in each grade cohort. Table 20.1 shows the distribution of the GLA sample data by enrolled grade (Grades 1–9) compared to the Provincial[2] distribution.

Students could have been coded as severely disabled, mild/moderately disabled, gifted, or English as a Second Language (ESL). Those students who were not coded as any of those categories are termed "non-coded." The non-coded students make up the largest proportion of the sample as shown in Table 20.2.

The distribution of students in each of the GLA results categories by subject is shown in Tables 20.3 and 20.4.

Table 20.1 Enrolled grade distribution.

Enrolled grade	Frequency	Percent of total	Province	Percent of total	95% confidence interval*
1	23,692	10.9	42,176	10.6	+/– 0.47
2	23,929	11.0	42,493	10.7	+/– 0.47
3	23,896	11.0	42,656	10.7	+/– 0.47
4	23,954	11.0	42,597	10.7	+/– 0.47
5	23,839	11.0	43,858	11.0	+/– 0.47
6	24,582	11.3	45,050	11.3	+/– 0.46
7	24,240	11.2	45,544	11.5	+/– 0.47
8	24,267	11.2	45,790	11.5	+/– 0.46
9	24,903	11.5	47,014	11.8	+/– 0.45
Total	217,302	100.0	397,178	100.0	+/– 0.15

* *Note:* The estimated confidence interval is expressed as a percentage and indicates how confident the researcher is (e.g. 95% confident) that the data collected accurately represent the results of the entire population. In this case sample sizes are very large and provide a high degree of confidence that sampling error is minimal.

Table 20.2 Frequencies of student codes.

Types of student codes	GLA frequency	Percent of total	Province	Percent of total	95% confidence interval
Non-coded	170,637	77.9	313,612	79.0	+/– 0.17
Severe disabilities	5,303	2.4	12,576	3.2	+/– 0.86
Mild/moderate disabilities	16,769	7.7	30,835	7.8	+/– 0.56
Gifted	3,314	1.5	5,221	1.3	+/– 1.31
ESL—Canadian-born	11,795	5.4	18,690	4.7	+/– 0.69
ESL—foreign-born	11,139	5.1	16,244	4.1	+/– 0.71
Total	218,957*	100.0	397,178	100.0	+/– 0.13

* Some students have double codes.

Severe Disabilities

There were 5,303 students coded as severely disabled who had GLA reported for English Language Arts and Mathematics. There were 69 students coded as severely disabled who had GLA reported for French Language Arts. Table 20.5 presents students having a severe disability code and their grade level of achievement.

More than half of students with a severe disability enrolled in mathematics have a GLA equal to their enrolled grade (55.1%). In Language Arts 53.5% of students have a GLA equal to their enrolled grade. Mathematics and Language Arts are fairly similar in their GLA distribution, each having approximately 53–55% of students achieving a GLA equal to their enrolled grade. A very low proportion of French Immersion or French as the language of instruction students were coded as severely disabled.

Table 20.6 provides information on all students who were on a graded curriculum

Table 20.3 All students, provincial.

All students—province

	Mathematics		English language arts		French language arts	
	Number of students	Percent of total enrolled	Number of students	Percent of total enrolled	Number of students	Percent of total enrolled
GLA below enrolled grade	21,348	9.8	24,116	11.1	741	5.8
GLA equal to enrolled grade	190,426	87.6	185,148	85.2	10,758	84.8
GLA above enrolled grade	1,027	0.5	540	0.2	45	0.4
GLA NA*	4,501	2.1	7,498	3.5	1,142	9.0
Total	217,302	100.0	217,302	100.0	12,686	100.0

* GLA NA refers to missing data, a "not applicable" situation, or "not available."

Table 20.4 Students non-coded, provincial.

	Mathematics		English Language Arts		French Language arts	
	Number of students	Percent of total enrolled	Number of students	Percent of total enrolled	Number of students	Percent of total enrolled
GLA below enrolled grade	10,443	6.1	11,248	6.6	587	5.1
GLA equal to enrolled grade	156,991	92.0	154,046	90.3	9,947	86.5
GLA above enrolled grade	619	0.4	452	0.3	36	0.3
GLA NA	2,584	1.5	4,891	2.9	936	8.1
Total	170,637	100.0	170,637	100.0	11,506	100.0

Table 20.5 Severe disabilities, provincial.

	Mathematics		English Language Arts		French Language Arts	
	Number of students	Percent of total enrolled	Number of students	Percent of total enrolled	Number of students	Percent of total enrolled
GLA below enrolled grade	2,022	38.1	2,101	39.6	14	20.3
GLA equal to enrolled grade	2,924	55.1	2,838	53.5	45	65.2
GLA above enrolled grade	11	0.2	9	0.2	0	0.0
GLA NA	346	6.5	355	6.7	10	14.5
Total	5,303	100.0	5,303	100.0	69	100.0

Table 20.6 GLA by type of severe disability.

Type of severe disability	Frequency	Percentage of total	Mathematics			English Language Arts		
			% at or above grade level	% below grade level	% GLA NA	% at or above grade level	% below grade level	% GLA NA
Severe cognitive disability	12	0.2	33.3	41.7	25.0	41.7	33.3	25.0
Severe emotional/behavioral disability	2,925	55.2	58.9	35.9	5.2	56.8	37.9	5.3
Severe multiple disability	204	3.8	28.9	56.4	14.7	27.0	56.9	16.2
Severe physical or medical disability	1,976	37.3	52.8	39.6	7.6	52.4	39.9	7.7
Deafness	117	2.2	46.2	46.2	7.7	35.9	54.7	9.4
Blindness	68	1.3	77.9	20.6	1.5	72.1	25.0	2.9
Total	5,302	100.0	55.4	38.1	6.5	53.7	39.6	6.7

Note: One ECS student was not shown on this table. Students are included in the remainder of the report as they are enrolled in a grade. Students at or above grade level were combined into a single category due to the small number of students achieving above grade level.

and were coded as severely disabled, by their disability type. The majority of students coded with a severe disability are those with an emotional/behavioral or physical/medical disability (92.4%). Students having severe multiple disabilities comprise the largest proportion of students attaining below their grade level in both Language Arts and Mathematics. Among the different types of severe disabilities (Table 20.6), the distribution of students among GLA categories varies more widely than the overall severe disability distribution (Table 20.5). When compared to the 2005–2006 data, gathered by Alberta Education, there is an increase in the number of students achieving at or above grade level in each of the disability areas. Of specific note are those relatively few students with a severe cognitive disability where currently one-third of the students are achieving at or above grade level compared to 0% in the previous year. Knowing the type of severe disability assists in understanding the student distribution throughout GLA categories.

Mild/Moderate Disabilities

There were 16,769 students in the 2006–2007 sample having mild or moderate disability codes in English Language Arts and Mathematics. In French Language Arts, 369 students were coded as having a mild or moderate disability. Table 20.7 shows the mild or moderate students' distribution across GLA categories.

In both Mathematics and Language Arts, a slim majority of students have a GLA equal to their enrolled grade (52–56%). Table 20.8 shows the breakdown of students on a graded curriculum having a mild or moderate disability by the type of disability. The largest proportion of students coded with a mild/moderate disability have a learning disability (46.1%). Students having a mild or moderate cognitive disability comprise the largest proportion of students attaining below their grade level in both Language Arts and Mathematics. It is interesting to note that aside from the students with a mild or moderate cognitive disability, over 50% of students in each of the other categories are achieving at or above their grade level. Compared to the 2005–2006 GLA data, there is an increase in the number of students achieving at or above

Table 20.7 Mild/moderate disabilities.

	Mathematics		English Language Arts		French Language Arts	
	Number of students	Percent of total enrolled	Number of students	Percent of total enrolled	Number of students	Percent of total enrolled
GLA below enrolled grade	6,693	39.9	7,430	44.3	93	25.2
GLA equal to enrolled grade	9,415	56.1	8,692	51.8	222	60.2
GLA above enrolled grade	25	0.1	17	0.1	2	0.5
GLA NA	636	3.8	630	3.8	52	14.1
Total	16,769	100.0	16,769	100.0	369	100.0

Table 20.8 GLA by type of mild/moderate disability.

Type of mild/moderate disability	Mathematics					English Language Arts		
	Frequency	Percentage of total	% at or above grade level	% below grade level	% GLA NA	% at or above grade level	% below grade level	% GLA NA
Mild cognitive disability	2,922	17.4	21.6	68.7	9.7	21.0	69.7	9.2
Moderate cognitive disability	93	0.6	11.8	64.5	23.7	9.7	67.7	22.6
Emotional/behavioral disability	1,766	10.5	69.6	27.9	2.4	72.1	25.8	2.2
Learning disability	7,726	46.1	60.3	37.4	2.3	55.1	43.0	1.9
Hearing disability	173	1.0	76.3	20.2	3.5	76.3	20.8	2.9
Visual disability	25	0.1	96.0	4.0	0.0	92.0	8.0	0.0
Communication disability	2,330	13.9	72.2	25.3	2.5	59.8	36.1	4.1
Physical/medical disability	870	5.2	70.2	26.8	3.0	67.7	28.6	3.7
Multiple disability	862	5.1	53.4	44.4	2.2	48.6	48.8	2.6
Total	16,767	100.0	56.3	39.9	3.8	51.9	44.3	3.8

Note: Two students coded as ECS Developmentally Immature were removed from this analysis. They have been included in the rest of the report.

grade level in most of the disability areas. This may indicate that as we move toward total reporting, the data are shifting toward a truer picture. As in Table 20.5, students who were "at or above grade level" were combined into a single category due to the small number of students who were achieving "above grade level."

Students Not on a Graded Curriculum (Modified Programming)

There were 3,380 students not on a graded curriculum in this study. The students were assessed based on the degree of achievement in their Individual Program Plans (IPPs) relative to their foundational skills, academic readiness skills, and life skills. The results reported below in Tables 20.9–20.11 should be considered preliminary data that will become more meaningful as multi-year trends become available.

Gifted

In this sample of students, 3,314 were coded as being gifted in English Language Arts or Mathematics. There were an additional 156 students in French Language Arts coded as gifted. Table 20.12 shows the grade level of achievement distributions for students coded as gifted.

The general assumption with gifted students is that they tend to perform better than the population of students as a whole. According to Table 20.12, we can see that the majority of gifted students are performing equal to their enrolled grade level.

Table 20.9 IPP foundation skills.

	Number of students	Percent of total enrolled
All skills attained	558	16.5
Most skills attained	1,078	31.9
Some skills attained	1,015	30.0
None of the skills attained	111	3.3
N/A	618	18.3
Total	3,380	100.0

Table 20.10 IPP academic readiness skills.

	Number of students	Percent of total enrolled
All skills attained	486	14.4
Most skills attained	1,087	32.2
Some skills attained	1,266	37.5
None of the skills attained	156	4.6
N/A	385	11.4
Total	3,380	100.0

Table 20.11 IPP life skills.

	Number of students	Percent of total enrolled
All skills attained	397	11.7
Most skills attained	995	29.4
Some skills attained	878	25.9
None of the skills attained	80	2.4
N/A	1,030	30.5
Total	3,380	100.0

Table 20.12 Gifted students, provincial.

	Mathematics		English Language Arts		French Language Arts	
	Number of students	Percent of total enrolled	Number of students	Percent of total enrolled	Number of students	Percent of total enrolled
GLA below enrolled grade	74	2.2	79	2.4	3	1.9
GLA equal to enrolled grade	2,962	89.4	3,198	96.5	126	80.8
GLA above enrolled grade	248	7.5	12	0.4	1	0.6
GLA NA	30	0.9	25	0.8	26	16.7
Total	3,314	100.0	3,314	100.0	156	100.0

Fewer than 3% of students are "below grade level" for each subject. Gifted students are performing better in Mathematics than in English Language Arts with approximately 7% more students having a GLA "above grade level" in math.

Gender

Students' GLA was broken down by gender in order to observe if any atypical patterns emerge. In this sample of students there was a larger number of males than females. Tables 20.13–20.15 show students' GLA by gender in each of the three subjects.

Tables 20.13, 20.14, and 20.15 show the frequency of female and male students in each of the GLA categories in Mathematics, English Language Arts, and French Language Arts. When testing for independence between genders, Chi square was used. Chi square is defined as "A nonparametric procedure for testing whether the observed frequencies of scores in different categories of a variable differ from the theoretically predicted frequencies" (Harris, 1995, p. 528). There is a statistically significant difference between the genders in both Math and English Language Arts, with a significantly higher percentage of males with GLA below enrolled grade in both subjects.

Table 20.13 Gender, mathematics, provincial.

Gender—provincial	Mathematics			
	Female		Male	
	Number of students	Percent of total enrolled	Number of students	Percent of total enrolled
GLA below enrolled grade	9,504	9.0	11,844	10.6
GLA equal to enrolled grade	93,918	88.7	96,508	86.7
GLA above enrolled grade	464	0.4	563	0.5
GLA NA	2,044	1.9	2,457	2.2
Total	105,930	100.0	111,372	100.0

Note: All of the above observed relationships were significant when measured by Chi square.

Table 20.14 Gender, English Language Arts, provincial.

Gender—provincial	English Language Arts			
	Female		Male	
	Number of students	Percent of total enrolled	Number of students	Percent of total enrolled
GLA below enrolled grade	9,335	8.8	14,781	13.3
GLA equal to enrolled grade	92,749	87.6	92,399	83.0
GLA above enrolled grade	308	0.3	232	0.2
GLA NA	3,538	3.3	3,960	3.6
Total	105,930	100.0	111,372	100.0

Note: All of the above observed relationships were significant when measured by Chi square.

Table 20.15 Gender, French Language Arts, provincial.

Gender—provincial	French Language Arts			
	Female		Male	
	Number of students	Percent of total enrolled	Number of students	Percent of total enrolled
GLA below enrolled grade	360	5.1	381	6.7
GLA equal to enrolled grade	5980	85.2	4778	84.4
GLA above enrolled grade	31	0.4	14	0.3
GLA NA	651	9.3	491	8.7
Total	7022	100.0	5664	100.0

Note: All of the above observed relationships were significant when measured by Chi square.

Next we consider gender difference using t tests in relationship to both GLA and Provincial Achievement Test (PAT) data patterns.

Tables 20.16 and 20.17 illustrate the gender differences in GLA and PATs across the enrolled grades. Considering GLA data, females outperform males to a statistically significant degree in both subjects in nearly all enrolled grades. Considering PAT results, a similar result is found for English Language Arts, where females outperform males to a statistically significant degree. Interestingly, however, the reverse is seen on the Math PAT results with males outperforming females to a statistically significant degree.

This phenomenon was also observed in an earlier study conducted at the high school level. Pope, Wentzel, and Cammaert (2003) conducted a study which showed that larger gender differences were found in school-awarded marks than in the diploma exam marks in favor of females in almost all DIP courses. Math courses (both Math 30 Pure and Applied) were among those subjects where boys, while being outperformed by girls in school-awarded marks, did better than girls in DIP exam marks. Given that these patterns were also observed in data from Grades 1–9 students this issue deserves further research including analysis of data for upcoming years.

Table 20.16 English Language Arts gender differences.

English Language Arts GLA gender differences					English Language Arts Provincial Achievement Tests gender differences					
Enrolled grade	Gender	05–06 N	05–06 Mean GLA	06–07 N	06–07 Mean GLA	Enrolled grade	Gender	05–06 N	05–06 Mean PAT	06–07 N	06–07 Mean PAT
1	F	3,562	1.01	11,525	0.93*						
	M	3,518	1.01	12,167	0.88*						
2	F	4,161	1.93*	11,704	1.90*						
	M	4,356	1.89*	12,225	1.85*						
3	F	4,236	2.89*	11,641	2.88*	3	F	4,088	71.03*	10,790	69.72*
	M	4,511	2.84*	12,255	2.83*		M	4,244	68.50*	11,537	66.72*
4	F	4,281	3.86*	11,608	3.87*						
	M	4,633	3.79*	12,346	3.79*						
5	F	4,535	4.81*	11,440	4.84*						
	M	4,664	4.75*	12,399	4.76*						
6	F	4,280	5.80*	12,114	5.82*	6	F	4,039	68.36*	11,451	69.79*
	M	4,689	5.71*	12,468	5.74*		M	4,304	64.90*	11,923	65.40*
7	F	4,127	6.87*	11,790	6.88*						
	M	4,350	6.75*	12,450	6.78*						
8	F	4,444	7.88*	11,849	7.88*						
	M	4,489	7.77*	12,418	7.77*						
9	F	4,466	8.87*	12,259	8.87*	9	F	4,154	71.42*	11,337	68.36*
	M	4,571	8.77*	12,644	8.76*		M	4,139	66.77*	11,742	63.25*

* Indicates a statistically significant difference between males and females.

Table 20.17 Mathematics gender differences.

Mathematics GLA gender differences						Mathematics Provincial Achievement Tests gender differences					
Enrolled grade	Gender	05–06 N	05–06 Mean GLA	06–07 N	06–07 Mean GLA	Enrolled grade	Gender	05–06 N	05–06 Mean PAT	06–07 N	06–07 Mean PAT
1	F	4,024	1.01	11,525	0.95*						
	M	4,080	1.01	12,167	0.93*						
2	F	4,293	1.95	11,704	1.93						
	M	4,495	1.96	12,225	1.92						
3	F	4,250	2.92	11,641	2.90	3	F	4,083	33.12*	10,790	30.60*
	M	4,530	2.91	12,255	2.89		M	4,240	34.07*	11,537	31.54*
4	F	4,274	3.88	11,608	3.89*						
	M	4,640	3.87	12,346	3.86*						
5	F	4,521	4.84	11,440	4.85*						
	M	4,660	4.83	12,399	4.82*						
6	F	4,266	5.83	12,114	5.82*	6	F	4,054	36.64*	11,451	34.47*
	M	4,670	5.80	12,468	5.80*		M	4,335	37.60*	11,923	36.03*
7	F	3,941	6.88*	11,790	6.87*						
	M	4,212	6.83*	12,450	6.82*						
8	F	4,197	7.89*	11,849	7.86*						
	M	4,254	7.80*	12,418	7.81*						
9	F	4,217	8.85*	12,259	8.82*	9	F	4,166	32.44	11,337	30.80*
	M	4,346	8.78*	12,644	8.76*		M	4,162	32.35	11,742	31.36*

* Indicates a statistically significant difference between males and females.

Student Mobility

When students change schools, they must learn to deal with a new physical, social, and learning environment—new teachers, new classmates, possibly different sets of rules, different learning expectations—and may start at a different point in the curriculum than that which they left behind. It also takes some time for teachers to determine the students' learning level, learning style, interaction skills, and so forth, and thus to define the optimal program for his/her ongoing learning.

These issues contribute to the findings within the research literature of a negative relationship between the number of times a student changes schools in a given period and his/her academic growth in that period. Other studies (Wasserman, 2001) of this relationship in an Alberta setting have supported these findings and suggest that additional research would be useful, to not only enrich the understanding of the relationship but to highlight any situations in which the negative impacts may have been mitigated by helpful strategies to support better transitions for students and schools. The GLA data provide such an opportunity for additional research. They permit an ongoing analysis of the relationship between the number of school changes students have made and their current level of achievement, thus allowing for an assessment of the cumulative impact of mobility.

Student registration data are collected from schools by Alberta Education, once at the end of September and again in March, and compiled in the Student Information System (SIS). The Student Mobility Indicator (SMI) provides an indication of the number of times a student has changed schools since entry into the Alberta school system. The SMI is calculated by counting the number of different school registrations each student has up until the most recent calendar year. Students could be changing schools more frequently than is captured; thus the numbers shown are a conservative estimate of student mobility. All students start with an SMI of 1 as they have all been registered in at least one school. Student mobility is then broken down into two categories—high and low. In Grades 1–3, high mobility students are those having a mobility indicator of 2 or more. Students having a mobility indicator of 1 are considered low mobility. In Grades 4–6, high mobility students are those having a mobility indicator of 3 or more. Students having a mobility indicator of 2 or less are considered low mobility. In Grades 7–9, high mobility students are those having a mobility indicator of 4 or more. Low mobility students have a mobility indicator of 3 or less. In the following figure the two categories of mobility include students on a graded curriculum in Grades 1–9.

Figure 20.1, based on the GLA data, illustrates the effect mobility can have on achievement.

As Figure 20.1 illustrates, there is a noticeable difference between the results of students with high and low mobility. There is a statistically significant difference between the mobility groups in Grades 4–9. This significance may indicate that mobility has a more pronounced, cumulative effect as students age.

Correlations Between SMI and GLA

Kendall's tau-b values were calculated in order to illustrate the relationship between SMI and GLA groupings. Kendall's tau-b is an alternative non-parametric form of rank correlations. The tau-b is used as an inferential statistic to show the strength of those relationships. Tau-b is used to measure the association between student mobility and GLA. This particular test was chosen as it uses ordinal level data based on pair by pair comparisons. Table 20.18 details the correlations.

The correlations in Table 20.18 between student mobility and GLA are significant

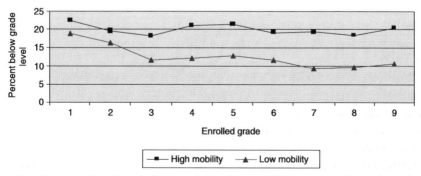

Figure 20.1 Percent of students below grade level by mobility category for each grade.

Table 20.18 SMI by GLA, tau-b calculations.

SMI by GLA—Grade and subject	05–06 Tau-b	06–07 Tau-b
Eng. LA and SMI	0.096*	0.103*
Math and SMI	0.126*	0.117*

* Correlation is significant at the 0.01 level.

at the 0.01 level in both years. They are relatively weak in strength, although this is to be expected as student mobility can affect a student's GLA but is only one of many determining variables. The correlations are similar between the two years of GLA data indicating the validity of the data.

GLA and Enrolled Grade

The relationship between GLA and enrolled grade was summarized and graphed in Alberta Education's (in press) full report on GLA 2006–2007 data. However, here we present only one summary graph that describes the number of students whose GLA is below grade level in each grade as shown in Table 20.19. From Grades 1–6 there are a higher number of students attaining below grade level in English Language Arts. In Grades 7–9 there are a higher number of students attaining below grade level in mathematics.

Birth Month-Combined Grades

Table 20.20 shows the breakdown of student birth month. The distribution was calculated by examining each grade individually and then combining all grades. Students in the January 1 and February 1 cohort are the oldest students in each grade, whereas students in the January 2 and February 2 cohort are the youngest in each grade.

GLA and PAT Results by Age Within Grade Cohorts

Previous Alberta Education studies have indicated that there is a relative age effect between average PAT scores and birth month within grade cohorts, whereby older students within the normal age range for the grade tend to have higher average test scores than the younger students when measured by the z score of average PAT results for each birth month group (Alberta Learning, 2001). An unpublished 2007 Alberta Education longitudinal study also found this effect to be prevalent. Further, this effect has also been noted in studies done in other countries such as New Zealand (Chamberlain, 2007) and the United Kingdom (Crawford, Dearden, & Meghir, 2007).

A similar analysis was undertaken using GLA data. The percentages of students "at or above" their grade level in English Language Arts were converted to z scores and

Table 20.19 Number of students below grade level by enrolled grade.

Grade level	ELA	Percent of total	Math	Percent of total
1	2,320	9.6	1,465	6.9
2	2,557	10.6	1,701	8.0
3	2,822	11.7	2,128	10.0
4	2,954	12.2	2,320	10.9
5	3,138	13.0	2,627	12.3
6	3,066	12.7	2,759	12.9
7	2,340	9.7	2,433	11.4
8	2,375	9.8	2,670	12.5
9	2,544	10.5	3,245	15.2
Total	24,116	100.0	21,348	100.0

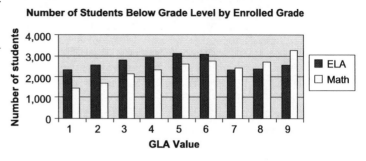

Number of Students Below Grade Level by Enrolled Grade

Table 20.20 Student birth month.

Student birth month Month	Frequency	Percentage
January 1	11,177	5.7
February 1	11,912	6.1
March	17,987	9.2
April	17,778	9.1
May	18,457	9.5
June	17,424	8.9
July	17,676	9.1
August	17,037	8.7
September	16,202	8.3
October	14,840	7.6
November	12,865	6.6
December	10,944	5.6
January 2	6,380	3.3
February 2	4,409	2.3
Total	195,088*	100.0

* Not all students were included in this table as some students were outside the parameters of analysis meaning they were much older than the students being examined in this table.

plotted (see Figures 20.2 and 20.3). There is a noticeable age effect in Grades 1–5, which is most pronounced in Grade 1. The following figures were produced using the z scores for Grades 1–5, English Language Arts GLAs for students in the GLA dataset.

In Grade 1, results for students born in each month from January 1 through October are statistically significantly higher than those for students born in January 2 and February 2.

In Grade 2, results for students born in each month from March through June are

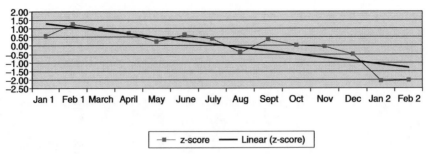

Figure 20.2 *Z* score of the percent of students at or above grade level in Language Arts, by birth month within cohort—Grade 1 students.

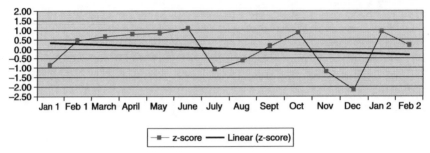

Figure 20.3 *Z* score of the percent of students at or above grade level in Language Arts, by birth month within cohort—Grade 2 students.

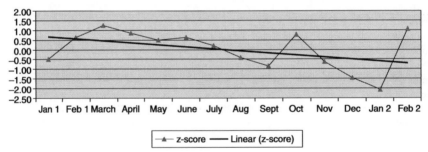

Figure 20.4 *Z* score of the percent of students at or above grade level in Language Arts, by birth month within cohort—Grade 3 students.

statistically higher than those for students born in November and December. Even though the results are more variable than for Grade 1, the downward trend is still evident.

In Grade 3, results for students born in each month from March through June are statistically higher than those for students born in December and on January 1. Even though the results are more variable than for Grade 1, the downward trend is still evident.

Figure 20.5 demonstrates that when Provincial Achievement Test (PAT) scores are recoded into "percent at or above acceptable" to employ the same concept as do the GLA data, the relative age effect remains. In Grade 3, March and April are statistically significant when compared to January 2.

In Grade 4, results for students born in each month from March through May are

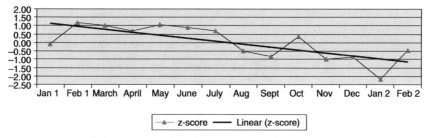

Figure 20.5 *Z* score of the percent of students at acceptable or above on the Language Arts Provincial Achievement Test, by birth month within cohort—Grade 3 students.

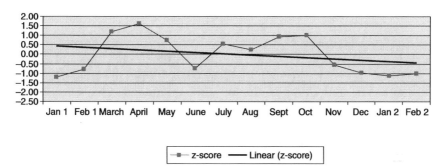

Figure 20.6 *Z* score of the percent of students at or above grade level in Language Arts, by birth month within cohort—Grade 4 students.

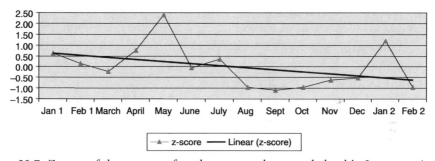

Figure 20.7 *Z* score of the percent of students at or above grade level in Language Arts, by birth month within cohort—Grade 5 students.

statistically significantly higher than those for students born in December, January 1 and February 1. Even though the results are more variable than for Grade 1, the downward trend is still evident.

In Grade 5, May is statistically significantly higher than August, September, and October. Although the trend is still present here, it is weakening, and analyses of results for later grades show no relative age effect.

One reason for the weakening of the effect in later grades has been documented in previous studies and may also be at work here—the greater tendency to retain those younger students who are within the normal age range for the grade. This tends to remove more of the less academically strong students from those later birth month groups, thus increasing their average results.

Discussion

The age effect, which illustrates that younger students (i.e., those born later in the year) achieve at a lower level than those students born earlier in the year, is apparent in English Language Arts in Grades 1–5. After Grade 5, the age effect tapers off and is no longer apparent. In this sample the age effect persisted longer than in previous analyses of GLA data, done by Alberta Education (2007b), where the effect dissipated by Grade 3.

GLA at a Glance

Table 20.21 shows all groups of students and their GLA in Mathematics and English Language Arts excluding students for whom GLA data were either not available or not applicable (GLA NA). The table is presented as an overall summary designed to provide ease when comparing groups of students. In this table asterisks indicate significant differences between a specific cohort of students and the non-coded cohort.

Correlations between PAT and GLA

Kendall's tau-b was used to measure the association between PAT and GLA. Table 20.22 details the correlations for 2005–2006 and 2006–2007. The PAT and GLA variables were re-coded into the dichotomous categories: either "Below acceptable" or "At or above acceptable" for PATs; and either "Below grade level" or "At or above grade level" for GLA, and then the two dichotomous variables were compared. All relationships tested were at the $p < .01$ levels meaning they were significant. The p value shows that the observed relationships are not due to chance. Table 20.22 shows all tau-b values for the relationships tested and from this one can conclude that the relationships are moderate in strength. A perfect relationship of 1.0 between GLA and PAT is neither an expected nor a desirable condition given the inherent differences in the evaluation designs which would underlie potentially different learning outcomes being measured with different assessment methods.

When comparing 2005–2006 to 2006–2007, the strength of the relationships has decreased. This decrease in strength may be attributed to the larger sample size in 2006–2007 and therefore may be a truer picture than the correlations of the previous year. The only exception is the increase in strength of the relationship between the Grade 9 PAT and GLA results for Math.

GLA by PAT Analysis—Comparisons Using Achievement Levels

In order to further examine the relationship between the GLA data and PATs and provide an additional perspective on these relationships, both PAT and GLA data were again re-coded into the categories of "Below grade level and GLA NA" and "At

Table 20.21 GLA overall summary table.

Student codes	Mathematics			English Language Arts		
	Frequency	Percent at or above	Percent below	Frequency	Percent at or above	Percent below
Provincial sample	212,801	90.0	10.0	209,804	88.5	11.5
Non-coded	168,053	93.8	6.2	165,746	93.2	6.8
Severe disability	4,957	59.2*	40.8*	4,948	57.5*	42.5*
—Emotional/behavioral disability	2,773	62.1	37.9	2,771	59.9	40.1
—Physical or medical disability	1,825	57.2	42.8	1,824	56.7	43.3
—Multiple disability	174	33.9	66.1	171	32.2	67.8
—Deafness	108	50.0	50.0	106	39.6	60.4
—Blindness	67	79.1	20.9	66	74.2	25.8
Mild/moderate disability	16,133	58.5*	41.5*	16,139	54.0*	46.0*
—Learning disability	7,549	61.7	38.3	7,578	56.1	43.9
—Mild cognitive disability	2,638	23.9	76.1	2,653	23.2	76.8
—Communication disability	2,271	74.1	25.9	2,235	62.3	37.7
—Emotional/behavioral disability	1,723	71.4	28.6	1,728	73.7	26.3
—Physical/medical disability	844	72.4	27.6	838	70.3	29.7
—Multiple disability	843	54.6	45.4	840	49.9	50.1
—Hearing disability	167	79.0	21.0	168	78.6	21.4
—Moderate cognitive disability	71	15.5	84.5	72	12.5	87.5
—Visual disability	25	96.0	4.0	25	92.0	8.0
Provincial sample	212,801	90.0	10.0	209,804	88.5	11.5
Gifted	3,284	97.7*	2.3*	3,289	97.6*	2.4*
ESL Cdn-born	11,350	87.0*	13.0*	11,059	82.8*	17.2*
ESL foreign-born	10,554	88.1*	11.9*	10,121	79.6*	20.4*
Gender						
—Males	108,915	89.1*	10.9*	107,412	86.2*	13.7*
—Females	103,886	90.9*	9.1*	102,392	90.9*	9.1*
Student mobility						
—High	56,541	84.1*	15.9*	56,220	83.1*	16.9*
—Low	156,254	92.1*	7.9*	153,579	90.4*	9.6*
Birth month						
—March to Sept	120,281	91.3*	8.7*	118,533	90.0*	10.0*
—Oct to Feb	48,429	90.7*	9.3*	47,765	89.1*	10.9*

* Denotes a significant difference at $p < 0.001$ when compared to the non-coded sample of students.

Note: The categories of "at grade level" and "above grade level" have been combined. There are not enough cases in the "above grade level" category to be shown separately.
Statistical testing was only done with the larger categories; disability types (severe and mild/moderate) were not tested against the non-coded sample.

or above grade level" for GLA; and "Acceptable or excellent" and "Below acceptable and excused or absent" for PATs. These groupings were chosen based on the current Alberta Education standard for cohort reporting. The groups were then cross-tabulated with the hypothesis being that students who score at or above the acceptable level on PATs tend to be at or above grade level, and likewise those who score below acceptable tend to be below grade level. Tables 20.23 and 20.24 show some support for the hypothesis, as 76–78% of the students in Language Arts and 65–80%

Table 20.22 PAT by GLA tau-b calculations.

2005–2006		2006–2007	
PAT by GLA—grade and subject	*Tau-b*	*PAT by GLA—grade and subject*	*Tau-b*
Gr. 3 Eng. LA	.378	Gr. 3 Eng. LA	.324
Gr. 6 Eng. LA	.406	Gr. 6 Eng. LA	.337
Gr. 9 Eng. LA	.338	Gr. 9 Eng. LA	.323
Gr. 3 Math	.388	Gr. 3 Math	.342
Gr. 6 Math	.403	Gr. 6 Math	.366
Gr. 9 Math	.399	Gr. 9 Math	.409

Table 20.23 Comparison of English Language Arts PAT and GLA.

Grade level of achievement—English Language Arts

		At or above grade level	Below grade level or GLA NA	Total
PAT—Grade 3 English Language Arts	Accept. or excellent	77.6% (17,304)	**5.7%** (1,276)	83.4% (18,580)
	Below accept., excused or absent	**8.1%** (1,801)	8.5% (1,905)	16.6% (3,706)
	Total	85.7% (19,105)	14.3% (3,181)	100.0% (22,286)
PAT—Grade 6 English Language Arts	Accept. or excellent	77.9% (18,173)	**5.4%** (1,266)	83.3% (19,439)
	Below accept., excused or absent	**8.1%** (1,887)	8.6% (2,014)	16.7% (3,901)
	Total	85.9% (20,060)	14.1% (3,280)	100.0% (23,340)
PAT—Grade 9 English Language Arts	Accept. or excellent	76.2% (17,489)	**4.3%** (982)	80.5% (18,471)
	Below accept., excused or absent	**10.8%** (2,483)	8.7% (1,999)	19.5% (4,482)
	Total	87.0% (19,972)	13.0% (2,981)	100.0% (22,953)

Note: All of the above observed relationships were significant when measured by Chi square. Percentages in bold represent inconsistent relationships between GLA and PAT data.

of the students in Math who are at grade level are also at or above the acceptable level on the PATs. The data in Tables 20.23 and 20.24 include all students from schools that submitted GLA data for 2006–2007 in Grades 3, 6 or 9.

It may be noted, in reviewing Tables 20.23 and 20.24, that more students are categorized as "below acceptable" in the PAT results than are categorized as "below

Table 20.24 Comparison of Mathematics PAT and GLA.

Grade level of achievement—Mathematics

		At or above grade level	Below grade level or GLA NA	Total
PAT—Grade 3 Mathematics	Accept. or excellent	79.6% (17,753)	**3.5%** (788)	83.2% (18,541)
	Below accept., excused or absent	**9.5%** (2,120)	7.3% (1,632)	16.8% (3,752)
	Total	89.1% (19,873)	10.9% (2,420)	100.0% (22,293)
PAT—Grade 6 Mathematics	Accept. or excellent	74.0% (17,279)	**3.0%** (701)	77.0% (17,980)
	Below accept., excused or absent	**13.4%** (3,134)	9.5% (2,226)	23.0% (5,360)
	Total	87.5% (20,413)	12.5% (2,927)	100.0% (23,340)
PAT—Grade 9 Mathematics	Accept. or excellent	65.8% (15,056)	**3.0%** (679)	68.7% (15,735)
	Below accept., excused or absent	**18.0%** (4,129)	13.2% (3,022)	31.2% (7,151)
	Total	83.8% (19,185)	16.2% (3,701)	100.0% (22,886)

Note: All of the above observed relationships were significant when measured by Chi square. Percentages in bold represent inconsistent relationships between GLA and PAT data.

grade level" in GLA ratings. This suggests that in terms of evaluating acceptable progress, the PAT is a more difficult standard to attain than is GLA. The two assessments are not expected to yield the same results, in that they are different forms of assessment, but both are designed to assess whether a student has met grade level standards. Therefore, one might expect that the variability would be seen as much in one direction as the other. The fact that this is not true suggests several possibilities:

(1) that it may be more difficult for teachers to assign a "below grade level" evaluation to one of their students than is the case for markers of the PAT assessments who are unaware of the student's identity,
(2) student performance on PATs may be depressed by test anxiety,
(3) students may perform better on many assessments over time than on a single paper and pencil test, or
(4) a combination of these factors.

At any rate, this analysis does point to potentially useful considerations in unpacking and gaining increased understanding of the meaning of achievement data from multiple sources.

Further Analysis of Students Below Grade Level

In this section the ratings given by teachers through the GLA are further compared to PAT results in Grades 3, 6, and 9. In each case, it is possible to identify the students who are rated as below grade level by their teachers (GLA) and those rated as below the acceptable standard by the PAT.

According to classical test theory (Crocker & Algina, 1986) all assessments are subject to some degree of test error. Given this fact the more achievement data available the clearer the true picture of a student's achievement becomes. One would expect some differences as well as complementary relationships in the designation of individuals in the two ratings provided by PAT and GLA data. Classroom assessment is based on an array of assessment methods over time for the GLA rating, ideally measuring the full and complete range of learning outcomes; whereas the PAT is a single, highly valid and reliable, selected and constructed response test that typically measures between 66% and 95% of the curricular outcomes in the tested subjects.[3] The PATs are very likely the single best criterion-referenced assessment instrument available to the classroom teacher. Since the objective of both methods is to measure and provide evidence on how well a student is achieving as compared to the learning outcomes in the program of studies, one would expect a generally positive relationship between the students identified as "below" by both methods, and that is what we see in this data set. Where anomalous or inconsistent relationships are observed it presents the occasion to ask why and to delve deeper into the data to help understand why the measures differ. A graphical depiction of the GLA pilot data for English Language Arts and Mathematics (Figures 20.8 and 20.9) shows that this assumption departs most dramatically for Math 9 and the difference increases with grade level in both subjects.

Discussion

A primary reason for provincial aggregation of Grade Level of Achievement data is evaluation of education programs such as special education, English as a Second

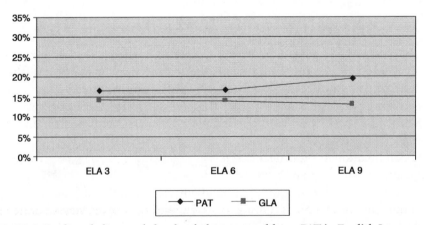

Figure 20.8 Students below grade level or below acceptable on PAT in English Language Arts.

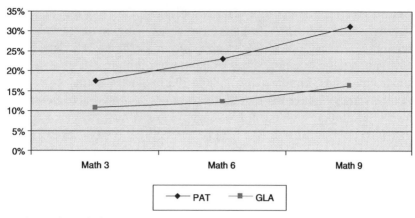

Figure 20.9 Students below grade level or below acceptable on PAT in Mathematics.

Note: The data presented in the above figures are discrete data points. The lines connecting the data plots were included to emphasize the patterns of the data.

Language, etc. This observation is particularly relevant for those grades that do not have PAT testing where GLA can provide data that would not otherwise be available. Additionally, it is useful to be able to supplement PAT data with GLA data in Grades 3, 6, and 9 as the added advantage would be broader and richer data to inform program planning and evaluation-related decisions.

Further, the fact that the tau-b values show moderate strength lends credibility to the process of collecting GLA. A perfect relationship of 1.0 between GLA and PAT is not an expected nor a desirable condition given the inherent differences underlying the evaluation designs. PAT data are derived from a single paper and pencil test whereas GLA data are based on numerous and more dynamic observations over time, and thus should be a much richer method of assessment, which one could reasonably assume to produce positively correlated albeit different data than a PAT result. The GLA by PAT analysis demonstrates that GLA data can supplement PAT data with reasonable reliability and validity.

Conclusions

This chapter described the processes and outcomes associated with the 2006–2007 Grade Level of Achievement (GLA) pilot data collection, data management, and data analysis in Alberta, Canada. Analysis of GLA data has demonstrated that GLA data can be collected and reported on a consistent basis. The analytical perspectives presented in this chapter confirm that GLA data contribute significantly to our knowledge base regarding student achievement. Among the key observations that have contributed to this knowledge base are the following findings regarding GLA data and student achievement patterns:

- The error rate for data submission was low with 2.2% of the files submitted having errors. Planned adjustments are intended to reduce this error rate to zero.

- Compared to the 2005–2006 data based on 81,430 students, the 2006–2007 data based on 217, 302 students have a very similar distribution. Patterns observed in 2005–2006 were also observed in the 2006–2007 data.
- The data analysis demonstrates notable variations in GLA between student subgroups. The GLA at a glance (Table 20.21) illustrates this.
- A much higher percentage of students coded as gifted achieve above grade level in Math than in English Language Arts or French Language Arts.
- When comparing GLA to PAT data, females outperform males to a statistically significant degree in nearly every grade on both English Language Arts and Mathematics GLA. When examining PAT data, males outperform females to a statistically significant degree in Mathematics in Grades 3, 6, and 9. In English Language Arts, females are outperforming males on the PATs.
- The age effect is apparent in English Language Arts in Grades 1–5. After Grade 5, the age effect tapers off and is no longer apparent. This relationship is more pronounced in the 2006–2007 data than in 2005–2006.
- There are moderate strength correlations between PATs and GLA (Grades 3, 6, and 9). This demonstrates the concurrent validity of the GLA data.
- Using GLA and PAT data, GLA can provide important information for students that would not otherwise be available.
- A greater proportion of high-mobility students (i.e., those who have changed schools more frequently than other students) have a GLA below their enrolled grade level.

How will GLA Information be used by Schools?

Education researchers (Crundwell, 2005; Fullan, 2006; Reeves, 2004; Volante & Cherubini, 2007) are beginning to understand that richer and more comprehensive data available to school and jurisdiction-based educational leaders provide opportunities for educators to effect greater ownership of accountability and school improvement processes. The implementation of GLA data collection and aggregation and production of school, jurisdiction, and provincial level reports will provide school jurisdiction and school staff with new ways to use data to better understand how school culture and community context influence student success. Examples of these opportunities include the following.

- Assisting jurisdiction staff to investigate issues identified in school or jurisdiction Annual Education Results Reports that point to areas where academic achievement for students may be further informed by analysis of GLA data. Jurisdictions may be able to identify what underlying factors are influencing their students' achievement such as gender-based differences or the effect of student age or student mobility on achievement in specific subjects.
- Using GLA data as a benchmark, jurisdictions may wish to compare their data over time or in relationship to provincial norms. This can lead to conversations regarding promising practices that have been demonstrated to improve student achievement in specific settings.

- In future reports, GLA data will be aligned with census data including mothers' level of education, family income and home ownership. School staff may use these data to understand how students' results are affected by variables external to the school.
- GLA data collected by Alberta Education will be available upon request to schools as a backup if a student's record is delayed or lost. This service will help teachers ensure that their instruction is geared to the student's instructional level and will help the student's transition to his or her new school.

Notes

1. The views expressed in this chapter are the authors' and not necessarily representative of Alberta Education.
2. In Tables 20.1 and 20.2, the "Province" columns refer to the data for the entire province. In the remainder of the report, provincial comparisons refer to the provincial sample of GLA data.
3. The percent of curricular outcomes measured by PATs were obtained from a discussion paper presented to the Program and Accountability Advisory Committee by Alberta Education, November 8, 2007.

References

Alberta Education (2005). *Beyond MIRS data—Technical report*. Edmonton, AB: Author.

Alberta Education (2007a). *GLA edulink manual*. Edmonton, AB: Author.

Alberta Education (2007b). *Grade level of achievement 2005–06 pilot data—Technical report*. Edmonton, AB: Author. Retrieved November 1, 2007, from http://www.education.gov.ab.ca/ipr/GLA/GLATechnicalReport.pdf

Alberta Education (2007c). *Guide to education: ECS to grade 12*. Edmonton, AB: Author. Retrieved December 1, 2007, from http://education.alberta.ca/admin/resources/guide07-08.aspx

Alberta Education (in press). *Grade level of achievement 2006–07 pilot data*. Edmonton, AB: Author.

Alberta Learning (2001). *Entry age, age within cohort, and achievement*. Edmonton, AB: Author.

Alberta Learning (2004). *Standards for special education*. Edmonton, AB: Author. Retrieved November 2, 2007, from http://www.education.gov.ab.ca/k_12/specialneeds/SpecialEd_Stds2004.pdf

Armstrong, D., Laird, A., & Mulgrew, A. (2006). *Grade level of achievement reporting: Teacher and administrator handbook*. Edmonton, AB: Alberta Education. Retrieved October 26, 2007, from http://www.education.gov.ab.ca/ipr/GLA/TeachAdminHandbook.pdf

Chamberlain, M. (2007). *Reading literacy: An overview of New Zealand's results from the Program for International Reading Literacy Study (PIRLS) 2005/2006*. Wellington, NZ: New Zealand Ministry of Education.

Crawford, C., Dearden, L., & Meghir, C. (2007). *When you are born matters: The impact of date of birth on child cognitive outcomes in England*. London: The Institute for Fiscal Studies.

Crocker, L., & Algina, J. (1986). *Introduction to classical and modern test theory*. New York: Holt, Rinehart & Winston.

Crundwell, M. R. (2005). Alternative strategies for large scale student assessment in Canada: Is value-added assessment one possible answer? *Canadian Journal of Educational Administration and Policy, 41*, 5.

Fullan, M. (2006). *Turnaround leadership*. San Francisco: Jossey-Bass.

Harris, M.B. (1995). *Basic statistics for behavioural science research* (2nd ed.). Needham Heights, MA: Allyn & Bacon.

Pope, G. A., Wentzel, C., & Cammaert, R. (2003). Relationships between gender and Alberta diploma scores. *Alberta Journal of Educational Research, 48*(4), 275–286.

Reeves, D. B. (2004). *Accountability for learning*. Alexandria, VA: Association for Supervision and Curriculum Development.

Volante, L., & Cherubini, L. (2007). Connecting educational leadership with multi-level assessment reform. *International Electronic Journal for Leadership in Learning, 11*(12). Retrieved December 20, 2007, from http://www.ucalgary.ca/~iejll/

Wasserman, D. (2001). *Moving targets: Student mobility and school and student achievement*. Edmonton, AB: Alberta Learning.

21

Collaborative Inquiry and Data-Based Decision Making

Douglas Huffman and Kelli Thomas
University of Kansas

Introduction

The educational reform movement and demands for public accountability have placed increased pressure on K-12 educators to help students perform on national, state, and local tests. Teachers and students are currently facing an onslaught of tests and assessments designed to judge whether or not they are making adequate yearly progress (AYP) in increasing student achievement. At the surface level, student data are gathered to meet the requirements of the federal, state, and local legislation and policies. At a deeper level, the increasing use of data to make decisions reflects a shift in the professional roles of educators. The focus on student test scores has forced educators to become more data driven as they attempt to analyze test scores and make decisions about curricular and instructional changes that will help students learn. The educational reform movement "broadened expectations for professional practice" calling for K-12 educators to be more than mere implementers of the policies and practices determined by others, and rather to be leaders responsible for school improvement (Kowalski, Lasley, & Mahoney, 2008, p. 3).

To some extent, the schools have become overwhelmed with data. State assessments, district assessments, school assessments, and classroom assessments have all led to more data than schools can easily manage. To help manage all these data, schools need to develop the capacity to conduct evaluations and assessments for data-based decision making (King, 2002; Kowalski et al., 2008). The purpose of this chapter is to describe a model of collaborative inquiry that is designed to engage educators in data-based decision making. Through the model, collaborative evaluation communities (groups of educators) use evaluation processes to facilitate data-based decision making in schools. Teachers typically do not have expertise in evaluation and therefore it is critical for university educators who have expertise in evaluation to respond to this need through professional collaborations with schools. Traditionally, collaborations have focused on developing teachers' ability to engage in action research or reflect on classroom practice; however, there is a need to go further and help teachers and schools begin to engage in a broader schoolwide evaluation of programs.

Numerous researchers have noted that educational growth can be optimized when teachers are supported by other education professionals (Darling-Hammond, 1997;

Fullan, 1993; Robb, 2000; Routman, 2000; Sarason & Lorentz, 1998). Unfortunately, the structures that support these types of professional long-term collaborations among educators still evade many K-12 teachers (Long, 2004). The daily work of classroom teaching does not typically promote collaborative inquiry. Teachers are so consumed with a wide variety of problems and concerns related to teaching and learning that they often do not have time in their schedules to develop meaningful working collaborations either with other teachers in their own building, or with outside groups such as university and community institutions. Teachers tend to have very little time during the day to work with other teachers, plan lessons as a team, or even talk with their colleagues (Peak, 1996).

Professional structures that engage teachers and university personnel in joint investigations create opportunities to share expertise and build interdependence in understanding instructional issues within a particular context (Elmore & Burney, 1999; Fullan, 1993; Little, 1999; Sarason & Lorentz, 1998). Furthermore, collaborations that stimulate teacher inquiry, reflection, and data-based decision making have all been shown to be powerful tools for influencing an individual's beliefs and theories of teaching and learning (Bissex, 1994; Cochran-Smith & Lytle, 1993, 1999; Huffman & Kalnin, 2003; Kalnin, 2000). To improve student achievement, Sarason (1996) urges districts and universities to create opportunities for partnering that move across current hierarchies. He concludes, "Teachers cannot create and sustain contexts of productive learning for students if those contexts do not exist for teachers" (pp. 253–254). Collaborative efforts that engage individuals across schools and universities in a shared evaluative process of data gathering and analysis not only give teachers a voice but can also lead to sustained improvements in learning.

However, collaborative efforts have not traditionally been used to engage teachers in inquiry by means of program evaluation. It is quite rare for teachers to engage in inquiry regarding schoolwide issues (Chval, Reys, Reys, Tarr, & Chavez, 2006). Action research and reflection are more common in the schools, and these are certainly worthwhile activities, but we would argue that there is a need to move teachers toward considering broader, more schoolwide evaluation of their work. Program evaluation has traditionally been deemed the realm of the district administration—not the realm of teachers' work. Also, teachers have not historically participated in systematic evaluation of educational issues as true partners (Henson, 1996). This leaves teachers with little or no voice in the questions that are considered, the data that are collected, or the way in which the data are analyzed and interpreted. We would argue that it is imperative for teachers to participate in collaborative inquiries using evaluation processes to develop the capacity for data-based decision making. Participating in these collaborative inquiries can help teachers become what Kowalski et al. (2008) describe as "evidenced-based decision makers" (p. 256). They contend that evidence-based decision makers not only know how to implement decisions, but also know how to examine school and classroom environments in a broader sense. Evidence-based decision makers "are not just looking at state test scores and standardized tests. They are looking at school, teacher, and student factors that might influence these scores" (p. 256). In this chapter we describe a unique model of collaborative inquiry that has been used to engage teachers in broader, more schoolwide program evaluation. Such efforts focused on program evaluation are rare and this chapter provides a unique case study of the impact of such efforts on developing teachers' ability to engage in data-based decision making. As participant observers, we studied how participation in a collaborative evaluation community (CEC team) affected teachers. In the following section we describe the link between collaborative inquiry, program evaluation, and data-based decision making.

Collaborative Inquiry and Evaluation to Build Capacity for Data-Based Decision Making

Individual teacher inquiry, reflection, and data-based decision making in the form of teacher research projects have been shown to be powerful tools for influencing an individual's beliefs and theories of teaching (Bissex, 1994; Cochran-Smith & Lytle, 1993; Kalnin, 2000). Noffke (1997) establishes that teacher research projects have personal, professional, and political purposes and benefits for teachers. Although individually conceptualized inquiry efforts may have substantial benefits for a teacher's learning and decision making, critics raise questions about whether such projects have any systematic impact on school change efforts (Elmore, 2000). Elmore claims that if teachers do not move toward collaborative designs addressing whole-school or district issues, their work will amount to no more than "playing in a sandbox" (Elmore, 2000). In contrast, professional structures that engage teachers and other educational personnel in joint inquiries create opportunities to share expertise and build interdependence in understanding educational issues within a particular institutional context (Elmore & Burney, 1999; Fullan, 1993; Little, 1999; Sarason & Lorentz, 1998).

A number of barriers have been noted to establishing data-based decision making as a feature of school culture, one of which is the lack of collaboration among educators when engaged in inquiry (Kowalski et al., 2008; Popham, 2006). Approaching inquiry from a collaborative, team-based approach potentially addresses the organizational structures in schools that have hampered school change efforts. Sarason (1996) urges districts and universities to create opportunities for collaboration that move across current hierarchies in order to improve student achievement. He concludes, "Teachers cannot create and sustain contexts of productive learning for students if those contexts do not exist for teachers" (pp. 253–254). Elliott (1991) specifically identifies inquiry-based efforts as critical to restructuring roles:

> Action research integrates teaching and teacher development, curriculum development and evaluation, research and philosophical reflection, into a unified conception of a reflective educational practice. This unified conception has power implications inasmuch as it negates a rigid division of labour in which specialized tasks and roles are distributed across hierarchically organized activities. (p. 54)

Engaging teachers in long-term collaborative inquiry coupled with participation in program evaluation can help schools build the capacity for data-based decision making. Kowalski et al. (2008) suggest that building this capacity involves four dimensions:

(1) proficiency generating data—the degree to which principals, teachers, and support staff are prepared to conduct assessment and related research,

(2) proficiency using data—the degree to which principals, teachers, and support staff are prepared to apply assessment outcomes to important decisions,

(3) resource adequacy—the degree to which principals, teachers, and support staff have access to data, time, equipment, and technical assistance.

(4) cultural acceptance—the degree to which principals, teachers, and support staff share values and beliefs supportive of data-driven decision making. (p. 17)

The Collaborative Evaluation Communities in Urban Schools Project (CEC Project) described in the following sections illustrates how these four dimensions of data-based decision making can be developed in schools.

Collaborative Evaluation Communities in Urban Schools

We received funding from the National Science Foundation to develop the ongoing CEC project. The purpose of the project is to help teachers in urban schools build assessment and evaluation capacity by engaging in long-term inquiry related to curriculum, instruction, and student learning in mathematics and science. The project provides a unique structure for immersing K-12 teachers, mathematics and science educators, and graduate students in the evaluation process in an attempt to improve teachers' capacity to use data and engage in continuous improvement through data-based decision making.

The CEC project provides long-term collaborative experiences in diverse settings as a means of developing the evaluation capacity of both K-12 schools and graduate students. The key concept behind the CEC project is that by immersing teachers in the evaluation process we can help build evaluation capacity and bridge the gap between district evaluation efforts and the teaching and learning of science and mathematics. Teachers need assistance in deciphering and understanding data to change practices and one way to do so is through a collaborative evaluation community.

Collaborate evaluation efforts between K-12 schools and universities can provide unique infrastructure developments that serve the needs of the schools by enhancing their evaluation capacity. Other forms of collaboration such as teacher inquiry, reflection, and data-based decision making have all been shown to be powerful tools for influencing an individual's beliefs and theories of teaching and learning (Bissex, 1994; Cochran-Smith & Lytle, 1993; Kalnin, 2000). Huffman and Kalnin (2003) reported that when science and mathematics teachers engaged in collaborative inquiry, they not only changed their instructional practices, but also began to make schoolwide changes. In their study, teachers also reported that the collaborative process helped their school engage in continuous improvement and to use data to make decisions. The CEC project provides professional growth activities for science and mathematics teachers. By engaging teachers in the evaluation process we are assisting school districts in the development of an evaluation culture designed to support teachers in the continual examination of programs with the ultimate intent of improving educational opportunities for all students.

One of the challenges in creating collaborative evaluation communities is organizing the wide variety of participants so that they can successfully achieve their goals. The goal is to involve all of the participants in significant and worthwhile evaluation activities. The participants come to the evaluation process with different expertise and background knowledge, along with different expectations and goals. The challenge is creating and sustaining a collaborative evaluation community that can bring these diverse views together in a way that is productive and useful for everyone. The key to sustainability is to design collaborative evaluation communities that serve the needs of the schools while at the same time serving the needs of faculty and graduate students. This means we must engage in evaluation that serves the everyday teaching and learning needs of science and mathematics teachers, while at the same time engaging in program evaluation that can address larger evaluation issues across schools. In her work with evaluation capacity building in schools, King (2005) highlights five key activities that, when implemented over several years, are important to developing a culture for evaluation. Among these activities are:

(1) creating an evaluation advisory group,
(2) beginning to build a formal evaluation infrastructure,
(3) making sense of test scores,
(4) conducting one highly visible participatory inquiry, and
(5) instituting action research activities.

(King, 2005, p. 90)

The CEC project employs activities similar to those which King used.

The Inquiry Cycle in Collaborative Evaluation Communities

The overview of the CEC given above provides insight into how the collaborative inquiry model operates. The formation of teams of participants is central to the collaborative nature of the CEC project. CEC teams comprised of teachers, school administrators, district personnel, graduate students, and university evaluators are established at schools to immerse participants in the process of evaluation. The CEC project uses an inquiry cycle developed by the National Research Council (NRC, 1999) to engage participants in the ongoing process of evaluation (see Figure 21.1). The cycle begins with a collaborative examination of student achievement data at the national, state, and local levels involving input from university evaluators, K-12 personnel, and science, technology, engineering, and mathematics (STEM) graduate students. Following the initial exploration of existing achievement data, CEC participants consider how the data might inform the evaluation of mathematics and science programs in the school district. The first two steps in the process are designed to help participants explore data and to think about the implications of the data for their own district. Exploring data typically produces many questions and serves as an excellent starting point for the evaluation process.

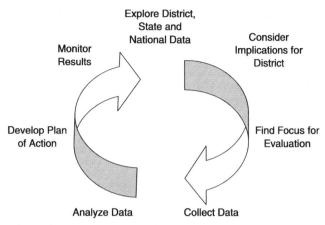

Figure 21.1 Inquiry cycle.

In the next step CEC participants establish a focus for an initial evaluation. Participants are asked to identify broad issues related to student achievement in mathematics or science drawing upon the data exploration from the first two steps of the inquiry cycle. Reflections on the issues lead the CEC participants to create evaluation questions that can serve as the focus for their upcoming investigations. The selection of focus areas is followed by the development of an initial evaluation plan to guide data collection and analysis. The next two steps in the inquiry cycle immerse the CEC participants in data collection and analysis. This involves developing data collection instruments and data analysis procedures that CEC participants use to answer the evaluation questions in their plan. The procedures used by the CEC teams in these two steps contribute to ECB by beginning to establish the infrastructures necessary for sustainable inquiry and evaluation in schools.

Based upon what is learned from the initial data collection and analysis, communities develop specific action plans to address the problems they identified. The action plans require continuous monitoring, more data collection, and analysis. This in turn typically leads to more questions, more data collection, and more analysis. In the end the process will help establish a continuous improvement cycle that can help the collaborative evaluation communities use evaluation as a tool to create change in their schools and empower the teachers to become leaders in their schools. The inquiry cycle we have described includes aspects of the evaluative inquiry process promoted by Parsons (2002) and reflects the working definition of evaluation capacity building (ECB) provided by Stockdill, Baizerman, and Compton (2002) emphasizing the importance of the "on-going, open-ended, and emergent nature of EBC work—sustaining evaluation and its uses" (p. 13).

A Case Study: The CEC Project in an Urban Elementary School

The elementary school described in this case study is located in an urban community situated in an industrial area of the city. The school serves approximately 300 students of which 58% are of Hispanic descent and 38% are of African American descent. Additionally, 89% of the students come from economically disadvantaged households. Of the 16 regular classroom teachers at the school, six were interested in participating on the CEC team along with the instructional coach and the principal. After the school was selected to participate in the project, the team of six teachers, the instructional coach, and the principal attended an organizational meeting conducted by the authors. The meeting served as a forum to begin the partnership between the school and university partners and to launch the inquiry cycle. In the following sections, we describe the progress of the CEC team through the phases of the inquiry cycle and present the results of the case study established through analysis of critical incidents.

Phases One and Two: Examining National, State, and District Data and Considering Implications

A kick-off meeting was held during an after-school time frame to accommodate the teachers' schedules. The session was organized by the university partners with the purpose of providing an overview of the CEC project and to begin the first phases of the inquiry cycle together with the school team. During the small group session the following goals of the CEC project were shared:

(1) create collaborative evaluation communities to examine teaching and learning of mathematics and/or science;
(2) use evaluation and assessment data to inform mathematics and science instruction and curriculum development; and
(3) engage in collaborative evaluation as a means of improving student achievement in mathematics and science.

The university partners then shared national data from the Trends in International Mathematics and Science Study (TIMSS). It was evident to the team that students in the United States have been outperformed by their counterparts in other countries. The question of why this might be occurring was raised. A presentation of findings from classroom video analysis research conducted by Stigler and Hiebert (1999) was shared through a short video clip. Stigler and Hiebert found that how students were taught and what they were taught were the predominant factors contributing to differences in student achievement. These results demonstrated for the teachers that the curricular and instructional decisions they make in their classrooms can have profound implications for student learning.

Next, the university partners presented state and district mathematics and science student test results from previous years. The team noted that the district test results in mathematics had improved slightly since the district had implemented a standards-based mathematics curriculum at the elementary level [*Investigations in Number, Data, and Space* (TERC, 1998)]. However, student achievement at the district level continued to fall below the state averages, highlighting the work that could be done to improve student mathematics achievement in the district. After examining the student data, the CEC team chose to focus on mathematics achievement.

Phase Three: Find a Focus for Evaluation

The CEC team agreed to meet every other week following the initial session in an effort to move forward in the inquiry process before the end of the school year. During the second group session the team generated potential factors that might contribute to student mathematics achievement that could become central to the evaluation inquiry process. The factors identified were discussed by the group to further clarify the meaning of each issue, particularly within the context of the school. The significance of the session became apparent as the team recognized several common issues that emerged through the discussion of mathematics teaching and learning. The issues the team found most important related to the recently adopted standards-based curriculum series that the teachers in the school were using for instruction. Specifically the team was interested in:

(a) curriculum alignment with state mathematics standards,
(b) pacing of instruction,
(c) instructional practices of teachers as they use the curriculum,
(d) teachers' mathematical knowledge of content contained in the curriculum, and
(e) curriculum alignment with the state mathematics assessment.

Consideration of curriculum alignment with the state mathematics assessment focused on two distinct aspects: (1) the mathematics content of assessment items and (2) the format of the assessment items (i.e., multiple choice). The emphasis on assessments in the discussion was particularly important to the school personnel as the state was preparing to implement a new mathematics test for elementary Grades 2 to 6. The teachers shared their concerns about low student scores on the state assessment and how important it is to increase student scores in ultimately increasing overall achievement. The teachers had the perception that one area of weakness for their students was computations, but there was a lack of evidence to confirm this belief. One teacher commented, "If our students truly have the depth of understanding number sense that *Investigations* supports then they would do well on the computation problems." She went on to say, "I don't think that every teacher in the school understands the connection between the activities, investigations, or games found in *Investigations* and concepts like number computations"; the other teachers in the group agreed. However, these perceptions were based on opinions without actual data. The CEC team decided to focus on gathering data related to instructional practices and curriculum alignment with assessments as the major areas for the evaluation work of the first inquiry cycle. The next few sessions were devoted to the development of a curriculum and instruction survey for teachers at the school and the examination of state assessment expectations.

Phase Four: Collect Data

The CEC team chose to focus on better understanding mathematics curriculum, instruction, and assessment, including: what was being taught in each grade; how topics were being taught; and how student learning was assessed at both the class-room level and through the annual state mathematics test. Few school districts have data about the instructional techniques used by teachers in their schools. As a start-ing point this team found it important to first understand not only how mathematics was being taught but also how the curriculum and their instruction aligned with the state mathematics standards and the state test before they could initiate change. As the teachers began to engage in the data collection process they needed more one-on-one assistance from the university partners to refine their data collection instruments and begin to implement the evaluation plan.

The first Phase Four session began with the university partners sharing samples of surveys they had used in their own research to address instructional practices, teacher self-efficacy for teaching, and confidence with particular mathematics content and processes. The university partners challenged the group with the task of reviewing the surveys and modifying items for use in a survey designed specifically for the school. Analysis of field notes from this session revealed that some of the teachers were hesitant about the task and actually began to question the value of surveying teachers in the building. A couple of the teachers were vocal about not wanting to do something that would not be useful in their own classroom. One teacher made it clear that she did not want to spend time creating a survey, she just wanted to work on something that she could use with her students in her classroom. The teachers' desire to focus on concrete issues related directly to their daily classroom work is not unique to this school. Cuban (1992) identified a common dilemma to building professional communities for systematic educational inquiry was the differences in the way teachers and researchers view the work. Cuban found that teachers wanted to pursue research in areas that seemed to have implications for the concrete tasks of their classrooms, while researchers were interested in implications of broader aspects of educational programs. Similarly, the CEC teachers began to question the value of conducting a survey because they believed that they already knew what they were doing in their own classrooms for instruction. The principal and the instructional coach commented that while teachers might know what happens instructionally in their own classrooms the school had little data about the instructional practices of all teachers in the school. The principal reminded the group that improving the mathematics program in the school was "larger than one teacher's classroom" and gathering data about these issues was important to the school as a whole. We encour-aged the teachers to think about how collecting instructional practice data would provide a baseline for future comparisons and might also lead to a greater under-standing of instruction in the school. As a result, the group refocused on its belief that understanding instruction in the school is an area that influences student learn-ing of mathematics. As the session ended, teachers returned to their focus on instructional practices and agreed on the value of surveying teachers in the school. They made suggestions for how survey items could be modified, changed, and cre-ated to benefit the inquiry process at the school, particularly by adding items that asked teachers about the curriculum. The university partners agreed to gather infor-mation on the new state mathematics assessments and to draft a survey instrument for the teachers to review at a future meeting.

Subsequent sessions were devoted to revising the survey, reviewing the changes in the state mathematics assessment, and to revisiting the broader issues and questions guiding the CEC inquiry cycle at the school. The teachers at the school completed the survey that was created by their colleagues and university partners. In an effort to continue to build trust among the university and school partners, the survey responses were anonymous. The CEC team determined that it was not necessary to connect responses to particular teachers because the focus of the evaluation was on the instructional practices of the teachers in the school collectively. During this phase the university partners also met with the district elementary mathematics coordinator who knew the latest information and changes related to the new state assessments. It was decided that data about the new assessments would be used by the CEC team in the data analysis phase of the inquiry cycle.

Phase Five: Data Analysis

The mathematics teaching and learning survey developed by the CEC team for the teachers at the school comprised items related to the mathematics curriculum, teacher efficacy, instructional practices, assessment practices, student learning outcomes, and teacher confidence with their own mathematics knowledge and understanding. The composition of the survey was consistent with a questionnaire, Inside the Classroom Mathematics Teacher Questionnaire, used by Horizon Research Corporation in a national study of mathematics instructional practices (Weiss & Pasley, 2004). Alignment between the CEC mathematics and teaching survey and the Inside the Classroom Mathematics Teacher Questionnaire helps establish validity of the survey. The teachers in the school completed the survey anonymously during a professional development session. The process was unique because the teachers were responding to the survey as a means of gathering data for their own inquiry and evaluation of the mathematics teaching and learning at the school. The survey request came from the partnership formed through the CEC project, which included teachers, rather than as a mandate from district administration or outside researchers.

For the purposes of data analysis, response frequencies were examined by the CEC team during a group session in which the results of several items materialized as relevant to the current inquiry process. It was clear from the responses to items related to the curriculum that teacher perceptions about the curriculum varied widely among teachers in the school. The divergent views of mathematics curriculum and teaching were quite intriguing to the team. While a majority of the teachers believed that their curriculum is better than traditional textbooks for helping students understand mathematics concepts, more than a third disagreed. When asked if the curriculum is better than traditional textbooks for teaching students about computation, a majority of the teachers either *disagreed* or *strongly disagreed* but more than a quarter of the teachers either *agreed* or *strongly agreed*. The responses from teachers were nearly equal between *agreeing* and *disagreeing* that the students learn mathematics better by using the curriculum and on whether or not teachers would prefer to use a different curriculum. Analysis of the opinions about instruction items showed that most of the teachers did *agree* that they had the ability to effectively teach mathematics. However, it is notable that none of the teachers felt strongly about this ability.

Group discussion related to the frequency distribution of responses to several questions about student learning, teacher assessment of student learning, and instructional practices led to an emphasis on the issue of assessment. For example, a majority of teachers in the school generally *agreed* that they are effective at embedding assessments into mathematics lessons but more than a quarter did not believe this to be true. Most teachers indicated that they use assessments embedded in class activities, as well as observations and questioning to assess student progress at least once or twice a week. However, more than 90% of the teachers reported that they never or rarely (a few times a year) used short-answer tests (e.g., multiple choice, true/false, fill in the blank) to assess student learning in mathematics. This result was significant to the work of the CEC team because the new state mathematics test consists of all multiple-choice items to measure student achievement. Analysis of the survey responses also indicated that a majority of the teachers in the school never have another colleague observe their students' academic performance or review their students' test scores. Consequently, the school partners wanted the plan of action to include adding common grade level embedded assessments into lessons from the curriculum that more closely align with the format and content of the state mathematics test.

Phase Six: Plan of Action

After the data analysis in Phase Five of the CEC inquiry process a plan of action was initiated by the CEC partners. The group decided that the plan of action for the first CEC inquiry cycle would be to write multiple-choice assessment items for teachers to use as embedded assessment throughout the school year while using *Investigations in number, data, and space* (TERC, 1998). The intent for these mini-assessments was to provide teachers with a means for gathering regular student assessment data aligned with the curriculum and the state mathematics standards.

Before writing the mini-assessments at each grade level the CEC team chose to study the new state test guidelines. With the assistance of the district elementary mathematics coordinator, the team participated in an analysis of the state mathematics test information and item analysis for Grades 3 to 5. The team reviewed the standard indicators from the state mathematics standards that would be assessed and considered the number of items that would be included for each standard indicator per grade level. Standard indicators that might not be assessed at an earlier grade level but that would be assessed in subsequent grades were also included in the analysis at each grade level. Therefore the partners considered standards indicators for grades K-5 in their review.

The teachers used released items from the National Assessment of Educational Progress (NAEP) and TIMSS as models for constructing multiple-choice items specifically aligned with units in their curriculum. Items written were then shared with the CEC partners at a follow-up session. The school and university partners discussed each item and evaluated the alignment with the intended standard indicator. The evaluation of items as part of the process of creating mini-assessments was significant because it helped the group establish a common understanding of how assessment items would be written. Once the CEC group had determined guidelines for writing items, pairs of teachers took responsibility for a grade level and began writing mini-assessment items to accompany specific units in the curriculum. The mini-assessment development work was undertaken by teachers during the summer with the mini-assessments to be implemented the following school year.

Phase Seven: Monitor Results

Continuous data analysis is a key component of building assessment and evaluation infrastructure in schools. The seventh phase of the inquiry cycle requires monitoring results of previous inquiry. The CEC team analyzed data from the mini-assessments to monitor student learning throughout the school year. One challenge faced by the CEC team was encouraging implementation of the mini-assessments schoolwide. During the first inquiry cycle described in this case, the use of mini-assessments was limited to the teachers (grade levels) involved in the project. The CEC team developed assessments for third, fourth, and fifth grade *Investigations in number, data, and space* (TERC, 1998) units but only third and fourth grade students completed mini-assessments during the first year. Even the teachers involved in the project struggled to embed the mini-assessments into their instruction, finding that some units passed without the administration of an assessment. To assist the teachers, the university partners worked collaboratively with the teachers to create databases that made recording and monitoring the assessment data more systematic. The databases contributed to increased infrastructure in the school for data collection and analysis. One positive outcome of the first cycle through the inquiry process is that teachers began meeting with each other to analyze results from the mini-assessments and collectively review students' academic performance. By the end of the first year of the project, the CEC teachers were committed to finding ways to ensure that all unit mini-assessments would be taken by students during the next school year and they were exploring options for including more teachers in the school in systematic analysis of mini-assessment data. On the survey of mathematics teaching and learning developed and administered by the CEC team the previous spring, more than 80% of the teachers in the building reported that they *rarely* or *never* engaged in this type of professional activity.

These collaborative evaluations of student learning led to changes in mathematics instruction and school programs across grade levels. For example, in the fall of 2005 the CEC team scored and analyzed results of a fourth grade mini-assessment on number sense and computation. Through item analysis, the team discovered that a majority of the fourth grade students were not able to successfully compute numbers represented as monetary values for the purpose of solving simple and complex problems. Discussions about these results focused on ways in which teachers can strengthen student understanding of number sense, particularly the representation of money. Field notes from the CEC team's work session captured the essence of the discussion including teacher comments such as, "We are doing so much surface teaching and we are not going deep enough with the concepts of number sense."

Another teacher concluded, "We have to build the bridge between the concepts in the curriculum and the representations of the concepts on the assessments." A third teacher added, "We also have to do the same thing between the manipulatives or concrete models and the concepts." As a result, changes in classroom practices were undertaken. At the first grade level, teachers in the school added three days to their instructional sequence for extended student exploration with multiple representations of the concepts of addition and subtraction of numbers. The students' work focused on computing monetary values and the connections between actual money, mental computations, and paper-pencil computations. The fourth-grade teachers engaged students in an analysis of the problems missed on the mini-assessment and incorporated additional experiences computing with money. The CEC team evaluations also led to the initiation of a schoolwide positive behavior support activity that involved students across all grade levels in using numbers represented as monetary values. The activity incorporated rewards for positive behavior in the form of earning "school money" during the last two months of school and the opportunity to spend money earned at an ice cream sundae reward party. As part of the activity, students recorded the money they earned, completed order forms for sundaes with various toppings, and calculated the amount owed, spent, and change received. This long-term activity engaged students in developing computational skills and understanding of numbers represented as monetary amounts.

Case Study Results

In a case study of her work with a large suburban school district, King (2002) acknowledged the challenges of building the capacity of schools to conduct and use evaluation for improving programs. Among the challenges are helping participants value the process of evaluation, the long-term time commitment for change to occur, and stimulating reflections on the evaluation process that lead to meaningful revisions in evaluation activities. As a result of her work in schools, she suggested the following aspects of effective evaluation capacity building:

(1) creating an evaluation advisory group,
(2) beginning to build a formal evaluation infrastructure,
(3) making sense of test scores,
(4) conducting one highly visible participatory inquiry, and
(5) instituting action research activities.

(King, 2005, p. 90)

In our work on the CEC project we have employed several of King's suggestions. For example, the CEC team serves, in part, as an evaluation advisory group; we have begun to build evaluation infrastructures through activities and products of the team (i.e., mini-assessments, schoolwide database for recording assessment data); the CEC team has examined test scores and made connections between those data and instructional practice; we have completed an initial collaborative inquiry focused on curriculum and assessment alignment (the inquiry cycle described in the narrative above). To make the collaborative inquiry more visible to other teachers in the school, the CEC teachers led two professional development sessions for the entire school during the first-year inquiry. The first session was structured around involving teachers at all grade levels in scoring and analysis of fourth-grade student mini-assessments. The second session extended the initial analysis of assessment data by having the teachers at all grade levels contribute to mini-assessment revisions. These two sessions not only made the work of the CEC team more visible, but they also began to broaden the evaluation work beyond the teachers on the CEC team. These sessions represent a good beginning for building the evaluation capacity of the school but any significant change at the school level will require a long-term partnership and continued collaborative evaluation activities. Through this case study we investigated how teachers on the CEC team were affected by their participation after one year of collaborative evaluation activities. The CEC project has not been exempt from challenges but the unique collaborative model we used to facilitate evaluation and assessment capacity building of urban elementary mathematics teachers has helped us face those challenges and influence the teachers in subtle yet significant ways. Critical incidents analysis of the qualitative data gathered during the first year of the project confirmed that our evaluation and assessment capacity-building efforts effected teachers through:

(1) better understanding of the link between curriculum and instruction;
(2) increased attention to the use of assessment to monitor student learning; and
(3) enhanced awareness of the mathematics program across grade levels.

Better Understanding of the Link Between Curriculum and Instruction

When the collaboration began, teachers seemed to relinquish responsibility for student learning to problems they perceived with *Investigations in number, data, and space* (TERC, 1998). They viewed the curriculum as something they had to use, but they did not believe that it was the best resource for the students in their classrooms. The focus of their discussions about the curriculum did not include the ways in which they could use *Investigations in number, data, and space* (TERC, 1998) to promote student learning but rather why using *Investigations* limited learning for students in their classes. This was evident through comments such as, "*Investigations* assumes students will have prior knowledge that our students just don't have," and "We usually have to move on to a new investigation before the students have time to understand the content because of the pacing guide (the timeline suggested by district leadership)." Initially, teachers did not discuss instruction in depth. When we asked about their instruction, the responses indicated that teachers did not believe that discussing instruction was relevant to the collaborative evaluation work. One teacher's comment was representative of the group's view: "We use *Investigations* so we already know what we are doing for instruction." It is important to note that these perceptions existed before teachers had the opportunity to actually participate in evaluation activities. At this point in the process, we were still helping teachers determine a focus for investigation.

After the teachers had actively participated in the evaluation process by (a) creating instruments for gathering data (i.e., mathematics teaching and learning survey and mini-assessments), (b) using those instruments to collect data from their colleagues and from students, and (c) examining the data as a group, our discussions about curriculum and instruction began to change. The teachers started to recognize and publicly acknowledge gaps between the curriculum, the state mathematics standards, and classroom instruction. For example, item analysis of the mini-assessments provided a context through which teachers could target specific areas (number sense, computations with monetary values) where they could take action through instruction. Having student data that they gathered and analyzed gave the teachers concrete examples to reflect on and discuss in meaningful ways. These student data differed from student data obtained from external sources (state tests, tests developed by national publishers) because the teachers had been involved in the decisions about what and how to assess mathematics learning. Now the CEC team teachers were not looking outside their classroom to explain student performance but rather considering improvements to their own classroom practices. During a focus group session in May 2006, a teacher summarized this by saying, "The mini-assessments definitely helped show areas for improvement. We could ask ourselves . . . Was it [the particular mathematics concept or skill] in *Investigations?* Was it missing from *Investigations?* Did I just miss it instructionally?" The teachers as a group were also more knowledgeable about how the curriculum could be a tool to guide their instruction rather than the device that defined their instruction. One teacher stated, "We all know that *Investigations* has gaps [areas that are not well aligned with state mathematics standards] and in the past we didn't have time to think about them, now I am more aware of them." Another teacher added, "Time is such a factor so in that way it [the evaluation inquiry process] shaped instruction because we looked at what could be cut out of a unit and what could be built upon in *Investigations*. I am more aware of *Investigations* and it made me more aware of my instruction and why I was using instruction."

Increased Attention to the Use of Assessment to Monitor Student Learning

The ways in which teachers viewed the topic of assessment evolved as the CEC team progressed through the inquiry cycle. The teachers' early discussions about assessment highlighted the concerns that many educators have about improving external test scores. The teachers wanted help to find ways to raise student test scores and questioned the alignment of *Investigations in number, data, and space* (TERC, 1998) with the state mathematics assessment. The notion that tests scores reflect overall student learning was not part of these early discussions, the main concern was increasing scores. At one meeting in an attempt to move the discussion beyond the emphasis on poor test scores, the principal reminded the group that scores in the school had been on the rise. We asked the teachers what they would credit for the increase and the response was "test prep" beginning two months before the test.

Discussions about the topic of assessment shifted to how assessment could be used to monitor student learning when teachers started writing mini-assessment items for

Investigations units at third, fourth, and fifth grade levels. First, the teachers were concerned with writing items in a multiple-choice format that would measure the key mathematics topics of a unit. Once the CEC team had actual student-completed mini-assessments to score and analyze, teachers' concerns focused on item analysis. The teachers used the results to discuss implications for instruction and student learning. As we described through the example of number sense and money in the narrative, the teachers began to connect assessment to instructional changes they could make to improve student learning. A teacher noted, "I created homework based on what the students did or did not understand." The teachers on the CEC team also increased their capacity to write and revise assessment items enhancing the value of the mini-assessments at the classroom level. The teacher's additional statement illustrates this change: "Now I know how questions [assessment items] are developed from standards and benchmarks, not simply by modeling off practice tests [tests from external sources]." This shift in thinking about assessment is a positive change for the teachers on the CEC team but this same value for classroom assessment has not yet transferred to other teachers in the school. A future goal of the CEC team is to expand the use of mini-assessments beyond the teachers on our team. The team plans to set aside several professional development times during future school years in which all teachers in the school score and analyze mini-assessments. The CEC teachers will serve as leaders, helping other teachers realize the benefits of collaborative evaluation activities such as the use of mini-assessments data to drive instruction.

Enhanced Awareness of the Mathematics Program Across Grade Levels

When the CEC project began, teachers had a general idea about the mathematics program at grade levels other than their own. They had spent time in the past looking at the state standards for all grade levels and had some knowledge of the *Investigations* units across grades. However, teachers had not been active participants in gathering data about multiple aspects of the mathematics program at the school. The collaborative evaluation activities were structured to guide teachers through a process of examining aspects of the mathematics program based on data they helped collect and analyze. As university partners, we wanted to involve the teachers in evaluation activities beginning with the first meeting. At the same time, we understood the importance of giving the teachers time to share their perceptions of the mathematics program with each other. We purposefully tried to help the CEC teachers balance between spending time focusing on concerns (some of which they could change and some of which they could not) and taking action through evaluation activities that could lead to positive changes. Through the process, teachers began to have increased awareness of both the mathematics program and of their colleagues' practices. One of the CEC teachers on the team teaches elementary students music, and her statement during the focus group illustrates this change: "I have more respect for my colleagues. I have a better understanding of how to help kids learn math. Now I know how important math vocabulary is and I can use math vocabulary in my classroom."

Having a variety of teachers on the CEC team was important to stimulate awareness of the mathematics program across grades. The combination of primary teachers, intermediate teachers, and even a fine arts teacher on the team enabled us to have cross-grade level discussions. It was common during meetings of the group for a teacher to respond to a colleague's contribution to the discussion by saying "I didn't know that was something the fourth graders do" or "I could do that same thing with my students." As one teacher summarized, "I've learned how I can support learning at other levels. I'm a primary person but now I can see how my instruction builds up to the intermediate grade levels." Another teacher concurred: "While we tried to do that in the past where we looked at standards at every grade level, it wasn't to the depth that we have this year. When we helped write assessment items for the fifth grade we could understand what fifth grade math is like." The increased awareness of the mathematics program across grade levels has and will continue to add depth and meaning to the collaborative evaluation activities.

As the CEC project progresses, we will continue to study teachers' instructional practices, attitudes, and beliefs as part of the evaluation CEC inquiry process. The group has discussed the importance of observing each other's classrooms to gather data and provide meaningful professional feedback to colleagues. Monitoring the results of collaborative inquiry typically leads to new questions and enhances the focus of program evaluation. As the CEC partnership continues to meet on a regular basis to discuss issues related to mathematics teaching and learning we will repeat the CEC inquiry process, in effect building a culture for sustained evaluation and assessment of educational programs in the school.

Discussion

In this chapter we described a collaborative inquiry model that was used to develop a partnership between university mathematics and science educators and urban schools. Through this collaborative inquiry model we were able to help develop capacity for K-12 teachers to make data-based decisions. The most powerful aspect of the process was that teachers themselves were equal partners in the evaluation process and decision making regarding their mathematics curriculum, instruction, and assessment. It was a bottom-up approach, rather than a top-down mandate from the district administration. This empowered the teachers to push for change, and in some ways, gave the teachers more credibility with their colleagues in the schools. They were able to take a leadership role in the schools and move toward using evidence to develop shared values and norms and to use the evidence to change practice. By participating as true partners in collaborative evaluation activities, a level of trust was created that helped teachers feel comfortable confronting aspects of their practice that could be improved. The teachers on the CEC team work in the demanding environment of an urban school in an era of public accountability. It could be argued that many of the changes the teachers made were things they should have been doing before the CEC project began. The reality is that what we know about effective mathematics teaching practice is not always part of teachers' day-to-day work (Weiss & Pasley, 2004; Weiss, Pasley, Smith, Banilower, & Heck, 2003). In addition, focusing on evaluation and data-based decision making is not traditionally considered part of teachers' job duties. The collaborative inquiry partnership established through this project provides a model that others can follow to help teachers improve programs in important and meaningful ways.

It is important in the fields of mathematics and science to build new cultures in schools for conducting and using results of inquiries (Chval et al., 2006). A system for school-based inquiries should be "one in which more research is motivated by practice; one in which changes in school practice are motivated by research; and one in which findings are expediently fed into the system, considered, and acted on" (Chval et al., 2006, p. 163). Collaborative investigations that focus on program evaluation and data-based decision making can help the field build an effective culture for integrating research and practice. The unique model for collaborative evaluation utilized through the CEC project has improved the teachers' ability to collect and analyze schoolwide data, facilitated collective examination of student assessment results, involved teachers in the evaluation of school and district mathematics and science programs, supported teacher analysis of instructional practices, and built infrastructure for data collection and analysis in the schools of the project.

The Collaborative Evaluation Communities model is a means of helping to create professional structures that can move beyond typical teacher inquiry or classroom-based action research and move toward addressing whole school and district issues. Sarason (1996) has urged school districts and universities to create opportunities for partnering, and the CEC project provides a unique model for creating such collaborations. The CEC partnership can break down the barriers to collaboration faced by schools and universities, it can help teachers develop the capacity to engage in data-based decision making, and it can help us work toward the ultimate goal of ensuring that all students achieve in mathematics and science.

References

Bissex, G. L. (1994). Teacher research: Seeing what we are doing. In T. Shanahan (Ed.), *Teachers thinking, teachers knowing* (pp. 88–104). Urbana, IL: National Council of Teachers of English.

Chval, K. B., Reys, R., Reys, B., Tarr, J. E., & Chavez, O. (2006). Pressures to improve student performance: A context that both urges and impedes school-based research. *Journal for Research in Mathematics Education, 37*(3), 158–166.

Cochran-Smith, M., & Lytle, S. (1993). *Inside/outside: Teacher research and knowledge.* New York: Teachers College Press.

Cochran-Smith, M., & Lytle, S. (1999). Relationships of knowledge and practice: Teacher learning in communities. *Review of Research in Education, 24,* 249–305.

Cuban, L. (1992). Managing dilemmas while building professional communities. *Educational Researcher, 21*(1), 4–11.

Darling-Hammond, L. (1997). *The right to learn: A blueprint for creating schools that work.* San Francisco: Jossey-Bass.

Elliot, J. (1991). *Action research for educational change.* Philadelphia: Open University Press.

Elmore, R. (2000, October). *Issues for teacher research.* Paper presented at the Spencer Foundation Teacher Research Symposium, Boston.

Elmore, R., & Burney, D. (1999). Investigations in teacher learning. In L. Darling-Hammond & G. Sykes (Eds.), *Teaching as the learning profession: Handbook of policy and practice* (pp. 263–292). San Francisco: Jossey-Bass.

Fullan, M. (1993). Why teachers must become change agents. *Educational Leadership, 5*(6), 12–17.

Henson, K. T. (1996). Teachers as researchers. In J. Sikula, T. J. Buttery, & E. Guyton (Eds.), *Handbook of research on teacher education* (pp. 53–66). New York: Simon & Schuster Macmillan.

Huffman, D., & Kalnin, J. (2003). Collaborative inquiry to make databased decisions in schools. *Teaching and Teacher Education, 19*(6), 569–580.

Kalnin, J. (2000). *Teachers learning: A cooperative research group in action.* Unpublished doctoral dissertation, University of California, Berkeley.

King, J. A. (2002). Building the evaluation capacity in a school district. *New Directions for Evaluation, 93,* 63–80.

King, J. A. (2005). A proposal to build evaluation capacity at the Bunche–Da Vinci Learning Partnership Academy. *New Directions for Evaluation, 106,* 85–97.

Kowalski, T. J., Lasley, T. J., & Mahoney, J. W. (2008). *Data-driven decisions and school leadership: Best practices for school improvement.* Boston: Pearson Education.

Little, J. W. (1999). Organizing schools for teacher learning. In L. Darling-Hammond & G. Sykes (Eds.), *Teaching as the learning profession: Handbook of policy and practice* (pp. 233–262). San Francisco: Jossey-Bass.

Long, S. (2004). Separating rhetoric from reality: Supporting teachers in negotiating beyond the status quo. *Journal of Teacher Education, 55*(2), 141–153.

National Research Council (1999). *Global perspectives for local action: Using TIMSS to improve U.S. mathematics and science education.* Washington, DC: National Academy Press.

Noffke, S. (1997). Professional, personal, and political dimensions of action research. *Review of Research in Education, 22,* 305–343.

Parsons, B. A. (2002). *Evaluative inquiry: Using evaluation to promote student success.* Thousand Oaks, CA: Corwin Press.

Peak, L. (1996). *Pursuing excellence: A study of U.S. eighth-grade mathematics and science teaching, learning, curriculum, and achievement in international context.* National Center for Educational Statistics, NCES 97–198. Washington, DC: U.S. Government Printing Office.

Popham, W. J. (2006). *Assessment for educational leaders.* Boston: Allyn & Bacon.

Robb, L. (2000). *Redefining staff development: A collaborative model for teachers and administrators.* Portsmouth, NH: Heinemann.

Routman, R. (2000). *Conversations: Strategies for teaching, learning, and evaluating.* Portsmouth, NH: Heinemann.

Sarason, S. B. (1996). *Barometers of change: Individual, educational, and social transformation.* San Francisco: Jossey-Bass.

Sarason, S. B., & Lorentz, E. M. (1998). *Crossing boundaries: Collaboration, coordination, and the redefinition of resources.* San Francisco: Jossey-Bass.

Stigler, J.W., & Hiebert, J. (1999). *The teaching gap: Best ideas from the world's teachers for improving education in the classroom.* New York: Free Press.

Stockdill, S. H., Baizerman, M., & Compton, D. W. (2002). Toward a definition of the ECB process: A conversation with the ECB literature. *New Directions for Evaluation, 93,* 7–25.

TERC (1998). *Investigations in number, data, and space.* White Plains, NY: Dale Seymour Publications.

Weiss, I. R., & Pasley, J. D. (2004). What is high-quality instruction? *Educational Leadership, 61*(5), 24–28.

Weiss, I. R., Pasley, J. D., Smith, P. S., Banilower, E. R., & Heck, D. J. (2003). *Looking inside the classroom: A study of K-12 mathematics and science education in the United States.* Chapel Hill, NC: Horizon Research. Retrieved January 15, 2008, from www.horizon=research.com/insidetheclassroom/reports/highlights/highlights.pdf

22

Evidential Reasoning and Decision Support in Assessment of Teacher Practice

Arthur M. Recesso and Sally J. Zepeda
University of Georgia

Introduction

Applications of evidential reasoning as an approach to assessment of teacher practices have gone unnoticed in education. Other sectors, such as law, use evidential reasoning methods for systematic interpretation of evidence to increase certainty and decrease doubt about events. Teaching is a complex series of events and it is difficult to explain what it means to enact effective teaching or standards-based practices, for example. Novice teachers, those who are preservice or in the induction phases, find it difficult to operationalize such global terms or understand what it means to enact standards-based strategies. Development of pedagogy and pedagogical content knowledge requires substantive feedback from those who assess and guide growth. Evidential reasoning methods and tools bring forward to education an opportunity to overcome this and other challenges. Deconstructing practice into its constitutive elements allows the assessment to be focused and manageable. Thus, an instructional leader is able to discuss collaboratively with a teacher the extent to which a standard of teaching is present or absent.

Our intent here is to present an instantiation of methods and a tool in the context of assessment of teacher practices for growth and support. Through close collaborations with educator preparation and now local schools, we have discovered ways in which principled approaches to systematic use of evidence inform continuous growth and support. We discuss a series of processes and a tool that enhance assessment of teacher practice extensible to all areas of educator preparation, educational assessment, and decision making. From our ongoing research to develop a methodology that tightly couples performance assessment with decision making emerges a principled and systematic approach to using evidence. First, our attention focuses on our purpose to examine teacher assessment and building leader decision making.

National Focus on Teacher Assessment

The No Child Left Behind (NCLB) accountability specifications require continuous monitoring and improvement of student achievement (NCLB, 2001). Much of this accountability falls to individual school principals, who assume many roles and responsibilities (Leithwood, 1994; Sebring & Bryk, 2000). Paradoxically, many of the provisions of NCLB force leaders to make decisions about the quality of teaching with a limited set, even sole source, of evidence (student achievement data). Leaders are handcuffed by the narrow definition of "evidence-based" adopted from the clinical trial methodologies used in medicine. Clearly, student achievement data are a valuable form of evidence that can explain learner progress toward expected outcomes. However, researchers have found other forms of evidence such as video capture of teachers' practice to have high levels of force in explaining what happened in the classroom leading to learning outcomes (Pea & Hoffert, 2007; Sherin & van Es, 2005; van Es & Sherin, 2002). Furthermore, NCLB requires the leader to train teachers in the uses of evidence-based instructional strategies. This assumes that the leader fully understands the problem based on an analysis of student achievement, and the leader is prepared to make a decision (selecting an appropriate intervention). Other sectors such as law have provided more powerful and useful ways to reach decisions with greater certainty in high stakes situations or making a more accurate diagnosis.

We are suggesting that we have the correct diagnosis—teachers need more support, but the mandated treatment (use of evidence-based interventions) is the very last step in the decision-making process. We propose that school-building leaders can make considerable improvements to the quality of teaching by using evidential reasoning and more appropriate tools to capture evidence to inform decision making. Selecting the most appropriate solution depends on how well informed the decision is. The probability of making the most appropriate decisions increases through the use of logical and systematic inquiry into the relationships between evidence and events and other evidence (Kadane & Schum, 1996; Schum, 1994). The very core of an argument is to increase the certainty of knowing what occurred during the act of teaching. Hence, this certainty allows a better choice of treatment aligned with explanations generated and more purposefully focused on needs. The certainty unfolds more clearly from not only the evidence but also through the methods of collecting and interpreting evidence. The utility of interpretation emerges from the validity of the instruments used to amplify fine grain elements of practice and apply a gradient (Kane, 1992, 2004; Messick, 1987).

Given effective leadership and opportunities to access a wide array of evidence of their influence on student achievement, teachers will improve daily implementation of effective instruction (Stigler, Gonzales, Kawanaka, Knoll, & Serrano, 1999; Teale, Leu, Labbo, & Kinzer, 2002; Zepeda, 2005). Typically, leaders are challenged by local capacity (e.g., funding) to provide support (e.g., instructional supervisors). Often the principal, for example, is overwhelmed with the sheer number of evaluations that must be conducted before the end of the school year. Hence, there are significant hurdles for implementing processes to clarify for the teacher which activities actually influence (or should influence) student learning priorities. Just as beginning teachers assume their approaches to be effective, school leaders assume that their support is helpful, lacking evidence of the impact of their teacher support on student achievement. The cycle becomes self-perpetuating as teachers teach and school leaders evaluate instead of assess—each fulfilling their respective roles without direct evidence of the link between teaching practice being implemented and defined student needs, and the collective impact of their respective practices on student learning. Leaders can no longer rely solely on informal observation, anecdotal recollection, and unsubstantiated perceptions in their interactions with teachers. We need to break this cycle.

Systemic reform through systematic use of a wide array of evidence can improve leadership quality, teacher quality, and student achievement (Spillane, Halverson, & Diamond, 2001). We propose Evidential Reasoning and Decision Support (ERDS), a systematic approach designed to link leadership, teaching practices, and student achievement, to provide tools through which these links can be made productive in the mutual support provided, and to use evidence of student learning and teaching practices as the cornerstones of planning, implementing, and assessing quality teaching-learning practices (Recesso et al., in press).

Using Evidence for Growth and Support

In this chapter, we focus on the integration of ERDS methods into teacher assessment. Through close collaboration with local schools and preparation programs, we elucidate how evidence-informed assessment practices that systematically identify, collect, and interpret evidence to assist in making decisions. Evidential reasoning methods are combined with instruments to measure progress and to delineate success or deficiency in classroom practices. Feedback is generated from interpretations of multiple pieces of convergent evidence known to embody critical attributes of effective practice presented in a teaching standards framework. Teaching standards that define what a teacher should know and be able to do are widely accessible including the Interstate New Teacher and Support Consortium (INTASC), National Board of Professional Teaching Standards (NBTS), and subject-specific standards such as the National Science Teaching Association (NSTA) and National Council of Teachers of Mathematics (NCTM) Standards. Using ERDS methods and a technology-based tool both teachers and instructional leaders can communicate growth or areas in need of improvement with greater certainty (e.g., Zepeda, 2005, 2006, 2007; Zepeda & Ponticell, 1998).

Foundations of Evidential Reasoning

Evidence is defined as all matter (physical or neurological) that can be detected by some device (organic or mechanical) for the purposes of explaining events linked to a hypothesis (Bentham, as cited in Twining, 1985; Schum, 1994). Something becomes evidence the moment educators passively receive it (someone tells the principal about discipline problems in a classroom) or purposefully seeks it out (classroom observation) to make sense of an event (classroom discipline) and build an argument (discipline rules are not being implemented). Evidence such as instructional practices and learning processes are what are captured through procedures such as classroom observations. Through our work, we have been able to enhance classroom observation through the use of video-capture and more extensive uses of data collection tools (Recesso, in press; Zepeda, 2005, 2007).

Four Stages of Evidence Methodology Related to Assessment

Evidential reasoning, drawing conclusions from multiple sources of evidence, has a complex history. What has become an approach to using evidence in many fields evolved from the early days of philosophers who were contemplating if the Earth was round to the contemporary psychology and Forensic sciences (Twining, 1985). During the last 100 years, health, intelligence, and legal sectors have experienced the greatest influence from the evolution of ideas, methods, and tools grounded in evidential reasoning. Schum (1994) presents one of the most well-articulated frameworks for studying and using evidence across any sector. Recently, educational researchers such as Mislevy, Steinberg, and Almond (2003) and Almond, Steinberg, and Mislevy (2002) have acknowledged the influence of Schum's work in developing innovative methods and technology-based tools for assessing student learning. Evidence Centered Design (ECD) has emerged as a principled way to structure student assessments embedded with tasks to generate evidence of learning (Mislevy, et al., 2003). Furthermore, ECD has been instantiated in Principled Assessment Designs for Inquiry (PADI), a technology-based tool that combines the theoretical foundations of assessment with technology applications. Making the design of quality assessments accessible to researchers and practitioners shows promise for increasing the education sector's capacity to generate evidence known to explain when and to what extent learning occurs.

Making sense of evidence in ways that inform growth and success is the foundation for the ERDS approach. Herein, we present a four-stage methodology for using evidence in systematic ways that inform decisions to improve or replicate effective teaching practices. After introducing the methods, we demonstrate how the stages are integrated into individual teacher performance assessments.

Stages of Evidential Reasoning and Decision Support

Stage 1. Trigger   A trigger is a signal or cue that emerges from an event that causes a person to think about support for teacher growth and success.

People do not just make decisions. There is always something, an event or a piece of evidence, which cues us to take notice, think, and then act. Principals do not just assess teachers' practice—they have acquired varying levels of sensitivity based on the source (e.g., report of student achievement data) and situation (e.g., school has not made Academic Yearly Progress) in which triggers are generated. Common sources of triggers associated with teacher assessment are multidimensional and can be categorized as follows.

> Intentional stimuli—these stimuli are emitted purposely and are directed at or sought by the receiver (may be solicited or unsolicited).
>> Directive—mandates, rules, laws, explicit directions, "you must"
>> Suggestive—unsolicited suggestions, "you should"
>> Implied—reports from others with the intention of precipitating decision; scores

Examples—NCLB mandates the use of student achievement test scores.
The School Board passes a policy to adopt new curricula.
Sixth-grade math scores have increased this year.
Unintentional stimuli—these stimuli are emitted without the intention of pre-cipitating a decision on the part of the receiver and are not directed purposely at the receiver (stimuli are unsolicited).
Incidental—observations, reports, experiences, unintentional learning
Natural stimuli—these are naturally occurring, unsolicited, undirected, and unalterable (e.g., demographics, time).
Examples—You observe an innovative way of teaching writing.
Newspaper article claims birth rates are on the rise.
Discipline reports are on the rise from one classroom.

The ability to manage and discriminate between levels of importance of each trigger helps gauge sensitivity to events. Principals must be attentive to the signals (i.e., student discipline problems on the rise) to provide assistance when teachers are in need. In contrast, reacting continuously to many triggers leads to constantly trying to put out fires and getting very little accomplished. The middle ground, finding the most appropriate level of sensitivity in an era of multiple simultaneous reform efforts, enables the principal to focus strategically on a few critical needs. In sum, the triggers linked to teacher assessment are important as they bring attention to what to focus on during a classroom observation. Managing triggers is a learned process and is critical to help one focus on explaining how a specific part of teaching practice is impacting student achievement.

Using a Common Framework to Frame Triggers in Practice

All 50 states have standards for teacher practice and student learning standards (Council of Chief State School Officers, 2003). Furthermore, each of the subject domains (e.g., science) has a standards framework espousing what are valued practices and integral knowledge to enact effective practice. These documents are useful resources for linking triggers to expected practices and generating clear focus—one that is centered on a fine grain attribute, the critical constitutive elements that make up a practice. Assessment of "effective teaching" or even inquiry-based instruction is too global. The concepts are so ambiguous that it is very difficult for teachers (especially novices) to grasp what is meant by effective teaching and, thus, nearly impossible to observe and determine if it occurred. Hence, using a standards document such as those available from national accreditation organizations (NCATE, SACS) and state agencies (Department of Education or Board of Regents) one is able to link a trigger (test scores show low assessment of new learning standards) to the domain-attribute-item (Planning and Instruction: teachers use instructional strategies reflecting a standards-based classroom) and establish the focus of the assessment (observe teachers' enactment of instructional strategies in the classroom). With a clear focus statement, an assessment becomes manageable and purposeful. Once both the prin-cipal and the teacher know what will be assessed, they can focus on how to capture evidence of the practice.

A principal might capture a trigger during an informal walkthrough of a classroom (see Figure 22.1). In this case, the principal has documented when the event took place and what was witnessed. Upon returning to the office, the principal was able to align the event to a specific attribute. The process refines what other teachers will be asked to replicate and show about this practice. It becomes clear about what in practice is important. In fact, other teachers can use the same instrument to observe their own or practices of others.

Stage 2. Marshalling Evidence   Marshalling evidence includes identifying, collecting, and using a wide array of evidence known to help explain events (Schum, 1994) such as planning (lesson plans), teaching (video of practice), and learning (student work samples or student achievement data). Evidence classification is based on its properties including credibility, relevance, type, and form.

Credibility of evidence rests primarily with the source (Schum, 1994). Self-assessment is often not a factor in recertification decisions because of the high stakes involved. In fact, in law and medicine evidence generated from human memory must be bolstered with other complementary or harmonious evidence to strengthen the direction of an argument. The force of evidence, the extent to which it explains an event with a known level of certainty, is attributed, in part, to knowing the credibility of the source. Video as evidence of an event is often free from bias and thus carries a high level of credibility.

Evidence is relevant when it is known to represent an event (Schum, 1994). A properly positioned video camera (back of the classroom) provides evidence (video of instructional strategies) with high relevance (video from back of the classroom is known to be appropriate for capturing whole class instruction). Student achievement data are evidence of student learning and therefore relevant. The same data are relevant to measuring the effectiveness of instruction but less than other evidence such as video capturing actual enactment of instruction. Hence, to the extent that

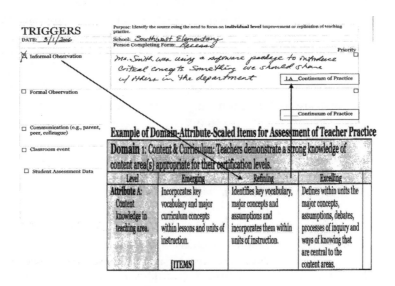

Figure 22.1 Trigger aligned to a common framework.

more relevant evidence is available it would be the first choice in the basis for decision making.

Very rarely does evidence provide absolute certainty (especially a sole source). Variance in levels of credibility of sources and relevance of evidence are important factors leading decision makers to consider how to marshal and combine evidence known to help explain events with a high level of certainty. An understanding of the types and forms of evidence further assists in selecting the best available evidence known to help explain the relationship between leadership decision making, teacher practice, and student performance. Table 22.1 provides a sample of the types and forms of evidence our school and teacher education program collaborators found to influence assessment of teacher practice.

Read Table 22.1 from bottom to top. You will notice a link between the leader's vision setting, teacher's enactment, and learner's demonstration of knowledge. Hence, the evidence is an embodiment of an event (vision setting, enactment, demonstrating learning). This is not to say that all of the evidence must be collected and analyzed. Depending on the question being asked, you may purposely select the best evidence to explain the events. Concentrating on the teacher's practice, for example, the principal may collect a lesson plan, video of enactment, and student work sample as evidence that can easily be shared with other teachers to see the success.

Stage 3. Interpretation: Making Sense of the Evidence Sense making can be enhanced by using instruments that are aligned with a common framework of teaching practices that amplify critical attributes known to influence student learning.

Interpretation extracts information from evidence to generate explanations. The power of an explanation increases through the use of instruments (tests, rubrics, observation forms) known to increase certainty and decrease doubt (Mislevy & Gitomer, 1996; Shafer, 1976; Yang & Singh, 1994). That is, through the use of well-designed valid instruments one can say with confidence that a classroom event (a teacher's use of software for students to construct knowledge about ratios) leads to student mastery knowledge. Using the metaphor of a lens to amplify attributes of practice or suppress the noise of extraneous information, we can operationalize how an instrument helps explain those parts of practice that need improvement (Hill,

Table 22.1 Evidence of teacher and learner performance.

Type	*Form*
Learner performance	Standardized test scores
	Student work samples
	Responses to open-ended questions
Teacher	Video enactment of strategies
	Lesson plan with strategies defined
	Pre-planning discussion about strategies to use
Leader practice	Observation of teacher's practices
	Funding professional learning on instructional strategies
	Vision for teaching and learning

Hannafin, & Recesso, 2008). Principals who assess teacher practice are often observing teachers outside of the subject domains in which they are familiar (Zepeda & Mayers, 2004). Even for principals who do have familiarity with a subject area, inquiry can look very messy where practices are non-traditional. Hence, using a lens created to focus on the attributes of a specific practice (students working in small groups and using simple machines to learn the concepts of mechanical advantage) improves the probability for quality feedback given to the teacher (Zepeda, 2005, 2007; Zepeda & Mayers, 2004). The power of interpretation is further enhanced when an instrument is applied to combinations of evidence, each contributing a given level of certainty, from which one derives an explanation that can be tightly aligned with an intervention (professional learning) or useful resource (appropriate instructional materials).

Stage 4. Course of Action   Select and implement intervention or resource appropriate for improving deficiencies and replicating success in teaching practices.

The final stage in the first iteration of the cycle is making the decision. A decision is the act of selecting an intervention and resource from existing knowledge and then implementing it in an effort to support changes in practice or replicate success. Interventions may involve focused professional development and other supports such as peer coaching. The decision is to link the teacher's needs (e.g., content knowledge, pedagogy, pedagogical content knowledge) with a support mechanism for learning and then enactment demonstrating progress toward meeting an expectation of increased knowledge and understanding about practice. A solution may be to adopt a new curriculum known to increase student achievement. It is critical not to operate from a deficit model. There are great successes in classrooms that are often not captured. Clearly, we need to do a better job of establishing processes for capturing and codifying through appropriate lenses what it means to enact standards-based practices in classrooms for others to see and learn. Having such a resource affords all teachers access to concrete deconstructed examples of success to support their learning and to improve teaching in ways that impact student learning and achievement.

Affordances of Video Evidence and Technology-Based Tools

Video is a powerful form of evidence for capturing actual events for live or post-event analysis. The utility of this and other kinds of evidence is realized through the use of Web-based technology to relieve the user's cognitive load when using an intricate methodology. Furthermore, the advent of user-friendly graphic interfaces and embedded guides aids in gaining efficiency. In this section we demonstrate how existing technologies give instructional leaders a tool to systematically link triggers, foci, and video evidence to understand with increased certainty and explain events as they really occurred. After providing an introduction to one type of tool for using ERDS methods and interpreting video we will present a case from our work in the field.

Video Capture Tools

Video capture equipment has been used in education since the 1960s. Video of classroom practices has since been a tool used in teacher education programs as a way of promoting reflection (Fuller & Manning, 1973). For example, student teachers often practice in front of the camera or even capture actual classroom practices to bring back to the university for collaborative reflection with peers and faculty supervisors. More recently, video has become a part of mentoring processes for beginning teachers (Pea & Hoffert, 2007; Sherin & van Es, 2005; van Es & Sherin, 2002). As advances in technology make video annotation easier and more affordable, the pace for developing tools also quickens. A catalyst for this work was the U.S. Education Department's Preparing Tomorrow's Teachers to use Technology (PT3) Program. Recesso and Hannafin (2003), for example, developed a video annotation tool with the intent that it be integrated into preservice preparation programs as an instrument to support assessment and continuous growth.

The Video Analysis Tool (VAT) implements standardized Web-based interface functions to populate a robust database and infinitely expandable storage system (Recesso et al., in press). Teachers have two options for getting their video into VAT. Video cameras connected to a computer network, called Internet Protocol (IP) video cameras, capture live events and immediately transmit video for live or post-event analysis. A great benefit of this technology is in the design of the camera. No tapes are required, there are no batteries to replace, and the teacher does not have to be concerned with the video camera configuration. Once the configuration of the camera is set through the interface in VAT, the video camera starts capturing, the video file is sent to storage, and the video camera turns off as stipulated in the teacher-defined settings.

As a second option, video of teaching and learning may also be uploaded manually into the system for analysis. This provides end users with flexibility to use any video recording equipment available to them. Teachers may choose to use any typical consumer-line video camera that is most readily available, capture the video, and upload it from tape or video camera embedded hard-drive to the VAT system. If the teacher chooses to use the live streaming functionality, the system permits the teacher to allow someone access (e.g., instructional leader) to view and code video of the practices live (as the events actually take place). Video uploaded post-event also requires that the teacher give permission to others (e.g., peer) who may simultaneously view and code the video. If the viewers so choose, they may code and annotate the video, all of which is stored in the database with the video. All of the metadata associated with segmenting video (e.g., coding using a rubric) into manageable parts (e.g., a three-minute video clip as compared to an hour), the video, and descriptions provided by users are stored in a database ready for search, retrieval, and analysis on demand.

Users access a video collection through the Web interface and choose to analyze or view videos. Clips are segmented through the *analyze video* function by depressing start time and end time (see Figure 22.2). Annotation of the clip is added through the standard text entry *comments* window on the right side of the browser. Users who have preselected a *lens* are also able to associate the *clips* (bottom left corner of browser) with attributes of practice and a level of performance (e.g., basic, advanced, proficient).

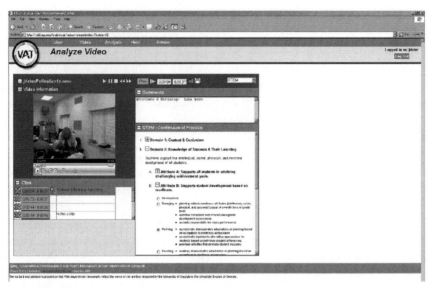

Figure 22.2 User analysis of video to segment clips in VAT.

Video owners may choose to view codified video themselves and/or share clips with others through the *view analysis* function. The principal and teacher, for example, may view the clips together or asynchronously each providing insight into the events as they actually unfolded in the classroom. Mentors may also request the use of the teacher's videos as exemplars (e.g., standards-based practices) to be shared with other preservice teachers. In VAT, teachers are owners of the video they capture, and they have complete control of who views or analyzes their practices. By accessing the *show analysis* function, teachers grant or deny permission for someone else to access the video (see Figure 22.3). With permission, other teachers are able to access the video and associated codes to see what constitutes practice (e.g., mastery of questioning strategies).

As a third option, users may compare and contrast events and/or the coding associated with video clips using the *view analysis* function and selecting two video files (see Figure 22.4). A multitude of uses have emerged for the dual-view function. Using VAT to create exemplars, videos coded by experts in the field, one can test his or her knowledge of practice (see if the same attributes of effective teaching) can be found or even compare his or her own practices. Teachers using VAT have uploaded a video of their classroom practice and multiple videos of students working in small groups. Using the view analysis function they can simultaneously view teaching and students' learning. This has been a powerful view for teachers to compare and contrast practice (e.g., expertly coded case compared to the teacher's coding of the same video) or even simultaneously view teacher practices in one window while students construct and apply knowledge in the other window. A teacher participating in one of our projects actually generated this idea—she wanted to see how the students reacted to her teaching as feedback about her use of strategies facilitating learning of mathematics. Teachers use VAT to see strategies *in situ* and to code discrepancies between espoused and actual practice.

In summary, the following illustrates how VAT directly supports ERDS:

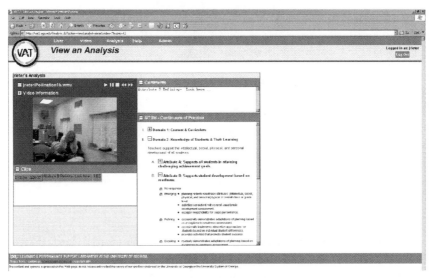

Figure 22.3 View analysis completed in VAT.

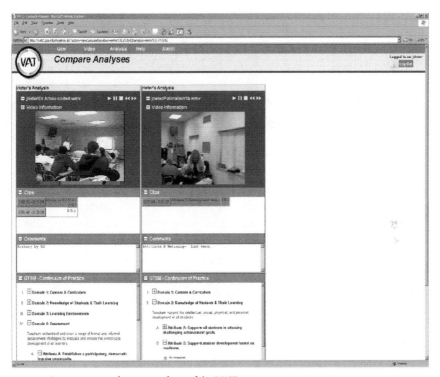

Figure 22.4 Compare analyses conducted in VAT.

VAT for Learning Triggers:

- Educators learn about triggers by watching pre-captured events (i.e., instructional strategies not aligned to expected practices) with an instructional leader who points out the specifics of an event that are important. Users also learn to gauge sensitivity to triggers and to act accordingly.

- Instruments within the VAT system assist educators' alignment of triggers to standards of practice—thus increasing granularity and clarifying the focus on improving a specific attribute of practice.

VAT for Collecting and Using Evidence:

- Live capture and post-event upload of video evidence is permitted for the user to see and share classroom practices. Users can capture evidence within close proximity of the actual event (e.g., camera focused on the student group conducting an experiment as it happens in the class). Furthermore, VAT allows for continuous replay and permanent storage for future access.

VAT for Interpretation and Explanations:

- Teaching frameworks (teaching and learning standards) and instruments (validated for measuring progress) can be uploaded into the system for subsequent codification of events. The process allows users to assess self and others' practices, gauge progress, and determine specific needs for support.

ERDS and VAT in Teacher Assessment

In this section, we present a case study in redesigning teacher assessment through the design of procedures informed by the principles and processes of ERDS. There are many complexities associated with the assessment of teaching and learning, and there are many ways to approach it (Danielson & McGreal, 2000; Wilkerson & Lang, 2007; Zepeda, 2005, 2007). Assessments vary for the purposes they serve. For example, testing for licensure at entry into the profession is a type of assessment. However, assessments are made across the career from the point of entry to the end of the career. Assessments can include standard evaluation of teaching using check-lists, classroom observations, and surveys. In this chapter, we are examining the assessment of teaching through the lens of evidential reasoning. The process is enhanced through VAT and its affordances to capture performance and enactments of teaching and student learning. Following what we know about the power of data collection through the uses of instructional supervision where a school leader conducts pre-observation conferences, observes teachers teaching, and then conducts post-observation conferences, we propose that there is a more reasoned and purposeful way to collect evidence for teachers and leaders to make sense. This approach is examined in this case.

Three pillars of the approach are anchored to what we know are critical aspects of effective instructional supervision (Zepeda 2005, 2006, 2007; Zepeda & Ponticell, 1998):

Pillar I.   Measure growth
Pillar II.   Provide continuous support
Pillar III.   Use highly collaborative processes

We add a fourth pillar; a deliberate focus on evidential reasoning to provide explanation and insight constructed by the teacher and leader to better understand the teaching and learning events.

Pillar IV.   Systematic use of evidence

To provide general parameters for the discussion, we describe the approach as it is implemented with individual induction teachers in order to make decisions using evidence to determine needs for and success of differentiated success support.

Case Context

We offer a case to illustrate how ERDS methods complement the work of the principal enacting instructional leadership and the practice of classroom observations vis-à-vis instructional supervision in a local school context. In brief, for the context of our illustration, instructional supervision is defined as the pre-observation conference, the classroom observation, and the post-observation conference. The clinical model of instructional supervision is a mainstay in assessment of teacher performance. Morton Middle School (MMS) is part of a large and fast growing school system located outside of a large metro area. MMS is implementing new statewide student performance standards in sixth-grade mathematics this year and sixth-grade science next year. The principal is new to MMS and has a successful track record in other buildings and is well respected in the school system. Thus far, the teachers have attended mandatory training about the standards provided by the state education department and the local system. Next school year, the schools will be implementing the standards. The school system's central administration has required all principals to report on implementation progress. The superintendent and Board want to know how successful teachers are in implementing new standards-based practices. Clearly, a decline in student performance will not be acceptable. The principal of MMS has added pressure of leading a school on the "needs improvement" list for two consecutive years. Furthermore, it is clear that the previous principal's teacher assessment processes were perfunctory; he used check-lists and spent little time in classrooms. The new principal began using the ERDS approach and created procedures for conducting teacher assessments.

Bringing Teacher Practice into Focus

MMS building-level performance has historically been lower than the school system and state averages. The principal has in hand the student achievement data reports from the previous years. There is a pattern of students doing poorly in sub-domain areas such as decimals and fractions. The principal has moved attention from the very global (school is underperforming) to the less ambiguous (new learning performance standards) to a more refined focus (sixth-grade mathematics: decimals and fractions). Yet, the principal knows the focus is not fine grain enough. The principal wants the focus to be observable (e.g., using computer software to teach decimals) and measurable along a continuum of growth (no evidence to exemplary practice) to fit into the plan for revitalizing the teacher assessment model. Hence, the principal engages faculty and staff to articulate what makes something standards-based teaching and to state specifically what standards-based teaching of decimals is and looks like. Together the principal and teachers ask if this expectation of standards-based practice is different from current practices and if so, how?

The principal uses the triggers (new state-mandated sixth-grade mathematics learning standards, low school performance in sixth-grade mathematics) to communicate schoolwide needs for improvement in a meeting with faculty and staff. The principal reiterates a commitment to revising the current teacher assessment procedures to define individual needs for growth and support. At the meeting, the principal presents the issues and uses a visual aid to highlight student performance standards (with data showing "needs improvement" based on existing test scores). Next, a version of the image shows the alignment of teacher performance standards (and the specific attributes that are critical elements of the practice) with the student learning standards. A rubric for assessing progress is shown and explained. It becomes clear there is a lot of work to be done, more than could be attended to in one year. The principal opens a discussion of what attributes all teachers will focus on first (they choose two to three for the year) and asks grade level subject area teachers (sixth-grade math) to add others as part of their assessment. As a final step, the principal and teachers state the foci and how they are aligned to teacher and learner performance standards. The principal announces that in the pre-observation conference there will be further discussion about how the interpretation of evidence will inform what types of differentiated support will be provided (Zepeda, 2007).

Individual Pre-observation Conference

A pre-observation conference is arranged with each sixth-grade mathematics teacher. Collaboratively, the principal and teachers write a focus statement for each of the two or three specific attributes they agreed to address this school year. Together, they develop an assessment plan including an evidence collection component. Many teachers choose to use the Video Analysis Tool (VAT) as a way to capture practices and student discourse.

Video Evidence of Teaching and Learning Events

The teacher refers to lesson plans to see when manipulatives will be used in class to teach fractions. Through VAT, the teacher is able to schedule the date for the Internet Protocol (IP) camera in the room to turn on automatically, record video of the teaching events, and audio of the discourse taking place. The IP video camera has been pre-mounted on the wall at the rear of the classroom. It has a sensitive mic to pick up the soft voices of the children and the video is very high quality. The camera requires no tapes or other settings. It turns on, captures the video, and streams it automatically across a secure network to mass storage. The teacher focuses on teaching and is able to view the video when she has time. In this case, the teacher permits the principal to view and code the live video through VAT.

Both the principal and the teacher access the video and code the events based on what they are viewing through VAT. They watch the video, look for important events defined by the foci, and place a digital marker at a place in time when they want to come back and visit later. The value of VAT is that the teacher can view the teaching by herself or in the company of the principal, perhaps a peer coach, or a mentor. The functions within VAT allow the principal and teacher to center their attention on the events while simply clicking a button to identify something of interest such as the use of manipulatives for teaching fractions. Later, they can return to these markers to annotate more refined feedback by using a lens that associates the events with a standard and a metric of quality of performance. In the present case, the use of manipulatives as a specific learner-centered strategy surrounding fractions is codified with NCTM standards and a 4-point growth scale of *not evident* to *mastery*. VAT allows the teacher to compare and contrast her own coding with the principal's coding through a dual-view window. Thus, feedback is very concrete and it is clear where there is success and needs for minor adjustments in the strategies that will benefit students.

Post-observation Conference: Making Sense of the Evidence

The principal and teacher have documents from the pre-observation conference, and the video capture of the teacher's classroom practices. During the post-observation conference, the teacher and the principal review the video capture and the annotations made on screen. Using the annotations and stopping at critical incidents, the teacher and the principal are able to discuss and interpret classroom practices. The principal and the teacher are able to pinpoint and assess instructional practices intended to support students' meeting content standards. Because VAT captures the totality of the room, the principal and teacher are also able to focus on how students respond to instruction. To support ongoing discussion and dialogue, the following guidelines are offered:

- Did the focus change during the process? If so, what effect did it have?
- Were there any discrepancies between your beliefs or recollection about practice and what the evidence says actually happened? If so, explain why.
- What was learned about progress toward goals and expectations established in the pre-observation conference?
- Is success or need for improvement defined in such a way that a course of action can be set?

Through these questions, the teacher and principal sit down at a computer and use VAT to watch a three-minute coded video clip and a five-minute video clip. Analyzing the evidence, they discover that the teacher did have access to resources appropriate for the age group and ability of the students. As they transition to talking about a course of action, the principal and teacher jointly agree that the teacher will attend a workshop on using manipulatives that is being supported through a grant awarded to the school system. They also agree that the teacher should observe coded videos of other teachers who have had success with this particular standard. The principal documents the feedback and discussion, and they agree to continue revisiting certain instructional strategies related to the standards.

Discussion

Using evidence-informed methods is a transformation in the way instructional leaders conduct teacher assessment and make decisions. Using evidential reasoning and the systematic interpretation of evidence are one way to address the uncertainty with which teachers' needs are defined and aligned with resources for improvement or replication of success. Currently, we are using the methods and tools in collaboration with those who assess prospective and practicing teachers in several different contexts as they develop and refine their professional knowledge and skills for teaching and their capacity to engage in continuous growth.

The instructional leaders and teachers with whom we have worked have gained greater self-knowledge of how to enact practices and goals for teaching in their domain areas. It is not easy for instructional leaders or teachers to confront and critique teaching, particularly new building level leaders who are in a phase of their career when certainty, self-confidence, and time to thoughtfully engage in assessment of teaching practices are limited. Providing both instructional leaders and teachers with opportunities early in their career to purposefully focus on assessment of practices will help them develop personal familiarity and comfort with looking for the most powerful and appropriate evidence, and building explanations from evidence in the process of making teaching- and learning-related decisions.

We have partnered with local schools to provide continuous access to VAT. In addition, educator preparation programs in the College of Education have integrated VAT/ERDS as a tool for assessing progress during field experiences. We expect our investigation with new populations of VAT users to reveal more systematic ways to support teachers' development and refinement of practice.

Technology to Support Decision Making

Multiple support mechanisms are often in place to assist with the building level and individual teacher assessment, success replication, and improvement procedures. Technology-based Support Systems are becoming more pervasive as usability and utility improve. State agencies, national organizations, universities, and research labs continue to develop Web-based versions of processes and tools to support the assessment processes. These systems often scaffold a form of structured assistance that can disappear as users become more proficient in the system. Built-in functions allow people to build cases that can be stored and contributed to by multiple people involved in the process. Users are able to upload and interpret evidence using a series of tools, build reports and portfolios, develop a growth plan, and enable expert review and assistance. Due to international standards set for programming it has become possible to connect multiple systems and share resources. A state agency may be developing a Web-portal, for example, to store lesson plans representing effective planning for standards-based classrooms. Another system that captures video of practices and aligns segmented clips with the same standards can be interconnected and viewed by users on a system. Such technology-based systems can only enhance and not supplant critical support mechanisms such as mentoring, coaching, critical friends, study groups, lesson study, action research, and growth plan development.

VAT Limitations/Considerations   While there are many positive aspects of VAT, there are also limitations and considerations to take into account. Perhaps the most common technical concern we encounter in using VAT with groups of teachers has to do with loading video into the system. If VAT users wish to load their own video into the system, they must know how to transfer video to their computer and convert the files to .wmv files before loading onto VAT. Often, an intermediary needs to be responsible for making sure the video is converted and loaded to VAT.

Second, in our work with area schools, we have uncovered technical challenges such as schools blocking video streaming into the school (hence, no video resources for teachers can be accessed); limited bandwidth, causing schools to be concerned about streaming across their networks; and limited expertise of school technology coordinators who are ultimately responsible for managing the school's network. Within a classroom, the viewing range of the video camera has been problematic at times. Mounted video cameras may limit the viewing area unless a wide-angle lens is attached to the camera. In addition, mounted cameras sometimes do not capture conversation clearly, nor are they able to record fine grain details of classroom events such as the writing on students' paper or white boards. Clearly, users can overcome all of these issues, but they may involve more time and effort than a user is willing to devote.

Finally, VAT is currently platform specific. VAT is accessible using a PC with a Windows operating system (XP, 2000, 98), Internet Explorer 6.0+, and Windows Media Player 9 or higher. Broadband internet provides the highest quality experience when a dedicated connection is available. Although wireless networks are widely accessible in public spaces, the experience of viewing video can be diminished if the bandwidth has been throttled by the provider. Any other required software such as Java-based applets is automatically downloaded when the user accesses the system. Given these limitations, we have been able to successfully use VAT in a variety of contexts with both individuals and groups of instructional leaders and teachers. When working with a group, we provide one session of group training for the use of VAT. We have been able to introduce VAT and allow for practice time within a 30-minute (or less) block of time. During these short VAT training sessions, we provide users with a "cheat sheet" that is downloadable from the VAT website.

Expanding the Use of VAT   VAT is undoubtedly a powerful tool in instructional leadership and assessment of teacher practices to encourage teachers to make purposeful and systematic inquiry a habit that will become increasingly valuable throughout their careers. In this chapter, we have focused on using VAT for the principal's assessment of teachers' practices. However, the use of VAT may be expanded to include opportunities for inquiry into one's own practice. VAT clips may be used as abbreviated video cases—"windows" into other teachers' classrooms that provide a means for learning others' practices in the process of defining and assessing one's own practice. The sixth-grade math teacher may choose clips of exemplary practices to demonstrate standards-based practices; for example, what instruction using investigations strategies looks like. By engaging in VAT analysis of others' practice, instructional leaders and teachers can clarify, confront, and revise their teaching practices in ways that impact student learning.

Conclusion

We have presented a series of processes and a technology-based tool that enhance decision making about teacher growth and development. ERDS is one conceptualization of how the principles and processes of a methodology (Recesso et al., in press) are translated into procedures for teacher assessment. Given evidence of supervisory support that influences classroom practice and student achievement, leaders can increase their understanding of the conditions that warrant various types and forms of assistance. Such an understanding of practice directly informs the next iteration of research and development on mechanisms of continuous support such as the next evidence-analysis tools to assist educational decision making.

References

Almond, R. G., Steinberg, L. S., & Mislevy, R. J. (2002). Enhancing the design and delivery of assessment systems: A four-process architecture. *Journal of Technology, Learning, and Assessment, 1*(5). Retrieved September 10, 2007, from http://escholarship.bc.edu/jtla/vol1/5

Council of Chief State School Officers (2003). *State content standards: A 50 state resource.* Retrieved January 20, 2008, from http://www.ccsso.org/content/pdfs/StateContentStandards.pdf

Danielson, C., & McGreal, T. L. (2000). *Teacher evaluation to enhance professional practice.* Alexandria, VA: Association for Supervision and Curriculum Development.

Fuller, F. F., & Manning, B. A. (1973). Self-confrontation reviewed: A conceptualization for video playback in teacher education. *Review of Educational Research, 43*(4), 469–528.

Hill, J., Hannafin, M., & Recesso, A. (2008). Creating a patchwork quilt for teaching and learning: The use of learning objects in teacher education. In P. Northrup (Ed.), *Learning objects for instruction: Design and evaluation* (pp. 261–280). Hershey, PA: Information Science Publishing.

Kadane, J. B., & Schum, D. A. (1996). *A probabilistic analysis of the Sacco and Vanzetti evidence.* New York: Wiley.

Kane, M. (1992). An argument-based approach to validity. *Psychological Bulletin, 112*(33), 527–535.

Kane, M. (2004). Certification testing as an illustration of argument-based validation. *Measurement, 2*(3), 135–170.

Leithwood, K. (1994). Leadership for restructuring. *Educational Administration Quarterly, 30*(4), 498–518.

Messick, S. (1987). *Validity.* Princeton, NJ: Educational Testing Service.

Mislevy, R. J., & Gitomer, D. H. (1996). The role of probability-based inference in an intelligent tutoring system. *User Modeling and User-Adopted Interaction, 5*, 252–282.

Mislevy, R. J., Steinberg, L. S., & Almond, R. G. (2003). On the structure of educational assessments. *Measurement: Interdisciplinary Research and Perspectives, 1*(1), 3–62.

No Child Left Behind Act of 2001, 20 U.S.C. 6301 et. Seq. (2001).

Pea, R., & Hoffert, E. (2007). Video workflow in the learning sciences: Prospects of emerging technologies for augmenting work practices. In R. Goldman, R. Pea, B. Barron, & S. J. Derry (Eds.), *Video research in the learning sciences* (pp. 427–460). Mahwah, NJ: Lawrence Erlbaum Associates.

Recesso, A., & Hannafin, M. (2003). *Evidence-based technology enhanced alternative curriculum in higher education (ETEACH)*. Project # P342A030009. Proposal funded by the U.S. Department of Education's Preparing Tomorrow's Teachers to use Technology (PT3) program office. Washington, DC: U.S. Department of Education.

Recesso, A., Hannafin, M., Wang, F., Deaton, B., Shepherd, C., & Rich, P. (in press). Direct evidence and the continuous evolution of teacher practice. In P. Adamy & N. Milman (Eds.), *Evaluating electionic portfolios in teacher education*. Greenwich, CT: Information Age Publishing, Inc.

Reilly, D. (2000). Linear or nonlinear? A metacognitive analysis of educational assumptions and reform efforts. *International Journal of Education Management, 14*(1), 7–15.

Schum, D. A. (1994). *The evidential foundations of probabilistic reasoning.* New York: John Wiley & Sons.

Sebring, P. B., & Bryk, A. S. (2000). School leadership and the bottom line in Chicago. *Phi Delta Kappan, 81*(6), 440–443.

Shafer, G. (1976). A theory of statistical evidence. In W. L. Harper & C. A. Hooker (Eds.), *Foundations of probability theory, statistical inference, and statistical theories of science, Vol. II* (pp. 365–436). Boston: Reidel Publishing Company.

Sherin, M. G., & van Es, E. A. (2005). Using video to support teachers' ability to notice classroom interactions. *Journal of Technology and Teacher Education, 13,* 475–491.

Spillane, J. P., Halverson, R., & Diamond, J. B. (2001). Investigating school leadership practice: A distributed perspective. *Educational Researcher, 30*(3), 23–28.

Stigler, J. W., Gonzales, P., Kawanaka, T., Knoll, S., & Serrano, A. (1999). *The TIMSS videotape classroom study: Methods and findings from an exploratory research project on eighth-grade mathematics instruction in Germany, Japan, and the United States.* Washington, DC: U.S. Department of Education.

Teale, W., Leu, D., Labbo, L., & Kinzer, C. (2002). The CTELL project: New ways technology can help educate tomorrow's reading teachers. *The Reading Teacher, 55*(7), 654–659.

Twining, W. L. (1985). *Theories of evidence: Bentham and Wigmore.* Stanford, CA: Stanford University Press.

van Es, E. A., & Sherin, M. G. (2002). Learning to notice: Scaffolding new teachers' interpretations of classroom interactions. *Journal of Technology and Teacher Education, 10*(4), 571–596.

Wilkerson, J. R., & Lang, W. S. (2007). *Assessing teacher competency: Five standards-based steps to valid measurement using the CAATS model.* Thousand Oaks, CA: Corwin Press.

Yang J. B., & Singh, M. G. (1994). An evidential reasoning approach for multiple attribute decision making with uncertainty. *IEEE Transactions on Systems, Man, and Cybernetics, 24*(1), 1–18.

Zepeda, S. J. (2005). *The instructional leader's guide to informal classroom observations.* Larchmont, NY: Eye on Education.

Zepeda, S. J. (2006). Classroom-based assessments of teaching and learning. In J. H. Stronge (Ed.), *Evaluating teaching: A guide to current thinking and best practice* (2nd ed., pp. 101–124). Thousand Oaks, CA: Corwin Press.

Zepeda, S. J. (2007). *Instructional supervision: Applying tools and concepts* (2nd ed.). Larchmont, NY: Eye on Education.

Zepeda, S. J., & Mayers, R. S. (2004). *Supervision across the content areas.* Larchmont, NY: Eye on Education.

Zepeda, S. J., & Ponticell, J. A. (1998). At cross-purposes: What do teachers need, want, and get from supervision? *Journal of Curriculum and Supervision, 14*(1), 68–87.

23

Data: The DNA of Politically Based Decision Making in Education

Bruce S. Cooper
Fordham University

John Sureau and Stephen Coffin
Montclair State University

Introduction

The politics and processes of making decisions in education are particularly complex, and at times, utterly confusing. While business policies, by contrast, are often based on a more limited set of concerns (e.g., viability, profitability, and availability) and are created apart from the larger political landscape, decision making for U.S. schools involves the interaction of three terribly complex areas, which are the topic of this chapter:

(1) the multiple governmental-jurisdictional *levels* at which politics flourishes and decisions are made (e.g., federal, state, local, and school-site);
(2) the complex *processes* of forming, instituting, and evaluating education decisions and policies; and
(3) the levels of educational policy *data* gathered by the nation, states, districts, schools, and students, creating a "double helix" of information that "flows up" from each child to the system to the country (and world); and in return "trickles down" to performance norms by system, school, and student.

No wonder that the politics of data-driven decision making can be confusing, if not confounding, and has been virtually ignored by researchers and political leaders. Recently, Slavin (2008) averred that "throughout the history of education, the adoption of instructional programs and practices has been driven more by ideology, faddism, politics, and marketing than by evidence" (p. 5). In comparison to the medical sciences, for example, education data are usually limited—meaning that educators and education policy makers often lack "evidentiary support" for what we do. As Hess (2008) explained:

> The tangled relationship between education research and policy has received little serious scrutiny, even as paeans to "scientifically based research" and "evidence-based practice" have become a staple of education policymaking in recent years. For all the attention devoted to the five-year-old Institute of Education Sciences, to No Child Left Behind's (NCLB) call for

"scientifically based research," to professional interest in data-driven decision-making, and to the refinement of sophisticated analytic tools, little effort has gone into understanding how, when, or why [or if] research affects education policy.

This chapter, acknowledging the levels of decision making, and the politics that occurs at each level (federal, state, local, school, classroom), seeks to explain the processes of decision making, and the use of data to influence the creation, implemention, and evaluation of education programs—and the differing roles of politics in each type of decision making.

We thus seek in this chapter to "unpack" and systematize the process, politics, and data management in the following three ways. First, the political levels of education are examined in four *policy arenas* (federal, state, local, and school-site), where we look at the macro-politics of federal-states with Congress and legislatures, the President and governors, and national lobbying groups; and the micro-politics of classrooms, schools and school systems (Helco, 1974; Mazzoni, 1993).

Second, the *policy process* involves a three-step effort to *formulate policy* with one set of political actors; to *implement* policy with key educators and constituencies; and to *evaluate* policy with yet another group of analysts and agencies gathering and analyzing data to see if the policy and program worked (see Nakamura & Smallwood, 1980). Or as Kennedy (1999) noted, "One could argue that, given the relatively recent entry of research into the education landscape, it has had a remarkable impact. Many of the ideas that motivate contemporary policies, and contemporary teaching, have come from research and evaluation" (p. 75).

Third, and finally, this chapter looks at the structure of education *data* as part of the data-driven decision-making effort, a *double helix* of data—often starting with the individual child (e.g., students' background, race, SES, attendance, academic program, achievement, special needs, English language acquisition, promotion, and graduation)—rising next to the school level (which makes for comparisons between locations), then aggregating to the school system, to the state, and finally to the national level, with the expectation that school systems, schools, and students demonstrate "adequate yearly progress" (AYP).

These three views (levels, processes, and data structures: the double helix) all come together to portray the difficulties of making decisions in a highly complex political environment, using data gathered and analyzed at different but related levels. By putting the three corners together—process, levels, and data-relationships—we can begin to understand how data-driven decision making works in the education political environments, particularly now that the national regime may be changing to a more moderate political leadership and education policy making.

The Process

Decision making in education, around key policy issues, is seen as a three-step process. Based on demands, needs and sets of data showing new problems, policy makers work to engage in political decision making in three phases. First, to *formulate* new education policies, often involving the passage of new laws and funding, at the federal, state, and/or local levels. The U.S. Congress, state legislatures, and local school boards all play a role in creating policies that affect schools, and members of the school community.

Second, these policy makers turn the programs over to key actors to *implement* the law and policies, at the local and school (classroom) levels. Active in this step are local school leaders, teachers, and students, as these new programs are organized and used in their schools and classrooms (Munro, 2008). Data at this point are often used to show the level of use and the changes in programs that result from the new policy and program.

And in the third "environment" (see Nakamura & Smallwood, 1984), efforts are made to *evaluate* the effectiveness of the program—involving a different group of people other than those who made and implemented the original program (Cooper, Fusarelli, & Randall, 2004), with more longitudinal data on program changes and possible student improvements. These outcome data then become the stimulus for school reform, and the politics of school policy formulation can start all over again (creating a demand "loop").

Data-Driving Decisions

Policy makers, administrators, and educators at all levels need sound, accurate, and appropriate data with which to make decisions. Quality information enables leaders to track results and to make decisions with greater accuracy. But the growing need for student achievement in the current standards-based environment has placed increasing demands on all of those involved with K-12 education to obtain sound data with which not only to more fully understand their school systems but also to improve the quality of education.

Yet in many ways, data analysis—purporting to be a highly statistical, rational, and even scientific process—may be contrary to the political process of decision making, which often involves the uses of power (e.g., votes, persuasion, lobbying) that are not usually very rational. Data-driven choices and decisions are best considered at the onset of the political process—as a means of stimulating interest and obtaining allies, and at the end of the political process when a new policy has been implemented, and people are ready to assess the effects of the new policy (e.g., on schools, children, and society).

Data that are collected and analyzed are often a way of getting political leaders to focus on a problem (e.g., drop-out, rising delinquency, violence in schools, declining graduation rates); and then again after the decisions are made and the policy is in effect, data-driven investigations and decision making may work to indicate how well the policy was implemented, and whether it is moving in the right directions.

While school-based data are not lacking, what seem to be missing are data that are generally agreed upon to be sound or of good quality. Discussions of data quality and their use with models usually brings to mind the adage of "garbage-in, garbage-out" because the quality of decisions made, the outcomes, is directly related to the quality of data used, the inputs. According to Kowalski, Lasley, and Mahoney (2008), unless those entering the data use exactly the same metrics, measures, or procedures, the realities of one school can be quite different from the realities of another, even though the data may look similar. Because all fifty states use different tests, measures, and approaches, a real absence of common metrics exists and that void makes it difficult for educators, even psychometrically astute ones, to make good judgments based on published data. (p. 148)

The key to school improvement is making data available, useful, and long-term, so that decision makers can track progress and change, using common measures and outcomes. Therefore, it is crucial to understand how data are collected, aggregated, analyzed, reported, and used around the politics of the three-step policy cycle (i.e., formulation, implementation, and evaluation). This process may sound easier than it is because data come in many forms, at many levels, and are often unconnected or disconnected from the individual district, school, classroom, teacher, and student. There are also different methods for data collection, aggregation, analysis, and reporting.

One good analogy is biological: the relationship between physical health and data such as DNA, defined as the location where the body's cells store coded information and the pairing of the DNA bases in the middle of the two strands or helices helps to keep the coded "data" intact. Because data, like DNA, are so intertwined in the formulation of educational policy such as decision making for funding formulas, the double helix that forms the structure of DNA might be the best way to depict our five-level model (State of New Jersey, Department of Education, 2008).

In our model the vertical dimension means relating each level to the one above and below it. The horizontal dimension includes the relationships within a level such as:

- Federal level: Comparisons of the American educational system with those of other nations.
- State level: Comparisons of school systems between and among states.
- District level: Comparisons of local education authorities (LEA) or school districts with one another especially ones that share similar characteristics.
- School level: Comparisons of different schools either within a state or across a number of states.
- Student level: Comparisons of students according to various factors such as socio-economic status, race, gender, subject matter, and grade level.

The dimensions and intersections of our model resemble those of DNA as data flow vertically, up and down the two congruent helices, as well as horizontally, across the base pairs as shown below for the double helix for DNA as well as for our model.

As Figure 23.1 indicates, the double helix of education politics in the USA runs across five levels or units (federal, state, local, school, and student), and the political behavior associated with each related level in the helix also varies.

Federal Politics

This level involves the U.S. President, Members of Congress, who do the voting and allocating, and the U.S. Department of Education which acts as the executive agency

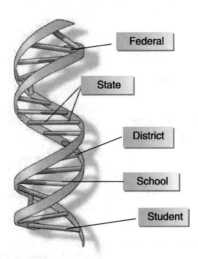

Figure 23.1 Structure/relations of education data as a double helix.

for carrying out federal policy and spending. Meanwhile, key "interest groups" such as AFT, NEA, NASSP, NAESP, CCSSO, AASA, and other associations act as political lobbyists, pressuring the President and Congress to provide funding and support for schools. The politics at the federal level is typically *macro-politics*, with large-scale interest groups at work. And the data used for federal politics are nationally aggregated, and are focused on national measures of student progress, percents of students graduating high school, and the changing populations of students affected by Title I (low income—free/reduced lunch students) and IDEA, and whether these students are being served—and how well—by these federal programs. Influencing decision making, therefore, is micro-political/interest group politics, working through the Congressional and Presidential levels, and the national Democratic and Republican parties.

State Politics, State Data

Similarly, each state has its own education system, and allocates states resources to educate its children. Data boil down by state, and politics involves analogous leaders: Governors, state Legislatures, and state education departments. The major difference between national and state politics and decision making is that each state has its own constitution, and under the 10th Amendment of the U.S. Constitution, education is the primary responsibility of the states, although the federal government's role has grown, as it seeks to balance differences in resources and performance across the 50 states and the District of Columbia.

This discussion poses a five-level model for data building and data use that is intended not only to help gather the right types and "levels" of information but also to put the information where it is needed most and best used. It examines the five key levels of education-based decisions as highlighted above, identifying the availability and limitations of data at those levels as well as how the data analysis might affect education at that level and throughout the system. While decision making depends on data, it is important to explain the limitations at each level and what might be done (for good or for bad) by creating more information at that level. Table 23.1 shows the three-step policy process (formulating, implementing, and evaluating), by the levels of the double helix (federal government down to the child) with the key agencies and agents in each cell.

A Case Model: Class Size as Policy and Program

We selected a hot policy issue, *class size* policies and programs, that helps to illustrate the decision-making process around the four levels of politics (federal, state, local, school/classroom), the bubbling and boiling of data from these levels, and the apparent controversy affecting the politics at these levels: decision making based on the apparent effects of *class size* as an outcome of policy reform, and as a stimulus for studying data effects (see Harris, 2007; Shrag, 2007).

This critical variable (number of students in the classroom for instruction) is by its very nature measurable, and variable, as school systems can reduce class size, presumably allowing teachers to have fewer students and more time for those they have. It has support from national groups such as the teachers' unions, and the American Education Research Association, which has been promoting studies of the class reduction programs and their effects for many years.

Table 23.1 Levels of political behavior against formulating, implementing, and evaluating education policy.

Levels of the double helix	Formulating policy	Implementing policy	Evaluating policy
Federal Politics and Data: NAEP, US DOE assessments, congressional and White House agencies	U.S. Congress, President, public interest groups	U.S. Dept. of Education, related agencies of government (health, science)	Bureau of Labor Statistics, National Center of Education Statistics
State Politics and Data: State tests and analysis	Governor, state Legislature, state lobbyists	State Dept. of Education, state interest groups	State Educ. Dept., state level associations and unions
Local Politics, Data and Assessments: local testing and analysis	School boards, mayors and city councils	School district superintendents, central office staff	Depts. of school districts, other groups
School Politics and Data: classroom and grade level, subjects	Principal and faculty councils	Teachers and administrators	Area chairs, and teachers
Student Level, Data and Politics: child's needs, background, interests	Teachers, and dept. chairs, grade level counselors, parents	Teachers and counselors	Dept. chairs, and area specialists, families

As Hess and Henig (2008) report:

> The push for class size reduction has benefited enormously from the findings of the famed Student Teacher Achievement Ratio project (STAR), a class size experiment conducted in Tennessee in the late 1980s. Educators spent $12 million on STAR between 1985 and 1989 to examine the impact of class size on student learning. Researchers found significant achievement gains for students in small kindergarten classes and additional gains in first grade, especially for black students, which persisted as students moved through middle school.

Similarly, Finn, Gerber, and Boyd-Zaharias (2005) wrote that "it is now established that classes of fewer than 20 students in grades K-3 have a positive effect on student achievement" (p. 215), again linking a policy (smaller classes) to some set of intervening conditions (e.g., more attention, better interactions, less misbehavior in class) to some better measurable data-based outcomes, say, in math and reading scores (see Robinson, 1990). A meta-analysis of the effects of class size, which has been extensively studied, found the following four effects:

(1) smaller classes benefited all students in every school subject area (Goldstein & Blatchford, 1998; Hedges, Nye, & Konstantopoulis, 2000);
(2) poor, minority, inner-city students were helped even more by smaller classes (Krueger & Whitmore, 2001) using STAR data;
(3) students were "more engaged" in learning in smaller classes (Evertson & Folger, 1989); and
(4) smaller classes worked better, generally, than larger classes with extra staff (teacher aides) or no extra staff.

Finn et al. (2005) took the analysis a step further, examining the sustained "enduring effects" of smaller classes, where students learned more and have better test outcomes. The advantages are:

- Improved classroom atmosphere, students may receive more individualized attention, and teachers showed flexibility to use different instructional approaches/assignments.
- Fewer students to distract each other; lower level of noise.
- Helped teachers to know the students better and can offer more extra help; recognize learning problems/special educational needs.
- Teachers had fewer discipline problems. By spending less time on discipline, teachers reported devoting more time to classroom instruction.
- Class size reductions were most effective when classes comprised between 15 and 19 students and certain schools were targeted, especially those with low-achieving and low-income students. However, smaller classes cost money, requiring more teachers (which the teacher unions support), and the controversy around cutting class size is a living example of the role of politics in education decision making.

Data on the effectiveness of smaller classes are not scientific, and are not based on a random field trial. While drug companies can usually get patients to try a new drug, while others use a placebo, few parents would allow their children to be placed into a class of 30 while children down the hall had classes of 19—to test the empirical effects of size. Thus, as Hess and Henig (2008) explain, "Organizational reforms relating to governance, management, compensation and deregulation are rarely precise and do not take place in controlled circumstances."

Research on class size is a useful case, as the Finn et al. study related class size at the lower grades to progress through high school, as they explained: "The analysis of achievement scores showed that both reading achievement and mathematics achievement in K-3 were significantly, positively related to the likelihood of graduating high school" (p. 219). Using odds ratios, they found that for every standard deviation (*SD*) improvement in reading (1.32) and in math (1.35) meant a one-third greater likelihood of graduating high school, for children in smaller classes. These findings illustrate the usefulness of comparative, *longitudinal* data as we track the effects of early treatment on later outcomes—and the possible implications for school funding and policies.

Does this mean that smaller classes always work, and for every child? Hardly. This one Tennessee study hardly generalizes to all students, in all states, in all schools and subjects. But these kinds of data do point a direction, and help policy makers to shape their ideas for changing and improving schools. A number of important researchers have argued that reduced class size makes little or no difference in student learning and performance (Dee, 2004; Turtel, 2006; Winerip, 2004).

Thus, the key role of data (and data-driven decision making) is not to end discussion or debate, but is a force to foster new ideas and provide information for reaching decisions. Again, Hess and Henig (2008) put it this way: "research as a collective enterprise—the clash of competing scholars attacking questions from different perspectives, with varied assumption and ideologies—can leave us wiser and better equipped to make good choices."

In fact, the role of politics in school decision making is to gather all this information, examine the competing and different findings and opinions, and put into motion the process of making policy—"satisficing" when the best solution or policy is not apparent. Thus, data "inform" decisions but cannot make them for us. The more democratic, engaging, and transparent are the issues and findings, the more likely the new policy will get passed politically and the greater the chance that the new policy will work. Thus, as this chapter shows, data do not end the political process; they can usually stimulate and inform it. Good data engage the public, the decision makers, and bring the situation to the attention of federal, state, and local decision makers. And once a decision is made at one level, the double helix goes to work, either bubbling information up the chain to give greater general results, or trickling down to individual schools, teachers, and classrooms, where best practices can be used.

The macro-politics in Washington, DC, and the state capitals, helps the major legislation (Title I, school desegregation, IDEA for the special education child) to pass into law; but it is always up to the district and school to carry out the policies—around the micro-politics of the community and the school. Politics, then, provides the platform, while data can challenge our assumptions, open our eyes to new ideas, and promote debate. Data in education will never end discussion or controversy; but they can open doors to new ideas, and give some feedback on new programs—in a quasi-experimental, limited scientific manner.

An example of a data analysis at the national, and state-by-state level, is Baird's (2008) study of school finance disparities and the role of federal program funding (Brimley & Garfield, 2008), showing how the double-data helix can work in evaluating a program. Baird explains that:

> federal initiatives direct resources to districts with children who are from economically dis-
> advantaged backgrounds (Title 1 and nutrition programs), who have limited proficiency in
> English (English Language Acquisition), who are "federally connected" (Impact Aid), and
> who are physically, emotionally, or mentally disabled (special education). (pp. 305–306)

She found that disparities in spending were reduced overall (nationally) by federal aid, in some states. But as sometimes happened, states reduced their own funding when federal resources are forthcoming—an unintended outcome of policies from Washington to the states to the local districts, to the child. Also, local education agencies (LEA) may reduce the level of property taxes needed for their school systems to the extent that a larger share of federal or state financial aid is made available.

We have a democratic education system—with school boards, state legislatures, state school boards, Congress—to give voice, and to engage the public. No one policy or approach will always work, with all children. So the politics of education decision making is the voicing, and the use of data, to make the best decisions possible and to help track and analyze the results over time, and space.

Data act as a stimulant to policy identification and creation, as shown in Figure 23.2. While the process is not now, nor will ever be highly scientific, as medical science decision making purports to be; but as Hess and others have argued, we need good data to start, direct, and evaluate the process of school decision making. These data are not *the* answer but are *possible* answers that deserve policy support and new program implementation. Each level of government, then, has a responsibility to supply and review data gathered at each level (child, school, district, state, and national) and to inform decisions at each level as policies are made, implemented, reviewed, and evaluated (see Figure 23.2).

 Across the levels of government and education activity shown in Figure 23.2, we see the rational process of gathering data on the problem and assessing political needs and processes (e.g., votes, support, lobbying), which leads to political action (passing new laws, writing new policies, allocating funds). Then, the new policies are implemented and data are useful in determining the extent of student access, the delivery of services, and the effects of these new policies on student progress, learning, graduation, and change.

It seems obvious that more data gathering should be built into new policies, if nothing more than to see if the programs ever get implemented, and whether they work over time. Small class size works, and we see it in wealthier public school systems, and in private schools nationwide. And we see it implemented in many poorer schools under Title I programs and special needs programs. So it is happening, as some data show, and may be working, as other information may show. So, data-driven decision making can help drive the policy process, and to see how it is working and being effective. Hess and Henig (2008) explain the case well, even as a critic of the so-called scientific approach to decision making in education, when they wrote:

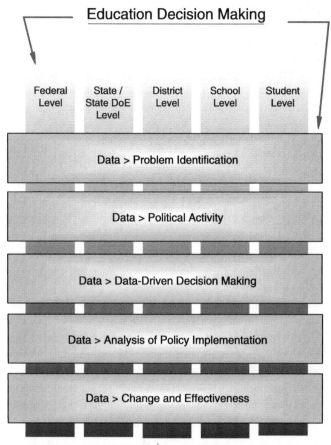

Figure 23.2 Levels and processes of data-driven decision making.

> Ultimately, the education community should seek to facilitate disciplined technical debate, encourage researchers to police the quality of their work, and help consumers make sense of the enormous variation in credibility of published research. This might include devising ways to support professional organizations or associations that encourage and reward self-policing; funding federally sponsored reviews of available research, as is being attempted by the U.S. Department of Education's "What Works Clearinghouse"; increasing foundations' attention to these considerations in the research that they fund; and fostering efforts by credible, competing institutions to assess the rigor of high-profile scholarship.

Reduced class size can have some important unintended results, which may have a negative effect on schools and students. First, smaller classes mean more teachers, such that to the degree that schools nationwide hire many more teachers, in some cases somewhat "less qualified" teachers may be hired while all teachers have to meet or exceed federal (e.g., NCLB) and state requirements. Would it be better to have fewer teachers who are perhaps more "outstanding" working more in larger classes, or more and smaller classes with somewhat "less qualified" teachers? Data should track the process and the effects of school systems and states as they institute smaller classes, and try to find and initiate new teachers.

Second, smaller classes will not always mean better classes, more relevant curriculum, and better-motivated students. Gilbert (1995) found that "instructor effectiveness has been found to be as good or better in large classes than in small classes. Thus, researchers have changed their focus from "does class size matter" to "what are the dimensions of effective teaching in large classes?" (p. 25). And third, good, effective classrooms are only marginally related to the "size" of the class; instead, "it would be better to develop measures that relate *what goes on in classes* to student learning and outcomes" (p. 27).

We see, according to Blatchford, Goldstein, and Mortimore (1998), that these various explanations may work in concert: that is, class size reduction may improve achievement because: (a) students enjoy more class time for learning, (b) get more attention from their teachers, and (c) receive a clearer, better introduction to classroom routine and activities—less distraction and more focused learning environments (Goldstein & Blatchford, 1998). And if teachers were trained to adapt their teaching in other ways that are suited to smaller classes, such as initiating different kinds of student activities that are possible in smaller classes, this might produce an additional benefit.

As early as 1999, Hanushek found in his examination of 277 studies of "class size" or "student–teacher ratios" that only about 15% of the studies found significantly positive effects, while 13% found negative results of the change. Thus, Hanushek's analysis of the critical relationships between funding and smaller class size and academic "output" has determined the relationship to be "weak" at best. Other analysts have contested Hanushek's findings, using different measures. One problem is how to determine *small class size*, as many studies use student–teacher ratios, with data aggregated to the school or even the district level. Perhaps a study with the student as the unit—the bottom of the double helix—could place children into larger versus smaller classes to study the effects, not only of the final output (a fourth grade test, for example), but how children behave, interact with both their teacher *and* with other children; and whether they tend to ask questions, concentrate, and "learn." Again, we see the problem of how to interpret the results of policies, and how these outcomes could affect the politics of federal, state, and local decision making.

Recommendations

Thus, data are hardly enough to drive quality, effective decision making. But data can help to frame the discussion and give policy makers a place to start their deliberations and set of findings to discuss. True, politics plays a key role in mediating and determining differences—because no perfect decision (e.g., how large or small, to require classes to be) can easily be made for all children in all settings. So, the politics of education is critical in providing through Congress, state Legislatures, and local school boards, for example, legitimate places and mechanisms for making and overseeing decisions.

Based on the model and research presented here, we propose the following five recommendations for education policy makers.

1. Consider Both Methods and Results

Many policy makers and advocates are quick to see the results and use them to their advantage. Recent political races show candidates quickly manipulating studies, delegate counts, and polls to support a particular position or stance. Policy makers, as the good of students should be an ultimate goal, should avoid this quick over-simplification of methods and findings, and consider not only the results but also the variety of methods used to learn about certain data at all levels of the double helix.

2. Encourage "Good" Research

Policy makers, particularly those affiliated with strong organizations, are in a position to demand, encourage, and bring about consistent, objective research methods that will produce stronger results. Models do exist for tracking the effects of policies over a period of time (e.g., "value added"), for comparing different treatments and pro-grams to determine their effects, and involving teachers and students in assessing their own experiences in school.

3. Make the Connections

It is to the advantage of policy makers, and the students and faculty who are working for them, to consider the important connections between the federal, state, local, school, and student levels of schools. What are the implications of data collected and analyzed at the local student level for politics of decision making at district, state, and federal levels? Keeping the DNA intact will help connect the levels and provide evidence for the politics at each and all levels. We need more data on how and why policies are created, how they are implemented, and how effective they are over time.

4. Avoid Partisanship but Recognize the Importance of Politics in Education Decision Making

However easy (and useful) it may be to only use subjectively "good" research, politics still comes into the process. Whenever resources and values are being allocated, politics will appear. So decision makers should resist the temptation to ignore the research of others who might disagree or contradict them. Rather, leaders should be informed of the latest research on all sides of an issue and allow it to inform their position.

5. Study Policies in Relationship to Each Other

Ferguson (2000) found significant relationships among teacher quality, class size, and student achievement, although he was unable to determine how well these variables would work alone. Often, research and policies need to look at a cluster of qualities—which are more powerful and effective together, where it is not easy to isolate and measure the effects of one variable (e.g., class size) alone. Wenglinsky (1997), similarly, shows how important it is to consider policy making, data analysis, and decision making at national, regional, and local levels, reinforcing the contention that data are a complex double helix, working at various levels, across various locations.

This chapter has shown that data can work to stimulate new policies, to help see how they are implemented, and importantly how the innovations are working and where—across different levels of government. *Macro*-politics uses macro-data (on state and national outcomes, such as the Baird (2008) study of funding equity nationally) to frame national policies. And important local *micro*-data may help teachers, parents, and school administrators to adjust their programs and teaching to the needs and growth of students, in particular settings for particular children's needs. Implementing new policies locally is a likely scene for micro-political processes and conflicts. If a district decided that it needed to save money, by increasing class size by 10%, the teachers union, in an alliance with the parent associations, might likely fight at school board meetings to keep classes smaller and to save jobs. Thus, education politics can range from the National Education Association lobbying for more Title I funding in Washington, DC, to the local NEA union pressing for smaller classes and more employment for its members.

Both macro- and micro-information is important in the data helix as we have discussed. And politics plays an important role in moving policies ahead, because rarely are data conclusive and clear—but rather research outcomes give indications of need, program activity, and effectiveness. In a democracy, with levels of government and diverse interest groups, the system functions to include groups and to make decision making complex (Essex, 2006). As Cooper et al. (2004) explain,

> the very process of decision making itself reflects democratic ideals and strengthens our democratic society. This pluralistic or shared decision making model allocates authority across society and also requires that education enable individuals to participate effectively in the ensuing dialogue and governance of schools. (p. 148)

Thus, the politics, while it makes the process of policy making more complex and public, has the benefit of often sharing decisions and governance among families, educators, and politicians across levels of government and systems of education. The political settings (Congress, state Legislative hearings, school board meetings, etc.) can help to build "firewalls" to encourage critical deliberation. And the future—with new technologies and methods for gathering and analyzing larger and larger data sets—promises even greater attention to data, showing the problems being addressed, the levels of implementation of new policies, and importantly, their effects and effectiveness.

Slavin (2008) states the purpose concisely when he writes: "A key requirement for evidence-based policy is the existence of scientifically valid and readily interpretable syntheses of research on practical, replicable education programs. Education policy [and the politics behind the policy] cannot support the adoption of proven programs if there is no agreement on what they are" (p. 5). Yet policy makers must make decisions, if we are to tackle the problems of education in the years ahead. That is where the politics of reality and compromise is needed and used, as politics is the "art of the possible," even in the complex, conflict-ridden world of American education.

References

Baird, K. E. (2008). Federal direct expenditures and school funding disparities, 1990–2000. *Journal of Education Finance, 33*(1), 297–310.

Blatchford, P., Goldstein, H., & Mortimore, P. (1998). Research on class size effects: A critique of methods and a way forward. *International Journal of Educational Research, 29*, 691–710.

Brimley, V., & Garfield, R. R. (2008). *Financing education in a climate of change* (10th ed.). Boston: Allyn & Bacon.

Cooper, B. S., Fusarelli, L. D., & Randall, E. V. (2004). *Better policies, better schools.* Boston: Allyn & Bacon.

Dee, T. S. (2004). Teachers, race, and student achievement in a randomized experiment. *Review of Economics and Statistics 86*(1), 195–210.

Essex, N. L. (2006). *What every teacher should know about No Child Left Behind.* New York: Allyn & Bacon Start Smart Series.

Evertson, C. M., & Folger, J. K. (1989, March). *Small class, large class: What do teachers do differently?* Paper presented at the annual meeting of the American Educational Research Association, San Francisco, CA.

Ferguson, R. F. (2000). Paying for public education: New evidence on how and why money matters. *Harvard Journal on Legislation, 28*(2), 465–498.

Finn, J. D., Gerber, S. B., & Boyd-Zaharias, I. (2005). Small classes in the early grades, academic achievement, and graduating from high school. *Journal of Educational Psychology, 97*(2), 214–223.

Gilbert, R. (1995). Small groups in music lessons: Creativity or cacophony? *Research Studies in Music Education, 5*(1), 24–31.

Goldstein, H., & Blatchford, P. (1998). Class size and school size: Taking the trade-off seriously. *British Educational Research Journal, 24*(3), 255–268.

Hanushek, E. (1999). Some findings from an independent investigation of the Tennessee STAR experiment and from other investigations of class size effects. *Educational Evaluation and Policy Analysis 21*(2), 143–163.

Harris, D. N. (2007). Class size and school size: Taking the trade-off seriously. In T. Loveless & M. Hess (Eds.), *Brookings papers on education policy: 2006/07* (pp. 137–161). Washington, DC: Brookings Institution Press.

Hedges, L. V., Nye, B., & Konstantopoulis, S. (2000). The effects of small classes on academic achievement: The results of the Tennessee class size experiment. *Educational Evaluation and Policy Analysis, 21*(2), 127–142.

Helco, H. (1974). *Modern social politics in Britain and Sweden: From relief to income maintenance.* New Haven, CT: Yale University Press.

Hess, F. M. (2008). When education research matters. *Education Outlook.* Retrieved February 4, 2008, from http://www.qei.org/publications/filter.all.pubID.27449/pub_detail.asp

Hess, F. M., & Henig, J. R. (2008). Scientific research and policy making: A tool not a crutch. Retrieved on February 7, 2008, from http://www.aei.org/publications/filter.allpubID.27484, filter.all/pub_detail.asp

Kennedy, M. (1999). Infusing educational decision making with research. In G. J. Cizek (Ed.), *Handbook of educational policy* (pp. 53–81). San Diego, CA: Academic Press.

Kowalski, T. J., Lasley, T. J., II, & Mahoney, J. W. (2008). *Data-driven decisions and school leadership: Best practices for school improvement.* Boston: Allyn & Bacon.

Krueger, A., & Whitmore, D. (2001). The effect of attending a small class in the early grades on college test-taking and middle school test results: Evidence from Project STAR. *Economic Journal, 111*(1), 1–28.

Mazzoni, T. L. (1993). The changing politics of state education policymaking: A 20-year Minnesota perspective. *Educational Evaluation and Policy Analysis, 15*(4), 357–379.

Munro, J. H. (2008). *Educational leadership.* New York: McGraw Hill.

Nakamura, R. T., & Smallwood, F. S. (1980). *The politics of policy implementation.* New York: St. Martin's Press.

Robinson, G. E. (1990). Synthesis of research on effects of class size. *Educational Leadership, 47*(7), 80–90.

Shrag, P. (2007). Policy from the hip: Class-size reduction in California. In T. Loveless & F. M. Hess (Eds.), *Brookings papers on education policy: 2006/2007* (pp. 253–261). Washington, DC: Brookings Institute Press.

Slavin, R. E. (2008). What works? Issues in synthesizing education program evaluations. *Educational Researcher, 37*(1), 5–14.

State of New Jersey, Department of Education (2008). *United States Library of Medicine, DNA Double Helix diagram.* Retrieved from http://www.coe.drexel.edu/ret/personalsites/2005/dayal/curriculum1_files/image001.jpg

Turtel, J. (2006). *Surprise—Public schools class size doesn't matter.* Retrieved October 21, 2006, from www.newswithview.com

Wenglinsky, H. H. (1997). *When money matters.* Princeton, NJ: Educational Testing Service (ETS) Policy Information Center.

Winerip, M. (2004). *Good teachers + small classes = quality education.* Retrieved March 5, 2008, from www.missouri.eduWeb.missouri.edu

24

Using Data to Assess School Culture

Theodore J. Kowalski
University of Dayton

and

Tricia Browne-Ferrigno
University of Kentucky

Across virtually all states, policy makers have shifted from centralized change strategies to tactics intended to produce improvements at the individual school level. This adjustment has been prompted by the realization that needs and resources among schools, even within most districts, are dissimilar—a condition that largely explains why federal and state generic reforms did not achieve their objectives (Baumann, 1996). Authors who have analyzed the drift toward decentralized school reform (e.g., Hall & Hord, 2001; Sarason, 1996; Spady, 2001) caution, however, that school-based initiatives will suffer the same fate if reformers ignore or fail to improve negative school cultures. This insightful conclusion has made culture change a core reform strategy (Fullan, 2001a); and consequently, diagnosing and altering counterproductive assumptions influencing educator behavior have become imperative tasks (Schein, 1992).

The purpose of this chapter is to demonstrate how two types of data, those derived quantitatively from inventories and those derived from a state accountability program, provide functional evidence that can be used to identify and analyze school culture. First, culture change is defined and its relevance to school reform explained. Then four examples of standardized assessment instruments and aspects of Kentucky's accountability programs are presented to demonstrate that these sources can generate relevant diagnostic data. Last, recommendations are made for broadening research on assessing and evaluating school culture.

Understanding and Assessing School Culture

Districts and schools are organizations; that is, they are social inventions (Johns, 1988) that have been deliberately designed to achieve specific goals (Reitz, 1987). Composed of people functioning independently and in groups, schools have often been compared to biological systems, most notably, the human body. Owens (2001), for example, wrote that groups and individuals function interdependently much like cells and molecules, and therefore, when one part of the system malfunctions, other parts are usually affected. Organizations have also been compared to mechanical systems. Morgan (1986), for example, explained that an organization's parts are purposely designed to interface with each other to ensure a minimum loss of energy. Both metaphors demonstrate that districts and schools are complex systems in which outputs are produced by an intricate and usually inconstant mix of causes (Weick, 1979).

Defining School Culture

Organizational climate is a concept that determines how people feel about organization (Hanson, 2003); it is an enduring quality experienced by organizational members that subsequently influences their behavior (Burton, Lauridsen, & Obel, 1999). This characteristic is the equivalent of a personality. According to Taguiri (1968), climate is composed of four elements: *ecology* (physical attributes), *milieu* (social attributes), *organization* (structural attributes), and *culture* (symbolic attributes). Culture, consisting of an invisible framework of norms emanating from shared values and beliefs, is commonly considered the vaguest but most important of these elements (Deal & Kennedy, 1982). Noted scholar Edgar Schein (1990) defined culture as:

> (a) a pattern of basic assumptions, (b) invented, discovered, or developed by a given group, (c) as it learns to cope with its problems of external adaptation and internal integration, (d) that has worked well enough to be considered valid and, therefore (e) is to be taught to new members as the (f) correct way to perceive, think, and feel in relation to those problems. (p. 111)

Through its norms, culture influences both how employees do their work (Schein, 1996; Trimble, 1996) and the degree to which employees promote and accept change (Duke, 2004; Leithwood, Jantzi, & Fernandez, 1994).

   Though all public schools share some aspects of a generic culture (Fullan, 2001a, 2001b; Sarason, 1996), the *strength* and the *quality* of individual school cultures vary. Culture strength refers to the extent to which norms and values are clearly defined and rigorously enforced (Cox, 1993). Maslowski (2001, 2006) explains that even if only a minority of employees shares the same convictions, a school could have a strong culture if a set of convictions is consistently and rigorously reinforced so that they influence group behavior. In weak cultures, sub-systems are usually balkanized, a specific set of convictions is not consistently reinforced, and individual responses to problems of practice are dissimilar. Culture quality, on the other hand, is defined by the extent to which dominant values and beliefs are supported by espoused and action theories. In a positive school culture, underlying assumptions guiding important pedagogical decisions are consistent with the established professional knowledge base (Kowalski, 2003). Studies of effective schools (e.g., Cotton, 2003; Purkey & Smith, 1983; Zigarelli, 1996) have commonly reported that highly successful institutions possess an atypical ethos manifested by traits such as decentralized authority, shared decision making, considerable parental involvement, high student expectations, and instructional leadership provided by principals.

Need to Assess Culture

Some elements of culture, such as artifacts and espoused beliefs, can be identified rather easily; however, they may not reveal a culture's true nature.[1] The greatest influence on organizational behavior is a set of *underlying beliefs* (Schein, 1992), but unearthing them is difficult and time consuming. Some teachers, for example, may be unable to discuss them because they are held at a sub-conscious level (Firestone & Louis, 1999). Suppressing fundamental assumptions is most likely when they are known to be (a) politically unacceptable, (b) professionally irresponsible, or (c) the source of intra-personal conflict (Schein, 1992). Over time, these assumptions go through a metamorphosis in which they become routine behaviors that organizational members encourage and reinforce. Thus, as new organizational members enter the organization, they are pressured to accept these norms through a process called socialization.[2]

Failed efforts to improve schools through staff development help us understand the power of culture. Often educators become enthusiastic about new programs or procedures immediately after attending workshops; but if the innovations prove to be incompatible with a school's culture, they almost always get discarded before being fully implemented (Fullan, 1999). This occurs because school culture influences how educators view the need for change and how they evaluate specific change initiatives. Consider a school in which teachers believe that they have little power to affect student learning. As changes are proposed, this assumption prompts the teachers to view them as uncomfortable, inconvenient, and risky ventures that have little or no prospect of improving learning (Hall & Hord, 2001). When change initiatives conflict with the prevailing culture, they usually fail unless culture is altered or severe penalties are imposed for non-compliance (Cameron & Quinn, 2006).

A deeper understanding of school culture reveals why it is essential for educators to accurately understand the culture in which they work (Conway, 1985). More precisely, reform at the school level requires them to first identify counterproductive assumptions and then to analyze them in relation to their effect on reaching an acceptable vision at some point in the future (Schein, 1992). Only then will they be able to pursue culture change as school-improvement strategy.

Culture Inventories

Studies that have reported associations between positive school cultures and higher student outcomes (e.g., Cavanagh & Waugh, 2004; Gaziel, 1997; Gruenert, 2005) have typically been conducted with quantitative surveys of teacher opinions and self-reported behaviors. The validity of such studies is challenged by the contention that culture must be "measured only by observation of the setting using qualitative methods" (Hall & Hord, 2001, p. 194). In large measure, this belief is nested in the realization that an organization's members are often incapable of identifying or unwilling to discuss their actual beliefs (Schein, 1992).

Though quantitative instruments do not identify underlying assumptions directly, they provide pieces of evidence relevant to institutional culture. Maslowski (2006) points out that after these elements are assessed, "behavioral aspects can be interpreted in terms of values and norms" (p. 28). One of the most popular concepts associated with quantitative assessments is the competing values framework developed by Quinn (1984) and subsequently revised by Cameron and Quinn (2006). After studying six quantitative instruments developed specifically to measure school culture,[3] Maslowski (2001) concluded that they were effective, efficient, and could be used to compare school cultures. He cautioned, however, that they did not produce a reliable measure of the strength of a school's culture.

A growing number of quantitative instruments are being developed for assessing aspects of school culture. Four such instruments are briefly summarized here to demonstrate their usefulness with respect to diagnostic work. Administrators should evaluate the merits of instruments in relation to their data needs, because these instruments vary in cost, complexity, and foci.

School Culture Survey (SCS)

The SCS was developed by Saphier and King (1985) as a diagnostic tool for educators pursuing planned culture change. The instrument was later revised by Edwards, Green, and Lyon (1996) and now contains three subscales: *teacher professionalism* (ten items), *professional treatment* (eight items), and *teacher collaboration* (six items). Response choices use a Likert scale ranging from 1 (*almost never*) to 5 (*almost always*). Reliability (Cronbach's alpha) ranges from .81 to .92.

An extensive study involving the SCS was conducted by Edwards et al. (1996). They administered this and two other instruments, the *Teacher Efficacy Scale* (Gibson & Dembo, 1984) and the *Vincenz Empowerment Scale* (Vincenz, 1990) to 425 teachers in the United States. They found all the SCS subscales to be correlated at a moderate level—an outcome supporting the contention that the instrument measures distinct facets of a commons construct. They also reported that all three SCS scales were significantly correlated with teacher efficacy and with five of the six empowerment scales.

School Work and Culture Profile (SWCP)

The SWCP, created by Snyder (1988), was based on the *Managing Productive Schools* model originated by Snyder and Anderson (1986). After pilot testing and input from a panel of experts, the instrument was reduced to a 60-item questionnaire. It consists of four subscales, each with 15 items: *Schoolwide Planning, Professional Development, Program Development,* and *School Assessment.* Intended to measure work-related behavior in a school, it uses a 5-point Likert response scale ranging from "strongly disagree" to "strongly agree." Maslowski (2006) reported that the instrument had been subjected to several validation studies, and "Cronbach's alphas for the four subscales were found to be between 0.88 and 0.93, with an alpha for the total scale of 0.97" (p. 16).

A study conducted by Bruner and Greenlee (2004) compared low-achieving schools and high-achieving schools in Florida using the SWCP. They found that the two groups of schools had dissimilar work cultures; on all four subscales, the high-achievement schools had higher means. The researchers noted that the effect size statistics suggested "notable differences between the two groups" (p. 42).

Organizational Culture Inventory (OCI)

The OCI is a quantitative, statistically normed, and validated survey that has been used primarily in business and industrial organizations. Developed by Human Synergistics International (Cooke & Lafferty, 1987), it addresses actual and ideal aspects of culture. With respect to actual conditions, the instrument assesses both individual normative beliefs (when the perspective of only one person is plotted) and shared behavioral expectations (when individual perspectives are combined). A picture of preferred culture is established by measuring 12 sets of behavioral norms associated with three general styles of organizational culture: (a) constructive, (b) passive/defensive, and (c) aggressive/defensive. It has been used most frequently to validate the need for change, planning, and monitoring organizational development programs, supporting programs designed to enhance member engagement, organizational learning, and measuring culture for academic and research purposes Though the OCI has been used primarily in large corporations and small businesses, it is advertised as being equally appropriate for governmental agencies, professional organizations, and non-profit organizations (Human Synergistics Incorporated, 2008).

The focus on behavioral norms is a characteristic that distinguishes the OCI from other surveys that assess more global aspects of culture such as shared values and beliefs. Though behavioral norms are related to beliefs and values, they arguably have greater influence on day-to-day activities and work situations (Cooke & Rousseau, 1988). As such, they "also have a relatively great impact on individual and organizational outcomes and are potentially indicative of environments that support organizational learning and knowledge management" (Balthazard, Cooke, & Potter, 2006, p. 713).

School Culture Quality Survey (SCQS)

Developed by Katzenmeyer (1999), the SCQS is a standardized instrument used to assess teacher perceptions of their work environments and it produces a school culture profile. The instrument has four subscales:

(a) *Shared Vision* (a collective awareness of an organization future members would like to share);
(b) *Facilitative Leadership* (the capacity to actively facilitate the work of organizational members);
(c) *Teamwork* (the capacity to work together productively toward common goals);

(d) *Learning Community* (a cadre of colleagues who are actively seeking and learning together the new skills and knowledge needed to achieve the desired organizational future).

Several studies have examined the relationship between school culture scores and student learning. One was conducted by Borman, Katzenmeyer, Barber, and Moriarty (2002). Comparing low and high math gain schools, they found that two-thirds of the high gain schools had moderate to high SCQS scores whereas only one-third of the low gain schools had such scores.

A more recent study (Herrmann, 2007) was conducted with all nine high schools located in Allen County Ohio. Results revealed that these schools had dissimilar culture profiles. Moreover, positive associations were found between a school's overall culture score (composite of the four subscales) and two performance variables: scores on Ohio's 10th Grade Graduation Test (high positive association) and a school's graduation rate (moderate positive association). This research demonstrates the usefulness of assessing culture in relation to state accountability programs (Kowalski & Herrmann, 2008).

School Culture as Accountability Measure

Transforming school cultures into dynamic learning communities is a recommended strategy to improve student achievement and school performance (e.g., Danielson, 2002: Elbot & Fulton, 2007; Zmuda, Kuklis, & Kline, 2004). A foundational requirement for sustainable organizational change is collaboration by broad-based stakeholder groups in schools that determine specific goals and then work collaboratively and strategically to achieve them (Beaudoin & Taylor, 2004; Fullan, 2005; Marazza, 2003). The required relational trust within such systemic initiatives develops capacity for individuals and schools to respond appropriately to changing student and community needs (Bryk & Schneider, 2002; Kochanek, 2005; Sergiovanni, 2007). Likewise, when action plans are assessed regularly and decisions are made based on diverse data, continuous improvement becomes imbedded in school cultures (Bernhardt, 2002; Phillips & Wagner, 2003). These concepts form the framework for statewide school reform and renewal initiatives in Kentucky (Browne-Ferrigno, Allen, & Hurt, in press).

Kentucky's School Accountability System

Passage of the Kentucky Education Reform Act of 1990 (KERA) introduced a dual system of *assessment* of student learning outcomes and *accountability* of school performance (Foster, 1999; Pankratz & Petrosko, 2000). Both cognitive measures (e.g., student scores on standardized tests) and non-cognitive measures (e.g., attendance, retention, and drop-out rates; successful transition to college or workforce following graduation) are used in assigning an annual academic index for each school. The index is then used to assess school improvement measured against state-assigned improvement goals. The Kentucky Department of Education (KDE) is required by law to audit schools that failed to meet their improvement goals and conduct voluntary formal reviews of a sample of schools that achieve or surpass their performance goals to gather data for comparison. A standardized accountability framework is used to support school improvement efforts and cross-school comparisons.

The *Kentucky Standards and Indicators for School Improvement* (SISI) are nine school standards grouped under three broad categories:

(a) *academic performance* (i.e., curriculum, classroom evaluation and assessment, instruction);
(b) *learning environment* (i.e., school culture, external support system, professional development and evaluation), and
(c) *efficiency* (i.e., leadership, organizational structure and resource allocation, comprehensive and effective planning).

Because the accompanying 88 indicators of school performance were developed after a comprehensive analysis of effective schools research literature (KDE, n.d.), the framework is appropriate for whole-school improvement at all P-12 levels.

KDE published a companion *School Level Performance Descriptors for Kentucky's Standards and Indicators for School Improvement* to assist building level personnel in preparing their annual improvement activities and portfolios required for accountability audits or reviews. Each SISI indicator in the *Descriptors* is presented separately with examples of appropriate supporting evidence listed (e.g., curriculum maps and instructional program plans, student performance reports, professional development activities, school governance and committee documents). A matrix is used to display descriptions of actions and activities within four performance levels (e.g., 4 = exemplary level of development and implementation; 3 = fully functioning and operational level of development and implementation; 2 = limited development or partial implementation; 1 = little or no development and implementation) for each of the 88 indicators. Appendix A presents a page about a school culture indicator from the *Descriptors* document.

Although all 88 indicators in the SISI framework are implied district requirements for guidance, assistance, and support to schools, 54 indicators have explicit district accountability responsibilities for oversight and monitoring their schools performance. KDE is required to audit any district that has any low-performing schools within the lowest third of that category (Level 3) for two consecutive accountability cycles (i.e., four years). KDE published a companion *District Level Performance Descriptors for the Kentucky Standards and Indicators for School Improvement*, presented in the same format as the one for schools, to assist district-office personnel in the preparation for an audit. Audited districts are accountable for all 88 indictors in SISI.

Data-Informed Planning and Action

Principals, teachers, and parents use the SISI framework to conduct self-studies about their schools' performance and use data collected to develop comprehensive improvement plans, a process similarly employed by superintendents and central office personnel to support district-wide efforts aimed at improving schools.

KDE uses the SISI framework to evaluate school progress toward goal achievement in the accountability system when sending teams of trained reviewers to conduct mandated audits and voluntary reviews. KDE-trained teams collect and analyze data from multiple sources of evidence (e.g., documents, interviews, observations) and then assign a numerical rating for each SISI indicator. One member of each team is assigned to input ratings into the central database maintained by KDE. At the conclusion of each accountability biennium, ratings for Level 3 schools and successful schools are compared. Chi-square and gamma computations on the most recent accountability data revealed statistical significance on 45 of the 88 indicators, which are collectively identified as *Variance Points 2004–2006* (see Appendix B).

School Culture

The highest number of variance points ($n = 10$) are located under the standard for school culture. Table 24.1 displays the 11 indicators under the school culture standard. All but one (i.e., effective assignment and use of staff strengths) emerged as variance points during the 2004–2006 accountability cycle, indicating the critical importance of school culture on student achievement and school performance.

External Application of Accountability Model

Although the SISI framework was developed for Kentucky schools, several states have adopted it without any modification or used it as a guide for developing their own statewide standards to guide school improvement efforts. Nine state departments of education have sought direct assistance from KDE to develop capacity for statewide

Table 24.1 SISI Standard 4: Learning environment—school culture indicators.

Effective learning community with climate . . .

4.1a	Leadership support for safe, orderly environment
4.1b	Leadership beliefs and practices for high achievement
4.1c	Teacher beliefs and practices for high achievement
4.1d	Teachers and non-teaching staff involved in decision making
4.1e	Teachers accept their role in student success/failure
4.1f	Effective assignment and use of staff strengths
4.1g	Teachers communicate student progress with parents
4.1h	Teachers care about kids and inspire their best efforts
4.1i	Multiple communication strategies used to disseminate info
4.1j	Student achievement valued and publicly celebrated
4.1k	Equity and diversity valued and supported

Source: Kentucky Department of Education (2004).

school improvement efforts. Copies of SISI documents are available from the KDE website.

Discussion

A myriad studies examining planned organizational change have found culture to be the most significant variable determining success or failure. Cameron and Quinn (2006) concluded that many as three-quarters of redesign efforts, including those focused on total quality management and involving strategic planning, either completely failed or created serious problems because they were incompatible with prevailing values and beliefs. Leading education scholars who have analyzed planned change and school improvement (e.g., Cotton, 2003; Duke, 2004; Fullan, 1999) conclude that culture has been no less influential in schools. Thus logically, school improvement seems probable in situations where leaders can (a) diagnose shared values and beliefs, (b) determine the extent to which these values and beliefs enhance or hinder school performance, and (c) forge a plan for changing or replacing counterproductive values and beliefs.

In his studies of public elementary and secondary schools spanning more than 20 years, Sarason (1996) found considerable inertia which he attributed primarily to administrators and teachers. He concluded that educators comprehended neither school culture nor organizational change, and consequently, they were incapable of reculturing schools.

Today, most principals recognize that culture change is difficult but necessary (Barth, 2002). The systemic approach to school improvement in Kentucky, which includes statewide use of the SISI and widely disseminated biennial reports of school audit and review results, has informed educators and parents about the critical influence school culture has on both school performance and student achievement. In fact, KDE regularly receives requests for voluntary audits. Additionally, all principal preparation programs and most professional development activities in Kentucky use the SISI as an instructional resource.

Nonetheless, many principals remain less than enthusiastic about engaging in this process. This reluctance stems from a mix of individual and organizational conditions, such as a lack of confidence, an aversion to change, and a preference for addressing other responsibilities. Their doubts and preferences not only prevent them from addressing culture, they prompt them to behave counterproductively, such as promoting culture change verbally while continuing to act in ways that sustain the prevailing culture (Kowalski, Petersen, & Fusarelli, 2007). Though teachers readily detect such contradictions, they are more prone to emulate the principal's behavior than to challenge it (Reeves, 2006–2007).

Premised on the conviction that understanding culture and diagnostic data lessens aversions to culture audits, this chapter examined the utility of standardized diagnostic instruments and state accountability programs. Both resources broaden our understanding of school culture and of the critical nexus between culture and school performance. They also generate essential evidence that should be used to solve existing problems by virtue of objective and informed decisions.

Given the essential nature of culture audits, surprisingly little research has been conducted on this topic. Additional research is needed in several critical areas including: (a) associations between culture profiles produced from standardized instruments and qualitative data stemming from observations (e.g., levels of collaboration and collegiality), (b) the feasibility of interfacing culture profiles with student performance data (e.g., student test scores, student grades), (c) identifying elements of state accountability programs that potentially contribute to diagnosing school culture, and (d) possible associations between culture profiles and data used to make summative school assessments (e.g., value-added components of state accountability programs).

Notes

1. Artifacts and espoused beliefs, such as those found in school philosophies and visions, may represent "ideal" rather than "real" underlying beliefs directing behavior.
2. Culture is also protected and preserved through the process of socialization—the use of routine and social pressures intended to make new organizational members comply with existing norms (Hart, 1991).
3. The instruments were: *School Culture Survey; Social Work Culture Profile; Professional Culture Questionnaire for Primary Schools; Organizational Culture in Primary Schools; School Values Inventory; School Cultural Elements Questionnaire.* Of these, only the first two were tested in the United States.

References

Balthazard, P. A., Cooke, R. A., & Potter, R. E. (2006). Dysfunctional culture, dysfunctional organization: Capturing the behavioral norms that form organizational culture and drive performance. *Journal of Managerial Psychology, 21*(8), 709–732.

Barth, R. S. (2002). The culture builder. *Educational Leadership, 59*(8), 6–11.

Bauman, P. C. (1996). *Governing education: Public sector reform or privatization.* Boston: Allyn & Bacon.

Beaudoin, M., & Taylor, M. E. (2004). *Creating a positive school culture: How principals and teachers can solve problems together.* Thousand Oaks, CA: Corwin Press.

Bernhardt, V. L. (2002). *The school portfolio toolkit: A planning, implementation, and evaluation guide for continuous school improvement.* Larchmont, NY: Eye on Education.

Borman, K., Katzenmeyer, W., Barber, J., & Moriarty, K. (2002, April). *Managing policy issues in carrying out systemic reform: Lessons for principals from Chicago, El Paso, Memphis and Miami.* Paper presented at the annual meeting of the American Educational Research Association, New Orleans, LA.

Browne-Ferrigno, T., Allen, L. W., & Hurt, P. (in press). Longitudinal reform and renewal efforts to improve public schools: Kentucky's standards and indicators for school improvement. *Leadership and Policy in Schools.*

Bruner, D. Y., & Greelee, B. J. (2004). Analysis of school work culture in schools that implement comprehensive school reform models. *Journal of Research for Educational Leaders, 2*(1), 33–53.

Bryk, A. S., & Schneider, B. (2002). *Trust in schools: A core resource for improvement.* New York: Russell Sage Foundation.

Burton, R. M., Lauridsen, J., & Obel, B. (1999). *Tension and resistance to change in organizational climate: Managerial implications for a fast paced world.* Retrieved July 10, 2007, from http://www.lok.cbs.dk/images/publ/Burton%20og%20Obel%20og%20Lauridsen%20tension%202000.pdf

Cameron, K. S., & Quinn, R. E. (2006). *Diagnosing and changing organizational culture: Based on the competing values framework* (rev. ed.). San Francisco: Jossey-Bass.

Cavanagh, R. F., & Waugh, R. F. (2004). Secondary school renewal: The effect of classroom learning culture on educational outcomes. *Learning Environments Research, 7*(3), 245–269.

Conway, J. A. (1985). A perspective on organizational cultures and organizational belief structure. *Educational Administration Quarterly, 22*(4), 7–25.

Cooke, R. A., & Lafferty, J.C. (1987). *Organizational culture inventory* (Form III). Plymouth, MI: Human Synergistics.

Cooke, R. A., & Rousseau, D. M. (1988). Behavioral norms and expectations: A quantitative approach to the assessment of organizational culture. *Group and Organization Studies, 13,* 245–273.

Cotton, K. (2003). *Principals and student achievement: What the research says.* Alexandria, VA: Association for Supervision and Curriculum Development.

Cox, T. (1993). *Cultural diversity in organizations: Theory, research and practice.* San Francisco: Berrett-Koehler.

Danielson, C. (2002). *Enhancing student achievement: A framework for school improvement.* Alexandria, VA: Association for Supervision and Curriculum Development.

Deal, T. E., & Kennedy, A. A. (1982). *Corporate cultures.* Reading, MA: Addison-Wesley.

Duke, D. (2004). *The challenge of educational change.* Boston: Allyn & Bacon.

Edwards, J. L., Green, K. E., & Lyons, C. A. (1996). *Factor and Rasch analysis of the School Culture Survey.* (ERIC Document Reproduction Service No. ED401 290).

Elbot, C. E., & Fulton, D. (2007). *Building an intentional school culture: Excellence in academics and character.* Thousand Oaks, CA: Corwin Press.

Firestone, W. A., & Louis, K. S. (1999). Schools as cultures. In J. Murphy & K. S. Louis (Eds.), *Handbook of research on educational administration* (2nd ed., pp. 297–322). San Francisco: Jossey-Bass.

Foster, J. D. (1999). *Redesigning public education: The Kentucky experience.* Lexington, KY: Diversified Services.

Fullan, M. G. (1999). *Change forces: The sequel.* Philadelphia: Falmer Press.

Fullan, M. (2001a). *Leading in a culture of change.* San Francisco: Jossey-Bass.

Fullan, M. (2001b). *The new meaning of educational change* (3rd ed.). New York: Teachers College Press.

Fullan, M. (2005). *Leadership and sustainability: System thinkers in action.* Thousand Oaks, CA: Corwin Press.

Gaziel, H. H. (1997). Impact of school culture on effectiveness of secondary schools with disadvantaged students. *Journal of Educational Research, 90,* 310–318.

Gibson, S., & Dembo, M. (1984). Teacher efficacy: A construct validated. *Journal of Educational Psychology, 76*(4), 569–582.

Gruenert, S. (2005). Correlations of collaborative school cultures with student achievement. *NASSP Bulletin, 89*(645), 43–55.

Hall, G. E., & Hord, S. M. (2001). *Implementing change: Patterns, principles, and potholes.* Boston: Allyn & Bacon.

Hanson, E. M. (2003). *Educational administration and organizational behavior* (5th ed.). Boston: Allyn & Bacon.

Hart, A. N. (1991). Leader succession and socialization: A synthesis. *Review of Educational Research, 61*(4), 451–474.

Herrmann, K. L. (2007). *The interface of school culture and selected demographic and school performance variables.* Unpublished doctoral dissertation, University of Dayton, Dayton, Ohio.

Human Synergistics Incorporated (2008). *Organization Culture Inventory.* Retrieved January 3, 2008, from http://www.humansynergistics.com/products/oci.aspx

Johns, G. (1988). *Organizational behavior: Understanding life at work* (2nd ed.). Glenview, IL: Scott, Foresman and Company.

Katzenmeyer, W. G. (1999). *The school culture quality survey.* Tampa, FL: The David C. Anchin Center.

Kentucky Department of Education (n.d.). *Research foundations: Standards and indicators for school improvement.* Frankfort, KY: Author.

Kentucky Department of Education (2004). *School level performance descriptors for Kentucky's Standards and Indicators for School Improvement.* Frankfort, KY: Author.

Kentucky Department of Education's 2004–2006 variance points. Retrieved December 1, 2007, from http://www.education.ky.gov/KDE/Administrative+Resources/School+Improvement/Standars+and+Indicators+for+School+Improvement/

Kochanek, J. R. (2005). *Building trust for better schools: Research-based practices.* Thousand Oaks, CA: Corwin Press.

Kowalski, T. J. (2003). *Contemporary school administration: An introduction* (2nd ed.). Boston: Allyn & Bacon.

Kowalski, T. J. (2006). *The school superintendent: Theory, practice, and cases* (2nd ed.). Thousand Oaks, CA: Sage.

Kowalski, T. J., & Herrmann, K. L. (2008). Evaluating the culture of high schools in relation to their demographic characteristics and performance. In W. K. Hoy & M. F. DiPaola (Eds.), *Improving schools: Studies in leadership and culture* (pp. 55–71). Charlotte, NC: Information Age Publishing.

Kowalski, T. J., Petersen, G. J., & Fusarelli, L. D. (2007). *Effective communication for school administrators: An imperative in an information age.* Lanham, MD: Rowman & Littlefied Education.

Leithwood, K., Jantzi, D., & Fernandez, A. (1994). Transformational leadership and teachers' commitment to change. In J. Murphy & K. S. Louis (Eds.), *Reshaping the principalship* (pp. 77–98). Thousand Oaks, CA: Corwin Press.

Marazza, L. L. (2003). *The 5 essentials of organizational excellence: Maximizing schoolwide student achievement and performance.* Thousand Oaks, CA: Corwin Press.

Maslowski, R. (2001). *School culture and school performance: An explorative study into the organizational culture of secondary schools and their effects.* Unpublished doctoral thesis, University of Twente, The Netherlands.

Maslowski, R. (2006). A review of inventories for diagnosing school culture. *Journal of Educational Administration, 44*(1), 6–35.

Morgan, G. (1986). *Images of organization.* Newbury Park, CA: Sage.

Owens, R. G. (2001). *Organizational behavior in education: Instructional leadership and school reform* (7th ed.). Boston: Allyn & Bacon.

Pankratz, R. S., & Petrosko, J. M. (Eds.) (2000). *All children can learn: Lessons from the Kentucky reform experience.* San Francisco: Jossey-Bass.

Phillips, G., & Wagner, C. (2003). *School culture assessment: A manual for assessing and transforming school-classroom culture.* Vancouver, BC: Agent 5 Design.

Purkey, S. C., & Smith, M. S. (1983). Effective schools: A review. *Elementary School Journal, 83,* 427–452.

Quinn, R. E. (1984). Applying the competing values approach to leadership: Toward an integrative framework. In J. G. Hunt, D. M. Hosking, C. A. Schriesheim, & R. Stewart (Eds.), *Leaders and managers: International perspectives on managerial behavior and leadership* (pp. 10–27). New York: Pergamon.

Reeves, D. (2006–07). How do you change school culture? *Educational Leadership, 64*(4), 92, 94.

Reitz, H. J. (1987). *Behavior in organizations* (3rd ed.). Homewood, IL: Irwin.

Saphier, J., & King, M. (1985). Good seeds grow in strong cultures. *Educational Leadership, 42*(6), 67–74.

Sarason, S. B. (1996). *Revisiting the culture of the school and the problem of change.* New York: Teachers College Press.

Schein, E. H. (1990). Organizational culture. *American Psychologist, 45*(2), 109–119.

Schein, E. H. (1992). *Organizational culture and leadership* (2nd ed.). San Francisco: Jossey-Bass.

Schein, E. H. (1996). Culture: The missing concept in organization studies. *Administrative Science Quarterly, 41*(2), 229–240.

Sergiovanni, T. J. (2007). *Rethinking leadership: A collection of articles* (2nd ed.). Thousand Oaks, CA: Corwin Press.

Snyder, K. J. (1988). *School work culture profile.* Tampa, FL: School Management Institute.

Snyder, K. J., & Anderson, R. H. (1986). *Managing productive schools: Towards an ecology.* Orlando, FL: Academic Press.

Spady, W. (2001). *Beyond counterfeit reforms: Forging an authentic future for all learners.* Lanham, MD: Scarecrow Press.

Taguiri, R. (1968). The concept of organizational climate. In R. Taguiri & G. H. Litwin (Eds.), *Organizational climate: Exploration of a concept* (pp. 11–32). Boston: Harvard Graduate School of Business Administration.

Trimble, K. (1996). Building a learning community. *Equity and Excellence in Education, 29*(1), 37–40.

Vincenz, L. (1990). *Development of the Vincenz empowerment scale.* Unpublished doctoral dissertation, University of Maryland, College Park.

Weick, K. E. (1979). *The social psychology of organizing.* Reading, MA: Addison-Wesley.

Zigarelli, M. A. (1996). An empirical test of conclusions from effective schools research. *Journal of Educational Research, 90,* 103–110.

Zmuda, A., Kuklis, R., & Kline, E. (2004). *Transforming schools: Creating a culture of continuous improvement.* Alexandria, VA: Association for Supervision and Curriculum Development.

Appendix A: Kentucky Standards and Indicators for School Improvement

Standard 4: School Culture

Indicator	Ratings of Performance			
	4 *Exemplary level of development and implementation*	3 *Fully functioning and operational level of development and implementation*	2 *Limited development or partial implementation*	1 *Limited or no development and implementation*
4.1c Teachers hold high expectations for all students academically and behaviorally, and this is evidenced in their practice. *Examples supporting evidence:* • Lesson plans • Walkthrough observations • Student, parent, staff interviews • School discipline plan • Student and parent handbooks • Posted behavior standards • Posted academic standards and rubrics • Perception surveys • School council policy • Individual growth plans • Student work	Meets criteria for a rating of "3" on this indicator plus: Students and staff members collaborate to establish, sustain, and demonstrate in practice schoolwide high academic expectations that are applicable to all. Students and staff members collaborate to research and adopt an effective program of schoolwide student behavior that emphasizes self-discipline and responsibility.	Teachers set high academic expectations for all students, challenge the students to set high expectations for themselves and provide the structure and support to ensure student success. Standards of student behavior collaboratively developed, clearly communicated to stakeholders, and equitably applied to all students.	Teachers set high academic expectations for some students, but not all. Standards of behavior are developed by staff members and communicated to students, but not equitably applied.	Teachers do not set high academic expectations for students. Standards of behavior exist, but are neither communicated to students nor equitably applied.

Appendix B: Variance Points 2004–2006*

Standard 1—Academic Performance—Curriculum
Rigorous, intentional and aligned . . .

1.1a Aligned with academic expectation, core content, program of studies ★(.82)

1.1b Discussions among schools regarding curriculum standards

1.1c Discussions among schools to eliminate overlaps, close gaps

1.1d Vertical communication w/focus on key transition points

1.1e Links to continuing education, life, and career options

1.1f Process to monitor, evaluate, and review curriculum

1.1g Common academic core for all students ★(.94)

Standard 4—Learning Environment—School Culture
Effective learning community with climate . . .

4.1a Leadership support for safe, orderly environment ★(.98)

4.1b Leadership beliefs and practices for high achievement ★(.97)

4.1c Teacher beliefs and practices for high achievement ★(1.0)

4.1d Teachers and non-teaching staff involved in decision making ★(.94)

4.1e Teachers accept their role in student success/failure ★(.94)

4.1f Effective assignment and use of staff strengths

4.1g Teachers communicate student progress with parents ★(.97)

4.1h Teachers care about kids and inspire their best efforts ★(.9O)

4.1i Multiple communication strategies used to disseminate info ★(1.0)

4.1j Student achievement valued and publicly celebrated ★(1.0)

4.1k Equity and diversity valued and supported ★(.93)

Standard 7—Efficiency—Leadership
Instructional decisions focus on support for teaching/learning, organizational direction, high performance expectations, learning culture, and developing leadership capacity . . .

7.1a Leadership developed shared vision

7.1b Leadership decisions are collaborative, data driven, performance ★(.95)

7.1c Leadership personal PD plan focused on effective skills ★(.71)

7.1d Leadership disaggregates data

7.1e Leadership provides access to curriculum and data ★(.96)

7.1f Leadership maximizes time effectiveness ★(.96)

7.1g Leadership provides resources, monitors progress, removes barriers to learning ★(.93)

7.1h Leadership ensures safe and effective learning ★(.83)

7.1i Leadership ensures necessary SBDM policies

7.1j SBDM has intentional focus on student academic performance

7.1k Leader has skills in academic performance, learning environment, efficiency ★(.93)

Standard 2—Academic Performance—Classroom Evaluation/Assessment

Multiple evaluation and assessment strategies . . .

2.1a Classroom assessments are frequent, rigorous, aligned

2.1b Teachers collaborate in design of assessment, aligned *(.89)

2.1c Students can articulate the expectations, know requirements *(.93)

2.1d Test scores used to identify gaps *(.87)

2.1e Multiple assessments provide feedback on learning *(.94)

2.1f Performance standards communicated and observable *(.83)

2.1g CATS coordination—building and district

2.1h Student work analyzed

Standard 5—Learning Environment—Student, Family, and Community Support

School works with families/community to remove barriers . . .

5.1a Families and communities active partners *(1.0)

5.1b All students have access to all curriculum

5.1c School provides organizational structure *(1.O)

5.1d Student instructional assistance outside of class-room *(1.0)

5.1e Accurate student record-keeping system

Standard 8—Efficiency—Organizational Structure and Resource

Organization maximizes time, space, resources . . .

Organization of the School

8.1a Maximizes organization and resources for achievement

8.1b Master schedule provides all students access *(.87)

8.1c Staffing based on student needs *(.93)

8.1d Staff's efficient use of time to maximize learning *(1.0)

8.1e Team vertical and horizontal planning focused on improvement plan

8.1f Schedule aligned with student learning needs *(.93)

Resource Allocation and Integration

8.2a Resources used, equitable

8.2b Discretionary funds allocated on data-based needs

8.2c Funds aligned with CP goals

8.2d State/Federal funds allocated with CP goals and data needs *(.88)

(Continued overleaf)

Appendix B: Continued

Standard 3—Academic Performance—Instruction	Standard 6—Learning Environment—Professional Growth, Development and Evaluation	Standard 9—Efficiency—Comprehensive and Effective Planning
Instructional program engages all students . . .	*Researched-based, professional development and performance evaluation to improve teaching and learning . . .*	*School improvement plan . . .*
		Defining the School's Vision, Mission, Beliefs
		9.1a Collaborative process
3.1a Varied instructional strategies used in all classrooms *(.96)	**Professional Development**	**Development of the Profile**
3.1b Instructional strategies/activities aligned with goals	6.1a Long-term professional growth plans *(.87)	9.2a Planning process involves collecting, managing, and analyzing data
3.1c Strategies monitored/aligned to address learning styles	6.1b Building capacity with ongoing PD *(.93)	9.2b Uses data for school improvement planning
3.1d Teachers demonstrate content knowledge *(.97)	6.1c Staff development aligned with student performance goals *(.96)	**Defining Desired Results for Student Learning**
3.1e Teachers incorporate technology in classrooms	6.1d School improvement goals connected to student learning goals	9.3a Plans reflect research/expectations for learning and are reviewed by team
3.1f Sufficient resources available *(.88)	6.1e PD ongoing and job embedded *(.87)	9.3b Staff analysis of student learning needs
3.1g Teacher collaboration to review student work	6.1f PD aligned to analysis of test data	9.3c Desired learning results are defined
3.1h Homework is frequent, monitored and tied to instructional practice *(.96)		**Analyzing Instructional and Organizational Effectiveness**
	Professional Growth and Evaluation	9.4a Data used to determine strengths and limitations
	6.2a School has clearly defined evaluation process	9.4b School goals are defined
	6.2b Leadership provides sufficient PD resources *(.86)	**Development of the Improvement Plan**
	6.2c Evaluations and growth plans effectively used *(.89)	9.5a School improvement action steps aligned with goals and objectives
	6.2d Evaluation process meets or exceeds statutes *(.78)	9.5b Plan identifies resources, timelines, and person responsible
	6.2e Instructional leadership needs addressed	9.5c Process to effectively evaluate plan
	6.2f Leadership provides evaluation follow-up and support *(.9O)	9.5d Plan aligned with mission, beliefs, school profile, desired results
		Implementation and Documentation
		9.6a Plan implemented as developed
		9.6b Evaluate degree of student learning set by plan
		9.6c Evaluate student performance according to plan
		9.6d Evidence to sustain the commitment to continuous improvement

Note: **Variance points** based on significant differences (chi square .001) between Level 3 and Successful Schools during 2004–2006 accountability cycle are identified by *(Gamma score).

25

Data-Based Teacher Selection
Viewed from a Planning, Recruitment, and Selection Perspective

I. Phillip Young
University of California-Davis

Teacher selection is an administrative process performed by public school districts on an ongoing basis throughout the calendar year. Driving this administrative process are several causes. Teachers must be selected to replace existing personnel due to retirements, to transfers within the district, to fill vacancies created by leaves, to voluntary resignations, and to non-renewals of probationary teachers.

Beyond replacement of existing personnel, teachers may be selected for other reasons. For school districts experiencing a growth in student enrollments, new teachers are needed. In other school districts, new teachers may be needed either to meet accreditation requirements or to staff a new organizational structure.

The importance of teacher selection is well noted in the research literature, in trade publications as well as in the popular press, and is catapulted to the forefront by federal legislation. Almost a century ago, Graces (1932) indicated "wise selection is the best means of improving the system, and the greatest lack of economy exits whenever teachers have been poorly chosen or inadequately adapted to their profession" (p. 191). These same sentiments stated by Graces continue to be echoed by recent federal legislation pertaining to the public school setting.

Most notably, the No Child Left Behind Act (NCLB) emphasizes the importance of teacher selection within the public school setting. Specifically addressed in this legislation is the employment of qualified teachers to staff America's classrooms. However, the employment of qualified teachers within the public school setting will come about most expediently from a data-based decision approach, or else issues as noted by Graces (1932) would have been resolved decades ago.

Delaying the practice of teacher selection from a data-based approach are past perceptions about this administrative activity. Largely overlooked in the past from a practice perspective in the field setting is that teacher selection is a process rather than an event (Delli & Vera, 2003). That is, selection decisions fail to be either a yes or no situation but must be grounded within a data-based decision context that considers multiple sources of information in a sequential manner (Heneman & Judge, 2005). Contained in Figure 25.1 is a model that should be followed by all public school districts with respect to the selection of teachers from a data-based approach. Important to note for this model is that attention is afforded to teacher selection

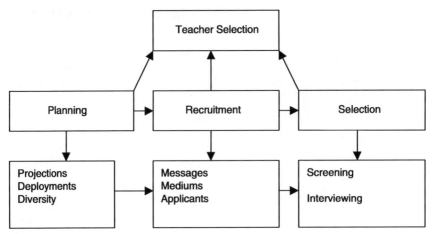

Figure 25.1 Teacher selection from a process perspective.

from a planning as well as from an implementation perspective relative to data-based decision making. Both planning and implementation perspectives are addressed in the following sections of this chapter relative to the different phases as depicted in Figure 25.1.

Teacher Selection as a Data-Based Process

Fundamental to the selection of teachers within the public school setting from a data-based decision mode are certain important questions to be resolved by all progressive school districts. Foremost, attention must be given to anticipated teacher needs. Anticipated teacher needs encompass both actual numbers as well as concerns about diversity of new hires and involves short- and long-ranging planning to provide data-based information.

After information is provided both about current and future needs for teachers within a public school district from a planning perspective, attention is redirected to recruitment, screening, and selection as other administrative processes. For all of these administrative processes, information exists to inform data-based decision making in the field setting. As such, within the following sections of this chapter, important information is provided from a data-based decision-making approach centering on teacher selection from a strategic planning point of view, from the perspectives of individuals as applicants within the recruitment process, and from the actions of public school districts as employers.

Planning for Teacher Selection

Without a doubt, public school districts that fail to plan may well be planning to fail. This adage is well sounded in the planning literature and is particularly applicable to public school districts when it comes to teacher selection. Planning for teacher selection is important because quality teachers are sought by all public school districts and because school districts entering the job market late forfeit a potential competitive advantage with respect to recruiting and to selecting the most qualified applicants.

Required by a strategic planning process relative to the selection of teachers are several types of information. Information is needed about anticipated teacher needs, about deployments of current teachers, and about diversity of individuals within the teacher workforce. Specific attention is afforded to each of these information needs from a planning perspective.

Anticipated Teacher Needs

To identify actual as well as potential needs for teachers within a public school district, a staffing plan must be formulated from a strategic planning perspective. Under-girding any staffing plan for teachers from a strategic planning process are two sources of data used to inform data-based decision making. At a minimum, one source of information involves enrollment projections for students, while the other source of data concerns current staffing deployments within a public school district.

Without a doubt, the number of actual or expected students for a school district has direct implications for the number of teachers needed to staff a public school district. For student enrollment projections, many models exist to guide informed decision making from a data-based perspective. However, these models differ in some important ways that have important implications for data-based decision making within the teacher selection context.

Most common among these enrollment projection methods is the survival ratio technique (SRT). The SRT is used by most state departments of education and by most public school districts from a strategic planning perspective. However, this model (SRT) considers only two sources of information to inform data-based decision making relative to needs for teachers, and this limitation to only two sources of information is a delimiting aspect associated with this planning technique as applied to teacher selection within the public school setting.

One source of data considered by the SRT is live birth rates for assessing entry to a public school district either at the kindergarten or at the first grade level. Live birth rates are obtained from established databases maintained by public school districts, county organizations, and/or state agencies. Assumed by this source of information as used by the SRT is that entry to a school district is restricted only to past demographic trends reflecting live births.

The other source of data considered by the SRT is movement (ascension) within a school district after students have been enrolled. Ascension of only students enrolled in a school across time is assessed and is incorporated within SRT models via survival ratios as a means for projecting future needs of a school district for teacher personnel. Students not born from a live birth perspective or not enrolled in a school district fail to be considered by the SRT method, and this limitation in enrollment projection has important implications for teacher selection at the local school district level when assessed by this particular method.

In contrast to the SRT method, other enrollment projection techniques exist that can inform better the teacher selection process from a data-based decision-making approach. Most notable among these techniques is the Bayesian estimation procedure (BES). Unlike the SRT relying only on live births and on ascension, the BES accommodates both subjective and objective information to capture the nuances of any public school district relative to needs for teachers as suggested by actual as well as anticipated student enrollments.

Beyond live birth rates and ascension data used by the SRT, Young (2008) noted different types of subjective information utilized by the BES enrollment projection method as applied to staffing needs of a public school district for teachers. Included among these other sources of information are openings of charter schools, tuition increases for parochial schools, and policy changes by a local board of education to mention only a few variables considered by the BES approach and found to impact student enrollments. Furthermore, these sorts of information can be tailored to specific school buildings within a public school district to capture unique needs for actual as well as anticipated teachers according to organizational structures.

Although all enrollment techniques provide an estimate for future teacher needs relative to student enrollments, these data fall short in a very important way. Information is provided about the number of teachers needed but is insensitive to the deployment of teachers and to the diversity of teachers from a data-based decision-making perspective. Both deployment and diversity warrant specific attention from a data-based decision-making approach involving the selection of teachers.

Deployment of Teachers

From a data-based decision-making perspective, attention should be given to deployment of teachers within any public school district. Deployment is defined by student–teacher ratios broken down by school building level and by instructional units. Of importance from a data-based approach are what these ratios should be and if these ratios should vary by organizational levels of a school district's academic programs and/or organizational structure. From a data-based perspective focusing on teacher selection, deployment is a policy decision based on informed knowledge driven by actual data assessed at the local school district level.

Informed knowledge to guide data-based decision making on the part of policy makers can be enhanced by a staffing analysis. For each school building as well as for each organizational unit, staffing ratios should be computed. Without a doubt, the ratios will vary according to organizational level and can inform data-based decision making for teacher selection.

For most public school districts, it is not uncommon to find that student–teacher ratios vary by organizational level. Elementary schools within any particular school district have typically lower student–teacher ratios than secondary schools with middle/junior high schools having lower student ratios than senior high schools. These differences among organizational levels for student–teacher ratios should reflect policy decisions based on informed data rather than on an equalization principle applied to all organizational levels of a particular public school district.

Even within a particular school building ratios may vary. For elementary school buildings it is not uncommon to have lower student ratios for K-2 and higher ratios for older students. At the high school level, ratios may be lower in science/math areas than in social science areas.

Beyond deployment of teachers within the data-driven decision-making process are other concerns that must be addressed by public school districts prior to recruitment and to selection. Of interest is the issue of diversity for the teacher selection process from a planning perspective as related to teacher selection. Concerns about diversity within the teacher selection process should be commingled with policy decisions, and actual data must be considered within the teacher selection process from a data-based decision approach.

Diversity of Teachers

Within the teacher selection process, diversity is an important topic for all stakeholders. From a policy perspective, public school districts should adopt a specific stance governing the teacher recruitment and the selection processes as this stance pertains to diversity. Within the teacher recruitment and selection processes, public school districts can be either an equal employment opportunity employer (EEO) or an affirmative action employer (AAE). Choices between these options have profound implications for the recruitment and for the selection of teachers from a data-based perspective.

Within the equal employment opportunity context, recruitment and selection of teachers should be facially neutral without any consideration of protected class status. That is, no attention is given to any protected status of teacher applicants when recruiting teachers, when delimiting applicant pools, and when selecting teachers. In contrast to the equal employment opportunity approach, the affirmative action perspective allows special consideration to teacher candidates of designated protected class groups (e.g., race, sex, national origin, etc.).

Guiding the decisions of public school districts relative to equal opportunity and to affirmative action from a policy point of view should be empirical data to inform decision making. From a data-based decision approach for teacher selection, several measures impart important information. These measures are (a) concentration statistics, (b) stock statistics, and (c) flow statistics.

Differentiating among these data-based measures is unique information about protected class groups either as employees and/or as potential applicants. Focusing only on employees within a public school district is concentration statistics. Concentration statistics reflect the current workforce independent of work assignment as distributed across different protected class groups within a particular public school district, and concentration statistics reflect diversity of the total workforce within a public school district.

On the other hand, stock statistics deconstruct the workforce within a public school district according to work assignments. Most generally, data are assessed for administrative assignments, instructional positions, and support staff relative to protected class groups within a public school district. Stock statistics, like concentration statistics, reflect current organization assignments for protected class groups from different perspectives relative to actual employees within a public school district.

Complementing this information about current staffing for protected class groups within the teacher selection process are flow statistics. Flow statistics address hiring ratios between protected and non-protected groups as defined by a relevant labor market comprised of potential applicants. Of concern for flow statistics are those eligible and those selected within a defined labor market independent of applicant pools.

Information as provided by concentration, stock, and flow statistics must be interpreted from a contextual perspective within the teacher selection process. This context involves a relevant labor market for a particular school district. A relevant labor market is defined from a geographical perspective and reflects the expected diversity of a public school district relative to a specific legal criterion measure.

Pivotal to this definition of a relevant labor market is the distance an applicant could be reasonably expected to travel for employment consideration as a teacher. Important to note in this definition of a relevant labor market for the teacher selection process are two distinctions. One distinction is traveling for consideration as compared to traveling for work once employed with only the former consideration (traveling) used to define a relevant labor market.

Indeed, a potential teacher applicant may be expected to travel several hundred miles for employment consideration, and this expected distance is moderated by local considerations of public school districts when defining a relevant labor market. For some less populated states with few institutions of higher education preparing teachers (i.e., Nevada) the distance is much greater than in other states (i.e., New York) with many institutions of higher education preparing teacher candidates. No doubt, the definition of reasonable distance for employment consideration varies greatly between Nevada and New York, but public school districts within any state should reflect the composition of a relevant labor market as defined from a contextual perspective with respect to the expected diversity of employees.

Another distinction often confounded from a data-based decision approach concerning diversity for the recruitment and the selection of teachers is the issue of student populations for a public school district. Important to note is that a relevant labor market for teachers is controlling and not the diversity of students within a school district when it comes to the selection of teachers. At first glance, the difference between a relevant labor market and the diversity of a student body within a public school district may seem contradictory for the teacher selection process; however, this is not the case.

For example, if the diversity of students within a public school district were indeed controlling for the teacher selection process rather than a relevant labor market, then many mono-ethnic school districts as found in some urban/suburban/rural school settings, albeit with different diversity representations, could fail to consider applicants of a different "like type" relative to students. Such a practice based on student body composition within the teacher selection process focusing on diversity of students rather than on a relevant labor market would promote segregation rather than desegregation. Thus, neither students nor potential teacher applicants would be well served from a legal or from an assimilation point of view if diversity of a student body rather than a relevant labor market is used as a criterion within the teacher selection process.

Once strategic planning issues pertaining to teacher demands suggested by enrollment projections, staffing requirements based on analyses of workforce allocations, and policy concerns relative to EEOC or affirmative processes relying on formal assessments of existing employment data (concentration, stock, and flow statistics) have been addressed, attention is redirected to other phases of the teacher selection process from a data-based perspective. Most importantly, teachers must be recruited, applicant pools must be screened, and teachers must be selected. For each of these administrative activities involving recruitment, screening, and selection special attention is provided from a data-based decision perspective.

Recruitment of Teachers

As an administrative activity, the focus of recruitment is on generating an applicant pool comprised of well-qualified teacher candidates. Without an adequate applicant pool from which to choose among candidates, selection is nonexistent, and assignment is the only available option for staffing teacher needs within the public school setting. To ensure that public school districts practice selection rather than assignment with respect to attraction as well as to selection of teachers, a data-based approach should be followed.

Data-based decision making from an organizational perspective relative to recruitment of teachers has been addressed only recently within the published literature. At one time in the recent past, decisions of applicants were taken as a given, and most research as well as practice focused on selection only from an organizational perspective. Indeed, few public school districts have followed a data-based approach to the recruitment of teachers sometimes at the expense of students by relying only on "walk-in" candidates.

To attract an able pool of job applicants and to select highly qualified teacher candidates, public school districts can no longer rely solely on walk-in candidates. For many identified teacher vacancies to be filled by public school districts, the demand for teachers exceeds the supply of potential candidates, especially in the areas of science, math, and special education (Hecker, 2004). As such, competition among school districts within the recruitment/selection process is high, and those public school districts utilizing a data-based approach for recruitment/selection are likely to enjoy a distinct advantage because supply favors a buyer's (applicants) rather than a seller's market (school districts).

Without question, teacher applicants like public school districts must make proactive decisions to consummate an employment contract. Enhancing the probability of teacher candidates to make proactive decisions is important data-based information revealed by empirical studies. Imparted by these studies is information about content of the recruitment message, the medium used for communicating this message, and characteristics of potential applicants.

Recruitment Messages

Communicated to teacher applicants within the recruitment process are a message about a public school district and information about particular job assignments. Potential recruitment messages have been deconstructed to reflect different content, and these messages have been assessed by studies relying on empirical data. As deconstructed in this body of literature, content of recruitment messages has been varied to emphasize financial incentives, psychological rewards, or job responsibilities as a means for attracting teacher applicants.

Underlying each of these potential recruitment messages are certain assumptions about individuals as applicants. When financial incentives are used as the content of a recruitment message, individuals are viewed as economic beings using the job search process as a means of enhancing one's quality of life. Emphasizing psychological rewards as a recruitment message for individuals as psychological beings is that the job search process serves to match applicant needs with organizational opportunities. With respect to communicating job responsibilities as a message within the recruitment process, individuals as applicants are viewed as rational beings seeking closure about particular job assignments.

Research within the teacher recruitment literature has addressed the viability of recruitment messages for each of these areas as can be used by a public school district from a data-based approach to attract potential teacher candidates within the recruitment process. Results from these studies addressing specifically teachers indicate that the message concerning economic incentives is the least favored. Information about both the psychological aspects associated with the organization and the job duties for an assigned position are important to potential teacher candidates within the recruitment process and should be used from a data-based approach for attracting teacher candidates as communicated through different mediums.

Recruitment Mediums

Recruitment messages are communicated through different mediums to potential teacher applicants. Foremost among these media are job postings via written messages and verbal communication as provided by organizational representatives within the recruitment process. For each of these mediums, data-based information exists for guiding practice in the field setting.

With few exceptions, most public school districts rely on written information to communicate with potential applicants about vacant teacher positions. Written information is communicated through job postings and job advertisements as a means for attracting individuals early within the recruitment and the selection processes. With respect to written information as imparted by different modes of communication, specific data exist relative to the attraction and to the selection of teachers.

For written information, insights are provided by Winter (1996) varying systematically the content of job advertisements from a procedural perspective. Specifically manipulated by this investigator for written information are contact information (general versus specific), grammatical tense of the message (first person versus third person), and follow-up processes (telephone contact versus written acknowledgement). Potential teacher candidates are found to be more likely to apply when a person rather than an office is listed as the contact source, when the tense of a recruitment message is written in first as opposed to third person, and when individuals receive a follow-up telephone contact in lieu of a letter as a result of their inquiry.

Another medium used to communicate recruitment messages at the attraction stage of the teachers selection process is an organizational representative of a school district. Organizational representatives of a school district serve as a communication source in several ways. Within the recruitment process, information to potential applicants is provided by organizational representatives in several settings.

These settings include interviews through college placement offices, recruitment fairs involving multiple school districts, and walk-in candidates at the local school district level. For each of these venues, important data-based information exists for guiding the recruitment and the selection process. Specifically addressed in these studies are demographic characteristics of organizational representatives as well as the knowledge base of these organizational representatives relative to particular job assignments for targeted positions.

With respect to demographic characteristics of organizational representatives, Young, Place, Rinehart, Jury, and Baits (1997) varied similarity of teacher applicants and of organizational representative relative both to race and to sex. These investigators found that similar race pairings are more important than similar sex parings for attracting teacher candidates at the recruitment phase of the teacher selection process. This information is important from a data-based decision approach for recruitment and for selection when related to policy adoption by a board of education (EEO or AAE) as discussed in an earlier section of this chapter, in that if specific groups of protected class applicants are sought, then organizational representatives should be so chosen accordingly but not without other considerations.

For organizational representatives chosen on the basis of race to represent a school district within the recruitment process, consideration must be given to their content knowledge about vacant focal teacher positions to be filled. Revealed further by the above research is that applicants for teacher positions are concerned about job-specific information and that they seek this information within the recruitment phase of the selection process. From a data-based decision approach for recruitment, it is important to provide potential applicants with specifics of actual job assignments (i.e., class size, curricular materials, student diversity, etc.).

Characteristics of Applicants

Not to be overlooked within this phase of the teacher selection process focusing on recruitment is that applicants vary in some important ways that have implications for data-based decision making. One way that applicants may vary is their human capital endowments, especially as related to on-job experience. Job experience of potential applicants has financial as well as practical implications for selection and for practice when recruiting potential new job incumbents.

Teachers represent a substantial cost to a school district with experienced teachers costing more than inexperienced teachers even when a cap on experience credit is used for new hires. However, in many instances school districts may seek experienced teachers to complement existing faculties or to address tailored program needs (e.g., reading recovery). Noted within this body of literature is that experienced teachers are more difficult to recruit than inexperienced teachers (Young, Rinehart, & Heneman, 1993), and from a data-based approach these data indicate additional cost as well as more effort from an organizational perspective to recruit experienced teacher candidates.

After attention has been afforded to organizational needs for teachers through systematic planning and after proactive efforts have been devoted to the recruitment of teacher candidates, concerns are directed to the actual selection of teachers. Selection is, however, a multistage decision-making process and should be driven by data-based decision making (Delli & Vera, 2003; Heneman & Judge, 2005). It involves screening an initial applicant pool and interviewing those surviving the screening phase; both of these administrative activities are addressed in the following sections of this chapter.

Selection of Teachers

The model depicted in Figure 25.1 reflects two different types of organizational decisions that occur within the teacher selection process. One type of decision involves screening the initial pool of applicants (Thoms, McMasters, Roberts, & Dombkowski, 1999). The other type of decision concerns interviewing of job candidates (Dipboye, 1992).

From the perspective of teacher candidates, screening decisions serve as an initial gatekeeping function relative to their probable success within the teacher selection process. For school districts as organizations, screening decisions optimize their time within the teacher selection process. As noted by Cable and Gilovich (1998), "Because interviews are time intensive and costly, interviewers generally prescreen job applicants on the basis of their resumés before granting interviews" (p. 501).

Important to note from a data-based decision approach is that screening decisions and interview decisions differ in non-trivial ways with implications for data-based decision making. One way that screening decisions differ from interviewing decisions is the type of candidate stimuli used to inform decision making. For the screening stage of the selection process, candidate stimuli are depicted largely by paper credentials involving resumés, placement files, and reference information.

In contrast to the screening stage of the teacher selection process, candidate information at the interview phase involves different stimuli. At the interview stage, information is provided through visual, verbal, and interpersonal interactions. Collectively, candidate stimuli availed to the decision maker at both stages of the teacher selection process differ in quantity as well as in quality.

Beyond information provided to organizational representatives at either stage of the teacher selection process (screening or interviewing) is a different decisional context. For screening decisions based on paper credentials, the outcome is either rejection or further consideration. However, the term "further consideration" should be interpreted literally because it fails to reflect any long-range commitment on the part of a public school district.

More binding than screening decisions are outcomes from interviewing decisions within the teacher selection process. Outcomes from interview decisions are definitive. Potential job candidates for vacant teacher positions are either rejected from further consideration or extended a job offer on the basis of their interview performance.

Because screening decisions differ from interviewing decisions relative to type of applicant stimuli and to type of organizational commitments with data-based implications for the selection of teachers, both types of decisions are addressed in the following sections of this chapter. Although most of the research has focused on screening decisions rather than on interviewing decisions, information exists that can be used to inform data-based decision making in the field setting for the selection of teachers.

Screening Decisions

Considerable information exists for informing public school districts about data-based decision making relative to the screening of potential teacher candidates as part of the selection process. This information is generated by empirical studies, and these studies mirror actual practice in the field setting. Within these studies (reviewed below) at least 95% of the principals surveyed indicate that they screen teacher candidates on the basis of paper credentials before extending an invitation to interview.

To capture screening decisions of practicing administrators in the field setting, a specific research protocol has been followed in this particular research stream. This research protocol involves the creation of hypothetical teacher candidates through the use of paper credentials. Candidate information, as provided by paper credentials and as used in these studies, is identical to information solicited by most public school districts as part of the teacher application process.

Paper credentials include resumés and letters of recommendation similar to those found in most college placement files requested by public school districts and to those issued by institutions of higher education as part of the actual teacher screening process used in the field setting to delimit initial applicant pools. Within these credentials for hypothetical teacher candidates, variables are manipulated systematically to assess screening decisions and to inform data-based decision making. For this particular research stream, screening decisions have been explored from a legal perspective and have been assessed with random samples of public school administrators.

From a legal perspective, compliance with several federal legislative acts is assessed at the screening stage of the teacher selection process. As addressed in this body of literature from a data-based decision-making approach are the following federal acts: Age Discrimination in Employment Act (ADEA), Americans with Disabilities Act

(ADA), and Title VII of the Civil Rights Act (Title VII). For each of these legislative acts, information exists for informing data-based decision making within the teacher selection process.

To illustrate, the ADEA forbids discrimination on the basis of chronological age at any stage of the selection process if applicants are over the age of 40. To assess likely age discrimination at the screening stage of the selection process, chronological age of teacher candidates is varied within the paper credentials to include those above 40 years of age and those below 40 years of age. Results across several studies indicate a disproportional impact for older teacher candidates at the screening stage of the teacher selection process.

At first glance it may seem that chronological age of teacher candidates serves as a proxy for other important variables because age correlates highly with job experience having cost implications, with recentness of educational preparation having academic implications, and/or with physical capabilities having to do with energy and enthusiasm. However, empirical data indicate that none of the above is a likely explanation for the age preference found to influence screening decisions within the teacher selection context, especially with school principals.

Pointedly, Young and Allison (1982) varied both chronological age and job experience of teacher candidates and found that organizational representatives (superintendents and principals) favored younger candidates over older candidates at the screening stage of the teacher selection process regardless of their teacher experience. Recentness of academic degrees as well as chronological age of teacher candidates are manipulated in another study (Young & Joseph, 1989), and only chronological age is found to influence screening decisions. Focusing on teacher positions (high versus low activity, physical education or physics) and chronological age of teacher candidates, results indicated again the importance of chronological age at the screening stage although these findings are counter to ADEA mandates (Young, Rinehart, & Baits, 1997).

Turning from the ADEA to the ADA, screening decisions have been investigated relative to handicapped status of teacher candidates at the screening stage of the selection process (Young & Prince, 1999). Handicapped status is varied within the paper credentials to include applicants using a wheelchair, requiring a walking cane, or no physical mobility problems (control group). Screening decisions are found to favor handicapped applicants as compared to non-handicapped applicants at the screening stage of the selection process.

Research addressing the protected status of applicants as defined by Title VII has explored sex and national origin of teacher applicants at the screening stage of the teacher selection process. Sex of teacher candidates has been found to exert little influence on screening decisions of public school principals (Reis, Young, & Jury, 1999; Stallard, 1990; Wallich, 1984; Young, 2006). However, national origin of teacher candidates appears to be an important factor within the screening stage of the teacher selection process.

National origin of teacher candidates is operationalized through surnames and by self-acknowledgment on resumés/placement type files. Principals favored Asian and Hispanic teacher candidates over Native American teacher candidates at the screening stage of the teacher selection process (Young & Fox, 2002; Young & Oto, 2004).

These findings emerged even though all these candidates were equally qualified for the teacher position under consideration.

Teacher candidates endorsed by school administrators at the screening stage of the teacher selection process are subjected to another hurdle (Delli & Vera, 2003; Heneman & Judge, 2005; Thoms et al., 1999). This hurdle involves a selection interview. Outcomes from selection interviews determine if a teacher applicant will receive an actual job offer or will no longer be considered for the particular focal position under consideration.

Interview Decisions

The final stage of the teacher selection process involves interview decisions. Although interviews are used universally by public school districts and are a very influential part of the teacher selection process, empirical research addressing this administrative procedure is sparse in this body of literature. No doubt, this research neglect can be attributed to several causes.

From an experimental perspective, interview research is inefficient as compared to screening research. To obtain a single observation addressing interview outcomes (interview decisions), visual, verbal, and interactional stimuli are needed. However, limited research does exist that explores interview decisions within the teacher selection context with implications for data-based decision making.

For example, Young and Pounder (1985) used video techniques and role-playing simulations to address the importance of chronological age of teacher candidates as detected by research addressing screening decisions. In a two-part study, chronological age of a single teacher candidate was manipulated cosmetically on video tapes (part 1), and chronological age of multiple teacher candidates was varied across subjects in a role-playing simulation (part 2). Within each of these experimental protocols (videos versus simulations), practicing educators acted as interviewers and evaluated a hypothetical teacher candidate.

For the video condition, interviewers were exposed only to verbal and to visual information as provided by a single candidate, albeit differing in perceived chronological age. Within the role-playing portion of their study, available to interviewers are verbal, visual, and interactional stimuli for multiple teacher candidates. Across both of these experimental conditions utilizing different research protocols, no effect for age discrimination was detected, and these findings for chronological age of teacher candidates differ from those involving screening decisions relying solely on paper credentials.

Implied by these findings from a data-based decision approach is important information. Unsurprisingly, screening decisions differ from interview decisions as can be anticipated because different types of applicant stimuli come into play and moderate the decision-making process. Also, any stereotype perceptions for age operating at the screening stage may well be overcome at the interview stage if applicants are afforded an opportunity to interview.

Additional experimental research involving role playing has varied the structure of the interview format within the teacher selection process (Young, 1983). The format was varied to include dyad interviews (teacher candidate and school administrator) or panel interviews (teacher candidate, faculty member, and school administrator). Interview outcomes are found to differ for the structure of the interview with those interviewed by multiple persons (panel condition) being more likely to be recommended than those candidates interviewed by a single administrator (dyad condition).

Because the format of the selection interview rather than qualifications of teacher candidates is found to influence teacher selection decisions, these findings have data-based implications for public school districts. Suggested by these findings is that public school districts should standardize their selection processes relative to an interview format. The type of interview format (either dyad or panel) is unimportant but the consistency of application of a particular format across the district is important to ensure all teacher candidates receive equal consideration within the teacher selection process.

More recently, teacher selection interviews have been investigated in the field setting involving actual teacher candidates and practicing school administrators (Young & Delli, 2002). This field-based research focuses on the Teacher Perceiver (Selection Research Incorporated, 1990) used by many school districts within the teacher selection process. Criterion measures relating to on-job performance of teachers as measured by principals' ratings for new hires and absentee rates for newly employed teachers were regressed on interview assessments obtained from the Teacher Perceiver, and these results offered little support for this process even though it is used by over 1,600 public school districts.

Young and Delli's (2002) findings from a data-based decision-making approach suggest the need to conduct validity studies at the local school district level. To assume that a single instrument is valid for all school districts implies an assumption that a universal teacher exists independent of contextual influences exerted by a particular school district. However, it is well known in practice that a teacher who is successful in a particular school district/building (urban-intercity) may well be unsuccessful in another school district/building (rural) due to contextual differences and to prevailing local norms.

Chapter Summary

Emphasized throughout this chapter is that teacher selection is a process rather than an event and that this process can be improved by relying on empirical information to drive data-based decision making. Fundamental to the teacher selection process is strategic planning. Strategic planning informs the teacher selection process by identifying actual as well as anticipated teacher needs through the use of projection techniques, provides information (concentration, stock, and flow statistics) to inform policy decisions about EEO and AAE concerns related to teacher diversity, and to address issues relative to the deployment of teachers within a public school district across organizational as well as instructional units.

Given that these basic issues are resolved from a data-based approach at the planning stage of the teacher selection process efforts are directed to recruitment both from an individual and from an organizational perspective. Without an adequate applicant pool from which to select teachers, assignment rather than selection comes into play for staffing a public school district. To increase the likelihood that public school districts will attract an able body of willing and of capable teacher candidates, attention is given to recruitment messages, recruitment mediums, and demographic characteristics of involved parties.

To delimit a pool of applicants and to employ only the best teachers for a public school district, selection is explored from two perspectives. Empirical information is provided for screening decisions and for interviewing decisions from a data-based decision-making mode. These decisions are found to vary for stages of the selection process and for the type of information availed to decision makers with implications for actual practice.

In closing, this chapter emphasizes the importance of data-based decision making within the teacher selection process. To guide this important administrative activity within the public school setting, teacher selection was examined relative to planning, to recruitment, and to selection as interconnected activities. Each of these components is important if public school districts are to employ only the most qualified candidates.

References

Cable, D. M., & Gilovich, T. (1998). Looked over or overlooked? Prescreening decisions and postinterview evaluations. *Journal of Applied Psychology*, 83, 501–508.

Delli, D.A., & Vera, E.M. (2004). Psychological and contextual influences on the teacher selection interview: A model for future research. *Journal of Personnel Evaluation in Education*, 17(2), 137–155.

Dipboye, R. I. (1992). *Selection interviews: Process perspectives.* Cincinnati, OH: South-Western College Publishing.

Graces, F. P. (1932). *The administration of American education.* New York: Macmillan.

Hecker, D. E. (2004, February). Occupational employment projections to 2012. *Monthly Labor Review*, 80–105.

Heneman, H. G., & Judge, T. A. (2005). *Staffing organizations* (6th ed.). Middleton, WI: Mendota House.

Reis, S. C., Young, I. P., & Jury, J. C. (1999). Female administrators: A crack in the glass ceiling. *Journal of Personnel Evaluation in Education*, 13(4), 71–82.

Selection Research Incorporated (1990). *The teacher perceiver interview* [Brochure]. Lincoln, NE: Author.

Stallard, J. B. (1990). *An investigation of factors in resumés that influence the selection of teachers.* Unpublished doctoral dissertation. The Ohio State University, Columbus.

Thoms, P., McMasters, R., Roberts, M. R., & Dombkowski, D. A. (1999). Resume characteristics as predictors of an invitation to interview. *Journal of Business and Psychology*, 13(3), 339–356.

Wallich, L. R. (1984). *The effects of age and sex on the prescreening for selection of teachers candidates.* Unpublished doctoral dissertation, University of Wisconsin-Madison, Madison.

Winter, P. A. (1996). Applicant evaluations of formal position advertisements: The influence of sex, job message content, and information order. *Journal of Personnel Evaluation in Education*, 10, 105–116.

Young, I. P. (1983). Administrators' perceptions of teacher candidates in dyad and panel interviews. *Educational Administration Quarterly*, 19(2), 46–63.

Young, I. P. (2006). Effects of "like type" sex pairings between applicants—principals and type of focal position considered at the screening stage of the selection process. *Journal of Personnel Evaluation in Education*, 18(3), 185–199.

Young, I. P. (2008). *The human resource function in educational administration* (9th ed.). Columbus, OH: Prentice Hall.

Young, I. P., & Allison, B. (1982). Effects of candidate age and experience on school superintendents and principals in selecting teachers. *Planning and Changing*, 13(4), 245–256.

Young I. P., & Delli, D. A. (2002). The validity of the Teacher Perceiver Instrument for predicting performance of classroom teachers. *Educational Administration Quarterly*, 38(5), 584–610.

Young, I. P., & Fox, J. A. (2002). Asian, Hispanic and Native American job candidates: Prescreened or screened with the selection process. *Educational Administration Quarterly*, 38(4), 530–554.

Young, I. P., & Joseph, G. (1989). Effects of chronological age, skill obsolescence, quality of information and focal position on evaluations of principals. *Journal of Personnel Evaluation in Education, 2*(3), 355–365.

Young, I. P., & Oto, T. (2004). The impact of age for Asian, Hispanic, and Native American teacher candidates on principals' screening decisions as viewed from a social distance perspective. *Leadership and Policy in Schools, 3*(4), 295–323.

Young, I. P., & Prince, A. L. (1999). Legal implications for teacher selection as defined by the ADA and the ADEA. *Journal of Law & Education, 28*(4), 517–530.

Young, I. P., Place, A. W., Rinehart, J. S., Jury, J. C., & Baits, D. F. (1997). Teacher recruitment: A test of the similarity–attraction hypothesis for race and sex. *Educational Administration Quarterly, 33*(1), 86–106.

Young, I. P., & Pounder, D. G. (1985). Salient factors affecting decision-making in simulated teacher selection interviews. *Journal of Educational Equity and Leadership, 5*(3), 216–233.

Young, I. P., Rinehart, J., & Baits, D. (1997). Age discrimination: Impact of chronological age and perceived position demands on teacher screening decisions. *Journal of Research and Development in Education, 30*(2), 103–112.

Young, I. P., Rinehart, J., & Heneman, H. G. (1993). Effects of job attribute categories, applicant job experience, and recruiter sex on applicant job attractiveness ratings. *Journal of Personnel Evaluation in Education, 7*(3), 55–65.

26

Issues of Recruitment and Selection from a Data-Based Perspective
Implications for Educational Leadership Programs

I. Phillip Young
University of California-Davis

and

Carol A. Mullen
University of North Carolina-Greensboro

Based on labor projections, the demand for and the supply of educational leaders is a topic of concern both for the public school setting and for educational leadership programs (Hecker, 2004; National Association of Elementary and Secondary School Principals, 1998). Public schools must re-staff existing positions vacated by turnovers as well as staff new positions created to accommodate increasing enrollments and organizational reconfigurations (Young, 2008). One vehicle for accommodating these needs is graduate education as provided by institutions of higher education.

Graduate education addresses these pressing needs in several important ways. First, graduate education provides a means to satisfy minimum certification requirements necessary for valid consideration as a candidate for leadership positions. For many leadership positions within the public school setting (e.g., principal, assistant superintendent, superintendent), advanced graduate coursework is required to meet state mandated certification requirements.

Second, performance of students within graduate programs may serve as a valid predictor for public school districts when selecting new employees. Empirical data are provided by grade point averages in graduate coursework, and experiential data are suggested by experiences encountered in practicum and supervised field projects. Subjective information can be obtained to inform data-based decision making within the selection context via references as provided by university and field supervisors.

To operate graduate level educational leadership programs, institutions of higher education must recruit and select potential students every year. Often overlooked in this operation of educational leadership programs is that recruitment and selection are related but separate administrative processes to be performed by most institutions of higher education. Student recruitment requires generating an applicant pool of potential program candidates.

In the past, recruitment may have been glossed over by many graduate programs. The modus operandi was to rely largely on "walk-in students" as the primary source for generating an applicant pool. In recent years, some graduate programs have begun to use recruitment fairs and information sessions to attract applicants through providing data to inform decision making from a data-based perspective.

Once applicants are attracted to a specific program, as evident by providing required information for consideration, faculty must make selections from among those applicants making formal application. From a data-based perspective, selection, like recruitment, is viewed as an administrative process as opposed to an organizational event. Initial applicant pools are delimited by faculty according to paper credentials submitted by applicants, and formal admission invitations are extended on the basis of invited interviews.

However, both administrative processes (recruitment and selection) can be enhanced by using data to inform decision making on the part of all stakeholders. Inadequate recruitment and selection serves neither potential applicants nor graduate faculty well. As noted by Ivankova and Stick (2007), inadequate recruitment and selection processes are "not only painful and expensive for a student, but [are] also discouraging for faculty involved, injurious to an institution's reputation, and result in a loss of high level resources" (p. 94).

Indeed, the adequacy of recruitment and selection processes is determined, at least in part, by program completion rates. However, some research suggests that program completion in U.S. institutions of higher education may be as low as 50% (D'Andres, 2002; Dorn & Papalewis, 1997; Marcus, 1997). No doubt, these percentages could be improved through more informed data-based decision making from the onset.

To provide empirical information bearing on these administrative processes (recruitment and selection) from a data-based perspective is the focus of this chapter. More specifically, existing literature is reviewed from an individual as well as from an organizational perspective relative to data-based decision making. Based on this review, specific recommendations are made that have important implications for recruitment and for selection from a data-based decision approach.

Related Literature

It is no longer a controversial notion that data should be used to support organizational decision making (Picciano, 2006). In recent years, this stance has become commonplace in public schools and universities alike, largely due to the emphasis placed on more rigorous accountability in American education (Darling-Hammond, 2004; Picciano, 2006). The educational literature dealing with data-driven decision-making processes mainly concerns schools and school districts, a focus that is commensurate with the standards expected of schools by federal laws, particularly the No Child Left Behind Act of 2001 (U.S. Department of Education, 2002), state education departments, local boards of education, and funding agencies (Picciano, 2006). In contrast, our somewhat original focus contributes to the higher education context and, more specifically, to graduate programs in educational leadership and administration. We assume the position that integrating data and information into the processes of student recruitment and selection will enable university faculty and administrators to make informed decisions that support a program's progress and goals.

Although recruitment and selection are separate but related administrative processes for all programs focusing on educational leadership, it is important to note that these administrative responsibilities rely on a common core of information. This information can be used to drive data-based decision making relative to the procurement of required certifications/qualifications and to replenish applicant pools for employment considerations. For recruitment, potential applicants for programs in higher education are concerned about program content as well as about admission requirements, while faculty within institutions of higher education must rely on certain information to make informed selection decisions about admission to an educational leadership program. Consequently, research addressing both concerns of applicants and concerns of graduate faculty are reviewed in the following sections.

Data Concerns of Applicants

Decisions of individuals, as potential applicants for a graduate program in educational leadership, have been explored relative to several personal orientations purported to influence data-based decision making. Differentiating among these orientations are specific needs and salient variables suggested to influence decision making from a data-based perspective as found in the general recruitment/selection literature and as captured by different theories: objective theory, subjective theory, work itself theory (see Young, Rinehart, & Place, 1989). These theories focus on the following constructs: (a) economic incentives, (b) psychological needs, and (c) program requirements.

Economic Incentives

The importance of economic incentives on data-based decision making for applicants in general is encapsulated within the objective theory of decision making (Behling, Laborita, & Gainer, 1968). According to the objective theory of decision making, potential applicants are economic beings who seek to maximize their financial status in life through informed decision making relative to career choices among alternatives. Particularly appealing from the objective theory perspective within the recruitment context are economic advantages associated with various alternatives (e.g., career advancement, better job, higher salary) that can be fulfilled by graduate education in an educational leadership program.

Psychological Needs

In contrast to the objective theory involving financial incentives and viewing individuals as economic beings is the subjective theory (Judge & Bretz, 1992). The subjective theory emphasizes the psychological needs of individuals as potential applicants for graduate education in educational leadership. Important for the subjective theory is graduate program content bearing on psychological needs of individuals as potential educational leaders. As psychological beings, individuals want to become enlightened about leadership, to increase their level of knowledge relative to this particular field of study, and to enhance their leadership skills in the field setting.

Program Requirements

Still different from either economic incentives or psychological needs are rational concerns of individuals within the recruitment process for educational leadership programs. That is, data are sought about admission and graduation requirements by individuals as potential applicants. Most importantly, potential applicants are concerned about what is required to be admitted and what is required to graduate relative to particular programs of study.

Research addressing these different theories (economic incentives, psychological needs, and program requirements) and different orientations of individuals as applicants (economic beings, psychological beings, or rational beings), as well as the salient variables (financial, program content, and admission criteria) purported to influence their decision making has received attention in the literature found in educational leadership publications. However, after reviewing this literature, only a single study was found addressing these variables within the graduate program context (i.e., Young, Galloway, & Rinehart, 1990), even though many studies have applied these theories to the attraction of employees in the public school setting (Newton, Giesen, Freeman, Bishop, & Zeitoun, 2003; Newton, Winter, & Keedy, 2000; Winter, Keedy, & Newton, 2001; Winter & Melloy, 2005). Within the single study addressing attraction for a graduate program in educational leadership, a recruitment brochure is used as an informational source to inform data-based decision making on the part of potential applicants (Young et al., 1990).

Manipulated specifically by Young and colleagues (1990) are both sex of potential applicants and contents of the recruitment brochure. Sex of potential applicants was manipulated to determine if females differed from males relative to their informational needs within the recruitment process. Contents of the recruitment brochure were varied to include the objective, subjective, or admission requirements.

No effect for sex of potential candidates was detected, suggesting that both females and males seek the same type of information to inform their decision making at the recruitment phase of the admission process for an educational leadership program. Most important for all potential candidates is the content of the recruitment brochure pertaining to admission requirements relative either to the objective theory or the psychological theory. Interestingly, these are the same data important to graduate faculty from a selection perspective relative to admission decisions.

Data Concerns of Faculty

Beyond these informational concerns of individuals, as applicants for recruitment, are those informational concerns of graduate faculty charged with gatekeeping functions relative to admission to an educational leadership program. To delimit an initial applicant pool for admission to an educational leadership program, graduate faculty members rely on specific information similar to information sought by potential applicants. Among these sources of data, Malone, Nelson, and Nelson (2001) listed standardized test scores, prior academic performance, and reference information as being among the most salient sources of information.

Standardized Test Scores

For admission to an educational administration graduate program, standardized tests, typically one of two, are most likely used within the recruitment and selection process. One test is the Graduate Record Examination (GRE). GRE scores are dis-aggregated according to a verbal subtest and to a quantitative subtest although other subtests exist (i.e., analytical) and new subtests are emerging for this particular standardized measure (i.e., writing).

Less frequently used but still popular for educational leadership programs is the Miller Analogies Test (MAT). Outcomes from the MAT are provided according to raw scores and to percentile measures allowing comparisons across applicants and testing situations. Although some graduate programs require a specific standardized test (GRE or MAT), it is not unusual for this choice between standardized tests as a means for satisfying admission requirements to be determined by an applicant from a personal preference point of view.

For these standardized tests, specific attention is given in the published literature relative to these measures within the educational leadership context. From a data-based decision-making perspective, much of this attention has focused on validity rather than on specific required performance. As noted by Smith and Garrison (2005), "The existing research most often relies on statistical technology concerning 'variance' to communicate the power of statistical tests" (p. 633) for specific predictors.

Variance is communicated usually by a coefficient of determination reflecting the amount of variance shared between a predictor and a criterion measure. For the GRE, Young (in press) found that only the verbal subtest of the GRE accounted for significant variance when both the GRE verbal and GRE quantitative subtests are considered. The criterion variable in the above-cited study includes those applicants rejected, those students admitted but failing to graduate, and those students graduated.

With respect to the Miller Analogies Test for educational leadership programs, data exist to inform decision making. Young (in press) regressed only admission decisions (rejected or accepted) on MAT percentile scores. Results indicate that a statistically significant amount of variance in admission decisions for an educational leadership program could be accounted for by performance of applicants on the MAT.

Not to be overlooked in the recruitment and selection processes for educational leadership programs is that standardized tests are only part of the admission process that informs data-based decision making, even though great difference is purportedly afforded these measures (Norton, 1994). Without a doubt, grade point averages and reference information come into play within the admission process from a data-based decision approach. Consequently, attention is refocused to these other sources of information relating to recruitment and to selection within the educational leadership context.

Grade Point Averages

As compared to standardized test scores, grade point averages provide additional information for data-based decision making. This point is echoed by publishers of the GRE: "Standardized test scores and prior grades measure overlapping but different aspects of educational attainment, and they have complementary strengths" (Educational Testing Service, 2004, p. 2).

Information about grade point averages is obtained from an analysis of transcripts submitted by applicants as part of the admission process. In conducting an analysis of transcripts for graduate program admission, grade point averages are computed several ways by programs in educational leadership. Attention is afforded to undergraduate (UGGPA) as well as to graduate grade point averages (GGPA) within the admission process, and this information is used to guide data-based decision making.

In general, undergraduate grade point averages are lower than graduate grade point averages and exhibit more variability. No doubt, this difference reflects, at least in part, maturational aspects of individuals as well as grading norms of universities. Undergraduates tend to be younger than graduate students, explore alternate majors, and become more focused as their educational career advances.

On the other hand, graduate students are experienced collegians, more directed on a specific area of study, and subjected to a different grading norm. Minimum acceptable performance for undergraduates is 2.0 in contrast with 3.0 for graduate education. This difference between undergraduate and graduate grade point averages has been noted in the professional literature as related to admission standards for graduate programs in educational leadership and administration.

In a survey of several hundred institutions ($n = 450$) addressing minimum admission requirements for graduate programs in educational leadership, Creighton and Jones (2001) found considerable variability across institutions of higher education. Indeed, 194 institutions require a minimum undergraduate grade point average of 3.00, 124 institutions require a minimum undergraduate grade point average of 2.75, and 132 institutions require a minimum undergraduate grade point average of 2.50. More recently, Dembowski (2007) surveyed 88 educational leadership programs about expectations for graduate grade point averages and reported "All of the programs required a Graduate GPA that ranged between 3.0–3.5" for admission.

Although standardized test scores and "grade point average represent quantitative measures in the decision making process" (Malone et al., 2001, p. 3), other variables (e.g., reference information) are considered by faculty members to delimit an initial applicant pool. With few or any exceptions most graduate programs collect reference information about potential candidates. In the following sections, we address this information.

Reference Information

Unlike scores from standardized tests (GRE or MAT) and grade point averages reported by official transcripts, reference information can be obtained through a variety of formats. Included among these formats are letters of recommendation and standardized reference forms. With respect to these sources of information used to guide data-based decision making within the recruitment and selection process for graduate programs in educational leadership, many differences have been identified in the professional literature that have important implications for data-based decision making.

Take, for example, letters of recommendation; content may vary considerably depending on the reference source. The reference source could address either personal characteristics of applicants or professional competencies of applicants within these free-flowing formats. These sources of variation (i.e., reference source and reference content) make it difficult, at best, to obtain similar information about all candidates comprising a common applicant pool for a leadership program within any given year.

To address this problem from a data-based decision-making perspective, many graduate programs in educational leadership rely on standardized reference forms rather than letters of recommendation. However, even among standardized reference forms, variations exist that have implications for data-based decision making. Many of these differences are noted (Young, 2005).

For example, reference information on a standardized form can be either criterion-related (how this person performs relative to established criteria) or norm-referenced (how this person performed relative to known individuals). Independent of the anchor source for evaluation (criterion or norm) content of the reference information can vary. Contained in Table 26.1 are specific norm-referenced items used to delimit an initial applicant pool for a particular program in educational leadership.

To assess the validity of these items as constrained by the norm-referenced process in Table 26.1, an empirical analysis is reported (Young, 2005). Results of this analysis indicated that only two of these items are found to differentiate between those accepted and those rejected: research ability and work habits. For data-based decision making, this is enlightening information derived from empirical results as assessed for a particular program focusing on educational leadership.

Furthermore, information as provided for all the predictors (standardized test scores, grade point averages, and reference information) described in this section has been assessed from a singular perspective largely concerning the issue of validity. Although validity is the *sine qua non* requirement for usage from a data-based decision approach, it falls short in an important way. That is, it fails to provide any insight about how to use this information from a data-based perspective via specific decisional models. We next address different decisional models.

Table 26.1 Descriptive statistics and correlations among variables.

	M	S.D.								
Intellectual ability	13.36	1.88	1.00							
Education knowledge	13.22	2.13	.76	1.00						
Motivation	14.09	1.70	.79	.78	1.00					
Research ability	13.17	2.63	.57	.64	.59	1.00				
Maturity	13.68	1.89	.77	.80	.84	.61	1.00			
Work habits	13.90	1.76	.79	.81	.90	.63	.87	1.00		
Problem solving	13.51	2.00	.79	.80	.80	.64	.81	.81	1.00	
Verbal ability	13.33	2.11	.75	.79	.75	.60	.80	.76	.83	1.00
Writing ability	13.02	2.25	.74	.77	.72	.67	.75	.76	.78	.85	1.00

Notes: All correlations are significant at the 0.01 level (2-tailed).
$N = 243$.

Source: Young, 2005.

Decisional Models for Data-Based Decision Making

Several decision models exist in the published literature that can be used to drive data-based decision making for attracting and selecting individuals as candidates in a graduate program focusing on educational leadership. All these models afford the ability to incorporate dissimilar information (standardized test scores, grade point averages, and reference information) to inform decision making on the part of graduate faculty performing a gatekeeping function. However, these models differ in important ways, have been used only recently for admission to educational leadership programs, and are labeled in the professional literature as follows: multiple cutoff model, compensatory model and eclectic model (Young, 2006).

Multiple Cutoff Model

Fundamental to the multiple cutoff method is that graduate education is a right rather than a privilege if all statutory requirements are met. That is, applicants must meet all minimum requirements to be considered admissible to an educational leadership program. According to this model, "performance on each dimension is examined separately, and underlying this model is the assumption that all must exhibit at least a minimum level of competency on each dimension" (Young, 2008, p. 224).

The multiple cutoff model is used frequently for certification programs and for admission to master's programs but less so for doctoral programs in educational leadership. It is particularly efficient when only statutory requirements as established by graduate schools and by specific leadership programs are set *a priori* (e.g., minimum requirements for standardized test scores, graduate grade point average [GGPA], undergraduate grade point average [UGGPA], and/or reference information) for recruiting and selecting candidates to a leadership program. Once pre-established standards are met for all academic predictors, admission is automatic although still data-based.

Compensatory Model

For the compensatory model, a different approach to admission is provided from a holistic perspective. That is, a low score on one predictor can be offset by a high score on another predictor used from a data-based decision approach. For example, a low undergraduate grade point average can be overridden by exceptional performance on any other predictor (i.e., standardized test results, graduate grade point average, and/ or reference information).

Of importance to the compensatory model is a single predicted score for each applicant across all predictors used to delimit an applicant pool. This score is based on the linear combinations of all predictor information used to delimit an initial applicant pool. However, this model fails to consider any statutory requirements that may have been established by graduate schools or by individual programs in educational leadership for admission considerations (i.e., minimum GPAs or minimum standardized test scores).

Eclectic Model

The eclectic model of decision making incorporates the strengths both of the multiple cutoff and the compensatory models. Within the eclectic model, specific statutory requirements can be included for some predictors (i.e., minimum GPAs and/or minimum standardized test scores) and variable performance outcomes can be included for other predictors with unspecified minimum performance expectations. This mixture of fixed and variable requirements for predictors is accomplished by considering admission to an educational leadership program as a process rather than as an event.

As a process, applicant pools are delimited initially on the basis of meeting all statutory requirements as per the multiple cutoff method. Subsequently, once these minimum requirements are met as per statutory requirements, further consideration is afforded to applicants from a compensatory model perspective utilizing a data-based decision-making approach for admission. Most importantly, if both statutory and variable standards exist for admission to a graduate program, then data derived from the eclectic model can be used by faculty to inform individuals of their likely acceptance as well as possible remedial actions for improving their likely acceptance when rejected.

Modeling the Eclectic Approach

To illustrate the utility of the eclectic model from a data-based decision-making approach, a specific example is used from the published literature that considers only quantitative measures involving GRE and GPAs as suggested by Malone and colleagues (2001) to reflect quantitative measures within the decision-making process. Within this example (Young, 2006), statutory requirements are established for grade point averages. These statutory requirements are rooted with mid-point values as reported by Creighton and Jones (2001) for undergraduate grade point averages (GPA = 2.75) and as suggested by Dembowski (2007) for graduate grade point averages (3.25).

Varying in this example, from the compensatory perspective, are standardized scores on the GRE as compensatory factors within the decision-making process. To determine the relative value of the GRE as measured by specific subtests (GRE Quantitative and GRE Verbal) for admission as a criterion variable (rejected or accepted), a regression analysis was performed. Results of the regression analysis indicate that the verbal subtest scores are more important than quantitative subtest scores in light of statutory requirements for grade point averages (UGGP 2.75 and GGPA 3.25).

As applied to the eclectic decision-making model involving data-based decision making for the purpose of illustration, different scenarios are presented in Table 26.2 for an applicant likely rejected given the statutory requirements for grade point averages. The first equation involves the specific linear combination of predictor variables found to differentiate between those rejected (coded as "0") and those accepted (coded as "1") based on their academic profiles (see Table 26.2).

Because those graduate students who are rejected after exhibiting satisfactory performance on statutory requirements (UGAP, 2.75 and GGPA, 3.25) can most likely improve their likelihood of acceptance by increasing their performance on the GRE, two different outcomes are assessed: increasing GRE quantitative subtest scores or increasing GRE verbal subtest scores (see Table 26.2). According to these data, as presented in Table 26.2, only one of these options is likely viable given these specific constraints. This means that the applicant in question must increase the verbal subtest score to 70% (new predicted score = .51) because a 99% performance on the quantitative subtest still renders this applicant as more similar to those rejected

Table 26.2 Illustration of the eclectic model (Young, 2006).

Normative data
Prediction equation: $Y = -.583 + .001(GRE\ Q\%) + .006(GRE\ V\%) + .045(UGGPA) + .172(GGPA)$.

Predicted outcome: $.44 = -.583 + .001(GRE\ Q\%, 42) + .006(GRE\ V\%, 45) + .045(UGGPA, 2.75) + .172(GGPA, 3.25)$.

Increases in GRE verbal (70%)
Predicted outcome: $.51 = -.583 + .001(GRE\ Q\%, 42) + .006(GRE\ V\%, 70) + .045(UGGPA, 2.75) + .172(GGPA, 3.25)$.

Increases in GRE quantitative (99%)
Predicted outcome: $.46 = -.583 + .001(GRE\ Q\%, 99) + .006(GRE\ V\%, 50) + .045(UGGPA, 2.75) + .172(GGPA, 3.25)$.

Source: Young, 2006.

(predicted score = .46) than to those accepted (minimum predictor score = .50) in light of satisfying minimum statutory requirements.

Conclusions

Within this chapter, data-based decision making is upheld as necessary to the functioning and progress of graduate programs in educational leadership and administration. We have addressed both the perspective of applicants and of graduate faculty. Common to both perspectives is a coalescence of informational needs to direct data-based decision making for these stakeholders within the recruitment and the selection process, albeit from different perspectives. Potential applicants are concerned about academic requirements for admission, and faculty members rely on this same information to delimit an applicant pool.

Most important among these requirements for guiding decision making are grade point averages, standardized test scores, and reference data. For each of these sources having implications for attraction as well as for selection, the existing literature was reviewed relative to current knowledge from a data-based decision perspective as applied to graduate education in educational leadership. As a means of using this information from an applied perspective in the field setting, different decisional models were addressed.

Included among these methods for processing data are the multiple cutoff, compensatory, and eclectic models. Differentiating among these decisional models is the ability to address statutory requirements as well as variable performances of applicants on the predictors used to attract and to delimit applicant pools. Most flexible among these decisional models is the eclectic approach. Within the eclectic approach, statutory requirements can be imposed early within the decision-making process, and other information can be considered after statutory requirements have been met by potential applicants.

To illustrate the application of the eclectic model for data-based decision making in the field setting, a specific case was provided. Contained in this example for applicants to a graduate program in educational leadership is information about probable acceptance as well as likely rejection; this was followed by recommended remediation if rejected on the basis of pre-established statutory requirements (e.g., GPAs) and/or variable performance on a standardized test (e.g., GRE). By using a data-based decision approach for applicants as well as for graduate faculty, decisions are depersonalized and hence objectified, and efficiency of decision making should be enhanced.

References

Behling, O., Laborita, G., & Gainer, M. (1968). College recruiting: A theoretical base. *Personnel Journal, 47*, 13–19.

Creighton, T. B., & Jones, G. D. (2001, August). *Selection or self selection? How rigorous are our selection criteria for educational administration programs?* Paper presented at the Conference of National Professors of Educational Administration, Houston, TX.

D'Andres, L. M. (2002). Obstacles to completion of the doctoral degree in colleges of education: The professors' perspective. *Educational Research Quarterly, 25*(3), 42–58.

Darling-Hammond, L. (2004). Standards, accountability, and school reform. *Teachers College Record, 106*(6), 1047–1085.

Dembowski, F. (2007). *An empirical description of doctoral programs in educational leadership. NCPEA Connexions* [National Council of Professors of Educational Administration]. Retrieved August 8, 2007, from http://cnx.org/content/coho427/1.2

Dorn, S. M., & Papalewis, R. (1997, April). *Improving doctoral retention.* Paper presented at the annual meeting of the American Educational Research Association, Chicago, IL.

Educational Testing Service (2004). *Guidelines for the use of GRE scores.* Retrieved July 16, 2007, from http://www.gre.org/scoreuse.html

Hecker, D. E. (2004, February). Occupational employment projections to 2012. *Monthly Labor Review,* 80–105.

Ivankova, N., & Stick, S. (2007). Students' persistence in a distributed doctoral program in educational leadership in higher education: A mixed methods study. *Research in Higher Education, 48*(1), 93–135.

Judge, T. A., & Bretz, R. D. (1992). Effects of work values on job choice decisions. *Journal of Applied Psychology, 77*(3), 261–271.

Malone, B. G., Nelson, J. S., & Nelson, C. V. (2001). *Completion and attrition raters of doctoral students in educational administration.* (ERIC Document Reproduction Service No. ED 457759).

Marcus, M. B. (1997, April 17). Half a doctor. *US News and World Report.*

National Association of Elementary and Secondary School Principals (1998). Over fifty percent of the principals in America's schools will retire in the next ten years. *Principal, 70*(4), 65.

Newton, R. M., Winter, P. A., & Keedy, J. L. (2000). Teacher attraction to school council service in Kentucky: Implications for national school reform. *Planning and Changing, 32*(1), 84–103.

Newton, R. M., Giesen, J., Freeman, J., Bishop, H., & Zeitoun, P. (2003). Assessing the reactions of men and women to attributes of the principalship. *Educational Administration Quarterly, 39*(4), 468–503.

Norton, M. S. (1994). *Student recruitment and selection in educational administration programs.* Arizona State University. (ERIC Document Reproduction Service No. ED 366 087).

Picciano, A. G. (2006). *Data-driven decision making for effective school leadership.* Columbus, OH: Pearson.

Smith, D. G., & Garrison, G. (2005). The impending loss of talent: An exploratory study challenging assumptions about testing and merit. *Teachers College Record, 17*(4), 629–653.

U.S. Department of Education (2002, January 16). *No Child Left Behind Act of 2001.* Washington, DC: Office of Elementary and Secondary Education. Retrieved August 9, 2007, from http://www.ed.gov/policy/elsec/leg/esea02/107-110

Winter, P. A., & Melloy, S. H. (2005). Teacher recruitment in a teacher reform state: Factors that influence applicant attraction to teacher vacancies. *Educational Administration Quarterly, 41*(2), 349–372.

Winter, P. A., Keedy, J., & Newton, R. M. (2001). Teachers serving on school decision-making councils: Predictors of teacher attraction to the job. *Journal of School Leadership, 10*(3), 249–263.

Young, I. P. (2005). Predictive validity of applicants' reference information for admission to a doctoral program in educational leadership. *Educational Research Quarterly, 29*(1), 16–25.

Young, I. P. (2006, November). *Predictive validity of the GRE and GPAs for a doctoral program focusing on educational leadership.* Paper presented at the annual conference of the California Educational Research Association, Monterey, CA.

Young, I. P. (2008). *The human resource function in educational administration* (9th ed.) Columbus, OH: Prentice Hall.

Young, I. P. (in press). Predictive validity of grade point average and of the Miller Analogies Test for admission to a doctoral program in educational leadership. *Educational Research Quarterly.*

Young, I. P., Galloway, C. M., & Rinehart, J. (1990). The effects of recruitment brochure content and gender of the reactor for doctoral programs in educational administration. *Educational Administration Quarterly, 26*(2), 168–182.

Young, I. P., Rinehart, J. S., & Place, A. W. (1989). Theories for teacher selection: Objective, subjective, and critical contact. *Teaching and Teacher Education, 5*(4), 329–336.

27

When Data are Insufficient to Make Group Decisions
A Case Study in Community College Administration

Diane M. Dunlap
University of Oregon

and

Renae E. Weber
Treasure Valley Community College

In practice, key decisions in all busy organizations are made with a mix of politics, personalities, and data in a complex milieu of competing interests and needs. The goal is to always rely on good data at the heart of important decisions (Kowalski, Lasley, & Mahoney, 2008). However, it is not always clear if collecting good data is sufficient for data to be used. Further, it is not always clear why available data are sometimes not used to guide decisions.

Both of the authors of this chapter have been administrators with substantial decision-making responsibilities and have seen and participated in a wide range of decision-making behaviors in different institutions over the decades. We have seen data used to clarify decisions, and we have seen data overlooked or bypassed to make decisions. We have seen good decisions made with bad data, and vice versa. We had become fascinated by that crossroads in theoretical space where decision theory and data-based decision making should come together to improve decisions with data, and equally fascinated about the kinds of things that keep them from coming together effectively in the shared perceptual and action space of key decision makers. We searched the research literature and found that few studies have been done in community colleges to determine when and why specific data are used, and not used, and how collected data are perceived by key decision makers. We decided to conduct a year-long study of data uses and non-uses in one community college to see if we could increase our understanding of how decisions and data interact in the actions and perceptions of key decision makers. This chapter describes the results of that year-long study.

We chose Treasure Valley Community College (TVCC) in Eastern Oregon as our research site both because it is typical in many ways of community colleges in general and also because the decision groups were enthusiastic and committed to helping us understand more about decision processes at TVCC. TVCC has several data collection and reporting strategies that are designed to inform decision makers and also meet the standards of regional and national accrediting bodies. The stated goals of

the institution included data-driven decision making, but we knew that actual practices did not always meet that goal. This difference between explicit goals and actual
practices is not unique to TVCC. In a 2001 study of information used in a university
setting, for example, Dhillon found that "tacit knowledge" about organizational
culture played a larger role in decisions than did extant data. The "way we do things"
or "what people expect" may play a more critical role than "what does the data
say." In Mintzberg and Rose's (2003) longitudinal study of McGill University, they
reported that little that resembled revolutionary change occurred over decades, and
that relevant data were not necessarily a key element in most major decisions. Access
to the TVCC key decisions over time would allow us to learn more about data uses in
a specific setting.

Review of the Literature

The collection and analysis of data is not a new managerial behavior in community
colleges. Data about the success of students and programs have always been essential
to managing limited financial resources. For example, recent studies of students have
included documentation of the value of attending community colleges (Paulsen,
1998; Rouse, 1998), the value of having graduated from a community college (Sanchez
& Laanan, 1999), documentation of graduate rates (Bailey & Weininger, 2002; Scott,
Bailey, & Kienzl, 2006), and documentation of results of programs for particular
student populations (Chang, 2005; Mellard & Byrne, 1993; Townsend & Wilson,
2006). However, most prior research and most prior data usage have been on the
specific application of one data set to one program instead of on organization-level
patterns of data usage.

Data use for decisions in the community college setting itself has not been as
extensively studied as in other educational settings, such as schools or four-year
colleges and universities. The few studies that exist support increased use of data to
make decisions. Poole and Denny (2001) found that employees of one community
college reacted positively to increased access to data and decision making. In data
collected from a random sample of North Carolina community college administrators, Hollar, Hattie, Goldman, and Lancaster (2000) found that administrators
were less likely to exhibit escalation behavior (repeated investment of time, money,
and other resources into a failing project) when they had ready access to related data,
and they had the training and background to make sense of the data available. Clark's
(1998) review of research on women in community college faculty found that timely
access to data and to decision making increased chances to succeed as campus leaders
and increased perceptions of competence.

Hawthorne and Smith (1993) looked at improving teaching and learning in community colleges. They produced a set of guidelines for academic leaders to use in
order to produce effective change. The research reported in this chapter replicated a
1987 survey of chief academic officers which was intended to "collect baseline data
on the existing level of commitment to instructional effectiveness and to suggest
areas that deserve attention so that substantive changes could be made" (Cochran,
1989, p. 34). It contained 712 chief academic officers from community colleges

located across the United States. Each participant was asked to complete a survey instrument with five areas: employment policies, campus environment, strategic actions, instructional enhancement, and instructional development. A series of questions in each of the five areas asked participants to rate each of the questions using a scale from 1 to 10 (with 1 indicating the *least commitment* and 10 representing the *most commitment*). Their findings were that the *highest commitment* by community college administrators was to campus culture and the *lowest commitment* was made toward promoting teaching effectiveness, research, and improving instruction. The intent of this study was to measure the level of commitment to instructional effectiveness and illuminate areas that deserve more attention. It was evident that if the culture was to become focused on academic excellence, more confidence in the use of data needed to be established as well as more attention given to research within the community college setting.

So, what little research had been conducted on using data to drive decisions indicates that community colleges, in general, use data at the program or student level on a regular basis and several studies demonstrated that leaders were willing to use more data that were available to them. What *is* new today are the accelerating demands that data and data documentation be "front and center" in all campus and program-level administrative decision making. In his 2003 survey study of 1,423 faculty and administrative staff of the 14 California systems of community colleges, for example, Smart noted that one of the most important roles performed by successful leaders is the management of data for decision making. However, he also noted that this management of data sources and information must be within the context of also successfully managing other, often conflicting roles. The role of analyzer of data must be in the context of successful management of other tasks, of setting and promoting the vision of the institution, and as being the motivator of self and others by building teams and using participative decision-making strategies.

Smart cited Birnbaum's earlier 2000 study that simply implementing "new" management systems when called upon to "improve" will not necessarily meet the leader's need to demonstrate command of data. Birnbaum argued that "management fads" (e.g., PPBS, TWM, BPR) typically have a short life cycle. Smart's results indicate that such a change in culture only comes when there is a healthy balance among attributes of all culture types, and campus leaders have command of the core competencies of their complex leadership roles.

In his 2005 survey and interview study of the 13 Tennessee community colleges and utilization and understanding of the institutional research function, Schulte identified multiple types of data, levels of data collection, and different uses of data. Types of data were management (budget, enrollment management, and external community), academic, student-oriented, information reporting, efficiency documentation, and external relations. Levels of data included individual, departmental, institutional, discipline, program and geographic area. Uses of data included managing budget, enrollment and staffing, managing political events, and documenting achievement. Schulte noted the absence of empirical research in this area and called for many additional studies of how data are actually used in particular types of decisions made in community colleges.

A Year-Long Research Study

Encouraged by Schulte's "mapping" of the data territory, we decided to identify what data were used during one academic year on one community college campus, with a particular focus on identifying rationales for when data were available but were not used (see Weber, 2006). The specific data users studied included the executive team (consisting of the president, dean of instruction, dean of students, and dean of finance), the board of directors, the directors group, and the department chairs. Each group was responsible for key decisions within the organization. Access to data, and an expectation to use data to make decisions, were part of the regular decision routines within the college. The purpose of our case study was to document and analyze how data were used (or not used) by key decision makers around specific decisions. We wanted to know when data were used by which groups, how they were used, and how data collection or reporting processes could be improved to increase data usage in making campus decisions.

We developed data collection instruments keyed to the specific data sources and decisions on this campus, using Schulte's (2005) data hierarchies to guide how we structured the questions. We worked to develop a triangulated case study informed by surveys and interviews with all key decision makers. Our goal was to have multiple inputs at each chronological stage of decisions, and at each decision group location within the decision structure hierarchy.

Description of the Site

Treasure Valley Community College is a two-year public institution of post-secondary education established in 1962 as part of the Oregon Community College System. The main campus is located in Ontario, Oregon, on the Oregon–Idaho border in Malheur County, named after the Malheur River which flows through it. The Oregon Trail passed through this geographic area, following the river. Dramatic contrasts between Alpine mountains, large expanses of federally owned rangeland, and desolate desert terrain contribute to an unevenly populated and difficult to serve geographic area. Average rainfall is less than 10 inches per year. It is one of the largest (49,428 square miles) and most sparsely populated (2.5 persons per square mile) community college service areas in the United States. Malheur County is the most impoverished county in Oregon. TVCC is one of its largest employers.

The College's vast service area in eastern Oregon (Malheur, Baker, Grant, Wallowa, Lake, and Harney Counties) also includes counties in southwestern Idaho (Payette, Washington, Owyhee, and Canyon Counties). The overall service area is slightly larger than North Carolina but has a relatively small population of just over 175,000. While nearby Idaho communities are not within the college's taxing district, they generate Oregon state reimbursable FTEs (as do all Oregon border states). The nearby Idaho communities are growing in population (while Southwestern Oregon is not), and Idahoans make extensive use of the college. More than 50% of TVCC's reimbursable FTEs now come from Idaho. No Idaho community college serves the region (there are only three in all of Idaho) and TVCC is the only two-year college in eastern Oregon.

Primary economic drivers are ranching of cattle and sheep, agriculture, and some mining. Food processing has been added to that mix in recent decades with the expansion of extensive irrigated agribusiness farming in the Jordan and Treasure Valley areas. One of the largest employers in the area is the Snake River Correctional Institute, Oregon's largest prison. The extensive federally owned desert lands are used for military waste storage and, during WWII, several Japanese internment camps were located in the most remote areas. Today, the entire geographic area is a destination site for hunters, fishermen, hikers, and rock and petroglyph seekers, and tourism has emerged as a leading economic force.

While TVCC has a unique rural location and cross-state funding situation, the size and program mix is like that of most community colleges. Like most community colleges, TVCC offers associate degrees and a variety of certificate programs with courses under several categories: transfer, professional technical, basic skills, adult education, and community outreach. The mission statement declares that TVCC is dedicated to providing "quality lifelong learning" to "our communities" within "available resources" (Treasure Valley Community College, 2008).

Around 10,000–12,000 students attend classes each year at TVCC. In 2005–2006, 176 associate degrees and 41 certificates were awarded. TVCC is accredited by the Northwest Commission on Colleges and Universities. The most recent full-scale accreditation review was conducted in October 2005. The Northwest Commission on Colleges and Universities (NWCCU) was originally founded in 1917 and is listed by the U.S. Secretary of Education as a nationally recognized accrediting agency for institutions offering programs of at least one academic year in length at the post-secondary level (Northwest Association of Schools and Colleges, 1994, p. 4). This commission continues to focus its assessment process on encouraging colleges to demonstrate decisions based on collected data and documentation as a key part of such assessment (NWCCU, 2003). In the formation of current assessment standards, the NWCCU drew on a growing consensus in the research and policy literature that data can and should be used to affect how decisions are made (Chand & Holm, 1998; Feldman & Tung, 2001; Kowalski et al., 2008; McLean, 1995; Rubenfeld & Newstrom, 1994). The emphasis on data-driven decisions at the accreditation level was an important factor in influencing the key decision makers at TVCC to participate in this research project as part of many efforts to improve data practices.

Decision Groups

There are four key decision groups at TVCC: the board of directors, the executive team (including the president), the program directors, and the department chairs. The TVCC board of directors comprises seven publicly elected individuals who each represent a specific voting district in Malheur County. The only qualification for standing for election is that the person must be an adult resident of the district and not be an employee of TVCC. The board meets on the third Tuesday of each month. One week prior to the meeting each board member is sent a packet of information from the president's office with a detailed agenda for the meeting. During the period of this research, there were six males and one female on the board. Their ages ranged from 30 to 60 years old. They had served on the board for between one and 25 years.

The executive team consists of the president, dean of finance, dean of instruction, and dean of students. During the period of this research, the executive team was made up of three males and one female, between 50 and 65 years old, who had served the organization between one and 25 years. The directors group was made up of 21 individuals: 13 females and eight males, who ranged in age from 25 to 65, and who had been with the institution for between six and 30 years. The chairs group consisted of 10 individuals: five men and five women, between 40 and 65 years of age, and with eight to 28 years within the institution.

The design of the study reported upon in this chapter included having all members of each group fill out an initial survey where each person was asked to identify what data they used to make decisions related to their TVCC responsibilities. These were open-ended questions. Respondents were also asked to rank importance of different reports in making decisions. This was followed by a second survey that listed specific data reports on campus and asked respondents to identify which reports they recognized, which reports they used, and how data usage was related to making specific decisions. The two surveys were followed by interviews with representative members of each decision group regarding how specific data were used by each individual.

Report of the Data

The participation rate in the initial survey was 81% (29 out of 33 possible participants returned completed surveys). This number included four board members (of seven, or 57%), three administrators (of four, or 75%), 13 directors (of 21, or 62%) and nine department chairs (of 10, or 90%). Thus, each group was well represented in the returned surveys. Each group identified the data sources and reports that they considered most and least useful. The board group reported the highest usage of budget data (75%), enrollment data (75%), and outside sources (75%). Assessment-strategic initiatives, information on faculty and staff, and student reports were used by only one of four members of the board. The administrative group responded that they used budget data (100%), enrollment data (100%), staff-faculty reports (100%), and student reports (100%). Outside sources (0%) and assessment-strategic initiatives (66%) were reported as least used. At the director level, student reports (85%) were used the most while budget data (69%), enrollment data (69%), and outside sources (54%) followed closely. The least reported as useful data by the directors included assessment-strategic planning (31%) along with staff and faculty information (23%). All the department chairs used student reports (100%), with budget data (56%), enrollment data (56%), staff and faculty information (44%) at lesser levels. Outside sources (22%) and assessment-strategic initiative data (0 %) lagged far behind. These patterns are listed in Table 27.1.

Without being given guidance as to what types of data were to be named, these decision makers reproduced the same categories reported earlier by Schulte (2005). The

Table 27.1 Results of first survey of data usage.

	Board %	Executive %	Directors %	Chairs %	Overall %
Budget	75	100	69	56	69
Enrollment	75	100	69	56	69
Outside sources	75	0	54	22	41
Student reports (satisfaction survey) completion, demographics, add/drop	25	100	85	100	83
Staff/faculty info (loads/leave/book orders)	0	100	23	44	34
Assessment strategies/initiatives	0	50	31	22	28

Source: Weber (2006)

category of "outside data" included such things named as newspapers, conversations with colleagues and constituents, professional organizations, and newsletters. During member checking, one member of the executive team noted that outside sources had not been named as the assumption had been that this research project focused only on internal reporting. A question was added to the forthcoming interview protocol to clarify this finding.

There was a contrast between board members and the other three groups with respect to use of staff and faculty information, or strategic planning data. The board spent little time looking at staff, faculty or student data, or strategic planning data. This suggests that the members of the board may have a different set of expectations regarding the planning and assessment process than the ones that are held internally by administrators, directors, and deans. The members of the executive group did not report using outside sources of data, but rather the other data sources used by the board, and also those used by the directors and department chairs.

The participants were also asked to rate their named data sources according to frequency of use, using a Likert scale from 1 to 5, with 5 representing the *most frequently used*. Budget information was named as used *most frequently* by the members of the executive team (average rating of 5), followed by the directors group (average rating of 3), members of the board (average rating of 2.75) and the chairs group (average rating of 1.78). Enrollment data were named as used *most frequently* by members of the executive team (average rating of 5), with average frequencies from the other three groups clustered under 3.0.

Student reports, including registration data and transcripts, student opinion surveys, add/drop data, and completion reports were reported as used *most frequently* by members of the executive team (average rating of 4), with lower average usage rates by the directors (average rating of 3.62), the chairs (average rating of 2.85) and members of the board (average rating of 1).

These data were useful to us in designing the second survey. When we reviewed the responses to the first survey, we concluded that not all decision makers could name each specific data report available to them. We decided to name specific reports for the second survey so our data would be more specific. Because of the consistency of responses within groups from the first survey, we also decided to direct the longer second survey to the interview sample rather than to the whole population. In fact, we asked on the second survey for the survey to be completed and ready for the interviewer at the start of the interview.

Table 27.2 is a copy of the second survey with specific reports named and response rates given.

The follow-up survey confirmed the information provided in the initial survey which was that financial data, including financial reports and budget reports, were the most consistently used by all groups. Each group identified specific reports that they found useful in order to make decisions. Full-time enrollment reports (14/16), financial reports (14/16), budget documents (14/16), and the annual campus climate report (13/16) were used most universally across campus. Data that are reported to the state and federal government [OCCURS (2/16) and IPEDS (2/16)] were the least used in making decisions within the organization. Student information, such as the quarterly success rate report (6/16) and academic history data reports (5/16) were used almost exclusively by the chairs.

The primary finding at this stage in our research, however, was that almost all of the 16 individuals scheduled to be interviewed had not completed their second survey by the time of the interview. In fact, we quickly discovered that having copies of each type of data report available to the individual was helpful to them in completing the survey because very few people knew all of the listed reports by name. Some

Table 27.2 Follow-up survey on data use.

Directions: Please complete the survey and have it available for the interviewer at the time of your scheduled interview on this research project. For each of the sources listed, check if you have used it, identify when and how in the spaces provided. If there is a data source you use that is not listed, please write it in the space provided.

	Board	Admin	Directors	Chairs	Total
FTE reports from registrar	2/4	4/4	4/4	4/4	14/16
Student Opinion Survey	2/4	4/4	1/4	4/4	11/16
Campus Climate Survey	2/4	4/4	3/4	4/4	13/16
Financial reports	4/4	4/4	3/4	3/4	14/16
Quarterly student success rate data	0/4	2/4	0/4	4/4	6/16
OCCURS data	0/4	2/4	0/4	0/4	2/16
IPEDS data	0/4	2/4	0/4	0/4	2/16
Student academic history data	0/4	1/4	0/4	4/4	5/16
Grade distribution	0/4	2/4	1/4	3/4	6/16
Assessment database	0/4	3/4	4/4	3/4	10/16
Budget information	3/4	4/4	3/4	4/4	14/16
Graduation follow-up survey data	0/4	3/4	0/4	0/4	3/16
Class evaluations	0/4	2/4	2/4	4/4	8/16
Load report	0/4	3/4	2/4	3/4	8/16
Room availability reports	0/4	2/4	1/4	0/4	3/16
Administrative evaluation	3/4	2/4	1/4	0/4	6/16
Inservice evaluation	1/4	2/4	0/4	1/4	4/16
SMART classroom survey	0/4	3/4	0/4	4/4	7/16

Source: Weber (2006).

had not completed the task because they were not sure what data were signified by which report title, or, when they could identify the report, they did not want to put down on paper that they did not understand the report well enough to use the data in the report. In almost all cases, the pre-interview discussion of the survey extended into an informal discussion and coaching session on the types of data available. It became very obvious to the interviewers that individuals appreciated the private opportunity to admit that they did not understand the data, appreciated a few words of coaching on how to use specific data, and would have been embarrassed to have had to admit their hesitancy in any public way.

One of the possible implications of this finding is that many people may not step forward and ask for assistance in understanding data. Rather than admit ignorance, they are more likely to follow the lead of others who appear more knowledgeable about what the data mean. However, when presented with a private, relatively "safe" opportunity to learn more about data reports, they will actively seek assistance. One of the possible implications of this research is that individual, one-on-one training on the use of particular data sets may be useful when a pattern of non-use is observed. This could be a particularly sensitive area if the non-user is a member of a public board who may not be as familiar with data reports in other aspects of his or her life, or is a key administrative leader who may be more comfortable with the mission and vision of the institution and less comfortable reading complex data tables or charts.

After completing the second survey and discussion of reports, each participant was then asked seven questions in order to identify how and what data had been useful to them in their respective roles over the past year. The interview sessions were tape recorded and the data subsequently transcribed and blind coded for themes by question and then by group. Member checking was done on the transcriptions, identified themes, and initial write-up of the findings in order to increase internal validity.

Members of the four groups responded very differently to the first interview question: "How do you get data that you need within the institution?" The four board members relied almost exclusively on the board packets that were mailed with information prior to each monthly board meeting.

Members of the executive team said that they requested data from the database manager on campus. All four chairs also identified the database manager as how they got data they needed within the institution to make decisions. The directors, on the other hand, said that they relied on their own report-writing skills and went directly into the information system on campus themselves to mine the data. This was a distinctly different response from the other three groups. One possible conclusion from these responses is that the database manager can play a very important role in influencing whether and how data are used and in how decisions are made. The database manager on this campus was a *de facto* decision maker. Yet, the person/role was not initially identified as a formal decision maker. It was also clear that many people depended heavily on a single person to supply critical data; this is perhaps an organizational weakness. Another aspect of the database manager's role is the many and perhaps sometimes conflicting demands for data that were directed to the manager. There seemed to be opportunity for overload and for difficulty in sorting the significance of particular requests within the overall decision structures of the campus.

The second question requested information on what decisions each individual made that were connected to data. The question generated a variety of responses that were consistent across groups and within each group. First, all four groups pointed to the importance of data in making decisions. This was a particularly interesting response as "importance" was not a direct part of the question. One director stated it succinctly:

> Having access to the information doesn't mean you will always use it [*sic*]. But when the decisions come about, you make better decisions pulling the data together.

A member of the executive team said:

> People have to see data whether they agree with them [*sic*] or not. You have to see it in order to believe it is good or not good, whether there are areas we can improve and whether it is realistic to try to improve.

Another chair cited how data had changed the program review process for accreditation, naming the program expansion in welding as a specific change that had been based on data from within the organization.

> Industry is asking or telling us that we need to expand the welding program. There is a great need for welding right now. So you have to use data. First of all you look at what is the forecast and what has happened in the last three years. We have had a waiting list and spent a lot of our overload (could have hired another part-time instructor with the funds we used in overloads). We used data in that respect to show that industry is right and we need to get something rolling. We have to expand, what does that expansion look like, can we justify it and what will it cost?

A director gave this example.

> Data can validate decisions. I am usually looking at individual pay and equity from program to program. The hiring rates pretty much conform group to group. Having the scores available gives me a better decision point to recommend when a wage is set on an offer. Having access to the information doesn't mean you will always use it. But when the decisions come about, you make better decisions pulling data together, rather than just approximating.

When the respondents were asked what data were *not* useful in their current role, the representative response was: "I don't think there are any. There are times and places where every one of these are important."

Members of all four groups shared the view that all forms of data were useful to the organization and they were not willing to identify any current data or reports as potentially not useful in the decision-making process.

The second most frequent category of data named was budgetary. The board members said they focused data usage first in budget decisions, and then on negotiations decisions and decisions about the college's future. The four executive team members reported that budget data were always in front of them. One of them made this statement.

Since I deal with the overall resources of the institution, whether people, place or things, money is really looking at enrollment and revenue. I try to look at those as a driver to see what is possible within the institution and what is feasible within the institution. Everything you have has a cost or replacement cost. So I look at what resources will I have to work with or how can I get more resources (either state, federal grant or what ever else is out there)? How you use it effectively, efficiently are somewhat subsequent.

One chair said:

Around here most everything is built around the budget: field trips, hiring adjuncts, overloads and supplies. I get a budget freeze on accounts in February and you have to kill anything that isn't absolutely necessary for the rest of the year. First of all you have to decide what is necessary and what isn't. When signing a requisition, I am afraid that someone up the line is going to say, "No you can't do this, it will look bad." The pressure from above makes you check budgets closer and make sure that the purchase is really necessary. With the new reports on budget, we can pull that information pretty quickly and find out how much money is left in each department. I sign requisitions on a daily basis so I continually need to know where the budgets are.

The third most frequently mentioned data category was student-related data. It was named by all four members of each of the three campus-based groups, and was not named by the board members. FTE reports were used regularly in all three groups to guide weekly meetings and discussions about program changes. Executive team members reported using FTE reports along with success rate data and accounts receivable that impacted class offerings as well as the financial aid policies regarding disbursement of funds. They said they used these reports in daily conversations with directors and chairs. Directors said they used FTE and class cancellations for directing class scheduling (adding or not). Several noted using data on distance learning, while chairs said they scheduled classes and hired adjuncts based on FTE reports.

Two chairs reported student evaluations to be useful, stating, "The student evaluations are great to help with scheduling classes, hiring adjuncts and continu[ing] to keep them employed." Two directors reported that census data and affirmative action data impacted daily operating procedures. One director stated:

My focus is our Access database report, because it deals with tracking and all of our accountability pieces for Adult Basic Skills, GED, etc. We are constantly looking at that and asking how the outcomes can be better. How can we get people to stay and achieve what they are here for?

A chair noted:

The data showing the candidate pool to actual registration showed that we really are doing a great job of turning the candidate into a real student. Some students are focused on coming here and we need to do a more efficient job of getting them information about TVCC. This data helps formulate what special events can be pulled together in order to move applicants from candidate to student.

Almost all of the reports listed in the second survey were named as important at one point in time by at least one respondent. Census data and affirmative action data were noted by several respondents as being specifically useful to them.

When the respondents were asked to identify specific data that had led to change, the board members reported campus climate survey data that had supported decisions regarding physical changes to campus that included parking and dorm construction. One member of the executive team said: "I was able to use data to dispute a misconception. It led to some curriculum changes and will lead to more."

Several directors also noted that modifications in the financial aid policies and practices had not only led to substantial changes in programs, but had also been almost completely driven by analysis of multiple data sources in making the decision to change the policies.

When asked the last two questions about how the data or reporting processes could be improved to increase the likelihood that data will be used to make decisions, the responses reflected specific group needs. Together with the information learned during the conversations around completing the second survey, we were able to pinpoint how and where specific reports could be modified to increase effective use. Requests for more explanatory and summary information were made from each group. Definitions of data, assuring reliability of data sources, and being able to access the information themselves, were themes that emerged around improving processes from members of all four groups. Most of these comments were made about specific data reports and were of immediate use to the institutional data managers in revising reports, formats, and timelines.

Conclusions

The findings of this case study indicate that data were used often by each decision-making group for a variety of decisions. As Supovitz and Klein pointed out in 2003, the bottom line is that systematically using data to make core decisions takes a commitment on many levels from various stakeholders. These commitments include time, training, technology, and discipline. Each of the TVCC groups demonstrated commitment as it identified a variety of sources it used and noted the frequency of use of each data source. The groups further identified skills in using data by making appropriate and useful suggestions for improvement of data formats and timing, and asking for on-the-spot training to improve their skills. While some participants may have been initially reticent to explore their questions about specific data, they readily gave suggestions about what would help them have a better understanding of specific data or data reports.

Prior research findings had pointed out that noticeable change within the culture occurred as the ownership of the data became more valuable for the individual (Dowd, 2003; Smart, 2003). Individuals who recognize their roles and responsibilities connected to specific data sources are more interested in the frequency, validity, and reliability of the data. Focusing attention on individual responsibility for data use, and individual understanding of the importance of the data to their job success, must be part of the cultural shift that has to take place in order for data to be useful to the organization, at all points in the organization. It appears that each group in this chapter valued data that they were connected to, valued but did not use data that they did not understand or saw no connection to, and were interested in more verification of data validity and usefulness to the institution when a data set was perceived as being useful to them in doing their jobs.

The decision makers whose work is reported upon in this chapter provided insight into what could be improved in data-reporting processes in order to increase the likelihood that data would be used effectively by all decision makers to make decisions. Like the participants in Poole and Denny's study (2001), these decision makers used data regularly and reacted positively to increased access to and understanding of data. These decision makers reflected the commitment to focusing on excellence through the use of data named by Hawthorne and Smith (1993) as essential to improving community colleges. And, like the findings of Smart's (2003) survey of California community colleges, these participants demonstrated that simply having the data available is not enough to guarantee that they will be used. Frequent data usage requires a broadly shared commitment to data-driven decisions, and also requires a subtle one-on-one monitoring process that allows those less confident in their data skills to build their skills in a discrete way.

References

Bailey, T., & Weininger, E. (2002). Performance, graduation, and transfer of immigrants and natives in City University of New York community colleges. *Educational Evaluation and Policy Analysis, 24*(4), 359–377.

Birnbaum, R. (2000). The life cycle of academic management fads. *Journal of Higher Education, 71*, 1–16.

Chand, S., & Holm, M. (1998). Managing for results through teams. *Community College Journal of Research and Practice, 22*(4), 1–9.

Chang, J. (2005). Faculty–student interaction at the community college: A focus on students of color. *Research in Higher Education, 46*(7), 769–802.

Clark, S. (1998). Women faculty in community colleges: Investigating the mystery. *Community College Review, 26*(3), 77–88.

Cochran, L. (1989). *Administrative commitment to teaching: Practical, research-based strategies to strengthen college teaching effectiveness.* Cape Girardeau, MO: STEPUP, Inc.

Dhillon, J. (2001). Challenges and strategies for improving the quality of information in a university setting: A case study. *Total Quality Management, 12*(2), 167–178.

Dowd, A. (2003). From access to outcome equity: Revitalizing the democratic mission of the community college. *Annals of the American Academy of Political and Social Science, 586*, 92–119.

Feldman, J., & Tung, R. (2001, summer). Using data-based inquiry and decision-making to improve instruction. *ERS Spectrum,* 10–19.

Hawthorne, E., & Smith, A. (1993, February). *Improving teaching and learning in community colleges: Guidelines for academic leaders.* Paper presented at the Second International Conference of Community College Chairs and Deans, Phoenix, AZ. (ERIC Document Reproduction Service No. ED354039).

Hollar, D., Hattie, J., Goldman, B., & Lancaster, J. (2000). Developing assessment procedures and assessing two models of escalation behavior among community college administrators. *Theory and Decision, 49*(1), 1–24.

Kowalski, T., Lasley, T., & Mahoney, J. (2008). *Data-driven decisions and school leadership: Best practices for school improvement.* Boston: Pearson.

McLean, J. (1995). *Improving education through action research: A guide for administrators and teachers.* Thousand Oaks, CA: Corwin Press.

Mellard, D., & Byrne, M. (1993). Learning disabilities referrals, eligibility outcomes, and services in community colleges: A 4-year summary. *Learning Disability Quarterly, 16*(3), 199–218.

Mintzberg, H., & Rose, J. (2003). Strategic management upside down: Tracking strategies at McGill University from 1829 to 1980. *Canadian Journal of Administrative Science, 20*(4), 270–291.

Northwest Association of Schools and Colleges (1994). *Accreditation handbook.* Seattle, WA: Commission on Colleges of the Northwest Association of Schools and Colleges.

Northwest Commission on Colleges and Universities (2003). *Accreditation handbook, 2003 edition.* Retrieved June 6, 2006, from http:www.nwccu.org/Pubs%20Forms%20and%20Updates/Publications/Accreditation%20Handbook%202003%20Edition%20Updated%20August%202007.pdf

Paulsen, M. (1998). Recent research on the economics of attending college: Returns on investment and responsiveness to price. *Research in Higher Education 39*(4), 471–489.

Poole, C., & Denny, E. (2001). Technological change in the workplace: A statewide survey of community college library and learning resources personnel. *College & Research Libraries, 62*(6), 503–515.

Rouse, C. (1998). Do two-year colleges increase overall educational attainment? Evidence from the states. *Journal of Policy Analysis and Management, 17*(4), 595–620.

Rubenfeld, S., & Newstrom, J. (1994). Caveat emptor: Avoiding pitfalls in data-based decision-making. *Review of Business, 16*(2), 1–6.

Sanchez, J., & Laanan, F. (1999). Postcollege earnings of former students of California community colleges: Methods, analysis, and implications. *Research in Higher Education, 40*(1), 87–113.

Schulte, R. (2005). *An investigation of institutional research in Tennessee community colleges: Functions, technology use, and impact on decision-making by college presidents.* Retrieved from ProQuest Digital Dissertations. AAT3188895.

Scott, M., Bailey, T., & Kienzl, G. (2006). Relative success? Determinants of college graduation rates in public and private colleges in the U.S. *Research in Higher Education, 47*(3), 249–279.

Smart, J. (2003). Organizational effectiveness of 2-year colleges: The centrality of cultural and leadership complexity. *Research in Higher Education, 44,* 673–703.

Supovitz, J. A., & Klein, V. (2003). *Mapping a course for improved learning: How innovative schools systematically use student performance data to guide instruction.* Philadelphia: Consortium for Policy Research in Education. Retrieved February 5, 2005, from http://www.cpre.org/Publications/AC-08.pdf

Townsend, B., & Wilson, K. (2006). "A hand hold for a little bit": Factors facilitating the success of community college transfer students to a large research university. *Journal of College Student Development, 47,* 439–456.

Treasure Valley Community College. *TVCC's mission and philosophy.* Retrieved January 6, 2008, from http://www.tvcc.cc.or.us/About_TVCC/mission.cfm

Weber, R. (2006). *A case study of data decisions at one community college.* Retrieved from ProQuest Digital Dissertations. AAT3251878.

28

How NCLB has Affected the Practice of School District Superintendents

George J. Petersen
Cal Poly San Luis, Obispo

and

Larry L. Dlugosh
University of Nebraska

Introduction

Since the mid-1960s, the state and federal governments have increased their intervention and scope of control over American schooling. Educational reforms such as higher standards, testing, and accountability seek to improve student achievement through tightened centralized control and more effective structures. Within the past 40 years, local control over America's schools has eroded, while at the same time, the federal and state governments exert ever-greater control over the educational process and outcomes (Wirt & Kirst, 2005). The enthusiasm among state and national leaders for greater levels of accountability and high-stakes testing has become part and parcel of election campaigns, sound bites, and funding streams. Federal and state policy makers have concluded, rightly or wrongly, that schools are in crisis and that one option for addressing this situation is reliance on federal mandates oriented at increasing educational outputs, especially those measured by standardized tests (Kowalski, 2006). Student achievement and closing the achievement gap have become the political *coin-of-the-realm* and powerfully mandated external pressures for educational accountability and school improvement have become the political tools of choice (Petersen & Young, 2004). In particular, the revised Elementary and Secondary Education Act (ESEA) (also known as the No Child Left Behind [NCLB] Act of 2001—Public Law 107–110) has sweeping implications for those who work in public education. As the newest incarnation of the ESEA, NCLB has expanded the federal role in education and become a focal point of education policy. The legislation also sets in place requirements that reach into virtually every public school classroom in America. NCLB seeks to ensure that all American students are proficient in math, reading, and science by 2014. NCLB represents a significant departure from past practice. Overriding two centuries of state primacy in K-12 education, the federal government requires that academic performance lead to concrete consequences for schools—and that children in inadequate schools have the opportunity to seek assistance or move elsewhere (Hess & Finn, 2004).

The current climate and emphasis on the reform and restructuring of the American educational system have placed an enormous amount of political pressure on schools to demonstrate effective leadership at the district level (Fusarelli, 2005; Morgan & Petersen, 2002). Federally and state supported initiatives, like charter schools, vouchers, parental choice, high-stakes testing, and decentralization, provoke substantive questions in the minds of many about the future of public education and those who staff and lead public schools. It is not uncommon to hear state and federal office holders portraying public education as feeble while articulating what many believe are root causes to the problems facing schools:

> Poorly trained teachers, undemanding curriculums suffused with political correctness and multiculturalism, the abandonment of drill and memorization and other traditional tools of learning and a general refusal on the part of a new generation of administrators to impose, and live up to, high standards of achievement.
>
> (Ferguson, 2007, p. 32)

It was thought that in order to reverse this trend, schools must be held accountable. Test the kids, publish the scores, and let parents, armed with the results, decide whether the teachers and administrators were doing the job they were hired to do. NCLB has done just that. This accountability-laden program has readjusted the spotlight of responsibility and focused it directly on district leaders. Superintendents are held responsible for the performance of children in their districts, and rewards and sanctions are in place to goad annual yearly progress. For example, if a district is not successful in raising the level of all students, immediately and steadily, to the state-defined level of proficiency, the district will lose control (Heath, 2003). Of course, adequate yearly progress (AYP) requirements vary by state. AYP punishes schools in one state for achievement levels that are defined as great successes in another (Sunderman, Kim, & Orfield, 2005). As a result, speculation and serious questions have been raised about the leadership of America's schools and the role superintendents will play in this *political mêlée* (Petersen & Barnett, 2005). As one California superintendent recently commented, "The [federal] government is attempting to *insult us into reform*" (Superintendent C1, personal communication, April 25, 2007). It is this issue that lies at the heart of our investigation. Our purpose is to examine superintendent attitudes and beliefs regarding the influence of the accountability movement and how it manifests itself on the professional life of the district leader. More specifically we investigate how the issues of assessment and accountability, parental choice, resource flexibility, and hiring highly qualified teachers play out in role realignment and decision making for district superintendents.

Theoretical Framework

Decision Making

In its simplest form, decision making can be defined as choosing between or among two or more alternatives (Picciano, 2006). Despite the fact that making decisions is the *sine qua non* of school leadership—it is not always as simple as choosing between "*option z*" or "*option y*." Far too often decision making in schools is a multifaceted process where complex and significant social problems cross paths with school policies and practices. It is at these intersections that school leaders examine and address problems and potential solutions (Bazerman & Chugh, 2006; Hoy & Tarter, 2008). While decision making may be *part and parcel* of the responsibilities of super-intendents, decisions affecting the larger organization are not typically made in isolation. Current conditions of unpredictability and uncertainty in highly inter-active and public settings coupled with increased demands for political, legal, pro-fessional, market, and bureaucratic accountability (Darling-Hammond, 2004) have resulted in school leaders taking more substantive measures to involve multiple actors who represent the larger social fabric (Kowalski, Petersen, & Fusarelli, 2007), as well as taking a more aggressive position in the integration of data-driven pro-cesses into all aspects of their operations (Picciano, 2006). Historically administrative operations like budgeting, inventory, and scheduling relied on data-driven processes; more recently educational reform initiatives such as NCLB have obligated school districts to develop and employ data delivery and data analysis support systems in order to accurately monitor and publicly report current information in the areas of instruction and student assessment (2006). School leaders find themselves using student assessment data and relevant background information, to inform decisions related to planning and implementing instructional strategies at the district, school, classroom, and individual student levels (Cradler, 2006).

No Child Left Behind and District Superintendents

Accountability

We find measures for greater accountability and laws designed to bolster how stu-dents and educational professionals are assessed are not new and in fact have played a significant part in the educational landscape. Historically, accountability legislation has been primarily aimed at finding methods to evaluate professional employees, to assess the achievement of students, and to evaluate and assess management methods (Gatti & Gatti, 1983). For example, in 1973 *Scheelhasse v. Woodbury Central Com-munity School District*, 488, F.2nd 237 (8th circuit), focused on the issue of student performance and teacher accountability. In *Scheelhasse v. Woodbury* the courts found that a student's performance on achievement tests could not be the basis of a teacher's dismissal and in essence the court deferred to local school board discretion when dealing with academic standards. Despite the fact that previous legal efforts to wed teacher accountability to student academic performance have not been success-ful, the increased scrutiny of NCLB legislation around issues of student proficiency significantly strengthens grounds for tort suits on educational malpractice.

> [S]tate and federal legislation making school districts accountable for ensuring student mas-tery of state standards may increase school districts' potential liability. Even though it seems unlikely that public schools in the near future will be held responsible for a specified quantum of student achievement, it is conceivable that schools will be held legally accountable for diagnosing pupils' needs, placing them in appropriate instructional programs, reporting their

progress to parents, and providing other educational options if they are not progressing in their current placements.

(Cambron-McCabe, McCarthy, & Thomas, 2004, p. 96)

O'Day (2002) points out that many of the current accountability policies make somewhat unrealistic assumptions about how public schools operate. In the case of NCLB and similar policies, the assumption is made that once schools possess current and accurate data about the achievement of their students, they will take whatever action is necessary to improve the learning outcomes. New accountability approaches, by their very nature, seek to influence from the outside what goes on inside schools. Moreover, such policies assume that external forces can play a determining role in changing the internal workings of schools. The limitations of such assumptions, however, have provided grist for the vast literature on policy implementation in education (Cambron-McCabe, Cunningham, Harvey, & Koff, 2005; Darling-Hammond, 2007; Lashway, 2001). NCLB has resulted in a dramatic shift in federal mandates for public schooling. NCLB affects almost every program authorized under the Elementary and Secondary Education Act, including Title 1 (Department of Education, 2003). Moreover, NCLB shifts the federal government's role *vis-à-vis* local schools. The stipulations of NCLB require school districts that accept Title 1 monies to publish detailed annual reports on the progress of all children within the district (Heath, 2003; Jennings & Renter, 2006). The significant difference here is that unlike previous accountability initiatives, schools must demonstrate their compliance and growth by adequate yearly progress in student achievement regardless of disability, race or ethnicity, limited English proficiency, or economic status.

Obviously, the superintendent's role as the instructional leader is more important now than ever. NCLB requires district administrators to have an increased philosophical and technical expertise in curriculum scope, sequence, and alignment. Building and district leaders will use student test data to make decisions about effective services and practices, develop school improvement plans and if necessary take corrective action when schools miss the mark. The new evaluation provisions have made student assessment high stakes for all districts. Proven results, extensive evaluations, and data-driven decision making have moved the role of the superintendent from the sideline to the frontline (Petersen & Barnett, 2005; Petersen & Young, 2004).

Recent research by the Center on Educational Policy indicates that there is an upside to the emphasis on accountability. As a result of NCLB, schools are paying closer attention to the achievement gap and the learning needs of particular groups of students. They are also spending more time on reading and math, sometimes at the expense of other subjects not tested as well as working at aligning school curriculum and instruction as well as utilizing test score data for district decisions (see Jennings & Rentner, 2006).

Highly Qualified Teachers

A compelling body of research makes it clear that classroom teachers are vital elements in achieving student learning and school progress. Cohen and Ball (1998) write that a teacher's "intellectual and personal resources influence instructional inter-actions by shaping how teachers, apprehend, interpret, and respond to materials and students" (p. 3). Instructors' knowledge, understanding of content, and flexibility of content understanding dramatically affect teacher interaction with students. Additionally, teacher resources are influenced by their relationships developed with students over time. Teachers must have an acquaintance with the students' know-ledge and have the ability to relate to, interact with, and learn about the student. Finally, a teacher's repertoire of means to represent and extend content and personal knowledge and to establish classroom environments combines to mediate how teachers shape instruction. Overall, a teacher's ability to use, develop, and extend his or her knowledge and capabilities can considerably affect instruction by how well they involve students around materials (Spillane & Louis, 2002; Spillane & Thompson, 1997).

One of the most important provisions of NCLB is that by 2006 all teachers of core academic subjects are required to be highly qualified. To mandate school districts to attract and retain better teachers and to improve the educational preparation of teachers' aides are very positive goals (Sunderman, Kim, & Orfield, 2005). Although NCLB leaves it to the states to define the terms of *high quality*, the National Confer-ence of State Legislators consider "highly qualified teachers" to be teachers who possess full state certification, successfully pass a state licensing exam, or meet the requirements of the state's public charter school laws (Jennings, Rentner, & Kober, 2002). Along with classroom teachers, NCLB required all teacher assistants in Title 1 schools to become "highly qualified" by January 2006. In the case of teaching assistants and tutors, highly qualified means they possess an associate degree, or two years of college credit, or have successfully passed a state-approved test (Petersen & Young, 2004).

Yet, a glaring caveat in NCLB is its failure to address the dilemma many school districts face in placing "highly qualified teachers" in all classrooms and teachers that may hold tenure. One of the fundamental issues facing concentrated poverty schools is their limited ability and resources to attract and retain highly qualified and experienced teachers. NCLB's requirement for highly qualified teachers has stimu-lated recruitment efforts in districts where traditionally underserved popula-tions (e.g., "poor" and "minority" students) have experienced a revolving door of inexperienced and marginally trained teachers (Darling-Hammond, 2007). Yet, No Child Left Behind's practice of labeling schools as failures often exacerbates efforts of district leaders to attract and keep qualified teachers. School districts plagued by such difficulties bound the superintendents to concentrate their efforts to work with and educate members of their communities. Yet, defining *high quality* in terms of creden-tials and certification creates an added burden for district leaders. It requires them to subject all existing and future district professional employees to higher levels of scrutiny. No more will an uncertified teacher be a simple red flag in the state super-visor's report. District administrators must ensure that current teachers strengthen and improve pedagogy using researched-based instructional strategies in their teacher development and continuing education programs. While districts may be in compliance with NCLB's teacher quality provision, current research indicates that it does not ensure dramatic increases in student achievement (See McMurrer, 2007).

NCLB requires superintendents to focus on the tasks associated with long-term, sustained success which begin from improving the quality of the novice teacher ensuring that teachers already in the classroom have the resources and learning opportunities they need to be most effective (Cicchinelli, Gaddy, Lefkowits, & Miller, 2003; Petersen & Young, 2004).

Resource Flexibility

The No Child Left Behind Act also has a dramatic effect on how district administrators receive, allocate, and maintain funding for programs focused on instruction and learning. Under current federal statute, districts and schools that do not make sufficient yearly progress toward state proficiency goals for their students first will be targeted for assistance and then be subject to corrective action and ultimately restructuring. Any school district identified for corrective action must reserve and spend up to 20% of their Part A Title 1 funding for students who exercise an option for choice-related transportation, and supplemental educational services. Although these funds do not have to be taken from Title I allocations, and may be provided from other allowable federal, state, local or private sources (see U.S. Department of Education, 2002), this provision inhibits the employment of district monies to spend on other, more pressing local educational issues. While this may be the most significant financial effect felt by districts, they do face other potential costs for corrective actions. NCLB also states that aside from choice-related transportation any school targeted for corrective action may have to do one or more actions such as replace the school staff, implement a new curriculum, decrease management authority at the school, appoint an outside expert to advise the district, extend the school day or year, and reorganize the school internally (Code of Federal Regulations, 2002, sec 200.42).

Even though NCLB is very specific on sanctions for schools that fail to make adequate annual progress, the statute does not operationally define the limitations or allowances for this type of "punitive result," therefore superintendents must step up their efforts to become advocates for the extraordinary costs posed by these types of situations. Moreover, they must be knowledgeable of the resources available, through the state, to assist low-performing schools. State funds should be available to provide low-performing schools with technical assistance for school improvement, corrective action, or restructuring, to provide school districts with funds for after-school and summer school programs, and to reward schools/teachers for closing the achievement gap over two consecutive years (Petersen & Young, 2004).

Parental Choice

NCLB mandates that parents are to receive information on the academic progress of their children, the performance of their schools, and to be involved in meaningful ways with school officials. Evidently, the authors of NCLB consider parents, "armed with data" and "schooling options," to be in the best position to guarantee their children a quality education. Unlike previous reform initiatives,

NCLB couples school choice with accountability measures to allow parents of children in under-performing schools the opportunity to choose higher-performing schools.

District leaders are keenly aware of the positive influence parental and community involvement has on improving the quality of schooling (Griffith, 1996), as well as increasing the academic achievement of children (Peterson, 1989; Xiato, 2001). NCLB also recognizes the importance of parents and offers parents of children in low-performing schools a range of educational options. Parents with children in schools that fail to meet state standards for at least two consecutive years may transfer their children to a better-performing public school, including a public charter school, within their district. If they do so, the district must provide transportation, using Title I funds if necessary. Students from low-income families in schools that fail to meet state standards for at least three years are eligible to receive supplemental educational services—including tutoring, after-school services, and summer school. In addition, the NCLB Act provides increased support to parents, educators, and communities to create new charter schools. After five consecutive years of inadequate progress, schools are required to restructure by:

(a) converting to a charter school,
(b) replacing staff relevant to the failure,
(c) hiring an external contractor to operate the school,
(d) inviting the state to take over the school, or
(e) another significant reform that fundamentally changes the school.

While the five options reflect specific means for change, they all potentially entail retaining the same students and, at a minimum, some of the staff, but quickly and substantially changing the academic performance of the school (see U.S. Department of Education, 2002).

Offering parents data and choices, on the surface, appears an important step in enabling them to make wise decisions about their children's education. However, due to a variety of factors, from access to information to a parent's ability to understand the information or data they have been given, few parental choice programs have been successful (Young, 1999). A recent investigation into the area of parent involvement in the wake of NCLB has found that many parents are not receiving clear and timely information, and not surprisingly, poverty, English proficiency, and varying cultural expectations remain significant barriers to meaningful parental participation (Coleman, Starzynski, Winnick, Palmer, & Furr, 2006).

For district superintendents, increased parental choice, whether accomplished at the levels stipulated by NCLB and state legislation, has a significant level of influence on their ability to lead. At a minimum, increased efforts and resources must continue to be reallocated toward parental outreach and education. More significantly, however, is the management of student transience. Superintendents who lead districts in which schools have been classified as failing or low performing are required to make difficult staffing and resource decisions, and in some cases they may even lose significant amounts of funding. Such a loss of control over one's district makes school improvement very difficult, if not impossible. The difficulties, however, will not impact only those superintendents with low-performing schools. District administrators of high-performing schools could see a significant influx of students from failing schools creating overcrowding in classrooms, numerous strains on district, school, and classroom resources, thus eroding the educational experience and performance of all students (see Education Commission of the States, 2004).

A lack of academic achievement is not the only stipulation that permits parents the option to transfer their children to another school. Under the *Unsafe Schools Choice Option,* NCLB requires states to establish and implement a statewide policy that provides parents the option to petition for transfer schools under two conditions:

(a) the child attends a persistently dangerous elementary or secondary school; or
(b) has been a victim of a violent criminal offense while in or on the grounds of the school he or she attends.

This exacerbates an already a complex situation faced by numerous school leaders in their attempts to make schools significantly safer than the streets leading to the schoolhouse door; while at the same time attempting to maintain an open atmosphere that emphasizes democratic principles and student learning (Petersen, 1997).

The Study

In this chapter we examined the influence of NCLB on the professional life of a district superintendent. Using four critical areas of the law, namely (a) assessment and accountability, (b) highly qualified teachers, (c) resource flexibility, and (d) parental choice. We asked superintendents if NCLB introduced significant role realignment for district leaders. The emphasis on academic achievement and accountability requires superintendents to move from the historical role of a comprehensive manager to a leader focused on learning and outcomes of all students. Through the examination of these areas separately, we speak to some of the challenges superintendents face in fully implementing and complying with this complex and sweeping federal mandate. These changes and challenges present implications for the daily practice of district leaders.

Data Collection and Analysis

The authors made use of a non-random selection method when choosing district superintendents for this investigation (Erlandson, Harris, Skipper, & Allen, 1993). This investigation was conducted using semi-structured ethnographic interviews with 15 district leaders, seven superintendents in California and eight in Nebraska (Bogdan & Biklen, 2003; Creswell, 2003). Similar protocols were used in all interviews (Seidman, 1991). Questions were primarily open-ended and were based on the four critical areas of the law. Interviews provided us with information regarding the attitudes, perceptions, and actual practices of district leaders that would be difficult to assess using a paper and pencil measurement. All interviews were tape recorded and verbatim transcripts were made. Systematic examination of each interview was conducted using a two-part domain analysis (Spradley, 1979). The first part required analysis of each interview across the question categories. Once each individual interview had been examined and categorized, responses were examined across districts. This helped to establish if themes or consistencies were apparent in the perceptions of the respondents. Preliminary data from interviews with district leaders provided a rich foundation of information from which to more clearly understand superintendents' perspectives on NCLB and the areas of assessment and accountability, parental choice, resource flexibility, and highly qualified teachers.

Findings

Examination of the data and review of interview transcripts indicate some interesting perceptions of the district leaders who participated in this investigation.

Accountability   Historically, teaching and learning in American classrooms have depended heavily on intuition, skills, and expertise of educators, albeit public schools have long been held accountable for compliance with state and federal regulations. Between 1997 and 1998, the California State Board of Education (SBE) adopted standards for the core curriculum areas of English language arts, mathematics, history/social science, and science and aligned tests to those standards, largely through the Standardized Testing and Reporting (STAR). The district leaders we interviewed indicated that schools have always been accountable for student learning on some level; they also indicated that NCLB now requires district leaders to "dive beneath the data," regarding who is and who is not learning. The superintendents we interviewed also agreed that NCLB had some important points directed at issues of equity and service to all children. "We have to be results oriented and we must pay closer attention to what the data is telling us about the learning needs of particular groups of students, especially those students who have traditionally underperformed" (Superintendent C2, personal communication, March 2, 2007). As part of this view, several superintendents said that discussion about serving all children had been answered. "The debate is over. We are now after results. NCLB has given us a common vocabulary" (Superintendent C4, personal communication, March 17, 2007). "The discussion of closing the achievement gap is over, we must get it done—period!" (Superintendent C7, personal communication, May 1, 2007).

In Nebraska, superintendents indicated that the combination of state accountability and assessment techniques along with NCLB increased their attention to the need for reliable assessment data on which they could make decisions about student learning and school improvement. The larger school districts in the sample (and those that were less rural in location) had assessment plans in place as far back as 1994–1995. While NCLB increased the attention on testing, the majority of superintendents interviewed insisted their schools had a vision for learning in advance of NCLB. One superintendent was quick to say, "Do not let NCLB become your school district's vision for excellence; it is not a vision aimed at excellence. A school's vision must be much more comprehensive than NCLB" (Superintendent N8, personal communication, September 21, 2007). Another superintendent was adamant about the vision for a successful school: "(Educators) must understand the connections among quality goal setting, quality instruction, and quality assessment—that is why we are here! The worst thing we can do is accept NCLB as the standard for learning— we cannot be lulled into narrowing student opportunities for learning in schools. NCLB is a restrictor, not an expander" (Superintendent N6, personal communication, October 1, 2007).

It is evident that NCLB was responsible for an increased awareness of the use of data for purposes of making sound educational decisions and it focused attention on the alignment of curriculum from elementary through secondary levels with all superintendents in this study. One superintendent's comment captures the sentiments of many of the participants around the issue of accountability and its influence on schools. "NCLB focused our attention on student achievement; everyone is talking about student achievement, even the board of education" (Superintendent N4, personal communication, October 4, 2007).

Resource Flexibility   Superintendents in this study were well aware of the specific sanctions for schools that fail to make adequate annual progress; they emphasized the importance of their role as district leader and spokesperson in the advocacy for available resources offered through states to assist low-performing schools. These superintendents indicated that while numbers of students eligible for "supplemental services" has increased somewhat over the last three years, the number of for-profit entities offering these services has also increased.

Superintendents talked about a reallocation of money when they spoke about the way NCLB impacted their spending. Seven of the eight superintendents in Nebraska said they invested a greater percentage of their budget in specific professional development programs to assist teachers and para-educators to improve instructional strategies, select and implement curriculum and instructional interventions, and align curriculum. Most said they had shifted resources toward professional development and curriculum development as a result of the state accountability system; however, when NCLB was added, the urgency to shift money to projects that improved teaching and learning strategies was heightened.

Parental Choice   The seven California districts participating in this study had open enrollment and home schooling policies in place well before the passage of NCLB. Provided this fact, superintendent responses focused on what they believed were the larger and more public meaning of parental choice. As one California superintendent said, "This law is discouraging, it indicates to our families that education is a broken and failed enterprise" (Superintendent C6, personal communication, March 5, 2007). Another superintendent indicated that her district had open enrollment for several years and there did not seem to be a great deal of dissatisfaction among parents in her district; although her view of parental choice is stipulated in NCLB, she saw it as "redefining the school and parent relationship in a negative way. Devaluing somehow this natural relationship and putting us in opposing camps" (Superintendent C4, personal communication, March 17, 2007). Other district leaders echoed these observations. Responses uniformly also suggested that the idea of choice is limited to individuals with the resources to move and therefore it may seem politically expedient but it is not a panacea: "We tell parents of their options. I don't see it [changing schools] as something that will automatically improve the students learning. There are too many factors involved in what a child needs to succeed. For NCLB to tell parents if they're dissatisfied they can change schools is short-sighted" (Superintendent C5, personal communication, April 2, 2007).

Option enrollment, home schooling, and parental choice have also been available to Nebraska parents for many years. Parents are afforded numerous options to change schools given a practical rationale for their request. In that respect, none of the superintendents viewed parental choice as anything new or threatening, although it is important to note that there are few choices to move to a nearby school in the less populated regions of the state because there is no nearby school.

The perspectives of Nebraska superintendents indicated that parents were generally not familiar with the finer points of NCLB and probably would not be until a school did not meet AYP; then concerns would be raised. One superintendent noted that new people who moved into an area where school choices existed were "excellent school shoppers." "They visited schools and asked questions about school and student performance" (Superintendent N8, personal communication, August 23, 2007).

Highly Qualified Teachers   Putting highly qualified teachers in classrooms ensures American schools will be able to meet the challenges of teaching in a rapidly growing and diverse student population. The extant literature indicates that in 2005–2006, 88% of school districts reported that all of their teachers of core academic subjects met the NCLB definition of "highly qualified" (Jennings & Renter, 2006). Even though districts may be in compliance with NCLB's teacher quality provision, this does not ensure increases in student achievement. As one superintendent stated, "There are common sense things like background, degree and teaching experience, but providing a rich and stimulating learning environment is much more complicated than that. There are multiple factors involved in working with and helping children learn, being highly qualified as stipulated by NCLB standard does not really address the really important stuff" (Superintendent C7, personal communication, May 1, 2007).

A Nebraska superintendent noted that ". . . the credentials of teacher applicants were examined closely to find candidates who had a background in assessment of learning and evidenced experience in curriculum design and curriculum alignment" (Superintendent N2, personal communication, October 5, 2007).

Placing a high-quality teacher in front of every child in the nation is the most important thing schools can do to improve student achievement. Although several superintendents stated that their districts continued to experience shortages of qualified teachers, especially in certain subject areas (e.g., math and science) as well as teachers of special education and in California particularly, teachers prepared to teach English learners. Many of them also pointed to the fact that as district leaders they had worked to increase the numbers of high-quality teachers in their schools, long before NCLB came into play. "Getting the best teachers with the proper degrees and background is just common sense. NCLB just mandates what we've been trying to do for years" (Superintendent C2, personal communication, March 2, 2007).

Conclusion

Much of what we can grasp from an overview of our interviews and multiple meetings with district leaders regarding the four areas of NCLB (i.e., accountability, teacher quality, resource flexibility, and parental choice) is that this relatively new legislation has created a new and more intense dynamic for district leaders. No Child Left Behind's accountability mandate, in essence, is about obligating school leaders to support the achievements of all children. Clearly this involves a number of different knowledge and skill areas (Clark, 1999; Van Meter, 1999), one of them, data-driven decision making (Picciano, 2006). For example, although these district leaders understood and clearly articulated the importance of their role and accountability in fostering the learning of students, their responses resonated that their state's adequate yearly progress (AYP) requirements were external factors that influenced their decision-making processes. They were now expected to meet and eventually exceed system requirements, which required them to use diagnostic data to drive effective instructional decisions and practices within a high-stakes environment (Cambron-McCabe et al., 2005; Petersen & Young, 2004). Responses also indicated that the increased emphasis on assessment required district leaders and their administrative teams to have a firm grasp of assessment instruments (e.g., what different types of assessments can and cannot tell you, what types of assessments are most useful for diagnostic purposes), develop the ability to analyze student achievement data, make yearly comparisons, and use those analyses as the basis for student achievement-centered decision making, resulting in different ways to enact their own leadership within highly public environments.

In terms of teacher qualifications, our interviewees indicated they had increased their recognizance in regard to the skills applicants enumerated when they applied for positions as classroom teachers. Potential new hires were carefully screened to determine whether they met the "highly qualified" designation. The screening processes naturally eliminated those who did not meet the criteria. The definition of highly qualified teachers is problematic as administrators seek to hire those who are most qualified. In addition to identifying highly qualified teachers by degrees held and training attained, Pianta suggests that "classroom visits to watch teachers teach [and] employing standardized assessments of good teaching could be used to accomplish this objective" (Pianta, 2007).

Some superintendents indicated they had indeed observed and reassigned teachers in an effort to place their most talented individuals at key grade levels. "Some teachers have been reassigned to meet the highly qualified designation, especially in Special Education and English Language Learners programs" (Superintendent N7, personal communication, September 27, 2007). One of the crucial decisions superintendents and their building level administrators contend with is the level at which teachers can take the pressure off increased public scrutiny. Another superintendent indicated that new teachers, those who were prepared in the past two or three years, "seemed to have a good grasp of assessment and accountability" and, if that held true, the district could provide the professional development they needed to operate effectively as a classroom teacher. "Some of the veteran teachers experienced high levels of stress with accountability in general and with NCLB specifically. Some have resigned or retired, and others have been reassigned" (Superintendent N4, personal communication, September 20, 2007).

The decisions about how to deploy limited resources may have been further complicated by NCLB. However, the superintendents we interviewed, by and large, indicated that they had a well-reasoned vision for learning in their school districts. One of the discoveries made in the interviews we conducted was the assertion by superintendents that they were confident about their knowledge of what the educational priorities were in their districts. They had a clear sense of what it took to assure student achievement at the classroom level and they deployed financial and human resources to that end. The decision-making process they used was related to the vision they held for learning and student achievement. They invested resources in four primary areas:

(a) good teachers,
(b) intervention strategies that had been carefully studied by teachers and administrators,
(c) alignment of curriculum, and
(d) targeted professional development to assist teachers with their work.

Those interviewed in this study perceived they had flexibility in terms of resource allocation, but wondered aloud how long that flexibility would be in place.

Parental choice was not a theme that engendered a great deal of discussion from the interviewees. While it is true that options exist for parents to request and expect transfers from poorly performing schools to other schools, the 15 superintendents in this study had not dealt with parental demands to change schools. The sample for the study was small and admittedly did not include schools which had previously been identified as poorly performing so we cannot generalize a response based on the information we collected. The option to move children from failing schools to better schools is a topic that should be investigated in further studies.

Suggestions for Future Research

With Congress stalled on revisions to NCLB and the presidential campaign in full swing, it may be reasonable to assume that a flawed law will not receive the adjustments it likely deserves. School leaders must contend with state and federal mandates to increase student achievement and leave no child behind without the benefit of a focused national dialogue regarding remedy or elimination of NCLB. Regardless of what happens or does not happen, the parents of children in classrooms expect their local schools to document student progress, hire the best and brightest teachers, and improve learning for all students—and so they should.

The swirling rhetoric of educational politics and the necessity to assure citizens that public schools are a good investment for them and the country will remain as schools strive to meet the demands placed on them.

Further information is needed about parental views of the efforts their local schools have made and are making to address the issues raised in the discussions that led to the No Child Left Behind Act. Is it possible for parents to move their children from low-performing schools to higher-performing schools? How many parents have exercised that option? What costs in terms of dollars and time have been incurred by parents and school districts? Are parents more cognizant of overall student achievement measures in America as a result of NCLB or is student achievement in elementary and secondary education more focused at the local and state levels rather than at the national level?

The matter of school district expenditures needs to be studied in light of the demands of NCLB. Have school district budgets been modified in any meaningful way in attempts to address issues raised by the passage of NCLB? Are veteran teachers resigning or retiring early as a result of the significant emphasis on accountability as stipulated in NCLB? Are newly prepared teachers more highly qualified than their more senior colleagues? Are districts allocating more resources to professional development programs for all teachers? Has there been an increase in expenditures for curriculum alignment, instructional interventions, testing and assessment materials, and new curricular materials?

Finally, the issue of whether American citizens perceive American Public Education to be best managed at the federal, state, or local levels should receive serious attention. Should an educational system that is rooted in state responsibility and local control be converted to a national system? If so, why, and if not, why not?

References

Bazerman, M. H., & Chugh, D. (2006). Decisions without blinders. *Harvard Business Review, 84*, 88–97.

Bogdan, R. C., & Biklen, S. K. (2003). *Qualitative research in education: An introduction to theory and methods* (4th ed.). Boston: Allyn & Bacon.

Cambron-McCabe, N. H., Cunningham, L. L., Harvey, J., & Koff, R. H. (2005). *Superintendent's field book: A guide for leaders of learning.* Thousand Oaks, CA: Sage & AASA Joint Publication.

Cambron-McCabe, N. H., McCarthy, M. M., & Thomas, S. B. (2004). *Public school law: Teachers' and students' rights* (5th ed.). Boston: Pearson.

Cicchinelli, L., Gaddy, B., Lefkowits, L., & Miller, K. (2003). No Child Left Behind: Realizing the vision [Policy brief]. Prepared for Mid-continent Research for Education and Learning (McRel) Denver, CO. Retrieved October 15, 2007, from http://www.mcrel.org/PDF/PolicyBriefs/5032PI_PBNCLBBrief.pdf

Clark, D. L. (1999). Searching for authentic educational leadership in university graduate programs and with public school colleagues. In J. Murphy & P. B. Forsyth (Eds.), *Educational administration: A decade of reform* (pp. 228–236). Thousand Oaks, CA: Corwin Press.

Code of Federal Regulations (2002, December 2). *Corrective action. In rules and regulations 34 C.F.C.§ 200.42.* Retrieved April 25, 2007, from http://www.ed.gov/legislation/FedRegister/finrule/2002–4/120202a.html

Cohen, D. K., & Ball, D. L. (1998). *Instruction, capacity and improvement* (RR-42). Philadelphia: Consortium for Policy Research in Education, University of Pennsylvania.

Coleman, A. L., Starzynski, A. L., Winnick, S. Y., Palmer, S. R., & Furr, J. E. (2006). *It takes a parent: Transforming education in the wake of No Child Left Behind.* Washington, DC: Appleseed Network.

Cradler, J. (2006). *Data-driven decision making and electronic learning assessment resources.* Retrieved January 28, 2008, from http://www.clrn.org/elar/dddm.cfm#A

Creswell, J. W. (2003). *Research design: Qualitative, quantitative, and mixed methods approaches* (2nd ed.). Thousand Oaks, CA: Sage.

Darling-Hammond, L. (2004). Standards, accountability, and school reform. *Teachers College Record, 106*(6), 1047–1085.

Darling-Hammond, L. (2007). Evaluating "No Child Left Behind." *The Nation.* Retrieved January 11, 2008, from http://www.thenation.com/doc/20070521/darling-hammond

Department of Education. (2003). *Improving the academic achievement of the disadvantaged. 34 Fed. Reg. 68697 Part III.* Retrieved October 15, 2007, from http://www.ed.gov/legislation/FedRegister/proprule/2003–1/032003a.pdf

Educational Commission for the States (2004, April 23). *Parent involvement: Action guide for parents and communities.* Retrieved January 11, 2007, from http://www.publiceducation.org/pdf/nclb/parental_involvement.pdf

Erlandson, D., Harris, E., Skipper, B., & Allen, S. (1993). *Doing naturalistic inquiry: A guide to methods.* Newbury Park, CA: Sage Publications.

Ferguson, A. (2007). No child left alone: An education reform run amok. *The Weekly Standard, 13*(2), 30–37.

Fusarelli, L. D. (2005). Gubernatorial reactions to No Child Left Behind: Politics, pressure, and education reform. *Peabody Journal of Education, 80*(2), 120–136.

Gatti, R. D., & Gatti, D. J. (1983). *New encyclopedic dictionary of school law.* West Nyack, NY: Parker Publishing.

Griffith, J. (1996). Relation of parental involvement, empowerment, and school traits to student academic performance. *Journal of Educational Research, 90*(1), 33–41.

Heath, S. (2003). *No Child Left Behind: What teachers, principals and school administrators need to know. Wrightslaw.* Retrieved October 15, 2007, from http://www.wrightslaw.com/info/nclb.teachers.admins.htm

Hess, F. M., & Finn, C. E. (2004). *Leaving no child left behind? Options for kids in failing schools.* New York: Palgrave.

Hoy, W. K., & Tarter, C. J. (2008). *Administrators solving the problems of practice* (3rd ed.). Boston: Pearson Education.

Jennings, J., & Renter, D. S. (2006). Ten big effects of the No Child Left Behind Act on public schools. *Phi Delta Kappan, 88*(2), 110–113.

Jennings, J., Rentner, D. S., & Kober, D. (2002, September). *A new federal role in education. A report prepared for the Center on Educational Policy.* Washington, DC. Retrieved October 17, 2007, from www.cep-dc.org/index.cfm?useaction=document.showdocumentbyid&documentid=60&c:/cfusionmx7/verity/data/dummy.txt

Kowalski, T. J. (2006). *The school superintendent: Theory, practice, and cases* (2nd ed.). Thousand Oaks, CA: Sage.

Kowalski, T. J., Petersen, G. J., & Fusarelli, L. D. (2007, November). *Understanding and applying civic engagement in relation to school improvement.* Paper presented at the annual convention of the University Council for Educational Administration, Washington, DC.

Lashway, L. (2001). *The new standards and accountability: Will rewards and sanctions motivate America's schools to peak performance?* Eugene, OR: (ERIC Document Reproduction Service No. ED 453589).

McMurrer, J. (2007, August). *Implementing the No Child Left Behind teacher requirements.* Washington, DC. Retrieved October 17, 2007, from www.cep-dc.org/index.dfm?fusseaction-page.viewpage&pageid=495&parentid=481

Morgan, C. L., & Petersen, G. J. (2002). The role of the district superintendent in leading academically successful school districts. In B. S. Cooper & L. D. Fusarelli (Eds.), *The promise and perils of the modern superintendency* (pp. 175–196). Lanham, MD: Scarecrow Press.

No Child Left Behind—Public Law 107–100 (2002, January 8). *107th United States Congress.* Washington, DC. Retrieved October 15, 2007, from http://www.ed.gov/policy/elsec/leg/esea02/107–110.pdf

O'Day, J. A. (2002). Complexity, accountability, and school improvement. *Harvard Education Review, 72*(3), 293–327.

Petersen, G. J. (1997). Looking at the big picture: School administrators and violence reduction. *Journal of School Leadership, 7*(5), 456–479.

Petersen, G. J., & Barnett, B. G. (2005). The superintendent as instructional leader: Current practice, future conceptualizations and implications for preparation. In L. G. Björk & T. J. Kowalski (Eds.), *The contemporary superintendent: Preparation, practice and development* (pp. 107–136). Thousand Oaks, CA: Corwin Press.

Petersen, G. J., & Young, M. D. (2004). The No Child Left Behind Act and its influence on current and future district leaders. *Journal of Law and Education, 33*(4), 343–363.

Peterson, D. (1989). *Parental involvement in the educational process.* (ERIC Reproduction Document Service No. ED312776).

Pianta, R. (2007). Measure actual classroom teaching. *Education Week, 27*(11), 30, 36.

Picciano, A. G. (2006). *Data-driven decision making for effective school leadership.* Upper Saddle River, NJ: Pearson Education.

Seidman, I. E. (1991). *Interviewing as qualitative research: A guide for researchers in education and social sciences.* New York: Teachers College Press.

Spillane, J. P., & Louis, K. S. K. (2002). School improvement processes and practices: Professional learning for building instructional capacity. In J. Murphy (Ed.), *The educational leadership challenge: Redefining leadership for the 21st century* (pp. 83–104). Chicago: University of Chicago Press.

Spillane, J. P., & Thompson, C. L. (1997). Reconstructing conceptions of local capacity: The local education agency's capacity for ambitious instructional reform. *Educational Evaluation and Policy Analysis, 19*(2), 185–203.

Spradley, J. P. (1979). *The ethnographic interview.* New York: Holt, Rinehart & Winston.

Sunderman, G. L., Kim, J. S., & Orfield, G. (2005). *NCLB meets school realities: Lessons from the field.* Thousand Oaks, CA: Corwin Press.

U. S. Department of Education (2002, September). *No Child Left Behind: A desktop reference.* Washington, DC: Author.

Van Meter, E. J. (1999). *The persistent saga: Changing instruction and curriculum to better prepare school leaders.* In J. Murphy & P. B. Forsyth (Eds.), *Educational administration: A decade of reform* (pp. 170–191). Thousand Oaks, CA: Corwin Press.

Wirt, F. M., & Kirst, M. W. (2005). *The political dynamics of American education* (3rd ed.). Richmond, CA: McCutchan Publishing Corp.

Xiato, F. (2001). Parental involvement and students' academic achievement: A growth modeling analysis. *Journal of Experimental Education, 70*(1), 27–61.

Young, M. D. (1999). Multifocal educational policy research: Toward a method for enhancing traditional educational policy studies. *American Educational Research Journal, 36*(4), 677–714.

About the Authors

Julie Alonzo earned her Ph.D. in Educational Leadership with a specialization in Learning Assessment/ Systems Performance from the University of Oregon in 2007. A National Board certified teacher, she has managed a variety of federally funded grants related to instrument development, educator use of data to guide instructional decision making, and response to intervention. Dr. Alonzo currently works as a Research Associate at Behavioral Research and Teaching where she manages three projects with a total annual budget of 1.2 million dollars. She has presented research papers on assessment at national conferences annually since 2004.

Paul T. Begley is Professor of Educational Leadership at Pennsylvania State University and Director of the Willower Centre for the Study of Leadership and Ethics of the UCEA. His teaching and research interests focus on all aspects of school leadership including the influence of values and ethics on school leadership practices, and international images of effective school leadership. Because of his extensive field development experience in Canada, Sweden, Hong Kong, and Australia, his work reflects a strong practitioner orientation. Recent publications include *The Ethical Dimensions of School Leadership* (2003) published by Springer Press.

Leanne R. Bettesworth earned her Ph.D. in Educational Leadership with a specialization in Learning Assessment/ System Performance from the University of Oregon in 2006. Currently a Director in the Central Okanagan School District in British Columbia, Canada, Dr. Bettesworth also consults internationally in English language development and assessment of English language learners. Her research interests include data-driven decision making, assessment of English language learners, and English language development. She has presented research papers on data-driven decision making and English language development at national and international conferences since 2004.

Tricia Browne-Ferrigno is an Associate Professor of Educational Leadership Studies at the University of Kentucky. She directed two sponsored leadership development programs that integrated data-based decision making. The Principals Excellence Program, supported by the U.S. Department of Education School Leadership Development Program, was featured in *Innovative Pathways to School Leadership*. The second, supported by the U.S. Department of Education, Improving Teacher Quality State Grant Program, developed broad-based leadership teams in rural high schools. She has published articles in *Educational Administration Quarterly, Journal of School Leadership, Leadership and Policy in Schools,* and *Mentoring & Tutoring: Partnership in Learning,* and chapters in other edited books.

Patricia Burch is an Assistant Professor in the Department of Educational Policy Studies at the University of Wisconsin-Madison. Her research interests are policy implementation and policy theory.

John M. Burger is a Senior Manager in the Accountability and Reporting Division of Alberta Education in Edmonton, Alberta, Canada. John obtained his B.A. and B.Ed. Degrees from the Ohio State University and his M.Ed. and Ph.D. in Educational Administration from the University of Alberta. He holds Adjunct Associate Professor appointments at the University of Calgary, where he has taught courses in Classroom Assessment and Educational Leadership, and the University of Alberta. His current interests focus on leadership development and the nexus between effective educational leadership and data-informed decision making.

Deborah Carran is an Associate Professor in the Department of Teacher Development and Leadership in the School of Education at Johns Hopkins University. She received her doctorate in Developmental

Psychology from the University of Miami, and then was a National Institute of Mental Health postdoctoral fellow in Psychiatric Epidemiology for two years in the Department of Mental Hygiene at Johns Hopkins School of Public Health. Dr. Carran has been a faculty member in the School of Education with JHU for the past 18 years with areas of specialization in research design, methodology, statistical analysis, and evaluation. Areas of research include longitudinal database linkage and tracking, program evaluation methodologies, and data-driven decision making for education.

John Castellani is an Associate Professor in the Department of Teacher Development and Leadership in the School of Education at Johns Hopkins University. He coordinates the Technology for Educators Program, which has an emphasis on technology leadership and data-driven decision making. He received his doctorate from George Mason University with an emphasis on instructional design and a cognate minor in reading and assistive technology. His current research interests are in the use of data mining for education research and the integration of technology into general and special education classes. He has been a faculty member at JHU for eight years, and most recently was a visiting research scholar at the National University of Ireland, Maynooth during his spring 2007 sabbatical.

Vincent Cho is a Ph.D. student in the Educational Policy and Planning Program at the University of Texas at Austin. He is a graduate of Boston College and an alumnus of Teach for America. He completed his M.Ed. in educational administration as a member of the University of Houston's urban principalship cohort. A former middle school teacher and assistant principal in urban Houston, he has also higher education policy and legislative experience serving on the staff of Texas Senator Judith Zaffirini.

Robin S. Codding is an Assistant Professor in the Counseling and School Psychology Program at the University of Massachusetts-Boston. Dr. Codding is a 2003 graduate of the School Psychology Program at Syracuse University. She was selected to be a member of the 2007 School Psychology Early Career Scholars Conference. Her research interests emphasize data-based decision making in schools, examining and comparing academic interventions, investigating strategies to enhance treatment integrity of intervention implementation, and improving academic success for students with ADHD.

Stephen Coffin, a former school business administrator, serves as an adjunct Professor of School Finance at Montclair State University, writes an education-focused column for a Blog entitled *Coffin's Corner on Education*, and provides consulting services particularly for K-12 public school districts as well as independent schools.

James E. Connell, Jr. is an Assistant Professor in the School Psychology Program at Temple University. Dr. Connell is a 2005 graduate of the Louisiana State University School Psychology Program, graduated Magna Cum Laude from Temple University, was selected to be a member of the 2007 School Psychology Early Career Scholars Conference, and is an author on the 2006 School Psychology Review article of the year. His research interests include curriculum-based assessment, functional behavioral assessment, universal screening and Response-to-Intervention, and school and classroom systems change through behavior analytic applications.

Bruce S. Cooper is a Professor of Education Leadership and Policy in the Fordham University Graduate School of Education, and the former president of the Politics of Education Association. His latest books include the *Handbook of Education Politics and Policy* (co-edited) and *The Rising State: Role of states in Education Politics* with Bonnie Fusarelli.

Michael A. Copland is Associate Professor of Educational Leadership and Policy Studies in the College of Education at the University of Washington, and has extensive experience with the preparation and professional development of school and district. His research interests include issues related to the preparation and professional development of school and district leaders, learning-focused leadership in school and district reform, central office transformation, transformation of comprehensive high schools, and distributed leadership in the context of whole school reform. Dr. Copland's recent publications include the book *Connecting Leadership with Learning*, as well as pieces in *Phi Delta Kappan, Journal of School Leadership, Educational Evaluation and Policy Analysis,* and *Educational Administration Quarterly*.

Amanda Datnow is an Associate Professor in the Rossier School of Education at the University of Southern California. Her research focuses on the politics and policies of school reform, particularly with regard to the professional lives of educators and issues of equity. She has conducted numerous prior studies of comprehensive school reform and studies of other related school change issues. She is currently conducting a study of data-driven decision making in four urban high schools.

Larry L. Dlugosh is Professor and Chair of the Educational Administration Department at the University of Nebraska-Lincoln. Prior to his university service, Dr. Dlugosh was a school Superintendent, Curriculum Director, and High School Principal for 25 years. His research and teaching interests are the school superintendency, school/community relations, and management of change. Dr. Dlugosh was co-author with M.S. Norton, L. D. Webb, & W. Sybouts (1996) of *The school superintendency: New responsibilities, new leadership*, Boston, MA: Allyn & Bacon. He has authored and co-authored articles about school leadership, strategic planning, distance education, and community involvement in schools.

Luke Duesbery earned his Ph.D. in Educational Leadership with a specialization in Learning Assessment/Systems Performance from the University of Oregon in 2007. He currently holds a position as Assistant Professor in the Department of Special Education at San Diego State University. Dr. Duesbery's research interests include educational measurement, data graphics in assessment, and the integration of technology in assessment and learning. He has presented research papers on appropriate use of measurement at national and state conferences annually since 2004.

Diane M. Dunlap is a Professor of Educational Leadership at the University of Oregon. She specializes in the study and practice of mastery learning experiences for novice researchers. She is the author or co-author of four books, numerous book chapters, and more than 60 professional articles and papers.

Meghann Eagle is a researcher with Alberta Advanced Education and Technology in Edmonton, Alberta. She completed her BA in Sociology at the University of Calgary, and enhanced her quantitative skills through work assignments with Statistics Canada and various community agencies. She became involved with the Grade Level of Achievement project during her internship with the System Improvement Group of Alberta Education, and was the lead Research Officer for the project. Her current research interests are related to the factors that determine students' decisions to access government-sponsored financial assistance and push/pull determinants for international students in Alberta.

Christine Carrino Gorowara currently serves as Director of Audits for the Teacher Education Accreditation Council, and has participated in the evaluation of over 30 educator preparation programs for TEAC. She is also a mathematics educator, and in this role has collaborated on curriculum design and instruction with colleagues at the University of Delaware and has coordinated assessment for the Mid-Atlantic Center for Mathematics Teaching and Learning. She is interested in models of continual improvement in the areas of teacher education generally and mathematics teacher education in particular.

Tracy Hayes was a graduate student in Educational Policy Studies at the University of Wisconsin-Madison.

Jane Hemsley-Brown is a Senior Lecturer, and Head of Department in the School of Management, University of Surrey, UK. Jane previously worked at the University of Southampton, UK as Senior Researcher, and as a Principal Researcher with the National Foundation for Educational Research (NFER) where she managed Local Government Association (LGA) funded projects and liaised with employers, professional organizations, and government departments (e.g., The Cabinet Office, London, UK). Her publications include: *Using Research for School Improvement* (NFER, 2003) and "The use of research to improve professional practice: A systematic review of the literature," published in the *Oxford Review of Education*, 29(4), pp. 449–470 (2004).

Douglas Huffman is an Associate Professor of Science Education at the University of Kansas. Dr. Huffman has a background in civil engineering, science education, and program evaluation. He has evaluated numerous National Science Foundation projects including the Collaborative for Excellence in Teacher Preparation (CETP), State Systemic Initiatives (SSI), and the Collaborative Evaluation Communities (CEC). He currently serves as an associate editor of the *Journal of Research in Science Teaching*, and has published his work in journals such as the *American Journal of Evaluation, New Directions for Evaluation*, and the *Journal of Research in Science Teaching*.

James M. Kauffman is Professor Emeritus of Education at the University of Virginia. He has published books on characteristics of emotional and behavioral disorders, behavior management, and the history of special education for children and youth with emotional and behavioral disorders. His book chapters and articles have included special education policy and practice, conceptual models, and commentaries on controversial issues. His email address is jmk9t@virginia.edu, and more information about him may be found at www.people.Virginia.EDU/~jmk9t/.

Michael S. Knapp, Professor of Educational Leadership & Policy Studies and Director of the Center for the Study of Teaching and Policy at the University of Washington, focuses on educational policy making, school reform, leadership development, and policy research methods, with emphasis on how policy and leadership connect to classroom and school improvement. His studies often concern the education of disenfranchised populations, mathematics and science education, and professional learning. Dr. Knapp has written extensively about his research, including eight books, among them, *School Districts and Instructional Renewal* (2002), *Self-Reflective Renewal in Schools* (2003), and *Connecting Leadership with Learning* (2006).

Timothy R. Konold is Associate Professor and Director of the Research, Statistics, and Evaluation program at the University of Virginia. He teaches introductory and advanced graduate level courses in psychometric theory and quantitative methods. He has served as the senior psychometric consultant for the Chartered Financial Analyst (CFA) international testing program for the past seven years. His research interests are in large-scale test use as it pertains to construction, interpretation, classification, and errors of measurement. He has authored and co-authored over 70 peer-reviewed articles, book chapters, tests, book/test reviews, and technical reports.

Stephanie A. Kotch is an Instructor at the University of Delaware. She supervises junior and senior teacher candidates in the Vertical Model of Field Experience. In addition, she instructs undergraduates in Educational Assessment. She has compiled 20 years of diverse educational experience that includes Child Care Director, Administrative Director for Delaware Adolescent Program Inc., Classroom Teacher, Professional Development Instructor, District Science Specialist, and State Science Assessment Item Writer. Her current research interests include improved field experiences through co-teaching, assessment practices of novice teachers, and novice teacher conversation groups.

Theodore J. Kowalski is Professor and the Kuntz Family Chair in Educational Administration at the University of Dayton. A former superintendent and college of education dean, he is the editor of the *Journal of School Public Relations*, serves on the editorial boards of two other journals, and is the author of over 150 professional publications including 31 books. His most recent books are *Effective Communication for School Administrators* (2007), *Case Studies on Educational Administration* (5th ed., 2008), *School Public Relations* (4th ed., 2008), and *Data-Driven Decisions and School Leadership* (2008).

Thomas J. Lasley II is Dean of the School of Education and Allied Professions at the University of Dayton. He has published in excess of 70 articles in professional journals and has authored or co-authored 11 books. He has served on a variety of regional and state level education commissions and boards including the Governor's Commission on Teaching Success and the Ohio Board of Regents' Planning and Accountability Committee. He co-founded the Dayton Early College Academy, a unique educational partnership between the University of Dayton and the Dayton Public Schools, and is co-chair of the Teacher Quality Partnership.

Gregory J. Marchant is a Professor of Psychology—Educational Psychology at Ball State University in Muncie, IN. He is a past president of the Mid-Western Educational Research Association, and has won College awards for his educational policy research. His research has explored the relations of students' contexts and demographic characteristics to their achievement on standardized tests. This research has established a number of adverse outcomes of standardized tests that are used for high stakes decisions. Most recently, he has developed a technique for assessing school performance using demographically adjusted scores.

Robert J. Marzano is President of Marzano & Associates in Centennial, Colorado, Senior Scholar at Mid-continent Research for Education and Learning in Denver, Colorado, and Adjunct Professor at Cardinal Stritch University in Milwaukee, Wisconsin. He is the author of a number of books, articles, and chapters in books translating research and theory into practical applications. During his 40 years in public education, Marzano has worked in every state multiple times as well as a host of countries in Europe and Asia.

Carol A. Mullen is a Professor and Chair, Department of Educational Leadership and Cultural Foundations, School of Education, the University of North Carolina at Greensboro. She specializes in mentorship and democracy, faculty and graduate student development, and curriculum leadership. She is editor of the refereed international *Mentoring & Tutoring: Partnership in Learning*, a Routledge/ Taylor & Francis publication. Her most recent book is *Write to the Top! How to be a Prolific Academic* (with W. B. Johnson, Palgrave Macmillan, 2007). Forthcoming is her edited book, *Leadership and Building Professional Learning Communities* (Palgrave Macmillan), along with two special issues of academic journals.

Vicki Park is a doctoral candidate at the University of Southern California's Rossier School of Education and is also a research associate with the Center on Educational Governance. She received her bachelor's degree in history, masters in education, and teaching credentials from the University of California, Los Angeles. Her research interests center on educational policy and administration with an emphasis on K-12 urban school reform, Asian American students' schooling experiences, and qualitative methodology. She is currently studying the reform of urban high schools and how educators use data to inform their decision making.

Sharon E. Paulson is a Professor of Psychology—Educational Psychology at Ball State University in Muncie, IN. She is a development psychologist with an expertise in adolescent development, specifically in the relations of family factors with school achievement. In addition, Dr. Paulson has been involved in educational program evaluation, working with local school districts, evaluating their programs for at-risk youth. Most recently, she has been engaged in educational policy research, examining the contributions of student and family demographics to standardized test scores, in particular high stakes test scores used in accordance with No Child Left Behind.

Brian Perry is a Senior Manager in Alberta Education, working in the Accountability and Reporting Division. In this role, he has conducted a variety of studies on the Alberta education system; has researched educational approaches in Alberta and other places; has developed and implemented a number of frameworks for the evaluation of the success of education programs and initiatives; has developed models for evaluation of the socio-economic status of schools; and has participated in the development of the Grade Level of Achievement measure. He has Master of Business Administration, Bachelor of Science, and Bachelor of Commerce degrees.

George J. Petersen is a Professor of Educational Leadership and Co-Director of the UCSB/Cal Poly Joint Doctoral Program at the California Polytechnic State University, San Luis, Obispo. His research and teaching interests are in the areas of the executive leadership of the superintendent, organizations, and communication. Dr. Petersen was co-author with T. J. Kowalski, & L. D. Fusarelli (2007), of the *Effective Communication for School Administrators: A Necessity in an Informaton Age*, Lanham, MD: Rowman & Littlefield Education. He has also authored and co-edited with L. D. Fusarelli (2004), *The Politics of Leadership: Superintendents and School Boards in Changing Times*, Greenwich, CT: Information Age Publishing.

Anthony G. Picciano is a Professor in the Graduate Program in Education Leadership at Hunter College of the City University of New York (CUNY). He is also a member of the faculty of the Ph.D. Program in Urban Education, the Program in Interactive Pedagogy and Technology and the Interdisciplinary Program in Communication and Culture at the Graduate Center (CUNY). Dr. Picciano has authored numerous articles and eight books including *Data-Driven Decision Making for Effective School Leadership* (2006, Pearson), *Educational Leadership and Planning for Technology*, 4th edition (2005, Pearson), *Distance Learning: Making Connections across Virtual Space and Time* (2001, Pearson), and *Educational Research Primer* (2004, Continuum). His most recent book was co-edited with Chuck Dziuban and is entitled *Blended Learning: Research Perspectives* (2007, Sloan Consortium).

R. Lance Potter is a research associate and Adjunct Professor at the Pennsylvania State University. He is working on a federal grant examining school resource links to student outcomes. He has a Ph.D. in Educational Leadership from Penn State and a J.D. from Georgetown University. Dr. Potter has been a teacher both in the United States and overseas as well as a practicing attorney. He teaches Educational Law for Teachers at Penn State.

James Raths is currently Professor in the School of Education at the University of Delaware. His Ph.D. degree in education research, evaluation, and statistics was from New York University in 1960. He has also held academic appointments at the University of Illinois, University of Maryland, the University of Vermont, and the University of Wisconsin, Milwaukee. He served as Executive Editor of the *Journal of Education Research* from 1975 to 2005 and co-edited (with Frank Murray) the *Review of Education*

Research. Dr. Raths has published widely, including co-editing a number of books and writing chapters for books on teacher preparation.

Arthur M. Recesso is Associate Research Scientist in the Learning and Performance Support Laboratory at the University of Georgia. His expertise is in educational policy, assessment, and decision making using evidential reasoning models. He also develops technology-based tools for collection and interpretation of evidence including the Video Analysis Tool (VAT). Dr. Recesso's research has most recently been funded through the US Department of Education.

Jacqueline A. Stefkovich is Associate Dean for Graduate Studies, Research and Faculty Development at the Pennsylvania State University. She holds an Ed.D. from Harvard University and a J.D. from the University of Pennsylvania Law School. Dr. Stefkovich began her career as a teacher and school counselor. She has published in peer reviewed journals and law reviews and has written the following books: *The Law and Education: Cases and Materials* and *Search and Seizure in the Public Schools* (both with Lawrence Rossow), *Ethical Leadership and Decision Making in Education* (with Joan Shapiro) and *The Best Interests of the Student.*

Terrell Lamont Strayhorn is Assistant Professor of Higher Education and Sociology and Special Assistant to the Provost at the University of Tennessee, Knoxville. Author of *Frameworks for Assessing Learning and Development Outcomes* and over 50 articles, chapters, and reviews, Professor Strayhorn has received numerous awards and recognitions for his research on the experiences of historically under-represented populations in American higher education and how educational disparities cascade over time into long-term inequalities in social life, graduate education, and labor market outcomes to name a few. He specializes in advanced quantitative data analysis, modeling techniques, and mixed methods studies.

John Sureau is a Minister at St. John the Baptist Diocesan High School (West Islip, NY), and a doctoral student at Fordham University.

Juli A. Swinnerton is a research associate at the University of Washington. Her research focuses on school district reform and educational leaders' learning in the context of reform efforts. She also works part-time as an Instructional Technology Specialist for Seattle Public Schools. She has been described as "bilingual" given her ability to understand district reform as both a researcher and an experienced practitioner.

Kelli Thomas is an Associate Professor of Mathematics Education at the University of Kansas. Dr. Thomas' research agenda focuses on issues related to mathematics education reform. She studies teaching, learning, and assessment of mathematics with a focus on better understanding mathematics education evaluation activities as they inform improved educational practices. She is currently a Co-PI for the Collaborative Evaluation Communities in one Urban Schools Project. Her research interests include work in urban contexts. She has published results of research in the *Journal of Educational Research, School Science and Mathematics, Teaching Children Mathematics, Action in Teacher Education,* and *New Directions for Evaluation.*

Jeffrey C. Wayman is an Assistant Professor in the Department of Educational Administration at the University of Texas at Austin. His research on data-based decision making includes efficient structures for creating data-informed school districts, effective leadership for data use among faculties, systemic supports that enable widespread, independent teacher use of student data, and software that delivers student data to educators. Prior to joining the UT faculty, Dr. Wayman conducted research at Johns Hopkins University, at Colorado State University, and was a junior high math teacher.

Renae E. Weber is a Mathematics Professor and Title III Coordinator at Treasure Valley Community College in Oregon.

I. Phillip Young is a Professor of Education and a Director of a Joint Doctoral Program for the University of California, Davis. His research interest is human resource management in the public school setting and he has recently published *The Human Resource Function in Educational Administration* (2008), now in its 9th edition. He has published numerous articles addressing compensation, recruitment, and selection.

Heather Zavadsky is the Director of Policy and Communication at the Institute for Public School Initiatives (IPSI) at the University of Texas system. Her 15 years of education experience includes work in urban district reform, data and accountability systems, teacher quality, and autism. Prior to coming to IPSI, she managed the Broad Prize for Urban Education for the National Center for

Education Accountability and served as a special education teacher for six years. She holds a B.A. in elementary education, an M.Ed. in special education, an M.Ed. in education administration, and a Ph.D. in educational policy and planning.

Sally J. Zepeda is Professor and Graduate Coordinator in the Department of Lifelong Education, Administration, and Policy and in the Program in Educational Administration and Policy at the University of Georgia. Her expertise is in instructional supervision, teacher evaluation, and professional development and the work of principals. She is a member of the Council of Professors of Instructional Supervision (COPIS) and serves on the Editorial Board of *Educational Administration Quarterly*. She has authored or co-authored 15 books and 60 articles and book chapters. Dr. Zepeda received the inaugural Master Professor Award from the University Council for Educational Administration in 2005.

Subject Index

Index of Names